Collectables
PRICE GUIDE 2003

Collectables
PRICE GUIDE 2003

Judith Miller

A DORLING KINDERSLEY BOOK

LONDON, NEW YORK, MUNICH,
MELBOURNE, DELHI

A joint production from DORLING KINDERSLEY
and THE PRICE GUIDE COMPANY

THE PRICE GUIDE COMPANY LIMITED

Publisher Judith Miller

Collectables Specialist Mark Hill

Publishing Manager Julie Brooke

Editor Carolyn Wilmot

Assistant Editors Megan Watson, Sara Sturgess

Editorial Assistants Emily Crane, Sonya Harvey, Sarah Wainwright

Design and DTP Tim Scrivens, TJ Graphics

Digital Image Co-ordinator Cara Miller

Advertising Julian Ellison

Photographers Graham Rae, Bruce Boyajian, John McKenzie, Mike Molloy, Byron Slater, Elizabeth Field, Dave Pincott, Martin Spillane

Indexer Hilary Bird

Workflow consultant Edward MacDermott

Business advisor Nick Croydon

DORLING KINDERSLEY LIMITED

Category Publisher Jackie Douglas

Managing Art Editor Heather McCarry

Managing Editor Julie Oughton

DTP Designer Mike Grigoletti

Senior Designer Mandy Earey

Jacket Designer Nicola Powling

Jacket Editor Beth Apple

Production Controller Joanna Bull

Production Manager Sarah Coltman**

First published in 2003 by
Dorling Kindersley Limited
80 Strand, London WC2R 0RL

A Penguin Company

The Price Guide Company (UK) Ltd
Studio 21, Waterside
44-48 Wharf Road
London N1 7UX
info@thepriceguidecompany.com

2 4 6 8 10 9 7 5 3

A CIP catalogue record for this book is available from the British Library.

ISBN 0 7513 6437 1

Printed and bound in Germany by GGP Media GmbH

See our complete catalogue at
www.dk.com

CONTENTS

Contents

WELCOME TO THE FIRST OF MY ANNUAL PRICE GUIDES TO COLLECTABLES, published in association with DORLING KINDERSLEY. The market for collectables has grown enormously in recent years and having been part of its growth, I can understand how hard it can be to spot the reason why two seemingly similar pieces can have such different values. One of the most important things I learnt early on is to look at an object. Not just a cursory glance, but a really good look. What shape is it? What colour is it? What is the design or pattern like?

This is why a full-colour, professionally illustrated guide is imperative. So much of what we all use to discern values is taken from the appearance of the object in front of us. This is one of the main reasons for our Closer Look features.

We can never hope to cover all collectable areas thoroughly in one book. For me, that's one of the most exciting attractions. By producing an annual guide, we hope to show you the enormous breadth of what is available over the years, but also to help you to learn more by showing you the most useful thing – the object itself – in full colour with descriptive caption, price range and code showing you where the item was sold.

Judith Miller.

List of consultants

Automobilia

Tony Wraight
Finesse Fine Art,
Fmpool Cottage,
West Knighton,
Dorset DT2 8PE

Ceramics

Judith Miller
The Price Guide Company (UK) Ltd

Dick Henrywood
Dreweatt Neate,
Donnington Priory,
Donnington, Nr. Newbury,
Berkshire RG14 2JE

Chess

Luke Honey
lukehoneyfineart@aol.com

Commemoratives

John Pym
Hope and Glory,
131a Kensington Church Street,
London W8 7LP

Computer Games

Hugo Lee Jones
electroniccollectables@hotmail.com

Costume Jewellery

John Wainwright
Vista 2000 Ltd

Steven Miners
Cristobal, 26 Church St.,
London NW8 8EP

Decorative Arts

John Mackie
Lyon and Turnbull,
33 Broughton Place,
Edinburgh EH1 3RR

Militaria

Roy Butler
Wallis and Wallis,
West Street Auction Galleries,
Lewes, East Sussex BN7 2NJ

Optical, Plastics and Scientific Instruments

Mark Hill
The Price Guide Company (UK) Ltd

Pens

Alexander Crum-Ewing
Author of *The Fountain Pen -
A Collector's Companion*
alexander@crumewing.fsnet.co.uk

Space Memorabilia

Victoria Campbell
Aurora Galleries International
30 Hackamore Lane, Suite 2,
Bell Canyon, California 91307

Toys

James Bridges
Glenn Butler
Wallis and Wallis,
West Street Auction Galleries,
Lewes, East Sussex BN7 2NJ

Category Heading
Indicates the general category as listed in the table of contents on pp.5–6.

The Object
All collectables are shown in full colour, which is a vital aid to identification and valuation.

Subcategory Heading
Indicates the subcategory of the main category heading and shows the general contents of the page.

Historical information
Provides background information on the designer, factory or make of the piece or style in question.

A Closer Look at...
Here, we highlight particularly interesting items or show identifying features, pointing out rare or desirable qualities.

A 1930s Carlton ware "springtime" dish.
6.75in (17cm) wide
£70–80   RH

The Caption
Describes the item and can include the maker, model, year of manufacture, size and condition.

The Price Guide
All prices are shown in ranges and give you a 'ball park' figure close to what you should expect to pay for a similar item. The great joy of collectables is that there is not a recommended retail price. The price given is not necessarily that which a dealer will pay you. As a general rule, expect to receive approximately 30% less. When selling, pay attention to the dealer or auction house specialist to understand why this may be, and consider that they have to run a business as well as make a living. When buying, listen again. Condition, market forces and location of the place of sale will all affect a price.

The Source Code
The image is credited to its source with a code. Use the 'Key to Illustrations' on pp.576-579 to check it against.

Find out more...
To help you seek further information, these boxes list websites, books, and museums where you can find out more.

Page Tab
Shows the first letter of the general category heading – for easy reference when using the book.

TINS

- The period from the 1860s to the 1930s is considered to be the 'golden age' of tins. Tins economically, practically and decoratively housed many perishable products from biscuits to tea and tobacco. The biscuit manufacturers Huntley & Palmers are the best-known name, but desirable tins were also made by Jacob's, Crawford of Edinburgh, Fry's and Macfarlane Lang & Co.
- Novelty shapes, such as carriages, boats and books, are highly sought after. Most had realistic rich external decoration and some had moving parts such as wheels.
- Tins that advertise products are popular, partly as they illustrate the evolution of graphic advertising from the late 19th to the mid 20th centuries. Commemorative tins can cross into other collecting areas, such as royal memorabilia.
- Avoid tins that have rust, dents, scratches, splits or missing parts, such as wheels or catches. Always buy in the best condition possible but near mint or mint condition tins (when found) will command an extremely high premium. Look inside and outside for damage.
- Never wash lithograph printed tins in water as this will damage the printed surface and the underlying tin considerably.
- Keep tins away from bright sunlight, which will bleach colours.

A Huntley & Palmers 'Literature' biscuit tin, in the form of eight finely embossed books with marble edges, titled on the spines: "History of England", "Pilgrim's Progress", "Burns", "Pickwick Papers", "Robinson Crusoe", "Gulliver's Travels", "Self Help" and "Shakespeare", bound together with a simulated leather strap and buckle, bookmark pull-tab missing.

These highly popular 'trompe l'oeil' tins were a best seller in their period, with different spines showing different ranges of books.

c1901

£50-100   **DN**

A Carr and Co 'Art Box' biscuit tin, of square aluminium construction pressed with a formalized Art Nouveau design of flower heads, impressed "Rd.No.709075" with maker's initials N.C.J. for N.C.

c1924

£40-80   **DN**

An early to mid-20thC William Crawford & Sons Ltd biscuit tin caddy.

6in (15.5cm) wide

£50-70   **SS**

A Huntley & Palmers biscuit tin.
c1868   8.5in (21.5cm) high

£300-350   **DH**

A Huntley & Palmers 'Bookstand' tin.
c1905   6.25in (16cm) high

£100-150   **DH**

A Huntley & Palmers 'Creel' biscuit tin, in the shape of an angler's fishing basket with belt loops, small handle, hinged lid, and small catch, marked "Regd. No. 486204" near base on back.
c1907

£100-150   **DN**

A William Crawford & Sons 'Lucie Attwell's Fairy House' money box biscuit tin, in the shape of a mushroom printed around the stem with typical Attwell characters, the domed roof with coin slot, some rusting, dent in roof, also another small circular money box tin in the form of a clock, the dial with the inscription "Save Time & Money" and the alphabet around the perimeter.

£130-180   **DN**

A Huntley & Palmers 'Maplewood Casket' biscuit tin, in the form of an octagonal veneered wood casket with inlaid stringing around edges, the hinged lid with a central oval hunting scene, with an inscription on the base including "No.4813".

1926-27

£40-60 DN

A Crawford's 'Sundial' tin.

c1926 9.5in (24cm) high

£100-150 DH

A pair of Huntley & Palmers 'Worcester Vase' biscuit tins, of tapered octagonal shape with removable necks forming the lids, marked "H.B. and S. Ltd. Reading" beneath the bases.

c1934

£100-150 DN

A Macfarlane Lang 'Wonderland Cottage' tin money box.

c1930 5.25in (13.5cm) high

£40-80 DH

A Huntley & Palmers 'Ginger Nuts' tin.

c1930 1.5in (4cm) wide

£20-40 DH

A J. Lyons biscuit tin, to commemorate the silver jubilee of King George V and Queen Mary.

c1935 10in (25.5cm) wide

£20-30 DH

A Peek Frean biscuit box tin.

c1950 2.25in (5.75cm) wide

£14-18 DH

A W. & R. Jacob & Co Ltd 'Coronation Coach' biscuit tin, in the form of the royal coach with tinplate wheels, the removable roof with crown-shaped knop.

c1936

£100-150 DN

A Carr & Company Ltd biscuit tin, to commemorate the coronation of Queen Elizabeth II.

1953 11.35in (29cm) high

£14-18 DH

A Cadbury's Dairy Milk Chocolate money box tin, in the shape of a milk churn with removable lid, the coin slot near the top of one side.

£20-30 DN

A 'Tatjana Needles' record needles tin.

c1910   *1.5in (4cm) wide*

£50-70   **DH**

A 'Herald Tango' record needles tin.

c1910   *1.5in (4cm) wide*

£50-80   **DH**

A 1920s HMV 'His Masters Voice, Loud Tone' record needles tin.

1.5in (4cm) wide

£5-10   **DH**

A Sem record needles tin.

1.5in (4cm) wide

£50-80   **DH**

A rare Art Nouveau olive oil tin, with inscription "A. Bennasser, Marcca registrada Mallorca".

c1905   *6in (15cm) high*

£150-200   **DH**

A Rowntree & Co Ltd tin, to commemorate the coronation of King George V and Queen Mary.

1902   *5in (12.5cm) wide*

£14-18   **DH**

A 'Three British Queens' tin, In the form of a brass bound carved wood casket, the surfaces embossed with Queen Mary's royal initials "R" and "M.I."

c1905

£20-30   **DN**

FIND OUT MORE...

Museum of Reading, Blagrave Street, Reading, RG1 1QH, England, www.readingmuseum.org.uk . This museum houses a display of over 300 tins made for Reading-based biscuit maker, Huntley & Palmers.

'Biscuit Tins 1868-1939: The Art of Decorative Packaging', by M.J. Franklin, New Cavendish Books, U.S.A.

'Decorative Printed Tins: The Golden Age of Printed Tin Packaging', by David Griffith, Studio Vista, 1996.

A J. S. Fry & Sons tin, to commemorate the silver jubilee of King George V and Queen Mary.

1935   *7.5in (19cm) wide*

£20-25   **DH**

A Queen Mary's Troops Christmas tin.

1914   *5in (13cm) wide*

£20-30   **MB**

A tin, showing George VI, Queen Elizabeth, and Princesses Elizabeth and Margaret.

5.25in (13.5cm) wide

£20-25   DH

A Mazawatte 'Old Folks at Home' tea tin.

3.75in (9.5cm) wide

£15-20   DH

A Matabele Tobacco tin.

3in (8cm) high

£200-250   DH

A Prince of Wales Cigarettes tin.

c1900   *3in (7.5cm) wide*

£200-250   DH

A Gaiety Girl Straight Cut Cigarettes tin.

3in (7.5cm) high

£300-350   DH

A Macdonalds Cut Golden Bar 'Kitty Brand' tin, Glasgow.

4in (10cm) high

£80-100   DH

A rare Johnson & Gluckstein Ltd 'King Rufus Cigarettes' tin.

c1950

£600-650   DH

A 1950s Salvation Army Collection tin, with inscription 'Where there's need there's The Salvation Army' with key, remains of paper label to base.

5in (12.5cm) high

£24-28   DH

A 1930s John Player & Sons 'Players Navy Cut' tin, with printed paper label.

2.25in (5.5cm) diam

£12-14   DH

A SPG Medical Missions collecting tin, in the shape of a medicine bottle, with inscription 'Society for the Propagation of the Gospel in Foreign Parts'.

c1910   *6.25in (16cm) high*

£12-16   DH

A Cunard Line tin.

c1920   *3.25in (8.5cm) wide*

£300-350   DH

- Card signs, also known as 'standees', were made as counter top displays for use in shops and department stores, using brightly coloured and stylish period designs to attract customers' attention.
- Usually more affordable than posters advertising the same product, collectors can build collections comparatively inexpensively.
- Card signs are smaller and easier to display and store than posters.
- They often had the same or similar artwork as the poster version of the same product by familiar poster artists, so collectors can still follow the changing fashions and styles of advertising through the ages.

A Salamander Brandy card sign.

15.75in (40cm) high

£100-150   DO

An Ovaltine card sign, 'Drink Delicious Ovaltine & Face the Winter with a Smile'.

14.5in (37cm) high

£50-70   DO

A Dubonnet card sign, 'Donne de l'appetit pour deux'.

14.5in (36.5cm) high

£40-60   DO

A Symons Devonshire Cider card sign.

13in (33cm) wide

£40-50   DO

An Edmondson's Toffee card sign.

18in (45.5cm) high

£40-50   DO

A Marquise Slumber & Setting Net card sign, 'In all Hair Pastel Shades, Made in England'.

12.5in (32cm) high

£35-45   DO

A Crème Mouson card sign, 'Agissant en Profondeur.'

12in (30.5cm) high

£50-70   DO

A Drocourt card sign, 'Desserts de la favorite desserts du roi'.

15.75in (40cm) high

£20-25   DO

A Pitralon card sign.

16.5in (42cm) high

£25-35   DO

A Meridian card sign, 'The Perfect Fabric for Sensitive Skins'.

9.5in (24cm) high

£3-4   DO

A Radiator Glace de Lingue card sign.

15.75in (40cm) high

£50-80   DO

A Japlac card sign, 'For Magic Colour Laquer Paint'.

14.25in (36cm) high

£30-50   DO

A Maëstro card sign.

17.25in (43.5cm) high

£50-70   DO

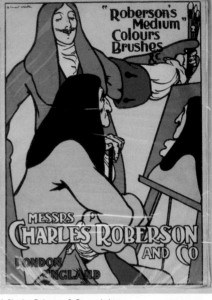

A Charles Roberson & Co. card sign.

17.75in (45cm) high

£40-60   DO

A Nuit à l'Arlequin card sign, Paris.

14in (35.5cm) high

£40-60   DO

A Jager Krüllschnitt Cruwell Tabak card sign.

15in (38cm) high

£40-50   DO

An Anggoer Obat Serravallo card sign.

11.5in (29.5cm) high

£30-50   DO

An Anggoer Obat Serravallo card sign.

16.25in (41cm) high

£30-50   DO

A 1930s Ashtead Potters Guinness ashtray, "Guinness is Good for You".

4.25in (11cm) diam

£40-50 DH

GUINNESS MEMORABILIA

- Guinness advertising started in 1928, with the famous toucan character by the artist John Gilroy (1898-1985) being introduced in 1935.
- The slogan 'Guinness is good for you' was thought up by the advertising company S.H. Benson Ltd., who employed Gilroy and worked with Guinness from 1928.
- In the 1950s, Carlton Ware were commissioned to make advertising ceramics for Guinness and produced a sought-after range of designs.
- Since the late 1920s a huge range of items have been produced and Guinness has become a collecting subject all of its own.
- Collectors should beware that many reproductions of ceramic Guinness memorabilia exist, especially the flying toucan wall ornaments. Although these are collectable, values should be much lower than for the originals.

FIND OUT MORE...

www.guinntiques.com

A Guinness poster, "See the Animals at Edinburgh Zoo".

30in (76cm) high

£300-350 DO

A pair of 20thC novelty Guinness pottery salt and pepper shakers, each in the form of a pint of Guinness.

2in (5cm) high

£70-100 J&H

A late 1940s Guinness blue and white plate, "My Goodness My Guinness".

6.75in (17.5cm) diam

£30-50 DH

A set of six 1950s Guinness buttons, "Guinness is Good for You".

Box 6.25in (16cm)

£70-80 DH

A Guinness rubber toucan advertising figure.

1950s 6.75in (17cm) high

£100-150 DH

A Guinness pocket calendar, "My Goodness My Guinness".

1959 3.5in (9cm) high

£20-30 DH

A 1950s Guinness paper cup, "Guinness is good for you".

4.5in (11.5cm) high

£5-10 DH

A Carlton Ware Guinness penguin table lamp, holding a plaque inscribed "Draught Guinness", the figure with original fitting and shade.

6.75in (17cm) high

£500-600 BAR

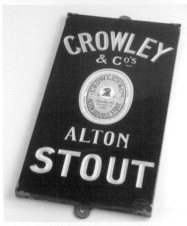

A Crowley & Co of Alton slate advertising sign, with copper reinforced corners and mounting brackets, with carved gilt lettering for "Alton Stout", inset brown-printed bottle label and maker's marks for "Dickson / Pyro Special / S. Bermondsey" in lower right corners.

20in (51cm) high

£350-400 — **DN**

1 A Foley advertising plaque, the rectangular-moulded frame enclosing a panel printed and painted in colours with classical pot making scene and bearing inscription "Depot for the Foley China England's Finest Porcelain" printed mark.

c1900 — *9.75in (25cm) long*

£1,700-2,300 — **L&T**

2 A Foley advertising plaque, the rectangular-moulded frame enclosing a panel printed and painted in colours with three crests for Dunbar and bearing inscription "Depot for the Foley Heraldic English Porcelain", printed marks.

c1900

£400-450 — **L&T**

An original Player's Navy Mixture advertisement, depicting HMS Diana ramming a whale.

c1906 — *18in (46cm) high*

£150-200 — **BAR**

A pair of Pratt's petrol cans, in copper and brass, with the Pratt's logo embossed on the sides, the name repeated on the front and on the brass caps, the tops embossed "Pratt's Petroleum Spirit, Highly Inflammable" and with the price 3/-, previously adapted as lamps with a single hole through each handle.

c1910

£50-100 — **DN**

A set of "Wills Star" cigarette dominoes, in tin.

7.25in (18.5cm) long

£10-20 — **WHP**

A 1920s Waterman's Oak counter top cabinet, glazed on all four sides, with plinth base and two lift-out trays for twelve pens each, cracks in glass.

16.5in (42cm) high

£250-300 — **GorL**

A Felix Pernod advertising tin hand.

These tin hands were placed flat on the table and spun, whoever the finger pointed at had to buy the next round of drinks.

c1910 — *2.75in (7cm) high*

£10-20 — **DH**

A Palmer's Donnington Pale Ales enamel sign, in white on a blue ground, with one edge folded for wall mounting, with rusting edges and some other faults, darkened with age.

c1915

£140-180 — **DN**

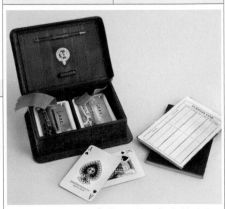

An advertising bridge case, for Furness Lines, fitted with playing cards printed with liners.

6in (16cm) wide

£50-100 — **LFA**

A 1920s Avon advertising sign.

8in (20.5cm) high

£30-60 left **BS**

A 1920s Globe Metal Polish advertising sign.

7in (17.5cm)

£180-230 right **BS**

A 1920s Pascals miniature chocolate dispensing machine money box.

5.25in (13.5cm) high

£80-130 **BS**

A 1920s/30s Sarony Cigarettes promotional tin, with original box.

12.5in (31.5cm)

£100-140 **BS**

A Macfarlane Lang Playmate's Biscuits advertising card, with movable eyes.

c1925 *4.25in (11cm high)*

£ 30-35 **DH**

A "Vimto" advertising display card, colour-printed with a girl out hiking with Vimto in her backpack.

14.5in (37cm) high

£60-80 **DN**

A Midland Bank money box, no. 458381.

1930 *3.25in (8cm) diam*

£15-20 **DH**

A 1930s Garant display, demonstrating fountain pen nib manufacture, with sixteen stages from blank to finished nib, including rolling, cutting, die-stamping, shaping, burnishing, splitting, polishing and plating, in plush-lined manufacturers' box with pull-off cover.

6.75in (17cm) wide

£700-750 **GorL**

A 1930s Grants Standfast Scotch Whisky advertising figure.

10.25in (26cm) high

£200-250 **DH**

A 1930s Worthingtons advertising ashtray, decorated with the scene from Dickens' "The Pickwick Papers", by Newhall Ceramics.

4.25in (11cm) diam

£20-25 DH

A 1930s Worthingtons advertising ashtray, decorated with the scene from Dickens' "Old Curiosity Shop" featuring Codlin and Short, by Newhall Ceramics.

4.25in (11cm) diam

£20-25 DH

A 1930s Bass advertising ashtray.

4in (10cm) diam

£20-25 DH

A Stolwerck chocolate vending machine.

c1950

£120-160 DH

A rare 1950s Parker Quink Station, in black Bakelite with central covered reservoir for Quink dispenser, two wells either side for customers to empty and wash their pen, lettering repainted, sealed crack on base at back.

7in (18cm) wide

£180-220 GorL

A Hovis Coronation periscope, to commemorate the coronation of Elizabeth II.

1953   12.5in (32cm) wide

£20-25 DH

A 1950s King George IV Old Scotch Whisky advertising figure.

8.5in (22cm) high

£55-65 DH

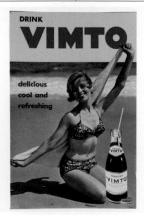

A Vimto card, 'Drink Vimto, Delicious, Cool and Refreshing'.

c1955

£20-25 DH

A 1950s Craven "A" Virginia Cigarettes tin calendar.

10.75in (27.5cm) high

£25-35 DH

A Johnny Walker whisky ashtray, with inscription 'Born 1820 Still Going Strong', by Magnier Blangy.

c1960   *4in (10cm) wide*

£8-10   **DH**

A Woodbine Virginia Cigarettes ashtray.

c1960   *4.5in (11.5cm) wide*

£4-6   **DH**

A 1960s Trumans advertising figure, with inscription 'Brewers of Good Beer'.

8in (20cm) high

£40-50   **DH**

A 1960s Carlsberg advertising figure, depicting a woman seated on a rock.

7in (18cm) high

£15-25   **DH**

A 1960s Tia Maria plastic advertising figure.

10.5in (27cm) high

£40-50   **DH**

A box of ten commemorative boxes of matches, to commemorate the wedding of HRH Princess Anne and Captain Mark Philips.

3.25in (8.5cm) wide

£4-6   **DH**

A set of three Biba cosmetics containers.

c1970   *Bottle 4.25in (11cm) high*

£10-15 each   **DH**

A plastic Nairn elephant, the plastic geometric form with removable lid enclosing a compartment for brochures on Nairn products and "the making of the elephant", by Eduardo Paolozzi, designed for Nairn Floors Ltd, no. 911 of 3000, signed on the base.

1972   *11.75in (30cm) high*

£600-700   **L&T**

A Warner Brothers Superman IV cardboard advertising placard, with a cut-out figure of Christopher Reeve, written inscription for Cannon Cinema, Reading, some minor damage.

1987   71.75in (182cm) high

£30-50   **DN**

Two American department store restaurant advertising display ice creams, ice cream soda and ice cream sundae.

c1990

£20-40 each   **BCAC**

An American department store restaurant advertising display chocolate cake.

c1990

£20-30   **BCAC**

A Nestlé 'Honey Queen' honey and almond milk chocolate bar.

4in (10cm) wide

£10-15   **DH**

An American department store restaurant advertising display of a slice of cake on a plate.

c1990

£20-30   **BCAC**

An American department store restaurant display banana split.

c1990

£20-30   **BCAC**

A Rothwell's Milk Chocolate Wafer bar.

4.75in (12cm) wide

£10-15   **DH**

A Middlemas & Son 'Middlemas Chocolate Wembley' chocolate bar.

£10-15   **DH**

A Galapeter milk chocolate bar.

4.75in (12cm) wide

£10-15   **DH**

A Patrick Thomson Ltd 'Chocolate Wembley' chocolate bar, made for the opening of Wembley Stadium.

c1915   4in (10cm) wide

£10-15   **DH**

A can of Lifeguard Extra Lustre Car Polish.

c1959 6.25in (16cm) high

£15-20   **DH**

A 1930s Jester Towel Soap box.

6in (15cm) wide

£10-15   **DH**

A box of Lever 'Sunlight' Soap.

1935   *6in (15.5cm) wide*

£14-16   **DH**

A 1930s Bell & Sons bottle of Chillexine for the Udder.

8in (20cm) high

£22-26   **DH**

A wartime pure dried whole eggs tin.

4in (10cm) high

£10-15   **DH**

A World War II Ovaltine tin.

5in (12.5cm) high

£15-25   **DH**

A wartime Clozone Concentrated Patent soap box, by J. Bibby & Sons.

5.5in (14cm) high

£6-12   **DH**

A 1940s Lever box of Wisk washing powder, with inscription 'For the Whole Family Wash'.

6in (15.5cm) high

£6-12   **DH**

A 1940s box of Rinso washing powder, with inscription 'Washes Whites Whiter than New'.

7in (18cm) high

£12-14   **DH**

A wartime C. Kunzle Ltd Mello chocolate bar.

6in (15cm) wide

£10-15 DH

A 1940s bottle of Evening in Paris, by Bourjois.

5.75in (14.5cm) high

£10-15 DH

A box of Oxydol washing powder, with inscription 'Super Soapy for Extra Whiteness'.

1950 *5in (13cm) high*

£6-12 DH

A Vim tin, with inscription 'For Safe Smooth Cleaning for Pots, Pans and Cookers'.

c1950 *8.75in (22.5cm) high*

£10-14 DH

A 1950s Cunard Line pamphlet, with inscription 'Tourist Class to USA'.

9in (23cm) high

£2-3 DH

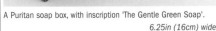

A Puritan soap box, with inscription 'The Gentle Green Soap'.

6.25in (16cm) wide

£12-14 DH

A 1950s box of White Tide washing powder.

7.75in (20cm) high

£6-12 DH

A Dr. Whites compressed sanitary towel box.

c1955 *2.75in (7cm) wide*

£2-4 DH

A Southhalls Travla compressed sanitary towel box.

c1955 *2.5in (6.5cm) wide*

£2-4 DH

A Boots Regaid compressed sanitary towel.

c1955 *2.25in (6cm) wide*

£2-4 DH

A Southhalls Travla compressed sanitary towel box.

c1955 *2.25in (6cm) wide*

£2-4 DH

A clear glass shell X-100 motor oil bottle.
c1955   *11in (28cm) high*

£15-20   **DH**

A clear glass Castrol bottle.
c1955   *0.5in (27cm) high*

£18-22   **DH**

A clear glass premium grade Staminol
Motor Oil bottle.
c1955   *13.5in (34cm) high*

£25-30   **DH**

A Cure-C-Cure tape repair outfit tin for car tyres, by Romac.
c1960   *5in (13cm) wide*

£6-12   **DH**

A Cure-C-Cure repair pack for motorbike tyres, by Romac.
c1960   *3.25in (8.5cm) wide*

£6-12   **DH**

A pot of Silvikrin hair cream.
c1960   *3in (7.5cm) high*

£12-14   **DH**

A box of Bibby Best soap.
c1935   *6in (15.5cm) wide*

£14-16   **DH**

A box of Robin starch.
c1960   *2in (5.5cm) high*

£4-6   **DH**

ANTIQUITIES

- An antiquity is the physical remains or a relic from Ancient times and usually originates from the Middle or Far East and some Mediterranean countries. Considering the age of the pieces, the antiquities market is very accessible, with many affordable prices. However, smaller pieces such as ushabti, amulets and jewellery, previously at the lower end of the market, now command higher prices.

- Many of the pieces available to the collector will be domestic in original use and will have been made in large quantities, such as oil lamps, vessels, or jewellery.

- Weapons are also commonly found and affordable. Luristan, in Western Iran, has become noted for its engraved bronze weapons, which are deemed sophisticated.

- Over the past ten years, the antiquities trade has been riddled with high profile stories involving looting of sites and fakes. Although this is not unusual, and has occurred for as long as the trade has existed, always buy from a reputable dealer or auction house who will be happy to demonstrate their expertise and probity.

- Despite its fragility, much Roman glass has survived and with its delicate colouring, makes a superb collection. In most cases, long periods of burial have altered the surface of the glass making uniquely and beautifully coloured pieces that have inspired designers such as Louis Comfort Tiffany and Christopher Dresser.

- Size, period and subject matter will affect value. Also look closely at the quality of manufacture and condition. Learn how to recognise styles and characters and motifs such as the gods which are depicted frequently.

Amulets

An Egyptian faience amulet, depicting Horus as a hawk.

c400 BC   1.5in (3.5cm) high

£80-100   **AnA**

A Egyptian blue faience amulet, depicting Horus with Solar disc.

c400 BC   1in (2.5cm) high

£100-150   **AnA**

An Egyptian faience amulet, of a papyrus scroll.

c400 BC   2in (5cm) high

£65-75   **AnA**

An Egyptian faience amulet, depicting the Eye of Horus.

c400 BC   1in (2.5cm) high

£55-65   **AnA**

An Egyptian steatite scarab amulet, with pharonic cartouche.

0.5in (1.5cm) long

£80-100   **AnA**

An Egyptian faience heart scarab amulet.

c400 BC   1in (2.5cm) long

£70-90   **AnA**

An Egyptian faience amulet, depicting a jackal-headed Anubis.

c400 BC   1.75in (4.5cm) high

£100-150   **AnA**

An Egyptian steatite scaraboid, with pattern and hieroglyph.

1.25in (3cm) long

£60-80   **AnA**

A large Egyptian heart scarab.

2.5in (6cm) wide

£250-300   **AnA**

An Egyptian faience amulet, depicting Thoth, Ibis-headed god.

2in (5cm) high

£400-450   **AnA**

An Egyptian faience amulet, of a Djed column, backbone of Isis.

c400 BC   1.5in (4cm) high

£65-75   AnA

An Egyptian faience amulet, depicting Bes standing.

c400 BC   2in (2.5cm) high

£55-65   AnA

An Egyptian New Kingdom faience mummiform ushabti, the figure with arms crossed over the abdomen, wearing a tripartite wig, the details in black glaze, including a single line of hieroglyphic text.

1200-1085 BC   5in (12.8cm) h

£350-400   SI

An Egyptian 22nd Dynasty faience ushabti, with black hair.

5in (13cm) high

£550-600   AnA

A Late Period Egyptian faience mummiform ushabti, depicted wearing a striated tripartite wig and curved false beard, the arms crossed over the chest holding hoes, a seed bag over the left shoulder, inscribed with nine lines of hieroglyphic text.

664-525 BC   8in (21cm) high

£1,500-2,000   SI

A Late Period Egyptian faience mummiform ushabti, depicted wearing a tripartite wig and a false beard, inscribed with hieroglyphic text.

664-525 BC   4.7in (12cm) high

£100-150   SI

A Late Period Egyptian faience mummiform ushabti, depicted wearing a tripartite wig and a false beard, inscribed with hieroglyphic text.

664-525 BC   4in (10.2cm) high

£140-180   SI

A Late Period Egyptian faience mummiform ushabti, depicted wearing a tripartite wig and a false beard, inscribed with hieroglyphic text.

664-525 BC   4in (10.2cm) high

£250-300   SI

Two Late Period Egyptian white and turquoise faience mummiform ushabtis, wearing tripartite wigs and false beards.

664-525 BC   3in (7.6cm) high

£140-180   SI

An Egyptian faience ushabti.

c400 BC   4in (10cm) high

£80-100   AnA

An Egyptian faience ushabti.

c400 BC   4.5in (11cm) high

£250-300   AnA

An Egyptian 26th Dynasty ushabti.

c400 BC   5.25in (13.5cm) high

£700-750   AnA

Jewellery

An Egyptian faience ushabti.
c200 BC   2.75in (7cm) high
£40-50   **AnA**

An Egyptian necklace.
c1800 BC 15.75in (40cm) long
£60-80   **AnA**

An Egyptian necklace, with blue faience beads and amulets.
c500 BC   *14in (36cm) long*
£1,000-1,300   **AnA**

An Egyptian necklace, with gold and blue faience amulets.
18in (46cm) long
£1,000-1,500   **AnA**

A Late Period Egyptian necklace, with faience beads and amulets, including mummy ring, cylindrical beads and a turquoise amulet.
305-30 BC
£200-250   **SI**

A Late Period Egyptian faience necklace, composed of mummy ring and cylindrical beads in numerous colours.
305-30 BC
£350-400   **SI**

A Late Period Egyptian necklace, composed of mummy ring and cylindrical beads and a turquoise amulet.
305-30 BC
£250-300   **SI**

A Late Period Egyptian necklace, composed of mummy ring and cylindrical beads and a turquoise amulet.
305-30 BC
£250-300   **SI**

A Pre-Dynasty Egyptian ovoid vase, with wavy line decoration in brown.
4in (10.5cm) high
£400-450   **AnA**

A Pre-Dynastic alabaster dish, probably for cosmetic use.
c3000 BC 4.5in (11.5cm) high
£150-200   **AnA**

An Egyptian Abydos ware jug in terracotta.
c3000 BC 7.75in (20cm) high
£180-200   **AnA**

An Pre-Dynastic Egyptian alabaster jar, with flaring body.
c3000 BC 4.5in (11.5cm) high
£450-500   **AnA**

A 1st Dynasty Egyptian terracotta vessel, of conical form, with everted rounded rim.
c3000 BC   8.5in (21cm) high
£650-700   **SI**

A Late Period Egyptian mask.

c500 BC   *5.5in (14cm) high*

£450-500   **AnA**

A Late Period Egyptian gilt wood figure of a sphinx, on a rectangular plinth, wearing a short wig.

730-16 BC *2.2in (5.7cm) long*

£450-500   **SI**

A Late Period Egyptian wood sarcophagus mask, wearing a tripartite wig.

730-16 BC *21in (53.3cm) high*

£5,000-6,000   **SI**

A Greek/Egyptian figure, carved from animal bone.

6.25in (16cm) high

£250-300   **AnA**

A Late Period Egyptian turquoise glass fragment, of circular form and moulded with a lion head.

730-16 BC *1.5in (3.5cm) diam*

£300-350   **SI**

An Egyptian mosaic glass fragment, with opaque black inlay and floral decoration.

3rdC BC - AD 1stC *2.5in (4cm) wide*

£250-300   **SI**

A Roman Period Egyptian faience bead mummy mask, composed of numerous ring beads.

AD 1st-2ndC 7.2in (18.4cm) high

£380-420   **SI**

An Egyptian frog-type terracotta oil lamp.

3.5in (9cm) wide

£60-80   **AnA**

Roman

A Roman translucent iridescent glass jar, with two handles and dimpled body.

AD c200   *3.5in (9cm) high*

£450-500   **AnA**

A Roman translucent blue glass double ungentarium, with handles at side, highly iridescent.

AD c200   *4in (10.5cm) high*

£340-380   **AnA**

A Roman translucent green glass flask, with handle and wheel cut lines to the body.

AD 1st-2ndC 4in (10cm) high

£700-750   **AnA**

A Roman translucent iridescent glass flask, with everted rim.

AD c300 *4.75in (12cm) high*

£250-300   **AnA**

A Roman translucent iridescent green glass beaker, with applied blue glass discs.

AD c300   *4in (10.5cm) high*

£450-500   **AnA**

Three Roman greenish-amber glass bottles, with broad pyriform bodies, flaring neck and rim; one pear shaped with cylindrical neck, from Egypt.

AD 3rd-4thC Lg 3in (7.6cm) high

£300-350   **SI**

Two Roman green glass bottles, one of globular form with a waisted neck, the other of pear shape with an elongated neck and a C-form handle.
AD c200-300   *Larger 5in (12.8cm) high*

£200-250   **SI**

A Roman single-handled translucent glass flask.
AD 400-500   *2.75in (7cm) high*

£200-250   **AnA**

A emerald green glass ungentarium or 'tear bottle'.
    4.75in (12cm) high

£250-300   **AnA**

A Roman amber glass ungentarium or 'tear bottle,' with good iridescence.
    3.5in (9cm) high

£250-300   **AnA**

Oil lamps

A Roman terracotta oil lamp, with a pair of rhytons.
AD 1stC   *4in (10cm) long*

£750-800   **AnA**

A Roman terracotta oil lamp, with Pegasus flying.
AD 1stC   *4.75in (12cm) long*

£650-700   **AnA**

A Roman terracotta oil lamp.
AD 1stC   *4.5in (11.5cm) long*

£50-70   **AnA**

A Roman oil lamp, in African red ware, with chi-rho symbol.
AD c400   *6in (15cm) long*

£100-150   **AnA**

A Roman oil lamp, in North African red ware, with profile bust of an Emperor.
AD c300   *5in (12.5cm) long*

£100-150   **AnA**

A Roman terracotta oil lamp, with female mark.
AD c200   *4in (10.5cm) long*

£200-250   **AnA**

A Roman terracotta mask.
AD c200   *5in (13cm) long*

£400-450   **AnA**

A large Roman patinated bronze appliqué bust, depicting Pan.
AD c200   *3.5in (8.5cm) high*

£1,800-2,000   **AnA**

A Roman bronze knife or dagger handle, in the form of a statue of the God Mars.
AD c200   *4.25in (11cm) high*

£2,000-2,500   **AnA**

A bronze knife handle, in the form of the head and shoulders of the Goddess Minerva.
AD c200   *3.5in (9cm) high*

£750-800   **AnA**

A
B
C
D
E
F
G
H
I
J
K
L
M
N
O
P
Q
R
S
T
U
V
W
XYZ

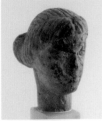

A Roman provincial marble head of a female.

AD c300　　3in (7.5cm) high

£400-450　　AnA

A Byzantine silver finial, in the form of an eagle with wings closed.

2in (5.5cm) high

£700-750　　AnA

A bronze mount, in the form of a bust of Alexander The Great, personified as Hercules with lion's skin drapery.

3.75in (9.5cm) high

£1,250-1,500　　AnA

A bronze applique, depicting a running cherubic figure.

1.5in (4cm) long

£80-100　　AnA

Jewellery

A pair of Roman gold earrings, with applied bosses.

AD c200　　1in (2.5cm) long

£150-200　　AnA

A large bronze brooch, inlaid with enamel.

AD c200　　2.75in (7cm) diam

£450-500　　AnA

A Roman bronze key ring.

AD c200　　1in (2.5cm) high

£50-60　　AnA

A bronze brooch, with four animal heads.

AD c300　1.75in (4.5cm) high

£80-100　　AnA

A Roman British trumpet-type brooch or fibula.

Fibula were used as fasteners to hold clothing together and come in a variety of shapes and sizes and designs.

2.75in (7cm) high

£60-70　　AnA

A Roman bronze phallic amuletic pendant.

1in (3cm) high

£80-100　　AnA

A Roman bronze gilt ring, with plain glass intaglio.

1in (3cm) wide

£125-150　　AnA

BYZANTINE JEWELLERY

■ Although Byzantine jewellery can be seen to represent a continuation of the Roman tradition, by the 4th century its own principles and styles are evident. Throughout the Byzantine Empire jewellery was valued by high-ranking officials at the court. Their signet rings were decorated with complicated monograms and jewellery became a sign of economic prosperity. Jewellery was also used for ceremonial purposes and objects include crosses, censers, rings, and buckles for ecclesiastical garments and they are often set with semi-precious stones.

A Byzantine cross, with setting.

AD 6th-7thC   1.5in (4cm) high

£65-75   **AnA**

A Byzantine bronze reliquary cross, with incised figures of Jesus and Mary.

AD c900   4in (10.5cm) long

£450-500   **AnA**

A Byzantine cross, with figure of Christ.

AD c1000   1.5in (4cm) high

£80-100   **AnA**

A Roman bronze medical/cosmetic instrument.
4.25in (11cm) long

£75-100   **AnA**

A Roman bronze medical/cosmetic instrument.
5.5in (14cm) long

£75-100   **AnA**

FIND OUT MORE...

Trade in Illicit Antiquities: The Destruction of the World's Heritage, by Neil Brodie, Jennifer Doole and Colin Renfrew, published by McDonald Institute for Archaeological Research, 2001.

The Art and Architecture of Ancient Egypt, by William Stevenson Smith et al, published by Yale University Press Pelican History of Art, 1999.

The Cambridge History of Ancient China, by Michael Loewe and Edward L. Shaughnessy, published by Cambridge University Press, 1999.

A Roman bronze medical/cosmetic instrument.
4.75in (12cm) long

£75-100   **AnA**

A Roman bronze medical/cosmetic instrument.
6.25in (16cm) long

£75-100   **AnA**

A Roman bronze medical scalpel.
3.25in (8.5cm) long

£80-100   **AnA**

A Roman North African red ware wine flagon.
AD c200   6in (15cm) high

£150-175   **AnA**

A Roman bronze tinned mirror.
c AD200   4.5in (11.5cm) diam

£100-150   **AnA**

A Roman North African red ware dish, with impressed decoration in centre.
c AD300   12.5in (32cm) diam

£250-300   **AnA**

A Roman pottery bottle, with pear-shaped body.
c AD200   5.25in (13.5cm) high

£40-50   **AnA**

A Roman North African red ware bowl, with flared sides.
c AD300   7.75in (20cm) diam

£75-100   **AnA**

Mesopotamia

A Luristan bronze arrow head.
c1000BC   4in (10cm) long

£30-50   **AnA**

A Luristan bronze arrow head.
c1000BC   4in (10cm) long

£30-50   **AnA**

A Luristan bronze arrowhead.
c1000BC 5.25in (13.5cm) long

£30-50   **AnA**

A Luristan bronze spearhead, with tang.
c1000BC   11.75in (30cm) long

£180-200   **AnA**

A Luristan bronze spearhead, with tang and shaft.
c1000BC   10.5in (27cm) long

£125-150   **AnA**

A Luristan bronze dagger, with integral grip, originally with inlay.
c1000BC   13in (33cm) long

£400-450   **AnA**

A Luristan bronze socketed spearhead, with decorated shaft.
c1000BC   11in (28cm) long

£180-200   **AnA**

A Luristan bronze pronged axe, with curved blade and socket.
c1000BC   8.25in (21cm) long

£400-450   **AnA**

A
B
C
D
E
F
G
H
I
J
K
L
M
N
O
P
Q
R
S
T
U
V
W
XYZ

CYLINDER SEALS

An Old Babylonian haematite cylinder seal, with presentation scene and cuneiform inscription.
c3000 BC   0.75in (2cm) long

£200-250   **AnA**

Cylinder seals are small (2-6cm) cylinder-shaped stones carved with a decorative engraved design. The cylinder was rolled over wet clay to mark or identify clay tablets, envelopes, ceramics and bricks. The seals were used as a signature, confirmation of receipt, or to mark building blocks. Inscriptions are mostly carved in reverse, so they leave a positive image on the clay with figures standing out, although some are directly carved and leave a negative imprint.

A Sumerian black stone cylinder seal bead, with animal freize.
c3000 BC   0.75in (2cm) long

£180-200   **AnA**

A Sumerian stone stamp seal bead, in the form of a lion's head.
c3000 BC   0.75in (2cm) long

£300-350   **AnA**

A Sumerian white stone amulet, in the form of a male head.
c3000 BC   0.75in (2cm) long

£250-300   **AnA**

An Old Babylonian cylinder seal blue bead, with presentation scene in lapis lazuli.
c1700 BC   0.5in (1.5cm)

£200-250   **AnA**

An Old Babylonian haematite cylinder seal blue bead, with presentation scene.
c1700 BC   0.75in (2cm) long

£200-250   **AnA**

A pair of Mesopotamian solid gold hoop earrings.
c1000 BC   0.5in (1.5cm) diam

£200-250   **AnA**

A Luristan bronze bangle, with animal headed terminals.
c1000 BC   3.5in (9cm) diam

£65-75   **AnA**

Vases

A Trans-Jordon terracotta Amphoriskos, with line decoration.
c3000 BC   3in (8cm) high

£40-50   **AnA**

An early Bronze Age Trans-Jordon red burnished jar.
c3000 BC   8.25in (21cm) high

£100-125   **AnA**

An Early Bronze Age Trans-Jordan jar, in burnished red ware.
c3000 BC   4.25in (11cm) high

£250-300   **AnA**

An Luristan bronze bowl.
c8thC BC   6in (15cm) diam

£150-200   **AnA**

A Mesopotamian terracotta fertility figure, with bird-like features.
2000-1000 BC 6.25in (16cm) long

£180-200   **AnA**

A Sumerian alabaster bowl, with flared sides.
c3000 BC   7.75in (20cm) diam

£450-500   **AnA**

A cuneiform nail of Gudea, King of Lagash.
c2000 BC   *4.25in (11cm) long*

£150-175   **AnA**

A Northern Wei Dynasty terracotta figure, depicting a servant woman.
AD *386-533*   *6in (15cm) high*
£450-500   **AnA**

A Tang Dynasty terracotta figure of an armoured soldier, with original paint pigment.
AD *618-907* *11.5in (29cm) high*
£450-500   **AnA**

A Tang Dynasty part amber-glazed figure of a hooded soldier.
AD *618-907*   *11in (28cm) high*
£450-500   **AnA**

A Tang Dynasty part amber-glazed figure figure of an attendant.
AD *618-907 7.75in (20cm) high*
£450-500   **AnA**

A Han Dynasty soldier on horseback, with original paint pigment, iron rings around legs.
11.5in (29cm) high
£1,250-1,500   **AnA**

A Han Dynasty terracotta horse, with painted decoration, would originally have had wooden legs.
11.75in (30cm) wide
£700-750   **AnA**

A Tang Dynasty horse and rider on base, horse with open mouth, original paint pigment.
AD *618-907*   *12.25in (31cm) high*
£1,250-1,500   **AnA**

A Northern Wei Dynasty terracotta figure, of a camel reclining.
AD *386-533*   *8.25in (21cm) wide*
£700-750   **AnA**

A Song Dynasty Jian stoneware tea bowl, with 'hare's fur glaze'.
AD *1127-1279*   *4.25in (11cm) diam*
£80-100   **AnA**

Two Quing Dynasty Chinese hair pins, one white jade, the other coral, each with carved finial.
AD *1644-1911 Larger 6in (15.2cm) long*
£450-500   **SI**

A
B
C
D
E
F
G
H
I
J
K
L
M
N
O
P
Q
R
S
T
U
V
W
XYZ

- Due to the enormous variety, collectors should focus on building a collection of a specific area, such as political figures or film stars, although it can be fun to build a collection in a book based on first hand meetings, such as autograph signing events, or by mail.

- Many very famous people, who could not cope with the enormous amounts of requests, used their assistants and secretaries to sign autographs, so beware.

- Personal dedications, unless that person is also notable or connected to the star in some way, often make an autograph less desirable on the open market.

- Authenticity is vital. If you did not obtain the autograph yourself in person, ensure that the seller is reputable. Look closely at condition too, as tears, fading and other damage affect value and desirability.

- Signed letters and documents can have a historical importance depending on their date and content, increasing the value of the autograph alone. Such documents that actually relate to the reason why the person is famous will be more attractive to collectors.

- Collectors should avoid fads and buy autographs of personal or long-lived public interest. Autographs from people who captured the public imagination on an enduring basis, or who are renowned for their life or an event, are always likely to be sought after by more people, ensuring a strong and consistent value.

ABBA, four matching album pages signed in blue and black inks by each of the members of this enduring pop band, Bjorn adding the band's name to his signature, mounted together with a photograph of the Swedish popular music artists in their prime.

£420-480　　　　　　　　　　　　　　　　　　**FA**

Woody Allen, a white album page with a clear signature in pencil, with a faint pencil dedication to Stanley.

£80-120　　　　　**FA**

Gillian Anderson, a 10x8 still of Anderson as "The X-Files" "Dana Scully", signed across the lower right corner of the image in bold blue ink.

10in (25.5cm) high

£80-120　　　　**FA**

Ursula Andress, a 10x8 photograph of Andress, clearly signed in blue ink across the image.

10in (25.5cm) high

£100-150　　　**FA**

Jennifer Aniston, a white card signed in bold blue ink by this popular actress, mounted together with a photograph.

£80-120　　　　　**FA**

Brigitte Bardot, an attractive postcard-size photograph of Bardot in her prime, signed across a lower portion of the image in bold black ink.

£120-180　　**FA**

Tallulah Bankhead, a strong fountain pen signature, in black ink on an off-white album page, mounted together with a black and white photograph, folded, otherwise in fine condition.

£120-180　　　　　　　　　　　　**FA**

Kim Basinger, a 10x8 photograph, signed across a lower portion of the image in bold blue ink, with trademark heart to the end of the signature.

10in (25.5cm) high

£80-120　　　**FA**

P. T. Barnum, a lined white page with a fountain pen inscription in black ink which reads 'Truly Yours P.T. Barnum. American Museum New York Feb 4th 1865. To Simmon W. Stone', in fine general condition with single fold and very light smudging, neither of which effect the signature itself.

This legendary U.S. showman (1810-91) was famed for his flamboyant and innovative publicity built upon his central philosophy that 'there's a sucker born every minute'. In 1871, after a varied career as a promoter, Barnum continued the success of his New York 'museum' by taking to the road with 'The Greatest Show on Earth' comprising a circus, menagerie and an exhibition of freaks including 'General Tom Thumb' all conveyed from city to city by 100 railroad cars.

4.75in (12cm) wide

£720-780   FA

John Betjeman, a white page signed in bold green ink, mounted together with a photograph of Betjeman who succeeded Cecil Day-Lewis as Poet Laureate in 1972.

£120-180   FA

The Bee Gees, three matching white cards signed in blue ink by Maurice, Barry and Robin Gibb, mounted together with a photograph of the band.

£220-280   FA

Dirk Bogarde, a white page signed and inscribed with "Best Wishes" in blue fountain pen ink by one of Britain's most prolific and respected actors.

£100-150   FA

Enid Blyton, a postcard featuring a colour illustration of "The Six Cousins" and a facsimile signature from the author, on the reverse is a printed letter of thanks for a donation to a children's home at the close of which is a genuine signature from Blyton in blue ink, beside the printed message Blyton has also added a handwritten line "What a good idea to have a toffee raffle!", with post cancellation stamp dated January 6, 1957, with a heavy fold across the card.

£300-350   FA

Two James Bond related signatures, including individual clipped autograph album pages, signed Sean Connery and Gert Frobe, matted with a black and white image of Bond (Sean Connery) and Auric Goldfinger (Gert Frobe) playing golf, from "Goldfinger".

16in (41cm) wide

£300-350   CO

Ten James Bond "You Only Live Twice" related signatures, including ten individual clipped signatures of Sean Connery (James Bond), Bernard Lee (M), Lois Maxwell (Miss Moneypenny), Desmond Llewelyn (Q), Charles Gray (Henderson), Karin Dor (Helga Brandt), Donald Pleasence (Ernst Stavro Blofeld), Cubby Broccoli (producer), John Barry (composer), and Roald Dahl (screenplay), matted with small reproduction colour poster.

23in (58cm) high

£450-500   CO

Lloyd Bridges, a pale blue album page featuring a vintage fountain pen signature in blue ink mounted together with a photograph of the stage and screen actor.

£80-120   FA

Pierce Brosnan, a 10x8 photograph of Brosnan posing as James Bond with a large signature in bold blue ink along the right hand edge of the image.

10in (25.5cm) high

£100-150   FA

Leonardo di Caprio, a white card signed in bold blue ink, sold together with a colour photograph.

£80-120   FA

Barbara Cartland, a black and white photograph of the late romantic novelist, signed in her customary pink ink across the upper left corner of the image.

5.75in (14.5cm)

£40-60   FA

Agatha Christie, a pink page signed in black ink.

£420-480   FA

Winston Churchill, a clear signature in black ink on an off-white page, mounted, framed and glazed, with a portrait photograph.

£1,200-1,500   FA

Winston Churchill, a photograph signed and dated "Winston Churchill 1947", in blue ink, mounted, framed and glazed.

13in (33cm) high

£1,500-2,000   CO

Arthur C. Clark, a magazine photograph of the science fiction writer, signed and dated "22nd June 98" across a lighter portion of the image in bold black ink.

9in (23cm) high

£100-150   FA

Montgomery Clift, a vintage, unposed snapshot of a young Clift in a suit and tie walking along a street, signed across a lighter portion of the image in black fountain pen ink, with some creasing which does not affect the signature.

4.25in (10.5cm) high

£820-880   FA

George Clooney, a white card signed in blue ink, mounted together with a head-and-shoulders length, colour photograph of the popular actor.

£50-80   FA

Noel Coward, a clear signature in blue ink on an off-white page, mounted together with a photograph of the celebrated wit, playwright and actor.

£150-200   FA

Charles Darwin, a clear signature in black ink on an off-white page clipped from the close of a letter, mounted, framed, glazed, with a portrait.

£2,000-2,500   FA

William Frederick Cody, "Buffalo Bill", a handwritten letter in black ink over two sides of a sheet of "Buffalo Bill and the 101 Ranch Shows" headed stationery, dated 12th October 1916.

£2,000-2,500   FA

David Duchovny, a white album page signed in black ink, mounted together with a photograph of the actor best known as "Fox Mulder" in "The X Files".

£70-100   FA

Doris Day, a 10x8 studio photograph clearly signed by the great Oscar-winning American actress and singer in bold black ink across a lighter portion.

10in (25.5cm)

£80-120   FA

Clint Eastwood, a 10x8 photograph signed in bold blue ink.

10in (25.5cm) high

£100-150   FA

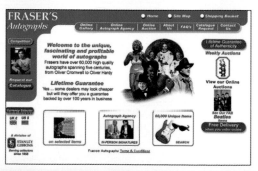

Britt Ekland, a white album page signed in blue ink.

£50-80 FA

Duke Ellington, a green album page dedicated to Linda, signed in blue ink by the great jazz musician and composer.

£200-250 FA

Douglas Fairbanks Jnr, a white page signed in blue ink by Fairbanks, the swash-buckling star of "The Prisoner of Zenda" and "Gunga Din".

£70-100 FA

Ella Fitzgerald, a white page signed "Sincerely Ella Fitzgerald" in blue ink mounted together with a photograph of the legendary jazz singer in her prime.

£220-280 FA

Errol Flynn, a hand-tinted publicity card of Errol Flynn and Olivia De Havilland in "The Adventures Of Robin Hood", signed "Hi, Errol Flynn" in black ink.

9in (23cm) high

£1,200-1,800 FA

Errol Flynn, an off-white album page signed and dedicated in black ink to Audrey, mounted together with a photograph of Flynn as he appeared in the 1935 swash-buckling adventure "Captain Blood".

£400-500 FA

Greta Garbo, a publicity photograph signed Greta Garbo in pencil, with additional printed signature, mounted, framed and glazed.

13in (33cm)

£500-600 FA

Jean Paul Gaultier, a hand-drawn sketch of a face in bold black ink on a white page, by the celebrated French fashion designer Jean-Paul Gaultier, signed and dated 98 by Gaultier below the sketch also in bold black ink.

9.75in (25cm)

£200-250 FA

Cary Grant, a yellow album page with a strong, clear signature in blue ink from Grant. Mounted, framed and glazed together with a photograph of this unique British actor.

£720-780 FA

William Randolph Hearst, American newspaper owner and inspiration for the Orson Welles film classic "Citizen Kane". A clear signature in black ink on an off-white album page. Mounted, framed and glazed together with a photograph of Hearst.

£700-1,000 FA

Ernest Hemingway, an envelope signed 'From E. Hemingway' in the return address (in Cuba), addressed to a gentleman in Copenhagen, Denmark, postmarked 31st December 1946. With two file holes not affecting the text or signature and some smudging affecting the 'g' and 'w' of Hemingway, a good example of a rare and sought-after signature, mounted, framed and glazed together with a photograph of the celebrated author best known for works such as "A Farewell to Arms", 1929 and "For Whom the Bell Tolls", 1940.

£2,000-3,000 FA

Alfred Hitchcock, a copy of the 1967 publication "Hitchcock" by Francis Truffaut. The book which documents Hitchcock's life and works through the form of interview transcripts is signed and dedicated to Harry Wilkinson by Hitchcock across one of the opening pages in black ink, Hitchcock has added his trademark self-caricature above the signature, also in black ink.

£1,500-2,000 FA

David Hockney, a 10x8, (landscape), half length, black and white photograph of the Bradford-born British artist associated with the Pop Art movement from his earliest work. Signed at the base of the image in bold blue ink. Mounted framed and glazed.

£300-500   **FA**

Bob Hope, a white card signed in bold blue ink by the veteran comedian. Mounted together with a half length, colour photograph of Hope in his prime.

£120-180   **FA**

Rock Hudson, a pale pink album page dedicated to Esther and signed in blue ink by Rock Hudson. With an undedicated signature in blue ink from American stage star Dolores Gray.

£150-200   **FA**

George Lucas, A white card signed in black ink. Mounted together with a photograph of the creator of 'Star Wars'.

£120-180   **FA**

Shirley Maclaine, A white card clearly signed in black ink by this unique, Academy Award-winning actress. Mounted together with a photograph.

£100-150   **FA**

Elle MacPherson, a white card signed with her first name only in bold blue ink. Mounted together with a photograph of the Australian supermodel.

£100-150   **FA**

Marilyn Monroe, a United Airlines DC-7 postcard, signed and dedicated on the reverse "To Judy Love & Kisses Marilyn Monroe", in blue ballpoint pen, matted together with a colour image of the actress.

16 x 12in (41 x 30cm)

£2,500-3,000   **CO**

Marilyn Monroe, a cheque drawn on the 'Bankers Trust Company' New York dated the 11th August 1961, made payable for the sum of one hundred and twenty seven pounds and ninety cents to a May Reis. Signed in blue ink by Monroe, the cheque is stamped as paid and has perforation holes which do not affect the signature. An excellent example of a highly sought after signature, mounted framed and glazed together with a photograph of the goddess of the silver screen.

£4,000-6,000   **FA**

Dudley Moore, an off-white card signed and inscribed in blue ink, 'With best wishes from Dudley Moore' by the late British actor and comedian.

£100-150   **FA**

Kate Moss, a white card signed in bold black ink mounted together with a photograph of the British supermodel.

£80-120   **FA**

Stirling Moss, a typed letter on a single side of a sheet of personalised stationery, the letter dated 4th May 1971, with folds to fit an envelope which do not affect the signature.

£120-180   **FA**

Ivor Novello, a clear signature in black ink on the back of a cheque dated 20th February 1950 made payable to Novello for the sum of one pound and eleven shillings from Esme Percy, popular British stage and screen actress of the 1930's and 1940's, appearing in films such as Hitchcock's 1930 classic "Murder". Mounted together with a photograph of Novello.

£70-100   **FA**

Al Pacino, a white card signed in bold blue ink by the famous Hollywood actor, star of films such as "Scarface" and "The Godfather". Mounted together with a photograph.

£100-150   **FA**

Nick Park, a white cotton handkerchief embroidered with a picture of Gromit the dog. Above, is an original drawing in bold black ink, of Wallace by the duo's Oscar winning creator Nick Park. Also signed by Park in black ink.

£600-1,000 FA

Brad Pitt, a white card signed in bold blue ink by Pitt mounted together with a photograph of the popular actor.

£100-150 FA

Cole Porter, the uniquely talented American composer and lyricist. A clear, fountain pen signature in blue ink on a pale green page.

£700-1,000 FA

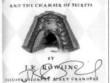

J. K. Rowling, a hardback copy of the 1998 publication "Harry Potter and the Chamber of Secrets" signed on the title page in black ink by author J.K. Rowling. In fine condition, a good example of a rare and extremely sought after signature on one her most popular publications.

£1,100-1,400 FA

Charles Schultz, a lined white index card (approx. 8.5x13cm) featuring a small original drawing of Snoopy in blue ink by his much admired creator. Clearly signed in same pen to the right of the sketch as 'Charles M. Schultz'.

£1,200-1,800 FA

Steven Spielberg, a white card signed in black ink, mounted together with a photograph of the massively successful film director.

£100-150 FA

Jerry Seinfeld, a 10x8, almost full length, colour photograph of actor and comedian Jerry Seinfeld jumping to reach a microphone. Signed across the lower right corner of the image in bold blue ink.

£100-150 FA

Peter Sellers, a mounted pale yellow card featuring a large fountain pen signature, dedicated to Terry, in blue ink from the great British comedian. A sought after signature.

£220-280 FA

Frank Sinatra, a yellow album page signed in blue ink by the great singer and film star. Mounted, framed and glazed together with a black and white head-and-shoulders length photograph of Sinatra.

£800-1,200 FA

Quentin Tarantino, a white card signed in black ink by the celebrated director, producer, screenwriter and actor, mounted with a photograph.

£100-150 FA

Star Trek, a collection of seven individual album pages signed by major Star Trek cast members: Shatner, Takei, Nicholls, Kelly, Koenig, Doohan and Nimoy (signed "Live Long and Prosper!"). Mounted, framed and glazed together with a cast photograph.

£700-1,000 FA

Mother Teresa, a postcard size, head and shoulders length, black and white photograph, signed and inscribed "God Bless You, M Teresa MC", in blue ink below the image.

£700-1,000 FA

John Travolta, a white card signed in bold black ink, together with a photograph.

£120-180 FA

CAR MASCOTS

- Car mascots were made to be screwed on top of car radiators. There are three main categories. Accessory mascots forms include animals, good luck symbols, figures and characters. Manufacturer mascots were mascots used by car manufacturers to adorn their cars, eg; Rolls Royce's 'Spirit of Ecstasy'. Finally, advertising mascots were used by parts manufacturers to advertise their products, such as Mr Bibendum, used by tyre maker Michelin.

- Although ships have long had figureheads to guide the ship onwards safely, the first car mascot is reputed to have been used by legendary car enthusiast Lord Montagu of Beaulieu on his 1899 Daimler.

- Most early mascots are accessory mascots with devils, elves and lucky horseshoes being popular forms. Many were satirical or whimsical in inspiration, or meant to bring good fortune. Characters such as Disney's Mickey Mouse are later extensions of these whimsical feelings.

- Many mascots represent and evoke certain attributes such as speed, usually portrayed by flying birds or nymphs. Lions represented strength. Postures are often heroic and 'point' forwards 'conquering' the oncoming roads.

- Early mascots are usually made from brass or bronze. More 'fragile' die cast mascots made from zinc and magnesium alloys came later, but the majority are made from long-lived metals. Glass was also used, with the most famous maker being Lalique. Other names who used glass to look for are Red Ashay and Sabino of Paris, which are generally less expensive than Lalique examples.

- Maker's marks are important, look for Souest, Ashay, Bazin, Finnigans and A & E Lejeune (AEL). Unmarked examples showing excellent modelling, detailing and a good pose will also be desirable.

- Details should be crisp with original plating. Replating and over-polishing removes original patination and will reduce value and desirability. Some of the die-cast mascots used a 'fragile' metallo bronze, which shows fatigue after 80 years. This should be minimal on the best examples. Clearly, fragile glass mascots should not show chips or cracks.

- Good quality, early mascots fetch very high prices today. Some of the more common types from the 1920s can be found for under $200, but attention is now turning to mascots from the 1940s and 1950s. Reproductions are common, which are usually heavier and less finely detailed than originals.

A rare 'Emily' car mascot, by Rolls-Royce Ltd.

£280-320   **TK**

A rare 'Femme-chauve-souris' mascot, by E. Famin, finished in heavy bronze, signed.

1922   *5.5in (14cm) high*

£2,000-2,500   **FFA**

A winged goddess car mascot, created by Ch. Soudant, finished in silvered bronze with Susse Fres. foundry markings.

Known under the name 'Prouesse', when originally retailed in France. An extremely rare mascot and the most impressive version of the two sizes produced. Used as an accessory mascot for the Rubay Automobile from 1922-1924 only.

1922-1924   *7in (18cm) long*

£5,000-7,000   **FFA**

A butterfly girl car mascot, by Red Ashay, in satin finish glass. This figure is one of five designs registered by Red Ashay between April 1928 and April 1931.

7.5in (19cm) high

£3,000-4,000   **FFA**

A winged nude Egyptian car mascot, by Coudray, signed to base "S. Coudray", marked "9" to rear on base.

1910   *9.5in (24.5cm) wide*

£9,000-12,000   **FFA**

A rare Icarus car mascot, by Colin George, silvered bronze, with foundry stampings from Cotenot & Lelièvre, cartouche and numbers to the rear of the base, also signed Colin George to side of lower drape.

c1925   6in (15cm) high

£1,800-2,500	**FFA**

A nude riding a broomstick car mascot, created by Franz Bergman, Austria, heavy bronze with original enamel highlight, signed "NamGreb", Bergman backwards.

This is one of the few mascots Bergman created and is unrecorded.

c1910   20.5in (52.5cm) high

£3,000-4,000	**FFA**

A 'Sirène' car mascot, by George Colin, silver-plated French nickel bronze, on original marble base, signed "G. Colin", foundry mark for Cotenot & Lelièvre and "2348" and "10" on the side.

This piece was marketed by Hermes in 1922-1925 and was awarded a medal by L'Auto in 1922.

1922-25   7in (18cm) high

£9,000-12,000	**FFA**

An Art Deco car mascot, by Varnier, silvered bronze, with period cap.

Two sizes were originally produced, this is the largest of them.

c1920   6in (15.5cm) high

£5,000-6,000	**FFA**

A glass Chrysis car mascot, by Red Ashay.

c1928   7in (18cm) high

£9,000-12,000	**FFA**

A glass Speed Head car mascot, by Red Ashay.

Based on Lalique's 'Victoire' design.

1929   5in (13cm) high

£3,000-4,000	**FFA**

A fine glass racing driver car mascot, by Red Ashay, mounted on filtered radiator cap with a propellor that rotates, turning the coloured filters within it.

c1930   5.5in (14cm)

£5,000-7,000	**FFA**

A Gregoire 'Archer Egyptienne' car mascot, by M. Guiraud Riviere, bronze, with full base markings, signature, date and "Depose French" stamp.

1918-1924 6.75in (17cm) high

£5,000-7,000	**FFA**

A rare Nostradamus car mascot, by A. Loir, heavy bronze.

c1920   8.5in (22cm) high

£4,000-5,000	**FFA**

An 'amour frileux' car mascot, by F. Bazin, heavy silvered bronze, signed 'F. Bazin'.

This design is usually seen as a deskpiece rather than a car mascot.

c1920   6in (15cm) high

£2,000-3,000	**FFA**

An American Indian car mascot, attributed to Frederick Bazin.

c1920

£5,000-7,000	**FFA**

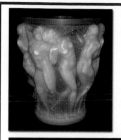

Finesse Fine Art

Empool Cottage, West Knighton,
Dorset, DT2 8PE, England.

Tel: +44 (0)1305 854286
Mobile: +44 (0)7973 886937

Email: tony@finesse-fine-art.com
Web: www.finesse-fine-art.com

LALIQUE & AUTOMOBILIA WANTED

● Exceptional signed metal and glass mascots, to include ALL René Lalique mascots. I am at present assembling the World's finest collection of car mascots on behalf of a private museum, and will pay exceptional prices for the very best pieces. Also required for major private collection - Pre-war motoring items and bronzes, deskpieces, finest automobilia, plus all pre-war René Lalique top glassware.

● Photos on this page show a few recent purchases, similar items ALWAYS required. If you have any piece you feel will interest me, please call. I am an enthusiastic and serious buyer.

● I have ample funds immediately available for the purchase of single items or complete collections and will travel anywhere in the world for the finest pieces. Absolute confidentiality and discretion always assured. Please phone anytime.

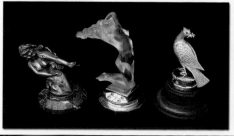

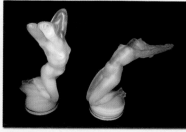

A rare satin glass female charioteer car mascot, by Red Ashay, mounted on original radiator cap.

A harlequin resting on a moon car mascot, by Mady, silvered bronze, signed.

c1920   *4.75in (12cm) high*

£5,000-6,000   FFA

A rare 'The Kid' car mascot, by Jean Verschneider, heavy nickel bronze with ivory face, deciptng Jackie Coogan, signed "J. Verschneider" on base with "The Kid" logo to the front, small chip to side of nose.

Car mascots with ivory faces are very rare.

1925   6in (15cm) high

£10,000-12,000   FFA

A racing driver car mascot, sculpted and designed by Boccazzi, in silver-plated bronze.

c1920

£5,000-7,000   FFA

Lalique made a similar mascot called 'Cinq Cheveaux' exclusively for Citroen and Red Ashay decided to incorporate a charioteer into their own design and made it three dimensional, based around five galloping horses pulling a chariot, created in semi Art Deco form.

c1928   6.75in (17.cm) wide

£8,000-10,000   FFA

A bird car mascot, by Bouraine, heavy bronze with ivory beak, signed with foundry stamping, age cracks to ivory.

PROVENANCE: This mascot came directly from the Bouraine family.

7.5in (19cm) high

£4,000-7,000   FFA

An Hispano Suiza car mascot, by Frederick Bazin, silvered bronze on a marble base.

c1919   9in (22cm) high

£3,000-4,000   FFA

An eagle car mascot, by Casimir Brau, nickel bronze, signed.

c1925   8.25in (21cm) high

£2,000-2,500   FFA

A 'Coq Gaulois' car mascot, signed by Charles Paillet, gilded bronze on original French radiator cap.

1920-24 6.75in (17.5cm) high

£2,000-2,500   FFA

An Art Deco horse car mascot, by Casimir Brau, heavy silvered bronze.

This is the larger and rarer of the two sizes produced. It was retailed by Hermes and featured in their 1925 catalogue.

A hare and tortoise car mascot, signed C. Seul, cast in bronze with integral cap, dated.

1911   5in (13cm) high

£2,500-3,000   FFA

A 1920s hare car mascot, by Henri Payen, two-tone bronze.

5.5in (14cm) high

£3,000-4,000   FFA

A hare on tortoise car mascot, by Petrilly, heavy silvered bronze, signed in base, with full base inscription.

c1920 6.75in (17.5cm) high

£3,000-4,000   FFA

1925   8.25in (21cm) long

£3,000-4,000   FFA

A horse's head car mascot, by Bregeon, silvered bronze, signed.

c1925   4.75in (12cm) high

£1,500-2,500   FFA

A Peugeot lion car mascot, by R. Baudichon, signed on the base.

1923   7.25in (18.5cm) long

£1,500-2,500   FFA

A butterfly car mascot, by Frederick Bazin, silvered bronze mounted on original French radiator cap, signed 'Bazin'.

c1920   5in (13cm) high

£2,500-3,500   FFA

A cat on the moon car mascot, by Etienne Mercier, mounted in period French radiator cap, signed on base.

This is an unrecorded variation, the cat usually sits on the base of the moon.

c1925   4.75in (12cm) high

£5,000-7,000   FFA

A 'La Sagesse' car mascot, created by A. Delm, depicting the three wise monkeys.

£8,000-10,000   FFA

A 1930s 'Mickey Mouse' car mascot, by Desmo, finished in bronze.

4.5in (11.5cm) high

£6,000-7,000   FFA

A late 1920s bronze Mickey Mouse car mascot, marked "Reproduced by Consent of Walter. E. Disney".

£9,000-12,000   FFA

A 'Felix the Cat' car mascot, produced by A. E. Le Jeune, heavy nickel bronze, with copyright stamp.

c1926   6in (15.5cm) high

£2,000-2,500   FFA

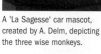

A Bibendum 'Scrutant L'Horizon' car mascot, by Ets Generes, Paris, heavily silvered metallo bronze, marked "Generes et Cie" and "Made in France" under the base and "Michelin Cable" on the tyre.

4.5in (11.5cm) high

£5,000-8,000   FFA

A devil car mascot, by Gelas, two-tone gilt on bronze highlighted with silver, signed on base.

c1920   4.5in (11.5cm) high

£10,000-12,000   FFA

A 'chat botte' car mascot, by Antoine Bofill, with Bofill signature and "MAM" foundry stamp.

£8,000-10,000   FFA

A racing Renault car mascot, sculpted by Verecke and produced exclusively for Garage Ponthieu, mounted on an original Renault radiator cap.

c1925   5.25in (13.5cm) long

£5,000-7,000   FFA

A 1920s Junior Racing Drivers' Club radiator badge, by the Birmingham Medal Company, mounted on an old racing car piston.

7.5in (19cm) high

£1,000-1,500   FFA

A
B
C
D
E
F
G
H
I
J
K
L
M
N
O
P
Q
R
S
T
U
V
W
XYZ

A rare pair of 1920s Carl Zeiss nickel plated fork-mounted head lamps.

These lamps are rare as they are fork mounted – the vast majority of Zeiss lamps had pillar mountings. These were made specifically for use on the Speed 6 Bentley.

12in (30.5cm) diam

£6,000-8,000　　　　　　　　　　　**FFA**

A pair of Lucas P100 lamps, restored.

1932-35

£2,500-3,000　　　**FFA**

A pair of Lucas QK596 hazard lamps.

Reproductions are common at present, and buyers should be aware that they are being passed off as original.

£5,000-6,000　　　**FFA**

A pair of Lucas sidelamps, restored.
c1910

£1,000-1,500　　　　　　　　**FFA**

A pair of 1930s Lucas long windtone trumpet horns, restored.

£900-1,200　　**FFA**

A pair of Lucas P100DB "bullseye" head lamps, restored.
1928-32

£5,000-6,000　　　**FFA**

A pair of Lucas R100 lamps, restored.

1938-39

£2,000-2,500　　　**FFA**

A rare pair of Zeiss spotlamps, restored.

Carl Zeiss of Jena, Germany is a renowned optical company that also made camera lenses and cameras, microscopes and binoculars.

1929

£6,000-8,000　　　　　　　　　**FFA**

A pair of Lucas sidelamps, restored.
c1910

£1,000-1,500　　　　　　　　　**FFA**

A pair of Lucas ST44/N rear lamps, restored.
1928-38

£1,500-2,000　　　　　　　　　**FFA**

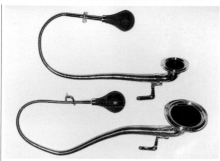

Two "boa constrictor" car horns.
1910-20

Smaller £1,000-1,500, Larger £1,500-2,000　　　　FFA

An early car radio, for General Motors, with loudspeakers and five valve-set for medium and short wave reception.

£30-40　　　　TK

A 1920s WMF inkwell and pen rest, in the form of a racing car.

£5,000-6,000　　　　FFA

A driving school demonstration model, with working engine, lights and steering mechanism.

51in (130cm) long

£300-350　　　　TK

An NBC (National Benzole Company Ltd) Lubricants oil can.

£25-35　　　　DH

A tobacco box, in the form of racing car driver with turned-up collar and goggles.
c1909

£1,000-1,500　　　　FFA

A 1930s tinplate Rolls Royce model, in box.

£1,500-2,000　　　　FFA

A Studebaker Carriages Trade Catalogue, with lithographed illustrations and printed paper wraps, minor soiling on cover.
1899

£160-200　　　　CHAA

A CLOSER LOOK AT A BRONZE SCULPTURE

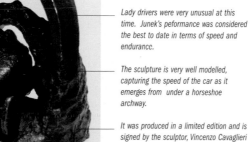

This fine sculpture was produced in 1928 to celebrate the racing achievements of the Czechoslovakian Elizabeth Junek in the Targa Florio race in 1927.

Lady drivers were very unusual at this time. Junek's peformance was considered the best to date in terms of speed and endurance.

The sculpture is very well modelled, capturing the speed of the car as it emerges from under a horseshoe archway.

It was produced in a limited edition and is signed by the sculptor, Vincenzo Cavaglieri on the rear.

A bronze sculpture of a Bugatti racing through a horseshoe bridge.
Provenance: Ex Raymond E. Holland Automotive Art Collection.
1928

£8,000-10,000　　　　FFA

The Modern Motorcar Magazine, with Maurice Beck on cover, produced by Shell.
1937　　*13.5in (34.5cm) high*

£30-35　　　　DH

Amis, Kingsley, "I Like It Here", first edition published by Gollancz, London, spine slightly darkened.
1958

£50-60 **PB**

Amis, Martin, "Success", first edition of the author's third book and signed on the title page, published by Jonathan Cape.
1978

£200-250 **PB**

Amis, Martin, "The Rachel Papers", first edition published by Jonathan Cape, minor spotting to some pages, slightly creased on back panel and spine, price clipped.

1973

£500-550 **PB**

Ballard, J.G. "The Disaster Area", first edition, published by Jonathan Cape, scattered foxing to edges, small red ink marks on front free endpaper and a few red scribbles on rear endpapers, spine faded and extremities rubbed.

1967

£30-50 **PB**

MODERN FIRST EDITIONS

- First editions represent the original version of the book and are widely collected. Some later editions are collected but these must have important additional material. Be careful that the book is a true first edition and not a later reprint or a book club version.
- Condition is vital when considering collecting – the most sought-after books are in as fine condition as the day they were sold.
- The presence of the original dust cover is highly important – values of the same book with and without the dust wrapper will usually vary widely.
- Creases and tears to the dust cover must also be considered and can affect value. A mint copy of a first edition may command a very large premium.
- Any notes, inscriptions and dedications will usually devalue a book – exceptions being if an inscription relates to or is by a famous previous owner or if the book is signed by the author.
- First editions of popular books that captured the public's imagination will generally be desirable. This includes Ian Fleming's James Bond, Agatha Christie's detective stories and J.K. Rowling's Harry Potter stories. A first edition of "The Philosopher's Stone", signed by J.K. Rowling, fetched £13,000.

Barber, Willetta Ann and Schabelitz, R.F "Murder Enters the Picture", first edition, published by Doubleday Crime Club, Garden City, NY, edges worn and chipped, back panel faded.
1942

£50-60 **PB**

Barnes, Julian (as Dan Kavanagh), "Fiddle City", first edition, published by Jonathan Cape, London, the second of the Duffy detective novels.

1981

£80-110 **PB**

Bentley, E.C., "Elephant's Work", first US edition, published by Knopf, New York, back panel slightly dusty.
1950

£40-50 **PB**

Berkeley, Anthony, "Not to be Taken", first edition, published by Hodder & Stoughton, London, published in the US by Doubleday as "A Puzzle in Poison", pale blue boards a little faded in places, very slightly cocked, top edge a trifle dusty with some faint foxing, short tears at spine, neatly repaired at foot, spine and back panel slightly darkened, a scarce book, especially in the dust jacket.
1938

£700-750 **PB**

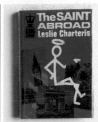

De Bernières, Louis, "Captain Corelli's Mandolin", first edition, published by Secker & Warburg, London, signed by the author on the title page, first issue white boards, usual tanning to edges, vertical crease to inner rear flap.
1994

£600-650 PB

De Bernières, Louis, "The Troublesome Offspring of Cardinal Guzman", first edition, published by Secker & Warburg, London, signed and dated by the author on the title page, usual faint browning to page edges.
1992

£200-250 PB

Burton, Miles (John Rhode), "The Cat Jumps", first edition, published by Collins Crime Club, light vertical crease to front free endpaper, spine slightly bumped, spine darkened, slight wear to top edge.
1946

£100-140 PB

Charteris, Leslie, "The Saint Abroad", first edition, published by Hodder & Stoughton, London.

1970

£100-150 PB

Christie, Agatha, "Destination Unknown", first edition, published by Collins Crime Club, London, margins of pages slightly browned, spine slightly rubbed, back panel dusty and faintly browning, price clipped.
1954

£40-50 PB

Christie, Agatha, "4.50 from Paddington", first edition, published by Collins Crime Club, London, top edge slightly browned, spine slightly darkened and one small closed tear at spine.
1957

£40-50 PB

Christie, Agatha, "Ordeal by Innocence", first edition, published by Collins Crime Club, London, spine very slightly bumped and faint offsetting to endpapers, small stain to top edge, back panel slightly soiled with small closed tear, slight wear to spine.
1958

£40-50 PB

Cornwell, Bernard, "Sharpe's Gold", first edition, published by Collins, London, signed by the author on the title page, edges slightly dusty, head of spine very slightly rubbed, inner flaps very faintly spotted.
1981

£200-250 PB

Cumberland, Marten, "The Man Who Covered Mirrors", first edition, published by Doubleday Crime Club, Garden City, NY, pages browned, spine and edges very slightly rubbed.
1949

£30-40 PB

Derleth, August, "In Re: Sherlock Holmes", The Adventures of Solar Pons, first US edition, published by Mycroft and Moran, Sauk City, the first hardcover collection of Derleth's Sherlock Holmes pastiches, spine and edges slightly browned, back panel dusty and price clipped.
1945

£80-110 PB

Dexter, Colin, "The Secret of Annexe 3", first edition, published by Macmillan, London, signed by the author on the title page, edges of pages sunning slightly, with minimal sunning to top edge.
1986

£300-350 PB

Dexter, Colin, "Last Seen Wearing", first edition, published by Macmillan, London, the second Inspector Morse novel, usual faint tanning to pages.
1976

£900-950 PB

Donleavy, J.P., "A Singular Man", first US edition, published by Atlantic-Little, Brown, Boston, precedes the UK edition, author's second novel, slight fading to boards, slight wear to top edge.

1963

£20-30 PB

Douglas, Norman, "Birds and Beasts of the Greek Anthology", first US edition, published by Jonathan Cape and Harrison Smith, New York, two small, closed tears and top of spine chipped and worn.

1929

£30-40 PB

Douglas, Norman, "In the Beginning", first US edition, published by John Day, New York, original white spine and decorated paper boards, fore-edge and tail uncut, half title page has a tiny nick to edge, very faint offsetting to endpapers.

1928

£80-100 PB

Farjeon, J. Jefferson, "Peril in the Pyrenees", first edition, published by Collins Crime Club, London, edges foxed, two small closed tears, extremities slightly worn.

1946

£60-70 PB

Faulks, Sebastian, "A Trick of the Light", first edition, published by Bodley Head, London, very slight wear to top edge.

1984

£500-600 PB

Fleming, Ian, "From Russia with Love", first edition, published by Jonathan Cape, London, extremities and spine slightly rubbed and chipped, back panel slightly soiled, price clipped.

1957

£450-500 PB

Greene, Graham, "A Sense of Reality", first edition, published by Bodley Head, London, price clipped.

1963

£70-80 PB

Gribble, Leonard R., "The Grand Modena Murder", first edition, published by Doubleday Crime Club, Garden City, New York, the third Inspector Slade Detective Story, slight foxing to fore-edge, slight wear at spine, a scarce title.

1931

£100-150 PB

Grierson, Edward, "A Crime of One's Own", first edition, published by Chatto & Windus, London, slight rubbing and browning to edges and spine with one small closed tear, from the library of Peter Apap Bologna with his bookplate on the front pastedown.

1967

£30-40 PB

Harris, Robert, "Fatherland", first edition, published by Hutchinson, London, signed by author on the title page, slightly sunned and very slight wear to top edge.

1992

£120-180 PB

Highsmith, Patricia, "This Sweet Sickness", first UK edition, published by Heinemann, London, previous owner's neat ink inscription on front free endpaper, edges and preliminaries slightly foxed, spine and edges of dust jacket sunned, very slight wear to top edge, back panel dusty.

1961

£40-50 PB

Highsmith, Patricia, "The Blunderer", first UK edition, published by Cresset, London, worn at extremities, back panel dusty.

Highsmith is well known for her homicidal character Tom Ripley who appeared in a series of books starting with "The Talented Mr Ripley".

1956

£120-180 PB

Irish, William (Woolrich, Cornell), "The Dancing Detective", first edition, published by Lippincott, Philadelphia, spine slightly bumped, tanning to edges of pages, extremities worn, head and foot of spine chipped with slight creases to head of front panel.

1946

£180-220　　　PB

Irish, William (Woolrich, Cornell), "Somebody on the Phone", first edition, published by Lippincott, New York, top edge very faintly tanned and head of spine very slightly bumped, back panel slightly dusty with faint foxing on the outer edge, a scarce title.

1940

£600-700　　　PB

James, P.D., "The Skull Beneath the Skin", first edition, published by Faber & Faber, London, signed by the author on the title page.

1982

£70-80　　　PB

Lees-Milne, James, "Midway on the Waves", first edition, published by Chatto & Windus, London, fourth volume of the author's diaries, covering his work for the National Trust in 1948 and 1949.

1985

£20-30　　　PB

Leon, Donna, "Death in a Strange Country" first edition, published by Chapmans, London, the author's second novel.

1993

£100-130　　　PB

Marsh, Ngaio, "Died in the Wool", first edition, published by Collins Crime Club, London, owner's tiny inscription on front free endpaper, edges tanned, back panel darned.

1945

£80-120　　　PB

Melville, James, "The Wages of Zen", first edition, published by Secker & Warburg, London, signed by the author on the title page, Melville's first novel featuring Inspector Otani, price clipped by the publisher with price sticker on the flap, it appears to have offset onto the front free endpaper leaving a faint mark.

1979

£50-60　　　PB

Mortimer, John, "Charade", first edition, published by Bodley Head, London, the first book from the creator of Rumpole of the Bailey, a review copy with the publisher's slip laid in, top edge very slightly darkened and rubbed.

1947

£100-160　　　PB

Murdoch, Iris, "The Italian Girl", first edition, published by Chatto & Windus, London, back panel dusty.

1964

£40-60　　　PB

O'Brian, Patrick, "The Fortune of War", first edition, published by Collins, London, the sixth Jack Aubrey novel, spine very slightly faded.

1979

£280-320　　　PB

O'Brian, Patrick, "H.M.S. Surprise", first edition, published by Collins, London, the third book in the Jack Aubrey series, very slight browning to top edge and spine slightly faded with one very small closed tear.

1973

£450-500　　　PB

Paretsky, Sara, "Indemnity Only", first edition, published by Gollancz, London.

1982

£100-130　　　PB

Peake, Mervyn, "Shapes and Sounds", first edition, published by Chatto & Windus, London, dust jacket designed by the author, fore and top edges foxed, spine tanned, lower covers slightly foxed and worn at edges.

1941

£200-240 PB

Peters, Ellis, "The Sanctuary Sparrow: The Seventh Chronicle of Brother Cadfael", first edition, published by Macmillan, London.

1983

£120-180 PB

Powell, Anthony, "Books do Furnish a Room", first edition, published by Heinemann, London, tenth in series "A Dance to the Music of Time".

1971

£50-80 PB

Rankin, Ian, "The Black Book", first edition, published by Orion, London, the fifth Inspector Rebus novel, signed by the author on the title page, an unpriced export copy.

1993

£100-150 PB

FIND OUT MORE...

www.abebooks.com

www.biblion.com

Antiquarian Booksellers' Association of America www.abaa.org

Antiquarian Booksellers' Association www.aba.org.uk

Rankin, Ian, "Westwind", first edition, published by Barrie & Jenkins, London, inscribed by the author on the title page with his hangman sketch, as new.

1990

£250-300 PB

Rendell, Ruth, "No More Dying Then", first edition, published by Hutchinson, London.

1971

£200-240 PB

Rendell, Ruth, "A Sleeping Life", first edition, published by Macmillan, London.

1978

£50-70 PB

Rendell, Ruth, "Shake Hands for Ever", first edition, published by Hutchinson, London, slight eraser marks on the front free endpaper, a trifle worn at corners and spine.

1975

£100-130 PB

Rowling, J.K., "Harry Potter and the Chamber of Secrets", first edition, published by Bloomsbury, London, one corner and spine very slightly bumped.

1998

£1,800-2,200 PB

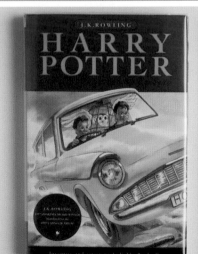

Salinger, J.D., "Franny and Zooey", first edition, published by Heinemann, London, white areas slightly dusty, spine sunned to blue with some very faint loss of colour at head and foot, one small closed tear on back panel.

1962

£40-60 PB

Seymour, Gerald, "Harry's Game", first edition, published by Collins, London, the author's first book.
1975
£100-125 PB

Smith, Zadie, "White Teeth" first edition, published by Hamish Hamilton, London, signed by the author on the title page, as new.
2000
£100-125 PB

Steinbeck, John, "Winter of our Discontent", first edition, published by Viking, New York, lightly sunned.
1961
£100-140 PB

Swift, Graham, "Waterland", first edition, published by Heinemann, London, nominated for the Booker Prize, as new.
1983
£100-130 PB

Vickers, Roy, "Murdering Mr Velfrage", first edition, published by Faber, London, corners and spine chipped, spine darkened.
1950
£40-50 PB

Walters, Minette, "The Ice House", first edition, published by Macmillan, London, the author's first novel.
1992
£550-650 PB

Walters, Minette, "The Sculptress", first edition, published by Macmillan, London, signed and dated by the author on the title page, the author's second book, very faint tanning to edges of pages.
1993
£70-90 PB

Waugh, Evelyn, "Brideshead Revisited", first edition, published by Chapman & Hall, London, boards slightly faded, spine and corners bumped and edges foxed, rather soiled, worn and chipped at the corners and spine but reinforced and presentable.
1945
£400-450 PB

Waugh, Evelyn, "Black Mischief", first edition, published by Chapman & Hall, London, slight stain to fore-edge, chipped and creased at head of spine but without loss to title, slight soiling and spine darkened, scarce in the dust jacket.
1932
£400-500 PB

Wilson, A.N., "The Sweets of Pimlico", first edition, published by Secker & Warburg, London, the author's first book.
1977
£180-220 PB

Wingfield, R.D., "Night Frost", first edition, published by Constable, London, as new.
1992
£300-400 PB

Winterson, Jeanette, "Sexing the Cherry", first edition, published by Bloomsbury, London, presentation copy signed by the author on the title page, as new.
1989
£80-120 PB

Attwell, Mabie Lucie, "Lucie Atwell's A B C Pop-up Book", Dean, illustrated glazed boards with simple pop-ups, colour illustrations throughout, very good condition.
1960

£30-40 | Bib

Awdry, The Rev. W., "The Little Old Engine – Railway Series No. 14", Edmund Ward, illustrations by John T. Kenney.
1959

£65-75 | Bib

Awdry, The Rev. W., "Very Old Engines - Railway Series No. 20", Edmund Ward, illustrations by Gunvor and Peter Edwards.
1965

£70-90 | Bib

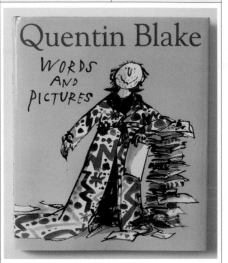

Barker, C.M., "Flower Fairies of the Summer", Blackie, with dust jacket, clean with little loss to head and tail of spine.
c1940

£55-65 | Bib

Blake, Quentin, "Words and Pictures", Chris Beetles Ltd, features pictures from 20 years of publication, signed, with very slight bumped spine, colour illustrations, large format.
2000

£35-45 | Bib

Blyton, Enid, "The Secret Seven", The Brockhampton Press Ltd, first edition with illustrations by George Brook.
1949

£80-120 | Bib

Blyton, Enid, "You Funny Little Noddy", Sampson Low, Marston & Co., first edition.
1955

£20-30 | Bib

Briggs, Raymond, "Father Christmas Goes on Holiday", Sir Joseph Causton & Sons, first edition.
1975

£40-60 | Bib

Browning, Robert, "The Pied Piper of Hamelin", Routledge & Sons, with illustrations by Kate Greenaway.

£120-180   Bib

De Brunhoff, Jean, "The Story of Babar, The Little Elephant", Methuen, with a preface by A.A. Milne.
1934

£100-155   Bib

Dickens, Charles, "The Magic Fishbone", Fredrick Warne & Co. Ltd, first published 1868, illustrations by F. D. Bedford.

£45-55   Bib

Disney, Walt, "Dumbo, Only His Ears Grew - The Better Little Books", Whitman Publishing, based on the motion picture, illustrated in black and white and with moving picture effect in the corner, with slight chipping at spine.
1941

£100-200   Bib

FIND OUT MORE...
George Edwards Library, E.H. Shepard Archive, University of Surrey, Guildford, GU2 7XH.

National Center for Children's Illustrated Literature: www.nccil.org

Crompton, Richmal, "William and the Witch", George Newnes Ltd, London, first edition with colour illustrations by Thomas Henry and Henry Ford, bumped at edges and corners, good green cloth boards.
1964

£80-110   Bib

Milne, A. A., "Winnie The Pooh" and "The House at Pooh Corner", Methuen, first edition, with decorations by E.H. Shepard.
1926

£3,500-4,500   Bib

Johns, Captain W.E., "Biggles Sets a Trap", Hodder and Stoughton, first edition with black and white illustrations by Stead, bumped at top and bottom, very good condition.

1962

£50-70   Bib

Norton, Mary, "The Borrowers Aloft", Dent, first edition of the second Borrowers book, illustrations by Diana Stanley, rubbed edges, inscription on front end paper.

1961

£45-55   Bib

Potter, Beatrix, "The Tailor of Gloucester", Warne & Co., first edition.

1903

£300-340   Bib

Ransome, Arthur, "Swallows and Amazons", Jonathan Cape.

1953

£180-220   Bib

Potter, Beatrix, "The Tale of Piggling Bland", Warne & Co., first edition with paper-covered boards, lettered in maroon, with pictorial onlay to upper cover, pictorial noticeboard endpapers, 15 colour plates and many line drawings, ownership inscription on half title and front blank, with modern protective box.

1913

£300-350   Bib

Seuss, Dr., "How The Grinch Stole Christmas", NY Random House, first edition, a scarce book with illustrations by the author.

1957

£800-1,200   Bib

Tourtel, Mary, "Rupert, Little Bear, More Stories", Sampson Low, Marston & Co.

1939

£750-850   Bib

Uttley, Alison, "Moldy Warp The Mole", Collins, first edition with illustrations by Margaret Tempest.

1940

£35-45   Bib

Tolkien, J.R.R., "The Hobbit," Allen & Unwin, third edition, seventh impression, illustrations by the author.

Due to Peter Jackson's recent films of The Lord Of The Rings, Tolkien books have seen an immense popular revival that extends far beyond devoted collectors and Tolkien fans. Condition is vital and collectors' or first edition copies of The Lord Of The Rings with dust jackets in fine condition have fetched prices exceeding tens of thousands of pounds at auction.

1972

£120-180   Bib

EARLY CAMERAS

- Most 19th century cameras had wooden bodies and brass fitments. Photography began to spread from c1840, with most cameras from this date being made in box-like forms using a 'wet plate' process involving glass plates with a film of light-sensitive chemicals. These cameras, dating from the 1840s-c.1880s are highly desirable. Bellows were introduced c1851.

- In 1864, attempts were made to develop a photographic plate that could be made in advance and taken to the field 'dry'. At first, these plates took longer to develop, but after experiments by many photographers, George Eastman set up the 'Eastman Dry Plate Company' (which eventually became 'Kodak') in 1880, producing such plates on a commercial scale.

- These plates were used in mahogany and brass 'folding' cameras with leather or fabric bellows which were still available up to the first decades of the 20th century. The back panel held a ground glass screen to check composition and a frame for holding the wooden plate holders.

- A large number of dry plate folding cameras survive today. Collectors should look for examples with manufacturers' names, especially Sanderson, Watson and Lancaster.

- They are often contained in leather bags containing shutters, lenses and other accoutrements such as cloths and wooden plate holders. Cameras accompanied by a range of accessories are likely to be more desirable.

A 19thC mahogany Lancaster International quarter plate camera, with rare blue bellows and rotary shutter.

£380-420 ColC

A 19thC mahogany Lancaster Extra Special quater plate camera, with see-saw shutter.

£380-450 ColC

A 19thC mahogany Lancaster Imperial Instantograph quarter plate camera.

£300-380 ColC

A mahogany Lizars Challenge quarter plate camera, needs restoration.

c1905

£100-150 TK

A 19thC mahogany London Stereoscopic Co. quarter plate camera, with Waterhouse stop and rectilinear lens.

£300-400 ColC

A mahogany J. F. Shew & Co. Eclipse quarter plate camera, shutter does not work.

c1890

£150-200 TK

A 19thC fiddle-back mahogany Sanderson quarter plate camera.

£400-500 ColC

A CLOSER LOOK AT A SANDERSON QUARTER PLATE CAMERA

The system used moving arms to allow the lens board to move more freely than before with a full range of rise, fall, swing and tilt.

The arms and board could be fixed in place with screws.

The photographer can monitor the composition via the glass panel at the back of the camera.

This example is for use in tropical climates. Teak is naturally resistant to insects and the bellows were also treated to deter attack.

A teak Sanderson tropical quarter plate camera, with Ross lens.

Sanderson cameras were innovative due to the way the lens board is mounted. Frederick Sanderson, an architect, needed a way to photograph buildings and the simple 'rising front' panel cameras of the time were not enough.

c1910

£350-450 ColC

A 19thC mahogany Watson tailboard half plate camera, with stereo sliding frame.

c1890

£400-500 ColC

LEICA CAMERAS

- Leica cameras are made by the optical company Leitz, based at Wetzlar in Germany. There are other factories, such as at Solms, also in Germany.

- The Leica was developed by the technician Oscar Barnack in 1913 and use compact 35mm cine film. Barnack's original prototype, known as the 'UR Leica', was launched in 1925 after brief testing of 31 hand-made prototypes known as 'Nullserie' cameras.

- The first Leicas (the Leica I(a) models) had non-interchangeable, fixed lenses and caught on quickly as they were small, light, easy to use, well built and used the high quality optics that Leitz were known for.

- Interchangeable lenses were introduced in 1930. These were screw fit, a system that did not change until the introduction of the 'M' series of cameras in 1954, which used a bayonet mounting.

- Today, Leicas are hotly collected all over the world. The accessories and lenses, usually contained in recognisable red card boxes, are also collected. Rare lenses and accessories can fetch very high prices. Many of these cameras are still useable today.

- All Leica cameras bear a serial number which allows precise dating to a year and also identification of a model, using tables found in specialist books. The model IIIa is perhaps the most common and fetches lower prices than other models.

- Condition is vital with Leica cameras. Collectors look for examples in as close to mint condition as possible. Scratches, scuffs and dents, modifications and damage to the mechanism all affect value seriously. Both the chrome plating and the black painted finish can show damage.

- Collectors particularly look for Leica cameras with unusual variations, such as those with different finishes, like an imitation 'sharkskin' covering to the body. Unusual engravings are very popular, and include those made for military purposes such as for the German Air Force, (engraved 'Luftwaffe Eigentum' – Luftwaffe Property), those used by Leitz for display (engraved Leitz Eigentum – Leitz Property) and other engravings such as 'Monté en Sarre'.

A Leica IA, with Elmar 3.5/50mm lens.

1930

£450-500 TK

A Leica IA near focus model, with Elmar 3.5/50mm lens, close focus to 1.5 feet, top and base plate restored professionally, with lens cap and camera case.

1929

£700-1,000 TK

A Leica Model C.

This was the first Leitz camera produced with an interchangable lens.

c1931

£300-380 ColC

A Leica IF converted from a IC, with Elmar 3.5/50mm lens, black dial.

1950

£400-500 TK

A black Leica II, with nickel Elmar 3.5/50mm lens.

1932

£300-400 TK

A black Leica II camera, Leitz, with nickel Elmar lens.

1928

£350-450 TK

A Leica IIIa, with rare sharkskin body and Summitar lens, engraved "Monté en Sarre", accessory shoe and some screws replaced, flash synchronization below shoe, certificate for service warranty.

Due to heavy tax duty, Leica licensed Saropitco in St Ingbert, Saare to produce Leicas for the French market from 1949 to 1951. These cameras were marked "Monté en Saare".

1949

£2,500-3,000 TK

A chrome Leica II, with nickel Elmar lens.

1939

£300-400 TK

A black Leica III, synchronized later with nickel Hektor 2.5/50mm lens, coated, no number, maker's case.

c1933

£400-500 TK

A Leica IIIa, with Summar 2/50mm lens, rewind knob damaged, with case.

1939

£250-350   **TK**

A Leica IIIb, with collapsible Summitar 2/5 cm lens, with "Leica" engraved in red, shutter needs help, with case.

1948

£300-400   **TK**

A Leica IIIa, with Elmar lens, flange "0" standardized.

1939

£220-280   **TK**

A Leica IIIf, factory converted from a 3C.

c1948

£300-350   **ColC**

A Leica IIIc, with Summaron 3.5/3.5 cm lens.

1949

£350-450   **TK**

FIND OUT MORE...

Dennis Laney, 'Leica Pocket Book', published by Hove Collectors Books, 1996.

Dennis Laney, 'Leica Collectors' Guide', published by Hove Collectors Books, 1992.

A Leica CL, with Summicron-C 2/40, lens hood, cap and maker's case.

1973-74

£320-380   **TK**

A Leica M2, with Summilux 1.4/50 lens, with self timer, protection film on base plate and lens cap.

1960

£600-700   **TK**

A Leica M3 body, single wind, with body cap.

1957

£320-380   **TK**

A black Leica M3 body, speed dial, accessory shoe and base plate probably restored, with body cap.

1961

£1,200-1,500   **TK**

A Leica M4, with Summaron 3.5/3.5 lens, filter and lens cap.

1970-71

£650-750   **TK**

A black Leica M6 body, as new, boxed.

1996

£800-1,000   **TK**

An American Al-Vista panoramic camera, with clockwork mechanism.

Standard cameras usually have an angle of view of 40-50 degrees, but the lens on a panoramic camera swivels by clockwork from pointing to the left to pointing to the right, enabling a wider 'panorama' image to be taken, without need for the camera itself to be moved.

c1903

£400-500   CoIC

An Anscoflex III, plastic body with twin lenses and flash, and with case and instructions.
c1958

£20-30   CoIC

A Bolsey B2 35mm camera, made in the USA.
c1950

£18-25   CoIC

An Italian Bilora Radix 35mm camera in tin, for 24x24 on rapid cassettes.

Collectors should look for the box for this camera as its presence can raise the value of the camera from £15-20.

1947-51

£60-80   OACC

A Canon L1, with Canon 1.8/50mm lens, lens cap and instruction manual.
1957

£350-450   TK

A 1960s Russian Cmena rapid load camera.

A Butcher's Reflex carbine 120 film camera, with case.
c1925 10.5in (26.5cm) high

£80-120   OACC

£5-10   CoIC

A chrome Canon P body, made in Japan, No. 728.655, chrome curtains not smooth, shutter runs well.
1958

£150-200   TK

A chrome Canon VL body, made in Japan, signs of use but no damage, metallic curtains not completely smooth but shutter runs reliably.
1958

£150-200   TK

A 1960s Fed 2 35mm camera, made in the USSR.

A 1950s Franke Solida 120 camera, with Schneider Radiana lens.

A Russian Hapyucc 16mm SLR camera, with removeable prism.
Early, white models were designed for use medical use.

1964

£30-40   CoIC

£25-35   CoIC

£180-250   CoIC

A
B
C
D
E
F
G
H
I
J
K
L
M
N
O
P
Q
R
S
T
U
V
W
XYZ

A German Goerz press-type camera, with Anchutz shutter.

If the mechanism is damaged, the value is greatly reduced. The Anschutz type camera was developed in 1896 and has four struts supporting the panel containing the lens. These can be collapsed allowing the camera to become flat.

c1910

| £75-100 | | ColC |

A Houghtons Ltd Ensign Reflex Model B SLR camera, shutter does not work.

1930

| £70-100 | | TK |

A teak Houghton Butcher Ensign Special Reflex tropical camera, brass bound with crown Russian leather bellows and viewing hood, FP shutter 15-1000.

c1935

| £400-500 | OACC |

A Russian Kiev IIIA, in working order.

This is a copy of a Contax camera. The Russians copied many Western styles and designs under their own name, the majority are of comparatively low value.

c1967

| £35-55 | ColC |

A Kodak Folding 4A camera.

This is the early version with a mahogany frame, the later versions have a metal frame.

1909

| £200-300 | ColC |

A brown No. 1A Pocket Kodak.

Brown is scarcer than the more common black version, which is worth about £20.

c1930

| £50-70 | ColC |

A Bakelite Kodak Baby Box Brownie camera, with box.

This example comes with its box, which adds value to the camera. Hundreds of thousands of Box Brownies were made with the majority having comparatively minimal values. The Box Brownie was designed by Frank Brownell for George Eastman (owner of the Eastman Kodak Co. of Rochester, New York) in 1900 and underwent design changes until the 1930s when it was phased out, although the name remained for some time afterwards, being used on similarly inexpensive and widely sold cameras. Named to draw on the popularity of 'brownie' characters by a well-known illustrator, it was aimed at the young and those who wanted to take photographs simply and inexpensively.

c1935

| £10-15 | OACC |

A Kodak Flash Brownie, with Bakelite body.

c1946

£12-15   ColC

A silver and cream 'Jersey' Kodak Brownie, with Bakelite body.

This model was launched as a prototype in Jersey in black and in this rare cream version. It was not a popular camera and was not available for general release.

c1955

£100-200   ColC

A Kodak Retina IIIc.

This model was produced in the Stuttgart factory, which was originally owned by Nagel.

c1957

£140-160   ColC

A Kodak Brownie Bullseye, with Bakelite body, made in the USA.

1958

£10-15   ColC

A Kodak Pony II.

c1959

£5-10   ColC

A Kodak Retinette 1B.

c1963

£12-15   ColC

A Kodak Instant, with original bag and papers.

Due to copyright infringement, Kodak was forced to withdraw this model at huge cost.

c1979

£8-12   ColC

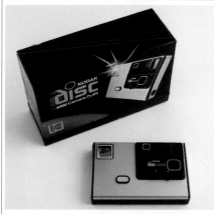

A Kodak Disc 4000, near mint and boxed.

The fashion for disc format cameras first hit manufacturers during the mid 1980s, spurred on by this model, Kodak's first. It was not successful and the format did not last. This was also the first mass produced camera with an aspheric lens.

c1985

£15-20   ColC

A Russian Leitz Leningrad 35mm camera, with spring-motor drive, with Leica mount.

c1960

£70-110   OACC

A Mamiya 6, with correct Olympus lens.

c1951

£80-100   ColC

A Mec 16 SB camera.

This was the first camera to feature TTL (through the lens light metering), despite Pentax advertsing that they had achieved this first.

c1960

£60-80   ColC

A CLOSER LOOK AT A MECAFLEX 35MM CAMERA

Although heavy, the Mecaflex has a compact size and clean lines when the top panel is closed. When flipped up, the top panel reveals a waist level view finder with magnifier, a lever film winding mechanism, a shutter release and the film rewind knob.

It has interchangeable lenses and allowed 50 exposures on 24mm x 24mm format film.

A Metz Mecaflex 35mm camera.

The Mecaflex, produced in the 1950s by Metz, was released in 1953 and was based on a prototype dating from 1947 designed by Heinz Kilfitt. It was not commercially successful and is now very rare.

c1953

£800-1,200 | **ColC**

A Micro Precision Products Microflex twin lens reflex camera, with Micronar 3.5/77.5 lens, with lens cap, case and instruction manual.

1959

£150-200 | **TK**

A German Minnigraph 35mm camera, with single speed shutter.

This is considered the first 35mm camera produced in Europe.

c1915

£700-800 | **ColC**

A Minolta 'A' 35mm camera, with coupled rangefinder, Chiyoda Kogaku shutter and 3.5 Chiyoko Rokkor lens.

c1956

£45-55 | **OACC**

A Minolta 110 zoom SLR camera.

This was the first Single Lens Reflex camera for 110 film.

c1976

£30-40 | **OACC**

A Nikon 'S' 35mm camera.

This was the second model that Nikon produced.

c1952

£500-600 | **ColC**

A Nikon SP camera.

This was the last model made by Nikon before they launched the 'F' series.

1957-63

£1,000-1,250 | **ColC**

A Nikon F photomic camera, with 50mm 1.4 lens.

The Nikon F was the first 35mm SLR (single lens reflex) camera that could take a motor drive.

c1965

£230-260 | **ColC**

A Nikon F Photomic FTN, made in Japan.

1968

£220-280 | **TK**

An Olympus Pen F half frame 35mm SLR camera, new rotary focal plane shutter synched to 1/500, lever codes shutter on first stroke, advances film on second.

c1965

£70-110   **OACC**

A silver Corfield Periflex I SLR camera, with periscope-finder, camera case.

The Periflex incorporated a small inverted periscope that was lowered into the film plane. This allowed the user to to see a very small part of the image about to be taken and then focus very finely. The periscope was drawn up and the optical viewfinder used to check composition before the shutter was released.

1955

£120-180   **TK**

A 1930s English Perma Special, with Bakelite body and gravity driven shutter.

£150-200   **ColC**

A Polaroid Miniportrait, made in Japan.

c1980

£80-120   **ColC**

A German Robot 1 camera, with Tessar 2.8 lens and spring motor drive.

The Robot used the first practical automatic film advance. The large knob on the top plate was wound, tensing a spring. Every time the shutter was released, the spring automatically advanced the film onwards.

c1936

£180-200   **ColC**

A Reflex-Kovelle camera, made by Kochmann, single lens reflex for 12 exposures on 120 film.

c1935

£50-60   **OACC**

A Franke & Heidecke Rolleicord I.

The Rollei TLR (Twin Lens Reflex) cameras were made by the German company Franke & Heidecke and their introduction was considered a great innovation.

Founded in 1920, Franke & Heidecke initially made stereoscopic cameras. The TLR was based on this model and was the first compact TLR camera. The photographer looked down onto the image which was composed through one lens, and the second was used to take the picture.

The first Rollei TLR camera was released in 1928 and took 117 film which was advanced with a knob. However the film format was changed shortly afterwards to 127 making those that hold the original film format scarce. Crank-wound mechanisms, introduced to deal with the new film format, became standard.

Rolleiflex cameras are still produced today. Collectors look for classic models and models with colour variations and rare lenses.

c1935

£120-180   **TK**

A grey Franke & Heidecke Rolleiflex T camera, excellent condition, with case.

1958

£200-300 TK

A Franke & Heidecke Rolleicord V b, with Xenar 3.5/75 lens Synchro-Compur X, shutter closes slowly, with lens cap.

1966

£150-200 TK

An early German Rollei 35 camera, shutter and light meter are working.

1967

£150-200 TK

A 1980s Chinese Seagull 35mm camera.

A copy of a Super Ikonta.

£50-60 ColC

A Russian 'Sputnick' stereoscopic camera, with viewer.

Without a viewer, this camera would be worth less. Condition is very important with this model as the Bakelite is often cracked. Stereoscopic cameras used two lenses a small distance from each other on the same plane to take two slightly different images of the same view. When these apparently identical images are viewed side by side in the viewer, the eye is tricked into seeing the image almost in '3D'. The third lens is the viewing lens, used to compose the image. Stereography had its heyday in the late 19th century, and although it largely died out by the turn of the century, it was still catered for by a very few manufacturers even as late as mid 20th century.

c1957

£180-200 ColC

A Thornton-Pickard Junior Special Ruby Reflex, SLR with focusing screen back and canvas bag.

1926

£100-150 TK

A Voigtländer Bergheil camera, with four part roll film back and cassettes, cased.

1925

£70-100 TK

A Voigtländer Vitessa II camera, with Color-Skopar 3.5/50 lens.

1955

£90-100 TK

A 1960s Voitlander Bessa II Rangefinder, with Color Heliar lens.

£380-420 ColC

A Voigtländer Bessa II, with Apo-Lanthar lens, with masks for 4.5 x 6cm and leather case.

The inclusion of the rare Apo-Lanthar lens on this model make it more desirable and valuable than similar models with different lenses.

1955

£1,500-2,000 TK

A Yashica 'J' 35mm camera.

c1962

£10-15 ColC

A Yashica Electro 35.

c1962

£20-25 ColC

∧ Zeiss Colibri camera.

As the 127 film used in this camera is no longer produced, the value has dropped recently as they cannot be used.

1930-35

£150-200　　　ColC

A 1930s Zeiss Ikarette 120 camera, with adjustable 10.5cm f4.5 Tessar lens.

£55-65　　　ColC

A Baby Ikonta 'Ikomat', with rare 3.5 Tessar lens.

This camera usually comes with a Novar lens.

c1935

£160-200　　　ColC

A 1930s Zeiss Adoro teak, nickel-plate and leather tropical camera.

£400-500　　　ColC

A Zeiss Ikon Contax II, with two lenses, shutter does not work correctly.

1936

£150-200　　　TK

An early Zeiss Ikon Contax III, with Sonnar 2/5cm lens, light meter does not work.

1936

£150-200　　　TK

A Zeiss Contaflex 35mm camera, with twin lens relex.

This was the first camera with a built-in light meter. If the shutter does not function or the meter is inoperative, the value will be lower.

c1936

£700-1,000　　　ColC

A Zeiss Ikon Contax II a, with Zeiss-Opton Sonnar 1.5/50 lens, lens a bit stained.

1952

£150-200　　　TK

A 1950s Ikonta 521, with Novar lens.

£25-35　　　ColC

A Zeiss Ikon Contarex I, with Planar 2/50 lens, lens hood and case.

1960-1967

£250-300　　　TK

A Zorki 35mm camera, made in the USSR.

c1974

£35-40　　　ColC

A
B
C
D
E
F
G
H
I
J
K
L
M
N
O
P
Q
R
S
T
U
V
W
XYZ

A 1930s Bell & Howell Filmo 16mm camera, with textured brown finish.

£30-40　　　　　　　　　　　　　**ColC**

A 1960s triple lens Bolex 8mm cine camera.

£70-100　　　　　　　　　　　　　**ColC**

A 1960s Bolex B8L 8mm cine camera, with seven speeds, two rotating lenses and TTL.

£30-40　　　　　　　　　　　　　**ColC**

A French Emel 8mm cine camera, with three lenses, two later.
1938-39

£80-120　　　　　　　　　　　　　**ColC**

A 1930s Ensign "Auto Kinecam" 16mm cine camera, with Taylor-Hobson lens and triple turrets to hold three lenses.

£70-100　　　　　　　　　　　　　**ColC**

A 1930s Ensign "Auto Kinecam" 16mm cine camera, with hand-cranked mechanism.

£80-120　　　　　　　　　　　　　**ColC**

A 1930s Siemens 16mm camera, with rare sliding turrets and three Schneider lenses.

£250-300　　　　　　　　　**ColC**

A 1930s Midas combined 9.5mm camera and projector, with Taylor-Hobson lens, lacks film magazine.

£60-70　　　　　　　　　　　　　**ColC**

A Zeiss 16mm Moviecon cine camera.

c1937

£120-180　　　　　　　　　　　　**ColC**

A 1960s brown Goerz Wien 16mm Minicord, with twin lenses and case.

£250-300　　　　　　　　　　　　**ColC**

A
B
C
D
E
F
G
H
I
J
K
L
M
N
O
P
Q
R
S
T
U
V
W
XYZ

A French Stylophot miniature camera.

c1955

£130-180 | **ColC**

A Minox BL subminiature camera, with feet dial, case and chain.

These Minox subminiature cameras were popularised as spy cameras after they appeared in a James Bond film, where Bond used a similar camera to photograph plans.

c1973

£220-280 | **TK**

A brown Bakelite Coronet Midget subminiature camera, with case.

This miniature camera came in a rainbow of Bakelite colours including mottled green and blue. These brighter colours fetch higher prices than the brown and black versions.

1936

£100-150 | **TK**

A silver-plated brass Kombi combined camera and graphoscope, by Alfred Kemper, USA.

c1893 | 2in (5cm) long

£180-220 | **ColC**

A Newman & Guardia London Special B Detective plate camera, with Zeiss Protar convertible lens.

This camera has a pneumatic action rather than an oil shutter and due to this unusual feature it was one of the cameras that Herbert Ponting took to the Antarctic with Scott's famous expedition in 1903 as the air was more reliable than oil at cold temperatures.

c1909

£240-300 | **ColC**

An R. J. Beck's Frena No. 0 Memorandum detective box magazine camera, with original box.

1901

£100-150 | **TK**

A Japanese Echo 8 novelty 'spy' camera, shaped as a Zippo lighter and usable as a lighter and camera.

c1954

£550-750 | **ColC**

A 1970s 'button-hole' spy camera.

£600-700 | **ColC**

A bronze C. P. Stirn 'button-hole' spy camera.

This camera was developed by A.D. Gray c1885-6. In July 1886, Carl P. Stirn of Berlin acquired the rights and patented the design across Europe. It was produced at a time when concealed and hidden cameras were very popular, being hidden in plain boxes or even handbags. This camera was worn under a waistcoat, with the lens protruding through a buttonhole. It was triggered by pulling on the loop on the bottom.

1886-1892

£900-1,200 | **ColC**

CANES

- Decorated canes first became popular during the 16th century but reached the apex of their popularity during the Victorian and Edwardian periods, primarily amongst the bourgeoisie and upper classes. Canes had largely gone out of fashion by the end of the First World War.
- A gentleman could have many canes, for either day or evening use. As well as a functional use, for support, the materials and quality of workmanship displayed the owner's wealth and social standing.
- Shafts are usually made from wood and may be carved or inlaid. Woods used include mahogany, fruitwoods and teak. Handles, or the round 'pommels', are most commonly found in carved wood or ivory. Precious metal covered handles are also common, which can be tooled or set with jewels.
- The metal tip often found at the other end is known as a 'ferrule' and is often missing. Although this will affect value slightly, it will not reduce it as much as other damage.
- Some canes have holes or 'eyelets' at the top of the shaft, under the handle and collar, which held a wrist cord.
- Most canes found will date from the mid-19th to the early 20th century and fall into three main categories – decorative, folk art and 'gadget'.
- Folk Art canes often use a whimsical or highly personal subject matter that was important to the carver or owner. Condition, subject and quality of carving, choice of wood and patina are important factors in determining the value of these pieces.
- Walking sticks made by sailors often use stacked shark vertebrae for the shaft and may have a handle carved from a type of ivory known as 'marine' or 'morse' ivory which is a very tight form taken from a walrus tusk.
- Materials and the level and quality of ornamentation and carving are the most important factors that affect values. Condition is important, with damage to carving, missing settings and cracks reducing value. Makers' marks are important, but not essential as many fine and valuable canes are not marked. Age is also important, with more modern sticks holding lower values.

A carved ivory figural cane, in the form of a running greyhound, with the collar decorated with scroll work borders, marked "Sterling", mounted on a briar wood shaft, slight chips on ears.

5in (12.5cm) high

£220-280   CHAA

A carved walrus ivory cane, in the form of a horse's head with glass eyes and gold-plated band decorated with floral designs, on a tapering malacca shaft.

1.5in (4cm) high

£350-450   CHAA

A carved ivory cane, in the form of a lizard climbing a branch, mounted on a black palm shaft with gold-plated collar.

3.25in (8.5cm) high

£600-700   CHAA

A carved stag antler cane, in the form of a greyhound with inset glass eyes and coin silver collar, unmarked.

4in (10cm) high

£120-180   CHAA

A carved cane, in the form of a dragon's head, with red rhinestone eyes, mounted on an ebonized black palm shaft with brass collar, ebonized finish worn.

£250-350   CHAA

A carved antler cane, in the form of two horses' heads, with wide gold-filled collar engraved "F.A.F." on an ebonized hardwood shaft.

2.25in (5.5cm) high

£600-700   CHAA

A carved walrus ivory cane, in the form of a Turk's head knot. mounted on a hardwood shaft, one inch vertical crack.

2.5in (6.5cm) high

£300-400   CHAA

A carved walrus ivory cane in the form of a lobster, mounted on an ebonized tapered hardwood shaft, ivory has very tight crack.

2in (5cm) high

£600-700   CHAA

A turned walrus ivory cane, with three inset silver wire bands, silver disk on top engraved "John Clapp / 1866" with Masonic compass in the centre and silver band engraved "Warwick, R.I.", very small drying crack on top.

1.75in (4.5cm) high

£700-800   **CHAA**

An ivory knobbed cane, with coin silver collar and stepped malacca shaft.

2in (5cm) high

£350-450   **CHAA**

A carved bone cane, with a lotus nut "knob" on a long bone handle, with wide nickel band joining the handle to the shaft, several small areas of bone loss, one leaf missing.

5.25in (13.5cm) high

£200-300   **CHAA**

A folk art one-piece carved hardwood cane, with root knob in the form of a human skull with a snake entwined in the eye sockets.

The skull is a popular 'memento mori' motif, acting as a reminder of ultimate death for all.

2in (5cm) high

£400-500   **CHAA**

A folk art two-piece carved cane, with burl knob in the form of a man's head, with two braids forming U-shaped loops and a winged cherub's head carved at the back, mounted on a tapered hardwood shaft, some chipping.

2.5in (6.5cm) high

£500-600   **CHAA**

A primitive one-piece carved rosewood cane, the handle in the form of a clenched fist handle with inlaid brass and ivory dots at the cuff.

The clenched fist is a popular motif for cane pommels.

£60-70   **CHAA**

A carved hazelwood cane, in the form of an otter's head.

£120-180   **MM**

A one-piece carved hardwood crook-handled cane, the handle in the form of a bust labelled "George V", also marked "Klam" and "S.N."

3.5in (9cm) high

£300-400   **CHAA**

A one-piece carved cane, the handle in the form of a hound's head, faded.

4.5in (11.5cm) high

£250-350   **CHAA**

A carved horn figural cane, in the form frigate bird's head, with a brass collar and tapered ebony shaft.

1.5in (4cm) high

£300-400   **CHAA**

An L-shaped cane, the metal handle in the form of bamboo on a birchwood shaft, a few dents.

2.5in (6.5cm) high

£180-220   **CHAA**

An L-shaped cane, with unmarked silver snake's head mounted in on a tapered exotic hardwood shaft.

2in (5cm) long

£180-220   **CHAA**

A silver knobbed cane, decorated with Japanese-style relief bamboo plants, with engraving plate, mounted in a tapered malacca shaft.

1.75in (4.5cm) high

£200-300   **CHAA**

A French silver knobbed cane, with hallmark for "LB" and other marks, shaft stamped "Beitalle".

1.75in (4.5cm) high

£150-200   **CHAA**

A Victorian gold knobbed presentation cane, with bright-cut floral and scroll decoration, on an ebony shaft.

2.75in (7cm) high

£200-300   **CHAA**

An Edwardian gold-plated presentation cane, with bright-cut scrollwork decoration, engraved "W.L.Griffin From J.H. Herald & Family 1-18-24", mounted on a tapered ebony shaft, light wear to top of plate.

£100-150 | **CHAA**

A Victorian gold-filled knobbed cane, with scroll and floral decoration and presentation engraving panel, mounted in an ebonized hardwood shaft.

2in (5cm) high

£120-180 | **CHAA**

A cast bronze figural cane, in the form of a bust of Hercules with a lion's skin draped over his shoulders, mounted on a tapered hardwood shaft.

3.5in (9cm) high

£150-200 | **CHAA**

An L-shaped agate handled cane, with engraved gold-plated collar, mounted on a tapered American walnut shaft.

£220-280 | **CHAA**

A Meissen-handled figural cane, with tau-shaped handle in the form of woman's bust, the body of handle decorated with a landscape with a courting couple and other vignettes, mounted on a tapered malacca shaft.

'Tau' is the name for the distinctively shaped handle which curves down at the back and up at the front.

3in (7.5cm) high

£750-850 | **CHAA**

Gadget canes

- As the cane's shaft is long and, like the handle, wide enough to hold items internally, many canes were made with specific uses or built-in gentleman's accessories – these are known as 'gadget' or 'system' canes.

- The simplest and most common have handles that unscrew to reveal items concealed in the shaft, such as drinking, smoking or writing accessories, but the variety of gadgets is huge, including camera tripods that use a split shaft as the stand, telescopes and even seats.

- On occasion, canes were also used as much for defence as for support and were adapted into sword sticks or gun canes with concealed weapons. Collectors should understand that some countries restrict the import or export of these pieces, and it is generally illegal to carry one in public.

- Most gadget canes date from the 1870s until the early 20th century, and must be intact. Ingenious or unusual designs and skilled workmanship are good indicators of high value pieces.

A 62 calibre percussion gun cane, with threaded round barrel and under hammer mechanism, woodworm damage to grip, paint worn, light surface rust, hammer repaired and missing barrel plug.

35in (89cm) long

£200-300 | **CHAA**

An unmarked 52 calibre percussion gun cane, two-piece burled walnut grip, the barrel segment with threaded front to attach barrel, cocking spur broken off, missing barrel plug.

37in (94cm) long

£250-300 | **CHAA**

A 9mm percussion gun cane, probably European, of all steel construction with L-shaped tubular handle, tapered barrel and pull-tab-cocking mechanism, light surface rust, does not appear to function.

£150-200 | **CHAA**

A malacca sword cane, with turned hardwood knob, nickel collar and double-edged steel blade.

36in (91.5cm) long

£150-200 | **CHAA**

A dagger cane, with blued steel blade and carved horn handle in the form of a hoof mounted on an ebonized hardwood shaft.

35.25in (89.5cm) long

£300-400 | **CHAA**

FIND OUT MORE...

Catherine Dike, 'Walking Sticks', published by Shire Publications, 1992.

Catherine Dike, 'Cane Curiosa: From Gun to Gadget', published by Les Editions de L'Amateur, Paris & C. Dike Publications, 1983.

Jeffrey Snyder, 'Canes: From the Seventeenth to the Twentieth Century', Schiffer Publishing, 1997.

A horn cigarette and match safe cane, with silver-mounted tau-shaped handle containing cigarette compartment and match holder and striker, mounted on a stepped, tapered bamboo shaft.

Handle 4.25in (10.5cm) long

£500-600   **CHAA**

A chrome-plated brass gadget cane, with stamped floral decoration, the hinged lid opening to reveal a cigarette compartment and a retractable candle holder, mounted on a tapered hardwood shaft.

Handle 4in (10cm) high

£350-450   **CHAA**

A brass monocular spy-glass cane, probably English, mounted on a tapered ebonized hardwood shaft with a brass ferrule.

36in (91.5cm) high

£200-300   **CHAA**

A gadget cane, the black-finished wooden knob in the form of a wind-activated siren/alarm with nickel mounts, mounted on a tapered hardwood shaft.

Knob 1.5in (4cm) high

£220-280   **CHAA**

A horse measuring cane, the carved root knob pulls up to reveal a marked maplewood measuring stick with spirit level, mounted on a bamboo shaft.

36.25 (92cm) high

£120-180   **CHAA**

A novelty figural gadget cane, the Britannia silver knob in the form of a man's head, with a threaded collar mounted on a bamboo shaft, a small button on the shaft forces water from the reservoir in the shaft out through the mouth of the figure.

Knob 2.5in (6.5cm) high

£150-250   **CHAA**

An Arcadian figure of a 'Bridesmaid', wearing a blue dress and black bonnet, with printed title and maker's marks and painted model number "16".

5in (13cm) high

£70-100   **DN**

An Arcadian figure of 'Doris', wearing a yellow dress and green bonnet, with printed title and maker's marks and painted model number "62".

5in (12.5cm) high

£80-120   **DN**

An Arcadian figure of a 'Bridesmaid', wearing a pink dress and green bonnet, with printed title and maker's marks and painted model number.

In the early 20thC, these colourful figures were produced by Arcadian, better known for its crested ware production (see Goss & Crested Ware), in the style of Doulton figurines.

15.5in (13cm) high

£100-150   **DN**

An Arcadian figure of 'Her Ladyship', seated wearing a pink dress, printed title mark and painted model number "2".

6in (15.5cm) high

£80-100   **DN**

An Arcadian figure of 'June', wearing a green crinoline and pink bonnet, with printed title and maker's marks and painted model number "75".

4.5in (11.5cm) high

£40-80   **DN**

An Arcadian figure of 'June', wearing a yellow crinoline and pink bonnet, with printed title and maker's marks and painted model number "73".

4.5in (11.5cm) high

£70-100   **DN**

An Arcadian figure of 'The Famous Monk of Lilleshall Abbey', in black robes, with printed title and maker's mark.

3.75in (9.5cm) high

£50-70   **DN**

A pair of Arcadian figures of 'Tulip Boy' and 'Tulip Girl', each in Dutch costume, with printed titles, maker's marks and painted model numbers "131" (girl) and "141" (boy).

5in (13cm) high

£200-250   **DN**

An Arcadian figure of 'Lady Bountiful', wearing a three-tone blue dress, printed title and maker's marks with painted model number "125".

6.75in (17.5cm) high

£100-150   **DN**

An Arcadian figure of 'Victorian Belle', wearing a maroon dress and green shawl, printed title and maker's marks with painted model number "160".

7.25in (18.5cm) high

£80-120   **DN**

An Art pottery jardinière, attributed to the Linthorpe factory and a design by Christopher Dresser, glaze obscures any visible makers marks, cracked on base.

8.5in (21.5cm) high

£120-180　　　**DN**

A Charles Vyse stoneware vase, of oviform with horizontally banded tapering neck, signed "CV" and dated.

1934　　5.75in (14.5cm) high

£200-250　　　**DN**

An early St. Ives Pottery plate, decorated by Bernard Leach, impressed St. Ives seal mark and signed in underglaze blue "BL".

Bernard Leach (1887-1979) was one of the most influential studio potters of the 20th century. He was born in Hong Kong and spent the first ten years of his life in Japan before moving to England. Leach attended The London School of Art and then returned to Japan to teach etching. During his ten years in Japan and China he became interested in ceramics and studied Japanese and Korean pottery. Following his return to England he set up the St Ives pottery in Cornwall in 1920 with the help of his friend Shoji Hamada.

Leach's wares fall into two broad areas: Those with an Oriental influence and those inspired by the English slipware tradition.

8in (20.5cm) diam

£1,200-1,800　　　**DN**

A Charles Vyse stoneware vase, of broad oviform with a short flared neck, incised "CV" and dated "1932".

Charles Vyse (1882-1971) was born in Staffordshire, England. He was apprenticed to the Doulton factory and subsequently won a scholarship to the Royal College of Art. He studied there from 1905 to 1910 and at the Camberwell School of Art in 1912. In 1919 he set up a studio in Chelsea with his wife Nell. They produced ceramic figures based on London characters, and later developed an interest in Chinese Sung pottery. Vyse retired in 1963 and died in 1971.

5.5in (14cm) high

£220-280　　　**DN**

A late 1930s Bullers porcelain bowl, Agnete Hoy mark.

8.5in (21.5cm) diam

£40-50　　　**OACC**

A bowl, by Bernard Charles.

Bernard Charles was head of Poole School of Art and had connections with Poole Pottery.

6in (15cm) diam

£40-50　　　**OACC**

A Briglin Pottery flowerpot holder.

c1970

£10-20　　　**OACC**

A bottle vase, by Julian Stair.

c1980　　6.75in (17cm) high

£30-40　　　**OACC**

A late 1970s bowl, by Sophie MacCarthy.

5.75in (14.5cm) diam

£20-30　　　**OACC**

A stoneware vase, by Paul Haber.

9.75in (24.5cm) high

£15-20　　　**OACC**

A Mike Dodd studio pottery vase.

c1989　10.75in (27.5cm) high

£200-250　　　**ADE**

BELLEEK

- The Belleek factory was founded by John Caldwell Bloomfield, David McBirney and Robert Armstrong in 1863 in Fermanagh, Northern Ireland.
- Belleek porcelain is of parian-type and is characterised by its iridescent glaze. Wares include vases, dishes and baskets. Openwork lattice designs were often applied with shamrocks, daisies and roses.
- The first three marks used from 1857 to 1946 were usually black. Marks include First Period printed mark with harp and wolfhound (1863-1890), 'Ireland' and 'Eire' were added after 1891 as well as Belleek, Co.
- The Third Green Period Fermanagh printed mark was used from 1965-1980. The Belleek factory is still operating today.

A Belleek thistle cup and saucer, first mark, slight nibble to saucer.
1863-1890
Saucer 5.25in (13.5cm) diam

£200-250   **OACC**

A pair of Belleek trinket dishes, encrusted with flowers.

2.5in (6.5cm)

£350-400   **GorL**

A Belleek shamrock salt.
1891-1926   *3in (8cm) wide*

£60-80   **OACC**

A Belleek cream jug and sugar bowl, with third black mark.

£60-80   **BAC**

A Belleek boat-shaped salt.
4.75in (12cm) wide

£100-130   **OACC**

A Belleek ivy cream jug, third period.
1926-46   *4in (10cm) high*

£70-100   **OACC**

A Belleek vase, with tinted Shamrock panels, fifth mark.
1955-65   *6in (15cm) high*

£100-130   **OACC**

A Belleek Tridacna coffee cup and saucer, sixth mark.
c1965 saucer 4.5in (11.5cm) diam

£60-70   **OACC**

A Belleek Shamrock vase.
c1965   *4in (10.5cm) high*

£40-50   **OACC**

A Belleek jug and saucer, sixth mark.
c1965 Saucer 5.5in (14cm) diam

£55-65   **OACC**

A Belleek jug, sixth mark.
c1965   *4.25in (10.5cm) high*

£80-100   **OACC**

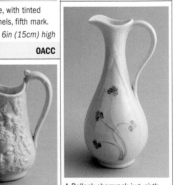

A Belleek shamrock jug, sixth mark.
c1965   *7in (18cm) high*

£30-40   **OACC**

A Beswick Beatrix Potter 'Mr Benjamin Bunny figure', with gold back stamp.

4.25in (11cm) high

£250-300 OACC

A Beswick Beatrix Potter 'Cottontail' figure.

c1985   3.5in (9cm) high

£50-60 OACC

A Beswick Beatrix Potter 'Mrs Flopsy Bunny' figure.

c1965   4in (10cm) high

£50-60 OACC

A Beswick Beatrix Potter 'Miss Moppit' figure, with gold back stamp.

3in (7.5cm) high

£80-100 OACC

A Beswick Beatrix Potter 'Peter Rabbit' figure, with gold back stamp.

4.5in (11.5cm) high

£100-120 OACC

BESWICK

- The John Beswick Studios were founded in 1894 at Loughton, Stoke-on-Trent, England, and initially produced tableware and ornaments, only later turning to animal figurines, primarily famed racehorses and champion dogs.
- In 1948, they began producing Beatrix Potter character figurines, with an initial range of ten figures, including Jemima Puddleduck (the first created) and Peter Rabbit, all modelled by the renowned chief modeller, Arthur Gredington.
- In 1952, after enormous success with the Beatrix Potter range, Beswick won the rights to produce Disney characters and later, in 1968, Winnie The Pooh characters.
- In 1969, Beswick was bought by The Royal Doulton Group .
- Collectors should look for the coveted 'gold' backstamp that was used on earlier pieces, before the brown and black stamps.

A Beswick Beatrix Potter 'Mrs Rabbit' figure.

c1951   4in (10cm) high

£50-60 OACC

A Beswick Beatrix Potter 'Ribby' figure.

c1951   3.25in (8.5cm) high

£50-60 OACC

A Beswick Beatrix Potter 'Tommy Brock' figure, with printed gold back stamp.

4in (9cm) high

£80-100 L&T

A Beswick Beatrix Potter 'Simpkin' figure, modelled as a tabby cat wearing a green coat, black boots and holding a bag and a mug, with brown backstamp.

4in (10cm) high

£40-80 DN

A Beswick Beatrix Potter 'Tabitha Twitchett' figure, no. "BP6a".

£40-60 PSA

A Beswick Beatrix Potter 'Tom Kitten' figure, no. "BP2", slight restoration.

£20-30 PSA

A Beswick Beatrix Potter 'Little Pig Robinson Spying' figure, no. "BP6a".

£60-100 PSA

A Beswick Beatrix Potter 'Tommy Brock' figure, no. "BP3c", second version, second variation.

£20-25 PSA

A Beswick Beatrix Potter 'The Old Woman who Lived in a Shoe' figure, no. "BP2".

£20-40 PSA

A Beswick Beatrix Potter 'Hunca Munca' figure, no. "BP4".

£30-50 PSA

A Beswick Beatrix Potter 'Tailor of Gloucester' figure, no. "BP2".

£80-120 PSA

A Beswick Beatrix Potter 'Old Woman Who Lived in a Shoe Knitting' figure no. "BP3b".

£40-60 PSA

A Beswick Beatrix Potter 'Mr Todd' figure, no. "BP6a".

£30-50 PSA

A Beswick Figures 'Pig Prom Band', including Daniel "PP5", Michael "PP6", James "PP7", Richard "PP8" and Christopher "PP9".

£80-100 PSA

A collection of Beswick Figures 'Little Loveables', including two 'To Mother' "LL5", 'God Loves Me' "LL3", 'Just For You' "LL11", 'I Love You' "LL9".

£100-120 PSA

Three Beswick Figures: 'Mrs. Tittlemouse', 'Mrs Tiggy Winkle' and 'Timmy Tiptoes', all with gold marks.

£150-180   **GorL**

A Beswick Figures Little Likeables 'On Top of the World', no. "LL5".

£15-30   **PSA**

A Beswick Figures Little Likeables 'Out at Last', no. "LL7".

£30-50   **PSA**

A Beswick Figures Little Likeables 'Treat Me Gently', no. "LL6".

£40-60   **PSA**

A Beswick Figures Little Likeables 'Hide and Sleep', no. "LL3".

£40-60   **PSA**

A Beswick Figures Little Likeables 'Watching the World Go By', no. "LL2".

£40-60   **PSA**

FIND OUT MORE...

'Beswick Quarterly', Laura Rock-Smith, 10 Holmes Court, Sayville, N.Y. 11782-2408, U.S.A..

Diana Callow, 'The Charlton Standard Catalogue of Beswick Animals', The Charlton Press, Toronto, Ontario, 1996.

Jean Dale, 'Royal Doulton Beswick Storybook Figurines' (6th edition), published by Charlton International Inc, U.S.A., 2000.

A Beswick Figures 'The Mad Hatter's Tea Party' tableau, limited edition number 533 of 1998, no. "LC001".

£80-100   **PSA**

A Beswick Birds 'Penguin Family', nos. MN800/801/802/803, some damage.

£30-50   **PSA**

A Beswick Wild Animals 'Small Giraffe', no. "MN853".

£40-60   **PSA**

A Beswick earthenware model of a Siamese cat, mould no.1559.

7in (18cm) long

£40-60   **GorL**

A set of four Beswick flying-duck wall ornaments, their bodies moulded in relief and naturalistically painted, printed marks "596-1" to "596-4".

Tallest 10.5in (26cm) long

£100-150   **Chef**

BLUE AND WHITE

- Blue and white patterns were first used by the Chinese during the Ming Dynasty where designs were hand-painted. The invention of under-glaze transfer printing in the late 18th century saw a massive expansion of blue and white ware. Here, a design was transferred to a warm copper plate using a cobalt (blue) oil and ink mix over which paper was pressed firmly, transferring the now reversed design to paper. This was then pressed onto the surface of the ceramic which was then fired and glazed and fired again.

- Plates, chargers and platters are desirable and highly collected as they are easily displayed and show off the pattern as much as possible. Collectors often concentrate on collecting one type of item, such as jugs.

- The type of pattern affects the value and desirability of the piece. The 'Willow' pattern is held as the most popular design, followed by 'Asiatic Pheasants' and 'Italian'.

- Restoration will affect value. Be careful with restored pieces which should be dipped in water only briefly to clean them. Do not use metal sprung grips to hang the plates as the grips can damage the plate's rim.

A Ridgway Angus Seats series plate, showing a view of Lumley Castle, Durham.

c1820   7.25in (18.5cm) diam

£120-160   **SN**

A 'Cowman' pattern plate, maker unknown.

c1820   9.75in (25cm) diam

£140-180   **SN**

A Spode 'The Lion in Love' pattern soup plate, from the Aesop's Fables series.

c1830   9.75in (25cm) diam

£280-340   **SN**

A Wedgwood Botanical series plate.

c1810   8in (20.5cm) diam

£130-180   **SN**

A Riley 'Dromedary' pattern plate.

1802-1828 10in (25cm) diam

£140-180   **SN**

A Copeland and Garratt 'Death of the Bear' pattern plate.

With its sad subject matter, this pattern is considered the most common of the 'Indian Sporting' series introduced by Spode in 1820.

1833-1847   9.75in (25cm) diam

£200-260   **SN**

A Spode 'Long Eliza' pattern plate.

c1815

£100-150   **SN**

A Minton Monk's Rock series soup plate, with watermill scene.

c1810   9.25in (23.5cm) diam

£150-200   **SN**

A Goodwin, Bridgewood & Orton 'Oriental Flower Garden' pattern plate.

1827-1829   7in (18cm) diam

£80-120   **SN**

An 1820s 'Russian Palace' pattern plate, maker unknown.

10in (26cm) diam

£130-180   **SN**

A 'Wild Rose' pattern dessert plate, maker unknown.

c1820   10in (26cm) diam

£120-180   **SN**

A Job Ridgway 'Curling Palm' pattern supper section dish.
1802-1808   *12.25in (31cm) wide*
£150-200   **SN**

An 1820s Minton 'Filigree' pattern dessert dish.
8.25in (21cm) diam
£160-220   **SN**

A Burleigh teapot stand.
c1900   6.25in (16cm) diam
£60-80   **SN**

A 'Ponterotto' pattern tureen stand, attributed to Rogers.
1815-1842   8.25in (21cm) w
£100-150   **SN**

A Rogers 'Camel' pattern plate.
c1815   7.75in (20cm) wide
£180-230   **SN**

An 1820s 'Family & Mule' pattern tureen stand, maker unknown.
17in (43cm) wide
£270-320   **SN**

An 1820s Minton 'Filigree' pattern platter.
15in (38.5cm) wide
£250-300   **SN**

An 1820s Rogers 'Greek Statue' pattern basket stand.
£250-300   **SN**

A Copeland 'British Flowers' pattern drainer.
c1850   12.25in (31cm) wide
£300-380   **SN**

An 1830s Maddock Sedders 'Fairy Villas' pattern drainer.
15in (38cm) wide
£250-300   **SN**

A Copeland and Garratt broth bowl.
c1833-1847
£250-300   **SN**

An 1820s 'India Flowers' pattern pickle set.
11in (28cm) wide
£500-600   **SN**

An 1820s 'Gleaners' pattern tea bowl and saucer, maker unknown.

Gleaners were poor farm workers or peasants who, after the harvest had been collected, scoured the fields for remaining corn to take home.

2in (5cm) high

£180-230 SN

A Copeland and Garratt 'Italian' pattern covered jar.

The 'Italian' pattern can also be found on Spode pieces, since Spode introduced it in 1816. From 1833, the pattern was used by Copeland and Garrett who bought the Spode pottery and continued to produce it. Between 1870 and 1970, Copeland ware carried a mark identifying the date of manufacture. The letter is the first letter of the month of manufacture and the two numbers represent the year. The Spode name was reintroduced in the 1970s.

c1833-1847 3.25in (8.5cm) h

£200-250 SN

An invalid's feeding cup, maker unknown.

The form of this cup allowed the invalid to drink while lying down.

2.75in (7cm) high

£110-160 SN

A Copeland 'Camilla' pattern sauce tureen, stand and ladle.

c1900   6.75in (17cm) high

£300-350 SN

A treacle jar, with fox-hunting scene, maker unknown.

c1850   6in (15cm) high

£300-400 SN

An 1820s mug, with Regency scene, maker unknown.

3in (7.5cm) high

£110-150 SN

A Minton 'Floral Vases' pattern mug.

c1825   3.5in (9cm) high

£230-280 SN

An 'Elephant' pattern child's chamber pot.

c1820   3in (8cm) high

£280-330 SN

A William Ridgway 'Oriental' pattern child's chamber pot.

1834-1854   5in (12.5cm) high

£260-320 SN

An Adams 'Bird and Basket' pattern loving cup.

c1900   4.25in (11cm) high

£240-280 SN

An 'Asiatic Pheasants' pattern sauce boat, maker unknown.

c1860   4.25in (11cm) high

£100-150 SN

A 'Woodman' pattern jug, maker unknown.
c1830   8.5in (22cm) high
£300-350   **SN**

A Wedgwood 'Ferrara' pattern jug.
c1900   5.5in (14cm) high
£150-200   **SN**

A Riley 'Dromedary' pattern sauce boat.
c1815   2.25in (6cm) high
£250-300   **SN**

A child's teapot, maker unknown.
c1815   3.5in (9cm) high
£180-240   **SN**

An 1820s Leeds Pottery coffee pot.
£300-350   **SN**

An Adams 'Bird and Basket' pattern tea caddy.
c1900   5.5in (14cm) high
£230-280   **SN**

A Minton 'Sicilian' pattern soup ladle.
c1830   11.75in (30cm) long
£130-170   **SN**

FIND OUT MORE...

R.K. Henrywood & A.W. Coysh, 'Dictionary of Blue & White Printed Pottery' 1780-1880 (Vols 1 & 2), published by Antique Collectors' Club, Woodbridge, 1982 & 1989.

R. Copeland, 'Transfer Printed Pottery', published by Shire Books, Princes Risborough, 1999.

The Spode Museum & Visitors' Centre, Church Street, Stoke-on-Trent, ST4 1BX.

An 1830s Davenport 'Muleteer' pattern pepper pot.
4.75in (12cm) high
£140-180   **SN**

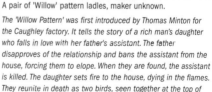

A pair of 'Willow' pattern ladles, maker unknown.

The 'Willow Pattern' was first introduced by Thomas Minton for the Caughley factory. It tells the story of a rich man's daughter who falls in love with her father's assistant. The father disapproves of the relationship and bans the assistant from the house, forcing them to elope. When they are found, the assistant is killed. The daughter sets fire to the house, dying in the flames. They reunite in death as two birds, seen together at the top of the design. The eponymous willow symbolises sadness.

c1830   7in (18cm) long
£80-100 each   **SN**

A 'Fitzhugh' pattern chestnut basket, possibly Spode.
c1800   7.5in (19cm) wide
£200-250   **SN**

An Adams 'Tendril' pattern egg stand.
c1810   6in (15cm) high
£250-300   **SN**

An 1870s Minton Hollins & Co scenic tile.
6.25in (16cm) wide
£45-65   **SN**

A 1960s Buchan Pottery coaster, hand-painted, unnamed pattern.

4in (10.5cm) diam

£10-15 FFM

A 1960s Buchan Pottery 'Hebrides' pattern coaster, hand-painted.

4in (10.5cm) diam

£10-15 FFM

A 1960s Buchan Pottery coaster, hand-painted, unnamed pattern.

4.5in (11.5cm) diam

£10-15 FFM

A 1950s Buchan Pottery milk jug with hand-painted stylized leaf decoration.

2.75in (6.75cm) high

£10-18 FFM

A 1950s Buchan Pottery milk jug with hand-painted stylized leaf decoration.

2.5in (6.5cm) high

£10-18 FFM

A 1960s Buchan Pottery jug, hand-decorated.

5in (13cm) high

£18-25 FFM

A 1960s Buchan Pottery jug, hand-decorated.

5in (13cm) high

£15-20 FFM

A 1960s Buchan Pottery jug, hand-decorated.

5in (13cm) high

£25-35 FFM

A 1960s Buchan Pottery tankard, hand-decorated.

4in (10.5cm) high

£10-15 FFM

A 1960s Buchan Pottery 'Sutherland' pattern jug, hand-decorated.

2.5in (6.5cm) high

£12-18 FFM

A 1960s Buchan Pottery 'Riviera' pattern tankard, hand-decorated.

4in (10.5cm) high

£10-15 FFM

A 1960s Buchan Pottery teapot, hand-painted.

8.75in (22cm) high

£20-30 FFM

A 1960s Buchan Pottery 'Riviera' pattern oil and vinegar cruet set, hand-decorated.

5in (13cm) high

£18-25 FFM

A Carlton ware yellow glazed fruit bowl.

1930s

£30-50 **AS&S**

CARLTON WARE

- Tradename used on china and earthenware from 1890 onwards by Wiltshaw & Robinson Ltd of the 'Carlton Works', Stoke.
- Crested souvenir ware may bear the name 'Crown China'.
- The name became 'Carlton Ware Ltd' in 1958.
- During the 1920s and 1930s the factory produced colourful geometric designs that are highly sought after, as are pieces made for Guinness in the 1950s.
- The richly decorated and coloured pieces with enamelled decoration on a dark glaze were inspired by the success of Wedgwood's lustrewares.
- A key style is chinoiserie with rich enamelled decoration including banded ornamentation. It was inspired by Oriental ceramics.
- Key chinoiserie motifs are birds, plant and tree forms, flowers and butterflies.
- Numerous manufacturers now make limited edition pieces under licence.

An unusual Carlton ware comical dog, decorated in black and white with a brown collar.

6in (15cm) high

£80-120 **PSA**

A Carlton ware "Egyptian Fan" vase.

7.5in (19cm) high

£800-1,000 **RH**

A Carlton ware "Barge" pattern bowl.

10in (25.5cm) diam

£340-380 **RH**

A Carlton ware "Heron and Magical tree" pattern coffeepot, milk jug and sugar server.

7.5in (19cm) high

£400-500 **RH**

A CLOSER LOOK AT CARLTON WARE

This wall charger is a large size which can be displayed easily with great visual impact.

There is no wear to the pattern, Carlton ware pieces were functional objects.

This rare pattern sums up the period well, with bold, bright colours and distinctive designs and is thus popular. The pattern and decoration is also highly typical of Carlton ware.

A 1930s Carlton ware "Floral Comets" wall charger.

12.5in (32cm) diam

£1,000-1,500 **RH**

A 1930s Carlton ware "springtime" dish.

6.75in (17cm) wide

£70-80 **RH**

A Carlton ware "lily pink" cruet set.

1.5in (4cm) high

£110-130 **RH**

A Carlton ware "Castle" pattern wall charger.

12.5in (32cm) diam

£400-500 | **RH**

Two Carlton Walking Ware mugs, hand-painted, unnamed designer.

1970s | *Left: 5in (12cm) high Right: 3.25in (8.5cm) high*

£30-50 each | **FFM**

A Carlton ware crimped edged dish, "Rouge Royale" design.

9.5in (24cm) diam

£70-100 | **OACC**

A Carlton ware "dog rose" teapot.

5in (12.5cm) high

£140-160 | **RH**

A Carlton ware "dog rose" tea cup and saucer.

3in (7.5cm) high

£35-45 | **RH**

An 'Old Charley' small character jug, no. D5527, glaze fault.

£20-30 | **PSA**

A Carlton ware box, "Rouge Royale" design.

5.5in (14cm) long

£70-100 | **OACC**

A Carlton ware vase, of octagonal section with chinoiserie reserves in black against a red/orange ground, gilt wear to rim.

9in (22.5cm) high

£70-120 | **FRE**

A Carlton ware lustre bowl, of deep form with everted rim and ring base, mottled orange glaze with reserves of frolicking children silhouetted against a blue sky, gilt highlights, a few scrapes to the glaze.

9in (22.5cm) diam

£100-150 | **FRE**

Four pieces of Carlton ware, including two octagonal trays, with painted fruit/floral motifs, chip to rim on both, a covered square box with embossed and painted oak trees on square blue ground, a few nicks, and a dish of similar oak tree pattern in the shape of an oak leaf.

£70-120 | **FRE**

CHARACTER JUGS

- Character jugs incorporate the head (and sometimes shoulders) of the character, whilst Toby Jugs show the full figure of the character.
- The first Toby jug was made in the 18th century, their name being derived from a popular song of the period. They became more popular after Doulton reintroduced them in the 19th century.
- Royal Doulton reinvented the Toby jug during the 1930s, creating the 'character jug'. The idea is popularly credited to Charles Noke who created jugs with bright colours and expressionistic faces that were full of character. His primary designs focussed on characters from English history, literature, song and legend. The first was released in 1934.
- During the 1950s, handles also became a more decorative part of the design with this feature telling more about the character.
- Withdrawn mugs were produced in smaller quantities and are highly desirable amongst collectors. Examples with colour variations are also sought after – for example, during the war certain colours could not be used.
- The popularity of the person depicted will also affect value and desirability. This is especially true if the character appeals to collectors in other areas, such as political or royal figures.

A large 'Beethoven' character jug, with box, no. D7021.

£55-65   PSA

A large 'Parson Brown' character jug, no. D5486, small fault to rim.

£45-55   PSA

A large 'Buddy Holly' character jug, limited edition number 1411 of 2500, with box and certificate, glasses broken.

£35-45   PSA

A large 'The Walrus and the Carpenter' character jug, no. D6600.

£80-120   PSA

A large Royal Doulton 'Jimmy Durante' character jug, D.6708, from the Celebrity Collection, by S. Biggs.

1985-1986

£80-120   DN

A large 'The Gardener' character jug.

£55-65   PSA

A large 'Desperate Dan' character jug, with box, no. D7006.

£45-55   PSA

A small Sandland 'Francis Drake' character jug, crazed.

£7-10   PSA

A large 'Sir Henry Doulton' character jug, limited edition number 0365 of 1997, with certificate, no. D7054, style three.

This character jug was made to commemorate the death of Sir Henry Doulton in 1887.

£50-80   PSA

A large 'Henry VIII' character jug, no. D6642.

£30-40   PSA

A small Sandland 'Robin Hood' character jug, crazed.

£7-10   PSA

A large 'Jarge' character jug, no. D6288.

£120-180 PSA

A large Royal Doulton 'Farmer John' character jug, by C. Noke no. D5788.

1938-1960

£40-60 DN

A large Royal Doulton character jug, 'Groucho Marx', D.6710, from the Celebrity Collection, by S. Taylor.

1984-1987

£40-60 DN

A large 'Glenn Miller' character jug, with box, no. D6970.

£120-180 PSA

A large 'Veteran Motorist' character jug, no. D6633.

£60-80 PSA

A large 'Jesse Owens' character jug, with box, no. D7019.

£60-80 PSA

A large 'Chelsea Pensioner' character jug, no. D6817.

£55-65 PSA

A large 'Punch and Judy' character jug, with certificate, no. D6946.

£120-180 PSA

A large 'Schubert' character jug, with box, no. D7056.

£70-100 PSA

A large 'Thomas O' Shanter' character jug, no. D6632.

£55-65 PSA

A large 'Queen Victoria' character jug, limited edition number 2742 of 3000, with box and certificate, no. D6788.

£30-50 PSA

A Burleigh ware 'General Smuts' character jug.

£400-500 PSA

A Burleigh ware white-glazed 'General Smuts' character jug.

£120-180 PSA

A large 'Izaak Walton' charater jug, with commemorative back stamp, with box, no. D6404.

£70-100 PSA

A large 'Dick Turpin' character jug, no. D6528.

£45-55 PSA

A large 'Dick Whittington' character jug, no. D6846.

£55-65 PSA

Toby Jugs

A Kevin Francis 'The Golfer' toby jug, limited edition of 1,000.

£80-120 PSA

A Kevin Francis 'President Gorbachev', toby jug, limited edition of 1,000.

£70-100 PSA

A Kevin Francis 'John Major' toby jug, limited edition of 750.

£60-80 PSA

A Kevin Francis 'Susie Cooper' toby jug, limited edition of 350.

£80-120 PSA

A CLOSER LOOK AT A TOBY JUG

A Kevin Francis 'The Shareholder' toby jug, limited edition of 1,500.

£120-180 PSA

Kevin Francis Ceramics started in 1985 after Kevin Pearson and Francis Salmon, who had studied together in Leeds, England, met by chance on the London Underground.

They initially published books, but when they met former Doulton modeller Geoff Blower, Pearson encouraged him to begin modelling again and commissioned the first Kevin Francis jug.

Later, Peggy Davies, a retired Doulton modeller, was brought on, along with her son Rhodri. At this point, the company got its own mark. 'The Shareholder' was one of its first designs.

As well as non-specific characters such as 'The Collector' and 'The Auctioneer', they produced jugs modelled on world leaders and a range based on famous potters was introduced in the early 1990s.

In 1993, The Kevin Francis partnership split up, but production in Stoke on Trent, England, has continued under Rodhri Davies.

A Kevin Francis 'Charlotte Rhead' toby jug, limited edition of 350.

£100-150 PSA

FIND OUT MORE...

David Fastenau & Stephen Mullins, 'Toby and Character Jugs of the Twentieth Century', Kevin James, 1999.

Graham McLaren, ' Toby and Character Jugs', Shire Books, 2000.

A Royal Winton Chintz 'Orient' trio.

c1954   *Cup 2.75in (7cm) high*

£50-70   **RH**

A Royal Winton Chintz 'Somerset' trio.

c1933   *Cup 2.75in (7cm) high*

£75-100   **RH**

A Wade Chintz 'Butterfly' trio.

c1955   *Cup 2.75in (7cm) high*

£70-90   **RH**

A Shelley Chintz 'Marguerite' teacup and saucer.

c1945   *2.5in (6.5cm) high*

£60-80   **RH**

A Shelley Chintz 'Blue Daisy' plate.

c1948   *7in (17.5cm) diam*

£20-30   **RH**

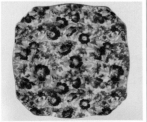

A Royal Winton Chintz 'Royalty' pattern plate.

c1936   *6in (15cm) diam*

£30-40   **RH**

CHINTZWARE

■ Chintzware is inspired by the bright and colourful floral patterns found on cotton fabrics imported from India from the late 16th century. Found on tea sets and dressing sets, it is viewed as quintessentially English. Chintzware has seen two 'golden ages' – the 1920s and the 1950s.

■ Over 200 patterns are known and popular manufacturers are Royal Winton, Lord Nelson Ware Ltd, James Kent Ltd, Shelley, Wade and Crown Ducal. Royal Winton is considered to be the first manufacturer to produce Chintz and the 'Marguerite' pattern, incorporating white daisies, yellow flowers and bluebells on a beige ground, was the first pattern designed.

■ Designs are not hand-painted but applied by lithographic transfer. Here the pattern is applied to paper which is stuck to the ceramic and removed, leaving the pattern, before firing. Joins are usually invisible, but those that show joins are either devalued or considered more individual due to this error, depending on the collector.

■ Familiarise yourself with the intricate patterns very carefully as some patterns appear the same but are different in minute and subtle ways. This is especially important when building up a set in one pattern. Some factories also used different pattern names for the same pattern.

■ Collectors usually either collect one or a number of patterns or selected items such as jugs or plates which show patterns off to their best advantage.

■ Examine pieces for signs of restoration, such as chips. Be aware of modern versions, which are not as desirable.

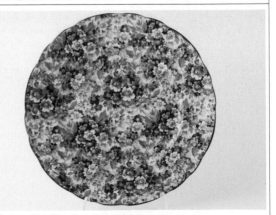

A 1930s James Kent Chintz 'Apple Blossom' plate.

8.75in (22cm) diam

£30-45   **RH**

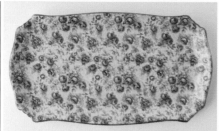

A Royal Winton Chintz 'English Rose' pattern tray.

c1951   *11.5in (29cm) wide*

£100-130   **RH**

A Grimwades Royal Winton 'Paisley' part tea service, comprising teapot, two cups, three saucers, five side plates and one cake plate.

£25-35 (service)   **AS&S**

A 1920s double-lipped vase with early 'Chintz' decoration, print and enamel, maker and designer unknown.

4.5in (11cm) high

£10-15   **FFM**

FIND OUT MORE...

Muriel M. Miller, 'Collecting Royal Winton Chintz', Wallace Homestead Book Co, 1996.

Susan Scott, 'Chintz: The Charlton Standard Catalogue' (3rd edition), Charlton International Inc, 1997.

A Royal Winton Chintz tea set for one, decorated in the 'Evesham' pattern, comprising teapot, cup, saucer, side plate, sugar bowl and jug.

£150-200   **PSA**

A 1920s Grimwades Chintz candlestick.

The Grimwade brothers owned the Royal Winton company and their name can often be found along with Royal Winton marks on the base of Chintz pieces. The Grimwades also devised a new lithographic transfer process using flexible paper to transfer the pattern to the ceramic surface. This allowed them to decorate ridged surfaces like this candlestick. The delicate paper used to do this previously was prone to tearing.

10.25in (26cm) high

£80-100   **RH**

A Royal Winton Chintz 'Hazel' three-bar toast rack.

c1934   *4.5in (11.5cm) long*

£120-150   **RH**

A 1950s Royal Winton Chintz 'Kew' pattern five-bar toast rack.

7in (18cm) long

£120-150   **RH**

A late 1940s Royal Winton Chintz lamp base.

9.5in (24cm) high

£150-200   **RH**

A Crown Clarence Chintz 'Briar Rose' biscuit barrel.

c1935   *6.5in (16cm) high*

£60-70   **RH**

CERAMICS

CLARICE CLIFF (1899-1972)

- She joined A.J.Wilkinson Ltd. Near Burslem, Staffordshire in 1916.
- In 1920, the firm acquired Newport Pottery and gave Cliff a studio there.
- Cliff and her decorators hand-painted biscuit-fired wares with brightly coloured enamels over a 'honey' glaze.
- She visited the Paris Exposition in 1925 and was influenced by Cubism and Art Deco.
- In 1928 the highly successful 'Bizarre' range was launched.
- Cliff designed over 500 shapes and 2000 patterns.
- Value is determined by shape, pattern, size, rarity and condition.
- There are fakes – so beware poor quality painting, smudged design, washed-out colours and a thick, uneven glaze.

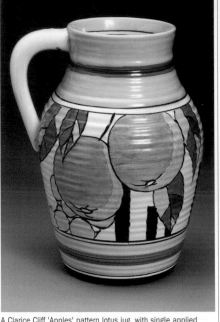

A Clarice Cliff 'Apples' pattern lotus jug, with single applied strap handle and ribbed body, with hand-painted decoration of apples, leaves and lines between yellow banding.

1931-32   11.5in (29cm) high

£2,500-3,000   **FRE**

A Clarice Cliff 'Autumn' pattern beehive honey pot.

4in (10cm)

£180-240   **GorL**

A Clarice Cliff 'Blue Chintz' pattern lotus jug, with abstract flowers in pastel colours, single strap handle.

This was an extremely popular pattern and was also produced in an orange colourway. The one to look out for is the rare 'Green Chintz'.

1932-33   12in (29.5cm) diam

£1,000-1,500   **FRE**

A rare Clarice Cliff 'Carpet' pattern cup and saucer.

Cliff copied this pattern from an illustration in a magazine of a carpet designed by Da Silva Bruhn.

c1930   2.25in (6cm) high

£650-750   **SCG**

A Clarice Cliff 'Broth' pattern large bowl, decorated with sunrays and bubbles in green, black, red and blue.

This pattern was originally called 'Fantasque 105', which, due to its success, was given the name 'Broth'. Bowls tend to be less popular with collectors, unless the pattern is very rare, as they do not show the pattern as well, nor are they as easy to display as chargers, jugs and vases.

1929-30   8.5in (21.5cm) diam

£400-500   **FRE**

A Clarice Cliff Biarritz 'Coral Firs' pattern plate.

c1935   7in (18cm) wide

£130-160   **RH**

A
B
C
D
E
F
G
H
I
J
K
L
M
N
O
P
Q
R
S
T
U
V
W
XYZ

A 1930s Clarice Cliff 'Cowslip' basket.

13.5in (34cm) high

£850-950 RH

A Clarice Cliff 'Crocus' pattern beehive honey pot.

3.75in (9.5cm)

£150-200 GorL

A Clarice Cliff 'Diamonds' pattern jardinière, with geometric decoration in blue, purple and orange, scrapes to rim.

1929-30   9.5in (24cm) diam

£1,000-1,400 FRE

A Clarice Cliff 'Crocus' pattern bowl.

£150-200 GorL

A Clarice Cliff 'Crocus' pattern octagonal fruit bowl.

9in (23cm)

£250-300 GorL

A Clarice Cliff 'Delicia Citrus' pattern Athens shape tea cup and saucer.

The colourway of this pattern to really look out for is the rare version where the fruit has a silver and gold lustre finish.

c1932 *cup 2.5in (6cm) high*

£250-300 RH

A Clarice Cliff 'Gayday' pattern cream jug and matching cup and saucer.

1930-34

£100-150 GorL

A Clarice Cliff 'Crocus' pattern conical sugar sifter.

5.75in (14.5cm)

£80-100 GorL

A Clarice Cliff Citrus 'Delicia' pattern flower ring.

1932-34   7in (18cm) diam

£320-380 SCG

A Clarice Cliff 'Etna' pattern vase, of squat form with ribbed body, hand-painted with stylized mountainous landscape.

6.75in (17cm) diam

£4,500-5,500 FRE

A Clarice Cliff 'Gayday' pattern vase, of lobed bulbous form with colourful daisies between yellow and brown bands.

1930-34   8in (20.5cm) high

£900-1,100 FRE

A Clarice Cliff 'Gibraltar' pattern milk jug, decorated with sailboats on a lake, mountains and clouds in pink, blue, yellow and green.

1931-35 4.25in (10.5cm) high

£500-1,000   **FRE**

A Clarice Cliff 'Honolulu' pattern side plate.

1933-34   7in (18cm) diam

£200-250   **GorL**

A Clarice Cliff 'Rudyard' pattern ribbed, tapered, cylindrical vase, shape 6028.

This is the blue and green version of Honolulu, named after Rudyard, near Stoke.

1933-34   7in (18cm)

£700-1,000   **GorL**

Nine pieces of Clarice Cliff 'Lightning' pattern, including two tea cups, a creamer and six plates, some wear to plates.

1929-30   7in (17.5cm) diam

£2,000-3,000 (set)   **FRE**

A Clarice Cliff 'Melons' pattern bowl.

6in (15cm) diam

£380-420   **RH**

A Clarice Cliff 'Oranges and Lemons' pattern plate.

1931-32   9.5in diam

£800-1,000   **SCG**

A Clarice Cliff 'Rhodanthe' pattern bowl.

This pattern took over from 'Crocus' as the best-selling design. It was produced by the etching technique.

1934-39   9in (22.5cm) diam

£260-300   **RH**

A Clarice Cliff 'Nuage' pattern conical bowl.

c1932   7.5in (19cm) diam

£850-950   **SCG**

A Clarice Cliff 'Solomon's Seal' cup and saucer, with solid triangular handle.

This pattern was named after the flower and was produced with a printed outline, which was then hand-coloured. This method lacked the spontaneity of the best Cliff designs, it was not a commercial success and the process was discontinued.

c1930

£180-240   **GorL**

A CLOSER LOOK AT CLARICE CLIFF

Collectors look for bold, geometric patterns.

The enamel paint was applied relatively thickly, leaving behind visible brush strokes, although by this period they were slightly less dominant.

Lotus jugs are popular because they show the pattern clearly – you get a lot of pattern for your money.

This piece is in perfect condition, with no scratches or rubbing on the enamels.

This piece is made more desirable because it epitomises the designs and style of Clarice Cliff.

A Clarice Cliff 'Sliced Circle' pattern lotus jug, with single strap handle and slightly ribbed body, decorated in an abstract circles pattern in orange, blue, green and yellow.

1929-30   *11.5in (29cm) high*

£5,500-6,500   **FRE**

A Clarice Cliff 'Sunray' pattern bowl, decorated with bright, vibrant abstract decoration.

1929-30 4.5in (11.5cm) diam

£500-600   **FRE**

A Clarice Cliff 'Sunrise' pattern cream pitcher, with reverse painting in green, orange, blue and brown, 2in (5cm) hairline crack at rim near handle, 1in (2.5cm) crack at rim.

3.75in (9.5cm) high

£250-400   **FRE**

A Clarice Cliff 'Tennis' pattern conical creamer, with stylized geometric design.

c1931   *4in (10cm) high*

£1,200-1,800   **FRE**

A Clarice Cliff 'Tennis' pattern 24 piece dessert service, including seven cups, nine saucers (two are not tennis pattern, one of these is repaired) one totally repaired, tiny chips to two, seven dessert plates, two with wear and one serving plate.

c1931   *serving dish 9in (22.5cm)*

£4,000-6,000   **FRE**

A Clarice Cliff 'Tulips' pattern vase, of spherical form on footring, with stylized trees and tulips against a yellow cloudy sky, restored.

Many of the elements of this pattern have been taken from earlier designs. The fact that it is painted in pastel shades tells us it is a later date.

1934-35   *6in (15.5cm)*

£650-750   **FRE**

A Clarice Cliff 'Woodland' pattern milk jug, with colourful abstract landscape.

4.25in (10.5cm) high

£250-300   **FRE**

A Clarice Cliff 'Woodland' pattern bowl, decorated with colourful flowers and trees in an abstract landscape, scrapes to interior, 1.25in hairline crack to rim.

7in (17.5cm) diam

£150-200   **FRE**

A Clarice Cliff 'Shape 362' vase, with colourful geometric and triangular design with blue borders.

7.75in (19.5cm)

£500-600   **GorL**

A Clarice Cliff conical banded jug.

1930s   7in (17.5cm) high

£180-220   **RH**

An extremely rare pair of Clarice Cliff 'Bizarre' bookends, each modelled with a kneeling North American Indian chief, with turquoise loin cloth and mocassins and long sand-coloured feathered headdress with orange tips, "Bizarre Wilkinson Limited" marks.

6in (15cm)

£3,500-4,500   **GorL**

A Clarice Cliff cocoa pot.

1930s   6in (15cm) high

£350-400   **RH**

A Clarice Cliff 'Chahar' wall mask, of a lady with an elaborate Egyptian headdress, the highly modelled mask has hand-painted details.

These masks, or wall medallions, as the factory called them, were produced from 1933. This mask was produced in small quantities and hence is desirable.

11in (28cm) high

£1,200-1,800   **FRE**

A 1930s Clarice Cliff 'Bizarre' pattern egg cup stand, modelled with a figure of a duckling, together with two egg cups.

£200-300   **GorL**

A Clarice Cliff Royal Staffordshire dish, of ovoid form with twin black ribbon handles and ivy chain decoration.

14in (35.5cm) high

£150-200   **FRE**

A Susie Cooper for Grays lemonade jug.
c1928   7.25in (18.5cm) high

£300-350   **SCG**

A Susie Cooper 'Cubist' pattern jug.
c1929   4.75in (12cm) high

£320-380   **SCG**

A Susie Cooper 'Moon and Mountain' pattern jug.
c1928   7.5in (12cm) high

£350-400   **SCG**

A Susie Cooper for Grays cup and saucer.
c1929   Saucer 5.5in (14cm) diam

£200-250   **SCG**

A Susie Cooper 'Geometric' pattern plate.
c1929

£650-750   **SCG**

A Susie Cooper for Grays 'Quadrupeds' pattern plate.
c1929   8.75in (22.5cm) diam

£180-220   **SCG**

Susie Cooper part coffee service, yellow decoration with black dot border, comprising coffee pot, six cups, six saucers, sugar bowl and jug, one cup badly damaged.
1930s

£100-150   **AS&S**

A Susie Cooper hand-painted coffee pot.
c1930   6in (15.5cm) high

£200-250   **SCG**

A Susie Cooper jug.
c1930   5in (12.5cm) high

£300-350   **SCG**

SUSIE COOPER (1902-1995)

- After abandoning her intended career in fashion, Cooper joined A.E. Gray & Co. in the Staffordshire Potteries in 1922 as a paintress. She was soon promoted, becoming a designer.

- In 1929 she set up her own company which decorated locally made white-ware blanks.

- In 1931 she moved production to the famous 'Crown Works', part of Woods & Sons.

- By 1932 she was designing her first shapes and adopted the famous Leaping Deer mark. The rounded and traditional 'Kestrel', 'Curlew' and 'Wren' shapes produced at this time are very collectable.

- Highly desirable decoration includes hand-painted or lithographed brightly coloured geometric shapes or polka dots. These are typical of the Art Deco period and were all produced before 1939.

- Post-War production is less brightly coloured and is inspired by organic and plant-like designs.

- In 1950 Cooper acquired a bone china manufacturer and began producing dinnerware, but these pieces are less desirable to collectors.

- Reproductions can be found. Examples include The Bradford Exchange which reproduced Cooper's geometric design plates in 1999, and Wedgwood, which re-released the Kestrel breakfast sets in 1987.

- Fakes are often found – primarily the miniature tea sets – check for irregular and fuzzy marks.

A Susie Cooper hand-painted 'Geometric' pattern biscuit barrel.
c1930   *5in (12.5cm) high*

£750-850   **SCG**

A Susie Cooper cup and saucer.
c1931   *4.25in (11cm) diam*

£150-180   **SCG**

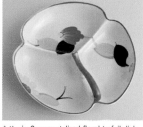

A Susie Cooper stylized floral trefoil dish.
c1932   *8.5in (21.5cm)*

£100-150   **SCG**

A Susie Cooper 'Studio Range' pink vase.
1932-1934   *7.75in (20cm) high*

£150-180   **SCG**

A Susie Cooper 'Studio Range' green fruit plate.
1932-34   *7in (18.5cm) diam*

£40-60   **SCG**

A Susie Cooper hand-painted floral plate.
c1932   *7.75in (20cm) diam*

£40-60   **SCG**

A Susie Cooper ladle.
c1932   *7.75in (20cm) long*

£70-100   **SCG**

A Susie Cooper 'Graduated Black Bands' pattern plate.
c1932   *5.25in (13.5cm) diam*

£20-30   **SCG**

A Susie Cooper 'Plaid' pattern fruit bowl.
c1933 9.5in (24cm) diam

£200-250 SCG

A Susie Cooper 'Tea for Two' set.
c1932 4.75in (12cm) high

£300-400 SCG

A Susie Cooper 'Galleon' pattern plate.
This pattern is rare.
c1933 11in (28cm) diam

£350-450 SCG

A Susie Cooper 'Noah's Arc' divided dish.
c1933 7.75in (20cm) diam

£200-250 SCG

A Susie Cooper 'Skier' mug.
1933-1934 3.75in (9.5cm) high

£200-250 SCG

A Susie Cooper 'Guardsman' plate.
This is one of the rarest Nursery Ware patterns.
c1933 6.25in (16cm)

£180-220 SCG

A Susie Cooper stylized floral gravy boat.
c1934 3in (8cm) high

£50-80 SCG

A Susie Cooper 'Modernist' pattern kestrel shape tureen, made for the Dorland Hall exhibition.
c1934 10.25in (26cm) wide

£80-130 SCG

A Susie Cooper Kestrel shape 'Dresden Spray' pattern tea set.
c1935 Teapot 4.75in (12cm) high

£350-450 SCG

A Susie Cooper hand-painted bowl with stylized leaves.
c1936 9.75in (25cm) diam

£250-300 SCG

A Susie Cooper hand-painted fruit plate.
c1936 11in (28cm) diam

£200-250 SCG

A Susie Cooper 'Angel Fish' table centre.
c1936   *10.75in (27.5cm) high*

£1,000-1,500   **SCG**

A Susie Cooper 'Crayon' pattern stylized floral plate.
c1937   *8.5in (22cm) diam*

£50-80   **SCG**

A Susie Cooper 'Turkey and Chicken' plate, with hand-painted outline on lithograph.
c1937   *17.75in (45cm) high*

£350-450   **SCG**

A Susie Cooper 'Scraffito Crescents' pattern breakfast tea set.
c1937   *Teapot 4.75in (12cm) high*

£550-650   **SCG**

A Susie Cooper 'Scraffito Chicken' pattern television cup and saucer, made for the American market.
c1938   *7in (18cm) long*

£80-100   **SCG**

A Susie Cooper 'Starburst' wall-charger.
c1938   *12in (30.5cm) diam*

£180-220   **SCG**

A Susie Cooper Pottery 'Chinese Fern' pattern plate, hand-painted.
c1947   *25cm diam*

£25-35   **FFM**

A Susie Cooper Falcon shape 'Asterix' pattern coffee set.
c1938   *Coffee pot 7.5in (19cm) high*

£400-450   **SCG**

A Susie Cooper Falcon shape 'Green Feather' pattern coffee set.
c1942   *Coffee pot 7.5in (19cm) high*

£300-350   **SCG**

A B C D E F G H I J K L M N O P Q R S T U V W XYZ

CORNISH WARE

- Cornish ware was produced by the T.G. Green Pottery in Church Gresley, Derbyshire, England, from the 1920s. Its popularity peaked in the 1940s and 1950s and declined in the 1980s. In that decade the rights to make Cornish ware were sold to Cloverleas of Swindon.

- Only pieces by T.G. Green are desirable to collectors. The company's marks were a church mark and black and green shield motifs. These are not associated with any particular date period.

- The mid-1990s saw a peak in collecting, with prices rising sharply, however, recently prices for common objects declined and have begun to level out.

- Collectors should look out for named jars – those bearing the name of a famous branded product or that have not been seen before can be valuable. T.G. Green undertook special commissions, often for unique pieces, so the scope is wide.

- Named jars always bear a black shield mark. If a piece bears a green shield, examine the lettering closely. If the varnish around the lettering is not even and flat, the letters are not original.

- Cornish ware was exported all over the world, so some special pieces were produced for national requests, such as a special butter dish and double egg cup for the U.S.A. These are still being discovered and are highly sought after, often fetching high prices.

- For a few years during the 1960s, a young designer called Judith Onion worked with T.G. Green. Her work is typified by streamlined shapes and the pieces designed by her bear a circular mark.

- Cornish ware is best known in blue and white, but after the 1960s was produced in black, navy blue, orange and dark green. The 1960s also saw a test range using red, although this was never put into production, making these pieces very rare.

A Cornish ware "olive oil" bottle, made by the Cornish Collectors Club, and with T. G. Green stamp to base.

7.25in (18.5cm) high

£45-55 GA

A Cornish ware "vinegar" bottle, with T. G. Green stamp to base, lacks stopper.

7.25in (18.5cm) high

£70-100 GA

A Cornish ware beaker, with T. G. Green stamp to base.

4in (10cm) high

£35-45 GA

A Cornish ware salt box, with wooden lid, and T. G. Green stamp to base.

4.5in (11.5cm) high

£80-100 GA

A Cornish ware cheese dish, with T. G. Green stamp to base.

8.5in (21.5cm) wide

£45-55 GA

A Cornish ware "loaf sugar" storage jar with lid, and T. G. Green stamp to base.

5in (12.5cm) high

£70-100 GA

A Cornish ware "icing sugar" storage jar with lid, and T. G. Green stamp to base.

5.5in (14cm) high

£100-125 GA

A Cornish ware "rice" storage jar with lid, and T. G. Green stamp to base.

4in (10cm) high

£55-65 GA

A Cornish ware "barley" storage jar with lid, and T. G. Green stamp to base.

5in (12.5cm) high

£90-110 GA

A Cornish ware "currants" storage jar with lid, and T. G. Green stamp to base.

5in (12.5cm) high

£45-55 GA

A Cornish ware "beans" storage jar with lid, and T. G. Green stamp to base.

5.75in (14.5cm) high

£120-150 GA

A Cornish ware "nutmegs" spice jar with lid, and T. G. Green stamp to base.

2.5in (6.5cm) high

£50-80 GA

A Cornish ware "ginger" spice jar with lid, and T. G. Green stamp to base.

2.5in (6.5cm) high

£70-100 GA

A Cornish ware "candied-peel" spice jar with lid, and T. G. Green stamp to base.

2.5in (6.5cm) high

£100-125 GA

A Cornish ware "flour" storage jar with lid, and T. G. Green stamp to base.

7in (17.5cm) high

£50-80 GA

A rare Cornish ware "meal" storage jar, with lid and T. G. Green stamp to base.

7in (17.5cm) high

£300-350 GA

A Cornish ware jug, with T. G. Green stamp to base.

4.5in (11.5cm) high

£35-45 GA

A Cornish ware measuring jug, with T. G. Green stamp to base.

4.75in (12cm) high

£50-75 GA

A Cornish ware rolling pin.

Barrel 9.75in (24.5cm) long

£70-100 GA

A Cornish ware mug, with T. G. Green stamp to base.

3.5in (9cm) diam

£5-10 GA

A Cornish ware plate, with T. G. Green stamp to base.

7.5in (19cm) diam

£10-15 GA

A Cornish ware plate, with T. G. Green stamp to base.

9in (22.5cm) diam

£15-20 GA

A Cornish ware sugar sifter.

5.5in (14cm) high

£40-60 GA

A Cornish ware teapot, with "Cloverleas" and T.G. Green stamp to base.

5in (12.5cm) high

£30-40 GA

A Cornish ware cafetière, probably 1960s, made for the Australian market.

7.5in (19cm) high

£70-100 GA

A yellow and white Cornish ware funnel, a special edition for the Cornish ware Collectors Club.

3.25in (8.5cm) high

£50-75 GA

Two Cornish ware egg cups.

2in (5cm) diam

£5-10 each GA

A Cornish ware butter dish with lid, by Judith Onion, with T. G. Green stamp to base.

5.5in (14cm) wide

£40-60 GA

A yellow and white Cornish ware plate, with T. G. Green stamp to base.

6.5in (16.5cm) diam

£8-10 GA

A yellow and white Cornish ware plate, with T. G. Green stamp to base.

9in (23cm) diam

£10-15 GA

A Domino jug, with T. G. Green stamp to base.

4in (10cm) high

£35-45 GA

A Domino toast rack, with T. G. Green stamp to base.

6.5in (16.5cm) wide

£40-50 GA

A Polo tea pot, with T. G. Green stamp to base.

6.5in (16.5cm) high

£30-35 GA

A Domino sugar bowl, with T. G. Green stamp to base.

3.75in (9.5cm) high

£20-30 GA

FIND OUT MORE...

www.tggreen.com, the proprietary website of the manufacturer T.G. Green Pottery.

'Cornish Ware: Kitchen & Domestic Pottery', by Paul Atterbury, Antique Collectors Club, March 1997, ISBN: 0903685485

A T. G. Green teapot, with stamp to base.

Although not classed as Cornish ware, this teapot was produced by T.G. Green.

4.25in (10.5cm) high

£70-100 GA

CERAMICS

CROWN DERBY

The Derby Crown Porcelain Co. was founded in 1876 by William Litherland and Edward Philips, in Derby England. It became Royal Crown Derby Porcelain in 1890. The wares are typically richly decorated and made of fine, thin porcelain. Artists at the factory included Albert Gregory, Cuthbert Gresley and renowned decorator Désiré Leroy. Leroy's work is typically painted, burnished, gilded and usually signed. It is highly collectable and commands high prices. The factory is still in operation today.

A Derby porcelain cake plate, with a cobalt blue rim, gilt highlights and painted with a central floral spray, red printed crown mark and "D" mark.

c1830   *11.75in (30cm) diam*

£300-400   **SI**

A Royal Crown Derby globular vase, painted by W.E.J. Dean, painted with a panel of fishing boats under sail, within a shaped gilt border, on a dark-blue ground, iron-red marks, date code for 1919, some minute scratches to the ground.

4in (10cm) high

£350-450   **DN**

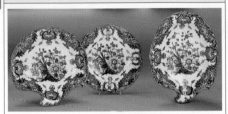

A Royal Crown Derby Imari part dessert service, printed and painted with pattern no. 4363, comprising: six dessert plates and three various fan-shaped serving dishes, iron-red printed marks, date code for 1900.

£350-450   **DN**

A Royal Crown Derby ovoid two-handled vase, with tall cylindrical neck, the shoulder decorated with printed, painted and gilt sprays of flowers on an ivory ground, iron-red printed marks, year cypher for 1892.

10.5in (27cm) high

£180-220   **DN**

A Royal Crown Derby cigarette box and cover, painted by W.E.J. Dean with a yacht, cover signed, iron-red printed marks, date code.

c1924.   *4.5in (11cm) wide*

£450-550   **DN**

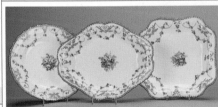

A Royal Crown Derby part dessert service, painted with sprays of pink roses, within a border of rose swags and gilt foliage, gilt gadrooned rims, comprising: twelve plates, two lozenge-shaped dishes, two shaped square dishes and a trefoil dish, iron-red printed marks, retailer's stamp for Osler, various date codes, two plates and the trefoil dish cracked.

c1909

£250-350   **DN**

A late 20thC Royal Crown Derby Solitaire miniature tea service, painted and gilt in the Imari palette, pattern number 1128, comprising: an oval tray, a teapot and cover, a milk jug, a sugar bowl and a teacup and saucer, iron-red printed marks, date code XLIV.

£300-350   **DN**

A Royal Crown Derby plate, painted by W.E.J. Dean with fishing boats, within gilt scroll rim, on a green ground, iron-red printed marks, date code circa 1933, slight surface scratches.

10in (25.5cm) diam

£180-220   **DN**

An Alcock bone china cup and saucer.
c1838

£50-80   MH

A William Alsager Adderley cup and saucer, with blue ground, pattern no. 5165.
c1910-20

£30-50   MH

A John Aynsley cup and saucer.
c1900

£30-50   MH

A John Aynsley cup and saucer, decorated with pink roses.
c1900

£50-80   MH

A John Aynsley cup and saucer, decorated with green leaves and daisies.
c1930-40

£30-50   MH

A Bishop & Stonier cup and saucer.
c1900

£30-50   MH

A Brown-Westhead & Moore cup and saucer.

£50-80   MH

A Brown-Westhead & Moore cup and saucer.
c1900

£30-50   MH

A Coalport cup and saucer.
c1940

£30-40   MH

A Coalport porcelain cup and saucer.
c1830

£60-80 | MH

A fine Coalport porcelain cup and saucer.
c1850

£140-170 | MH

A Coalport cup and saucer.
c1840

£30-50 | MH

A Coalport plate, cup and saucer, pattern no. 4562.
c1920

£40-60 | MH

A Collingwood plate, cup and saucer, pattern no. 775.
c1900

£40-60 | MH

A Crown Derby porcelain cup and saucer.
c1949

£30-50 | MH

A Crown Derby cup and saucer, pattern no. 2451.
c1914

£30-50 | MH

A Crown Ducal plate, cup and saucer.
1930s

£20-30 | MH

A Crown Staffordshire cup, saucer and plate.
c1906

£50-80 | MH

A Henry Daniels cup and saucer.
c1825

£80-120 | MH

A Daniels Savoy-shape cup and saucer, painted with scenes, pattern no. 450.
c1840

£120-180 | MH

A Daniels cup and saucer.
c1850

£80-110 | MH

A Davenport cup and saucer, pattern no. 356.
c1860

£80-120 MH

A Crown Derby porcelain plate, cup and saucer.
c1880

£70-100 MH

A Royal Doulton cup, saucer and plate, pattern no. 2588.

£30-50 MH

A Doulton Lambeth stoneware cup and saucer, applied with graduated rows of florets picked out in pale brown and deep-blue borders.

Cup 3.25in (8cm) high

£50-70 DN

A Hilditch cup and saucer.
c1830-35

£80-120 MH

A Hilditch & Hopwood cup and saucer.
c1844

£70-100 MH

A Hilditch cup and saucer.
c1845

£50-70 MH

A George Jones cup and saucer, decorated with roses.
c1900-20

£30-40 MH

A George Jones plate, cup and saucer.
c1909

£30-50 MH

A C.J. Mason cup and saucer.
c1835-45

£50-80 MH

A C.J. Mason cup and saucer.
c1835-45

£80-100 MH

A B C D E F G H I J K L M N O P Q R S T U V W XYZ

A Meyer & Sherratt (Melba china) plate, cup and saucer.
c1935-41

£30-40 MH

A Minton cup and saucer.
c1910

£50-80 MH

A Minton cup and saucer.
c1863

£40-50 MH

A Minton cup and saucer, with butterfly handle, pattern no. G599.
c1860

£120-180 MH

A Nautilus plate, cup and saucer.
c1896

£80-100 MH

An Osbourne cup and saucer, decorated with pansies.
1940s

£40-50 MH

A Paragon plate, cup and saucer, pattern no. 11.
c1930

£30-40 MH

An RH & SL Plant plate, cup and saucer.
c1930

£30-50 MH

An A.G. Richardson cup and saucer, pattern no.439.
c1928

£20-30 MH

A John Ridgway cup and saucer.
c1850

£50-80   MH

A John Rose Coalport cup and saucer.
c1815

£200-250   MH

A Royal Albert cup and saucer, decorated
with roses, pattern no. 1341.

£20-30   MH

A Ridgway 'London-shape' cup and saucer.
c1820

£80-110   MH

A Shelley pale blue 'Vogue' shape trio.

Cup 2.5in (6.5cm) high

£120-160   RH

A Queen Ann Shelley 'Sunset and Trees'
trio.

£100-120   MH

A Shelley cup and saucer.

£40-50   MH

A Spode cup and saucer.

c1827-30

£100-140   MH

A B C D E F G H I J K L M N O P Q R S T U V W XYZ

A Spode porcelain cup and saucer.
c1815

£200-250   MH

A Spode cup and saucer, with 'Imari' pattern, pattern no. 471.
c1820

£120-180   MH

A 'Vogue' shape "Horn of Flowers" trio.
Cup 2.5in (6.5cm) high

£400-500   RH

A Thomas Wild (Royal Albert) plate, cup and saucer.
c1940

£30-40   MH

A Wileman & Co. plate, cup and saucer.
c1890

£100-120   RH

A Wileman & Co. cup and saucer.
c1897

£50-70   MH

A Wileman & Co. plate, cup and saucer.
c1890

£50-70   MH

A Grainger Worcester porcelain cup and saucer.
c1835

£150-200   MH

Lambeth

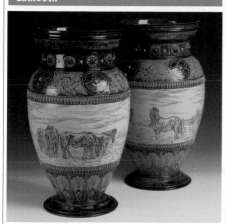

A massive pair of Doulton Lambeth stoneware vases, decorated by Hannah Barlow, each of shouldered ovoid form incised with a frieze of ponies within bands of incised and applied leaf and flowerhead motifs, the cylindrical neck and convex rim similarly decorated, the glazes in shades of blue and green, impressed marks and incised initials.

c1885   18.5in (47cm) high

£3,500-4,500   **L&T**

A Doulton Lambeth stoneware ewer, by Eliza Simmance, the oviform body having a cut-out shaped neck and foliate handle, carved with scrolling foliage and incised with florets picked out in pale greens and browns against dark green within a beaded panel, the neck and base in streaked amber, factory marks and "ES" monogram, numbered "203", some glaze losses and small repair on neck.

9in (23cm) high

£180-220   **DN**

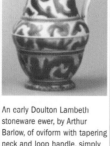

An early Doulton Lambeth stoneware ewer, by Arthur Barlow, of oviform with tapering neck and loop handle, simply decorated with blue and dark brown foliage against a greyish ground, oval factory mark, dated and with "ABB" monogram.

This piece was purchased from the Doulton Reserve Collection at Phillips Auctioneers in London, November 1999.

1874   10.5in (26cm) high

£500-600   **DN**

A Doulton Lambeth stoneware 'seaweed' vase, by George Tinworth, of ovoid form and decorated with meandering horizontal bands of beaded aquatic foliage applied with florets and picked out in blue against a streaky amber-coloured ground, impressed factory marks, dated and with "GT" monogram on side, restored on base.

1875   11in (27.5cm) high

£250-300   **DN**

A Doulton Lambeth silver-mounted stoneware pitcher, various incised and impressed marks, tapering cylindrical vessel incised with leafage between beaded borders, strap handle with scale decoration and a silver rim, together with another Doulton Lambeth globular gold-swirl ground three-handled footed vase.

1878-79   Highest 9.5in (24cm) high

£220-280   **SI**

A pair of early Doulton Lambeth stoneware candlesticks, by Frank A. Butler, oval factory marks and with "FAB" monogram, some restoration to bases.

10in (25.5cm) high

£320-380   **DN**

A Doulton Lambeth stoneware jardinière, in 'Natural Foliage' design of brown oak leaves on a mottled amber ground.

7in (18cm) high

£70-100   **BAR**

A Doulton footwarmer, registration date 1892.

c1892   9.5in (24cm) wide

£70-90   **BS**

A Royal Doulton Series Ware jug, 'The Pickwick Papers', in low relief by C.J.Noke.

£120-180   **DN**

A B C D E F G H I J K L M N O P Q R S T U V W XYZ

CERAMICS

A Doulton Burslem 'Holbeinware' oviform vase, painted by W. Hodkinson, in naturalistic colours with a sunset scene of cattle drinking from a stream and flanked on the banks by trees, factory marks and signed on side "W. Hodkinson", restored.

12.25in (31cm) high

£100-150 **DN**

A stoneware cachepot, probably Doulton Lambeth, modelled with six reserves of differing animal portraits in relief within scroll frames on a brown ground, unmarked except incised "WH" monogram.

6.5in (16.5cm) high

£180-220 **BAR**

Royal Doulton

A pair of large Royal Doulton vases, each of baluster form with cobalt glazed body, floral reserves, celadon neck and leaf-decorated everted rim, stamped marks.

16.5in (42cm) high

£700-800 **FRE**

A pair of Royal Doulton vases, each with bulbous body moulded with floral panels against a cobalt ground, tapering neck with floral collar and flat evereted rim, stamped marks.

15.25in (38.5cm) high

£350-450 **FRE**

A pair of Royal Doulton vases, with floral panels.

9in (23cm)

£150-200 **GorL**

A pair of Royal Doulton stoneware vases, each of a footed ovoid form with tall baluster necks, decorated in tube-line with floral panels and painted in green, blue and brown glazes, impressed and incised marks.

15.35in (39cm) high

£250-350 **L&T**

A pair of Royal Doulton stoneware vases, each of shouldered ovoid form, painted in colours with wisteria on an olive ground, impressed and incised marks.

10.75in (27cm) high

£250-350 **L&T**

A Royal Doulton stoneware tobacco jar and cover, painted in colours with a landscape on mottled blue ground.

4.75in (12cm) high

£200-300 **L&T**

A pair of Royal Doulton vases, of tapered cylindrical form with heart-shape motifs, on marmalade grounds, one badly damaged.

7in (18cm)

£150-200 **GorL**

A Royal Doulton stoneware twin-handled oviform vase, by Mark V. Marshall, factory marks, initialled "M.V.M" numbered "269" and with date code.

1906 *12.25in (31cm) high*

£350-400 **DN**

1 A pair of Royal Doulton Lambeth stoneware vases, each of baluster shape, tube-line decorated with clematis pendant from the shoulders and picked out in naturalistic colours, factory marks and "BN" for Bessie Newberry.

13in (32.5cm) high

£280-320 DN

2 A Royal Doulton Lambeth stoneware oviform vase, decorated around the shoulders in naturalistic colours with grapes and vine leaves, against an off-white and beige ground and another Doulton stoneware vase, similarly decorated with grapes, leaves and blossom, both with impressed factory marks.

Largest 7in (18cm) high

£200-250 DN

3 A pair of Royal Doulton stoneware vases, each painted in colours around the slightly swollen shoulders with stylised flowers and leaves against greeny-grey ground with an area of mottled purple and mauve below, impressed factory marks.

9in (22.5cm) high

£150-200 DN

A Royal Doulton ovoid vase, with Slater's patent panels.

8in (20.5cm)

£100-150 GorL

A Royal Doulton jardinière, with wavy rim and floral palmette panels.

9in (23cm)

£150-200 GorL

A Royal Doulton stoneware tobacco jar and cover, made to commemorate the Centenary of Nelson's death, bearing inscription "England expects that every man will do his duty", impressed factory marks.

1905   5in (12.5cm) high

£250-300 DN

1 A Royal Doulton Lambeth stoneware baluster vase, painted around the shoulders with square-edged flowers in mauve flanked by olive-green foliage above a band of vertical black lines, impressed factory marks on base.

10.75in (27cm) high

£200-250 DN

2 A Royal Doulton Lambeth stoneware oviform vase, tube-line decorated with three groups of narcissi with white petals and blue centres, having green foliage against a streaky greyish ground, impressed factory marks.

6.75in (17cm) high

£180-220 DN

3 A Royal Doulton Lambeth stoneware vase, decorated by Eliza Simmance, of slender oviform with a cup-shaped neck and painted highly stylized Art Nouveau tulips, buds and foliage in mauve, olive green and deeper green against a milky pinkish-grey ground, impressed factory marks and incised "ES" monogram, numbered "349" and date code for 1910, flaw on base glazed over.

1910   14in (35.5cm) high

£450-500 DN

4 A Royal Doulton Lambeth stoneware jardinière, decorated by Eliza Simmance, of compressed globular shape, painted around the shoulders with a trellis and thorny branches of roses in milky-pink and olive-green tones against a shaded pale blue ground, impressed factory marks, incised "ES" monogram, numbered "323" and date code.

1916   6.5in (16cm) high

£350-400 DN

5 A Doulton Lambeth stoneware oviform jug, decorated by Edith Lupton, carved with scrolling panels of stylised foliage in blues and brown, flanking oval panels delicately painted in pate-sur-pate technique with scrolling foliage and florets against a greeny-brown ground, factory marks with initials "EDL" numbered "422" and dated.

1800   9in (22.5cm) high

£450-500 DN

6 A Royal Doulton Lambeth stoneware globular vase, decorated by Margaret Thompson, in naturalistic colours with blossom and foliage against an apple-green and streaked blue glaze, impressed factory marks and "MET" artist's monogram.

5.25in (13cm) high

£120-150 DN

A Royal Doulton silver-mounted whisky bottle, with Art Nouveau buds on a dark blue ground.

9.5in (24cm)

£120-180   **GorL**

A Royal Doulton Brangwyn Ware 'Harvest' pattern jug, of oviform with strap handle painted in colours with wheatsheaves, fruit and foliage against a shaded ground, factory marks on base, date code and marked "D 6120".

1940   7.5in (19cm) high

£80-120   **DN**

A set of eight 20thC Royal Doulton luncheon plates, purple printed factory mark, retailed by Tiffany & Co., each printed in green, brown, black and gilt with a border of stylized flowers round a central rosette and vine.

9in (23cm) diam

£100-150   **SI**

Figures

PEGGY DAVIES

- Davies worked as a freelance designer on a contract basis with Doulton, producing her first model in 1946.
- Her first figures were girls and figures in contemporary dress and styles, but she went on to produce a diverse range of figures including dancers, historical characters and studies of children.
- Davies was responsible for around 250 figure designs during her 40 year career with Doulton.

A Royal Doulton figure, 'Town Crier', HN2119, by Peggy Davies.

1953-1976 8in (20.5cm) high

£180-220   **DN**

A Royal Doulton figure, 'Sweet Dream', designed by Peggy Davies, introduced 1971.

5in (12.5cm) high

£100-150   **OACC**

A Royal Doulton figure, 'Noelle', HN2179, by Peggy Davies.

1957-1967 7in (17.5cm) high

£150-200   **DN**

A Royal Doulton figure, 'Teenager' HN 2203, by Peggy Davies.

1957-1962   7.5in (18.5cm) h

£100-150   **DN**

A Royal Doulton figure, 'Lily', HN 1798, by Leslie Harradine.

1936-1971   5in (13cm) high

£60-80   **DN**

A Royal Doulton figure, 'Maureen', HN1770, by Leslie Harradine.

1936-1959 7.75in (19.5cm) h

£120-180   **DN**

A rare Royal Doulton figure, 'All a blooming', by Leslie Harradine, this figure has not been given an HN number but is a colour variant of HN1466.

c1931   6.25in (16cm) high

£900-1,200   **DN**

LESLIE HARRADINE

- Harradine worked for Doulton's Lambeth factory from 1902-1912 before leaving for Canada. He returned to work as a freelance designer, releasing his first figure in 1920.

- Over the next 30 years, he sent at least one model per month to be produced, including stylishly dressed ladies and excellent studies of Dickens' characters. His work dominated 1930s' production, particularly fashionably dressed ladies and notable stars of the time. Harradine retired in 1956.

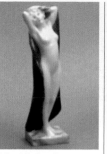

A Royal Doulton figure, 'Susanna' (HN 1288), by Leslie Harradine.

1928-36   6in (15cm) high

£800-900   DN

A Royal Doulton figure, 'Windflower' HN 1763, by Leslie Harradine, date code for 1937.

1937   8in (18cm) high

£200-250   DN

A Royal Doulton figure, 'The Orange Lady', HN1759, by Leslie Harradine.

1936-1975   8.75in (22cm) h

£150-200   DN

A Royal Doulton figure, 'Harlequinade' HN 585, by Leslie Harradine, repaired at neck.

1923-38   6.75in (17cm) high

£420-480   DN

A Leslie Johnson hand-painted figure, modelled as a young woman wearing a mauve bonnet tied with a green ribbon, a scarlet jacket painted with roses and other flowers and a pink skirt, painted with roses, signed "Leslie Johnson" on base.

Johnson was a decorator at Royal Doulton so it is conceivable that this is by the same artist but on his own account.

10.25in (26cm) high

£60-80   DN

A Royal Doulton figure, 'Cobbler' HN 1706, by C.J. Noke.

1935-69   8in (20.5cm) high

£80-120   DN

A Royal Doulton Ships' Figureheads series 'Benmore Full Rigged Ship' figure number 614 in a limited edition of 950.

1870-1924 10.5in (27cm) high

£280-320   OACC

C.J. NOKE

- Previously a modeller at the Worcester factory, joined Doulton in 1889 and during his later career, was influenced by the early work of Harradine.

- Preferring to work on figures, he released his first figural design in 1892 after modelling vases.

- He led a revival of Staffordshire style figurines, along with a team of artists, launching the range in 1912.

- Noke retired in 1941.

A large Royal Doulton flambé 'Tiger'.

13in (33cm) long

£250-300   PSA

CERAMICS

A Royal Doulton flambé 'Rhinoceros', seated and rearing his head, with red flambé glaze and a veined bluish-orange glaze to base.

9in (22.5cm) high

£700-800   **FRE**

A Royal Doulton flambé sculpture 'Gift Of Life', of a mare and her foal seated on a circular base, under a red flambé glaze.

1987-1996 9.5in (24cm) high

£450-550   **FRE**

A 20thC Royal Doulton model of a cat, with white fluffy fur and bright yellow eyes, factory marks on base, numbered "2539".

5in (12.5cm) high

£55-65   **DN**

Three 20thC Royal Doulton model, Bunnykins 'Grandpa's Story' DB14, by Walter Hayward, a Bunnykins 'Busy Needles' DB10 and a 'Mr Bunnykins 'Autumn Days', by Walter Hayward.

Largest 4.25in (10.5cm) high

£180-220   **DN**

A Royal Doulton 101 Dalmations series 'Cruella De Vil' DM1, with box.

£45-55   **PSA**

A Royal Doulton 101 Dalmations series 'Pongo' DM6, with box.

£30-40   **PSA**

A Royal Doulton 101 Dalmations series 'Perdita' DM7, with box.

£10-20   **PSA**

A Royal Doulton The Winnie the Pooh collection 'Christopher Robin and Pooh' WP10, with 70th anniversary backstamp.

£15-25   **PSA**

A Royal Doulton 101 Dalmations series 'Penny', 'Roly', and 'Lucky', all with box, nos. DM2, DM4 and DM8 respectively.

£30-50   **PSA**

A Royal Doulton 101 Dalmations series 'Patch, Roly and Freckles' DM5 tableau, limited edition number 273 of 3500, boxed with plinth.

£80-120   **PSA**

A Royal Doulton Snowmen series 'Snowball' money box.

£20-30   **PSA**

A Royal Doulton 'Grumpy's Bathtime' SW20, with box, number 2009.

£25-35   **PSA**

A Beatrix Potter musical box.

£25-35   **PSA**

FORNASETTI

- Piero Fornasetti was born in Milan in 1913 and entered the Brera Art School in 1930. After being expelled for insubordination, he joined the Scuola Superiore d'Arti Applicate all'Industria in Milan in 1932, and had his first public exhibition at Milan University a year later.

- Fornasetti's love of opulent surface ornamentation and decoration set him apart from his contemporaries who concentrated on linking form and function. Disregarded and dismissed by Modernists, but popular in the 1950s, his work underwent a renaissance during the 1980s.

- Popular motifs are flowers, suns, fish, classical architecture, classical faces and playing cards. Colouring is highly distinctive, usually being black, white and gold, although he did occasionally use other strong primary colours.

- During the 1940s and 1950s he established his reputation as an interior decorator, painting interiors including the San Remo casino, and opened a shop in Milan.

- In 1980, he opened the 'Themes and Variations' shop in London, which started a popular reappraisal of his work. In 1988, Fornasetti died during a surgical operation.

- The 1990s saw increased interest in his work, including an exhibition at the Victoria & Albert Museum, London in 1991-1992 and a Christie's auction dedicated to his work in 1998.

- His son Barnaba Fornasetti has taken over the company and continues to produce some of the most popular pieces, some in association with the manufacturer Rosenthal.

A Fornasetti Balarms ceramic pot.

1958

£80-100 FM

A Fornasetti limited edition plate, made to celebrate the 45th annual international automobile exhibition at Turin, Italy, 3rd-16th December 1967.

7.75in (20cm) diam

£50-85 FM

A Fornasetti calendar plate.

1969   9.5in (24cm) diam

£80-125 FM

A Fornasetti Astronomers plate, made for annual Christmas release.

1969   9.5in (24cm) diam

£100-135 FM

A Fornasetti limited edition plate, made to celebrate the 3rd international exhibition of industrial vehicles, Turin, Italy, 3rd-11th November 1974.

7.75in (20cm) diam

£50-85 FM

A commemorative Fornasetti plate, made to celebrate 50 years of the company (1925-1975).

9.5in (24cm) diam

£80-125 FM

One of a series of Fornasetti opera plates, featuring José from George Bizet's 'Carmen'.

10.25in (26cm) diam

£120-160 FM

One of a series of Fornasetti Italian artists plates, featuring Andrea Mantegna.

10in (25.5cm) diam

£100-135 FM

A Fornasetti ceramic paperweight, with crossed keys motif.

3.5in (9cm) wide

£80-125 FM

A set of Fornasetti 'Vini & Legumi' coasters, with original box.

4.25in (10.5cm) wide

£150-200   **FM**

A pair of Fornasetti kidney-shaped dishes.

£45-55   **FM**

A Fornasetti 'crème de cocu' ashtray.

6in (15cm) diam

£80-120   **FM**

FIND OUT MORE...

'Fornasetti – Designer of Dreams', by Patrick Mauries, Thames and Hudson Ltd, London, 1991. ISBN: 0500280517

www.fornasetti.com

A set of six Fornasetti cups.

2in (5cm) high

£180-220 (set)   **FM**

A Fornasetti 'Al Merito' (For Merit) teacup and saucer.

Saucer 5.5in (14cm) diam

£160-180   **FM**

A pair of Fornasetti dishes.

5.5in (14cm) long

£50-85   **FM**

A rare Fornasetti dish, with sun motifs.

6.75in (17cm) diam

£100-145   **FM**

A pair of Fornasetti pen holders.

2.75in (7cm) high

£80-125   **FM**

A Fornasetti ceramic biscuit barrel.

9.5in (24cm) high

£650-750   **FM**

GOSS & CRESTED WARE

- W.H. Goss was founded by William Henry Goss at the Falcon Pottery at Stoke-on-Trent in late 1850s and produced fairings. In 1888, having gained permission from UK towns to reproduce their arms on miniature porcelain pieces, his son Adolphus Goss began production of inexpensive souvenirs.

- Production was extremely large but was matched by demand amongst people who were able to travel, often for the first time, for leisure purposes due to the expansion of the railways and the introduction of public bank holidays in 1871.

- Due to Goss' immense success, imitators also made similar pieces during the late 19thC and early 20thC. Companies include Arcadian, Crescent, Carlton, Grafton, Queens, Shelley and Swan, but some of these show inferior modelling. They are fully marked with the maker's name and the crests are flush with the surface, not raised as with Goss.

- From the 1930s until 1940 quality of production fell and public tastes changed. By the early 1940s the Goss mark, and those if its competitors, fell into disuse.

- Pieces in the form of gun placements, tanks, naval vessels, military aircraft and ammunition shells usually date from between 1914 and 1920. Tanks are the most common, with ships and despatch riders being less so.

- Goss cottages and buildings (modelled after existing well-known buildings) are very desirable as are character figures and World War One pieces commemorating particular battles and campaigns.

- Cracks and chips devalue crested pieces by a half or more. Look carefully for hairline cracks.

- Crested ware should not be wrapped in newspaper as the ink oxidises the paint leading to faded colours.

An Arcadian model of a despatch rider, with the crest of Arundel.

£70-80   DN

An Arcadian model of a black cat in a well, with the crest of Slough.

£70-80   DN

An Arcadian model of a battleship, inscribed "HMS Queen Elizabeth" (Upper Norwood).

£30-50 each   DN

An Arcadian model of a charabanc, numbered 7734, with the crest for York.

An Arcadian model of 'Tommy and his Machine Gun', the base with the Ancient Arms of the Burgh of Stirling.

£50-60   DN

A Bazley & Co crested china pot with lid and arms for Plymouth, stamped on base "Bazley & Co Plymouth".

2.25in (6cm) diam

£4-6   OACC

A Carlton model of a motorcycle and sidecar, with arms of Sheffield.

£170-200   DN

A Carlton crested china boot with the crest for Rochdale, stamped on base "Carlton China W+R Stoke on Trent".

4in (10cm) long

£7-10   OACC

A W.H. Goss model of Thomas Hardy's cottage, coloured but unglazed, black-printed Goshawk mark and inscription "Model of Birthplace of Thomas Hardy, the Wessex Poet, Dorchester and Copyright".

4in (10cm) long

£140-160   DN

A Carlton model of a racehorse and jockey, a rectangular base with the crest of Newmarket.

£70-100   DN

A W.H. Goss model of the cottage from "A Window in Thrums", coloured but unglazed, black-printed Goshawk mark with inscription "A Window in Thrums, Rd. No.322142".

2.25in (6cm) long

£80-100 DN

A Goss model of Ann Hathaway's cottage, a coloured night-light version with impressed mark and black-printed Goshawk mark with inscription "Model of Ann Hathaway's cottage, Shottery, Stratford-on-Avon, Rd.No. 208047, Pub. by W. Pearce, Stratford-on-Avon", with a tiny nick to one chimney.

6in (15cm) wide

Price for two: £80-120

A large-size Jack with two matching arms for the City of Winchester and Winchester College.

4.75in (12cm) high

DN

A W.H. Goss model of a Swiss cow bell.

3in (7.5cm) high

£30-50 OACC

A W.H. Goss model of the Old Manx Pot at Peel.

2.75in (7cm) diam

£18-22 OACC

A W.H. Goss parian bust of Queen Victoria, wearing a mob-cap, on a square base titled "Victoria R", impressed mark "Copyright as Art Directs / W.H. Goss / Stoke-on-Trent / November 30 1881" date indistinct, a Crested China grandfather clock, British Empire Exhibition and a small footed vase.

Largest 6.25in (16cm) high

A crested china coal scuttle with royal coat of arms.

3.5in (9cm) wide

£5-10 OACC

A crested china trunk with arms for Chelmsford.

2.25in (6cm) wide

£10-15 OACC

£90-100 DN

A crested china elephant jug, with crest for Thorpe on rear.

2.5in (6.5cm) high

£20-30 OACC

A crested china cruet set, with a crest on the rear and stamped "King Alfred born at Wantage AD 811-901".

£14-16 OACC

Five pieces of Great War crested china, comprising "Tommy and his Machine Gun", with the crest of Dunstable, an Arcadian tank, with the crest of Ramsgate, a Botolph battleship, with the crest of the City of London, a Diamond trench mortar, with the crest of Glasgow and a Grafton "Jack Johnson" shell, with the crest of Southsea.

£150-200 DN

HUMMEL

- Franz Detleff Goebel and his son, William Goebel founded the Goebel Company in 1871, in Bavaria. The company introduced the first Goebel porcelain figures in 1890. By 1933, there was an extensive line of porcelain figures. Later pieces were influenced by the artist Sister Maria Innocentia Hummel, a member of the Sisters of the Third Order of St. Francis, at the Convent of Siessen. In 1934, Franz Goebel wrote a letter to her proposing that Goebel artists translate her two-dimensional drawings into three-dimensional figurines. She eventually agreed and in 1935 the factory introduced the first Hummel figures based on these designs, many of which are still in production.

- Early Hummel pieces generally command the highest prices. Figures from the 1930s and 1940s bear a 'V' mark surmounted by a large bumble-bee in blue. On later pieces the bee sits within the 'V'.

A 1940s Hummel figure, "Weary Wanderer", restored.
6in (15cm) high
£80-90   OACC

A Hummel figure, "Sister", small restoration to hair.
5.5in (14cm) high
£80-100   OACC

A Hummel figure, "Mother's Darling".
1940-56   6in (15cm) high
£80-100   OACC

A Hummel Club figure, "Forever Yours", first issue 1996/7.
4in (10cm) high
£60-70   OACC

A Hummel figure, "For Mother", dated.
1963   5in (12.5cm) high
£55-65   PSA

A Hummel ashtray, "Joyful", withdrawn in December 1984.
£60-70   OACC

A Hummel figure, "Merry Wanderer".
4in (10cm) high
£60-70   OACC

A Hummel figure, "Meditation".
4.5in (11cm) high
£40-50   OACC

A Hummel figure, "Cuddles", dated.
1997   3.5in (9cm) high
£45-55   OACC

A Hummel Club figure, "Garden Treasures", membership year 1998/99.
3.5in (9cm) high
£45-55   OACC

A Hummel figure, "My best friend", first issue 1998.
3.5in (9cm) high
£45-55   OACC

A German Hummel-style figure, modelled as a boy with an umbrella, black painted marks to base.
£5-10   PSA

MASON'S IRONSTONE

■ Miles Mason founded the Mason porcelain works in 1802 in Lane Delph, Staffordshire, England. The factory produced a hybrid hard paste porcelain, using both English and Chinese designs. In 1813 Mason passed the business to his sons, George and Charles James Mason. Charles James introduced the Patent Ironstone China, for which the company has become renowned.

■ Ironstone China is a hard white earthenware, slightly transparent but very strong. It is made by adding ironstone slag to the porcelain mix, and is dense and durable. The strength of the china meant it could withstand heat and so it was popular for dinner services. Other wares include large vases and fireplaces. The pieces were most commonly decorated in Oriental patterns in bold colours, with flower and bird motifs.

■ In 1848 Charles James Mason went bankrupt and subsequent Mason shapes and patterns have been produced under many company banners including George Ashworth & Brothers and, since 1973, the Wedgwood Group.

A pair of Mason's Patent Ironstone China tea plates, enamelled in colours with a table and vase pattern, single-line impressed marks, one also with brown-printed crown and drape mark.

1813-25   *7.25in (18.5cm) diam*

£80-120   **DN**

A Mason's Ironstone china footbath jug, glue-filled firing crack to body.

1820-40   *12in (30.5cm) high*

£1,500-2,000   **DN**

A Mason's Ironstone 'Blue Pheasants' pattern vegetable tureen and cover.

c1825   *9.5in (24cm) wide*

£100-150   **DN**

A Mason's Ironstone octagonal sauce tureen.

c1830 Stand 8in (20cm) long

£120-180   **DN**

A Mason's Ironstone 'Imari' two-handled vase, of octagonal section with flared neck and foot, applied with two gilt serpent handles, impressed mark.

c1825   *8in (20cm) high*

£280-230   **DN**

A mid-19thC Jonathan Lowe Chetham Stone China 'Amherst Japan' pattern ewer and basin, with oriental buildings and flowering shrubs, together with a similar ovoid two-handled pot pourri vase and pierced cover.

    Basin 14.5in (37cm) diam

£400-450   **DN**

1 An English ironstone octagonal jug, of Fenton-type shape with moulded dragon's head upper terminal to the handle, decorated with a typical Japan pattern, unmarked except for red-painted pattern number 7322.

1825-50   *6.25in (16cm) high*

£220-280   **DN**

2 An English ironstone drainer, possibly Mason's, decorated with a typical Japan pattern, unmarked, hair crack from centre hole, together with a small Mason's Ironstone dish with combed base and a different Japan pattern, printed crown and drape mark, small area of restoration to rim.

c1820-30   *Largest 13.25in (33.5cm) wide*

£250-300   **DN**

A Mason's Ironstone scent bottle and stopper, of globular form, gilt with floral sprays beneath broad gilt rims, on a dark blue ground, restoration to the rim.

c1830   *4.75in (12cm) high*

£150-200   **DN**

A Midwinter Fashion shape 'Alpine Pink' pattern plate, unnamed designer, transfer-printed.

This pattern was also produced in blue.

c1960   6in (15.5cm) diam

£3-6   FFM

A Midwinter Stylecraft shape 'Blue Domino' pattern sugar bowl, designed by Jessie Tait, hand-painted.

The blue version is rarer than the 'Red Domino' pattern.

c1954   2.25in (6cm) high

£12-15   FFM

A Midwinter Fashion shape 'Cannes' pattern plate, by Sir Hugh Casson, with printed and enamelled decoration.

This is a later version of the 1954 'Riviera' pattern.

c1960   8.5in (22cm) diam

£10-20   FFM

A Midwinter Fashion shape 'Capri' pattern TV cup and plate, designed by Jessie Tait, with printed and enamelled decoration.

This was also produced as the 'Bolero' pattern using different colours.

1955 Plate 8.5in (22cm) diam

£30-45   FFM

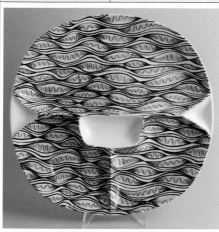

A Midwinter Fashion shape 'Caribbean' pattern buffet or TV plate, with recessed area in one corner for cup, designed by Jessie Tait, with printed and enamelled decoration.

c1955   12.25in (31cm) diam

£75-85   FFM

MIDWINTER

- Founded in 1910 in Burslem, Stoke-on-Trent, England, by William Robinson Midwinter.
- Early production was of standard tea sets and dinnerware with typical Art Deco patterns and shapes.
- Midwinter excelled at producing nurseryware with printed images by William Heath Robinson. These are now highly sought after and valuable.
- Roy Midwinter (the founder's son) joined in 1946 and proceeded to revolutionize British tableware with his innovative designs. During the 1950s, factory output was immense with many different designs.
- Aimed at a younger market, pieces could be bought separately and had multiple uses. Shapes were squared off and patterns often came from up-and-coming designers of the time including Sir Terence Conran, who designed the colourful 'Plant Life' and the 'Nature Study' patterns, Sir Hugh Casson and Jessie Tait.
- The first range in February 1953 was 'Stylecraft', which was followed in 1955 by the 'Fashion' range.
- 1957 saw the release of Midwinter's 'Melanex' range – a break-resistant material made from melamine.
- Collectors should look for pieces that sum up the design fads of the time – in terms of shape, design and colouring.
- Condition is important as these were functional pieces and often show signs of wear or damage through use, which affects value.

A Midwinter Fashion shape 'Cassandra' pattern plate, unnamed designer, transfer-printed.

c1957   9.5in (24.5cm) diam

£5-8   FFM

A Midwinter Fashion shape 'Cassandra' pattern salt and pepper pots, unnamed designer, transfer-printed.

c1957   2.75in (7cm) high

£10-15   FFM

A Midwinter Fine shape 'Cherry Tree' pattern coffee set, designed by Nigel Wylde, transfer-printed.

c1966   Pot 7.75in (20cm) high

£35-45   FFM

A Midwinter Fashion shape 'Cherokee' pattern trio, designed by Jessie Tait, hand-painted.

c1957 *Plate 6in (15.5cm) diam*

£30-40 FFM

A late 1950s Midwinter Fashion shape 'Contemporary' pattern meat plate, unnamed designer, transfer-printed.

13.75in (35cm) diam

£18-25 FFM

A Midwinter Stylecraft shape 'Cottage Ivy' pattern milk jug, designed by Jessie Tait, hand-painted.

c1953 *2.25in (5.5cm) high*

£15-20 FFM

A Midwinter Stonehenge 'Day' pattern trio set, possibly by Eve Midwinter, transfer-printed.

1970s *6.75in (17.5cm) diam*

£12-18 FFM

A Midwinter Stylecraft shape 'Domino Variant' pattern trio set, designed by Jessie Tait, hand-painted.

This variation is rarer than the 'Red Domino' pattern.

c1954 *16in (15.5cm) diam*

£25-30 FFM

A hand-painted Midwinter Stylecraft shape 'Fantasy' pattern plate, designed by Jessie Tait.

c1953 *8.5in (22cm) diam*

£20-25 FFM

A hand-painted Midwinter Fashion shape 'Festival' pattern dinner plate, designed by Jessie Tait.

c1955 *8.75in (22.5cm) diam*

£15-30 FFM

A Midwinter Fine shape 'Focus' pattern meat plate, designed by Barbara Brown, transfer-printed.

c1954 *15.5in (39.5cm) diam*

£15-20 FFM

A hand-painted Midwinter Fashion shape 'Festival' pattern egg cup, designed by Jessie Tait.

c1955 *1.75in (4.5cm) high*

£20-25 FFM

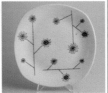

A Midwinter Fashion shape 'Flower Mist' pattern plate, designed by Jessie Tait, with printed and enamelled decoration.

c1956 *8.5in (22cm) diam*

£20-35 FFM

A Midwinter Fashion shape 'Happy Valley' pattern plate, designed by Jessie Tait, with printed and enamelled decoration.

c1959 *6in (15.5cm) diam*

£8-12 FFM

A Midwinter Stylecraft shape 'Homeweave' pattern trio set, designed by Jessie Tait, hand-painted.

This is the rare version with coloured holloware.

c1960 *Plate 6in (15.5cm) diam*

£25-30 FFM

A Midwinter Fashion shape coffee pot with later version of 'Happy Valley' pattern, designed by Jessie Tait, blue transfer-printed decoration on white glaze.

c1961   8.5in (22cm) high

£25-45   **FFM**

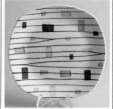

A Midwinter Fashion shape 'Magic Moments' pattern plate, designed by Jessie Tait, hand-painted.

c1956   6in (15.5cm) diam

£15-25   **FFM**

A Midwinter Fashion shape 'Marguerite' pattern coffee set, unnamed designer, transfer-printed.
This pattern was also made in yellow.

c1958   Coffee pot 9.75in (20cm) high

£30-50   **FFM**

A Midwinter Fashion shape 'Melody' pattern trio set, unnamed designer, transfer-printed.

c1958   6in (15.5cm) diam

£35-45   **FFM**

A Midwinter Stylecraft shape unusual 'Mimosa' pattern trio set, unnamed designer, transfer-printed.

c1953   6in (15.5cm) diam

£15-20   **FFM**

A Midwinter Fashion shape 'Monaco' pattern plate, designed by Jessie Tait, transfer-printed.

c1956   8.5in (22cm) diam

£8-15   **FFM**

A Midwinter 'Nature Study' pattern plate, designed by Sir Terence Conran, transfer-printed.

c1955   9.5in (24.5cm) diam

£20-35   **FFM**

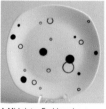

A Midwinter Fashion shape 'Pierrot' pattern plate, designed by Jessie Tait, transfer-printed.

c1955   6.25in (16cm) diam

£25-35   **FFM**

A Midwinter Fashion shape 'Plant Life' trio set, by Terence Conran, transfer-printed.
This is the later version of the original 1954 design.

c1960   6in (15cm) diam

£40-50   **FFM**

A Midwinter Fashion shape 'Plant Life' pattern plate, designed by Sir Terence Conran, transfer-printed.

c1956   7.75in (19.5cm) diam

£20-30   **FFM**

A Midwinter Fashion shape 'Primavera' pattern plate, designed by Jessie Tait, hand-painted, extremely rare, minor crack.

c1954   12.5in (32cm) diam

£20-30   **FFM**

A B C D E F G H I J K L M N O P Q R S T U V W XYZ

A hand-painted Midwinter Fashion shape 'Primavera' pattern TV set plate, designed by Jessie Tait, originally with tea cup.

c1955   *8.5in (22cm) diam*

£15-20   **FFM**

A Midwinter Fashion shape 'Quite Contrary' pattern plate, designed by Jessie Tait, transfer-printed.

c1959   *6in (15.5cm) diam*

£5-8   **FFM**

A hand-painted Midwinter Stylecraft shape 'Red Domino' pattern plate, designed by Jessie Tait.

c1953   *8.5in (21.5cm) diam*

£10-20   **FFM**

A Midwinter Fashion shape 'Saladware' pattern tea plate, designed by Sir Terence Conran, with printed and enamelled decoration.

c1955   *6in (15.5cm) diam*

£12-25   **FFM**

A Midwinter Fashion shape 'Riviera' pattern plate, designed by Sir Hugh Casson, with printed and enamelled decoration.

The 1950s saw a huge boom in foreign holidays as flying by air became affordable for many more people. Seen as very fashionable and even glamorous, people were able to travel to Europe and beyond for comparatively short periods. Patterns like Hugh Casson's 'Riviera' and 'Cannes' designs represented an evocative memory of past holidays.

c1954   *8.5in (22cm) diam*

£15-25   **FFM**

A Midwinter Fashion shape 'Savanna' pattern plate, designed by Jessie Tait, with hand-painted yellow detail and printed and enamelled decoration.

c1956   *9.5in (24.5cm) diam*

£18-25   **FFM**

A Midwinter Stylecraft shape 'Shalimar' pattern plate, designed by Jessie Tait, with printed and enamelled decoration.

c1953   *9.5in (24.5cm) diam*

£15-25   **FFM**

A Midwinter Fine shape 'Sienna' pattern milk jug and sugar bowl, designed by Jessie Tait, transfer-printed.

c1962   *2.25in (5.5cm) high*

£8-10   **FFM**

A Midwinter Stylecraft shape 'Silver Bamboo' pattern teapot, designed by Jessie Tait, hand-painted, damage to inside of lid.

c1953   *5in (13cm) high*

£20-25   **FFM**

A Midwinter Fashion shape 'Stardust' export pattern meat plate, designed by Jessie Tait, hand-painted speckled glaze, chipped rim.

This pattern was made for export to Canada.

c1958   *13.75in (35cm) diam*

£15-20   **FFM**

A Midwinter Stonehenge shape 'Wild Oats' pattern milk jug, designed by Eve Midwinter, transfer-printed.

c1974   *4in (10cm) high*

£5-8   **FFM**

A Midwinter Fashion shape 'Zambesi' pattern trio set, designed by Jessie Tait, hand-painted.

c1956   *Plate 6in (15.5cm) high*

£25-30   **FFM**

A Minton baluster vase, designed by Christopher Dresser, applied with ring 'handles', painted in gilt and coloured enamels with floral motifs in a faux cloisonne style on a turquoise ground, impressed marks.

9.5in (24cm) high

£900-1,200   L&T

A Minton framed tile, printed and painted in coloured enamels with the figures of Ferdinand and Ariel, in a floral landscape, impressed and incised marks verso.

7.75in (20cm) wide

£250-350   L&T

A Minton cloisonné porcelain vase, the design possibly by Christopher Dresser, the cylindrical vessel supported on four bracket feet with gilded base and collar, painted in colours in the Persian manner with formalised flowers and foliage against a rich turquoise ground, impressed "Minton" and date code for 1869, cracked.

1869   7.5in (18.5cm) high

£350-450   DN

A framed three tile panel by Minton & Hollins, painted in coloured enamels with figure of a young man, in saintly pose with halo around his head, walking through a grassy meadow, bears indistinct inscription.

17.75in (45cm) long

£450-550   L&T

A Minton porcelain flower-encrusted miniature teapot and cover, and another, smaller blue crossed swords marks, minor damage.

c1840

£350-450   DN

A Minton flower-encrusted teapot.

c1835   1.75in (4.5cm) high

£350-450   Gro

A large Minton jardinière, of shaped ovoid form, decorated with shaped panels of flowering poppies and painted in colours, moulded mark "Mintons England", inciscd no "3434".

13in (33cm) diam

£350-450   L&T

A Minton pottery Japanaiserie garden seat, of barrel-shaped form, date code, some small cracks through the footrim, minor wear.

c1881   17.5in (44.6cm) high

£550-650   DN

A Moorcroft MacIntyre Florian ware vase, with blue flowers against a white ground.

4in (10cm)

£1,200-1,800 GorL

A Moorcroft MacIntyre Florian ware slender baluster vase, with dark blue poppies against a pale blue ground, small area of restoration on rim.

9.75in (25cm)

£650-750 GorL

A pair of Moorcroft MacIntyre 'Yellow Iris' pattern vases, with frilled rims, slender stems and bulbous bases, tiny foot rim chips on one vase.

12.25in (31cm)

£2,000-2,500 GorL

A Moorcroft Florian ware baluster vase, in an unusual reverse painted style with yellow poppies and blue flowers.

7in (18cm) high

£2,200-2,800 GorL

A Moorcroft MacIntyre green and gold Florian ware two-handled vase, cover missing.

7in (18cm)

£700-800 GorL

A Moorcroft MacIntyre Florian ware two-handled inverted baluster vase, with sprays of spring flowers on a cream ground, restored rim.

8.75in (22cm)

£700-800 GorL

A Moorcroft Art Deco peacock feather design pitcher, in orange and browns.

9.5in (24cm)

£500-700 GorL

A Moorcroft columbine bowl, hand-decorated flowers to well, deep green ground, with paper label, flaw to rim.

5in (12.5cm) diam

£100-150 FRE

A Moorcroft ovoid vase, with clematis on a blue ground.

5.25in (13.5cm)

£200-250 GorL

A Moorcroft orchid cabinet vase, with hand-decorated flowers on a deep cobalt ground, paper label.

4in (10cm) high

£200-300 FRE

A Moorcroft 'Tudor Rose' pattern vase, of bellied form decorated in pinks and blues against a rare turquoise ground, registered no. 431157, crack to rim.

8in (20cm) high

£1,500-2,000 GorL

Two Moorcroft hibiscus cabinet vases, one with a cobalt ground, the other green.

Tallest 4.25in (11cm) high

£120-180 FRE

An unusual Moorcroft vase, of irregular tapered oval form with ribbed body in blues and greens, possibly an experimental piece.

8.75in (22cm)

£130-180 GorL

A Moorcroft baluster vase, with wisteria within palmette-shape leaves against a dark blue background.

7in (18cm)

£700-800 GorL

A Moorcroft magnolia ashtray and leaf/berry dish, each with hand decoration to well against a cobalt glaze.

Ashtray 6in (15cm) diam

£100-150 FRE

Three Moorcroft cabinet vases, two hibiscus, one with a blue ground, the other green, and clematis on a cobalt ground.

Tallest 4in (10cm) high

£170-220 FRE

A Moorcroft ovoid vase, with hibiscus on a yellow green ground.

7.25in (18.5cm)

£160-200 GorL

A Moorcroft vase, painted with cornflowers against a white ground, blue script signature.

9in (23cm)

£2,500-3,000 GorL

A Moorcroft pomegranate cabinet vase, hand-decorated in soft tones, cobalt interior.

3.25in (8cm) high

£250-300 FRE

A Myott ware scroll-handle jug.

8in (20.5cm) high

£250-300   RH

MYOTT, SON & CO.

- Founded by Ashley Myott in Staffordshire, England, in 1897. It is still in operation today as part of the Churchill Group.
- Few original documents survive as factory records were destroyed in a fire in 1949.
- Although it produced a huge range of tableware, it is mainly the brightly and highly coloured Art Deco styled vases, jugs, planters and wall pockets made in the 1930s that are desirable today. Look for bright reds, blues, oranges and black glazes.
- Mainly hand-painted, but also lithographed, value is dependent on condition as the decoration has a tendency to flake and wear off which reduces value considerably.
- The more common jugs are known as 'pinch jugs' as the rim is strongly crimped to form the spout.
- The most sought after forms are Ragtop, Beaky and Bowtie jugs and Petal, Fan, Torpedo and Diamond vases.

A Myott ware jug.

8in (20.5cm) high

£70-90   RH

A Myott ware Bowtie jug.

8in (20.5cm) high

£150-200   RH

A Myott ware jug.

8.25in (21cm) high

£90-110   RH

A Myott ware oval jug.

8.25in (21cm) high

£100-140   RH

A Myott ware oval jug.

8.75in (22cm) high

£70-90   RH

A Myott ware oval jug.

8.5in (21cm) high

£75-90   RH

A Myott ware square neck jug.
7.75in (19.5cm) high

£130-150 RH

A Myott ware square neck jug.
7.25in (18.5cm) high

£80-100 RH

A Myott ware star vase.
8.5in (21.5cm) high

£120-140 RH

A Myott ware star vase.
8.75in (22cm) high

£140-160 RH

A Myott ware spiderweb jug.
6.5in (16cm) high

£130-160 RH

A Myott ware Bowtie vase.
8in (20.5cm) high

£180-210 RH

A Myott ware diamond planter, without insert.
6in (15cm) high

£100-130 RH

A Myott ware round jug.
6.5in (16cm) high

£180-200 RH

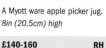

A Myott ware apple picker jug.
8in (20.5cm) high

£140-160 RH

A Myott ware castle vase.
8.5in (21.5cm) high

£250-300 RH

A Myott ware cat jug.
8.25in (21cm) high

£1,000-1,500 RH

A B C D E F G H I J K L M N O P Q R S T U V W XYZ

CERAMICS

POOLE

- In 1873 Jesse Carter (1830-1927) bought James Walker's tile company, in Poole, Dorset. The pottery became known as Carters in 1901. Owen Carter died in 1919 and two years later the Carter pottery became Carter, Stabler and Adams. Charles Carter, Owen's brother continued the business with Harold Stabler and John Adams, a potter from Stoke.
- A subsidiary was formed in 1921 to make domestic artistic ceramics. Carter's son Owen developed the production of art pottery with different glazes. Wares were hand-thrown and hand-decorated, often with stylized floral motifs.
- The Thirties saw a boom at the pottery, with some of the most memorable Poole designs being produced. Truda Carter, Charles Carter's wife, and John Adams produced a succession of outstanding patterns that have become classics.
- The Forties saw a slump in production as a result of wartime recession, but by the Fifties the pottery was at the forefront of contemporary design. In 1962 the factory became Poole Pottery Ltd and the following years saw an abundance of abstract patterns in orange, yellows and browns that corresponded with the fashions of the Sixties and Seventies. Today the pottery is still active and Poole Pottery has become highly collectable.

A Carter, Stabler & Adams Poole two-handled vase, painted with wild birds and stylized foliage in polychrome, impressed mark.

c1925   7in (18cm) high

£220-280   GorL

A Carter, Stabler and Adams Poole Pottery footed fruit bowl, incised "464", blue hand-painted "OT & H" in foot rim, small chip to foot rim, and with stained crazing.

8in (20.5cm) diam

£100-150   AS&S

A Carter, Stabler & Adams square honey pot and cover, impressed mark and "TK" signature.

5in (12.5cm) wide

£60-70   AS&S

A large 1920s Carter, Stabler and Adams Poole Pottery jug.

8.5in (21.5cm) high

£100-150   OACC

A Poole Pottery 'Blue-bird' pattern jug, designed by Truda Carter, painted in vivid colours with two blue-birds in flight amid flowers and trellises, between formal bands, impressed "Carter Stabler & Adams Ltd" mark, "316/PN".

4.5in (11cm) high

£150-200   DN

A Poole Pottery vase, painted by Ruth Paveley to a Truda Carter design, of compressed globular shape with a broad frieze of stylized flowers and foliage, impressed "Carter Stabler Adams" and "Poole England" numbered "338/ZX".

8.25in (21cm) high

£180-220   DN

A Poole Pottery shallow bowl, decorated with a geometric band.

8in (20.5cm) diam

£60-80   GorB

A Poole Pottery compressed round bowl, painted by Rita Curtis to a design by Truda Carter, the rounded sides showing a broad band of large stylized blooms interspersed with foliage impressed "Carter Stabler Adams Ltd. Poole England" with painter's mark and "0564/OT".

9in (23cm)

£250-350   DN

A Poole Pottery water jug, impressed "Poole England".

7.75in (20cm) high

£50-60   AS&S

A Poole Pottery vase, painted with a stylized array of foliage in polychrome.

4.5in (11.5cm) high

£60-70   **GorL**

A Poole vase, decorated with birds and flowers.

6in (15cm)

£150-200   **GorL**

A 1930s-60s Poole Pottery four egg cup set on stand, "seagull" and turquoise glaze decoration, unnamed designer.

Stand 6in (15.5cm) wide

£15-25   **FFM**

A Poole Pottery cylindrical vase, painted in coloured glazes in shades of iron-red, brown and ochre with a stylized interwoven leaf band, incised mark for Carol Cutler together with a Poole Pottery 'Aegean' conical bowl, painted script mark for Andree Fontana.

Tallest 10.5in (26.5cm) high

£70-100 (both)   **DN**

A Poole Pottery 'Aegean' circular wall plate, designed and decorated by Carolyn Wills, showing a landscape at sunset with tall trees in the foreground in muted colours with an autumnal coloured sky, impressed "Poole England" and signed "C.Wills".

13in (32.5cm) diam

£250-350   **DN**

A set of four 1980s Poole Pottery dishes.

£8-12 (set)   **AS&S**

A 1970s Poole Pottery bowl.

6in (15cm) diam

£20-30   **AS&S**

A 1970s Poole Pottery fruit bowl, chipped and repaired, rim losses.

8in (20.5cm) diam

£10-20   **AS&S**

A CLOSER LOOK AT A POOLE PLATE

Robert Jefferson, a designer at Poole, introduced the Delphis 'studio ware' range in 1958.

Brightly coloured decoration and individual styling are characteristic of the Delphis pattern.

The Delphis range tends to have a finer texture than that of the Aegean range, which was made to complement Delphis.

An impressive Poole Pottery 'Delphis' circular wall plate, painted with a large owl perched on a branch against a moonlit sky and having brightly coloured geometric plumage, "Poole England" and Dolphin mark and painter's mark which resembles that of Carolyn Bartlett.

16.25in (41cm) diam

£450-550   **DN**

A B C D E F G H I J K L M N O P Q R S T U V W XYZ

A Portmeirion Potteries 'Talisman' pattern mixing bowl, transfer-printed, designed by Susan Williams-Ellis.

c1962   *11in (28cm) diam*

£20-35   **FFM**

A Portmeirion Potteries 'Talisman' pattern cigarette box, transfer-printed, designed by Susan Williams-Ellis.

c1962   *5.25in (13.5cm) wide*

£20-30   **FFM**

A Portmeirion Potteries 'Talisman' pattern jug, transfer-printed, designed by Susan Williams-Ellis.

c1962   *6.75in (17cm) high*

£20-35   **FFM**

A Portmeirion Potteries 'Talisman' pattern dinner plate, transfer-printed, designed by Susan Williams-Ellis.

c1962   *10in (25.5cm) diam*

£10-15   **FFM**

A set of three Portmeirion Potteries 'Talisman' pattern storage jars with lids, transfer-printed in three colourways, designed by Susan Williams-Ellis.

c1962   *4.75in (12cm) high*

£40-60 (set)   **FFM**

Two Portmeirion Potteries 'Talisman' pattern storage jars, transfer-printed, designed by Susan Williams-Ellis.

c1962   *6.25in (16cm) high*

£15-25 each   **FFM**

Two Portmeirion Potteries 'Totem' pattern soup goblets, designed by Susan Williams-Ellis.

1963   *Tallest 5in (12.5cm) high*

£15-25 each   **FFM**

▶ A Portmeirion Potteries 'Totem' pattern meat plate, blue glaze, designed by Susan Williams-Ellis.

This pattern was available in a variety of colourways. It was made until the mid-1970s.

c1963   *13.5in (34.5cm) diam*

£20-35   **FFM**

A Portmeirion Potteries cylinder shape 'Totem' pattern coffee pot, white glaze, designed by Susan Williams-Ellis.

1963 (and produced until mid-1970s, and again from 2002)

13in (33cm) high

£40-60   **FFM**

A Portmeirion Potteries meridian shape 'Botanical Garden - Night-Flowering Cactus' pattern plate, transfer-printed, designed by Susan Williams-Ellis.

1972 (made to present day)
8.25in (21cm) diam

£20-25 FFM

A Portmeirion Potteries Meridian shape 'Botanical Garden - Citron' pattern plate, transfer-printed, designed by Susan Williams-Ellis.

1972 (made to present day)
7.25in (18.5cm) diam

£20-25 FFM

Two Portmeirion Potteries cylinder shape 'Greek Key' pattern coffee pots, transfer-printed on white and orange glazes, designed by Susan Williams-Ellis.

1968 to 1970s
13in (33cm) high

£25-35 each FFM

A Portmeirion Potteries 'Greek Key' pattern sugar or flour sifter, transfer-printed, designed by Susan Williams-Ellis.

1960s 6.5in (16.5cm) high

£20-25 FFM

A Portmeirion Potteries serif shape 'Cypher' pattern coffee pot, olive green glaze, designed by Susan Williams-Ellis.

1963 12in (30cm) high

£20-30 FFM

A Portmeirion Potteries serif shape 'Jupiter' pattern tureen with lid, petrol blue glaze, designed by Susan Williams-Ellis.

1963 9in (23cm) wide

£20-30 FFM

A Portmeirion Potteries serif shape 'Magic City' pattern coffee cup and saucer, transfer-printed, designed by Susan Williams-Ellis.

1966 to 1970s
Cup: 3.5in (8.5cm) high

£5-8 FFM

A Portmeirion Potteries 'Pantomime' pattern plate, transfer-printed.

The characters for this series were adapted from Pollock's Theatre Drawings. It was also available in other colours, including black and white.

c1966 10in (25.5cm) diam

£30-40 FFM

A Portmeirion Potteries 'Sailing Ships' pattern wall plate, transfer-printed, designed by Susan Williams-Ellis.

c1966 8in (20.5cm) diam

£12-18 FFM

A Portmeirion Potteries 'Tivoli' pattern herb jar, transfer-printed, designed by Susan Williams-Ellis.

1964 4.25in (10.5cm) high

£5-12 FFM

A Portmeirion Potteries 'Monte Sol' pattern storage jar, transfer-printed, designed by Susan Williams-Ellis.

1966 6.25in (16cm) high

£18-25 FFM

A Portmeirion Potteries cylinder shape 'Velocopedes' pattern plate, transfer-printed, designed by Susan Williams-Ellis.

c1968 7.25in (18.5cm) diam

£8-10 FFM

A
B
C
D
E
F
G
H
I
J
K
L
M
N
O
P
Q
R
S
T
U
V
W
XYZ

A Royal Albert Beatrix Potter figure, 'Mother Ladybird', with box.

£55-65　　　**PSA**

A Royal Albert Beatrix Potter figure, 'Babbity Bumble'.

£45-55　　　**PSA**

A Royal Albert Beatrix Potter figure, 'Christmas Stocking', with box.

£100-150　　　**PSA**

A Royal Albert Beatrix Potter figure, 'Mittens and Moppet', second.

£35-45　　　**PSA**

A Royal Albert Beatrix Potter figure, 'Thomasina Tittlemouse'.

£600-800　　　**PSA**

A Royal Albert Beatrix Potter figure, 'Old Mr Pricklepin'.

£500-700　　　**PSA**

A Royal Albert Beatrix Potter figure, 'Lady Mouse'.
c1989　　　*4in (10cm) high*

£65-75　　　**OACC**

A Royal Albert Beatrix Potter figure, 'Benjamin ate a Lettuce Leaf'.
4.75in (12cm) high

£45-55　　　**OACC**

A Royal Albert Beatrix Potter figure, 'Mr Alderman Ptolemy'.
c1973 3.25in (8.5cm) high

£45-55　　　**OACC**

A Royal Albert figure, 'Susan'.

£1,700-2,000　　　**PSA**

A Royal Copenhagen figure, by Bing and Grondahl, modelled as a salmon trout, with Bing and Grondahl factory mark and "2366 FL" in green, top fin re-glued.

c1915 8.5in (21.5cm) long

£100-140 PSpA

A Royal Copenhagen figure, modelled as a pheasant on a rocky base, with factory marks in blue and "1881" marked in green.

c1960 7.75in (19.5cm)

£300-350 PSpA

A Royal Copenhagen figure, by Bing and Grondahl, modelled as a pheasant, now out of production, with Bing and Grondahl factory mark and "2389 BJ" marked in green and "B & G" marked in blue.

c1969 8.5in (21.5cm) high

£300-350 PSpA

A Royal Copenhagen figure, modelled as a partridge, with "FO" and factory marks in blue and "Royal Copenhagen", "Denmark" and "2261" in green.

c1950 3.75in (9.5cm) high

£50-80 PSpA

A Royal Copenhagen figure, modelled as a kingfisher, marked with a crown and 'Denmark 3234" in green and with three waves and "DH" in blue.

c1969 3.75in (9.5cm) high

£50-100 PSpA

A Royal Copenhagen figure, by Bing and Grondahl, modelled as a sparrow, now out of production, with "Bing and Grondahl" and "1869 BG" in green and 'B & G' in blue.

c1948 4.75in (12cm) high

£100-200 PSpA

A Royal Copenhagen figure, by Bing and Grondahl, modelled as a rice-bird, marked with "Denmark, 2361 SV" and with a castle in green and "B & G" in blue.

c1948 3.5in (8.5cm) high

£50-100 PSpA

A Royal Copenhagen figure, by Bing and Grondahl, modelled as a titmouse marked with "Bing and Grondahl" and "1635 LA" in green and "B & G" in blue.

c1948 2in (5cm) high

£45-55 PSpA

A Royal Copenhagen figure, modelled as a starling, marked "Denmark, 3270" and with a crown in green and with factory mark and "FO" in blue.

c1969

£80-120 PSpA

A Royal Copenhagen figure, modelled as a pigeon, with Bing and Grondahl factory mark in green, "2540" and "BJ" painted in green and impressed B & G mark.

c1970 2.5in (6.35cm) high

£50-100 PSpA

A Royal Copenhagen figure, by Bing and Grondahl, modelled as a bullfinch, now out of production, with Bing and Grondahl factory mark in green, "B & G" in blue and "170 AS" painted in blue.

c1902 2.5in (6.35cm) high

£50-100 PSpA

A Royal Copenhagen figure, modelled as a pair of owls, with crown, "Denmark" and "834" in green and factory mark and "CK" in blue.

c1980 3.5in (8.5cm) high

£80-120 PSpA

A Royal Copenhagen figure, modelled as a turkey, now out of production, with "Denmark" printed in green and factory mark in blue and painted "4784".

c1969   2.75in (7cm) high

£80-120   **PSpA**

A Royal Copenhagen figure, modelled as a panda and cub, with factory marks, "666" and "YA" in green.

c1989   5in (12.5cm) high

£100-150   **PSpA**

A Royal Copenhagen figure, by Bing and Grondahl, modelled as a spaniel, with factory marks and "3116".

c1984   5.25in (13.5cm) high

£80-120   **PSA**

A Royal Copenhagen figure, by Bing and Grondahl, modelled as a dachshund, with factory marks, painted "1603 B".

c1948   7.75in (19.5cm) high

£120-180   **PSA**

A Royal Copenhagen figure, by Bing and Grondahl, modelled as a beagle, with factory marks and painted "2565 SA".

c1970   4.75in (12cm)

£100-150   **PSA**

A Royal Copenhagen figure, modelled as a cockerel and hen, with factory marks and painted "1094".

c1980   9.5in (24cm) high

£400-500   **PSpA**

A Royal Copenhagen figure, by Bing and Grondahl, modelled as a penguin, with factory marks and painted "1822 SA".

c1965   9.75in (24.5cm)

£200-250   **PSpA**

A Royal Copenhagen figure, modelled as a penguin, with factory marks and painted "417".

c1960   9.5in (24cm) high

£100-150   **PSpA**

A Royal Copenhagen figure, by Bing and Grondahl, modelled as a Great Dane, now out of production, with factory marks and painted "1773F".

c1952   11.5in (29cm) high

£200-250   **PSpA**

A Royal Copenhagen figure, modelled as Pan on a turtle, now out of production.

c1969   6in (15.5cm) high

£150-200   **PSpA**

A Royal Copenhagen figure, modelled as Pan with a bear, now out of production.

c1944   6in (15.5cm) high

£300-350   **PSpA**

A Royal Copenhagen figure, modelled as a sitting moose, with "Royal Copenhagen", "Denmark" and "2813" in green and factory mark and "hfx" in blue.

c1956   8.75in (22.5cm) high

£350-450   **PSpA**

A Royal Copenhagen figure of 'A Boy with Two Calves', with factory marks, painted "1858".

c1968   *9.25in (23.5cm) high*

£300-400   **PSpA**

A Royal Copenhagen figure, modelled as a herder with his dogs, with factory marks and "785" painted and impressed.

c1945   *7.75in (19.5cm) high*

£180-220   **PSpA**

A Royal Copenhagen figure, by Bing and Grondahl, modelled as a girl and Mastif, with factory marks and painted "1790 ML".

c1948   *4in (10cm) high*

£150-200   **PSpA**

A Royal Copenhagen figure of 'Friends', by Bing and Grondahl, modelled as a girl with a cat, with factory marks and painted "2249 HR".

c1948   *4in (10cm) high*

£100-150   **PSpA**

Two Royal Copenhagen dishes, decorated with ducks in shades of brown.

£25-35   **PSA**

A Royal Copenhagen vase, with crown, "Royal Copenhagen" and "Denmark 2629, 2129" printed in green and factory mark in blue.

c1969 *11.25in (28.5cm) high*

£100-150   **PSpA**

A Royal Copenhagen vase, with crown, "Royal Copenhagen" and "Denmark" printed in green, factory mark and "Lg" in blue and "2680 47c" painted in green.

c1955   *7in (17.5cm) high*

£50-100   **PSpA**

A Royal Copenhagen plate, entitled "XXII Olympiade Mockba 1980", decorated with a gymnast in a Russian scene, in shades of blue.

8in (20cm) diam

£15-25   **PSA**

A Royal Copenhagen porcelain dish, moulded with 'Foliate' designs, with various painted marks.

c1939   *3.25in (8.5cm) high*

£70-80   **MHT**

A Royal Copenhagen plaque, made to commemorate the first man landing on the moon.

1969   *7.25in (18.5cm) diam*

£40-60   **H&G**

Three Royal Copenhagen Modernist dishes, two with matte brown squeezebag decoration, the other with swirled pods under a high gloss glaze, various marks.

10in (25.5cm)

£80-120   **FRE**

Two Royal Copenhagen Modernist vases, the smaller abstract, the larger featuring stylized fish, various marks.

5.25in (13.5cm)

£60-100   **FRE**

Two Royal Copenhagen Crackleware dishes, both porcelain with high-fired craquelature, various marks.

7in (17.5cm) diam

£40-80   **FRE**

Three Royal Copenhagen Modernist bowls, each with abstract and stylized floral designs, various marks.

Largest 7.75in (19.5cm) diam

£150-200   **FRE**

CERAMICS

A pair of Ruskin spill vases, in original EPNS stands, impressed mark for 1911, some faults.

6in (15.5cm) high

£60-70 **OACC**

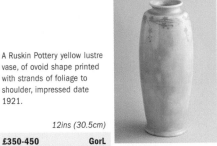

A Ruskin Pottery yellow lustre vase, of ovoid shape printed with strands of foliage to shoulder, impressed date 1921.

12ins (30.5cm)

£350-450 **GorL**

A Ruskin Jian shallow bowl, in original EPNS cradle, impressed mark for 1912, small repair.

8in (20cm) diam

£60-70 **OACC**

A Ruskin Pottery fruit bowl, in orange lustre, the perimeter moulded with foliage.

10in (25.5cm) diam

£550-650 **GorL**

A Ruskin Pottery yellow lustre oviod vase and cover, impressed date 1923.

8.25in (30cm)

£220-280 **GorL**

A Ruskin Pottery ovoid vase, glazed in mottled mauve lustre, impressed date 1925.

10in (25.5cm)

£350-450 **GorL**

Rye

A 1950s Rye Pottery hand-thrown abstract pattern pot, unnamed designer.

3.5in (9cm) high

£20-30 **FFM**

A 1950s Rye Pottery hand-thrown abstract pattern pot, unnamed designer.

3.25in (8cm) high

£20-30 **FFM**

A 1950s Rye Pottery hand-thrown abstract pattern pot, unnamed designer.

2.5in (6cm) high

£20-30 **FFM**

A 1950s Rye Pottery hand-thrown abstract pattern vase, unnamed designer.

3in (7.5cm) high

£40-60 **FFM**

A 1950s Rye Pottery hand-thrown bowl, with hand-painted abstract wheel decoration.

3.25in (8cm) high

£30-40 **FFM**

A Shelley 'Floral' trio, no. 11564.

Largest plate 5.5in (14cm) diam

£80-120 SCG

A Shelley 'Iris' trio, no. 2160.

1927-29 Largest plate 6in (15.5cm) diam

£100-140 SCG

A Shelley 'Garden' trio, no. 11607.

1927-29 Largest plate 5.5in (14cm) diam

£80-120 SCG

A Shelley 'Garland of Flowers' trio, no. 11504.
1927-29 Largest plate 6in (15.5cm) diam

£70-100 SCG

A Shelley 'Blue Iris' trio, no. 11561.

1927-29 Largest plate 6in (15.5cm) diam

£80-120 SCG

A Shelley 'Sunrise and Tall Trees' trio, no. 11670.
1927-29 Largest plate 6.25in (16cm) diam

£70-100 SCG

A Shelley 'Urn' trio, no. 11565.

1927-29 Largest plate 6.25in (16cm) diam

£100-150 SCG

A Shelley green 'Vogue Shape' trio, no. 114740.
1931 Largest plate 6.25in (16cm) diam

£200-250 SCG

A Shelley orange 'Vogue Shape' trio.

1931 Largest plate 6.25in (16cm) diam

£200-250 SCG

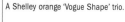

A Shelley 'Sun Ray Vogue Shape' coffee pot and six cups, no. 11742.
c1931 *Jug 7in (18cm) high*

£1,000-1,500 SCG

A Shelley Intarsio ware character teapot and cover, modelled as Austin Chamberlain wearing a green jacket, printed marks, some damage.

7.5in (19cm) long

£150-200 WW

CERAMICS

STAFFORDSHIRE

■ From the early 17th century Staffordshire has been pre-eminent in the ceramics industry. The area has abundant supplies of clay, salt and lead for glazing, and coal, used to fire the kilns. Staffordshire potteries were made up of five towns, Stoke-on-Trent, Burslem, Hanley, Longton and Tunstall. Other areas involved were Fenton, Lane Delph, Longport, Shelton, Cobridge and Newcastle-under-Tyne.

■ By the 19th century there were over 1,000 firms in production in the Staffordshire region. The expansion of the canal system in the beginning of the 19th century and the proximity of the port at Liverpool meant that English ceramics spread far and wide. By the late 19th century the railway system aided the ceramics trade even further and as a result Staffordshire had become the pottery centre of the world. The factories produced figures, dinner services and various domestic wares in earthenware and stoneware.

■ Today Staffordshire is still at the forefront of the British ceramic industry, and is the largest clayware producer in the world.

One of a pair of mid-19thC Staffordshire models of King Charles spaniels, sitting up and decorated with red patches, moulded '4' marks, one with base cracks.

7.5in (19cm) high

£100-150 (pair)   **WW**

One of two similar mid-19thC models of poodles with pups, with extruded clay clipped coats, on blue gilt-line bases, sparsely coloured and gilt.

5.75in (14.5cm) high

£150-200 (both)   **DN**

A pair of mid-19thC models of spaniels, facing left and right, seated on their haunches, painted with iron-red patches, gilt collars and black chains.

8.75in (22cm) high

£350-450   **DN**

A pair of mid-19thC models of spaniels, facing left and right, seated on their haunches, iron-red patches and gilt collars, some slight enamel flaking.

7.5in (19cm) high

£200-300   **DN**

A pair of mid-19thC models of spaniels facing left and right, seated on their haunches, painted with black patches and gilt collars separate from legs, enamel flaking.

6.75in (17cm) high

£250-300   **DN**

A mid-19thC group of two spaniels, each seated on its haunches, one on a barrel, painted with iron-red patches and with gilt collars, on a gilt line and flecked base.

8.25in (21cm) high

£180-220   **DN**

One of a pair of mid-19thC spaniel and pup groups, modelled facing left and right, the spaniels painted with iron-red patches, the pups with black patches, on blue gilt-line bases, one with small chip to the base.

6.25in (16cm) high

£400-500 (pair)   **DN**

One of a pair of Staffordshire spaniels, with green and lustre decoration.

This pair is desirable for two reasons, firstly, their front legs are separate from their bodies which is a sign of quality and the use of green and lustre paint is unusual.

c1880   *7in (15cm) high*

£100-150 (pair)   **OACC**

Three 19thC Staffordshire seated spaniels, comprising a pair of spaniels holding flower baskets and King Charles spaniel, imperfections.

Tallest 4.75in (12cm)

£120-180   **SI**

A pair of Staffordshire seated spaniels, pink noses, gilt decoration.

13in (33cm) high

£100-150   **OACC**

A pair of mid-19thC recumbant hound penholders, painted with black patches and gilt collars, on blue gilt-line bases, one head glued.

6in (15cm) long

£300-400   **DN**

A pair of late 19thC recumbant greyhound penholders, painted in iron-red with gilt collars, on blue gilt-line bases, one has small chips to nose and ears.

6in (15.5cm) wide

£150-200   **DN**

A pair of greyhound models, seated on their haunches facing left and right, painted in iron-red with gilt collars, on blue gilt-line bases, both worn.

c1860   *6in (15.5cm) high*

£180-220   **DN**

A pair of Victorian earthenware models of greyhounds, holding dead game.

7.5in (19cm) high

£150-200   **GorL**

A pair of Victorian Staffordshire models of recumbant sheep.

3.5in (9cm) high

£100-150   **GorL**

A Staffordshire model of a ram, standing four square on a gilt-lined base, its shaggy coat of grated porcelain.

4.5in (11cm) high

£150-200   **Chef**

A mid-19thC Staffordshire model of a ram, standing on a green gilt lined base.

4in (10cm) wide

£300-400   **WW**

A late 18thC Staffordshire figure of a seated deer, with bocage back and mound base.

5.5ins (14cm)

£250-300   **GorL**

A late 18thC Staffordshire group of a cow and calf, with bocage back and scroll mound base.

4.5ins (11.5cm)

£400-500   **GorL**

Two similar 20thC William Kent Ltd models of cats, seated on cushion bases, painted with iron-red patches and seated on green and pink cushion bases, some enamel flakes, chips to ears.

7.25in (18.5cm) high

£250-300 | **DN**

A Crown Staffordshire pintail duck, from a limited edition of 250, modelled by Peter Scott, with plinth and certificate, small hairline crack to base.

£250-350 | **PSA**

A late 18thC Walton Staffordshire group of a lady and gentleman musician, "Rural Past Time" on square base, drum stick replaced, minor fretting.

7.75in (19.5cm)

£250-350 | **GorL**

A Walton bocage group of a boy fighting off two girls, a hat full of grapes at his feet, modelled standing before flowering bocage, on a scroll-moulded base, painted with coloured enamels, some damage and losses.

c1820 *7.75in (20cm) high*

£250-350 | **DN**

A Walton 'Tenderness' group, typically modelled with a shepherd and companion before bocage, on a scroll-moulded titled base, the reverse with Walton banner mark, repaired.

c1820 *8.25in (21cm) high*

£550-650 | **DN**

An early 19thC Staffordshire bust of Elijah, with floral bocage back on square base.

£250-350 | **GorL**

An Obadiah Sherratt-type 'tithe pig' group, the vicar and his parishioners standing before a leafy tree, on a scroll-moulded base, painted with coloured enamels, top section of tree lacking.

c1825 *6.25in (16cm) high*

£500-600 | **DN**

A 19thC Staffordshire flat-back model, of a hunter on horseback.

10in (25.5cm) high

£150-200 | **WW**

A 19thC Staffordshire flat-back model, of a lady and gentlemen on a boat with a spaniel at their feet.

8.5in (21.5cm) high

£150-200 | **WW**

Two small 19thC Staffordshire groups, one of two figures in a boat, the other of a woman and child standing on a rocky base, the latter with a crack to the reverse.

7in (18cm) high

£100-150 | **WW**

Two large 19thC Staffordshire groups, one of Colonel Peard, titled, the other of George Rignold in the character of Henry V.

15.5in (39.5cm) high

£400-500 **WW**

A mid-19thC Staffordshire figure of two soliders, with a clock and a deer.

9in (23cm) high

£80-120 **SI**

A Walton hollow-base figure of a gardener, with urn of flowers and spade, bocage damaged.

5.5in (14cm)

£90-100 **GorL**

A pair of Victorian Staffordshire figures of Scottish dancers, playing a triangle and tambourine, together with a spill vase group with children.

Figures 7in (18cm) high

£80-120 (set) **GorL**

A Staffordshire tithe pig group.

5.5in (14cm)

£100-150 **GorL**

A pair of Staffordshire seated snuff taking figures.

5in (12.5cm)

£180-220 **GorL**

A pair of large Staffordshire figures, fitted as table lamps.

26.5in (67cm) high

£350-450 **SI**

A late 19thC Staffordshire group, titled "Prince and Princess".

c1890   15.75in (40cm) high

£100-200   **OACC**

An early Staffordshire spill vase, 'Grape harvest'.

11in (28cm) high

£100-150   **OACC**

A Staffordshire spill vase, of a musician with goat, restored.

£120-180   **OACC**

A mid-19th century Staffordshire toby jug of Nelson.

c1850   12.25in (31cm) high

£300-400   **OACC**

A pair of Staffordshire spill vase groups, each modelled with two poodles and a colourful cat perched upon a branch, raised on blue oval bases.

c1860   7.25in (18.5cm) high

£1,500-2,000   **WW**

A spill vase group of a stag and doe, of Kent and Parr types, some small areas of damage and loss.

c1880   9.25in (23.5cm) high

£550-650   **DN**

A novelty Staffordshire earthenware plate, printed in blue with reversible portraits of a man and woman, entitled 'Courtship' and 'Matrimony', Rd No. 497086.

8.25in (21cm) diam

£45-55   **HamG**

A Staffordshire pearlware part dessert service, printed in manganese and painted in green and brown with fruiting vine, comprising: a square pedestal bowl with turnover corners, a pair of sauce tureens, integral stands and cover, a pair of trefoil serving dishes, a quatrefoil serving dish and 17 plates, some damage and restoration.

c1810

£3,000-3,500   **DN**

A Staffordshire pottery 'Pekin' pattern part dinner service, printed in black and painted in colours with Chinese figures in a garden landscape, comprising: a soup tureen, ladle, cover and stand, an oval serving plate, another smaller, an oval drainer, a sauce tureen and cover, a sauce boat, an oval deep dish, a spoon tray, 14 soup plates, 15 entrée plates, and 30 dinner plates, some damage.

c1880

£800-1,000   **DN**

SYLVAC

■ In 1894 William Shaw and William Copestake founded the Shaw and Copestake factory in Stoke-on-Trent, Staffordshire, England. The factory initially produced decorative vases, jugs, and jardinières. The 1920s saw a move away from these more traditional wares and the company began to produce novelty items and ornaments. Pieces were finished or painted in a cellulose glaze, and by the 1930s animals were produced in this style as 'novelties and fancies' for the seaside and fairground gift shop market.

■ As demand increased a new green matt glaze was introduced and it is during this period that the familiar green rabbits and dogs were created. One of the directors named this line SylvaC. The name went on to become the name of the factory.

■ In the 1940s and early 1950s a glossy glaze finish was introduced. This was a gloss finish that was used on the majority of the company's products including domestic wares such as vases, pots, jugs and bowls as well as the popular animal ornaments. This was the most prolific period of production.

■ At the end of the 1970s production began to deteriorate. In 1982 the Shaw and Copestake factory ceased production. The company was subsequently run by Crown Windsor but eventually closed in 1989. Portmeirion bought the company but have not resurrected the SylvaC line, adding to its collectability. However, because of this there are some fakes on the market.

A SylvaC gnome jug.
8.75in (22.5cm) high
£60-80   OACC

A SylvaC stork jug.
10.25in (26cm) high
£60-80   OACC

A SylvaC squirrel jug.
£10-20   PC

A SylvaC squirrel jug.
8in (20cm) high
£60-80   OACC

A SylvaC rabbit jug.
8.75in (22.5cm) high
£70-90   OACC

A SylvaC rabbit.
This rabbit has a pale brown glaze. The same model in the rarer dark brown glaze is worth up to three times as much.
5in (12.5cm) high
£40-50   OACC

A SylvaC rabbit, lop eared.
5.5in (14cm) high
£20-30   OACC

A SylvaC blue squirrel.
6.75in (17cm) high
£80-120   OACC

A SylvaC spaniel, lying down, model no. 114.6.
6.5in (16cm) long
£40-50   PSA

A SylvaC dog, with sore paw.
£15-20   PC

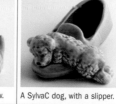

A SylvaC dog, with a slipper.
£15-20   PC

A SylvaC pig.
4in (10cm) long
£25-35   OACC

A pair of 1930s Wade Heath vases, with inserts.

5.25in (13cm) high

£150-180   **RH**

Two Wade Natwest pig money boxes, 'School Girl' and 'Baby'.

£10-20   **PSA**

A Wade Hat Box series, including 'Lady', 'Jock coat', 'Jock no coat', 'Tramp', 'Trusty', 'Peg' and 'Scamp'.

£80-120   **PSA**

Six Wade Minikins figures.

£40-50   **PSA**

A Wade Wynken figure, first version, minute chips.

£50-70   **PSA**

A Wade 'Kissing Rabbits' posy bowl, slight damage.

£20-30   **PSA**

A Wade Blynken figure, first version, minute chips.

£50-70   **PSA**

A Wade Blynken figure, second version, minute chips.

£70-100   **PSA**

Three Wade ABC cats.

£180-220   **PSA**

Three Wade farm animals: 'Cow', 'Goat' and 'Dog'.

£15-20   **PSA**

A Wade 'Faust Lang Panther on Rock', with green base and unusual colourway.

8in (20cm) high

£750-850   **PSA**

Six Wade Lilliput Lane Cottages, including 'Victoria Cottage', 'Woodman's Retreat', 'Old Mother Hubbard's', 'Anne Hathaway's Cottage' and 'Sadler's Inn'.

£100-150   **PSA**

Keith Murray

A Wedgwood Keith Murray moonstone-coloured fluted shallow bowl, signature mark.

10.25in (26cm)

£150-200   GorL

A Wedgwood Keith Murray moonstone-coloured pedestal fruit bowl, with fluted body, crack, Etruria and monogram mask.

10in (25.5cm)

£60-80   GorL

A Wedgwood Keith Murray moonstone-coloured pedestal fruit bowl, with fluted body, monogram mark.

10.25in (26cm)

£220-280   GorL

A Wedgwood matt green dinner plate, with fluted border, a matt green two-handle soup bowl and stand, both Keith Murray designs.

Dinner plate 10.25in (26cm)

£80-120   GorL

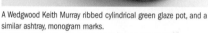

A Wedgwood Keith Murray ribbed ovoid vase, in a dark green signature mask, small crack to foot rim.

10in (25.5cm)

£320-380   GorL

A Wedgwood Keith Murray ribbed cylindrical green glaze pot, and a similar ashtray, monogram marks.

£120-180   GorL

A Wedgwood Keith Murray moonstone-coloured salt or small bowl, on tapered fluted conical pedestal and a miniature mug with fluted body, both with monogram marks, small rim chip.

Bowl 3in (7.5cm) high

£80-120   GorL

A Wedgwood Keith Murray rectangular inkstand, with pen depression and well with liner but no cover, signature mark.

10.5in (26cm)

£180-220   GorL

A pair of Wedgwood Keith Murray green tankards, signature marks.

5in (12.5cm)

£120-180   GorL

A pair of Wedgwood Keith Murray moonstone-coloured dwarf candlesticks, signature marks, one restored.

3in (7.5cm)

£120-180   GorL

Two Wedgwood Keith Murray green circular ashtrays, with fluted bodies, one with monogram, one with signature.

4.5in (11.5cm)

£120-180   GorL

A Wedgwood Keith Murray moonstone-coloured mug, with blue printed badge for the Royal Highland Regiment of Canada, monogram mark and three plain mugs, all with signature marks.

4.75in (12cm)

£180-220   GorL

A Wedgwood Keith Murray bowl and cover, with silvered lustre knop and fluted decoration.

3.5in (9cm)

£120-180   GorL

Two Wedgwood Keith Murray moonstone-coloured circular ashtrays, both with signature marks, both chipped.

4.5in (11.5cm)

£80-120   GorL

A small Wedgwood Keith Murray moonstone-coloured cream jug, with a broken silver lustre handle and ribbed body, signature and moonstone marks.

3in (7.5cm)

£80-120　　　　　　　　　　　　**GorL**

A Wedgwood Keith Murray moonstone-coloured semi-circular fluted wall pocket, signature mark.

8.5in (21.5cm)

£120-180　　　　　**GorL**

A Wedgwood Keith Murray green semi-circular fluted wall pocket, signature mark.

8.5in (21.5cm)

£180-220　　　　　**GorL**

A Wedgwood Keith Murray fruit bowl, with lightly fluted rim in an unusual blue grey colour, signature mark, small internal chip.

9.5in (24cm)

£180-220　　　　　**GorL**

A Wedgwood Keith Murray moonstone-coloured fluted tapered cylindrical vase, monogram Etruria mark.

11.5in (29cm)

£400-500　　　**GorL**

A Wedgwood Keith Murray moonstone-coloured fluted tapered cylindrical vase, signature and moonstone marks, two large cracks and area of glaze damage.

11.5in (29cm)

£80-120　　　**GorL**

KEITH MURRAY (1892-1981)

- Keith Murray was a New Zealand born architect and glass and ceramic designer, who became a pioneer of Art Deco styling.
- He designed glass for Stevens & Williams and, from 1933, ceramics for Wedgwood. His designs are typically modern, with bold, simple and streamlined forms, often with fluted or ribbed designs.
- Colours are muted, including duck-egg blue, straw, light green, ivory white and pale grey. Glazes are matt, semi-matt and celadon-satin.
- All his pieces are marked and highly desirable today. His vases in particular are highly sought after.

A Wedgwood Keith Murray fluted ovoid vase, in a rare turquoise colour, monogram and Etruria marks.

6in (15cm)

£350-450　　　**GorL**

A Keith Murray ribbed globular vase, with beige glaze.

£220-280　　　**GorL**

A Wedgwood Keith Murray matt green pedestal bowl, with banded decoration.

£250-350　　　　　　　　　　　　**GorL**

A Wedgwood matt straw coffee set with ribbed bodies comprising coffee pot, cream jug, sugar bowl and six cups and saucers, (sugar bowl cracked, one side chipped).

£400-600 GorL

A Wedgwood matt straw square ashtray (each corner chipped on the underside).
7.25in (18.5cm)

£70-100 GorL

A set of six Wedgwood matt green side plates with fluted borders.
7in (18cm)

£200-250 GorL

A Wedgwood moonstone two-handle sugar bowl and cover with fluted body, Etruria and Moonstone marks.
7.5in (19cm) across the handles

£150-200 GorL

A Wedgwood gilt-decorated jasperware vase, impressed "Wedgwood", decorated with floral sprays.
19thC 6in (15cm) high

£180-220 SI

A Wedgwood 'Water Lily' pattern jug, of tall Dutch shape with strap handle, printed in blue with the composite botanical pattern and with the usual cut-reed stringing adapted for use as a border around the neck, inside the rim and down the handle, impressed mark, cracked, glaze rubbing to spout.
1811-20 6.5in (16.6cm) high

£180-220 DN

A Wedgwood basalt plaque, made to commemorate Winston Churchill's centenary.
1974 6.25in (16cm) wide

£50-65 H&G

A Wedgwood 'Garden Pattern' plate, designed by Eric Ravilious.
c1939 9.25in (23.5cm) diam

£100-150 REN

A Wedgwood 'Queensware' Veilleuse and fittings, painted in the Dutch style in shades of iron-red, blue and green with oriental flowering shrubs, birds and insects, impressed marks, date code, repaired.

c1884   11in (28cm) high

£100-150   DN

A Wedgwood dragon lustre vase, variegated blue background with a dragon encircling the vase, inside of vase shades from bluish-purple to green and the inside rim is decorated with three panels of Oriental village scenes, alternating between the panels are gold stylized flowers, some minor wear to the gold floral trim on the inside of the vase.

8.5in (21.5cm) high

£500-800   JDJ

A Wedgwood 'Heartsease' pattern plate, produced for the Orient Shipping Line, designed by Edward Bawden.

c1952   6in (15cm) diam

£70-90   REN

A Wedgwood plate, produced for the Orient Shipping Line, designed by Robert Gooden.

c1960   8.5in (22cm) diam

£20-40   REN

A Wedgwood sporting souvenir black basalt Jasperware mug, designed by Professor Richard Guyatt.

c1969   4.25in (11cm) high

£250-300   REN

A Wedgwood Anniversary mug, designed by Professor Richard Guyatt.

1984   4.25in (11cm) high

£100-150   REN

A Wedgwood lemonade jug, with four matching beakers, produced for Liberty's of London, designed by Professor Richard Guyatt.

1953   7.5in (19cm) high

£1,000-1,500 (set)   REN

A Wedgwood bone china limited edition plate, from a series depicting historic British castles and country houses, here "Warwick Castle", designed by David Gentleman, with original box and certificate.

c1980 10.75in (27.5cm) diam

£60-90   REN

A Wedgwood bone china limited edition 'Ashdown House' plate, designed by David Gentleman, from a series depicting historic British castles and country houses, with original box and certificate.

c1980 10.75in (27.5cm) diam

£60-90   REN

A pair of Wedgwood bone china vases, pattern number Z3620.

3.75in (9.5cm) diam

£200-250   WW

A Wedgwood Fairyland Dana series lustre bowl, designed by Daisy Makeig Jones, of octagonal form, printed and painted in gilt and coloured enamels to the exterior in the 'Castle on a Road' pattern and to the interior with 'Fairy in a Cage' pattern, with an all-over lustre wash, printed and painted marks Z4968.

10.75in (27cm) diam

£2,000-£3,000   L&T

A CLOSER LOOK AT A WEMYSS PIG

Pigs are a popular Wemyss design. In Bohemia, the birthplace of Karel Nekola, the Wemyss painter, pigs are symbols of good luck.

Wemyss ware is renowned for its distinctive style and high quality paintwork.

Bold floral decoration such as the flowering clover on this pig is typical, and usually botanically accurate.

A Wemyss pottery pig, seated on its haunches, painted with pink roses, impressed "WEMYSS" and with ochre script mark "MYS", one ear and a foot restored.

Wemyss ware was produced at the Fife Pottery in Kirkcaldy, Scotland, from the mid 1800s. Wares include jug-and-basin sets, large pig doorstops, inkstands, tablewares and candlesticks, all hand-painted with brightly coloured fruit, flowers, cats and birds in the distinctive Wemyss style. In 1930, the Bovey Tracey pottery took over the manufacture of Wemyss ware until 1942.

6.25in (16cm) long

A Wemyss Lady Eva vase, painted with thistles.

6.5in (16.5cm) high

£850-950	DN	£250-350	GorL

A large Wemyss pottery pig, painted with pink flowering clover, marked "Wemyss, Made in England", fine crack on forehead and tiny glaze chips to tips of ears.

16.5in (42cm) long

A Wemyss pottery pig, painted with three-leaf clover, marked "Wemyss" in yellow, one ear chipped.

6.25in (16cm)

A small Wemyss honey pot, painted by Nekola, with bees and hive.

c1890 *2.75in (7cm) high*

A small Wemyss early morning preserve pot, painted with plums, minor restoration to chips on lid.

c1890 *2.75in (7cm) high*

£1,800-2,200	GorL	£400-450	GorL	£200-300	RdeR	£100-200	RdeR

A Wemyss commemorative mug, with motto "Nae Sic Queen Was Ever Seen" minor restoration to original handle.

This piece was part of a series of Wemyss ware produced to commemorate Queen Victoria's diamond jubilee in 1897.

1897 *5.75in (14.5cm) high*

A Wemyss fern pot, painted with sweet peas, minor restoration to rim.

c1890 *3.5in (8.5cm) high*

£400-500	RdeR	£100-200	RdeR

A Hadley's Worcester baluster vase, painted with roses.

3.75in (2.5cm)

£100-150 GorL

A pair of Worcester small jugs, printed with floral sprays on an ivory ground, gilt loop handles, puce-printed mark, shape number "1094".

c1891 *4.75in (12cm)*

£150-200 BonS

A Royal Worcester blush vase, painted with roses, no.991.

3in (7.5cm)

£70-100 GorL

A mid-19thC Kerr & Binns Worcester two-handled vase, painted with butterflies above foliage, raised on a fluted socle base and square foot, printed mark.

7.25in (18.5cm) high

£200-300 WW

A Royal Worcester blush globular vase, painted with a bird on gilt branches.

2.75in (7cm)

£150-200 GorL

A Grainger Worcester reticulated teapot and cover, pierced with scrolling foliage, within gilt band borders, printed marks.

c1880

£300-500 DN

A Royal Worcester baluster vase, painted with blackberries, no.285.

4.25in (10.5cm)

£180-220 GorL

A Royal Worcester floral-painted miniature tyg, a similar basket and a trinket dish.

£120-180 GorL

A Royal Worcester 'The French Cook' candle-snuffer.

2.75in (7cm)

£120-180 GorL

A set of eight Royal Worcester fish plates, retailed by Tiffany & Co., each painted with a fish and marine plants on a basket weave-moulded ground, with purple-printed mark.

c1865 *9.5in (24cm) diam*

£350-400 SI

A Royal Worcester candle-snuffer, in the form of a nun.

1949

£35-45 DN

A pair of Royal Worcester gilt blush figures of musicians, boy's pipe broken.

1803 *6in (15cm)*

£350-400 GorL

CROWN DEVON

The Crown Devon pottery was founded in 1870 in Staffordshire by S. Fielding and Co. It was initially called the Railway Pottery, but in 1911 became Crown Devon. The company produced mainly earthenware and majolica pieces. Wares included toby jugs, wall plaques, novelty items, figurines and vases. From 1930 the pieces carried a printed Crown Devon mark. The factory closed in 1982.

A 1930s Crown Devon Malta jade fairy castle vase.
6.25in (15.5cm) high

£500-600 RH

A 1930s Crown Devon lustre vase.
7.5in (18.5cm) high

£250-350 RH

A 1930s Crown Devon 'Matilda' fairy castle vase.
8in (20.5cm) high

£600-700 RH

Two 1930s Crown Devon green glazed dogs.

£20-25 AS&S

A 1930s Crown Devon wall charger.
12in (30.5cm) diam

£550-650 RH

A Crown Devon geometric jug.
3.5in (8.5cm) high

£85-95 RH

An unusual mid-19thC Alcock bone china relief-moulded milk jug, modelled with witches in a wood fanning a cauldron, the reverse with figures in a tent beneath trees, moulded mark, a crack across the top of the handle.
5.5in (14cm) high

£100-150 WW

A Mable Lucy Attwell elf-form milk jug, modelled saluting, painted in green with rosy red cheeks, printed facsimile signatures, factory marks and RD No "724421", part of "Boo-Boo" nursery tea set.
c1926   6in (15.cm) high

£80-100 BonS

A Mable Lucy Attwell mushroom-form teapot and cover, printed in black as a house, an elf and a mouse at one door and painted in green and orange, restored cover, part of "Boo-Boo" nursery tea set, printed facsimile signatures, factory marks and RD No 72442.
c1926   5in (12.5cm) high

£150-200 BonS

A Mable Lucy Attwell mushroom-form sucriere, painted with red spots and green grass at the base, part of "Boo-Boo" nursery tea set, printed facsimile signatures, factory marks and RD No 724421.
c1926   4in (10cm) high

£60-70 BonS

A B C D E F G H I J K L M N O P Q R S T U V W XYZ

CERANICS

A Mable Lucy Attwell nursery bowl, printed with an illustrated verse "Fairies, fairies everywhere, Dancing in the sun, Flying here and flying there, Yet - I can't catch one", printed marks, RD number 72156, some wear.

7.75in (20cm) diam

£45-55 **BonS**

A Mable Lucy Attwell canted square cake plate, with foliate moulded handles, printed with an illustrated verse, "To work in the garden is ever such fun, With fairies to help you to get the job done", printed marks, RD number 721562.

9.5in (24cm) diam

£45-55 **BonS**

An Ault Pottery vase, shape designed by Christopher Dresser and probably decorated by Clarissa Ault, of conical shape tapering to a slender neck, and simply painted in naturalistic colours with a kingfisher carrying a fish in its beak, and flanked by pink flowers and leaves, impressed facsimile designer's signature, restored patch on base.

8.25in (21cm) high

£180-220 **DN**

An Ault Pottery ewer, designed by Christopher Dresser, the vessel of shouldered oviform with an extended elliptical neck decorated with geometric banding and palmette on the spout beneath a streaked bright green and browny-pink glaze, raised Ault mark and numbered "176".

9.5in (24cm) high

£400-450 **DN**

A pottery whiskey flask, by the Bennington Company, Vermont, in the form of a book, flint enamel glaze.

c1845   5.5in (13.5cm) high

£350-400 **RAA**

A Bennington Company pitcher.

£80-100 **BCAC**

A Booth's silicon china miniature teapot, decorated in the first period Worcester-style with exotic bird reserves on a blue scale ground.

£120-180 **Chef**

A pair of Berlin double sweetmeat dishes, surmounted by putti and painted with birds.

5.5in (14cm)

£300-400 **GorL**

An American B.P.O.E. flask, hairline crack in neck.

B.P.O.E. stands for the Benevolent & Protective Order of Elks which is an American fraternal organisation. The clock on one side signifies it's always the right time for a drink.

£30-40 **BAC**

A 1930s Burleigh ware parrot vase, with liner.

7.5in (19cm) high

£650-690 **RH**

A large Brannam pottery oviform vase, by James Dewdney, modelled in high relief on the shoulders with two shells that form handles flanked by seaweed spreading on to the body, beneath a bright olive-green glaze, signed "C.H. Brannam Barum" and "JD", dated, cracked and with some glaze losses.

1904   16.25in (41cm) high

£180-220   **DN**

A Bretby silver overlay pottery vase, of classical form with blue glaze, yellow interior, and hammered silver floral overlaid motifs, stamped sun mark.

8.75in (22cm) high

£100-150   **FRE**

A 1930s 22-piece Burleigh ware zenith-shape 'vine' pattern tea set.

6in (15cm) high

£500-600   **RH**

A Copeland earthenware jug, with frieze of classical figures against a green ground, and a matching beaker.

5.5in (14cm)

£80-100   **GorL**

A Burmantofts earthenware stove, of Moorish design, the domed cover similarly decorated with flue aperture, the whole raised on moulded base with arcaded bracket feet, impressed marks.

34.25in (87cm) high

£650-750   **L&T**

A Cauldon goblet, the semi-oval bowl boldly printed with floral sprays and entwined gilt handles, printed mark.

7in (18cm) high

£350-450   **LC**

A Cauldon goblet, the semi-oval bowl boldly printed with floral sprays and entwined gilt handles, printed mark.

7in (18cm) high

£400-450   **LC**

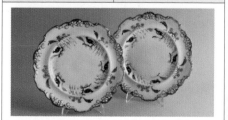

A pair of early 19thC plates, possibly Davenport or Ridgway, each painted with five pheasants in gilt trees within the rims moulded with pairs of flowerheads,

8.25in (21cm) diam

£18-22   **Chef**

A late 1960s Carol Daw Pottery small pot.

£70-90   **V**

A Davenport caneware baluster water jug, with independent decoration attributed to Robert Allen, painted with a figure before a bathing machine, coastal shipping in the distance and to one side indistinctly inscribed "Trifle Lowestoft", above an engine-turned basketweave lower section and blue enamel rims and borders, impressed mark, extensive wear, some stains and restoration.

See Sheena Smith, Lowestoft Porcelain in the Castle Museum Norwich Vol. 2 for an almost identical scene on a Lowestoft flask, pl. 21a. Robert Allen (1745-1831), seems to have been established as an independent decorator in Lowestoft following the closure of that factory c1800.

c1810   5.5in (14cm) high

£50-60   **DN**

A Denby 'Burlington' pattern vase, hand-painted, unnamed designer.
c1959 11.25in (28.5cm) high

£25-35 FFM

A Denby 'Arabesque' pattern coffee pot, hand-painted, designed by Gill Pemberton.
1964 to 1970s
12.25in (31cm) high

£15-25 FFM

An 18thC Derby figure of a shepherd girl, in pink dress on pierced gilded rococo base with floral encrusted bocage back.
6in (15cm)

£70-100 GorL

An 18thC Derby figure of a lady, amidst floral bocage and a sheep at her side.
5.75in (14.5cm)

£120-180 GorL

A late 19thC Dresden circular floral encrusted box and cover, with bird decoration.
5in (12.5cm)

£45-55 GorL

A pair of T. Forrester & Sons double gourd vases, floral painted in blue against a gilded ground, necks restored.
12in (30.5cm) high

£250-350 GorL

A Goebel wall pocket, in the form of a horse and rider, decorated in shades of brown, black and orange, heightened with gilt.
5in (12.5cm) high

£60-80 PSA

A Goebel decorative ornament, modelled as two budgies on a perch, one decorated in green and one in blue.

£45-55 PSA

A Goebel figure of a lady.

£35-45 PSA

A 1960s Isle of Wight Pottery jug, hand-painted, designed by Jo Lester.
3.5in (8.5cm) high

£6-10 FFM

A 1960s Isle of Wight Pottery pencil pot, hand-painted, designed by Jo Lester.
4.75in (12cm) high

£5-8 FFM

A Robert Jacob porcelain coffee set.

Coffee pot 9.5in (24cm) high

£55-65 CA

Three Liliput Lane Figures, comprising a Land of Legend figure, 'Mr. Bronzer', 'Ranol' and 'The Swamp Bird', with box.

£20-25 PSA

A Liliput Lane Under the Hedge figure, "Deck the Halls" Ltd edition.

£20-30 PSA

A 1960s Stig Lindberg high-fired earthenware bowl, transfer-decorated with geometric leaf design pattern. *Part of a table range Bohus "Bersa", in production until 1974.*

6.35in (16cm) diam

£35-45 MHT

A Linthorpe Pottery jardinière, of compressed globular shape with wavy rim and dimpled sides and applied with six double loop handles, moulded with florets, the red clay streaked with a milky greenish amber glaze, only number "179" visible on base.

5.25in (13cm) high

£200-250 DN

A Linthorpe pottery bowl, of compressed form on spreading circular foot painted in naturalistic colours with branches of pink blossom against a ground shading from yellow to grey, impressed "Linthorpe", printed "FB" monogram and numbered "466", having a metal neck rim.

10.75in (27cm) diam

£180-220 DN

A Maling earthenware two-handled vase, painted in lustre enamels.

6in (15cm) high

£70-90 GorL

A pair of Maling earthenware vases, relief-moulded and painted with flowers and leaves.

8in (20.5cm) high

£120-180 GorL

A Martin Brothers stoneware "double-face" jug, modelled on one side with the face of a man whistling, the other side shows a man with a grimacing visage in rich biscuit-brown tones, the eyes picked out in white, with overhead handle and spout, signed on base "Martin Bros., London & Southhall" and dated "5-1910", repaired on spout.

5.25in (13cm) high

£1,800-2,200 DN

An early 20thC Martinware oviform vase, decorated with vertical bands of short incised lines alternating direction beneath a shaded glaze, signed "Martin London".

5in (12.5cm) high

£200-300 DN

An Alfred Meakin "Gay Nineties" transfer-printed plate.
c1960   *22.5cm diam*

£8-12   **FFM**

A 19thC Meissen two-handled sweetmeat basket, pierced and painted with flower sprays, painted mark, incised numeral.
10.25in (26cm) long

£450-550   **GorL**

A 20thC Meissen chaffinch No.798, restored tip of wing.
4in (10cm)

£70-100   **GorL**

A pair of late 19thC Meissen blue and white 'onion' pattern sweetmeat dishes, flanked by reclining figures in period costume, No.2872 and 2875, chips to fingers and toes.
6.75in (17cm)

£900-1,000   **GorL**

A Mettlach plaque, with castle scene and boats, numbered "2195".
7.5in (19cm) diam

£300-350   **JDJ**

A Mettlach plaque, with castle scene and boats, numbered "2196".
7.5in (19cm) diam

£350-400   **JDJ**

Three Moore Bros. figural table centre pieces, each modelled as a putto playing a musical instrument, seated beside a blackberry incrusted bowl, chips and losses.
c1880   *6.25in (16cm)*

£250-350   **DN**

A New Hall porcelain bowl, "oriental" decoration on the outside with small painted decoration on the inside bottom of the bowl, some wear to inside decoration.
6in (15cm) diam

£120-180   **JDJ**

A Nippon four-handled vase, panelled decoration of two birds on a branch with dogwood blossoms, blue and white handled decoration of grapes and leaves, signed on base, handpainted "Nippon".
12.5in (31.5cm) high

£1,300-1,500   **JDJ**

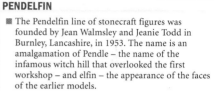

A Pendelfin rabbit, 'Peeps'.
c1970   *4in (10cm) long*

£25-35   **PC**

A Pendelfin rabbit, 'Rocky'.
c1970   *4in (10cm) high*

£20-30   **PC**

An Omega Workshops circular tin-glazed pottery plate, painted in the centre with a red spiral and on the everted rim with four further spirals alternating with green banding, against a milky off-white ground, impressed on the underside with an Omega symbol in a square.

9.75in (24.5cm) diam

£650-750   **DN**

PENDELFIN

■ The Pendelfin line of stonecraft figures was founded by Jean Walmsley and Jeanie Todd in Burnley, Lancashire, in 1953. The name is an amalgamation of Pendle – the name of the infamous witch hill that overlooked the first workshop – and elfin – the appearance of the faces of the earlier models.

■ The first items produced were myth and legend figures, nursery rhyme characters and ducks which are now highly prized by collectors. Later Pendelfin produced the rabbit figures for which they have become world renowned.

■ Pendelfin models are made from a durable stone-based compound and then hand-painted. The company continues to produce stonecraft figures today.

A Pendelfin rabbit, 'Bongo'.
c1970   *3in (7.5cm) high*

£30-50   **PC**

A Pendelfin rabbit, 'Margo'.
c1970   *3in (7.3cm) high*

£100-150   **PC**

A Pendelfin rabbit, 'Squeezy'.
c1970   *3in (7.5cm) high*

£100-150   **PC**

A Pinder Bourne plaque, hand-painted with bulldog lying in woodland, edged with gilt, slight crazing.
6.5in (16.5cm) high

£120-180   **PSA**

A Plichta model of a seated cat, with thistle decoration and a smaller cat.
5.5in (13.5cm)

£180-220   **GorL**

A 20thC Potschappel figure of a grape harvester, printed marks.
5.5in (14cm) high

£25-35   **Chef**

A Pratt Belle Vue Pegwell Bay paste pot.

£70-100   **GorB**

A Pratt pot, decorated with a scene of "Belle Vue Pegwell Bay".
5.25in (13.5cm) diam

£150-200   **PSA**

A Pratt pot, decorated with a scene of "The Room in which Shakespeare was born".

4.25in (10.5cm) diam

£75-85   **PSA**

A Pratt pot, decorated with a scene of "The Times".

4.5in (11cm) diam

£65-75   **PSA**

A Pratt pot lid, signed Mayer, decorated with a scene of bears on a rock.

3.75in (9.5cm) diam

£70-80   **PSA**

A Pratt pot lid, decorated with a scene of Osbourne House, restored.

£70-80   **PSA**

A Quimper oval platter, decorated with a mother and baby in soft colours and a geometric border, marked "Briec" on lower edge.

c1880   *15.75in (39.5cm) high*

£1,000-1,500   **FLA**

QUIMPER

- Rustic faience pottery has been made in the town of Quimper, on the South West coast of Brittany, France, since the late 17th century. The first factory was called the 'Grande Maison' and enjoyed modest success through to the late 18thC.

- The lifting of a tariff on imported English creamware and the French Revolution brought about the end of most French potteries. Quimper, however, survived due to Brittany's isolation and because it did not rely on the aristocracy to buy its wares.

- Pieces are typically decorated with local flora and fauna and depictions of local Breton life, which made them popular as tourist wares during the late 19th and early 20th centuries.

- Quimper is still produced today.

A rare Quimper demi lune vase, decorated with a Breton and Bretonne on one side, a basket of flowers on the other and with a border of florals and cross hatching, marked "HR".

c1905

£800-1,200   **FLA**

A Quimper scalloped plate, painted with a Breton couple in muted colours and with a wide green décor border.

10in (25cm) diam

£400-500   **FLA**

A pair of Quimper urn-shaped vases, marked "Henriot Quimper".

c1922   *15in (37.5cm) high*

£2,000-2,500   **FLA**

An Odetta vase, decorated with a man smoking a pipe, signed by Fouillex HB Quimper.

c1925   *10in (25cm) high*

£750-850   **FLA**

CERAMICS

Two 19thC German oval porcelain plaques, painted with a lady warrior and a violinist, labelled "Maz Ravissa, Munchen".

7in (18cm)

£700-800 GorL

A Ridgways pitcher, relief-moulded to resemble bamboo.

c1835

£50-60 BAC

A Rorstrand Sweden 'Picknick' pattern tureen with lid, printed and hand-painted, designed by Marianne Westmann.

c.1954 14.5in (22cm) high

£40-60 FFM

Three Rorstrand cups and saucers.

c1965

£35-40 MHT

A Rorstrand Sweden 'Picknick' pattern serving dish, printed and hand-painted, designed by Marianne Westmann.

c.1954 14.25in (36cm) wide

£35-55 FFM

A Royal Bayreuth apple jug.

£100-150 BAC

Two Royal Bayreuth devil and card pitchers

Large: **£300-400** Small: **£100-200** BAC

A Gunnar Nylund for Rorstrand porcelain pitcher, with green semi-matte glaze, engraved "R" and crown mark, "G. N." initials.

13.5in (34.5cm) high

£280-320 FRE

A Royal Bayreuth lobster jug.

£70-100 BAC

A Royal Bayreuth elk jug.

£100-200 BAC

A Royal Dux porcelain figure, modelled as a partially nude woman with cobalt blue skirt, applied triangle mark.

11in (28cm) high

£300-400   **FRE**

A Royal Dux porcelain centrepiece, maiden kneeling beside foliated pond, applied pad mark, chipped.

10in (25.5cm) high

£250-350   **GorL**

A Royal Dux Art Nouveau mirror, the bevelled plate flanked by a lady in flowing gilt dress over a tray base, surmounted by water lilies, No.1097.

23.5in (59.5cm)

£450-550   **GorL**

A Royal Dux camel and rider group, with a boy holding carpet bags below, on a natural base, No.1725.

19.5in (49.5cm)

£1,800-2,200   **GorL**

A set of six late 19thC Sarreguemines pig jugs, the pink tinged snouts forming the spout, the tails forming the handles.

8.75in (22cm) high

£220-280   **Chef**

A Sevres wall sconce.

c1890

£800-1,000   **ACM**

A 19thC Sevres card tray, with pink border decorated in centre with roses, cherries and strawberries surrounded by a gold enamel wreath, topped in the border with a Royal Crest, ormolu stand.

12in (30.5cm) long

£650-750   **JDJ**

A 1980s Janice Tchalenko Vessel vase, for Next.

8.75in (22cm) high

£60-100   **MHT**

A Royal Stone China covered vase, by Ralph Stevenson & Williams, red-printed royal arms mark with maker's initials.

c1825   *16in (40.5cm) high*

£150-200   **DN**

A 1980s Janice Tchalenko Vessels bowl, for Next.

4.75in (12cm) high

£60-100   **MHT**

A 1950s pitted glazed earthenware bowl by Vallauris, France, stamped "Vallauris".

8in (20.5cm) wide

£100-120   **MHT**

A Reginald Fairfax Wells "Soon" vase.

c1919-51 7.25in (18.5cm) high

£250-350   **ADE**

A Wilkinson Memory Lane jardinière, with abstracted trees and landscape in the style of Clarice Cliff.

8.5in (21.5cm) diam

£150-200   **FRE**

A Willow model of John Knox's house, coloured version with inscription "model of the house in Edinburgh where John Knox, the Scottish reformer, died, 24th Nov. 1572".

£45-55   **DN**

A Withersea rabbit jug.

8in (20cm) high

£20-30   **OACC**

A 1930s ceramic model of two deer, by Zsolnay Pecs.

6.25in (16cm) wide

£200-260   **OACC**

A fairing, "Two Different Views".

c1890 .5in (9cm) high

£60-80   **OACC**

A fairing, untitled.

c1890 4in (10.5cm) high

£60-70   **OACC**

A fairing, untitled, crack to base.

c1890 4in (10cm) high

£45-55   **OACC**

A fairing, "Paddling His Own Canoe".

c1890 4in (10cm) high

£80-90   **OACC**

A fairing, "The Power of Love".

c1890 3in (8cm) high

£80-90   **OACC**

A mid-19thC porcelaineous pastille burner and separate stand, modelled as a turreted house.

£400-450   **DN**

A mid 19thC porcelaineous pastille burner and separate stand, modelled as a cottage.

4.25in (11cm) high

£180-220   **DN**

A mid-19thC porcelain pastille burner and separate stand, modelled as a gothic church, with tower.

5.5in (14cm) high

£400-450   **DN**

A pair of mid-19thC porcelain models of cottages, with moss-encrusted gables and with two large flowers in the garden.

4.25in (11cm) wide

£280-320 (pair)   **DN**

A 19thC English biscuit porcelain group, of three children at play on an oval base, tiny chips.
5.75in (14.5cm) high

£250-300   **WW**

A mid-19thC English biscuit porcelain model of a girl, with her dog sitting up and wearing a bonnet, all on a moulded base.
5.75in (14.5cm) high

£80-120   **WW**

A pair of Continental porcelain figures, of a lady and gentleman in period costume with sheep at their sides.
c1890 10.5in (26.5cm) high

£150-250   **GorL**

A pair of 20thC German porcelain figures, one seated with a dog and the other with a cat.
5.25in (13.5cm) high

£70-100   **GorL**

A pair of late 19thC German porcelain figures, of lady and gentleman in period costumes with lambs at their feet.
7in (18cm)

£120-180   **GorL**

A 19thC porcelain-handled desk seal, with pastoral landscape and gold-coloured base, set with a cornelian engraved with a coronet and "G&R".

£850-950   **GorL**

An American Boy Scout mug
c1910-1920

£120-180   **BAC**

A pair of 19thC American chalkware decorated dogs.

£800-1,000 (pair)   **BCAC**

A pair of late 19thC Austrian Secessionist green-glazed vases.
9.75in (25cm) high

£80-120   **AS&S**

A creamware mug, scroll handle, black printed hunting scene within silver resist lustre border.
c1820 3.75in (9.5cm) diam

£80-100   **OACC**

A small Continental ceramic figure, probably Austrian, in the manner of Preiss, modelled as a naked female child sucking her finger and sitting on a large book, incised only with number "6227" on base.
3.25in (8.5cm) high

£250-300   **DN**

A Victorian bone china centrepiece, two semi-nude children.
9in (23cm) high

£350-450   **GorL**

A late 19thC faience plate, painted mark "RD" and "1756".
9.25in (23.5cm) diam

£35-45   **Chef**

An Edwardian pink lustre moustache cup, with view of The Pier, Hastings.
3.5in (9cm) diam

£40-50   **OACC**

A 19thC majolica candlestick, modelled as a cherub.

9.5in (24cm) high

£120-180 GorL

A 19th C Staffordshire pastille burner.

5in (13cm) high

£120-180 OACC

A Danish pottery money box, in the form of a seated King Charles spaniel, the coin slot in the back of the mottled ochre and brown animal.

5.25in (13.5cm) high

£30-40 Chef

A 19thC American spongewear pitcher.

8.25in (21cm) high

£220-280 BCAC

A 1970s stoneware studio vase, unsigned.

£180-220 V

Two Rococo-style vases, applied with colourful flowers on a blue ground, some restoration.

c1830   8.75in (22.5cm) high

£50-60 WW

A mid-19thC floral encrusted vase, the two-handled baluster-shape heavily applied with various flowers on a deep blue ground.

10.75in (27.5cm) high

£45-55 Chef

A 20thC scallop-shaped dish.

9in (23cm) high

£12-15 WW

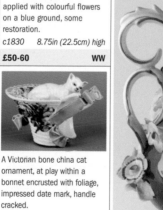

A Victorian bone china cat ornament, at play within a bonnet encrusted with foliage, impressed date mark, handle cracked.

1878   7in (18cm) high

£150-200 GorL

A framed pot lid, depicting New St Thomas's Hospital.

£40-50 GorL

A turtle and shell mustard pot, unmarked, chip to base.

£80-120 BCAC

COMICS

COMICS

- Condition is vital as comics are often damaged and worn when read. Early comics were also not 'made to last', being printed on inexpensive paper. The paper darkens with age and its colour affects the value. Look for doodles and scrawlings by previous owners, detached (or missing) covers, tears and lost pages or areas. Restoration is possible and is considered necessary on some of the rarer comics found.

- Major superheroes, such as Superman and Spider-Man, are likely to be interesting to collectors. Popular interest in some superheroes is reawakening due to the 2002 release of the 'Spider-Man' film, soon to be followed by many more, including 'The Incredible Hulk'. Widely popular characters are always likely to be more desirable.

- The first issue of any comic is likely to be the most valuable, but prices will drop considerably for any later issues.

- As well as collecting by 'age', publisher, superhero or character, the work of individual comic book artists is often collected. Some artists are better known than others, such as Bob Kane (Batman), Jerome Siegel & Joe Shuster (Superman), Carl Banks (Donald Duck), Steve Ditko (early Spider-Man) and Harvey Kurtzman (early M.A.D.).

- Many comics are moralistic or patriotic in their themes and stories and are intended as a form of proaganda to educate the young. Themes such as America battling 'evil forces' like Nazi Germany is a good example.

- Comics are usually divided into three eras:

  Golden Age: 1938-c1955. Began with the first Superman story in 'Action Comics' No.1 in Spring 1938. New characters appeared regularly as the market boomed, such as Batman in 'Detective Comics' No.27 in May 1939. Wonder Woman, the Green Lantern, and the Flash were also popular characters introduced at this time.

  Silver Age: c1956-c1969. Saw the rebirth of many superheroes after a lull in the 1950s. This period saw the arrival of Spider-Man and the Incredible Hulk. Comic collecting also began in earnest during this period.

  Bronze Age: c1970-c1979 and beyond. More modern classics, some targeted at serious readers, and a continuation of surviving popular characters. Comic collecting is now a well-established activity.

'Action Comics' #100 by DC Comics, fine condition, off-white pages.

1946

£150-200   HC

'America's Greatest Comics' #1, by Fawcett Comics, very good condition, cream to off-white pages.

1941

£350-450   HC

'Animal Comics' #6, by Dell Comics, near mint condition, cream to off-white pages.

1944

£150-200   HC

The Avengers' #3 by Marvel Comics.

This is the first Sub-Mariner crossover issue.

1964

£35-45   HC

'The Avengers' #4, by Marvel Comics, very fine condition, off-white pages, top edge of cover trimmed.

This is the first Silver Age appearance of Captain America, with Jack Kirby cover artwork.

1964

£320-380   HC

'The Avengers' #9, by Marvel Comics, off-white pages.

1964

£80-120   HC

'Batman' #130, by DC Comics, water stain on the bottom of the first few pages.

1960

£10-15   HC

'Batman' #18, by DC Comics, with Hitler, Tojo and Mussolini cover.

1943

£120-180 **HC**

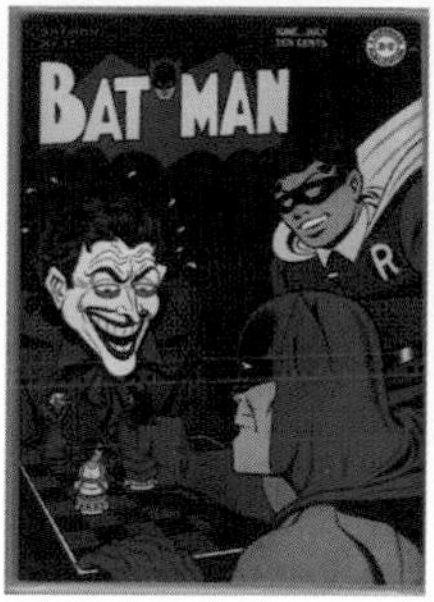

'Batman' #23, DC Comics, off-white pages, with Joker cover, very fine condition.

1944

£1,000-1,500 **HC**

'Batman' #25, DC Comics, very fine condition, white pages.

This is the only Golden Age Joker/Penguin team-up, the first team-up between two major villains.

1944

£700-1,000 **HC**

'Batman' #3, DC Comics, fine condition, off-white to white pages.

This is the first appearance of the Puppet Master and the first Catwoman in costume.

1940

£800-900 **HC**

'Captain America Comics' #13, Timely Comics, cream to off-white pages, classic cover, very fine condition.

1942

£1,200-1,500 **HC**

'Captain America Comics' #19, by Timely Comics, cream to off-white pages, with Human Torch story, good condition.

1942

£200-250 **HC**

'Batman' #67, by DC Comics, fine condition, off-white to white.

1951

£120-180 **HC**

'Black Cat' #25, by Harvey Comics, very fine condition.

1950

£70-100 **HC**

'Captain America Comics' #62, by Timely Comics, off-white pages, very good condition.

1947

£160-200 **HC**

Captain America Comics #4, by Timely Comics, cream to off-white pages, Alex Schomburg cover, Simon and Kirby artwork, fine condition.

1941

£550-650 **HC**

Walt Disney's Comics and Stories #1 Rare Star Copy, by Dell, off-white pages.

Note the black star printed at the spine, to the left of "Walt".

1940

£800-1,200 HC

'Dandy Comics' #1, by EC Comics, off-white pages, very good condition.

1947

£80-120 HC

'Daredevil Comics' #1, by Lev Gleason's Comic House, off-white pages, with Hitler cover, near mint condition.

1941

£5,000-6,000 HC

'Detective Comics' #53, by DC Comics, with double cover and off-white to white pages, very fine condition.

1941

£400-500 HC

'Detective Comics' #66, by DC Comics, off-white to white pages, origin and first appearance of Two-Face, near mint condition.

1942

£600-700 HC

'Green Lantern' #8, by DC Comics, very good condition.

1961

£25-35 HC

'The Incredible Hulk' #2, by Marvel Comics, white pages, Jack Kirby and Steve Ditko artwork, fine condition.

1962

£300-400 HC

'Dick Tracy Monthly' #1, by Dell Comics, first issue, inside cover edges are tan, fine condition.

1948

£80-120 HC

'Flash Comics' #21, by DC Comics, off-white pages, staples cleaned, with classic Hawkman cover, very fine condition.

1941

£320-380 HC

'The Incredible Hulk' #1, by Marvel Comics, off-white to white pages, fine condition.

This premiere issue features the origin and first appearance of the Hulk by Jack Kirby. It is one of the most sought after of all the Marvel Silver Age keys, and one of the toughest to find in any condition.

1962

£1,500-2,000 HC

'The Incredible Hulk' #6, by Marvel Comics, off-white to white pages, all Steve Ditko artwork in this issue, very good condition.

1963

£180-220　　HC

'Mad' #1, by EC Comics, cream to off-white pages, very fine condition.

1952

£1,200-1,500　　HC

Mad #18, by EC Comics, good condition, centrefold and next page detached from top staple, water stains.

1954

£20-30　　HC

'Marvel Mystery Comics' #55, by Timely Comics, off-white to white pages, cover and centrefold detached, Schomburg cover, good condition.

1944

£90-120　　HC

'Marvel Super-Heroes' #1, by Marvel Comics, fine condition.

1966

£12-15　　HC

'Silver Surfer' issues #1, #4, #5 and #14, by Marvel Comics.

1968

£250-350　　HC

'The Amazing Spider-Man' #1, by Marvel Comics, Winnipeg pedigree, white pages, very fine condition.

1963

£7,000-8,000　　HC

'The Amazing Spider-Man' #17, Marvel, good condition, water damage.

1964

£35-45　　HC

'The Amazing Spider-Man' #13, Marvel, very good condition.

1964

£55-65　　HC

'The Amazing Spider-Man' #2, Marvel, white pages, very fine condition.

This is the first appearance of the Vulture and the Terrible Tinkerer, with a Steve Ditko cover and artwork.

1963

£1,000-1,500　　HC

An earthenware memorial plate, for the inventor of the Penny Post, Sir Roland Hill, K.G.B., printed with a full-length portrait within green foliate-banded border.

c1880   *9.25in (23.5cm) diam*

£50-60   **HamG**

A Doulton bone china jug, made to commemorate the death of Tennyson.

1892   *6.25in (16cm) high*

£325-375   **H&G**

A Robinson and Leadbetter parian bust, depicting Beethoven.

c1900   *7.5in (19cm) high*

£90-110   **H&G**

A Caverswall Earl Mountbatten of Burma *in memoriam* plate, from a limited edition of 500.

1979   *10.5in (27cm) diam*

£75-95   **H&G**

COMMEMORATIVE WARE

■ Commemorative memorabilia became available on the mass market with the advent of transfer printing in the late 18th century, and became enormously popular in the 19th century with the Industrial Revolution and its improved manufacturing, communication and distribution methods. Queen Victoria's Diamond Jubilee in 1897 is a good example, where many thousands of items were produced and collected – many have survived.

■ Collectors should restrict themselves to a single topic or manufacturer from the start, otherwise the sheer volume can be too considerable to collect – even single reigns can have many thousands of objects associated with them.

■ Unless an item is extremely rare, condition is vital. Most items were produced in extremely large volumes and were carefully kept by their owners, so only those in the best condition are more likely to hold value.

■ Apart from noted personalities, collectors should look for items that display a certain quality and sum up a period or era through styling or design. Items related to Margaret Thatcher, and the British union struggles during the 1980s, are good examples.

■ As values are not comparatively high, there are very few reproductions or copies on the market. However, collectors should be aware of 'waisted' mugs (where the rim and base are wider in size than the middle) celebrating coronations, including Queen Elizabeth II's, as these are reproductions.

A Buffalo Pottery blue-on-white George Washington pitcher, Stuarts' portrait of Washington and Mt. Vernon, excellent condition, some staining at rim which extends into body, retains much of its original gilded lip decoration.

c1910   *7.5in (19cm) diam*

£300-400   **TWC**

A Caverswall Earl Mountbatten of Burma *in memoriam* mug.

1979   *3.75in (9.5cm) high*

£40-50   **H&G**

A Spode mug, to commemorate the visit of Pope John Paul II to Great Britain.

1982   *3.25in (8.5cm) diam*

£20-30   **OACC**

A Panorama Earl Mountbatten of Burma *in memoriam* mug.

1979   4in (10cm)

£40-50   **H&G**

A Crown Chelsea bone china oval portrait plaque, depicting Lord Kitchener.

c1900   6.75in (17.5cm) high

£175-200   **H&G**

A Continental bone china plate, made to commemorate the Boer War.

c1900   8.75in (22cm) diam

£75-90   **H&G**

A Carlton Ware bone china dish, made to commemorate the Boer War.

c1900   4.25in (11cm) diam

£100-150   **H&G**

A Shelley bone china mug, made to commemorate World War I.

c1916   3in (7.5cm) high

£55-65   **H&G**

A Shelley bone china cup and saucer, made to commemorate World War I.

c1914-1916 Cup 2.5in (6.5cm) h

£150-180   **H&G**

A Royal Doulton earthenware mug, made to commemorate World War I.

1919   3in (8cm) high

£65-75   **H&G**

A Lord Nelson ware plate, printed with "There'll always be an England" and with a portrait of Churchill.

c1942   9.5in (24cm) diam

£65-85   **H&G**

A Fieldings Crown Devon musical chamber pot, made during World War II, printed with "Have this on Old Nasty".

1940-42   8.5in (22cm) diam

£800-950 (with music) £500-600 (without music)   **H&G**

A wartime 'War against Hitlerism' teapot, printed with "This souvenir was made for Dyson & Horsfall of Preston to replace aluminium stocks taken over for Allied armaments 1939".

During World War II, people were encouraged to give up metal household items, such as aluminium saucepans, which could then be used to make weapons and machinery for the war effort. In reality, these items were often not used and the initiative was simply to make people feel that they were making a contribution. These teapots were given in exchange for these items to further augment this feeling.

5.75in (14.5cm) high

£145-165   **DH**

A Caverswall mug, made to commemorate victory in the Gulf.

1991   3.75in (9.5cm) high

£35-45   **H&G**

A Royal Kendall plate, made to commemorate the liberation of Kuwait.

1991   8in (20.5cm) diam

£30-40   **H&G**

An earthenware octagonal plate, by Wallace Gimson, made to commemorate the Marquis of Salisbury.

1884   9.5in (24cm) high

£130-160   **H&G**

An octagonal earthenware plate, printed with "Lord Randolph Churchill, Chancellor of the Exchequer 1886" and "rd No.4050".

9.75in (24.5cm)

£120-180   **HamG**

An earthenware mug, made to commemorate the death of William Gladstone.

Hawarden Church, where Gladstone was buried, is printed on the reverse of the mug.

1898   4in (10cm) high

£125-145   **H&G**

A Booths silicon china plate, printed in black with a photographic portrait of Neville Chamberlain, within a flower-moulded border, printed mark and date code.

1936   10.5in (27cm) diam

£25-35   **HamG**

A small Lancaster Winston Churchill toby jug.

1940   2.75in (7cm)

£50-65   **H&G**

A Copeland jug, made to commemorate Winston Churchill.

1940-41   6.75in (17.5cm)

£250-300   **H&G**

A Champion of Democracy beaker, with Winston Churchill and President Roosevelt.

1942   4in (10cm) high

£55-65   **H&G**

A Sylvac bust of Winston Churchill, *in memoriam.*

1965   7.75in (20cm) high

£225-275   **H&G**

A B **C** D E F G H I J K L M N O P Q R S T U V W XYZ

A Copeland Spode Winston Churchill toby jug.

As well as this white version, which was made for the home market, there is a coloured version.

c1942   8.25in (21cm)

£145-170   **H&G**

A Panorama bone china plate, made to commemorate Harold Wilson's second term as Prime Minister, from a limited edition of 50.

1974   10.5in (26.5cm) diam

£70-85   **H&G**

A Caverswall plate, made to commemorate Margaret Thatcher's election on 3rd May, 1979, from a limited edition of 1,979.

1979   10.5in (27cm)

£65-85   **H&G**

A Caverswall mug, made to commemorate the convening of the first European Parliament.

1979   3.75in (9.5cm) high

£25-35   **H&G**

A Royal Doulton bone china loving cup, made to commemorate Margaret Thatcher's election as the first female Prime Minister of Great Britain.

1979   4in (10cm) high

£25-45   **H&G**

A mug depicting Margaret Thatcher, made to commemorate the 50th annual Conservative Women's conference.

1980   3.75in (9.5cm) high

£35-45   **H&G**

A Coalport bone china goblet, made to commemorate Margaret Thatcher's second election victory, from a limited edition of 500.

1983   4.5in (11.5cm)

£95-110   **H&G**

A Norfolk China bone china mug, made to commemorate New Labour's election victory.

1997   3.75in (9.5cm) high

£15-25   **H&G**

A Norfolk China Anti-Euro mug.

c1999   3.5in (9cm) high

£15-20   **H&G**

A Caverswall Winston Churchill plate, made to commemorate 50 years since Churchill first became prime minister.

1990   8.5in (22cm) diam

£30-40   **H&G**

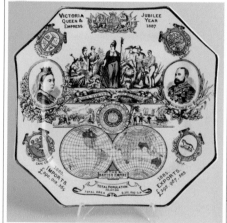

A papier-mâché plate, commemorating the coronation of Queen Victoria.

1838   *8in (20.5cm) diam*

£40-60   **OACC**

A rare Prince Albert memorial earthenware plate, printed in brown with a profile portrait within a panelled border depicting the achievements of his reign, rim chipped, restored, printed with "published by J.T. Close".

c1862   *11in (28cm) diam*

£200-250   **HamG**

An octagonal Golden Jubilee earthenware plate, printed in black with Victoria's portrait, chips to rim.

9.75in (24.5cm) diam

£50-80   **HamG**

An octagonal earthenware "Balance of Payments" plate, made for Queen Victoria's Golden Jubilee.

This plate was made to commemorate the Golden Jubilee of Queen Victoria and illustrates the Commonwealth by means of a map of the world on two globes in the bottom centre of the plate. The plate also cites the figures in 1885 (although this plate was produced in 1887) for the population (303,347,924) and total area of the British Empire (9,101,699 miles). It also shows the total value of imports (£390,18,569) and exports (£295,967,583). These plates were produced in large numbers but it is rare to find one in mint condition today.

1887   *9.5in (27cm) high*

£110-140   **H&G**

A Coalport Diamond Jubilee plate, printed in blue with the standing figure of Victoria within a border naming dominions of the British Empire, rim cracks, green printed mark.

10.5in (26.5cm) wide

£55-65   **HamG**

A Doulton earthenware beaker, made to commemorate Queen Victoria's Golden Jubilee.

1887   *3.75in (9.5cm) high*

£110-140   **H&G**

A Doulton bone china plate, made to commemorate Queen Victoria's Diamond Jubilee.

1897   9in (22.5cm) high

£135-160   **H&G**

A Royal Worcester bone china plate, made to commemorate Queen Victoria's Golden Jubilee.

1887   10.5in (27cm) diam

£100-140   **H&G**

An Aynsley bone china mug, made to commemorate Queen Victoria's Diamond Jubilee.

1897   3in (7.5cm) high

£125-165   **H&G**

A Doulton earthenware mug, made to commemorate Queen Victoria's Diamond Jubilee.

1897   3.25in (8.5cm) high

£100-135   **H&G**

An earthenware beaker, made for Queen Victoria's Diamond Jubilee and presented by Sir Henry Doulton.

1897   3.75in (9.5cm) high

£175-200   **H&G**

A Copeland earthenware mug, made to commemorate Queen Victoria's Diamond Jubilee.

1897   3in (8cm) high

£110-140   **H&G**

A Doulton three-handled vase, made to commemorate Queen Victoria's Diamond Jubilee.

1897   6.5in (16.5cm) high

£325-375   **H&G**

A Copeland earthenware jug, made to commemorate Queen Victoria's Diamond Jubilee.

1897   6.25in (16cm) high

£220-250   **H&G**

A Doulton earthenware silver rim jug, made to commemorate the coronation of Edward VII.

1902   7.5in (19cm) high

£250-290   H&G

A Radford bone china mug, made to commemorate the coronation of Edward VII.

1902   3in (7.5cm) high

£65-75   H&G

A Crown Staffordshire bone china jug, for Thomas Goode, made to commemorate the coronation of Edward VII, from a limited edition of 500.

Thomas Goode Ltd, founded in 1827, is a well known retailer of ceramics and holder of the Royal Warrant, located in Mayfair, London.

1902

£650-725   H&G

A Bros bone china mug, made to commemorate the coronation of Edward VII.

Most of these mugs are dated 26th June, the planned date for the coronation. Before this date, Edward was struck down with appendicitis and the coronation was delayed until August 9th. Those items that display both dates or the August postponement will usually command a premium.

1902   3.25in (8.5cm) high

£110-135   H&G

A pair of Wedgwood plates, made to commemorate the coronation of Edward VII.

1902   10.25in (26cm) diam

£325-375   H&G

An Royal Doulton earthenware mug, made to commemorate the coronation of George V.

1911   3.25in (8.5cm) high

£65-75   H&G

An earthenware pub advertising jug, with "Ask for Worthington in a Bottle" printed on the side, made to commemorate the coronation of George V.

1911   4.75in (12cm) high

£110-135   H&G

An Aynsley bone china mug, made for the coronation of King George V.

1911   2.75in (7.5cm) high

£75-85   **H&G**

A Royal Doulton bone china plate, made to commemorate the coronation of George V.

10.25in (26cm) diam

£110-130   **H&G**

An earthenware vase, made to commemorate the Allies during World War I.

1914-16   8.25in (21cm) high

£75-125   **H&G**

An Aynsley bone china beaker, made to commemorate the Silver Jubilee of George V.

1935   4in (10cm) high

£60-75   **H&G**

A Wedgwood creamware beaker, made to commemorate the Silver Jubilee of George V.

1935   4.5in (11.5cm) high

£70-80   **H&G**

A Mason's earthenware jug, made to commemorate the Silver Jubilee of George V.

1935   6.75in (19.5cm) high

£230-280   **H&G**

A Radfords Crown China loving cup, to commemorate the coronation of Edward VIII.

1936-37   3.25in (8cm) diam

£60-70   **OACC**

A Crown Ducal earthenware mug, designed by Charlotte Rhead, made for the proposed coronation of Edward VIII.

1936-37   4.75in (12cm) high

£135-160   **H&G**

A Royal Doulton bone china beaker, with a green ground, made to commemorate the proposed coronation of Edward VIII.

1936-1937   3.75in (9.5cm) h

£275-325   H&G

A Coalport cobalt-blue bone china plate, made to commemorate the coronation of George VI.

1937   9.5in (24cm) diam

£175-195   H&G

A Wedgwood earthenware mug, designed by Eric Ravilious, made to commemorate the proposed coronation of Edward VIII.

Eric Ravilious (1903-1942) was a well-known and influential designer and book illustrator, often using wood block designs. He was lost at war whilst acting as an official war artist during World War II.

1936   4in (10cm) high

£650-750   H&G

A Royal Doulton bone china mug, with G-handle, made to commemorate the coronation of George VI.

1937   3.25in (8.5cm) high

£160-185   H&G

A Hammersly bone china mug, made to commemorate the coronation of George VI.

1937   3in (8cm) high

£65-75   H&G

A Pountney & Company Ltd earthenware mug, made to commemorate the coronation of George VI.

1937   4.25in (11cm) high

£70-80   H&G

A Fieldings Crown Devon earthenware musical "super jug", made to commemorate the coronation of George VI.

1937   11.75in (30cm) high

£1,750-2,000   H&G

A small Paragon china plate, made to commemorate the coronation of George VI, printed and over-enamelled with "The Royal Coat of Arms" within an inscribed border, printed marks.

1937   8.75in (22cm) diam

£40-60   HamG

An English transfer-printed mug, made to commemorate the coronation of King George VI.

1937   3.5in (9cm) high

£25-30   PC

A Wedgwood green band earthenware mug, designed by Eric Ravilious, made to commemorate the coronation of King George VI.

1937 *4in (10cm) high*

£550-650 H&G

A Wedgwood blue band earthenware mug, designed by Eric Ravilious, made to commemorate the coronation of King George VI.

1937 *4in (10cm) high*

£500-650 H&G

A Royal Doulton loving cup, made to commemorate the 80th birthday of Queen Elizabeth the Queen Mother.

1980 *3.75in (9.5cm) diam*

£20-30 OACC

A Spode bone china mug, made to commemorate the 80th birthday of H.M. Queen Elizabeth the Queen Mother.

1980 *3.5in (9cm) high*

£35-50 H&G

A Caverswall bone china loving cup, made to commemorate the 80th birthday of H.M. Queen Elizabeth the Queen Mother and the 50th birthday of Princess Margaret, from a limited edition of 100.

1980 *3.5in (9cm) high*

£75-95 H&G

A Spode for Mulberry Hall bone china plate, made to commemorate the 80th birthday of H.M. Queen Elizabeth the Queen Mother, from a limited edition of 1,000.

1980 *10.5in (27cm) diam*

£60-75 H&G

A Royal Crown Derby bone china loving cup, made to commemorate the 90th birthday of H.M. Queen Elizabeth the Queen Mother, from a limited edition of 500.

1990 *3in (7.5cm) high*

£200-250 H&G

A Coalport bone china plate, made to commemorate the 90th birthday of H.M. Queen Elizabeth the Queen Mother, from a limited edition of 5,000.

1990 *10.5in (27cm) diam*

£75-100 H&G

A Caverswall bone china plate, made to commemorate the 90th birthday of H.M. Queen Elizabeth the Queen Mother, from a limited edition of 250.

1990 *10.75in (27.5cm) diam*

£75-95 H&G

A Bradmere House bone china mug, made to commemorate the 99th birthday of H.M. Queen Elizabeth the Queen Mother, from a limited edition of 99.

1999   3.5in (9cm) high

£35-45   **H&G**

A Caverswall bone china lionhead beaker, made to commemorate the 100th birthday of H.M. Queen Elizabeth the Queen Mother, from a limited edition of 500.

2000   4.25in (11cm) high

£45-50   **H&G**

A Chown bone china mug, made to commemorate the 101st birthday of H.M. Queen Elizabeth the Queen Mother, from a limited edition of 70.

2001   3.75in (9.5cm) high

£50-75   **H&G**

A Caverswall bone china lionhead beaker, made to commemorate the life *in memoriam* of H.M. Queen Elizabeth the Queen Mother, from a limited edition of 2002.

2002   4.25in (11cm) high

£35-45   **H&G**

A china mug, made to commemorate the coronation of Queen Elizabeth II, illegible mark, ink stains inside.

1953   3.25in (8cm) diam

£10-15   **OACC**

A Royal Doulton bone china beaker, made to commemorate the coronation of Queen Elizabeth II.

1953   4in (10cm) high

£40-50   **H&G**

A Salisbury bone china mug, made to commemorate the coronation of Queen Elizabeth II.

1953   3in (7.5cm) diam

£15-25   **OACC**

An English transfer-printed mug, made to commemorate the Silver Jubilee of Queen Elizabeth II.

1977   3.25in (8.5cm) high

£5-10   **PC**

An Aynsley mug, made to commemorate the Silver Jubilee of Queen Elizabeth II, with a list of the kings and queens of England on the reverse.

1977   3.25in (8.5cm) diam

£30-40   **OACC**

A Wedgwood print band earthenware mug, designed by Eric Ravilious, made to commemorate the coronation of Queen Elizabeth II.

Ravilious was dead by this time, but Wedgwood resurrected his 1936-37 design for the coronation. This piece is worth less as it was produced after the designer had died.

1953   4in (10cm) high

£175-225   **H&G**

An earthenware "Ajax" mug, made to commemorate the Silver Jubilee of Queen Elizabeth II.

1977   3.25in (8.5cm) high

£25-35   **H&G**

An Ovaltine pottery earthenware mug, for Woman's Own magazine to commemorate the Silver Jubilee of Queen Elizabeth II.

These mugs were sent to women who had had a baby in Silver Jubilee week.

1977   4.5in (11.5cm) high

£25-35   **H&G**

A large Wedgwood earthenware mug, made to commemorate the Silver Jubilee of Queen Elizabeth II.

1977   4.5in (11.5cm) high

£25-35   **H&G**

A Sunderland China for the Royal Collection bone china lionhead beaker, made to commemorate the Golden Jubilee of H.M. Queen Elizabeth II, from a limited edition of 2,500.

2002   4.75in (12cm) high

£45-60   **H&G**

A Royal Doulton earthenware loving cup, made to commemorate the Queen's Silver Jubilee, from a limited edition of 250.

1977   10in (26cm) high

£900-1,250   **H&G**

A large Wedgwood earthenware mug, made to commemorate the investiture of Prince Charles.

1969   4.75in (12cm) high

£40-45   **H&G**

A Royal Worcester mug, made to commemorate the marriage of Prince Charles and Lady Diana Spencer.

1981   3.25in (8cm) diam

£20-30   **OACC**

A Rye Pottery hand-painted half-pint tankard, made to commemorate the Golden Jubilee of H.M. Queen Elizabeth II.

2002   3.75in (9.5cm) high

£25-35   **H&G**

A Denby mug, made to commemorate the marriage of Prince Charles and Lady Diana Spencer.

1981   *3.5in (9cm) diam*

£18-23   **OACC**

An Elizabethan Bone China royal commemorative mug, the marriage of Prince Charles and Lady Diana Spencer.

1981

£15-20   **OACC**

A Spode bone china mug, made to commemorate the wedding of Prince Charles to Lady Diana Spencer.

1981   *3.5in (9cm) high*

£40-50   **H&G**

A Kiln Cottage Pottery earthenware teapot, made to commemorate the wedding of Prince Charles to Lady Diana Spencer.

1981   *6.75in (17.5cm) high*

£125-175   **H&G**

A Kevin Francis 'Charles and Diana' Spitting Image mug, from a limited edition of 350.

£50-80   **PSA**

A bone china mug, by Chown, to commemorate the divorce of the Prince and Princess of Wales, limited edition of 150.

1996   *4in (10.5cm) high*

£75-85   **H&G**

An Aynsley footed bowl, made to commemorate the marriage of Princess Anne and Captain Mark Phillips.

1973   *5.5in (14cm) diam*

£20-30   **OACC**

A Clokie and Company earthenware mug, made to commemorate the visit of Princess Viscountess Lascelles to Castleford.

1925   3.25in (8.5cm) high

£150-175   **H&G**

A Caverswall bone china lion head beaker, made to commemorate the birth of Prince William.

This mug was a limited edition of 1,000.

1982   4.5in (11.5cm) high

£55-65   **H&G**

A Coalport bone china mug, made to commemorate the bestowing of the title 'Princess Royal' on H.R.H. Princess Anne, from a limited edition of 2,000.

1987   3in (7.5cm)

£45-65   **H&G**

A royal commemorative mug, celebrating the birth of Prince William. Made for the National Trust by Cardigan Pottery.

Following the Princess of Wales' death, commemorative wares related to her children are now a growing collecting area.

1982   3in (8cm) diam

£20-30   **OACC**

An Aynsley small bone china loving cup, made to commemorate the birth of Prince Henry.

1984   2.25in (6cm) high

£55-65   **H&G**

A bone china mug, made to commemorate Buckingham Palace.

1996   2.75in (7cm) high

£20-25   **H&G**

A Chown bone china loving cup, made to commemorate the life *in memoriam* of H.R.H. Princess Margaret, from a limited edition of 70.

2002   2.75in (7cm) high

£45-60   **H&G**

A bone china mug, to commemorate *in memoriam*, H.R.H. Princess Margaret.

Only a very small number of these mugs were commissioned.

2002   3.5in (9cm) high

£20-25   **H&G**

DOG COLLARS

- Rare dog collars dating from the 15th century to the 18th century are usually made from iron and bear spikes as they were designed to protect the vulnerable throats of hunting dogs from attacks by wolves and boars, as much as to restrain them.

- German and Austrian collars are more richly made than British ones. They are usually made from ornately engraved and embossed precious metals and lined with fabrics and were as much a display of the wealth and status of the owner as utilitarian items.

- 19th century dog collars are generally less ornate than earlier examples and are made from silver or brass with rolled edges to prevent chafing. They commonly bear engraved names or wording used for identification.

- Collars often bear the popular decorative motifs of the period they were made in, which helps when dating them.

- Dog collars are often misidentified as slave or prison collars, which are much scarcer.

- There is a comprehensive collection of historic dog collars at Leeds Castle, Kent, England.

A plated chain link dog collar, with rectangular panel and initials M.R.

£100-150   LFA

A plated chain link dog collar, with rectangular panel inscribed 'J Usher, Keynsham'.

£100-150   LFA

A brass dog collar, with a panel inscribed 'John Jones,' and bearing the date 1847, flanked by chain link panels.

£600-1000   LFA

A mid 19th century plated and leather bound dog collar, with plaque inscribed 'Won by Dick at Birmingham, in a sweepstakes, 12 rats each, dogs of all weight, Nov. 10'.

1852   *3.75in (9.5cm) diam*

£600-800   LFA

A plated chain link dog collar, with rectangular panel with initials M.R.

£100-150   LFA

A 19th century brass plain dog collar, with padlock.

5.5in (13.5cm) diam

£150-200   LFA

A brass dog collar, with padlock and inscribed 'W. Smith, Rushenden,' within a scroll band.

4.5in (11cm) diam

£250-400   LFA

A 19th century plated dog collar, with leather mounts, inscribed 'J. F. Fell, Kilburn Wells'.

5in (13cm) diam

£250-350   LFA

An unusual 19th century white metal cat collar, inscribed 'Tiny Tim'.

3in (8cm) diam

£200-400   LFA

EPHEMERA

- Ephemera is the collective term for many different types of printed or handwritten objects, usually on paper or card, that were made for specific, often short term, purposes and discarded thereafter. This includes Valentine and Christmas cards, postcards, trade cards, catalogues, invitations, calendars and all forms of paper advertising and packaging.

- Condition of ephemera is very important. As they are primarily made from paper or card, damage can easily occur over the years. This includes tears, creases, crumples and folds, missing portions and tatty edges. All of these factors will affect the value of a piece detrimentally. Some level of discolouration is to be expected, but fading and stains are to be considered seriously.

- Storing of ephemera is important to protect the often delicate paper or card. This is best done in acid free card, paper or high quality plastic folders. Keep ephemera away from strong light, both natural and artificial as this will fade and discolour pieces and can make them more brittle. Damp conditions are unsuitable.

- Always handle ephemera with clean hands and keep ink and other substances that may stain them away from it. Never trace or write on ephemera, or stick "Post-It" notes or other adhesives on pieces as this can stain and discolour them.

An English Valentine, with embossed lace paper, with a hand-painted silk centre of flowers and hand-coloured circle.

c1855   *6.75in (17cm) high*

£70-80   **PC**

An English Valentine, with embossed lace paper and background of silk netting, silk and linen flowers and leaves and hand-painted flowers, maker unknown.

1850-1860

£60-70   **PC**

A gold and white English Valentine, with embossed lace paper, silk background and gold die-cuts with hand-coloured die-cut flowers.

c1855   *10in (25.5cm) high*

£180-220   **QUAD**

An English Valentine, on unusual lace paper with background of silk-mesh and hand-painted flowers, dated, slight fading.

1851

£90-120   **PC**

An English Valentine, with embossed lace paper, with cut-out on silk background, the main body of work in a heart-shaped frame.

c1855   *6.75in (17cm) high*

£80-100   **QUAD**

An English Valentine, with embossed lace paper, with hand-painted die-cut detail, by Wood.

c1855   *6.75in (17cm) high*

£90-100   **PC**

An English Valentine, made with rare embossed lace paper, unusually decorated underneath silk gauze, hand-painted with flowers, fruit, shells, leaves and feathers, with gilt-edged flags showing "Constancy will Triumph", and "Love is my Shareland", by Dobbs Bailey & Company.

c1855

£240-280   **PC**

An English Valentine, with superb embossed lace paper of the finest quality, with hand-coloured die-cut flowers and leaves, by Kershaw & Sons.

   6.75in (17cm) high

£85-100   **PC**

An English Valentine, with embossed lace paper and original hand colouring, made by Dobbs & Company.

c1855   *5.25in (13.5cm) h*

£50-60   **PC**

An unusual English Valentine, with embossed lace paper, silk background and hand-coloured die-cut flowers, silk leaves and glass stones, maker unknown.

c1855   6.75in (17cm) high

£180-220   **PC**

A pair of Valentine poetry booklets, written by English Valentine writers, in mint condition.

c1840-50 7in (17.5cm) high

£120-150 each   **QUAD**

A German Beidermeier friendship Valentine card, with gold leaf die-cuts and original hand-colouring, made in Dresden, Germany.

c1820   3.25in (8.5cm) w

£400-500   **QUAD**

A German Beidermeier friendship Valentine card, with gold leaf die-cuts and original hand-colouring, made in Dresden, Germany.

c1820   3.25in (8.5cm) w

£400-500   **QUAD**

VALENTINE CARDS

- The first references to tokens given on Valentine's Day can be dated to the 15th and 16th centuries, in Samuel Pepys' famous 'Diary' (although these were mainly trinkets) and in documents describing the giving of religious 'devotional' tokens at various events throughout the year. These were intricately cut from paper and it is perhaps from here that the exquisitely cut paper cards of the 19th century date.
- Most handmade Valentine's tokens made during this period show high levels of craftsmanship. In America, German immigrants introduced 'fraktur' (paper designs using German imagery and lettering) and 'scherenschnitte' (paper cutting).
- Paper making methods soon began to improve and by 1834, techniques for creating designs in impressed open work 'lace' paper had been developed which remained popular until the 1860s. Cards of this period were beautiful, often finished by hand with gilt, painted and cut decoration using different silks, lace, ribbons and card as materials.
- As the Industrial Revolution spread in Europe and the USA, people spent less time making cards. Chromolithographic images also took over from the intricate lace-like cards, with coloured Victorian 'die-cut' scraps and heavy layers becoming popular.

An English Valentine, with embossed lace paper and a cut-out of a lady with a gauze and silk overskirt, original hand-colouring and an unusual blue border, maker unknown.

c1855   6.75in (17cm) high

£85-100   **QUAD**

An early wood-cut comic Valentine card, depicting a cricketer with original hand-colouring.

c1840   7in (18cm) high

£60-70   **QUAD**

An early English Valentine, printed and with original hand-colouring, published by A. Park, Leonard Street, London.

c1840   10in (25.5cm) high

£120-150   **PC**

A comic Valentine, with inscription "All the way from Manchester and got no work to do".

c1840   7in (18cm) high

£40-50   **PC**

An English Valentine, with embossed lace paper, showing glove motif, with silvered die-cut leaves.

Gloves have been given as a token of love since the late 16th century.

c1855   6.75in (17cm) wide

£120-150   **PC**

A very rare early English chromolithographic Valentine, printed in colour by F. Scherick, Edinburgh, published by B.F. Lloyd & Co., Edinburgh, drawn by Adolf Schrodler.

c1850   10in (25.5cm) high

£220-250   **PC**

FIND OUT MORE...

Robert Brenner, 'Valentine Treasury: A Century of Valentine Cards', published by Schiffer Publishing, 2000.

Katherine Kreider, 'One Hundred Years of Valentines', published by Schiffer Publishing, 1999.

An unusual English Valentine, showing a galleon in sail.

c1840   10in (25.5cm) h

£220-250   **PC**

CHRISTMAS CARDS

- Although handwritten messages of best wishes have been sent at Christmas time to family and friends for many centuries, it was not until 1843 that the Christmas card was first used.

- Sir Henry Cole, the first director of London's Victoria & Albert Museum, wanted to save time sending best wishes to his family, friends and acquaintances. Rather than use festively decorated headed paper for personalized messages, he commissioned John Calcott Horsley, a member of the Royal Academy, to design and produce a lithographed card, of which 1,000 copies were produced, the spare copies being sold in a shop.

- Sending messages this way soon caught on and was aided by the introduction of the 'Penny Post' in 1840, allowing letters to be sent anywhere for one penny. 1844 saw another card being produced, by W.C.T. Dobson, symbolising the 'Spirit of Christmas'.

- By the 1850s, improved colour lithographic printing processes allowed coloured cards to be produced inexpensively. The 1880s saw millions of cards sold as the fashion took hold and the industry grew, with cards being sold in tobacconists, toy and other shops.

- Cards produced during the 1860s to 1890 are the most commonly found and present great variety to the collector. Cards can have delicate cut edges or designs, embossed patterns and the addition of materials such as silk.

A Christmas card, by Ernest Nister, printed in Bavaria.

c1890 4.5in (11.5cm) high

£10-12 PC

A Christmas card, depicting Pierrot seated on snowball, by Raphael Tuck & Sons.

c1890 4.75in (12cm)

£10-12 PC

An English chromolithographic Christmas card, by Raphael Tuck & Sons.

c1890 5.25in (13.5cm) high

£8-10 PC

A Christmas card, with three babies, published by Hagelbrag, Berlin.

c1890 5in (13cm) high

£10-12 PC

A fine chromolithographic Christmas card, by Shidesheimer & Company.

c1890 6in (15cm) high

£10-12 QUAD

An unusual moveable Christmas card, showing girls with pigs.

c1890 4.25in (11cm) high

£15-20 QUAD

A die-cut English Christmas card, dated.

1892 5in (12.5cm) high

£10-12 QUAD

A De la Rue Christmas card, showing a woman with a candle, looking at the moon.

De La Rue, founded by Thomas de La Rue in London, England in 1821 are also very well known for printing British stamps from 1855 and various banknotes from 1860 as well as for making the famous 'Onoto' range of fountain pens. As one would expect from a company that printed money and stamps, the quality of lithography, and printing in general, is very high with sophisticated and very well coloured pieces.

c1895 2.75in (7cm) high

£8-10 QUAD

Two early English moveable Christmas cards, by Goodall.

c1870   4.75in (12cm) high

£40-50 each   PC

An unusual pull-out Christmas card of a dog.

c1890   4in (10cm) high

£12-15   QUAD

An unusual die-cut English Christmas card, depicting a robin, by Ernest Nister.

c1895   4.75in (12cm) h

£10-15   PC

An unusual early chromolithographic Christmas card, in four parts.

c1870   4in (10cm) high

£35-40   PC

An unusual German die-cut card, printed in England, dated.

1891   4.25in (11cm) high

£15-20   PC

An unusual die-cut Christmas card, depicting a policeman.

c1890   4.25in (11cm) high

£10-12   QUAD

LITHOGRAPHY & CHROMOLITHOGRAPHY

■ Lithography (from the Greek 'lithos' for 'stone') was developed in Germany by Aloys Senefelder in 1798 and spread to other parts of Europe and the USA over the following 20 years. A design is drawn on the surface of a highly polished stone using a grease 'lithographic' crayon. Where the crayon adheres to the stone, the ink also adheres so that when the stone is pressed onto paper, the design is transferred in ink.

■ Chromolithography uses many colours rather than a single colour. For every colour used a new stone is drawn on. Providing the paper remains at the same 'register' or positioning, each stone with a different colour is successively pressed down, resulting in a multi-coloured image.

■ It was developed during the 1840s and popularised during the 1860s. The most successful American chromolithographer was Louis Prang, who produced scenes of Civil War battles as well as reproductions of art works.

■ The development of chromolithography allowed the production of many intricately designed and coloured cards.

■ Cards from the 1870s onwards tend to lose the simplicity of colour that is found in earlier cards and are very heavily coloured with great detail.

An unusual set of four embossed chromolithographic cards, with various fruits, each with the image of a child inset, made for any occasion with no wording.

c1880   5in (12.5cm) high

£40-50   PC

A set of three award winning cards, for "Exposition Palais d'Industrie", Champs Elysées, Paris, by Raphael Tuck & Sons.

1882

£40-50   PC

An unusual die-cut card, in the form of a tambourine with cat.

c1895

£10-12   QUAD

A moveable card, in the form of a posy of flowers, the flowers lift up to show the greeting inside.

c1865

£125-150   QUAD

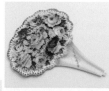

An unusual chromolithographic Lifeboat card, sold in aid of the National Lifeboat Institute for the Christmas season.

c1895   6.75in (17cm) w

£45-50   QUAD

A rare moveable card, from Germany, die-cut with cherubs in a tree and two lovers on a park bench.

Moving parts can be damaged in themselves, but also cause wear to the surrounding area. Condition is imperative, with damaged and worn cards being worth much less.

c1870

£220-250   QUAD

An unusual German moveable card, in the form of a table, made for the English market.

c1870

£250-280   QUAD

An unusual moveable peep-show appearance card.

These cards are particularly prone to damage due to their delicate nature. Although they fold flat, protruding elements and folds can easily be damaged. Collectors should look for examples in the best condition with strong, vibrant colours and intact details. Damage will reduce value.

c1865

£150-180   QUAD

TRADE CARDS

- Trade cards were used to advertise the services or products of tradesmen and manufacturers. The earliest cards date from the early 17th century and come from London, but these are extremely rare.
- The woodcut or letterpress method was used to print very early trade cards. Then, in the 18th century, copperplate engraving was introduced. Printing during this period was still monochrome.
- Cards often contained complicated graphic designs, in ornate script with detailed lettering, others used block letters and simple designs. Illustrations and motifs of the products or services offered were also incorporated. If the maker held a Royal Warrant this would also be proudly displayed. Names would usually take a prominent position.
- Custom-made cards were printed specifically for individual tradesmen but cards with standardized designs and blank spaces for a tradesman's stamp were also available and are often known as 'stock cards'.
- The spread of colour lithography in 1870 led to a boom in advertising. Companies began manufacturing their own cards for products and there was a decline in trade cards for individual tradesmen. Late Victorian advertising cards are more readily available and affordable than earlier trade cards.

A trade card, for Robert Vincent, scale maker, "At the Hand and Scales on London Bridge the Second Door from the Bear Tavern".

Robert Vincent, the scale maker worked from 1751 until 1793, based mainly around the Southwark area of London. The address listed on this card is his earliest known location.

c1751   6.25in (16cm) high

£1,500-1,800   PJC

A trade card for Thomas Ripley & Co., scientific instrument makers.

Thomas Ripley is listed as working as a maker of scientific and optical instruments from 1765-1790.

c1760

£1,800-2,200   PJC

A trade card, for John Grant, son of the late Mrs. Ann Pitman, a brushmaker, the shop was on London Bridge.

The shops on London Bridge were demolished in the 1750s.

c1750   7in (18cm) high

£1,200-1,500   PJC

A trade card, for Maydwell & Windles of London, cut glass works.

1751-1778 11.25in (28.5cm) h

£2,200-2,500   PJC

A trade card, for Jacques Songy, instrument maker, made with a plate dating from c1690 overprinted with new wording and dated in1732

£1,000-1,200   QUAD

A trade card, for Henry
Hastings, night-watchman.

c1745   9.75in (25cm) high

£1,200-1,500   **PJC**

A trade card, for Richard Hand,
"The oldest original Chelsea
bun maker", by William
Hogarth, dated.

1718   8.75in (22cm) high

£1,200-1,500   **QUAD**

A trade card, for Thomas
Norris, gold chain and swivel
maker, trimmed.

c1720   6.25in (16cm) high

£750-850   **PJC**

A trade card, for Harrison,
Norwich, saddler and harness
maker.

1800-1810   3.5in (9cm) high

£120-150   **QUAD**

A trade card for Blair &
Company, makers of guns and
pistols, printed in blue.

c1790   4.5in (11.5cm) h

£350-400   **QUAD**

A trade card, for Le Blond &
Company, engravers, copper
platers, lithographic printers,
letter press and account book
maintainers, London.

c1860   4.5in (11.5cm) wide

£120-150   **QUAD**

A CLOSER LOOK AT A TRADE CARD

*This extremely fine quality trade card was printed with a lithographic
stone by R. Martin of 124 High Holborn, London, during the 1830s and
is arguably one of the finest cards found. It is not in the usual format
of a trade card with the name being hidden within the design and it
almost has the appearance of a print rather than an advertising card.*

A trade card for J. Southby,
artist in fireworks, Vauxhall
Gardens, main theatre.

c1820   4.5in (11.5cm)

£400-500   **QUAD**

A trade card for a C.L. Wulcko,
manufacturer of tobacco and
snuff, Covent Garden.

c1820   3.5in (9cm) wide

£120-150   **QUAD**

*The detail is of extremely high quality, showing an
attention to fine detail, with a range of shades and
good handling of perspective. The small 'stone
plaque' in the centre reads 'A SPECIMEN OF INK
LITHOGRAPHY FROM R.MARTIN 124 HIGH
HOLBORN' revealing that this was a trade card
produced by the tradesman himself to display the
skill and quality of his work to potential clients.*

*Many of the objects depicted have been chosen, not only for their
ability to show the virtuosity and skill of the lithographer, but also as
they were indicative of popular fashions of the time such as the 'Grand
Tour', Palladian and Classical architecture, anatomy and Egypt.*

A trade card, for Thomas
Pritchard, a chimney sweep
and night-watchman.

c1760

£800-1,000   **PJC**

A trade card, for J. F. Salter, hat
maker.

c1790   6in (15cm) high

£1,000-1,200   **PJC**

An early lithographic trade card, designed, drawn on stone and
printed at the Robert Martin Lithographic Establishment, dated.

1830

£1,200-1,500   **PJC**

FUNERAL EPHEMERA

- The Victorian period saw the high point of funeral ephemera. The Victorian preoccupation with death, mourning and remembrance is illustrated by their jewellery which includes mourning rings and lockets, often containing the hair of dead relatives. This national sentiment increased further after the death of Queen Victoria's husband, Prince Albert, in 1861.

- Funerals of high profile figures were often public affairs and the Victorian predilection for organisation and formal approach to grieving dictated the production of tickets and programmes in many instances.

- However, the printing of invitations is not unusual and had been in existence in the 18th century. Invitations were not usually issued publicly, so few were made. As with trade cards, standard designs were offered with blank spaces upon which the specific details could be handwritten or printed.

- Despite this morbid subject matter, this type of ephemera is sought after, with collectors looking for invitations, programmes and announcements associated with renowned historical figures and items with fine artwork and printing.

A ticket to the funeral of prime minister Mr. William Pitt, the Younger.
1806   10.25in (26cm) wide

£850-1,000   **QUAD**

A ticket to the funeral of Sir Joshua Reynolds, by Bartolozzi, dated.
1792   8.75in (22cm) wide

£1,200-1,500   **QUAD**

A funeral ticket, for a Mr. Richard Mackleston, dated.
1732   8.5in (21.5cm) high

£1,200-1,500   **QUAD**

A blank funeral ticket, also an advertisement for C. Jennings, undertakers.

c1740   9.5in (24cm) wide

£1,000-1,200   **QUAD**

ST. PAUL'S CATHEDRAL.
ADMIT BEARER TO
Service of Solemn Supplication
AT THE HOUR OF THE FUNERAL
OF HER LATE MAJESTY
QUEEN VICTORIA.

A ticket to the funeral of Queen Victoria, at St. Paul's Cathedral, with inscription "Admit the Bearer to Service of Solemn Supplication".
1901   3in (7.5cm) high

£60-70   **QUAD**

A memorial card, in memory of HRH Prince Albert, embossed by Windsor, on an original black velvet background.
1861-1862   10in (25cm) high

£250-300   **QUAD**

In Memoriam.
In Memory of
**OUR BELOVED QUEEN,
VICTORIA.**

A Queen Victoria memorial card, detailing her death on 22th January 1901 at Osborne House, the Isle of Wight.
1901   5in (13cm) high

£15-20   **QUAD**

An advertisement for patent iron coffins, with inscription "Safety for the Dead!".
Metal coffins were made in order to prevent grave robbers. There is an example of this coffin in St Bride's Church, London.
1800-1820   10in (25.5cm) h

£250-350   **PJC**

A page of certificates of proof of burials.
The act for "compelling the burying of corpses in Woollen" was passed in 1679 to help the wool market. All corpses had to be buried in woollen garments.
c1700-1775

£400-750 each   **PJC**

A ticket for the coronation of William IV and Queen Adelade, at Westminster Abbey.

Despite the importance of the event and the richly ornate decoration on comparable tickets to coronations, this ticket is extremely plain. The reason for this was that William was shocked by the expense and extravagance of his brother's coronation and vowed not to be so lavish with his.

1831

£120-150 PJC

A ticket to the Guildhall, for a dinner given by the Lord Mayor, with steel engraving.

1788   9.5in (24cm) high

£250-350 PJC

A ticket to the Guildhall City of London, in honour of the coronation of Queen Victoria, embossed by Dobbs.

1837   7.5in (19cm) high

£250-350 QUAD

An invitation to The Corporation of London, for the inauguration of the Metropolitan Cattle Market, (today Caledonian Market), HRH Prince Albert in attendance.

1855   11.5in (29.5cm) high

£150-200 PJC

A ticket for a reception by the City of London, for his Imperial Majesty Alexander II, Emperor of all Russias.

1874   7in (18cm) high

£250-350 PJC

A chromolithographic ticket to the Guildhall for International Municipal Entertainment, by F.J. Fitch, printed with the names of the Lord Mayor and Aldermen of London.

The removable coupon that should have been retained at the Guildhall is intact.

1875   7.25in (18.5cm) high

£150-200 PJC

A chromolithographic ticket for a banquet, given by the Lord Mayor, by Blades, East & Blades.

1878   7.25in (18.5cm) high

£100-150 PJC

A ticket for the reception of HRH Prince of Wales, to celebrate his return home from India, printed by S.W. Rowsell & Son.

1876   8.5in (21.5cm) high

£150-175 PJC

A ticket for the "Visit of the National Corporation of London to Epping Forest", with photographs.

An actual photograph is attached to the ticket because there was no way of reproducing photographs until the 1890s.

1875   8.25in (21cm) high

£120-150 PJC

A benefit ticket, with all the proceeds going to Mr Grimaldi the clown, held at Sadler's Wells, North London.

1813   3in (7.5cm) high

£300-400 PJC

A Christmas calendar, die-cut in one piece, printed in Germany and made for the Davidson brothers, New York, dated.

1909   13.25in (34cm) high

£70-80   **QUAD**

A broadside advertisement, for the New Vauxhall Gardens, printed by W. Mason.

1826   20in (51cm) high

£1,200-1,500   **PJC**

A broadside detailing Mr. Green's 109th Ascent with his balloon, dated 1832, printed by T. Wilson, Whitehaven.

It is unusual to find such a high quality of printing outside London during this period. Memorabilia relating to ballooning is extremely popular amongst a band of devoted collectors and can fetch very high prices. Ballooning was very popular in the late 18th century when, as well as being followed and developed seriously by its early proponents, it almost became a 'sport' for aristocratic adventurers. It was also popular through the 19th century, with pieces from the 18th and early 19th centuries tending to be the most popular and, due to their scarcity, fetching high prices when offered. Mr Charles Green (1785-1870) the aeronaut, ascended in his balloon for the 109th time on 29th August 1832 at Whitehaven. His balloon was 100 feet in circumference and was made of alternate panels of crimson and gold silk cloth.

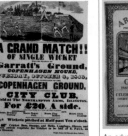

An advertisement for a cricket match, Northampton Arms, Islington, dated Tuesday October 6th.

1846   15.75in (40cm) high

£1,500-2,000   **PJC**

An advertisement for the grand opening of the Argyll Rooms, (what is today the Trocodero), lithograph by Day & Sons, proprietor R.R. Bignell.

1850   16.25in (41cm) high

£750-1,000   **PJC**

1832   19.75in (50cm) high

£1,200-1,500   **QUAD**

An unusual advertisement for a cricket match, in two-colour printing.

It is rare to find two-colour printing at this date.

1854   15in (38cm) high

£1,200-1,500   **PJC**

An unusual advert for Rimmel's perfumed Valentines, showing the range of Valentines and prices, dated.

Rimmel are still making cosmetics today.

1871

£35-40   **PC**

An advertising leaflet, for the Lumiere Cinematograph's first screening before a paying audience, it opened on Regent Street Polytechnik on 20th February.

1896   4.75in (12cm) high

£2,000-3,000   **PJC**

An advertisement for British cinema in Piccadilly Circus.

This was Britain's first attempt at establishing a permanent cinema, after a few weeks it was destroyed by a fire.

1896   8.5in (21.5cm) high

£1,200-1,500   **PJC**

An English fan-shaped calendar, made with coated paper, dated.

1874   *4.5in (10.5cm) high*

£70-80   **QUAD**

A skip note, made to look like a bank note and designed to dupe those who could not read into thinking that they were real, with inscriptions "Bank of Folly" and "Fool".

1847   *5in (12.5cm) high*

£120-150   **QUAD**

A hairdressing skip note, with inscriptions "promise to cut any lady or gentleman's hair superior to any man in England or forfeit on demand the sum of ten thousand pounds" and "Bank Of Elegance", by C.B. Macalpine.

1823   *5in (12.5cm) high*

£120-150   **QUAD**

A penny dreadful leaflet, describing the arrest of Dr. Crippen and girlfriend Le Neve aboard the S.S. Montrose, for the brutal murder of his wife.

c1910   *10in (25.5cm) high*

£200-300   **PJC**

Four of a set of twelve German calendar cards, with superb chromolithographic printing, published by Sackett, Wilhelms and Betzig, New York, dated.

1884   *7in (18cm) high*

£200-300 (set)   **PC**

A skip note, made to look like a bank note and in protest against hanging, by George Cruikshank.

The penalty for producing counterfeit bank notes was death by hanging. Cruikshank campaigned against hanging and was horrified that people, including women, could be hung for passing a false banknote. He designed these skip notes in ironic protest.

1819   *5in (13cm) high*

£200-250   **PJC**

POLICE NOTICE.

TO THE OCCUPIER.

A rare leaflet, issued by the police requesting information regarding Jack the Ripper, dated 30th September.

1888   *8.75in (22cm) high*

£250-300   **PJC**

LONDON MURDER MYSTERY.

Mutilated Body found in a Cellar

A broadside detailing the murder of Maria Marten. The murderer, William Corder, was later apprehended in Ealing.

The woodblock engraving and hand-colouring make this particular piece very rare.

1828   *18.5in (47cm) high*

£1,200-1,500   **PJC**

A German calendar, for the "Calendria Antikamnia" Chemical company, USA, depicting macabre skeleton figures, designed in 1899 for the calendar of 1900, made for English, French and German distribution.

1899-1900 *10in (25.5cm) high*

£340-380   **QUAD**

A set of three coupons, with the head of George IV, from Atlas newspaper, embossed by Dobbs.

These were the first ever free offers in a publication.

1821   *5in (12.5cm) high*

£250-350   **QUAD**

FIFTIES AND SIXTIES

■ Collectors should look for pieces that have a strong 'retro' feeling that sums up the period. This can be represented in terms of form or in the decorative motifs used.

■ Many new forms were introduced during the period, some with an exaggerated streamlined and 'modern' feel that was inherited from the 1930s. Man-made materials such as vinyl and Dralon were very popular.

■ The 1950s also saw the emergence of 'Popular' music, the birth of the teenager as a social and economic force and a move away from the austerity of the post-war years. Colour, frivolous motifs and a return to a preoccupation with glamour are some of the hallmarks of the period.

■ Popular motifs of the 1950s include diamonds, spades, clubs and hearts from playing cards and 'glamorous' scantily clad ladies posing. Cats were also popular subjects and there are many thousands of ceramic cats available on the market, mostly with elegantly elongated forms.

■ Items connected to household names, such as 'I Love Lucy' and stars, musicians and celebrities, are also desirable and often cross collecting fields making them desirable to different collectors.

■ Due to the 'throw away' nature of modern society, once styles changed, pieces in then 'old-fashioned' styles were thrown away, meaning selective pieces can be scarce. 'Retro' styles are still currently fashionable and decorating your interiors in a 1950s style is still largely affordable and easy, as well as possibly being a good investment!

■ As many items were produced in great numbers, condition is vital to make a piece desirable. Sets should be complete and individual items undamaged as damage will seriously affect value.

A Ridgways 'Homemaker' series plate, transfer-printed, designed by Enid Seeney.

The 'Homemaker' series of tableware is perhaps one of the most recognisable objects from the 1950s. Sold in vast numbers through 'Woolworths', they gave any home an inexpensive, but very fashionable, table setting. As so many were made, they are commonly found now, but are now worth much more than they sold for during the period, if in excellent condition. Both the simple forms and the highly characteristic motifs used sum up the essence of 1950s styling.

c1957 (made to early 1970s)   25.5cm diam

£12-18   **FFM**

A Ridgways 'Homemaker' series side-plate, transfer-printed, designed by Enid Seeney.

1957-1970s   7in(18cm) diam

£8-10   **FFM**

A Ridgways 'Homemaker' series trio, transfer-printed, designed by Enid Seeney.

This range was only available with black cups with white interiors.

1957-1970s   7in (18cm) diam

£20-25   **FFM**

A Ridgways 'Homemaker' series cereal bowl, transfer-printed, designed by Enid Seeney.

1957-1970s 6in (16cm) diam

£10-15   **FFM**

A Ridgways 'Parisienne' pattern plate, transfer-printed.

c1957   9.75in (25cm) diam

£10-15   **FFM**

A 1950s pin-up girl glass, decorated on both sides with transfers.

4.25in (11cm) high

£18-22   **CVS**

A Ridgways 'Barbeque' pattern meat plate, print and enamel, unnamed designer.

1958   11in (28cm) diam

£15-18   **FFM**

Four 1950s playing card glasses.

Playing card symbols were highly popular motifs during the 1950s.

4.5in (11.5cm) high

£40-50   **MA**

A stainless steel Danish teapot.
c1965   5in (13cm) high
£40-50   MHT

Six Alveston coffee spoons, by Robert Welch (RCA), for Oldhall, in original box, each stamped.
c1963   4.5in (11.5cm) high
£50-60   MHT

A 1960s serviette holder and salt and pepper set, with reindeer motif.
£6-8   MA

An electrical mixer, by Excelsior.
1955
£80-120   TK

A Robert Welch five-piece cruet set, by Old Hall, stamped "Old Hall".
c1965   7.75in (20cm) wide
£40-45   MHT

A set of Venus salt and pepper shakers.
c1950   4in (10cm) high
£50-80   SM

A 1950s Prince Pineapple string holder, some damage.
£80-120   DAC

A Dutch boy laundry sprinkler.
£120-180   DAC

Two Robert Welch toast racks, for Old Hall.

Robert Welch first became interested in stainless steel while visiting Scandinavia during the 1950s.

Largest 9.5in (24cm) wide
£20-30   MHT

A set of six 1930s Australian pale blue Bakelite kitchen canisters.

A full set of these canisters in blue is extremely rare, although separate pieces are found. Blue is a very sought after colour for Bakelite.

Largest 9.5in (24cm) high
£120-180   MA

A 1950s picnic set, with four settings.
19in (48.5cm) wide
£50-70   MA

A 1960s picnic set, with plastic flower motif carrier.

16in (40.5cm) wide

£35-45　　　　　　　**MA**

LADY HEAD VASES

■ 'Lady Head Vases' are rapidly becoming a sought after collectable. The earliest examples from the 1940s are often marked 'Glamour Girl', from which the vases of the 1950s, 1960s and early 1970s derive. However, these early examples are not as stylish or sought after as those from the 1950s. They were made to display flowers and some examples have decorative features such as jewellery and hands with painted nails resting against the faces. The most desirable vases are those modelled on personalities of the period such as Marilyn Monroe, Jackie Kennedy and Lucille Ball. Some are hard to recognise, so refer to a book for guidance.

■ Many 'Lady Head Vases' were made in Japan and the U.S.A. with manufacturers names including 'Napco' or 'Napcoware' (National Potteries Company), Enesco, Relpo, Ruebens and Betty Lou Nichols. In many instances however, the styling of the vase is more important than the maker, so a mark does not necessarily make a vase more valuable.

A 1950s Lady Head Vase.

£70-100　　　　　**DAC**

A 1950s Lady Head Vase, marked "INARCO" (registered symbol) on base.

£80-120　　　　　**DAC**

A 1950s Lady Head Vase.

£80-120　　　　　**DAC**

A 1950s Lady Head Vase.

£20-30　　　　　　**PC**

A CLOSER LOOK AT A LADY HEAD VASE

This example has delicately rouged cheeks and a good hairstyle. Collectors look for features such as well-modelled and well-painted hair and good quality painting, especially on the 'made-up' face. Also look for applied eyelashes.

The way the head is modelled is also important, with many having an attractive tilt to the head.

Condition is very important. Clean interiors attract a premium, as do examples with no chips to the rim or base and paint that has not crazed or flaked. Colours should be bright and not faded.

The applied flowers that stand out from the body of the vase are another feature that makes this example desirable. They are easily damaged, but the flowers on this example are not. The earrings and 'pearl' necklace are also original and intact.

A 1950s Lady Head Vase.

£60-80　　　　　　**PC**

A 1940s plaster wall mask.

11in (28cm) high

£50-70　　　　　　**MA**

A 1940s plaster reproduction face wall mask.

10in (25.5cm) high

£45-55　　　　　　**MA**

Two 1950s ceramic cat vases and matching fan vase, made in Western Germany.

The fan vase is not as commonly found as the cats.

Fan £30-35, cats £20-30 each   **MA**

A 1960s ceramic Siamese cat.

11.5in (29cm) high

£10-20   **MA**

A 1960s ceramic Siamese cat.

14.5in (36.5cm) high

£30-40   **MA**

A 1950s Pilkingtons ceramic free-form bowl, designed by Mitzi Cunliffe.

10.5in (26.5cm) diam

£100-150   **REN**

A 1950s alabaster vase, with musical theme design.

9.75in (25cm) high

£100-135   **V**

A Robert Welch candlestick, made from vitreous cast iron at Chipping Campden.

c1964 5.75in (14.5cm) high

£45-50   **MHT**

A 1950s 'bridge' cigarette lighter and ashtray, made in China.

3.5in (9cm) high

£30-40   **MA**

A Poul Henningsen PH5 hanging lamp, produced by Louis Poulsen, Denmark, designed 1958, tiered, enamelled metal shade with red and blue interior.

c1958   *19in (48cm) diam*

£350-450   **FRE**

A Gae Aulenti Pipistrello lamp, designed in 1967, produced by Martinelli-Luce in Italy, with black enamelled metal base, telescoping stainless steel shaft and white methacrylate shade, labeled.

36in (91.5cm) high

£1,000-1,500   **FRE**

A 1960s bronze and Baccarat crystal chandelier, with nickelled bronze dome over an illuminated interior with stepped rows of 80 crystal teardrop pendants, stamped "BACCARAT Bronze".

16in (40.5cm) diam

£1,800-2,200 FRE

A 1950s Lightolier table lamp, with plastic shade, enamelled metal shaft and base.

19in (48cm) high

£250-350 FRE

A 1950s table lamp, with plastic shade.

39in (99cm) high

£50-80 MA

A rare Fornasetti 'magic' mirror.

c1950 11.75in (30cm) diam

£1,200-1,600 FM

A psychedelic pop mirror triptych, two panels with bubble border framing mirror plate, a third panel with 'Saturn Ring'.

Largest 36in (91.5cm) high

£320-380 FRE

A pair of Dralon-upholstered and wire constructed dressing table chairs.

31.5in (80cm) high

£40-60 CA

A 1950s artist's easel table, by Dennis & Robin Portslade SX D&R products.

This table is rare. The legs are detachable and can be clipped to the base and whole hung from the wall to resemble an artists easel with 'brushes'. This also acts as a useful 'space-saving' device, which was another popular theme during this period.

19.75in (50cm) high

£70-90 MA

A 1940s Hoover.

£25-35 MA

A Photoplay magazine, featuring Elvis Presley on the cover, November edition.

1962 11.5in (29cm) high

£20-25 CVS

A Picture Goer magazine, featuring Sal Mineo on the cover, March edition.

1960 11.75in (30cm) high

£5-8 CVS

A Picture Goer magazine, featuring Valerie Alan, March edition.

1957 11.75in (30cm) high

£5-8 CVS

A Tit Bits magazine, featuring Zsa Zsa Gabor, January edition.

1954 12.5in (31.5cm) high

£3-5 CVS

An 'I Love Lucy' comic no. 18, published by Dell.

1958

£15-25 HC

A 1950s 45rmp record case.

The 1950s saw both the explosion of the pop music movement and the emergence of the 'teenager'. For the first time, young people had music aimed specifically at them that was different to other popular music. With freedom growing, teenagers were able to work in their spare time to earn money with which they bought 'singles'. These inexpensively produced, brightly coloured bags were produced to store collections, but as they were heavily used and not made to last, many have not survived.

9.5in (24cm) high

£12-18   **MA**

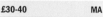

A 1950s 45rmp case, with a jiving couple.

£20-25   **MA**

A 1960s 45rmp record case.

7.5in (19cm) high

£15-20   **MA**

A Bush transistor radio.

1959

£40-50   **MA**

A radiogram musical cigarette box.

9in (23cm) wide

£30-40   **MA**

A 1950s pin-up girl lighter.

£8-10   **CVS**

A 1950s pin-up girl lighter, with box.

£40-60   **CVS**

An English toffee tin.

c1960   4.25in (11cm) diam

£10-15   **DH**

A 1960s tin money box, with outer space scene.

4.5in (11.5cm) high

£10-15   **DH**

A 1950s battery-powered Moon Rocket toy.

The 1960s saw a growing fascination with outer space, which reached its high point with the first man landing on the moon in 1969.

9.5in (24cm) wide

£200-270   **DH**

A 1950s 'Elvis is King' badge.

1in (2.5cm) diam

£10-15   **CVS**

A 1950s 'I Love Lucy' badge.

1.75in (4.5cm) diam

£12-18   **CVS**

A Warner Brothers animation art cel from "Another Froggy Evening", featuring Michigan J. Frog, fourth cel in series, limited edition 673/750, signed by Chuck Jones, with Warner Brothers, Certificate of Authenticity, framed.

1995   *21in (53.5cm) high*

£650-750   **SI**

A Warner Brothers animation art cel from "Another Froggy Evening", featuring Michigan J. Frog, CJ02-070-006, with Certificate of Authenticity 24238, signed "Chuck Jones 1995 Warner Brothers", framed.

1995   *18in (45.5cm) wide*

£2,000-3,000   **SI**

A Warner Brothers animation art cel, featuring Bugs Bunny as a knight, signed by Chuck Jones, framed.

1980   *19in (48.5cm) wide*

£2,000-2,500   **SI**

A Warner Brothers animation art cel no. 200696, depicting Bugs Bunny, Marvin Martian and a dog hanging from the moon, limited edition 377/500, signed by Chuck Jones, framed.

1998   *21.25in (54cm) high*

£1,000-1,500   **SI**

A Turner Entertainment Company animation art cel no. CJ75-257-007 from "How The Grinch Stole Christmas!", featuring the Grinch carving the "Christmas Beast", with Certificate of Authenticity 17955, signed by Chuck Jones, framed.
1966   *21in (53.5cm) wide*

£2,000-3,000   **SI**

A Turner Entertainment Company animation art cel no. CJ75-332-013 from "How The Grinch Stole Christmas", featuring the Grinch holding onto Max's foot, with Certificate of Authenticity 21412, signed by Chuck Jones, framed.
1966   *21in (53.5cm) wide*

£2,000-2,500   **SI**

A Turner Entertainment Company animation art cel no. CJ75-329-010 from "How The Grinch Stole Christmas", featuring the Grinch discovered stripping decorations, with Certificate of Authenticity 29598, signed by Chuck Jones, framed.
1966   *21in (53.5cm)*

£2,000-2,500   **SI**

An MGM animation art cel no. CJ75-093-018 from "How The Grinch Stole Christmas", featuring the Grinch on a sled with Max, with Certificate of Authenticity 05593, signed by Chuck Jones, framed.
1966   *21in (53.5cm)*

£2,000-2,500   **SI**

An MGM animation art cel no. CJ75-153-011 from "How The Grinch Stole Christmas", featuring the Grinch holding Max, with Certificate of Authenticity 16903, signed by Chuck Jones, framed.
18in (45.5cm) wide

£2,000-2,500   **SI**

Two Lone Ranger animation cels, depicting Indian chiefs, one showing the head of "Chief Running Water", pegbar punched on the bottom edge, the other a colour model sheet showing chiefs "Devil Spirits" and "Running Water", extensively annotated, also pegbar punched on the bottom edge, each framed and glazed.
Both 11in (28cm) wide

£120-180   **DN**

Two Lone Ranger animation cels, depicting the character "Sheriff Twogun", pegbar punched on the bottom edges, each framed and glazed.

Largest 13in (33cm) wide

£120-180   **DN**

Two Lone Ranger animation cels depicting the character "Town Tamer Jake", pegbar punched on the left hand side, each framed and glazed.

13in (33cm) wide

£120-180 DN

Two Lone Ranger animation cels, depicting the characters "Farmer Fred" and outlaw "McLeod", the first pegbar punched on the right hand side, the other pegbar punched on the bottom edge, each framed and glazed.

Largest 13in (33cm) wide

£120-180 DN

Two Lone Ranger animation cels, depicting the characters "Wallace Volunteer" and "Honest Abe", pegbar punched on the left hand sides, each framed and glazed.

Largest 13in (33cm) wide

£120-180 DN

Two Lone Ranger animation cels, one depicting a hunter wearing a pith helmet and holding a shotgun, the other a blond-haired man with knife and rifle, pegbar punched on the left hand sides, each framed and glazed.

13in (33cm) wide

£120-180 DN

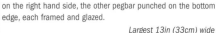

Two Lone Ranger animation cels, one depicting three outlaws with guns drawn, pegbar punched on the top edge, the other showing "Clarence Undertaker (called Terrible Tiny Tom)", pegbar punched on the bottom edge, each framed and glazed.

12in (30cm) wide

£120-180 DN

Two Lone Ranger animation drawings, one in colour depicting a young girl in three poses, pegbar punched on the bottom edge, the other a black and white sketch titled "Sheriff" and numbered LR511, pegbar punched on the bottom edge, each framed and glazed.

13in (33cm) wide

£120-180 DN

Two Lone Ranger black and white animator's models, one depicting "Soldier Sam (hero of Gettysburgh), two-stripe soldier", numbered LR516/130 and S1, the other showing "Colonel Wakefield, congressional medal, Victor at the Battle of Charlestown", annotated "clean-up as this" and numbered LR9/139 and G1, each cut to shape and pegbar punched on the lower edges, each framed and glazed.

13in (33cm) wide

£120-180 DN

Three Lone Ranger black and white animator's model drawings of bandits, variously inscribed "Cecil, Bandit One, one tough hombre", "Bandit Two, trace as this clean-up", numbered LR1, and "Girlie Jackson, Bandit Three", pegbar punched on the lower edges, each framed and glazed.

13in (33cm) wide

£220-280 DN

A Peanuts animation cel, depicting Charlie Brown, shown reading a letter with simple colour landscape background, framed and glazed.

10.25in (26cm) high

£70-90 DN

A Peanuts animation cel, depicting Lucy, shown wearing a yellow dress and seated on a sketched chair, framed and glazed.

8.75in (22cm) square

£70-90 DN

A Peanuts animation cel, depicting Schroeder, shown looking anxious and wearing an orange shirt, pegbar punched on the bottom edge and annotated "Reg to BG", framed and glazed.

10in (25.5cm) wide

£70-90 DN

A Warner Brothers animation art cel no. CJS 27 - 156024 for "Pullet Surprise", featuring Foghorn Leghorn, with Certificate of Authenticity 32464, signed by director Darrell Van Citters, framed.

1996 *20in (51cm) wide*

£650-750 SI

An animation art cel featuring Sylvester, framed.

21in (53.5cm) wide

£5,500-6,500   **SI**

A Warner Brothers animation art cel, featuring Tweety in a sailor's hat, framed.

21in (53.5cm) wide

£2,000-3,000   **SI**

A pair of Yellow Submarine animation cels, featuring Paul, one where he is falling (only the top half of his body visible), the other of him landing, gouache on celluloid on an orange and black background

c1968   *Overall 12in (30cm) high*

£600-800   **CO**

Two animation cels from the Beatles "Yellow Submarine", depicting clowns, each with a half-side view and a rear view, both peg bar punched near the bottom edge, one titled "The Clown", the other untitled, separately framed and glazed.

1968   *Largest 13in (33cm) wide*

£1,000-1,500   **DN**

PROPS AND MEMORABILIA

- Authenticity and provenance are vitally important, so always buy from a reputable dealer or auction house. If the item is a prop, ensure that it comes with a good provenance or a letter of authenticity guaranteeing it is what it claims to be. Try to find out how the item was obtained.

- Look for props that can be clearly seen in the film, preferably having been used in key scenes or if they represent an important facet of an actor's or an actress' character. Costumes are often very popular and can command high prices.

- Unless there are personal reasons for collecting a particular film, collectors should buy props and memorabilia that come from films that captured the public imagination or are classed as popular or period classics. "Star Wars", "James Bond" and "Titanic" are good examples. Props from unpopular, largely unsuccessful films or films that pass out of public interest will command lesser values and be less likely to retain a value.

- Large, bulky or cumbersome props that are difficult to display and store, or parts of props, generally command lesser prices for these reasons.

- Condition is also important, with some props being treated badly during or after the film. Do not be surprised if the prop is not of high quality production. Unless they had a specific function, many were made only to appear visually correct on screen, often seen only from a distance.

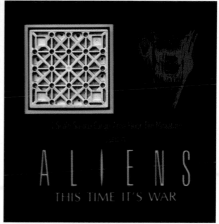

A 1:4 scale Sulaco cargo area floor tile from "Aliens", metal effect plastic mounted on card with the film's logo die-cut into it.

1986   *Overall 12in (30cm) wide*

£120-180   **CO**

Four prop Smylex products from "Batman", comprising three boxes and an aerosol can used as set dressings in the Joker's Smylex commercial, together with a colour image of the scene where the Joker (Jack Nicholson) can be seen with similar items, and a Certificate of Authenticity.

£400-500   **CO**

A painted latex Alien claw from "Aliens", of a complete alien costume worn in the film.

1986

£250-300   **CO**

A prop diamond from "Batman & Robin", clear cast special effects diamond used by the character Mr Freeze (Arnold Schwarzenegger) and kept in his backpack, mounted over a custom-made background featuring digital stills from the film together with descriptive text, in a perspex display case.

1997   *11in (28cm) wide*

£280-320   **CO**

Two prosthetic model pig facial parts from "Babe – Pig In The City", comprising the end of the snout and a mouth palate, box framed with a small version of the movie poster.

This piece is accompanied by a certificate of authenticity explaining the items' origins.

1998   *18in (46cm) high*

£180-220   **CO**

A brown cocktail dress from "Batman & Robin", as worn by Poison Ivy/Dr. Pamela Isley (Uma Thurman), unlabelled, together with a matching clutch purse, labelled "Saks New York" inside, with a one paper label reading "paisley drk brn." sample purse only do not use!" and another numbered "232", with two Certificates of Authenticity, the first from Warner Bros. Studios, the second from the original purchaser of the costume.

1997

£600-700   **CO**

An Army camouflage hat and trousers from "Black Hawk Down", as worn by Specialist Danny Grimes (Ewan McGregor), hat inscribed on the interior in black marker pen "Gordon, Delta Master Sgt." and additionally inscribed "EMcG", together with trousers also inscribed "Gordon" and a black cast-rubber stunt rifle.

Nikolaj Coster-Waldau who played Delta Master Sergeant Gary Gordon and Ewan McGregor swapped costumes as this one fitted McGregor better and McGregor then gave the costume to the vendor.

2001

£400-500 | **CO**

A stunt rifle from "Black Hawk Down", believed to have been used by Sgt. Matt Eversmann (Josh Hartnett), mounted with a signed colour still of Hartnett in character on a custom-made background with digital stills and descriptive text, in a perspex display case.

475in (1205cm) wide

£280-300 | **CO**

A rubber stunt machine gun from "James Bond – Tomorrow Never Dies", as used by Colonel Wai-Lin (Michelle Yeoh), sold together with an index card signed by Yeoh in blue marker pen.

1997   17in (43cm) wide

£300-350 | **CO**

A prop satellite wing from "James Bond – Tomorrow Never Dies", forming part of Elliot Carver's 'Carver Media Group News' satellite, made of white-painted wood with applied blue mirrored tiles and red lettering, some scratches and minor marks.

Bond is clearly seen battling past and around two of these wings in fight scenes in the film, which was set in a high tech building actually located in Hamburg. Props from key, memorable scenes such as this have added value, particularly if they are clearly visible in the film.

1997   55in (140cm) wide

£550-650 | **CO**

A teaser and illegal release warning poster for "James Bond – The Living Daylights".

During the last few weeks of production, unedited footage was stolen and circulated, masquerading as the new film. This poster advises the public that illegal copies are available, but that the authorised version opens in British cinemas on 30th June.

1987   30in (76cm) high

£100-150 | **CO**

A central console from "James Bond – Tomorrow Never Dies", forming part of Bond baddie Elliot Carver's (Jonathan Pryce) black stealth boat, the silver-painted console with one of the original screens fitted and features wiring, switches and lights, inscribed on the interior in black marker pen "Ops Room Ceiling Command Console", obtained from the Bond stage at Pinewood Studios, where the boat was built.

1997

£220-280 | **CO**

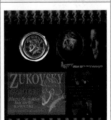

A Zukovsky caviar jar and box label from "James Bond – The World Is Not Enough", comprising a glass jar, one of many visible in Zukovsky's caviar factory scenes and box label, both featuring the profile of Zukovsky (Robbie Coltrane), mounted in a display including digital stills featuring Coltrane with the jars in the background together with descriptive text, in a perspex case.

1999   11in (28cm) high

£70-100 | **CO**

Three prop casino chips and a cheque from "James Bond - The World Is Not Enough", in denominations of $25, $100 and $1000, together with a Casino D'Or Noir client cheque made payable to Electra King, both mounted with digital stills featuring similar chips and cheques together with descriptive text, the whole in a perspex clip frame.

1999   16.5cm (42cm) high

£180-220 | **CO**

A $25 casino chip from "James Bond – The World Is Not Enough", mounted on a custom-made display with digital stills and descriptive text, in perspex clip frame.

1999   8.5in (22cm) high

£60-80 | **CO**

A prop axe head from "Braveheart", a special effects axe-head painted to resemble steel and used in the production of the film, mounted over a custom-made background featuring digital stills and descriptive text, in a perspex display case.

1995   11in (28cm)

£200-300   **CO**

A rubber stunt weapon from "Braveheart", a wide-bladed, falchion-like weapon, painted to resemble steel, used in battle sequences in the film, mounted on a custom-made background with descriptive text, in a perspex display case.

40in (102cm) wide

£120-180   **CO**

A prop New York State police badge from "Drowning Mona", as worn by Wyatt Rash (Danny DeVito), Chief of the town of Verplanck, matted with a signed colour photo of DeVito in character, and two on set polaroid images from the film's production, box framed and glazed.

22in (56cm) high

£250-300   **CO**

A large prop parchment document from "Elizabeth", an illuminated document on parchment-style paper with stylized script beginning "Omnibus Christi Fidelibus...", Elizabeth I's coat of arms, a large gold-coloured seal and the royal insignia.

1998   27in (68cm)

£120-180   **CO**

A full Scottish warrior costume from "Braveheart", comprising a large tartan kilt which wraps over to form a shawl, brown cotton padded breast plate, brown heavy woollen tunic, two belts (one plastic), leg wraps, a pair of knee high brown suede boots and a black long-haired wig, as worn by an extra in the film, also includes a wooden shield with handles on the back and written instructions and a diagram on how wear the costume.

1995

£450-550   **CO**

A prop dagger with knuckle duster handle from "Cutthroat Island", painted to look like steel with a brass handle, the latter doubling as a knuckleduster in the shape of a skull, mounted on a custom-made background featuring digital images from the film and descriptive text, in a perspex display case.

1995   11in (28cm) wide

£70-100   **CO**

A montage of images from "Enter the Dragon", signed by John Saxon (Roper), mounted with "Enter the Dragon"-style graphics, framed and glazed.

30in (76cm) wide

£120-180   **CO**

A Paper Street Soap wrapper from "Fight Club", as featured in the soap factory scene, mounted with a letter of authenticity from 20th Century Fox, framed and glazed, together with a letter of authenticity from Pinewood Studios.

1999   14in (36cm) high

£70-100   **CO**

A prop New York Post newspaper front page from "15 Minutes", with the headline "Double Homicide – Eddie's On It!" and an image of Detective Eddie Fleming (Robert DeNiro), mounted with a descriptive plaque, framed and glazed, accompanied by a letter of authenticity from New Line Cinema.

2001   21in (53cm) high

£80-120   **CO**

A large flail-like weapon from "Gladiator", the large spiked rubber ball painted to resemble iron, attached to a wooden handle by a length of plaited leather, used in arena fight scenes in the film.

2000   54in (137cm) long

£120-180   **CO**

A prop Barbarian sword and scabbard from "Gladiator", resin painted to resemble steel with wooden handle ornately carved with the figure of a head accompanied by a leather scabbard with brass detail, used in the Germania battle scenes in the film, mounted on a custom-made display, in a perspex case.

2000   *40in (102cm) wide*

£180-220   **CO**

A special effects Barbarian sword and holder from "Gladiator", used in early scenes in the film, mounted on a background featuring an image of General Maximus Decimus Meridus (Russell Crowe) and digital stills with descriptive text, in a perspex display case.

2000   *39in (99cm) wide*

£220-280   **CO**

A prop Roman sword from "Gladiator", a Gladius-style wood and steel sword, the blade painted to resemble steel with blood on the tip, together with its accompanying scabbard used in Arena scenes in the film, both mounted on a custom-made background with descriptive text, in a perspex display case.

2000   *40in (102cm)*

£350-400   **CO**

A oversized Harry Potter promotional postcard, signed by author J.K. Rowling in black marker pen, together with a copy of a letter from Rowling's PA to the charity this item was originally donated to.

10in (25cm) high

£450-500   **CO**

A prop wand box from "Harry Potter and the Philosopher's Stone", used as set dressing in Ollivander's Wand Shop where Harry purchases his wand prior to entering Hogwarts School, with green faux lizard skin top with brass-look studded loop on one end, a gold and black label reading "Ollivander's Makers of Fine Wands since 382BC. This is to certify that the wand box is a genuine Ollivander's article".

These props were given as gifts at the UK premier of the film and can be seen in their hundreds when Harry is choosing his wand in Ollivander's shop in one of the early parts of the film.

2001   *14in (36cm)*

£550-650   **CO**

A Red Army Bell Bolas prop from "Planet of the Apes", consisting of a strap made of three plaited leather strips, individually connected to foam bell shapes, conicals at one end, matted with an image of a member of the Red Army, and a die-cut card of the film title/logo, box framed.

27in (68cm) high

£300-400   **OD**

A large fighting net from "Gladiator", with black rubber crab/spider-like creatures attached, used in arena fight sequences.

2000

£120-180   **CO**

A gold coloured ingot from "The Mummy", with the impression of a scarab beetle used in production, mounted in a perspex display case.

11in (28cm)

£50-80   **CO**

A prop Sankara Stone from "Indiana Jones and The Temple of Doom", solid resin with chiselled, incised markings, with a colour image from the film.

This item was previously sold at Christie's in London.

1989   *6in (15cm) high*

£4,000-5,000   **CO**

Two solid rubber prop hand guns from "Resident Evil", one marked "Smith & Wesson TZS6614 Mod 596", the other "Springfield Armory G422", mounted with an image of Alice/Janus Prospero, box framed and glazed.

27in (68cm) high

£1,200-1,800   **CO**

An original painted foam and leather axe from "Robin Hood: Prince of Thieves", mounted on a custom-made background with descriptive text, in a perspex case.

1991   *40in (102cm)*

£120-180   **CO**

A 19thC-style lady's day dress from "Sleepy Hollow", comprising a bodice of black sheer fabric embroidered with gold floral detail trimmed with lace over a gold full skirt, with bustle.

1999

£180-220   **CO**

A special effects severed limb from "Saving Private Ryan", a realistic, mud-splattered silicone cast human arm and hand with hand-punched hair detail, used in the Normandy landing scenes, mounted on a custom made background, in a perspex display case.

1991   *40in (102cm)*

£200-300   **CO**

A current flow filter from "Star Wars: Episode I - The Phantom Menace", used in the Pit Droid scenes, juggled by the animated character Jar Jar Binks in Watto's shop, mounted over a custom-made background featuring digital stills and descriptive text, in a perspex display case.

1999   *11in (28cm)*

£220-280   **CO**

A small prop crystal from "Superman", used in the Fortress of Solitude, mounted over a custom made background featuring digital stills with descriptive text, in a perspex display case.

1978   *11in (28cm) high*

£380-420   **CO**

A prop Daily Planet newspaper from "Superman III", with the headline "Superman Scandal", featuring a photograph of Superman (Christopher Reeves), framed and glazed.

5in (63cm)

£200-250   **CO**

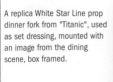

A montage of digital images from "Terminator 2: Judgment Day", signed by Edward Furlong (John Connor), in silver ink, mounted with a descriptive plaque, framed and glazed.

1991   *29in (74cm)*

£200-250   **CO**

A replica White Star Line prop dinner fork from "Titanic", used as set dressing, mounted with an image from the dining scene, box framed.

1997   *13in (33cm) high*

£120-180   **CO**

An 1:8 scale model ship's whistle from "Titanic", mounted with an image of the film's stars Leonardo DiCaprio and Kate Winslett and a descriptive plaque, box framed and glazed.

1997   *19in (48cm)*

£300-350   **CO**

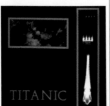

A replica White Star Line Moët & Chandon champagne bottle from "Titanic", labelled "White Star Moët & Chandon Eperney".

1997   *12in (30cm) high*

£180-220   **CO**

A part of the replica ship's hull and a section of bench from "Titanic", both mounted on a custom-made background featuring digital stills from the film together with descriptive text, in a perspex display case.

For certain scenes in the film, director James Cameron built a scale model of the Titanic at Rosarito Beach in Mexico. After filming had finished and the crew had left, the area was littered with left over parts and 'props'. This piece was collected from the beach at this point.

1997   *11in (28cm)*

£70-100   **CO**

A rare French cast aluminium Mickey Mouse penny bank, by Depeche Company.

6in (15cm) high

£150-200   **TK**

A pair of 1930/40s Mickey and Minnie toothbrush holders, marked "copyright Walt Disney".

4in (10cm) high

£240-280   **RH**

A ceramic Mickey Mouse figure, together with two smaller figure, by Severn China.

c1970   *3.25in (8cm) high*

£40-50   **WHP**

A Walt Disney's Mickey Mouse "Maestro Michel Mouse" figure.

1993

£100-150   **MSC**

A 1930s Walt Disney's Pinocchio figure, made by Knickerbocker.

£550-650   **FRA**

A Walt Disney's Pinocchio "I'll Never Lie Again ..." figure.

2000

£120-180   **MSC**

A pair of 1950s Walt Disney's Snow White and the Seven Dwarfs ceramic toothbrush holders, by Walt Disney Designs.

Snow White 6in (15cm) high

£180-220   **WHP**

A Walt Disney's Sneezy from Snow White and the Seven Dwarfs felt toy.

£120-180   **FRA**

A Walt Disney's Snow White and the Seven Dwarfs "Soup's On" group.

2000

£1,000-1,300   **MSC**

A Walt Disney's The Lion King "Pals Forever" figure.

1995

£80-120   **MSC**

A Walt Disney's Toy Story Buzz Lightyear "To Infinity and Beyond" figure.
1998

£80-120   **MSC**

A Walt Disney's Peter Pan Tinkerbell "A Firefly! A Pixie! Amazing!" figure.
1993

£250-350   **MSC**

A Walt Disney's 101 Dalmations Cruella De Vil "Anita Daahling!" figure.
1995

£200-250   **MSC**

An original Disney Studios "Mickey Mouse" printing slate, with two original gift box samples featuring six images of Mickey in different poses.
29in (73.5cm) long

£500-550   **TK**

Barks, Carl, "The Fine Art of Walt Disney's Donald Duck", published by Rainbow Publishing, Inc., hardcover edition featuring glossy prints and fold-outs of the work of "the good Duck artist", autographed by the author, limited edition 0096/1875.
1981

£700-800   **HC**

A boxed set of Mazda Disneylights, manufactured by the British Thomson-Houston Co, consisting of 12 bell-shaped Christmas tree lights, each printed with Disney characters including Mickey Mouse, Dumbo, the Seven Dwarfs, and Bambi, complete in original colour printed box.

£45-55   **DN**

A typed letter signed by Walt Disney, a personal letterhead, boldly signed "Walt Disney", dated December 29, 1964, written to John Hurt of the Curtis Publishing Company, with a letter of authenticity.
1964

£1,800-2,200   **HC**

Left: A Walt Disney Blow-Up Thumper figure, by Royal Albert.
1961-1965

£150-200   **PSA**

A 1970s Mickey Mouse Disneyland promotional badge.
3.5cm (9cm) diam

£15-20   **CVS**

A Wadeheath six piece nursery tea set, transfer-printed by Walt Disney Designs.
Teapot 3.25in (8cm) high

£15-20   **WHP**

Right: A Walt Disney Blow-Up Bambi, by Royal Albert.
1961-1965

£100-120   **PSA**

DAUM

- In 1878, Jean Daum (1825-1885) bought a glass factory at Nancy, France. After his death, it was run by his sons, Antonin and Auguste and was known as 'Daum Frères'. After being inspired by the work of Emile Gallé at the Paris Exhibition in 1889, they started to produce art glass.

- Under influence of Antonin Daum, the factory produced work in the Nancy style of Art Nouveau, using wheel carving, engraving, etching and enamelling. In 1893, the first acid-etched cameo glass was shown at the Chicago World's Fair. Technically sophisticated, 'vitrification' was developed which resulted in a cloudy, mottled effect through reheating enamel particles.

- Decoration was typically organic, incorporating flowers, foliate designs, fish and leaves, and a common shape is the 'Berluze' vase with its elongated neck.

- 'Pate de verre' was produced from 1906-1914 with figures and small vases in the shape of insects and birds. In 1909 Auguste's son Paul took over and after World War I, seeing the decline of the Art Nouveau style, he introduced transparent vases. These were typically made with embedded bubbles or silver or gilt decoration. Some were decorated with lines and dots or trailing vines and berries over coloured, opaque glass.

- Pioneering the Art Deco styling in glass, low relief vases with stylized flowers were produced, some with gilded details. As the 1920s progressed, forms became simpler with more stylised and formal designs and textured surfaces.

- The designer Maurice Marinot was a strong influence during the 1920s, leading to production in single colours with slightly rough surfaces combined with polished surfaces and bold 'deco' style acid-etched patterns.

- After World War II, the factory produced clear, uncolored lead glass. Designed by Michel Daum, pieces were organic and spiky in form.

- In 1962, the name of the factory changed to 'Cristallerie Daum' and production centred on juxtaposing areas of smooth, polished glass with deep-cut, abstract, rough and textured patterning.

- The factory is still in existence today, producing coloured glass and high quality clear lead crystal.

A Daum vase, with applied enamelled red glass berries, cameo leaves and vines, signed in cameo "Daum Nancy"

21.75in (55cm) high

£12,000-15,000   **JDJ**

A rare enamelled and gilt Daum bumble bee vase, decorated with leaves and flowers surrounded by twenty bees, signed on the bottom "Daum Nancy".

8.75in (22cm) high

£6,000-7,000   **JDJ**

A Daum summer scene vase, with green trees and foliage against an orange background, possibly cut down from a taller vase, two burst bubbles in the background, one ground, possibly during manufacturing, signed "Daum Nancy".

7in (18cm) high

£360-400   **JDJ**

A Daum day lily vase, the diamond-shape waisted vase with acid-cut day lilies and stems on all sides, each enamelled in rich orange and yellow tones, signed in cameo "Daum Nancy", very good to excellent condition.

4.5in (11.5cm) high

£1,300-1,500   **JDJ**

An early Daum cameo vase, red acid etched background with deeply cut purple cameo flowers, etched into the base "Daum Nancy".

5in (12.5cm) high

£620-680   **JDJ**

A Daum cameo and enamel sugar bowl, rim fitted with silver collar, probably added to cover possible damage.

7in (18cm) long

£480-520   **JDJ**

An unusual Daum cameo and enamelled lamp, signed "Daum Nancy".

Shade 6in (15cm) diam

£3,000-,4000   **JDJ**

A Daum cameo lamp, the base is impressed "MADE in FRANCE".

Shade 8.5in (21.5cm) diam

£3,200-3,800   **JDJ**

A Daum Nancy cameo bowl, decorated with leaves and berries on mottled glass, signed in decoration "Daum Nancy".

6.25in (16cm) diam

£720-780   **JDJ**

A Daum cameo enamelled and gilt salt.

2in (5cm) diam

£750-850   **JDJ**

A miniature Daum tumbler, acid-cut and enamelled violets, signed in cameo "Daum Nancy FRANCE".

2in (5cm) high

£750-850   **JDJ**

A Daum cameo bucket salt, with acid-cut and enamelled bellflowers, stems and leaves on a yellow and purple ground, signed "DAUM NANCY FRANCE".

1.75in (4.5cm) diam

£850-950   **JDJ**

A signed Daum cameo and enamelled salt, with cameo and enamelled sailing ships on a yellow and orange ground, one tiny chip to the rim.

2in (5cm) diam

£1,000-1,500   **JDJ**

FIND OUT MORE...

Clothilde Bacri, Noel Daum, Claude Petry, 'Daum: Masters of French Decorative Glass', published by Rizzoli, 1993.

Musée des Beaux Arts, 3 Place Stanislas, 54000 Nancy, France. A collection of over 600 pieces partly built from donations from the Daum factory.

A rare miniature Daum vase, signed "Daum Nancy" on the base.

2.5in (6.5cm) high

£1,800-2,200   **JDJ**

A Daum cranberry cameo tumbler, signed on the bottom "CRISTAL Nancy FRANCE", one small chip at the base.

3.5in (9cm) high

£350-400   **JDJ**

A signed Daum mini tumbler, with acid-cut gilt leaves and stems on a green ground and gilt trim to lip.

2in (5cm) high

£300-400   **JDJ**

A signed Daum miniature tumbler.

2in (5cm) high

£750-850   **JDJ**

A signed Daum Nancy toothpick holder, some very minor wear to gilt.

2in (5cm) high

£120-180   **JDJ**

An early miniature Daum pitcher, signed on the base "Daum Nancy".

3.25in (8.5cm) high

£280-320   **JDJ**

A miniature Daum long neck vase, with acid-cut and enamelled Dutch winter scene, signed on the base "Daum Nancy".

3in (7.5cm) high

£750-850   **JDJ**

EMILE GALLÉ (1846-1904)

- The origins of the Gallé factory date back to a mirror glass workshop founded by Charles Gallé in the 1840s, in Nancy, France. After studying glass making, his son Emile established a workshop there and began to design glass.
- Emile initially produced transparent glass with coloured enamelled or engraved designs.
- Soon, he became interested in natural motifs and, influenced by the coloured glass of Rousseau at the Paris Exhibition of 1878, he began experimenting with coloured glass.
- In 1884, he publicly displayed glass with opaque and translucent enamels and by the late 1880s had mastered cameo glass techniques. Pieces included up to seven layers which were cut back by acid and then by carving. Some had enamelled or gilt decoration and had added decoration in the form of insects.
- A major influence in the developing Art Nouveau movement, Gallé's work was shown at the Paris Exhibition in 1889. In 1894, he built his first factory at Nancy and produced three ranges. These were one off, often experimental, pieces; high priced limited editions and more standard pieces. Gallé personally oversaw all designs produced.
- He won the 'grand prix' at the Paris Exhibition of 1900. After his death in 1904, his widow Madame Gallé ran the factory. All production between 1904 and 1914, when the factory closed for the war, is marked with a star.
- The factory reopened in 1919, but production was limited to less sophisticated two or three layer pieces, mainly vases and lamps in cameo glass. Pale colours and animal motifs dominated the 1920s, including elephants, seagulls, otters, polar bears and penguins. The factory is still in production, making particulary high quality limited editon pieces. However, it is important that collectors beware reproductions.

A large Gallé enamelled green glass vase, the tapering cylindrical vessel painted with lady slipper blossoms and ferns, with moulded and engraved signature.

c1900   *17.5in (44cm) high*

£1,200-1,800   **SI**

A Gallé enamelled vase, cylindrical smoky amber vase decorated with enamelled thistles and cross of Lorraine on the back, signed on the bottom "E. Gallé Nancy", base restored.

10in (25.5cm) high

£80-120   **JDJ**

A Gallé cameo vase, peach-coloured cameo decoration of chrysanthemums on a frosted white background. signed on the side in cameo " GALLE".

13.5in (34.5cm) high

£1,300-1,500   **JDJ**

A Gallé enamelled glass tall vase, the cushion base with long cylindrical vessel painted with thistles and the cross of Lorraine, enamelled on base "E. Gallé". c1900

17.5in (44.5cm) high

£1,600-1,800   **SI**

A Gallé cameo stick vase, decorated with green and purple columbine blossoms and leaves, signed in decoration "GALLE".

11in (28cm) high

£700-800   **JDJ**

A Gallé cameo glass banjo vase, with purple acid cut flowers, leaves and buds on a yellow-green background, signed in cameo "GALLE".

6.75in (17cm) high

£1,500-2,000   **JDJ**

A Gallé enamelled glass vase, onion-shaped with slender cylindrical neck, with pale smoky tone acid-etched with leaves and enamelled in naturalistic colours with stems and flowerheads, centres applied in relief as bosses, finely painted on base "Cristallerie d'Emile Gallé a Nancy" and "Modele et decor déposé".

7.75in (19.5cm) high

£700-1,000   **DN**

A large Gallé scenic cameo vase, with amethyst, green and blue trees and mountains, signed within the decoration "GALLE".

14in (10cm) high

£4,000-5,000   **JDJ**

A Gallé scenic cameo vase, with brown and green acid-cut trees, shrubs, and a boat on a pond, with background colour shading from blue to green.

A Gallé cameo scenic vase, with overall panoramic scene of a lake, trees and a boat, on a frosted yellow and grey background, signed "Gallé" in script on the side.

A small Gallé cameo fern vase, decorated with ferns on a frosted ground shading from amber to green, signed "GALLE" in cameo, slight damage.

A small Gallé cameo vase, decorated with hanging trumpet lilies and buds with leaves and branches on a raisin-coloured ground.

13in (33cm) high

12.75in (32.5cm) high

7in (18cm) high

6.5in (16.5cm) high

£2,300-2,800   JDJ

£2,200-2,800   JDJ

£500-800   JDJ

£550-650   JDJ

A Gallé cameo vase, decorated with lavender bellflowers, stems and leaves on a frosted ground, signed in cameo "Gallé" with a star.

A signed Gallé scenic cameo vase, with trees, pond and bridge in shades of brown on a rich orange background.

A Gallé cameo vase, amethyst over frosted glass with amethyst flower blossoms, leaves and stems on a frosted ground, signed in decoration, possible bruise to lip of vase.

A large Gallé French cameo glass vase, with deep purple tiger lilies over opalescent yellow.

8.25in (21cm) high

15.5in (39.5cm) high

6.5in (16.5cm) high

18in (45.5cm) high

£600-800   JDJ

£2,000-3,000   JDJ

£500-800   JDJ

£1,500-2,000   JDJ

A Gallé iris vase, with amethyst irises on frosted amber glass, signed "Gallé" within the decoration, ground top, two minor flakes to the base.

A Gallé cameo glass vase, with purple floral stems, on a frosted gray glass shaded pink, signed in cameo "Gallé".

A Gallé enamelled vase, translucent brown vase with applied enamelling of flowers, leaves and branches, signed on base "E. GALLE DEPOSE".

A Gallé cameo vase, amethyst over pastel blue cameo decoration of flowers and leaves, signed on side "GALLE".

11.5in (29cm) high

c1900

5.5in (14cm) high

3.75in (9.5cm) high

£2,000-3,000   JDJ

£420-480   SI

£800-1,000   JDJ

£450-550   JDJ

FIND OUT MORE...

Tim Newark, 'Art of Emile Gallé', published by Books Sales, 1989.

Francois-Therese Charpentier, 'Gallé', published by Harry N. Abrams, April 1988.

Musee de l'Ecole de Nancy, 36-38 Rue du Sergent Blandan, 5400 Nancy, France.

The Corning Museum of Glass, One Museum Way, Corning, New York 14830, U.S.A.

A small Gallé cameo vase, green over blue over frosted pink glass with a blue blossom and green branches and leaves, signed on side " GALLE".

6in (15cm) high

£1,000-1,500   JDJ

A small Gallé cameo vase, burnt orange glass over oyster white, fire-polished cameo decoration of leaves, signed in the decoration.

4.75in (12cm) high

£400-600   JDJ

A small Gallé cameo vase, peach-coloured cameo decoration of lily pads and blossoms, signed within the decoration.

3.75in (9.5cm) high

£420-480   JDJ

A rare Gallé fire-polished cameo decanter, with green cameo leaves, vines and berries, highlighted with gilt, silver collar on the neck with grapes engraved, signed on the bottom "EMILE GALLE".

10in (25.5cm) high

£1,500-2,000   JDJ

A rare early Gallé carved decanter, smoky amber colour, carved with a roaring lion and a stylized fleur-de-lis, four flat knobs applied on either side, signed on the bottom "GALLE DEPOSE" with an engraved flower, small bruise to the ground pontil, near signature, minor staining to the inside of the decanter.

9.5in (24cm) high

£650-750   JDJ

A Gallé enamelled smoky glass bottle and stopper, of flattened teardrop shape with applied ribbons of glass and painted en grisaille with a hunting scene and embellished with floral sprays in coloured enamels, finely signed on the base "E. Gallé Nancy déposé".

8.5in (21.5cm) high

£450-550   DN

An early Gallé tumbler, signed on the underside "E. GALLE NANCY", an unusual signature.

4.5in (11.5cm) high

£220-280   JDJ

A miniature fire-polished Gallé tumbler, with red fire-polished leaves, vines and berries, signed.

2in (5cm) high

£450-550   JDJ

A signed Gallé chandelier, red acid-cut flowers, leaves and foliage on a shaded green and cream background, signed in cameo "GALLE", supported by three cast brass chains with decorative Art Nouveau motif.

Shade 12in (5cm) diam

£2,500-3,000   JDJ

A Gallé cameo glass bowl, cameo leaves and vine on a frosted background, signed "GALLE" in the design, bowl appears to have been ground on the lip as well as the base.

4in (10cm) long

£220-280   JDJ

A Gallé cameo glass tazza, acid-etched flowering orchids on grey glass overlaid with yellow and ruby glass, raised on a turned foot, cameo signature, crack to foot.

8in (20cm) diam

£500-800   L&T

RENÉ LALIQUE

- René Lalique (1860-1945) was born near Reims, France. Lalique began his career designing popularly acclaimed jewellery. A pioneer of the Art Nouveau movement, his clients included stars such as the actress Sarah Bernhardt.

- In the 1890s he began to experiment with glass, both for jewellery and for small vessels, using the lost wax technique. In 1905 he opened a shop in Paris and began to make glass perfume bottles.

- By 1911, he had ceased making jewellery to concentrate on glass, establishing three factories by the 1920s.

- Using moulded glass, his pieces could be clear, frosted or opalescent. Opalescent glass is particularly desirable amongst collectors. Translucent milky glass was one of Lalique's specialities. Some pieces were stained with colour.

- Most of his designs were modernistic and clean. Repetition of an animal or plant motif or abstract design that covers the entire surface in a sophisticated pattern is common.

- Marks are important and help with dating. Marks for Lalique can be both etched and moulded. Before his death in 1945, marks used an 'R' before Lalique's name. This could appear with or without the word 'France' and was sometimes in script and sometimes in capitals. After 1945 the mark is simply 'Lalique, France' with no 'R'.

- Due to the popularity of Lalique's work, there are fakes. Crude production often identifies them, so familiarise yourself with authentic Lalique by viewing and handling as many pieces as possible. Other signs are wrong colours, thick rims and examples that are lighter in weight than genuine Lalique.

A Lalique 'Actina' pattern opalescent shallow bowl, signed "R.Lalique, France".

10in (25.5cm) diam

£450-550 GorL

A Lalique 'Vaguest No.1' pattern clear glass bowl, signed "Lalique, France".

9.5in (24cm) diam

£220-280 GorL

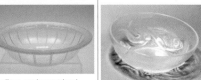

A Lalique opalescent bowl, designed by Cremieu, moulded mark "R. LALIQUE FRANCE" with inscribed "No. 400", small scratches to the well and two bruises to the lip, one appears to have been ground.

1928   *12in (30.5cm) diam*

£650-750 JDJ

A Lalique 'Ondines' pattern opalescent bowl, moulded on the exterior with a group of six mermaids swimming amid bubbles, signed "R. Lalique France" and numbered "380".

8.25in (21cm) diam

£900-1,000 DN

A mid-20thC Lalique bowl, tapered towards the foot and cut with a design of thistle heads divided by thorned canes, engraved script "Lalique France" mark.

10.25in (26cm) diam

£250-350 BonS

A mid-20thC Lalique opalescent bowl, moulded in a spiral with serrated edged leaf motifs, moulded "R. Lalique France" mark.

8in (20.5cm) diam

£200-300 BonS

A small Lalique clear glass bowl.

£80-120 GorL

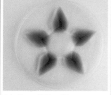

A Lalique dish, with green petal and cut decoration, signed "Lalique, France".

12in (30.5cm) diam

£450-550 GorL

A Lalique 'Poisson' clear glass dish, signed "Lalique, France".

14ins (35.5cm) diam

£500-600 GorL

An R. Lalique 'Fauvettes' pattern clear glass ashtray.

7in (18cm) diam

£80-120 GorL

A Lalique moulded glass 'Oeillets' pattern tray, the rim moulded with stylized blossoms, stamped "R. LALIQUE/FRANCE".

1936 15.75in (40cm) wide

£450-550 SI

A Lalique ashtray, decorated with a galleon, signed "Lalique".

7ins (18cm)

£70-90 GorL

A Lalique clear glass ashtray, decorated with impressed frosted flowerheads.

£80-120 GorL

An octagonal Lalique bowl, with petalled rim, signed "Lalique, France".

8.5in (21.5cm) diam

£120-180 GorL

A frosted Lalique fan-moulded ovoid bowl, signed "Lalique, France".

8.5in (21.5cm) diam

£150-200 GorL

A CLOSER LOOK AT A LALIQUE VASE

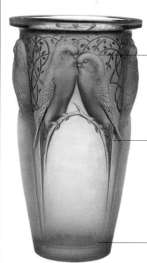

Opalescent glass was produced by adding phosphates, fluorides and aluminium oxide. This was followed by carefully controlled amounts of pigment to give very subtle hints of colour.

As in this example, colours are typically delicate, becoming part of the design.

Animals are a typical form of imagery used by Lalique. As well as birds, he used fish, reptiles and insects.

A mid-20thC cylindrical Lalique vase, moulded with long leaves and berries towards the rim, stained in blue, moulded "R. Lalique France" mark to side of vase.

7in (17.5cm) high

£500-600 BonS

A Lalique 'Rampillon' pattern frosted and clear glass vase, engraved "R. LALIQUE".

5.25in (13cm) high

£250-350 GorL

A Lalique 'Ceylan' pattern frosted and opalescent vase, of tapering cylindrical form with broad rim, moulded with a frieze of budgerigars, blue staining, wheel etched marks.

9.75in (25cm) high

£3,500-4,500 L&T

A square Lalique 'Roses' pattern bowl, signed "Lalique, France".
9.5in (24cm) wide

£280-320   GorL

A Lalique 'Bagatelle' pattern frosted glass vase, the sides with birds in foliate compartments, inscribed with "Lalique, France".
6.75in (15.5cm) high

£250-350   SI

An R. Lalique opalescent vase, all-over fish decoration with waves, signed on underneath side "R. Lalique".
5.5in (14cm) high

£1,400-1,600   JDJ

An R. Lalique 'Ronces' pattern opalescent vase, with moulded thorny vines, engraved "R. Lalique France" retailer's label.
9.25in (23.5cm) high

£1,800-2,200   FRE

An R. Lalique 'Archer' vase, frosted amber glass with a blown-out moulded decoration of ten archers and ten birds, signed in block letters on the underside as well as in script.
10.5in (26.5cm) high

£8,500-9,500   JDJ

A green coloured R. Lalique vase, with moulded design of leaves, signed on base "R. Lalique FRANCE H984".
6.5in (16.5cm) high

£3,000-4,000   JDJ

A Lalique crystal vase, of urn-form with moulded and frosted sparrows, engraved "Lalique France".
4.75in (12cm) high

£180-220   FRE

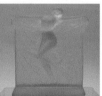

An R. Lalique 'Ornis' pattern opalescent vase, with two applied bird handles, signed "R. Lalique, FRANCE".
7.5in (19cm) high

£150-200   JDJ

An R. Lalique frosted glass 'Thais' figure, signed "R. LALIQUE".
8.5in (21.5cm) high

£6,000-7,000   JDJ

A Lalique frosted glass 'Chrysis' figure, signed on base "LALIQUE FRANCE".
6.25in (16cm) long

£1,000-1,500   JDJ

An R. Lalique 'Grape' pattern decanter set, with six matching tumblers and tray, all signed in block letters "R LALIQUE", slight damage to tray and tumblers.

Decanter 10.5in (26.5cm) high

£650-750   JDJ

A Lalique 'Eventail' pattern moulded glass ice cream cup.
1928   3in (7.5cm) diam

£60-80   SI

A Lalique opalescent atomizer, with ten moulded nudes, signed on base "R. LALIQUE FRANCE 2654".
9in (23cm) high

£400-500   JDJ

SCANDINAVIAN

- Scandinavian glass designs are typically very 'modern', often with strong angular elements and with clear lines. Pieces were aimed at being aesthetically pleasing but also affordable and were produced in large amounts. As such, they are still affordable today as this area has only begun to be appreciated by collectors.
- Production centred around mould blown glass which can be machine made or free-blown into a mould by a blower. It was highly popular during the 1960s and 1970s when glass was improving due to increased competition between factories.
- The striking clarity of Swedish glass is highly sought after, so beware of scratched or scuffed examples.
- Collectors should look for pieces that were designed by famous designers working at well-known factories.
- The Riihimaki Glassworks, based in Finland and founded 1910, is considered a key factory. Examples of glass production are often known as 'Lasi' after the factory's full title, 'Riihimäen Lasi Oy', meaning 'Riihimäen Glass Company'.
- During the 1940s and 1950s, a team of skilled designers including Nanny Still and Helena Tynell joined forces. Their collective improved methods in glass blowing ensured the company took a leading role in post-war glass production.
- In 1976, glass making went fully automatic and blown glass was discontinued. After a small series of sales to different companies and a merger, the factory was closed in 1990.
- Iittala was another key factory. It was based in Finland and founded in 1881, initially making household glass. The early 1930s saw competitions bringing in new modernist designers.
- From 1945, Iittala's production was confined to container glass, with Tapio Wirkkala joining in 1946 as Chief Designer. Timo Sarpaneva joined in the 1950s and, with a team of innovative designers, Iittala became Finland's largest art glass maker and merged with Nuutajarvi glassworks in 1987.

A Nanny Still vase, for Riihimaën Lasi Oy.

7.75in (20cm) high

£50-60   MHT

A Nanny Still vase, for Riihimaën Lasi Oy.

11.75in (30cm) high

£100-110   MHT

Three Nanny Still vases, for Riihimaën Lasi Oy.

1970s   11in (28cm) high

£70-80 each   MHT

NANNY STILL

- Born 1926 in Finland and trained in Helsinki. She worked for Riihimaki from 1949-1976 and is considered one of their chief designers, working in ceramics, enamels, jewellery, glass and other materials.
- Her earliest designs exploited the plastic nature of glass, but during the 1950s, her designs became more geometric with strong colours. In 1954 won the 'diplome d'honneur' at the Milan Triennale.
- She had great success in 1963 with her 'Flinari' decanters which were decorated with a diagonal grid-like relief pattern. From then her designs became more textural, starting with these 'Fantasma' and 'Kehra' vases of the late 1960s and 1970s.
- Elongated bottle shaped vases designed by her are commonly found and are affordable.

A Nanny Still cased vase, for Riihimaën Lasi Oy, pattern no. 1436 and acid stamp "Riihimaën Lasi Oy" with polar bear on base.

7.75in (19.5cm) high

£50-60   MHT

Two Nanny Still still-mould blown vases, for Riihimaën Lasi Oy.

8.25in (21cm) high

£35-45 each   MHT

A Nanny Still cased vase, for Riihimaën Lasi Oy, pattern no. 1339 and acid stamp "Riihimaën Lasi Oy" with polar bear on base.

7.75in (21.5cm) high

£50-60 MHT

Two Nanny Still 'Tiimalasi' vases, for Riihimaën Lasi Oy.

1970s 7in (18cm) high

£55-65 each MHT

A Nanny Still cased vase, for Riihimaën Lasi Oy, pattern no. 1436 and acid stamp "Riihimaën Lasi Oy" with polar bear on base.

6in (15cm) high

£50-60 MHT

Three Tamara Aladin vases, for Riihimaën Lasi Oy.

c1976 9.75in (25cm) high

£35-45 each MHT

Two Tamara Aladin large undulating vases, for Riihimaën Lasi Oy.

1960s 11in (28cm) high

£55-65 each MHT

TAMARA ALADIN

- She was born 1932 in Finland and joined Rihiimaki in 1959. She is considered one of their chief designers.

- Her designs are typical of the period with bright, jewel-like and strong colours and simple, clean designs, often using geometrical features.

- Her work is typified by these vases where the vertical line is cut with undulating sections, either with rippling ribs or stronger, horizontal flanges.

A Tamara Aladin large undulating vase, for Riihimaën Lasi Oy.

1960s 11in (28cm) high

£55-65 MHT

A Tamara Aladin undulating vase, for Riihimaën Lasi Oy.

1960s 9.75in (25cm) high

£65-70 MHT

A Tamara Aladin undulating vase, for Riihimaën Lasi Oy.

1960s 7.75in (20cm) high

£45-55 MHT

A Tamara Aladin 'Tuulikki' vase, for Riihimaën Lasi Oy.

c1976 7.75in (20cm) high

£35-45 MHT

Two Tamara Aladin vases, for Riihimaën Lasi Oy.

c1970s 7.75in (20cm) high

£35-45 each MHT

A Vicke Lindstrand vase, for Kosta, randomly decorated with pale blue, red and amethyst threads, signed "Kosta LH 1089".

6.75in (17.5cm)

£300-350 MHT

A Vicke Lindstrand dish, for Kosta, internally decorated, signed "Kosta LH 1386".

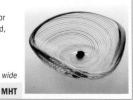

6.25in (16cm) wide

£120-140 MHT

A Vicke Lindstrand vase, for Kosta, Sweden, internally decorated, signed "_KOSTA LH 1260".

c1960   *6.25in (16cm) high*

£250-280   **MHT**

Two Vicke Lindstrand "Dark Magic" vases, for Kosta, signed to base "Kosta LH 1605".

5in (12.5cm)

£280-300 (each)   **MHT**

A coloured Vicke Lindstrand vase, for Kosta, with trapped air bubble from the 'Mambo' range, signed "Kosta LH 1889".

9in (23cm) high

£180-200   **MHT**

A small ovoid Vicke Lindstrand 'Moonshine' bowl, for Kosta, signed "Kosta LH 1316/90".

3in (7.5cm) high

£75-85   **MHT**

VICKE LINDSTRAND

- Born in 1904, Lindstrand began working for Kosta in 1950 as Chief Designer after twelve years at Orrefors. He held the position until 1973 and died in 1983 after a successful and varied career.
- Many of his designs use trees as inspiration or as motifs. He also worked as a book illustrator and this experience helped him with his decorative abilities in glass.
- He captured contemporary feelings during the 1950s with natural, bud-shaped forms. He is well known for his use of colour and organic forms. His inventive use of asymmetrical figural or abstract designs also make him noteworthy.

A Tapio Wirkkala 'Pinus' vase, for Iittala, signed "TW" on base.

8.75in (22.5cm) high

£100-120   **MHT**

TAPIO WIRKKALA

- Born in 1915 in Finland, Wirkkala studied sculpture at Helsinki from 1933-36.
- He was inspired by the Finnish and Laplandish countryside and the patterns of nature such as those found in wood and bark.
- He worked for Iittala from 1946-1985 and Venini from 1959-1985.
- He won the first prize at the Iittala glass competition in 1946 after which he took the position of Chief Designer. This was followed by gold medals at Faenza all during the 1960s. After a successful career, he died in 1985.

A Tapio Wirkkala 'Cog' vase, for Iittala, acid etched and polished, signed "Tapio Wirkkala 3552".

6.5in (16.5cm) high

£260-300   **MHT**

A Tapio Wirkkala kanto (tree stump) vase, for Iittala, signed "_3241 Tapio Wirkkala".

4.5in (11.5cm) high

£110-130   **MHT**

Two Tapio Wirkkala 'Ultima Thule' tankards, for Iittala, still-mould blown, designed by Wirkkala for Finnair's transatlantic flights.

1968   *4.75 in (12cm) high*

£65-70   **MHT**

A Helena Tynell vase, for Riihimaën Lasi Oy.

1970s 7.75in (21.5cm) high

£65-75   **MHT**

HELENA TYNELL

- Tynell started designing for Riihimaën Lasi Oy in 1946 and became known for her household glass designs.
- Forms are organic, often with undulations and wavy optical designs.
- During the late 1960s, her work became more geometric and surfaces became more textured.

A 1930s Alvar Aalto-style 'Savoy' vase, for Iittala

The Finnish designer Alvar Aalto (1898-1976) is better known for his architectural, interior and furniture designs. As well as glass, he also worked in lighting and textiles.

A Helena Tynell 'Pala' vase, for Riihimaën Lasi Oy.

c1969-76   4.5in (11.5cm) high

£35-45   **MHT**

A Helena Tynell 'Sun' juice carafe, for Riihimaën Lasi Oy.

'Sun' bottles were available in four different sizes.

c1964-74   9in (23cm) high

£75-95   **MHT**

1990s   4in (10cm) high

£50-60   **MHT**

A Swedish green Elis Bergh 'Ribbed Optic' vase.

c1948   7.75in (20cm) high

£80-90   **MHT**

An Otto Brauer "Gul" white cased vase, for Kastrap/Holmegaard.

1960s

£80-90   **MHT**

A selection of Otto Brauer "Gul" vases, for Kastrap/Holmegaard.

1960s

£50-120 (each)   **MHT**

A Kiejl Engman vase, for Kosta, with abstract landscape on white ground, signed "Kosta Boda 48638 K Engman".

9.5in (24cm) high

£80-100   **MHT**

A Boda Sun Catcher, by Eric Hogland, with impressed abstract animals, signed "H866/F".

11.75in (30cm) wide

£80-100   **MHT**

A Paul Kedelv still-mould blown vase, for Reijmyre.

c1965   8.25in (21cm) high

£45-55   **MHT**

A Holmegaard ice bucket, by Per Lutken, signed "Holmegaard 8715".

6in (15cm) high

£40-45   **MHT**

A Strombergshyttan Free Form vase, by Gunnar Nylund, signed to base "Strombergshyttan G. Nylund".

c1955 *54.25in (11cm) high*

£80-90 MHT

A late 1950s Aimo Okkolin Free Form vase, for Riihimaën Lasi Oy, with air-bubbled decoration around the base, signed "AIMO OKKOLIN Riihimaën LASI OY" on base.

9.25in (23.5cm) high

£80-100 MHT

A Bengt Orup vase, for Johansfors, graduated colour, signed to base "J Fors Orup".

16.6in (42cm)

£120-140 MHT

A Bengt Orup olive green tail glass, for Johansfors, signed "Johansfors Orup".

16.5in (42cm) high

£120-140 MHT

An Orrefors 'Selena' dish, by Sven Palmqvist, signed "Orrefors Pu 3092/31".

6in (15.5cm) wide

£50-60 MHT

An Orrefors vase, by Sven Palmqvist.

6.75in (17.5cm) high

£70-90 MHT

One of a set of four Timo Sarpaneva 'Klinka' whiskey glasses, for Iittala, with box.

3.5in (8.5cm) high

£55-65 (set) MHT

Three Timo Sarpaneva 'Festivo' candlestick holders, signed "TS" to base.

Largest 8.5in (21.6cm) high

£110-120 (set) MHT

A Boda vase, with abstract celestial motifs, signed "Boda Artist B Vallien 48330".

5.75in (14.5cm) high

£65-75 MHT

A Finnish ruby red carafe and a turn-mould blown tumbler, for Nuutajatui Notsjo.

1962-63 *7.5in (19cm)*

£80-90 MHT

A Kosta vase, decorated internally with amethyst swirls, signed "_KOSTA LH 1405".

c1960 *6.25in (16cm) high*

£160-180 MHT

FIND OUT MORE...

Jennifer Opie, 'Scandinavian Ceramics & Glass in the Twentieth Century, Victoria & Albert Museum, 1989.

A Mona-Morales-Schildt vase, for Kosta, signed "Kosta".

4.5in (11.5cm) high

£50-60 MHT

A Tiffany gold iridescent dish, with blue highlights and a scalloped edge, signed on base "L.C.T. FAVRILE".

5in (12.5cm) diam

£250-350   **JDJ**

A signed Tiffany gold iridescent bowl, with ruffled and fluted top edge with a ribbed outside design, signed on the bottom "L.C.T FAVRILE", a few minor scratches to the interior of the bowl.

7in (18cm) diam

£350-450   **JDJ**

A Tiffany gold iridescent shallow bowl, with pulled out feet, signed "L.C.T. M 9142".

5.5in (14cm) diam

£450-550   **JDJ**

A Tiffany green and gold iridescent bowl, with a gold and beige exterior, applied iridescent foot, signed on foot "L.C. TIFFANY FAVRILE".

7.5in (19cm) diam

£600-700   **JDJ**

A Tiffany gold iridescent stretched glass compote, with applied pedestal and foot, signed on base "L.C.T.".

8in (20.5cm) diam

£620-680   **JDJ**

A signed footed Tiffany bowl, with creamy yellow rolled rim, clear opalescence bowl and cupped foot with swirled panels of opalescence, signed on the bottom "LC Tiffany FAVRILE 1839", some very minor scratches to the inside of the bowl.

10in (25.5cm) diam

£1,800-2,200   **JDJ**

TIFFANY

- The son of an American jeweller, Louis Comfort Tiffany (1848-1933) traveled widely and was inspired by the different decorative styles he encountered.
- He founded 'Tiffany Glass & Decorating Co.' in 1892 and became chairman of his father's jewellers, Tiffany & Co, in 1902. 'The Tiffany Glass Company' was set up in 1885 and he became further interested in glass as a medium after seeing the work of Emile Gallé at the Paris Exhibition in 1889.
- In 1902, the 'Stourbridge Glass Company', run by his employee A. Douglas Nash, was renamed 'Tiffany Furnaces'.
- Tiffany began to produce lamps in 1890, the shades coming to be made from many pieces of his patented glass, 'Favrile'. Favrile, originally called 'Fabrile' means 'made by a craftsman or from his craft' and was patented in 1894. The glass was treated with metal oxides and exposed to acidic fumes to give it its particular appearance.
- The iridescence and lustre of many Tiffany pieces was produced by spraying surfaces with metallic salts. This style was inspired by excavated Roman glass and became very popular.
- Tiffany produced many different types of glass, including 'Cypriote' which was produced from 1896-1927 and has a lustrous but rough surface, 'Lava' glass with lustrous drips running down the surface and 'Agate' glass, opalescent coloured glass. He also produced glass that included sections of millefiori to represent flowers.
- In 1924, Tiffany dissolved the glass company and it was bought by A.D. Nash. Although Tiffany would not allow his name to be used, many of his styles continued to be produced. The A. Douglas Nash Corporation finished production in 1931.

A Tiffany gold iridescent footed bowl, with ruffled top and applied foot, signed on base "L.C.T.".

6in (15cm) diam

£500-600   **JDJ**

A Tiffany pastel gold iridescent compote, with oyster-white iridescent exterior finish, signed on base "L.C. TIFFANY FAVRILE V234".

8.25in (21cm) diam

£550-650   **JDJ**

A Tiffany Favrile glass dish, of bulbous form, with flared rim, etched "L.C.T.".

3.75in (9.5cm) diam

£350-450   **FRE**

A Tiffany pastel pink finger bowl and underplate, both signed "LCT FAVRILE".

Underplate 7in (18cm) diam

£700-800 JDJ

Two Tiffany Favrile glass salts, one circular with ruffled rim, signed "L. C. T.", the other roughly octagonal on four feet, signed "L. C. T.", chips to feet.

First 2.5in (6.5cm) diam

£200-300 FRE

A Tiffany gold intaglio-cut finger bowl and underplate, with green, blue and purple iridescence, both bowl and underplate intaglio-cut with grapevines, grapes and leaves, signed "LCT" on the bottom of the underplate.

Underplate 5.75in (14.5cm) diam

£750-850 JDJ

A Tiffany Favrile glass compote, with circular pedestal, bulbous body and wide ruffled rim, signed "1529-5633 K L C Tiffany - Favrile".

4.25in (10.5cm)

£650-750 FRE

A Tiffany gold iridescent floriform vase, with green and blue highlights and ruffled top, signed on base "L.C.T. W5977".

5in (12.5cm) high

£550-650 JDJ

A Tiffany gold iridescent floriform vase, with a stretched ruffled top and an applied foot, signed on base "L.C.T. 4872B", some interior staining.

11in (28cm) high

£2,000-3,000 JDJ

A Tiffany gold iridescent floriform vase, with ruffled top, signed on base "L.C.T. W1737".

4.75in (13cm) high

£600-700 JDJ

A Tiffany iridescent vase, with gold and green finish, vertical ribs and pinched in sides, button pontil, signed "L.C.T. U970".

4.75in (12cm) high

£1,500-2,000 JDJ

A Tiffany gold iridescent ribbed vase, with uneven ribs from top to base, marked on the base "7314C".

3.5in (9cm) high

£650-750 JDJ

A Tiffany gold iridescent floriform vase, of melon ribbed design with slightly domed foot, marked on the base "48788", some staining to the interior.

6in (15cm) high

£750-850 JDJ

A Tiffany iridescent vase, with brown, gold and beige striped decoration and gold collar, signed on base "TIFFANY FAVRILE B-522", ground pontil.

11.25in (28.5cm) high

£2,800-3,200 **JDJ**

A Tiffany iridescent vase, blue-grey background with silvery blue pulled leaves and vines, signed on the bottom "LCT F698", base drilled and patched.

21in (53.5cm) high

£6,500-7,500 **JDJ**

TThis example is made from Agate glass, which was produced from the mid-1890s and is highly desirable. Sometimes known as 'laminated glass', the stunning effect was produced by mixing carefully chosen, often contrasting, colours together in a pot with heat reactive glass that changed colour after being cooled and reheated.

Pieces were finished for display or sale by cutting and polishing the glass to show the sophisticated striations in the glass.

This piece bears the original paper label and is signed on the base " L.C. Tiffany INC FAVRILE EXHIBITION piece in 5545M".

A Tiffany agate exhibition piece, green, brown and beige with allover faceting, original Tiffany paper label, very minor chips to the side, two small holes in the centre of two of the cane panels, done in the making.

This piece was made to exhibition quality and would have been used to demonstrate and represent Tiffany's glassmaking skills.

4.5in (11.5cm) high

£8,000-9,000 **JDJ**

A Tiffany Favrile glass loving cup, with three applied handles, etched "L. C. Tiffany - Favrile 2684 D".

7.25in (18.5cm) high

£1,200-1,800 **FRE**

A Tiffany blue iridescent covered compote, with purple highlights, signed on base "L.C. Tiffany FAVRILE 5679M", cover is signed "L.C. Tiffany Inc FAVRILE 5679M".

9.5in (24cm) high

£1,500-2,500 **JDJ**

A Tiffany turquoise iridescent vase, dark blue bands on a light blue ground, button pontil, signed on underneath of base "L.C. TIFFANY FAVRILE PANAMA PACIFIC EXHIBITION 9439".

7.25in (18.5cm) high

£2,500-3,500 **JDJ**

A Tiffany gold iridescent stick vase, in a brass and green and gold enamelled metal holder, signed on base "LOUIS C TIFFANY FURNACES INC 152", some interior staining.

16.5in (42cm) high

£900-1,000 **JDJ**

A Tiffany gold iridescent candle lamp, of ruffled stretched shade with gold and purple iridescence, the swirled base signed on the bottom "LCT" and supporting the original candle holder.

15in (38cm) high

£2,000-3,000 **JDJ**

A Tiffany Favrile glass lamp, with twisted vasiform base, cylindrical pulled glass electrified bobeche and ruffled stretch glass shade, base and shade signed "L. C. T. Favrile".

14in 35.5cm) high

£1,200-1,800 **FRE**

WHITEFRIARS & GEOFFREY BAXTER

■ A glassworks was founded in Whitefriars, London, in the 17th century. In 1834 it was acquired by James Powell and became known as 'Powell & Sons' until 1962 when its name reverted to 'Whitefriars Glassworks'.

■ During the 19th century, designs included pieces by renowned designer William Morris. The 20th century saw a move towards more Art Deco designs and coloured and textured glass.

■ In 1954 the talented Geoffrey Baxter was employed and during the 1960s designed ranges that injected a new impetus into Whitefriars. Today they are highly sought after. His designs varied between those that were unusually shaped, had textured finishes or resembled the pure and brilliant colours found in Scandinavian glass of the time.

■ Textured finishes were fashionable during the 1960s and Baxter initially used nature as his inspiration.

■ Mould-blown pieces such as those with bark-like textured exteriors were produced from 1967. Other popular textured pieces were made using carpet nails hammered into the wooden moulds so that the nail heads left an impression.

■ Baxter was also influenced by man-made subjects, as can be seen in the innovative and asymmetric 'Drunken Bricklayer' vase.

■ As moulds were slightly burnt by the hot glass each time they were used, look for pieces that were produced early in the mold's life and show a fine and varied level of texture.

■ Despite being highly popular during the 1960s and 1970s, the difficult economic climate meant that Whitefriars began to decline, until its eventual closure in 1980.

A large ruby Geoffrey Baxter for Whitefriars vase, with bulbous pinched form.

10.5in (27cm) high

£60-80   MHT

A pair of Geoffrey Baxter for Whitefriars ruby bud vases.

c1960s   7.85in (20cm) high

£20-25 each   MHT

A Geoffrey Baxter 'Kingfisher' blue bud vase.

c1960s   8.5in (21.5cm) high

£25-30   MHT

A Geoffrey Baxter for Whitefriars textured 'Nailhead' vase, pattern 9683.

c1967   6.75in (17cm) high

£30-40   MHT

Above left: A Geoffrey Baxter for Whitefriars "Drunken Bricklayer" glass vase, of rectangular section formed as three blocks with the central portion dislodged and in "pewter" toned glass.

13in (33cm) high

£1,000-1,500   DN

Above right: A Whitefriars "ribbon-trailed" glass lamp base, designed by Barnaby Powell, the body of pale green tone and decorated with a horizontal spiralling band.

8.25in (21cm) high

£180-220   DN

A Geoffrey Baxter for Whitefriars, amethyst soda glass vase.

1962-64   4in (10cm) high

£45-55   MHT

Two Geoffrey Baxter for Whitefriars small shadow green soda glass vases, pattern no.9548.

4in (10cm) high

£35-45 pair   MHT

A Geoffrey Baxter for Whitefriars willow cased bowl, pattern no "9660".

c1965   11.5in (29.5cm) wide

£60-80   MHT

A Geoffrey Baxter for Whitefriars cased dish.

c1960s   5.25in (13.5cm) high

£25-30   MHT

A Geoffrey Baxter for Whitefriars ruby dish, with splayed rim.

c1960s   6.25in (16cm) high

£25-30   MHT

SOWERBY

- The 'Gateshead Stamped Glass Works' was the first factory devoted exclusively to making pressed glass and was founded by John Sowerby in 1846. It was replaced by the purpose-built 'Sowerby Ellison Glass Works' in 1852. The Vitro-Porcelain range of opaque pressed glass was introduced in 1877 and included decanters, cruets, bowls and jugs.

- Between the wars new colours and styles were introduced and during the 1920s Carnival glass was produced in iridescent orange and blue. Pastel shades and a basic Art Deco style characterised the 1930s with dishes, table centres and fruit sets being typical examples.

- After World War II the company suffered against competition and after a series of take-overs, it closed in 1972.

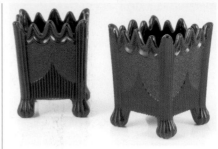

A pair of square Sowerby jardinières, factory marks.

£60-70   WW

One of a pair of Sowerby jardinières, factory marks.

£45-55 (pair)   WW

A Sowerby dish, factory marks.

£25-30   WW

A light blue Sowerby flower trough, modelled in lavender blue, factory marks.

£40-50   WW

A Sowerby cream jug and sugar bowl, factory marks.

£40-60   WW

LOETZ

- Founded by Johann B. Eisner von Einstein at Kostermuhle in Austria in 1836, the factory was bought by Susanna Gerstner, the widow of glassmaker Johann Loetz and renamed 'Loetz-Witwe', in 1851.

- Gerstner's grandson Max Ritter von Spaun took over in 1879. Assisted by Eduard Prochaska, a glass technician, together they produced new designs in iridescent art glass and in Art Nouveau-styles.

- Inspired by Tiffany's 'Favrile' range they used stronger, unusual and sophisticated colour combinations, incorporating reds, cobalt blues and golds.

- Forms were inspired by Tiffany's pieces, but Loetz also produced other new forms with applied ribs, metal mounts and numerous handles.

- After 1905, production moved away from Art Nouveau styles with forms becoming more regular, colours brighter and silver became the dominant metallic colour in use.

- In 1906, Josef Hoffman joined and the factory was reinvigorated, with new designs using stylized leaf and geometric patterns .

- After 1914, the factory produced pieces for Weiner Werkstatte, including those by designers such as Arnold Nechansky, Michael Powolny and Dagobert Peche.

- The 1930s saw a serious fire at the factory and the 1939 Wall Street Crash. Although it was declared bankrupt in 1939, the factory carried on until 1948 when it finally closed.

A pair of Sowerby turquoise 'malachite glass' candlesticks, the spiral-moulded columns with Corinthian capitals, factory marks and registration marks, ground chips to the base.

1877   *7.5in (19cm) high*

£50-80   WW

A Loetz decorated and silver overlay vase, with light blue iridescent pattern, topped with silver overlay in a flowing Art Nouveau pattern.

5.25in (13.5cm) high

£2,000-3,000   JDJ

A Loetz 'Papillon' glass vase, possibly designed by Michael Powolny, lobed form with ruffled rim on three ball feet, "CZECHOSLOVAKIA" in oval stamped mark, minor scratches in interior.

c1920   *5in (12.5cm) high*

£550-650   FRE

A Loetz 'Candia Papillon' nautilus shell, designed 1898, unsigned.

7.5in (19cm) long

£400-500 FRE

A Loetz iridescent 'King Tut' vase, the gold body swirled with blue lines.

4in (10cm) high

£550-650 JDJ

A Loetz 'Phaomen' vase, of classical form, etched signature "Loetz Austria".

5.25in (13.5cm) high

£1,000-1,500 FRE

A Loetz 'Octopus' vase, brown glass with air-trapped scrolls highlighted with gold enamelling, pink interior.

10in (25.5cm) high

£1,500-2,000 JDJ

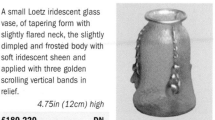

A small Loetz iridescent glass vase, of tapering form with slightly flared neck, the slightly dimpled and frosted body with soft iridescent sheen and applied with three golden scrolling vertical bands in relief.

4.75in (12cm) high

£180-220 DN

A Loetz oil spot and silver overlaid vase, brown and blue oil spot design with silver overlaid snap dragons on the front.

8.75in (22cm) high

£450-550 JDJ

A Loetz iridescent glass vase, of conical shape with random splashes of silvery blue lustre, further decorated with a sinuous floral appliqué, cracked on neck and with added collar.

4.5in (11.5cm) high

£100-150 DN

A Loetz iridescent bottle, with light blue iridescent free-form threading, chip to edge of base.

7in (18cm) high

£80-120 JDJ

A rare Loetz glass bowl, peach-coloured shading to raspberry at the base, entirely threaded with fluted rim.

10in (25.5cm) diam

£450-550 JDJ

A Loetz glass footed bowl, with ruffled edge and three curved feet, in clear glass with iridescent oil spot decoration, unsigned, falsely inscribed "Tiffany".

c1900 8.5in (21.5cm) wide

£150-200 SI

A Loetz floriform vase, shades from green base to red top with blue-green iridescence

13.5in (34.5cm) high

£150-200 JDJ

An unusual iridescent green Loetz vase, with green snake wrapped around the body, several tiny chips to the lip.

9in (23cm) high

£80-120 JDJ

An unusual glass 'creature' pouring vessel, attributed to Loetz and a design by Richard Techner.

7in (18cm) high

£250-300 DN

A red Loetz vase, with pinched body, ribbed shoulder and bulbous mouth with irregular silver iridescence.

5.5in (14cm) high

£120-180 JDJ

CRANBERRY GLASS

- As its name suggests, cranberry glass has a characteristic ruby pink colour. This comes from the addition of copper oxide or gold chloride to the glass mix. Although it was produced by the ancient Romans, it became most fashionable in Victorian England, where the centre of production was at Stourbridge. In America it was widely produced, primarily at the Boston & Sandwich Glass Co. (1826-1888) in Sandwich, Massachusetts.

A cranberry glass two-handled vase, slight damage.

6in (15cm) diam

£60-90   OACC

Two opalescent cranberry glass vases, comprising a triple tree trunk vase with a clear fluted base and a light amber green glass vase with cranberry opalescence at the heavily fluted rim, clear glass rigaree spirals down the body.

Largest 10in (25.5cm) high

£150-200   JDJ

A religious cranberry glass bowl, with white enamel decoration "IHS" (In His Service).

2.75in (7cm) diam

£40-50   OACC

An American freeblown cranberry glass apothecary's shop trade sign, wooden base.

Apothecary's shops had two of these signs: one red and one blue. If the blue sign was in the window visitors knew there was disease in the town. A red sign meant it was safe to visit.

c1840   *15in (38cm) high*

£1,000-1,300   RAA

A Victorian cranberry glass sweet basket.

4.5in (11cm) diam

£80-120   OACC

A cranberry glass tankard, engraved "To Madame Fontana as souvenir from Mr Voisin, 1840".

c1840   *5.5in (14cm) high*

£120-180   OACC

A Victorian cranberry glass jug, gilded and hand-painted.

c1870   *4in (10cm) high*

£80-120   OACC

A pair of cranberry glass tumblers.

4in (10cm) high

£45-55   OACC

A cranberry glass wine glass.

5in (12.5cm) high

£12-16   OACC

CARNIVAL GLASS

Carnival glass is an inexpensive decorative glass characterized by its bright colours and iridescence. It is most commonly found in orange (marigold), through to green and blue. Red is very rare and and is the most valuable. Often known as the 'poor man's Tiffany', the iridescence was produced by spraying the moulded glass with metallic salts suspended in oil. It was popular in England from the late 19th century and in America from around 1900. It was produced in vast quantities and was often given away as prizes at fairs, hence its name.

A Carnival glass marigold dish.

£10-20   **OACC**

A Carnival glass bowl, with rose and dragon decoration, peacock colour.

8in (20.5cm) diam

£10-15   **AS&S**

A Carnival glass punch bowl.

12.25in (31cm) diam

£70-100   **OACC**

A Carnival glass bowl.

7.5in (19cm) diam

£10-15   **OACC**

A Carnival glass boat-shaped dish.

7in (18cm) long

£25-30   **OACC**

Pressed Glass

A late Victorian moulded glass dish.

c1900   *7.75in (20cm) diam*

£15-18   **OACC**

A pressed glass chamber stick, bearing the motto 'Good Night'.

c1900   *5.25in (13cm) diam*

£35-45   **OACC**

A pressed glass tazza.

7.75in (20cm) diam

£8-12   **OACC**

Two small 19thC green pressed glass plates, decorated with flowers and foliage.

Largest 10.5in (26.5cm) diam

£50-80   **WW**

A tall Clutha green glass vase, by James Couper & Sons, designed by George Walton, the body of tapering cylindrical form, with a broad rim and trailing opaque inclusions.

15.75in (40cm) high

£2,500-3,000   **L&T**

A Clutha green glass vase, by James Couper & Sons, the ovoid body with knopped and tapering neck and everted rim, the body having aventurine and trailing opaque inclusions.

9in (23cm) high

£280-320   **L&T**

An Etling moulded opalescent glass vase, moulded with stylized blossoms, moulded "ETLING".

Etling is commonly seen as influenced by, and an imitator of, Rene Lalique.

c1930   *7in (18cm) high*

£200-250   **SI**

An Etling opalescent bowl.

Edmond Etling & Cie, active 1920s and 30s, produced moulded opalescent glass comparable in standards of design to Sabino, the figures of draped female nudes are especially collectable.

1920-30   *9in (23cm) diam*

£300-400   **OACC**

A Higgins striped glass bowl, in beige, white, and grey, with gold striped accents, marked.

9.5in (24cm) diam

£150-200   **CR**

A 1970s Mdina vase, by Michael Harris.

1970s   *5.25in (13.5cm) high*

£35-45   **MHT**

MDINA

■ Mdina Glass was founded by Michael Harris, an ex-tutor at the Royal College of Art, in 1967, on the island of Malta. Its output is characterised by the colours of the coast and sea such as marine blues and greens, amethyst decorated with ochres, golds and sandy colours. Common forms include large, shallow dishes and bottle shaped vases. Harris left in 1972 and set up the Isle of Wight glass factory in the same year, although the Maltese factory continued. Today there are three glassworks on the island, all still producing designs by Michael Harris.

A Monart glass vase, of tapering cylindrical form, with wide flaring rim, the mottled green body and pale blue rim joined with a band of swirls.

7in 17.5cm high.

£300-350   **L&T**

A Monart tapering cylindrical vase, the mottled turquoise body with blue and aventurine inclusions to the rim.

7.75in (20cm) high

£80-120   **PC**

A 1970s Mdina vase, in greens and blues, by Michael Harris.

9in (23cm) high

£35-45   **MHT**

A 1970s Mdina vase, in greens and blues, by Michael Harris.

7in (18cm) high

£35-45   **MHT**

A Monart shallow glass bowl, of circular form with applied foot, the mottled powder blue body graduating to clear rim with aventurine inclusions.

10.5in (27cm) diam

£150-200   **PC**

A Nazeing blue tricorn bowl, with clear glass flower holder.
1970s   *6.5in (16.5cm) diam*

£6-12   **NBen**

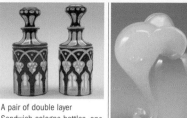

A pair of double layer Sandwich cologne bottles, one marked "48" on the pontil and the other marked "2", a few chips to the underside of one and minor chips to the base of the other, some wear to the gold decoration.

7in (18cm) high

£550-600   **JDJ**

A blue and white glass elephant, attributed to Seguso, etched "Seguso Murano", unmarked.

6in (15cm) high

£80-120   **CR**

A pair of clear two-tier 'Sheringham' candlestick, by Ronald Stennett-Willson, for Wedgwood Glass.

c1968   *5.25in (13.5cm) high*

£60-70   **MHT**

Three Brancaster candlesticks, by Ronald-Stennett-Willson, amber/peach coloured glass with hollow stems and applied splayed feet.

c1960 Tallest 11in (28cm)high

£120-140 set   **MHT**

An unusual 1960s Wedgwood vase, by Ronald Stennett-Willson, dark blue glass with acid stamp to base.

8.75in (22cm) high

£80-100   **MHT**

A Stevens and Williams red cameo glass vase, ovoid with white dogwood branch and bleeding heart decoration.

c1890   *7in (18cm) high*

£900-1,000   **SI**

A Stevens & Williams bowl, pink and green candy-striped.

7in (18cm) diam

£60-70   **MHT**

Two 1960s Dartington daisy jars, by Frank Thrower, with daisy flower motif to each side.

Tallest 7in (18cm) high

£45-60 each   **MHT**

A group of Dartington vases, by Frank Thrower.
c1970   *5in (13cm) high*

£45-55 each   **MHT**

A contemporary art glass vase, floriform with pulled orange, blue and yellow petal decoration, signed Vandermark, dated.
1978   *16in (40.5cm) high*

£150-200   **SI**

A 1930s Vaseline glass spill vase, of Neo-classical design with silver-plated stand.

13in (33cm) high

£55-65   **AS&S**

A pair of 'Ming' vases, by Frank Thrower, for Wedgwood, each stamped "Wedgwood" to base.

5.5in (14cm) high

£45-55   **MHT**

An early 20thC vaseline glass bonbon dish, in Walker & Hall silver-plated stand.

6.75in (17cm) diam

£80-120   **AS&S**

Six vaseline glass items, including an inverted thumprint pitcher, a hobnail vase and tumbler, a daisy and button goblet with opalescent rim and small vase and bowl, some chips to hobnail vase at base.

£70-100 (set)   **JDJ**

Six vaseline glass decanters, including a pair of diamond quilted decanters, a small 'daisy and button', one with cut design, one square and one faceted decanter, 'daisy and button' shows stains to interior.

£150-200 (set)   **JDJ**

A Vasart dessert set, comprising a large serving bowl and six smaller individual bowls (two shown).

c1940 Largest 9in (23cm) diam

£300-400 (set)   **REN**

A 1970s Zweisel blue vase, by Heinrech Loffelhardt, internally decorated with profuse bubbles.

7.5in (19cm) high

£70-120   **MHT**

A 1970s Zweisel green vase, by Heinrech Loffelhardt, internally decorated with profuse bubbles.

37.5in (9.5cm) high

£70-120   **MHT**

A late 19thC French art glass vase, with a flared neck.

6in (15cm) high

£35-45   **AS&S**

A late 19thC French hand-blown vase, with bubble decoration.

6in (15cm) high

£60-80   **AS&S**

A French art glass vase, with twisted decoration.

6in (15cm) high

£45-55   **AS&S**

An enamel-decorated art glass vase, probably French, green shading to clear iridescent glass, painted with yellow and white irises, inscribed in enamel "F.H. 493/3 H146".

c1900   *8in (20.5cm) high*

£250-350   **SI**

A gold iridescent Austrian art glass vase, with clear free-form lines.

28.5in (72.5cm) high

£900-1,000   **JDJ**

A late 19thC art glass vase, yellow cased in white with gold leaves and branches and four jewelled bugs, the collar with Egyptian type lettering.

6in (15cm) high

£350-450   **JDJ**

A French art glass vase, with mottled green and blue metallic decoration, pinched rim.

4in (10cm) high

£45-55 AS&S

A late 19thC French Art Nouveau glass vase, applied with green glass mouldings and with a wide flat rim.

5in (12.5cm) high

£80-120 AS&S

An art glass vase, blue shading to clear inverted thumbprint. decoration

6.5in (16.5cm) high

£250-350 JDJ

A 1920s hand-blown blue art glass vase, with wave decoration to waist.

7.75in (20cm) high

£45-55 AS&S

A grey glass vase, with abstract flower motifs.

c1960 *11.75in (30cm) high*

£50-60 MHT

An English green glass vase, with applied teardrop decoration.

8in (20.5cm) high

£150-200 AS&S

Two Italian art glass vases, one of cylindrical form with bands of orange, green and blue, unmarked, together with a vase of bulbous form with alternating yellow and white stripes, small fracture to foot.

Tallest 11.5in (30cm) high

£280-320 FRE

Two Whitefriars-style paperweight vases, both with concentric millefiori paperweight bases with clear flutes, rough pontils.

8.25in (21cm) high

£300-400 JDJ

A Murano presentation goblet, with floral design, accented in gold, unmarked, some losses to gold.

10in (25.5cm) high

£150-200 CR

An Art Deco opalescent green glass bowl, circular with moulded "V" geometric panels between three supporting legs.

5.25in (13.5cm) high

£90-100 FRE

An art glass centre bowl, with a pierced rim.

11in (28cm) diam

£17-20 AS&S

A 1960s art glass bowl.

9in (22cm) diam

£18-22 AS&S

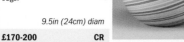

An Italian 'Canedece' glass bowl, with polychrome swirled design, unmarked, fleck to one edge.

9.5in (24cm) diam

£170-200 CR

A 1960s Murano glass dish, unsigned.

17in (43cm) high

£120-180 V

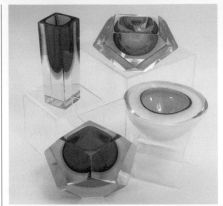

Four pieces of American studio art glass, including two faceted low vases, one vertical square vase, and one opalescent bowl.

Tallest 6in (15cm) high

£200-300 FRE

A Continental glass bowl and stand, the vessel of compressed form with lobed sides, crackle-textured surface chased silver banding, the lobed flower form stand with chased silver rim and "swag" decoration.

7in (18cm) diam

£150-250 DN

An art glass dresser box, iridescent blue with applied enamelled decoration of pink and white flowers.

4.75in (12cm) diam

£150-250 JDJ

A late 19thC art glass sugar and creamer, amethyst shading to emerald green with applied floral decorations.

Creamer 5.75in (14.5cm) high

£350-450 JDJ

A pair of engraved Edwardian tumblers.

c1905   4.5in (11cm) high

£5-10 OACC

A hinged art glass dresser box, with enamelled pansies and green leaves on a beige background, original metal hardware.

8in (20.5cm) diam

£120-180 JDJ

A Georgian glass, with facet-cut stem and base of bowl, broken pontil.

c1800   5in (13cm) high

£80-110 OACC

A Victorian waisted liquor glass, with engraved fruit on bowl, small chip on bowl.

c1870   3.5in (9cm) high

£35-45 OACC

An early 20thC cut glass celery vase.

9in (23cm) high

£45-55 OACC

A pair of Edwardian engraved sherry glasses.

c1905   *3.75in (9.5cm)*

£5-10   **OACC**

A Victorian glass celery vase.

c1870   *11in (28cm) high*

£15-25   **OACC**

A 1960s blue brandy glass, with internal jewelling.

10in (25.5cm) high

£5-8   **AS&S**

A large Murano lamp, by Cenedese.

c1960   *18.5 in (47cm) high*

£250-300   **MHT**

A free-blown 'end-of-day' glass punch ladle, with white powder sulphide lining.

c1890   *14.5in (37cm) long*

£150-200   **RAA**

A pair of Bohemian amber-flashed candlesticks, engraved with grapes, leaves and strawberries.

13.5in (34.5cm) high

£250-350   **JDJ**

A late 19thC glass cruet set.

£200-300   **BAC**

A pair of Italian glass figures in pale blue, clear and gold-flecked glass.

c1940

£150-200   **SI**

A milk glass rabbit, bearing mark "pat 1886".

£120-180   **BCAC**

An 'end-of-day' glass dump.

'End-of-day' pieces were made at the end of the working day by craftsmen and makers and are not included within the standard production of the factory. A 'dump' is a doorstop, which is the most common form of 'end-of-day' work. The green tint is 'natural', but only seen in such examples as the glass is usually rolled into thinner sheets for windows and the colour is lost. They usually have bubble decorations as seen in this example.

5in (12.5cm) high

A pair of 19thC 'end-of-day' dumps, with internal flower design, some chips.

2.75in (7cm) high

£45-55   **PSA**

£40-60   **PSA**

JEWELLERY

CHRISTIAN DIOR

- Christian Dior started making costume jewellery at the end of World War II as part of his extravagant New Look.
- Early designs were made to look deliberately 'fake' and showy, using unconventional stones such as aurora borealis and petal-shaped glass.
- Soon, Dior started using these 'new' stones in conventional 18thC designs and the company's trademark costume jewellery look was born.
- Early designs are couture pieces, made by craftsmen to complement a particular outfit for one client. Later pieces were made in greater numbers, but not mass-produced, for the company's boutiques.
- Dior's designs were produced by Kramer in the US until 1955 and by Mitchell Maer in England from 1950-52. Then in 1955, the German firm Henkle & Grosse was given an exclusive licence to produce Dior's designs.
- Collectors look for pre-1970 evening necklaces and earrings, although there is a growing market for more affordable pieces from the 1970s.

A mid-late 1950s Christian Dior rhinestone and paste unicorn brooch, by Mitchell Maer.

£60-85   RG

A mid-late 1950s Christian Dior clear paste and faux pearl flower brooch, by Mitchell Maer, signed Christian Dior.

£80-120   RG

A Christian Dior necklace and earrings, set with iridescent glass and aurora borealis stone, signed by Christian Dior.

c1958

£300-350   RG

A mid-late 1950s Christian Dior necklace and earrings set with clear paste stones and green marble effect cabochons, by Mitchell Maer.

£350-420   RG

A Christian Dior pin, set with royal blue and aurora borealis stones, signed and dated 1958.

£80-120   RG

A Christian Dior necklace and earrings, set with faux rubies and diamonds.

1959 Earrings 1.5in (4cm) long

£320-380   Rox

A 1960s Christian Dior necklace, bracelet and earrings, by Kramer.

Earrings 1in (3cm) long

£150-200   Rox

A Christian Dior pearl and diamanté pin.

1963   4in (9cm) long

£120-180   Rox

A Christian Dior abstract apple brooch, set with red, blue and clear rhinestones and faux pearls, signed "Christian Dior", made in Germany.

1962

£250-300   RG

A 1960s Christian Dior heart-shaped brooch, set with clear stones with pink or white inclusions and pastel yellow, blue and green stones, signed Christian Dior.

£120-150   RG

A Christian Dior necklace, earrings and brooch,set with faux emerald and lapis stones, signed "CD Germany".

1966

£300-350   RG

A rare Christian Dior circus seal pin.

1966   *3in (8cm) long*

£120-180   Rox

A Christian Dior necklace and earrings,set with emerald green and clear paste, signed Christian Dior.

1967

£300-350   RG

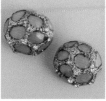

A pair of Christian Dior earrings.

1967   *1in (3cm) diam*

£50-100   Rox

A 1970s Christian Dior pin.

3in (7cm) long

£40-60   TR

A 1940s Miriam Haskell pearl and diamanté pin and earrings.

Earrings 1in (3cm) long

£200-300   Rox

A 1940s Miriam Haskell pearl, diamanté and gold flower pin.

3.25in (8cm)

£180-220   Rox

A Christian Dior Indian influence necklace, set with faux pearl and faux lapis beads, signed and dated.

From the the estate of the singer and actress, Vivienne Blaine.

1970

£220-280   RG

A pair of 1930s Miriam Haskell pink and diamanté drop earrings, unmarked.

2.25in (6cm) long

£80-120   Rox

MIRIAM HASKELL

- Miriam Haskell's jewellery is always handmade using glass beads and simulated seed and baroque pearls threaded onto brass wire and secured to filigree backings. Another common feature are rose montée – clear paste stones set closely together.

- She only started signing her jewellery in the late 1940s, but earlier unsigned pieces can be identified by the quality of the workmanship and materials.

- Haskell opened her boutique at the McAlpin Hotel in New York in 1925 and sold the company in the early 1950s. The company continues to produce reproductions of classic designs from the 1940s and 50s today.

- Collectors of vintage pieces should learn to tell reproductions from originals. An inspection of the metal can help. The metal used in vintage pieces – known as 'antique Russian gold' – has a warm matt finish. Modern pieces look yellower in comparison.

- Buyers should also inspect the faux pearls closely. Poor storage often chips the surface irreparably and perfume, soap and creams will also erode the finish.

A Miriam Haskell pin, with matching earrings.

Pin 2.5in (6cm) high

£100-200   Rox

A 1940s Miriam Haskell pearl and diamanté necklace.

Drop 2in (5cm) long

£250-300   Rox

A pair of 1940s Miriam Haskell gold and diamanté flower earrings.

1.5in (4cm) long

£100-150 Rox

A pair of 1940s Miriam Haskell pearl and diamanté flower earrings.

1.5in (4cm) long

£100-150 Rox

A 1940s Miriam Haskell "cherry" design pearl and diamanté pin and earrings.

Earrings 2in (5cm) long

£300-400 Rox

A 1940s Miriam Haskell necklace, bracelet and earrings, with faux pearl and brass spacers and beads.

£300-350 RG

A 1940s Miriam Haskell faux pearl and brass necklace.

£140-160 RG

A 1940s Miriam Haskell pink flower brooch.

2.5in (6.5cm) long

£200-300 Rox

A 1940s Miriam Haskell red and clear glass bead brooch.

2in (5cm) long

£140-180 Rox

A pair of 1940s Miriam Haskell earrings, with large pink stones.

1.25in (3.5cm) long

£100-150 Rox

A 1940s Miriam Haskell pink and pearl bead bracelet.

Clasp 1.5in (3.5cm) long

£100-150 Rox

A 1940s Miriam Haskell bird of paradise stick pin, set with blue, green and pink beads.

£40-60 RG

A 1940s Miriam Haskell necklace.

£180-220 Rox

A 1940s Miriam Haskell multi-coloured bead bracelet and earrings.
Earrings 2.25in (6cm)

£300-400   **Rox**

A pair of 1940s Miriam Haskell yellow flower earrings.
1.25in (3.5cm) long

£100-150   **Rox**

A pair of 1940s Miriam Haskell earrings.
1in (2.5cm) long

£80-120   **Rox**

A 1940s Miriam Haskell gold, blue and green pin.
3in (7.5cm) long

£80-120   **Rox**

A 1940s Miriam Haskell white bead pin.
3in (7.5cm) long

£100-150   **Rox**

A 1940s Miriam Haskell amber and gold necklace.
Drop centre 2in (5cm) long

£200-300   **Rox**

A 1940s Miriam Haskell amber and gold necklace.
Drop centre 2in (5cm) long

£200-300   **Rox**

A 1940s Miriam Haskell amber and pearl bead pin and earrings.
Earrings 1in (3cm) long

£180-220   **Rox**

A 1950s Miriam Haskell blue and white bead necklace and earrings.
Earrings 1.75in (4.5cm) long

£280-320   **Rox**

A 1950s Miriam Haskell stick pin, with baroque pearls and filigree stampings.
2.75in (7cm) long

£50-100   **CRIS**

A 1960s Miriam Haskell pearl pin and earrings.
3.5in (9cm) long

£120-180   **Rox**

A 1960s Miriam Haskell pink and white necklace.
15.75in (40cm) long

£120-180   **Rox**

A 1960s Miriam Haskell tutti-frutti necklace.
16in (41cm) long

£120-180   **Rox**

A 1960s Miriam Haskell necklace, with brass chains and faux pearls.

£180-220   **RG**

An early Joseff of Hollywood pin, set with faux emeralds and diamonds.

c1930 *2.5in (6cm) high*

£120-180 **Rox**

A pair of Russian gold and amethyst glass butterfly earrings, by Joseff of Hollywood.

c1940

£70-100 **PC**

A pair of Russian gold and diamanté star earrings, by Joseff of Hollywood.

c1940

£40-60 **PC**

A 1940s star pin, by Joseff of Hollywood.

4.5in (11cm) wide

£300-350 **CRIS**

A pair of 1940s Art Deco-style red cabochon earrings, by Joseff of Hollywood.

2.5in (6cm) long

£50-75 **CRIS**

A monarch butterfly pin, by Joseff of Hollywood.

3.5in (9cm) wide

£200-250 **CRIS**

A 1940s bee chatelaine pin, by Joseff of Hollywood.

Large bee 2.25in (5.5cm)

£200-250 **CRIS**

A 1940s horse chatelaine pin, by Joseff of Hollywood.

Shortest chain 7in (18cm) long

£100-150 **CRIS**

A 1940s French bull dog pin, by Joseff of Hollywood.

1.5in (3.5cm) diam

£40-60 **CRIS**

A pair of 1940s French bull dog earrings, by Joseff of Hollywood.

2.75in (7cm) long

£75-85 **CRIS**

Three 1940s fish pins, by Joseff of Hollywood.

1.5in (4cm) wide

£20-25 each **CRIS**

A pair of 1940s owl earrings, by Joseff of Hollywood.

2.25in (5.5cm) high

£100-150 **CRIS**

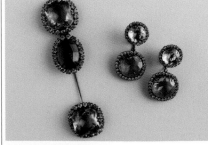

A set of Kenneth J. Lane earrings and pin.

Pin 5in (2cm) long

£500-700 set **TR**

A rare 1950s/60s Kenneth J. Lane pin.

5in (13cm) long

£320-380 **Rox**

A 1950s Kenneth J. Lane necklace.

£30-50   TR

A Kenneth J. Lane bracelet.

1in (2.5cm) wide

£80-100   TR

A Kenneth J. Lane necklace.

Longest drop 7.75in (20cm)

£650-750   TR

A Kenneth J. Lane bracelet and earrings.

Earrings 1in (3cm) long

£300-350   TR

A Kenneth J. Lane bracelet.

3.25in (8.5cm) wide

£280-320   TR

A Kenneth J. Lane bracelet.

3.25in (8.5cm) wide

£280-320   TR

A pair of Kenneth J. Lane earrings.

1in (3cm) long

£80-120   TR

A pair of Kenneth J. Lane earrings.

1.5in (4cm) long

£40-60   TR

A pair of Kenneth J. Lane earrings.

1.5in (4cm) long

£20-30   TR

A pair of Kenneth J. Lane earrings.

1in (3cm) long

£25-30   TR

A 1930s Mazer rhodium-plated floral brooch, set with rhinestones and claret and lilac stones.

£150-200   RG

A late 1930s Mazer rhodium-plated brooch, set with rhinestones.

£120-140   RG

A late 1940s Joseph Mazer rhodium-plated necklace and earrings, set with rhinestones.

£150-180   RG

A 1940s Mazer sterling silver and gold-plated bow brooch, marked "Mazer Sterling".

£150-180   RG

A 1940s Mazer sterling silver and gold-plated retro brooch and earrings, set with faux emeralds and rhinestones.

£200-250   RG

A 1960s Joseph Mazer necklace, bracelet and earrings, set with faux turquoise, pearls and rhinestones, marked "Jomaz".

Joseph Mazer started out with his brother Lincoln in the 1930s, they split in 1947 and Joseph carried on as Joseph Mazer and Jomaz. Early pieces are marked Mazer or Mazer Brothers.

£250-350   RG

A pair of 1960s 60s z gold-plated clip earrings, set with cranberry cabochons and rhinestones.

£50-75   RG

A 1960s Jomaz gold-plated brooch and earrings, set with faux emeralds and lapis cabochons.

£80-120   RG

A 1960s Jomaz gold-plated double-flower brooch, with faux coral-coloured glass and yellow rhinestones, signed "Jomaz".

£30-50   RG

A late 1960s Jomaz necklace, brooch and earrings, set with red, blue and green cabochons and rhinestones.

£150-200   RG

A 1960s Jomaz leaf brooch, with faux turquoise and lapis stones.

£60-80   RG

A Jomaz jester pin.

3.25in (8.5cm) high

£100-150   Rox

A 1960s Jomaz gold-plated brooch and earrings, set with faux turquoise pearls and rhinestones.

£70-90   RG

A rare early Réja flower pin.

Réja jewellery was only produced in 1940s-50s, and this short production period makes pieces hard to find.

3.25in (8.5cm) long

£300-400   Rox

A 1940s Réja sterling silver blackamore pin and earrings.
Pin 2.25in (6cm) long

£400-500 Rox

A Réja sterling silver and gold-plated bracelet, brooch and earrings, set with clear rhinestones and opaque pink cabochons, signed and dated "Réja Sterling".
1947

£180-220 RG

A 1940s Réja sterling silver brooch, set with rhinestones, faux sapphires and pearls, signed "Réja Sterling".

£150-200 RG

A 1940s Réja sterling silver and gold-plated turtle brooch, set with green and clear rhinestones, signed "Réja Sterling".

£120-150 RG

A 1940s Réja sterling silver and gold-plated stork pin, with faux emeralds, rhinestones.

£80-110 RG

A 1940s Réja sterling silver and gold-plated leaping stag brooch, set with rhinestones and a large faux aquamarine, signed "Réja Sterling".

£120-140 RG

A 1940s Réja sterling silver and gold-plated bird brooch and earrings, set with rhinestones and faux citrines.

£180-220 RG

SANDOR

- Sandor was founded in New York, USA, c.1938 by Sandor Goldberger and made jewellery until 1972.
- Very little is known about the company, but it is believed to have been the first to use enamel to decorate costume jewellery.
- Pieces rarely come on to the market and are therefore highly collectable.
- When buying any enamelled costume jewellery, do check the condition. Enamel can chip and peel and while small areas can be retouched, large areas of damage significantly reduce the value of a piece.

A 1930s Sandor enamel and diamanté pin.
4.25in (10.5cm) long

£550-650 TR

A 1930s Sandor pin, with yellow flowers and a green pot.

3in (7.5cm) long

£550-650 TR

A 1930s Sandor pin, with blue and pink flowers.

3.5in (9cm) long

£550-650 TR

A 1930s Sandor ribbon and flowers pin.

3.5in (9cm) long

£300-400 TR

A 1930s Sandor yellow flower bouquet pin.

3.25in (8cm) long

£320-380 TR

A 1930s Sandor flower pin, with purple petals.

4in (10cm) long

£750-850 TR

A 1950s Schiaparelli necklace and earrings, with Bakelite cabochons and aurora borealis crystals.

Earrings 1.25in (3cm) long

£200-250 CRIS

ELSA SCHIAPARELLI

A 1930s Sandor pin.

3.5in (9cm) long

£800-1,000 TR

A 1940s Schiaparelli gold and pearl bracelet.

3in (7.5cm) wide

£80-120 TR

- Elsa Schiaparelli (1890-1973) was an Italian-born fashion designer who worked in Paris and America.
- She is famous for introducing brightly coloured fabrics to the austere world of Post War Parisian Haute Couture – especially the shocking pink which has come to bear her name.
- From the late 1930s, Jean Schlumberger designed a limited number of unsigned pieces for Schiaparelli. These are highly sought after today.
- Signed pieces from the 1940s and 50s are coveted for their stunning use of unusual stones.
- Schiaparelli's avant garde style embraced Surrealism and Dada and her artist friends, including Salvador Dali and Jean Cocteau, designed pieces for her.
- In the 1950s Schiaparelli moved to America where she designed jewellery using aurora borealis and frosted glass beads. These pieces are more common than her earlier designs and popular with collectors.

A 1950s Schiaparelli bracelet, with light sapphire and aurora borealis beads and leaf motif.

6.25in (16cm) long

£200-250 CRIS

A 1950s Schiaparelli bracelet, brooch and earrings, gilt metal and green stones, signed "Schiaparelli".

£300-350 RG

A 1950s Schiaparelli bracelet and earrings, with iridescent blue and aurora borealis stones, signed "Schiaparelli".

£200-250 RG

A 1950s Schiaparelli bracelet, brooch and earrings, set with aurora borealis stones and faux pearls, signed "Schiaparelli".

£200-250 RG

TRIFARI

- Trifari was founded in New York by Gustavo Trifari and Leo Krussman in 1918. The firm was known as Trifari and Krussman until 1925 when Carl Fishel joined and its name was changed to KTF.
- Its early success can be attributed to its successful imitation of the Art Deco jewellery being produced at the time by firms such as Cartier and Van Cleef and Arpels.
- In the 1940s its 'jelly-belly' animal jewellery – which featured large Lucite stones – was the perfect antidote to wartime shortages. Jelly bellies are still popular with collectors today, although later examples are less valuable.
- In the 1950s Trifari developed Trifanium, an ultra-shiny, non-tarnishing metal alloy. Complete Trifanium parures, set with richly coloured stones, are highly collectable.
- The firm's success was sealed in 1952 when America's First Lady, Mamie Eisenhower, commissioned a faux pearl and rhinestone parure for the presidential inauguration ceremony. She repeated her request in 1956.
- Trifari won a landmark legal case in 1954 when it gained a ruling that costume jewellery is a work of art and therefore copyrightable. The aim was to prevent competitors stealing its designs. Jewellery made after 1954 bears a copyright mark.

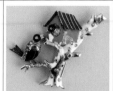

A 1930s Trifari white metal and enamel birds on a branch pin.
2.25in (6cm) long

£200-300 Rox

A 1930s Trifari enamel and white metal pea pod pin.
2.5in (6.5cm) long

£120-180 Rox

A Trifari enamel and white metal sailor pin.
2.25in (6cm) long

£150-250 Rox

A very rare 1930s Trifari elephant's head pin.
2in (5.5cm) long

£200-300 Rox

A rare 1930s Trifari enamel, diamanté and faux topaz pin.

£300-400 Rox

A 1930s Trifari enamel pin.
4in (10cm) long

£300-400 Rox

A 1930s Trifari bug pin.
1.5in (4cm) long

£100-200 Rox

A 1930s Trifari enamel pansy pin.
2.75in (7cm) long

£140-180 Rox

A very rare 1930s Trifari lantern pin.
2.75in (7cm) long

£450-550 Rox

A 1930s Trifari bunch of flowers pin.
4.75in (12cm) long

£1,000-1,500 Rox

A 1930s Trifari pin.
4in (10cm) long

£250-350 Rox

A 1930s Trifari diamanté pin.
3in (8cm) long

£180-220 Rox

A 1930s Trifari "fruit salad" pin and earrings.
Earring 1in (2.5cm) diam

£200-250 Rox

A Trifari "jewels of India" pin.
2in (5cm) high

£250-300 Rox

A 1930s Trifari white metal bunch of flowers pin.
3.75in (9.5cm) long

£140-180 Rox

A 1930s Trifari bunch of grapes pin.

£140-180 Rox

A 1930s Trifari duet pin.
3.25in (8.5cm) diam

£200-300 Rox

A very rare 1930s Trifari bug pin.

3in (7.5cm) long

£500-600   **Rox**

A 1930s Trifari turtle pin.

2.25in (6cm) long

£180-220   **Rox**

A 1930s Trifari fish pin.

2.25in (6cm) long

£150-200   **Rox**

A 1940s Trifari smooth metal necklace, bracelet and earrings, one stone missing.

£200-300   **Rox**

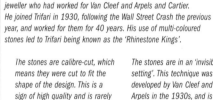

A 1940s Trifari pin and earrings.

Earring 1in (3cm) long

£200-300   **Rox**

A CLOSER LOOK AT A TRIFARI PIN AND EARRINGS

This pin and earrings were designed by Alfred Philippe, a French-born jeweller who had worked for Van Cleef and Arpels and Cartier. He joined Trifari in 1930, following the Wall Street Crash the previous year, and worked for them for 40 years. His use of multi-coloured stones led to Trifari being known as the 'Rhinestone Kings'.

The stones are calibre-cut, which means they were cut to fit the shape of the design. This is a sign of high quality and is rarely seen in costume jewellery.

The stones are in an 'invisible setting'. This technique was developed by Van Cleef and Arpels in the 1930s, and is used here 10 years later.

The clear rhinestones offset the brightly coloured stones.

A 1940s Trifari flowers pin and earrings.

Earring 1.25in (3.5cm) diam

£600-800   **Rox**

A 1940s Trifari pin and earrings.

Earring 1.25in (3.5cm) long

£450-550   **Rox**

A 1940s Trifari pin and earrings.

Earring 0.75in (2cm) diam

£250-350   **Rox**

A 1940s Trifari American flag pin.

2.25in (6cm) long

£150-200   **Rox**

A 1940s Trifari American eagle pin.

1.75in (4.5cm) long

£140-180   **Rox**

A 1940s Trifari American eagle pin.

2in (5cm) long

£50-100   **TR**

A Trifari 'Jelly Belly' chick in egg pin.
2in (5cm) long

A Trifari 'Jelly Belly' fly pin.
2in (5cm) long

A Trifari 'Jelly Belly' crab pin.
3in (7.5cm) long

£700-800 **TR** | £600-700 **TR** | £600-700 **TR**

Three Trifari duck pins and a duck emerging from egg pin.
Largest 1.45in (2.5cm)

A 1940s Trifari sterling silver and gold-plated bird of paradise pin, designed by Alfred Philippe.

A 1940s Trifari sterling silver and gold-plated bird on a branch pin.

£200-300 **Rox** | £200-250 **RG** | £120-140 **RG**

A very rare 1940s Trifari swan pin.
2.75in (7cm) wide

A 1940s Trifari bug pin.
2.25in (6cm) long

A 1940s Trifari leaf and bug pin.
2.75in (7cm) long

A 1940s Trifari bug pin.
1.75in (4.5cm) long

£500-600 **Rox** | £180-220 **Rox** | £140-180 **Rox** | £120-180 **Rox**

A 1940s Trifari Alfred Philippe sterling silver butterfly pin, with red and blue cabochons.
2.5in (6cm) long

A 1940s gold-plated Trifari pin, with blue and green stones.

A 1940s Trifari rose pin.

£100-125 **CRIS** | £80-120 **RG** | £120-180 **Rox**

A rare Trifari crab pin.

3.25in (8.5cm) wide

£1,000-1,500   Rox

A 1950s gold-plated Trifari snake pin and earrings, with simulated ruby and emeralds.

£120-150   RG

A 1950s gold-plated Trifari pin, set with red, blue, green and clear stones.

£60-80   RG

A 1950s Trifari "jewels of India" necklace and earrings.

Earring 1in (3cm) long

£180-220   Rox

A Trifari crown pin, set with pearls.

2.25in (5.5cm) long

£180-220   TR

A early 1950s Trifari blue and gold stylized fruit pin.

2in (5cm) long

£50-100   CRIS

A 1950s Trifari peapod pin, with faux pearls mounted in cold enamel on gilt metal.

2.75in (7cm) long

£80-120   CRIS

A 1950s Trifari emerald and crystal rhinestone fruit pin.

2.5in (6cm) long

£55-65   CRIS

A 1950s Trifari shell pin, decorated with cold enamel.

3.25in (8cm) long

£80-120   CRIS

A 1950s sea motif Trifari pin and earrings, set with cabochon imitation rose-pink and white moonstones.

Pin 3.5in (8.5cm) long

£100-150   CRIS

A 1950s Trifari owl pin, set with faux coral cabochons and pavé-set crystals.

3.75in (5.5cm) long

£55-65   CRIS

A 1950s Trifari toadstool pin, decorated with faux angel skin coral.

1.5in (4cm) long

£55-65   **CRIS**

A 1950s Trifari balloon pin, with satin finish.

2.25in (5.5cm) long

£35-45   **CRIS**

A 1950s Trifari enamel bee pin.

1.5in (3.5cm)

£20-30   **CRIS**

A 1950s Trifari small cat pin, with a Bakelite turquoise belly and glass eyes.

1.75in (4.5cm) long

£30-40   **CRIS**

A 1950s Trifari seahorse pin, with Bakelite turquoise cabochons.

1.75in (4.5cm) long

£20-30   **CRIS**

A 1960s Trifari watch ring, face under diamanté panel.

Head 2in (5cm) long

£120-180   **Rox**

A 1950s Art Christmas tree pin, in enamel with multi-coloured crystal rhinestones, with copyright mark.

2.5in (6cm) high

£30-40   **CRIS**

A 1950s Art Christmas tree pin, set with multi-coloured crystal rhinestones.

2.5in (6cm) high

£30-40   **CRIS**

A Cadora Christmas tree pin, with cherubs set with pearls.

2.75in (7cm) high

£50-75   **Rox**

A Cristobal-designed Christmas tree pin, using 1950s Swarovski crystals, with peridot and emerald green glass.

3.25in (8cm) high

£20-25   **CRIS**

A Cristobal-designed Christmas tree pin, set with ruby-red and emerald-green stones.

2.75in (7cm) high

£20-25   CRIS

A Cristobal Christmas tree pin, set with emerald, ruby-red and green glass stones.

4in (10cm) high

£55-65   CRIS

A 1980s Eisenberg Ice Christmas tree pin, with multi-coloured crystal rhinestones on gold-plated casting, with copyright mark.

2in (5cm) high

£10-15   CRIS

A 1980s Eisenberg Ice Christmas tree pin, with emerald-green navette, with ruby-red and clear crystal rhinestones.

2.25in (5.5cm)

£20-25   CRIS

A 1950s Hollycraft Christmas tree pin, with multi-coloured crystal rhinestones.

2.25in (5.5cm) long

£35-45   CRIS

A 1960s English Sphinx Christmas tree pin, with green enamel leaf with ruby-red crystal rhinestones.

2.25in (5.5cm) long

£20-30   CRIS

A Mylu Christmas tree pin, set with pink and green stones.

2.75in (7cm) long

£200-250   Rox

A 1960s English Sphinx Christmas tree pin, with green enamel and diamanté.

2.75in (7cm) high

£25-35   CRIS

A 1950s Trifari Christmas pin.

This is one of three designs that Trifari made.

2in (5cm) high

£55-65   CRIS

A Trifari Christmas tree pin.

2in (5.5cm) long

£40-60   Rox

A Trifari partridge in a pear tree pin.

2in (5cm) long

£40-60   Rox

A 1980s French 'bijoux stern' Christmas tree pin, with green enamel and crystal rhinestones.

2.5in (5cm) long

£30-35   CRIS

A 1980s French 'bijoux stern' Christmas tree pin, with multi-coloured crystal rhinestones.

2.75in (7cm) high

£25-35   CRIS

An Emporio Armani bead necklace, from the Spring/Summer 1997 collection, with original box, storage bag and certificate of authenticity.

£30-50   PC

A 1950s American Art turtle pin, set with Bakelite cabochons, coral moonstones and faux lapis stones.

2.25in (5.5cm) long

£35-45   CRIS

A 1950s Marcel Boucher rose pin and earring set, the carved ebony rose on rhodium-plated pavé rhinestones.

Pin 4.25in (10.5cm) long

£100-150   CRIS

A 1930s Marcel Boucher rhodium-plated and pearlised enamel sweet pea brooch, signed "Sterling" and with Marcel Boucher logo.

£300-350   RG

A 1950s Marcel Boucher brooch, gold-plated, rhinestones and faux sapphires, signed "Boucher".

£60-90   RG

A late 1990s Butler and Wilson brooch.

£5-8   PC

A 1950s Hattie Carnegie Bakelite pin.

3in (5.5cm) wide

£100-150   CRIS

A 1950s-60s Hattie Carnegie seahorse pin and earrings.

4.35in (11cm) long

£180-220   Rox

A 1960s Hattie Carnegie necklace and earrings.

Earrings 1in (3cm) long

£70-100   Rox

A pair of 1980s Chanel gilt earrings.

£40-60   RG

A 1940s Coroduette jelly belly pin, by Corocraft, studded with crystals.

A rare 1950s-60s Hattie Carnegie merman pin.

4.25in (11cm) long

£150-200   Rox

A 1950s-60s Hattie Carnegie lionhead pin.

4in (10.5cm) long

£180-220   Rox

Coroduette pins are comprised of two pieces that may be taken apart to be worn individually.

1.75in (4.5cm) long

£320-380   CRIS

A Corocraft fish brooch in sterling silver, enamel and Lucite/Perspex, signed "Corocraft Sterling America".

Designed by Adelpho Katz. During World War II designers used less metal and more plastic.

1942-45

£150-250   RG

A Corocraft sterling silver and gold-plated starfish baby brooch, signed "Corocraft Sterling".

1942-45

£150-190   RG

A 1940s Corocraft sterling silver and gold-plated rose brooch.

£200-250   RG

A 1940s Corocraft sterling silver and gold-plated rose pin.

£200-250   RG

One of a pair of 1940s De Rosa sterling silver and gold-plated fur clips, set with red and clear rhinestones.

The De Rosa company was owned by Ralph de Rosa and its head designer was his wife, Elvera de Rosa.

£200-250 pair   RG

A 1940s De Rosa sterling silver gilt and blue enamel bracelet, set with rhinestones.

£150-180   RG

A 1940s De Rosa sterling silver brooch, with rhinestones and faux sapphires.

£80-110   **RG**

A 1930s Eisenberg pearl and diamanté pin.

3in (7.5cm) long

£480-520   **TR**

A pair of Eisenberg earrings.

2in (5cm) long

£300-400   **TR**

A 1930s Fahrner pin.

2.25in (6cm) long

£2,500-3,000   **TR**

A 1960s Stanley Hagler poinsette flower pin, with murano glass leaves and petals, and a wired filigree base.

4in (10cm) wide

£120-180   **CRIS**

A 1960s Stanley Hagler Murano glass fruit pin.

2.56in (6cm) long

£40-50   **CRIS**

A 1990s Histoire de Verre pin, with poured glass in metal frames.

3.5in (8.5cm) long

£120-180   **CRIS**

A 1940s Hobé sterling bow pin, set with faux peridot, rose quartz, jonquil and amethyst.

4in (10cm) long

£100-200   **CRIS**

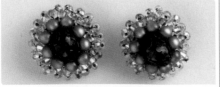

A pair of Hobé earrings, set with blue and clear crystals.

1in (3cm) long

£15-25   **TR**

A 1940s Hobé sterling heart pin with a faux amethyst stone.

2.5in (6.5cm) long

£200-250   **CRIS**

A pair of mid-1990s Christian Lacroix gold and imitation pearl clip earrings.

£30-50 PC

A 1930s Robert pin.

3in (7.5cm) long

£550-650 TR

A 1940s Nettie Rosenstein crab fur clip, gold-plated silver and enamel, signed "Nettie Rosenstein" and "Sterling".

£100-120 RG

A rare 1940s Nettie Rosenstein sterling silver, gold-plated and enamel butterfly fur clip, signed.

Nettie Rosenstein was a couturier who made jewellery, and pieces by her are quite rare.

£250-300 RG

A 1940s Vogue gold-plated sterling silver blackamoor pin and earrings.

£200-250 RG

A 1940s Warner mechanical day and night flower pin, with petals which open and close.

2.5in (6cm)

£50-60 CRIS

A 1950s costume jewellery pin, unmarked.

£20-25 PC

A mid-1980s costume jewellery pin, from Miss Selfridge.

1983

£3-5 PC

A 1950s costume jewellery pin, unmarked.

A 1930s basket of flowers pin, set with channel-cut ruby and pavé crystals, unsigned.
5in (7.5cm) long

A 1930s American rhodium-plated silver brooch, with prong-set fruit salad stones, unsigned.
2in (5cm) long

£50-55   **PC** | £100-200   **CRIS** | £200-300   **CRIS**

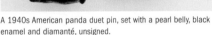

A 1930s French pin, rhodium-plated silver with prong-set fruit salad stones, unsigned.
1.75in (4.5cm) long

An early hand-beaded pin, with matching earrings, unsigned.
Pin 6in (15.5cm) high

A 1940s American panda duet pin, set with a pearl belly, black enamel and diamanté, unsigned.
1.5in (4cm) long

£200-300   **CRIS** | £250-300   **Rox** | £100-150   **CRIS**

A pair of 1940s American sterling silver and gold-plated wing pins.

A 1940s American sterling silver and gold-plated 'jelly-belly' penguin pin, set with rhinestones and Lucite.

An American sterling silver and gold-plated blackamoor clip, the black glass face set with clear rhinestones.

£120-150   **RG** | £60-80   **RG** | £60-80   **RG**

A French Art Deco chrome-plated shield dress clip.

A 1940s American pin, sterling silver and gold-plated, with coloured faux pearls.

£60-80   **RG** | £100-120   **RG**

A 1930s enamel lobster pin, claws on springs.

1930s   *3.25in (8cm) long*

£40-60   **TR**

An enamel and diamanté lobster pin.

4.25in (11cm) long

£60-80   **TR**

A 1940s American blackamoor pin, with black enamel head and gold-plated turban.

1.75in (4.5cm) long

£200-300   **CRIS**

A 1930s clear Lucite "Scotty dog" pin.

3in (8cm) long

£200-250   **Rox**

A 1930s black Lucite "Scotty dog" pin.

3in (7.5cm) long

£100-150   **Rox**

An extremely rare 1930s-1940s apple juice Bakelite figural pin.

£1,500-2,000   **Rox**

A 1930s Lucite parrot pin.

3.5in (9cm) long

£70-100   **TR**

A CLOSER LOOK AT A BAKELITE FISH CUFF

In the 1930s, when the use of plastics was new, Bakelite was seen as the material of the future and craftsmen used it to great effect – treating it with far more respect than we do plastic today. This witty fish design is typical of the creativity put into Bakelite jewellery.

Each fish has been hand-carved from the plastic to give a three-dimensional effect.

The fish have been hand-painted to give the illusion of movement as they 'swim' around the wrist.

This pale orange Bakelite is known as 'apple juice'.

An 1940s apple juice Bakelite fish cuff.

2.5in (7cm) wide

£700-1,000   **Rox**

A "Scotty dogs" pin.

£150-200   **Rox**

A Victorian 18ct gold, turquoise and pearl brooch and matching screw-on drop earrings, in original box.
c1870

£650-750 SSp

A Victorian tortoiseshell, gold and silver pique demi-parure, comprising a brooch and a matching pair of drop earrings.
c1870

£400-500 SSp

A Victorian three-piece demi-parure, comprising matching gold earrings and brooch, set with cabouchon garnets.

£1,000-1,500 GS

A Georgian 18ct gold foil link and barrel bracelet.

£800-900 SSp

A Victorian 15ct gold and platinum horseshoe bracelet.
1870

£400-500 SSp

A gold bracelet, set with diamonds and emeralds.

£4,000-4,500 GS

A diamond and platinum rectangular brooch, by Mappin & Webb, London.

£6,000-7,000 GS

A white gold and diamond rose brooch, set with a sapphire.

£3,000-4,000 GS

A gold and diamond brooch, of a leaping stag with ruby stones.

£800-1,000 GS

A blue enamelled silver butterfly brooch.

£30-50 SSp

A circular micromosaic gold brooch, with beetle design.

Micromosaics are currently enjoying a revival in popularity.

£300-350 GS

A late Victorian silver lizard brooch, marked "Sterling".
c1880

£120-150 RG

A Victorian silver brooch.

2in (5cm) long

£20-30   PC

An Art Nouveau enamelled silver pansy brooch. c1890

£50-100   SSp

A diamond-set portrait of a woman, on ivory.

£1,000-1,250   GS

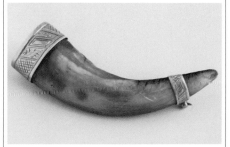

A 1920s Italian cameo brooch, made for the tourist market.

2in (5cm) long

£20-30   PC

A Victorian silver "Bella" name brooch.

£30-40   SSp

A Victorian silver "Bertha" name brooch.

£30-40   SSp

A Victorian silver "Clara" name brooch.

£30-40   SSp

A Victorian silver "Ethel" name brooch.

£30-40   SSp

A Victorian silver "Lilian" name brooch.

£30-40   SSp

A Victorian silver and blue enamel "Mother" name brooch.

£30-40   SSp

A horn brooch.

2in (5cm) long

£10-15   OACC

A cameo, with a scene of a mother with children and cherubs.

£400-500   GS

A
B
C
D
E
F
G
H
I
J
K
L
M
N
O
P
Q
R
S
T
U
V
W
XYZ

A cameo, with a woman's head.

£600-700   **GS**

A cameo, with a woman's head in two colours.

£400-500   **GS**

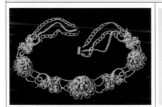

An elaborate Georgian seed pearl necklace.
c1800

£800-1,000   **SSp**

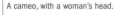

A Victorian yellow amber bead necklace.

32.25in (82cm) long

£100-140   **SSp**

A row of cultured pearls, with an 18ct white gold, diamond and sapphire clasp.

24in (61cm) long

£700-800   **SSp**

A row of cultured pearls, with a 18ct white gold and diamond chip ball clasp.

1960s   12in (30.5cm) long

£800-850   **SSp**

A Victorian silver, diamond and star sapphire pendant.
c1870

£700-800   **SSp**

An Edwardian platinum, diamond and citrine pendant.

£200-300   **SSp**

A small diamond pin, of a flying pheasant.

£800-1,200 GS

An important Georgian 18ct gold rosecut diamond ring, set with three diamonds on either side.

£1,000-2,000 SSp

A stylish ring, probably Italian, with alternating ribbed and plain curved bands enclosing a garnet-topped doublet, stamped "750" and an indistinct mark.

£50-80 DN

An 18ct white gold ring, with an exeptionally large white South Sea pearl in the centre, surrounded by diamonds.

South Sea pearls are cultured pearls from Australia or the Philippines. They usually grow up to 0.75in (1.5cm).

£2,000-2,500 SSp

FIND OUT MORE...

'Understanding Jewellery', by David Bennett & Daniela Mascetti, published by Antique Collectors' Club, 2000.

'Jewels and Jewellery', by Clare Phillips, published by V&A Publications, 2000.

'Earrings' by Daniela Macetti & Amanda Triossi, published by Thames and Hudson, 1999.

A set of three 18ct gold press studs, with Greek Key decoration and set with seed pearls.

c1870/1880

£100-200 Wim

An Art Deco dress set, set with square cut rubies, in fitted case.

c1930

£1,000-1,250 Wim

A late 19thC baby's gilt whistle, with coral teether, bells missing, maker TH.

With all its bells this would be worth £200-250.

£100-150 PC

A pair of Victorian 9ct gold and enamel cuff links.
c1870

£200-300 — SSp

A pair of 9ct gold oval cuff links, in a fitted case.
c1885

£180-220 — Wim

A pair of 18ct gold and enamel oval cuff links, in a fitted case.
c1900

£500-800 — Wim

A pair of 15ct gold "coffee-bean" cuff links, in a fitted case.
c1900

£180-220 — Wim

A pair of 9ct gold "bowling" cuff links and pin, in a fitted case.
c1900

£200-300 — Wim

A pair of Edwardian 18ct gold and enamel bar cuff links, set with sapphires, in a fitted case.
c1905

£700-1,000 — Wim

A pair of Edwardian 18ct gold and enamel bar cuff links, set with sapphires, in a fitted case.
c1905

£700-1,000 — Wim

A pair of 15ct gold and mother-of-pearl cuff links, with enamel decoration and set with seed pearls, in a fitted case.
c1915

£300-500 — Wim

A pair of 18ct gold and mother-of-pearl cuff links, decorated with enamel and gold "button threads", in a fitted case.
c1915

£400-600 — Wim

A pair of 18ct gold and guilloche enamel cuff links, in a fitted case.
c1915

£800-1,200 — Wim

A pair of green bakelite Eloware cuff links, manufactured by Birkby's of Liversedge, England.
c1920

face 0.75in (2cm) long

£20-30 — MHC

A pair of enamel double-sided cuff links.

1920-30s

£70-100   **CVS**

A pair of French black and white enamel double-sided cuff links.

1920-30s

£50-80   **CVS**

A pair of green and blue double-sided cuff links.

1920-30s

£70-100   **CVS**

A pair of 18ct gold and lapis lazuli square cuff links, in a fitted case.

c1930

£700-1,000   **Wim**

A pair of 1950s black and Bakelite oversized dice cuff links.

£50-80   **CVS**

A pair of 1950s leather and metal gun-in-holster cuff links.

1.5in (4cm) wide

£40-60   **CVS**

A 1950s bowling motif tie bar and cuff links set.

2.5in (6.5cm) wide

£20-30   **CVS**

A pair of sterling silver Volkswagen cuff links and tie pin.

$80-100   **Koz**

A pair of silver Georg Jensen cuff links, marked "Georg Jensen", "925 S Denmark" and "114".

1961

£150-200   **SSp**

A pair of 1960s silver Georg Jensen cuff links, decorated with a horseshoe, marked "Georg Jensen", "925 S Denmark" and "123".

£120-280   **SSp**

A pair of 1960s 18ct gold Kutchinsky "D" cuff links.

£300-500   **SSp**

A pair of 18ct gold, onyx and citrine cuff links.

1970

£100-150   **SSp**

A pair of 1980s silver gilt, lapis lazuli and pearl bar cuff links, by Mappin & Webb.

£80-110   **SSp**

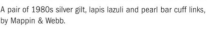

- Jelly probably originates from medieval England, where food was cooked in a pot over a fire, resulting in many soft-pounded mixtures. Early versions of blancmange were concocted from boiled milk and ground almonds, flavoured with savoury additions such as fish.

- The Elizabethans devised imaginatively shaped foods known as 'sotelties' (meaning 'wit') which were modelled into various animal shapes for the amusement of the Court. Flummery, made from boiled oatmeal seasoned with wine, beer or honey, was perhaps the first recipe to be set in moulds.

- The late 18th century and Victorian era saw a rise in numbers of cookery books which included jelly recipes and the latter period coincided with potteries such as the Staffordshire potteries being able to make deeper and more varied moulds.

- Major manufacturers were Copeland, Minton and Davenport who produced cream and white wares. Minton pieces often have a bluish colouring to the glaze. Shelley also produced a huge variety of moulds which are highly collectable.

- Moulds are often inspired by architectural motifs of buildings, leaving an architectural feel to the final jelly. The Art Deco period with its clean lines provided good inspiration to jelly mould makers.

- Animals and flora and fauna are popular motifs and as well as often having symbolic meanings in themselves, they may have originally hinted at the contents of the jelly in early periods.

- Jelly moulds saw their 'golden age' during the Victorian period and the first quarter of the 20th century. After this, jelly declined in popularity and moulds, now being made primarily in aluminium, became less inventive.

A ceramic Brown & Polson's blancmange mould, printed with a recipe for cornflour blancmange.
1916   *6.75in (17cm) wide*
£40-50   **SSc**

A mid- to late-19thC Cetem Ware ceramic jelly mould, with shell motif.
£45-55   **SSc**

A Copeland ceramic individual jelly mould, with pineapple motif.
4.25in (11cm) wide
£25-35   **SSc**

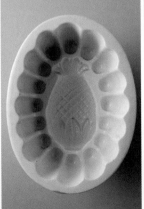

A late 19thC Copeland ceramic jelly mould, with pineapple motif.
7.75in (19.5cm) wide
£40-50   **SSc**

A 1920s/30s Greens Newstyle Jellies earthenware chicken shape jelly mould.
6.25in (16cm) wide
£40-60   **SSc**

A 1930s Grimwades ceramic rabbit shaped jelly mould, with printed mark for "Grimwades Stoke-on-Trent England".

Animal moulds are particularly collectable.

8.75in (22cm) wide

£30-40 SSc

A rare mid-18thC ceramic creamware jelly mould, possibly Leeds, with peg feet and sheep and lamb motif.

6.75in (17cm) wide

£125-150 SSc

A 1920s Malin ceramic jelly mould, with swan motif.

This item is of special interest to collectors because of its highly desirable swan motif and because pieces by the manufacturer, Malin, are collectable too.

6.75in (17cm) wide

£60-70 SSc

A Minton ceramic jelly mould, with bunch of grapes motif, impressed mark "MINTON No 20"

1862-1871 6.75in (17.5cm) wide

£40-50 SSc

A Minton ceramic jelly mould, with wheatsheaf motif, with printed marks for "Minton no 42".

£40-50 SSc

A Shelley 'Acanthus' design jelly mould.

The acanthus leaf is a popular historical decorative motif and has been used since antiquity.

1912-1925 5.74in (14.5cm) wide

£40-50 SSc

A Shelley 'Carlton' design, small cream centre mould.

The deep indentation on the top surface left an area for cream to be poured over the jelly.

1912-1925 6in (15cm) wide

£50-60 SSc

An early Shelley 'Ritz' design jelly mould.

The popular Ritz hotel in London was opened in 1906 to widespread acclaim.

c1912 7in (18cm) wide

£60-70 SSc

A Shelley 'Queens' design jelly mould, with printed mark.

1912-1925 6.75in (17cm) diam

£30-35 SSc

A Shelley 'French' design jelly mould, with printed mark.

1912-1925 6.75in (17cm) w

£50-60 SSc

A Shelley 'Round Ornamental' design individual jelly mould, with shell motif and printed mark.

1912-1925 2.75in (7cm) w

£30-35 SSc

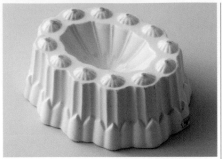

An early Shelley 'Savoy' design cream centre jelly mould.
c1912   *7.5in (19cm) wide*

£60-70   **SSc**

A ceramic octagonal jelly mould, possibly Spode, with basket of flowers motif.
6in (15cm) wide

£75-85   **SSc**

A Wedgwood ceramic jelly mould, with pineapple motif.

Pineapples traditionally represent hospitality and friendship.
6in (15.5cm) wide

£45-55   **SSc**

A Shelley 'Victoria' design ring jelly mould, with printed mark.
1912-1925   *7.5in (19cm) diam*

£50-60   **SSc**

A late 19thC Wedgwood individual ceramic mould, with bunch of grapes motif, impressed marks "66 Wedgwood".
3.5in (9cm) wide

£35-45   **SSc**

An octagonal individual jelly mould, with bunch of grapes motif.
4.75in (12cm) wide

£35-45   **SSc**

A late 19thC ceramic jelly mould, possibly pearl ware, with asparagus motif.
6.5in (16.5cm) wide

£40-50   **SSc**

A late 19thC cream coloured earthenware 'Lily' design.
7.75in (19.5cm) wide

£45-55   **SSc**

A late 19thC cream coloured earthenware 'Lily' design.
7.75in (19.5cm) wide

£45-55   **SSc**

A ceramic asparagus motif jelly mould.
7.5in (19cm) wide

£30-40   **SSc**

A pair of early 19thC Davenport individual jelly moulds, with pattern motif.
5.25in (13cm) wide

£35-45   **SSc**

An Edwardian stoneware jelly mould, with pattern.

7.75in (20cm) wide

£25-35   SSc

A stoneware jelly mould, with lion motif.

1840-1850   6.5in (16.5cm)

£20-30   SSc

A salt-glazed jelly mould, with rabbit motif.

6.5in (16.5cm) wide

£25-35   SSc

An early salt-glazed jelly mould, with chrysanthemum motif.

8in (20.5cm) wide

£30-40   SSc

A salt-glazed jelly mould, with acanthus motif.

7.5in (19cm) wide

£20-30   SSc

A mid- to late 19thC copper jelly mould.

6.75in (17cm) wide

£125-175   SSc

A mid- to late 19thC copper jelly mould.

6in (15.5cm) wide

£100-125   SSc

A copper jelly or cake mould.

1880-1900   11.5cm wide

£125-175   SSc

A mid- to late 19thC copper jelly mould.

6.25in (16cm) wide

£125-175   SSc

A mid- to late 19thC copper cylindrical Charlotte mould.

Charlotte was a 19th century dessert.

4.25in (11cm) diam

£75-85 SSc

Two late 19thC copper Charlotte jelly moulds.

Larger 4.25in (11cm) diam

£75-85 SSc

An individual copper jelly mould.

3.25in (8cm) diam

£50-60 SSc

An individual copper jelly mould.

3in (7.5cm) diam

£50-60 SSc

An 1920s/30s aluminium jelly mould.

6.75in (17.5cm) wide

£5-7 SSc

A 1920s/30s aluminium jelly mould.

5.25in (13cm) wide.

£5-7 SSc

An 1920s/30s enamel diamond shape jelly mould.

7.75in (20cm) wide

£7-10 SSc

An extremely rare mid-18thC sycamore wood flummery mould.

6in (15cm) diam

£100-150 SSc

An 1920s/30s enamel jelly mould.

6.25in (16cm) wide

£7-10 SSc

An early American knife box.

£180-230   **BCAC**

An American skewer set, in hand-forged iron, all original. c1740

£500-800   **RAA**

An American potato masher, made from turned maple. c1810   9.75in (24.5cm) long

£20-30   **RAA**

An American pierced tin foot-warmer, in wooden frame and decorated with multiple heart designs, with original tray and bail handle, good finish worn on frame. c1820

£50-80   **TWC**

A 19thC painted leather fire bucket, with brass-studded rim and two handles cast with masks.
15in (38cm) high

£450-550   **DN**

A 19thC walnut pestle.
9in (22.5cm) long

£60-80   **BS**

A walnut and brass-banded string barrel, with tap and cutting blade. c1850   3.5in (8.5cm) wide

£100-150   **MB**

A 19thC ceramic jelly mould, in the shape of a dairy maid.
7.75in (19.5cm)

£200-250   **BS**

A 19thC fold-down brass plate warmer.
19in (48cm) long

£100-125   **BS**

Two 19thC brass saucepans.
Top: 6in (15cm) diam. Bottom: 5.5in (14cm) diam

Top: £35-45 Bottom: £60-70   **BS**

A 19thC Gilpin vegetable cutter.
6.5in (16.5cm) wide

£50-70   **BS**

A 19thC lemon squeezer.
11in (28cm) wide

£100-200   **BS**

A 19thC crimping machine, with heating bars.

12.5in (31.5cm) high

£400-450 BS

A 19thC Moore's patent knife sharpener.

2.75in (7cm) wide

£40-50 BS

A pair of 19thC curling tongs, with unused gas heater.

10in (25.5cm)

£60-80 BS

A 19thC Benham & Froud copper bain-marie.

5.5in (14cm) high

£140-180 BS

A 19thC copper coffee pot.

12.5in (31.5cm) high

£500-550 BS

A 19thC copper kettle, engraved "Good Luck".

11in (28cm) high

£300-350 BS

A 19thC copper ale muller.

10in (25.5cm) long

£100-130 BS

A 19thC copper 'bunch of grapes' jelly mould, by Mary Benham & Frord.

6in (15cm) wide

£400-450 BS

From left to right:
A three-pint copper-bellied saucepan, by Benham and Froud, with lid and boxwood handle.

£320-370 BS

A two pint copper-bellied saucepan, with lid and ebonized handle.

£300-350 BS

A one pint copper-bellied saucepan, with lid and ebonized handle.

£300-350 BS

A copper and steel 'wheatsheaf' jelly mould.

5in (12.5cm) wide

£200-230 BS

Two 19thC copper grocer's scoops, dated 1882 and 1885.

10.5in (26.5cm) long

£80-100 each BS

A 19thC Wright's Patent brass and boxwood pastry brush.

8in (20cm) long

£50-70 BS

A 19thC brass pastry crimper and cutter.

5.5in (14cm) long

£40-60 BS

A 19thC ginger beer bottle.

c1870 7in (17.5cm) high

£45-55 BS

A Grant's Special whisky water jug.

4.25in (10.5cm) high

£200-230 BS

A set of 19thC Salter's scales.

13.5in (34cm) high

£180-230 BS

A mid-to late 19thC wooden pantry box, with swing handle and metal trim, maker unknown, old finish worn on top.

9in (23cm) diam

£50-80 TWC

A pair of 19thC Mochaware ale measures, one quart, one pint.

Largest 6in (15cm) high

£400-450 BS

A 19thC cast-iron fish scaling grip and scraper, patented USA 1889. 16in (40.5cm) long

£200-250 BS

A 'The Everett' raisin seeder, patented USA.

1889 3.25in (8cm) high

£75-125 BS

A Kent's knife cleaner, with circular wooden case and brass fittings mounted on cast-iron legs, the case bearing a brass maker's plate inscribed "Kent/Patentee & Manufacturer/199 High Holborn/London" together with another ceramic plate "Kent's/Knife Cleaner/Latest Patents/1895-1902 and 1903", the legs also with embossed inscription "Kent's Patent, 199, 200 & 201 High Holborn, London".

Case 19.25in (49cm) wide

£80-100 DN

An early "Star" vacuum cleaner, of cylindrical shape with tinplate body surmounted by hand-operated canvas bellows, the red body printed with inscription "Star Vacuum Cleaner, Pat.18899, British Made".

£40-60 DN

A copper crumb tray and brush.

c1900 Brush 13.5in (34cm)

£80-100 BS

KITCHENALIA

Left: A sycamore 'thistle' butter stamp, replaced grip.
c1900   5in (12.5cm) diam

£50-70   **BS**

Centre: A 19thC sycamore "strawberry" butter stamp, replaced grip.
                         5in (12.5cm) diam

£80-100   **BS**

Right: A sycamore 'tulip' butter stamp, replaced grip.
                         5in (12.5cm) diam

£60-80   **BS**

Left: A Burgess anchovy paste pot and lid.
c1900   5in (12.5cm) diam

£25-35   **BS**

Middle: A Woods areca nut toothpaste pot lid.
c1900   4in (10cm) diam

£40-50   **BS**

Right: A cold cream of roses pot lid.
c1900   3in (7.5cm) diam

£50-70   **BS**

An A. Kenrickson & Son cast-iron coffee grinder.
c1900   5in (12.5cm) high

£400-450   **BS**

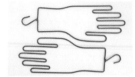

A pair of steel glove-drying frames.
c1900   11.5in (29cm)

£50-70   **BS**

A tin flour dredger.
c1900   5.25in (13.5cm) high

£50-70   **BS**

A Duva cast-iron knife cleaning machine, with original box and instructions.
                         7in (17.5cm) wide

£80-100   **BS**

A cast-iron coffee mill, marked Beatrice, registration date 1908, with original paintwork.
                         4.5in (11.5cm) high

£80-100   **BS**

A 1920s soda syphon, with old replacement spout.
                         12in (30.5cm) diam

£150-180   **BS**

A 1920s bull's head can opener.
                         6.5in (16.5cm) long

£10-20   **BS**

A Peerless can opener, patented
1900   6.25in (15.5cm) long

£10-20   **BS**

A 1920s can opener.
                         5.5in (14cm) long

£25-35   **BS**

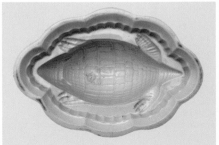

A Shelley ceramic jelly mould, in the shape of an armadillo.
1912-25   7in (17.5cm) wide

£150-200   **BS**

A 1920s brass wafer ice cream dispenser.
4in (10cm) wide

£50-70   **BS**

A 1920s 'Gladstone Bag' hot water bottle.
9in (23cm) wide

£120-160   **BS**

A ceramic jelly mould, in the shape of a dog seated on a cushion, with registration mark.
1929   *6.5in (16.5cm) long*

£60-90   **BS**

A footwarmer, dated 1939.
10in (25cm) long

£40-50   **BS**

A 1920s Simplex no. 2 copper washing posser.
30in (76cm) high

£60-80   **BS**

A 1920s Carlisle Old Brewery Co Ltd Extra Double Stout bottle.

£20-30   **BS**

A 1920s Coomer's Stone Ginger Beer bottle.

£20-30   **BS**

A 1930s Bakelite lemon squeezer.
6.25in (15.5cm) high

£45-55   **BS**

A 1930s pub water jug.
5.5in (14cm) high

£80-100   **BS**

A 1920s North & Co Ltd Home Brewed Ginger Beer bottle.

£15-25   **BS**

A six pint 'Blow' butter churn, registration date 1948.
13in (33cm) high

£60-80   **BS**

A Singer sewing machine, with fresh decoration in excellent condition.

Despite their often decorative finishes, with many ornate gilt and coloured transfers, Singer sewing machines do not fetch high prices as they were made in enormous quantities. Only examples in the very best condition will be of interest to collectors but compared to other machines the prices will be low.

£40-60 | **TK**

An extremely rare French sewing machine, "Paris-Louvre", similar to "Todd Champion", circular shuttle, missing its winder.

c1890

£520-580 | **TK**

A 19thC sewing machine, with scroll-moulded cast-iron base and frame japanned with gilt foliate decoration, the work table bearing the serial number "63431".

11.25in (28.5cm) long overall

£40-60 | **DN**

A very rare French sewing machine, by Thabourin.

c1880

£350-450 | **TK**

An extremely rare French Peugeot No. 0 sewing machine, no shuttle.

c1883

£800-1,000 | **TK**

An original metal sign for Pfaff vintage sewing machine, signed "E. Doepler".

c1920   21.75in (55.5cm) high

£120-180 | **TK**

A CLOSER LOOK AT A SEWING MACHINE

The Maine-based American company Shaw & Clark made sewing machines between 1857 and 1866. Amongst a range of chain-stitch and running-stitch models, they made the 'Monitor' from 1860-1864. In 1867, the company moved to Cicopee, Mass., adopting the name 'Cicopee Sewing Machine Company' but closed one year later. This example dates from just before the relocation occurred. It is in good condition but shows some wear to the paint and ornate transfers. If its condition were better, the value would be higher. Despite this, it was produced by a short-lived company and so is more valuable than most machines.

A decorative American chain-stitch sewing machine, by Shaw and Clark, in very good condition.

c1865

£450-550 | **TK**

An original Gritzner sewing machine metal sign.

c1920   29.5in (75cm) high

£80-120 | **TK**

Two 19thC oblong necessaires, one in an ivory case, the other in a gilt metal case.

Largest 5.5in (14cm) long

£400-500 | **DN**

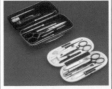

A mid-18thC gilt scissors case, engraved with rococo scrolls, flowers and cartouches, and a pair of scissors.

4.25in (11cm) long

£350-450 | **DN**

MECHANICAL MUSIC

- Mechanical music devices take a number of forms; a musical box with a revolving cylinder, the disc musical box, the phonograph and the gramophone. The majority were produced during the second half of the 19th century and were driven by winding springs which drove gears to operate the mechanism.
- Musical boxes using cylinders with embedded protruding pins striking metal teeth of different lengths on a 'comb' to produce sounds were popular from the Great Exhibition of 1851 until the 1880s. The centre of production was Switzerland, and desirable names include B.A. Bremond, Paillard and Nicole Freres.
- Disc musical boxes, often known as 'Symphonions' after the most popular manufacturer, reached the height of their popularity around the 1890s, which lasted until the first few decades of the 20th century.
- Look closely for damage to the mechanism or the 'comb' used to produce sounds. Missing or broken teeth and seized mechanisms can be expensive to repair. Take care not to damage the springs and gears by overwinding or winding a seized mechanism.
- The gramophone, the precursor to the last century's record player, which could play specially recorded discs, was developed by Emile Berliner in 1887, with the format becoming popularised around the turn of the century on both sides of the Atlantic.
- Gramophones use a needle and 'soundbox' to pick up sound from the grooves on the disc and a horn, which can be built in or applied, to amplify the sound. As well as the desirable and decorative table mounted horn gramophones, there are many portable gramophones which are usually more affordable.

A Victor Three gramophone, with original oak horn and in full working order.

£1,500-2,500   **ACM**

An unmarked brass horn gramophone, with oak case and Fidelio reproducer.

£200-300   **TK**

A gramophone, wooden body with inlaid decoration to front, reproducer marked 'Polyphon Concert', original horn, minor repairs.

c1910

£380-420   **TK**

A portable gramophone, with original horn soundbox, in working order.

£180-220   **TK**

A Mikiphone clockwork pocket gramophone, nickled case, needs some restoration.

This was the smallest commercial gramophone ever produced and all the parts fold up compactly into a portable instrument the size of a large, thick pocket watch.

4.5in (11.5cm) diam

£350-450   **TK**

A novelty Excelda portable gramophone, in the shape of a Kodak 'Autographic' camera, case repaired, working well.

£120-180   **TK**

A Swiss Thorens 'Excelda' portable gramophone in the form of a folding camera.

c1930

£150-250   **OACC**

A small German Symphonion disc musical box, playing 6.25in discs, with original seaside scene in lid.

c1890

£850-950   **AMM**

A German Symphonion disc music box, playing 10 5/8in discs, with walnut cabinet, 84 teeth in double comb, with 12 discs, complete but needs small regulation.

£650-750   **TK**

A Symphonion Style 28 hand-cranked musical box, plays 5.75in discs, with 40 teeth comb, one broken, black finished case with decals on top, with 19 discs.

£250-350   **TK**

A late 19thC mahogany-cased disc musical box, the comb mechanism marked with a windmill trademark and serial number 48274, the lid with inset reverse-painted glass panel named "Alice Butcher", with a collection of 30 discs by Kalliope.

11.25in (28.5cm) wide

£350-450   **DN**

A Swiss bells and drum in sight cabinet musical box, playing six airs on 52 teeth with four bells and drum with nine hammers, Stop/Play levers to side recesses, bird's-eye maple veneered two-door cabinet with ebonised band and box-strung inlaid panel fronts, ogee-moulded base with block feet.

c1880   *20in (53cm) wide*

£1,500-2,000   **BAR**

A Swiss musical box, with brass cylinder for 12 tunes and 62 notes, in wooden case with inlaid top, original tune-sheet, zither attachment, one tooth missing, not working.

c1880

£450-550   **TK**

A National musical box, made in Switzerland, with six tunes, lever wind, painted wood box with ebonised edges, with original tune sheet. .

c1900   *13in (33cm) wide*

£1,200-1,600   **AMM**

A French clockwork singing bird snuff box, in composition case with snuff compartment and animated singing bird with moving beak, tail and wings, with a repoussé scene of putti releasing a caged bird on the lid.

c1880   *4in (10cm) wide*

£2,000-2,400   **AMM**

441

A mechanical singing bird cage, brass cage, mechanism with small bellows, operated slide whistle created a warbling sound, not working but complete.

£250-350   **TK**

A continental silver singing bird music box, with repoussé decoration, box has fine detailing with griffins, faces, birds and scrolls, hallmarked on the bottom "E B" in an oval and "925".

4in (10cm) long

£2,500-3,000   **JDJ**

A Crystal radio set by Regent.

c1920

£35-45   **OACC**

An American 'Colonial Globe' radio.

c1930

£1,000-1,500   **TK**

A Pillow Speaker Radio model no. 413-S, by the Dahlberg Company, Minneapolis.

c1955

£150-200   **TK**

An Ultra R906 Coronation twin deluxe receiver, with hinged back panel and twin sliding doors concealing speaker aperture and controls.

£70-100   **DN**

FIND OUT MORE...

Benet Bergonzi, 'Old Gramophones & Other Talking Machines', published by Shire Books, 1995.

Arthur W.J.G. Ord-Hume, 'The Musical Box, A Guide for Collectors', published by Schiffer Publishing, 1995.

- During the 19th century, there were no chemists and doctors may have been located far from certain houses, so medical chests containing medicines and drugs were common in the homes of families who could afford them.
- They take many forms, from the very simple to the very large and sophisticated, complete with accessories such as balances and pestles and mortars. The more sophisticated and larger chests will fetch higher prices than smaller, simpler ones.
- Some have concealed compartments behind panels at the rear of the chest to hold poisons and dangerous drugs. These are sometimes only opened by operating a small lever or bar located in a unusual place, such as inside a drawer.
- When buying chests, check that the bottles match and are not replaced, as this can devalue a chest. Medical bottles of all sizes are in themselves highly collectable. They are often very decorative, particularly leech jars.
- When considering post mortem sets or surgeon's instruments, there are three factors to consider. Firstly, the maker – a set will be more valuable if it is made by a noted maker. Secondly, the set should be as complete as possible as missing pieces will devalue a set considerably, although some collectors will buy an incomplete set with a view to completing it over time. Thirdly, condition is important. Damage and rust will affect the value.

Four 19thC apothecary jars with paper labels, all with original stoppers, all in good condition, some loss to labels.

8.5in (22cm) high

£50-80 TWC

Three 19thC apothecary bottles, with original stoppers, paper labels, varying condition, from poor to good.

9in (23cm) high

£40-50 TWC

Three 19th/20thC apothecary jars, original stoppers, good condition.

Tallest 9.5in (24cm) high

£30-50 TWC

Three ceramic medicine jars, with applied printed labels.

Largest 9.5in (24cm) high

£120-180 BA

A large apothecary bottle, with original stopper, good condition.

13in (33cm) high

£40-50 TWC

A 19th/20thC apothecary bottle, polished bottom with 'poison' type stopper.

9in (23cm) high

£30-50 TWC

A 19thC mahogany apothecary's box, the doors holding six glass stoppered bottles each and opening to reveal five pull-out drawers containing an assortment of glass vessels under a recess holding five further bottles.

14in (35.5cm) high

£1,000-1,500 BA

A 19thC mahogany apothecary's box, the top lifting up to reveal eight glass stoppered bottles, over a pull-out drawer with five compartments containing an assortment of glass vessels and a glass pestle and mortar.

12in (30.5cm) wide

£600-800 BA

A 19thC mahogany apothecary's box, with nine compartments holding glass stoppered bottles, six with printed labels reading "Dandelion Pills, C. H. Booth, Chemist, Kings Road, Chelsea SW" and pull-out drawer to base.

6in (15.5cm) wide

£300-500 BA

A late 19thC apothecary set, possibly American, in a leather trunk.

c1890-1910

£220-280 BAC

A large 19thC French marine surgeon's instrument set, with two layers in padded, fitted wooden case with printed paper label.

Case 22.75in (58cm) wide

£7,000-8,000 BA

A 19thC cased surgeon's set, with stainless steel blades and black stained wooden handles, case with ivory label marked "Evans & Wormull, 31 Stamford Street, Blackfriars, London".

Case 18in (46cm) wide

£800-1,200 **BA**

A cased postmortem set, with stainless steel blades and black stained wooden handles, blades marked "J. Gray & Son, Sheffield".

Box 9.5in (24cm) wide

£650-750 **BA**

A 19thC lacquered brass and glass cupping set, in velvet-lined, fitted mahogany case, including a glass medicine bottle with printed label "Godfrey".

£700-900 **BA**

An "Improved Patent Magneto-Electric" machine, in fitted mahogany case with printed paper label.

A great many 'amazing' benefits were promised from regular treatment with minor electric shocks during the 19th century. These included more rapid recovery from illnesses, prevention of hair loss and all manner of physiological ailments. The machine would be wound using the handle to generate a charge and electrodes applied to deliver the shock to the right area.

Box 8.75in (22.5cm)

£100-150 **BA**

A pessary mould.

c1900   *6.75in (17cm)*

£40-60 **BS**

A steel folding corn razor, with original case.

c1900   *5in (12.5cm)*

£20-40 **BS**

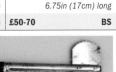

A 19thC gum lancet, with tortoiseshell cover.

6.75in (17cm) long

£50-70 **BS**

An early 19thC steel cranium rasp.

7.5in (19cm)

£50-70 **BS**

A late 18thC "Heys" steel cranium saw, with ebony grip.

6.75in (17cm)

£100-140 **BS**

FIND OUT MORE...

Keith Wilbur, 'Antique Medical Instruments', published by Schiffer Publishing, 1998.

A CLOSER LOOK AT A TOOTHKEY

A 19thC steel toothkey, with horn grip, marked "Charriere, Paris".

Toothkeys, used to extract teeth, were first mentioned in records in 1742. They are also known as 'clef de Garegeot', 'Fothergill key', 'English key' and 'French key'. The first examples had a straight shaft and were made from iron. Handles were initially plain and shaped like a turnkey, but were made later on from horn, ivory and other material over time, sometimes incorporating instruments, such as this example which contains screwdrivers, to adjust the grip or claw.

7in (17.5cm) long

£60-100 **BS**

A selection of 1920s-30s glass eyes.

Glass eyes were used as false eyes by people who had lost an eye. They were stored in large quantities as every patient had a differently shaped eye and the colour had to be matched as closely as possible to the other eye. Today, they are sought after by collectors, with large collections in original cabinets fetching very high prices at auction.

£20-30 (each) **BS**

A CLOSER LOOK AT A CANDLESTICK

This candlestick was designed by Christopher Dresser (1834-1904) and is indicative of his work with its clean lines and simple design.

Ornamentation is minimal, and the style of the piece is very modern. Dresser is credited with being the first 'modern' industrial designer.

The angled position and design of the handle is typical of his designs.

The pared down 'Moroccan' or Middle Eastern feel of the piece is also indicative of Dresser, who was skilled at combining the best elements of designs from other cultures with an understanding for mass production and machines.

A Buffalo Art Craft Shop three-sided chamberstick, with stylized flowers in green, red and black, some dents, stamp marked.

4.5in (11cm) high

£350-400   **CRA**

A large Stickley Brothers hammered copper coal scuttle, with two riveted handles, a few minor dents, lip slightly bent, stamped "406" on base.

Gustav Stickley (1857-1942) was a prominent and renowned furniture maker in the American Arts & Crafts style. He founded 'The Craftsman Workshops' under the name 'Gustav Stickley Company' in 1898, mostly making oak furniture. In 1916, his brothers took over and renamed the company 'L & JG Stickley'. The family ended its association with the company in 1974, but it still retains the Stickley name

14.5in (37cm) wide

£600-700   **CRA**

A Keswick School of Industrial Arts copper tray, of rectangular form, repoussé decorated with a band of fruiting Arbatus, stamped mark, together with a Keswick School of Industrial Arts brass bowl, of ovoid form with repoussé decoration, stamped marks, also a small Celtic design copper tray.

Largest 20.5in (52cm) wide

£250-300   **L&T**

A Kardofan brass chamber candlestick, designed by Christopher Dresser, for Richard Perry, Son & Co., the dished drip tray above cylindrical neck on a domed base with curved cylindrical mahogany handle, bears factory mark.

56.25in (143cm) high

£420-480   **L&T**

A Dirk Van Erp hammered copper bowl, with scalloped rim.

7.5in (19cm) diam

£400-500   **CRA**

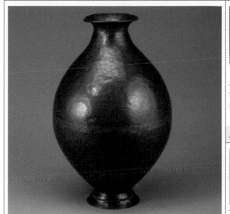

An oval twin-handle brass tray, the rim and handles decorated in Celtic inspired repoussé.

29.5in (75cm) wide

£300-400   **L&T**

Two Heintz silver-on-bronze verdigris pieces, some wear, stamped mark and patent.

Ashtray 8in (20cm) diam

£200-250   **CRA**

An Arts and Crafts silver overlaid copper desk set, comprising a calendar frame, a pen tray, a rolling blotter and four blotter corners, each with geometric overlay.

c1900 Pen tray 9in (23cm) high

£120-180   **SI**

A large Stickley Brothers hammered copper bulbous vessel, with rolled rim, stamped "83".

16in (40.5cm)

£600-700   **CRA**

A pair of Tudric pewter candlesticks, designed by Archibald Knox, each with broad drip trays and tapered supports with three flared brackets on a broad circular base cast with entwined tendrils, stamped mark "0221".

5.75in (14.5cm) high

£1,000-1,500   L&T

TUDRIC WARE

- Tudric is the trade name for decorative and table ware made by William Haseler of Birmingham and marketed by Liberty & Co. of London from 1903.
- It is made from a form of pewter with a high proportion of silver, and accompanied Haseler's solid silver range which was called 'Cymric'.
- Decoration is typically Art Nouveau, and uses many interlaced Celtic motifs as well as stylised leaves and flowers. Pieces also often have enamelled decoration.
- The designer Archibald Knox (1864-1933), an exponent of the Celtic interpretation of the Art Nouveau movement, designed many pieces.

A pair of Tudric pewter candlesticks, the scrolled drip trays above moulded tapering columns on circular spreading bases cast with leaves and set with turquoise enamel roundels, stamped marks "023".

5.5in (14cm) high

£850-950   L&T

A Liberty's Tudric two-handled comport, pierced and embossed with shamrocks, impressed numeral "0287".

11in (28cm) wide

£100-150   GorL

A Tudric pewter cake tray, designed by Archibald Knox, cast with stylised fruiting branches and centred by a Moorcroft panel, painted in the 'pomegranate' pattern, stamped mark "0357", and a similar twin-handled bowl the body pierced and cast with stylised bands, stamped marks "0350".

Tray 12in (30.5cm) wide

Tray £1,000-1,500, Bowl £400-600   L&T

A Liberty's Tudric sugar bowl, with single handle, cast with stylised organic forms, stamped "BOM 0231".

4.5in (11.5cm)

£45-55   GorL

A Liberty & Co. Tudric pewter timepiece, from a design by David Veasey, of square section with a spreading base and top surmounted by a squared dome with cross-banding, the sides and back hinged door panel embellished with branches of stylised honesty, the front copper dial embossed with Roman numerals and with pewter hands, stamped "Tudric" and numbered "0159".

The original design for this timepiece was an elaborate silver tea-caddy. For that design and a Liberty version of a pewter caddy see 'The Designs of Archibald Knox for Liberty & Co.' by Adrian J. Tilbrook, Ornament Press, 1976, p.58 figs. 29 & 30.

6.5in (16.5cm) high

£1,600-2,000   DN

Two Scottish School brass jardinières, the first decorated with polychrome enamel hearts and panels of stylized dragonflies, the second with broad rim over flaring sides, decorated with Celtic galleons and roundels of swimming fish.

L £900-1,000, R £200-300 L&T

A Scottish School brass and enamel inlaid stationery rack, with shaped back above divided interior, inlaid with a roundel of a downcast maiden in coloured enamels.

11.5in (29cm) wide

£800-1,200   L&T

From left to right:
A Scottish School brass wall mirror, the rectangular frame repoussé decorated with entwined Celtic mythical beasts, bears inscription "Wool Prize, Gargunnoch Show, the gift of F.H. McLeod & Sons, 1927".

15.5in (39.5cm) high

£300-350   **L&T**

A Scottish school brass wall mirror, of rectangular outline, the rectangular mirror enclosed within repoussé decorated frame depicting stylized roses on a hammered ground, bears inscription "Wool Prize: Killearn Show 1921, The Gift of F.H. McLeod & Sons".

14in (36cm) high

£300-350   **L&T**

A Scottish school brass picture frame, possibly by Agnes Bankier Harvey, of rectangular outline, repoussé decorated with a band of flowering stems.

13.5in (34.5cm) high

£400-500   **L&T**

A German pewter easel mirror, attributed to Kayser, of arched shape embellished at the top with rose blooms and thorny branches, the sides extending to form feet and further embellished with roses, having a brass wire hinged support.

£500-600   **DN**

A WMF style pewter dressing mirror, cast with classical maiden and foliage.

14in (35.5cm) high

£180-220   **GorL**

A WMF pewter soda-syphon coaster, of openwork cylindrical shape embellished with geometric plant form motifs, and sinuous twin handles, maker's marks on base.

2.75in (20cm) high

£200-250   **DN**

An Art Nouveau copper gimbal lamp and tray, the tray is with flowing silver designs, which extends up to form the frame, tray monogrammed "RL" and signed on back "SHREVE & CO. sterling & other metals"

10in (25.5cm) long

£900-1,000   **JDJ**

An Art Nouveau WMFB silver calling card tray, with a maiden standing in the middle, her flowing gown drapes to the ground and flows out to form the tray on either side of her.

13.75in (35cm) wide

£500-600   **JDJ**

Three Art Nouveau patinated metal table articles, comprising a candlestick of tapering square shape with green slag glass panels held by stylized foliage, on a similar square base, a tall bud-shaped candleholder on a circular base, and a mother-of-pearl and brass inkstand, the first stamped "Apollo Studios".

Candlestick 14in (35.5cm) high

£250-350   **SI**

An Austrian Art Nouveau rosewood and inlaid desk set, comprising a letter rack, the domed lid enclosing a divided interior, the sides with brass tendril straps, the whole with whiplash foliate inlay, also an inkwell, with two glass wells and inlaid lids on an inlaid twin-handled tray with pen rests, a blotter of rectangular form with inlaid panel, and a pair of table candlesticks.

11.5in (29cm) high

£1,000-1,500   **L&T**

An Art Nouveau copper jardinière, probably English, cylindrical form riveted with three stylized cast handles and paw feet, stamped "Emantee" underneath.

c1900   12.75in (32.5cm) high

£200-250   **FRE**

A collection of Chase Art Deco chromeware, comprising a pair of bubble candlesticks, a mint and nut dish with banded middle, designed by Ruth and William Gerth, a mustard jar with frosted glass liner, all with stamped archer mark, together with a Revere chrome creamer, sugar and tray set, stamped mark.

Dish 8.5in (21.5cm) wide

£50-60 **FRE**

A Chase chrome Art Deco breakfast set, designed by Ruth and William Gerth, with semi-spherical creamer and lidded sugar with black Bakelite handles, on a tray with concentric circle design, stamped archer marks.

The Chase Brass & Copper Company was founded in Waterbury, Connecticut in 1876. The bulk of production was for industrial uses, until the 1930s when they released a range of homeware. Primarily in chrome, but available in other finishes, its clean lines and Art Deco styling made it immensely popular. Renowned period designers such as Walter von Nessen, Russell Wright, Ruth and William Gerth and the in-house designer Harry Laylon were employed to work on the range. The war effort in the 1940s meant that production of the range ceased and after the war, the company chose not to revive the range. Produced for a short period, Chase domestic metalware is now highly collectible.

£50-60 **FRE**

A Chase Diana Art Deco chrome console set, designed by Harry Laylon including a flower bowl with ribbed white plastic base and sawtooth rim, and a pair of matching candlesticks, stamped and moulded archer mark.

Bowl 10in (25.5cm) diam

£60-80 **FRE**

A Chase Diplomat coffee service, designed by Walter Von Nessen, including coffee pot, sugar and creamer, copper with black plastic handles and knobs, stamped archer mark, , chip to handle of pot.

c1932

£100-150 **FRE**

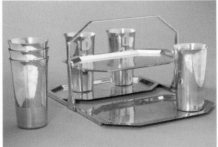

A Chase chrome Art Deco metalwork triple collapsible tray, designed by Harry Laylon, with scribed concentric design and six iced drink tumblers with scribed lines, stamped archer marks.

Tray 7in (17.5cm) high

£100-150 **FRE**

Three Chase Art Deco boxes, a divided candy dish with black metal base, glass insert and nickel lid with black metal finial, designed by Ruth and William Gerth, a one-tray box in chrome with shell finial designed by Harry Laylon and a dolphin box with brown Bakelite base and brass lid designed by Helen Bishop Dennis, tiny chip to base, stamped archer marks.

Largest 7in (17.5cm) diam

£40-50 **FRE**

A Chase copper pretzelman, designed by Lurelle Guild, cutout silhouette design with brass rod and tray, stamped mark.

16in (40.5cm) high

£100-150 **FRE**

A Chase Connoisseur Art Deco cigarette box, designed by Ruth and William Gerth, in a satin nickel finish with scribed geometric designs, wood lining, chip to lining.

6.75in (17cm) wide

£50-80 **FRE**

A Chase copper Art Deco bud vase, designed by Ruth and William Gerth, together with a copper napkin holder with orange Bakelite handle, designed by Harry Laylon, stamped archer mark.

First 9in (23cm) high

£40-50 **FRE**

An Art Deco chrome appetizer stand, in the shape of a swan with red Bakelite head and body pierced to hold toothpicks, on a dished base.

7in (17.5cm) high

£60-80 FRE

A Max Le Verrier Art Deco pelican lamp, bronze figure on a marble base, unwired, signed "FRANCE LE VERRIER".

c1930   7.25in (18.5cm) high

£150-200 FRE

A pair of European pewter domed base candlesticks.

c1680-1720   7in (18cm) high

£1,000-1,500 JDJ

Two hog scraper pushup candle holders.

6.5in (16.5cm) high

£120-180 TWC

An Art Deco pewter caddy.

6in (15cm) high

£20-30 OACC

A Machine Age chrome coffee service, designed by Michael W. McArdle for Sunbeam, including a pitcher, creamer, sugar and tray, executed in chrome with black Bakelite handles and line inlay.

1934 Pitcher 9.5in (24cm) high

£100-150 FRE

A pair of mid 19thC brass beehive-type push-up candle holders.

Many candlesticks have scratches from where solidified wax has been cleaned off over the years. Beware of sticks in pristine condition and in bright yellow coloured brass, as these are likely to be modern reproductions.

10in (25.5cm) high

£30-45 TWC

A 19thC hog scraper candlestick, with side ejector.

7in (18cm) high

£60-70 OACC

A silver-plated Mappin & Webb Art Deco three-piece tea service, monogrammed initials, stamped "MAPPIN & WEBB PARIS FAB. ANGLAISE".

5.5in (14cm) high

£70-100 FRE

A pair of 19thC small brass push-up candlesticks.

11in (28cm) high

£120-180 JDJ

A 1950s table lamp, with chrome stem with Lucite leaves and large spherical bulbs

38in (96.5cm) high

£150-200 FRE

A pair of Victorian brass candlesticks.

8.25in (21cm) high

£100-200 OACC

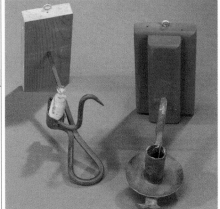

Two 18thC/19thC American wrought iron candle holders, with jamb spikes.

£150-200 SI

A set of three early copper measuring jugs, comprising a half gill, one gill, and one-and-a-half gills.
Largest 4.5in (11cm) high

£150-200 OACC

A set of six graduated English pewter lidless bellied measures, from a quarter gill to a quart, some dents and imperfections.

£300-400 JDJ

A Mexican silver and copper Modernist pitcher, the spherical body with applied silver band, simple strap handle and stylised silver ice guard to spout, unmarked.
8.25in (21cm)high

£100-150 FRE

A vintage cream can.
11.5in (29cm) high

£25-35 OACC

A Victorian brass hot water can.
11.5in (29cm) high

£40-50 OACC

A Victorian brass hot water can.
14.25in (36cm) high

£60-70 OACC

A 19thC American pierced tin hanging candle lantern.

14in (35.5cm) high

£80-120 SI

A Norwegian enamelled metalware bowl.

£35-45 V

Top: A large 19thC Martingale horse decoration, comprising cast and pattern brasses, surmounted by various small boss-like studs, including heart, cross, crescent and shield patterns, leather work in generally good condition.
38.5in (98cm) long

£80-120 HamG

Middle: A large 19thC Martingale horse decoration, comprising cast brasses including a plough, chained bear and a brass of North Eastern Railway, surmounted by a small brass with maker's name "J. Watson, Maker, Pickering", leather work in generally good condition with some perishing.
16.25in (41cm) long

£70-80 HamG

Bottom: A group of four Martingale horse decorations, comprising three small and one large, all of 19thC period, including anchor pattern and bell, the large Martingale consisting of cast barrels denoting brewery transport, all in generally good condition with some perishing.
Longest 37in (94cm) long

£100-150 HamG

A set of three 20thC steel fire irons, with gilt metal baluster handles.

£450-550 DN

An early 20thC cast bronze figure of a Boy Scout, on square base, staff missing.
7.75in (19.5cm) high

£100-150 GorL

MILITARIA

PISTOLS

- Pocket pistols, used by journeymen to protect themselves, are the most affordable form of pistol. Duelling pistols are more expensive, with cased pairs fetching the highest prices.
- Makers' names are important as those by good makers are of higher quality. Look for pistols made by Manton and Mortimer.
- Reproductions are found, usually originating from Spain. These low quality pieces are easy to spot when compared to an authentic weapon or firearm.
- Pay close attention to firearm licensing laws, with details available from your local police station. Sometimes a licence is needed simply to own a piece.
- Handle the metal parts as little as possible. Natural acids on fingers cause small red spots known as 'finger rust' to appear. To avoid this and spots caused by air pollution, apply a thin protective layer of beeswax.

An early 18thC flintlock holster pistol, signed "John Harman" on the lock and "Harman, London" on the breech of the three-staged swamped barrel.

John Harman was made a freeman of the Gunmakers Company on 15th April 1714. Appointed gunsmith to HRH Frederick Prince of Wales in 1729.

c1725   16in (40.5cm) long

£1,500-2,000   **L&T**

An English Sea Service standard issue pistol, dated.

1800

£1,500-2,000   **CS**

A percussion duelling pistol, the octagon barrel with gold inlaid legend "Canon A. Rubens D'Acier", with side loading breech and foliate engraving.

14.25in (36cm) long

£700-800   **SI**

A mid-18thC flintlock Caucasian holster pistol, in the English tradition, the lock signed "CjC Burrij", the stock split at the pistol grip.

19in (48.5cm) long

£700-800   **L&T**

A percussion pistol, .68 calibre, Pedro Eibar, with snaphaunce lock.

£650-750   **SI**

A mid-18thC side-by-side double-barrelled flintlock box lock tap-action carriage pistol, by Bond of London.

9.5in (24cm) long

£1,800-2,200   **L&T**

A Tower Wharf proofs pistol, by John Barber London.

£550-650   **CS**

A flintlock box lock tap-action under-over turn-off barrel pocket pistol, signed "G Wallace" within a trophy of arms, the barrels numbered "3" and "4".

8in (20.5cm) long

£450-550   **L&T**

An 18thC brass under-over flintlock overcoat pistol, by Ketland & Co., Birmingham.

£750-850   **CS**

A mid-19thC percussion six-barrelled revolving pepper-box pistol, with engraved round action lock, Birmingham proof marks, finely chequered butts, engraved steel butt plate trigger guard and butt strap.

8.5in (21.5cm) long

£350-450   **L&T**

A second model trenter pistol, by Deane & Sons, London Bridge.

£500-700   CS

A late 19thC Continental 10-shot pin fire revolver, with engraved action, captive sliding extractor chequered walnut slab butt with lanyard ring.

10in (25.5cm) long

£450-550   L&T

A single-barrel under-lever falling block .360 centre fire hammer rifle, by Alex Henry Edinburgh, No.2648, the barrel signed "Alex. Henry 12 South St.Andrews St, Edinburgh".

£1,800-2,200   L&T

A pair of late 18thC English Dragoon officer's holster pistols, by Henry Nock, the locks signed "H. Nock, London", minor damage to the fore end of one pistol and missing barrel tang screw and stock pins.

14.5in (37cm) long

£1,500-2,000   L&T

A pair of early 19thC flintlock Officer's pistols, the locks signed "Davidson", engraved steel furniture.

12in (30.5cm) long

£2,000-2,500   L&T

A pair of mid-18thC brass flintlock box lock turn-off pocket pistols, by Hampton, with folding triggers and reeded turn-off steel barrels, chequered walnut rounded butts with blank silver escutcheons and engraved silver butt caps.

8in (20.5cm) long

£350-450   L&T

A pair of Charles I Smith single shot duelling pistols, with octagon barrels and foliate engraved mounts.

£900-1,000   SI

A single-barrel under lever 10-bore hammer wild fowling gun, the barrel engraved "G. Jeffries Norwich" on the top flat, the back action lock signed "G. Jeffries".

£700-800   L&T

A single-barrel .290 under-lever falling block hammer sporting rifle, by Adams, the barrel engraved "Adams & Co. 32. Finsbury Pavement London".

£350-450   L&T

A single-barrel under lever 10-bore hammer wild fowling gun, the barrel engraved "G. Jeffries Norwich" on the top flat, the back action lock signed "G. Jeffries".

£700-800   L&T

A single-barrel .600 under-lever falling block big game rifle, by Westley Richards, No. 309, the barrel engraved "Henry's patent rifling", a spurious silver plate on the butt reads "Edwin Landseer and his true friend Victoria R".

£1,500-2,000   **L&T**

A single-barrel top-lever box lock ejector rook rifle, converted to .22 calibre, the barrel engraved "Holland and Holland, 98 New Bond Street, London".

£650-750   **L&T**

A single-barrel .450 falling block sporting rifle, by W.W. Greener, London, signed "W.W. Greener", the butt plate trap engraved with "VR" surmounted by a crown, the plate engraved "Sir Edwin Landseer".

Greener's records confirm that this rifle serial No. 014996, was built in 1905. Since Sir Edwin Landseer died in 1873, it is possible that the butt plate is from another rifle.

Barrel 27in (68.5cm) long

£2,500-2,800   **L&T**

A single-barrel top lever sidelock 16-bore sporting shot gun, by Woodward, No 5440. the barrel with scroll engraving signed "J. Woodward".

£1,800-2,200   **L&T**

A single-barrel .303 falling block sporting rifle, by John Wilkes, serial no.8883, the barrel engraved "John Wilkes 1 Golden Square, London W".

£1,200-1,800   **L&T**

A single-barrel side-lever ejector .300 hammer sporting rifle, by Beesley London, No.2452, the barrel engraved "F. Beesley .300, 2 St. James's Street, London".

£450-550   **L&T**

A rare Scottish silver-mounted 12-bore flintlock single-barrel sporting gun, in mid-European fashion, by William Heriot of Edinburgh, the moulded border signed "W. HERIOT".

c1760 Barrel 44in (120cm) l

£2,800-3,200   **L&T**

A pair of 12-bore single trigger over-and-under sidelock ejector guns, by Gebruder Merkel, in Suhl No.15411/2, locks signed in gold "Suhler Waffenwerk Gebruder Merkel, Suhl".

Barrel 28in (71cm) long

£2,200-2,800   **L&T**

A single barrel bolt action mod 98.270 calibre sporting rifle, by David Lloyd, No.188, with Habicht 4 telescopic sight.

£1,500-2,00   **L&T**

A double-barrel .450 under-lever rifle, by Alex Henry Edinburgh, No. 3452, the barrels engraved "Alexander Henry Edinburgh & London".

Barrel 26in (66cm) long

£1,500-2,000   **L&T**

A double-barrel .600 under lever pin-fire hammer big game rifle, by Garden, No. 7649. *c1860*

£1,000-1,200   **L&T**

A double-barrel 12-bore under-lever hammer ejector shotgun, by Boss of London, No.3150, the barrels engraved "Boss & Co., 73 St. James's Street London", the locks signed "Boss & Co.", nitro proof right barrel out of proof built in 1874, ejectors fitted later.

Barrel 30in (76cm) long

£4,200-4,800   **L&T**

A double-barrel top lever side-by-side boxlock ejector 12-bore shotgun, by Gow of Dundee, No. 36539, the barrels engraved, in leather case with accessories.

Barrel 30in (76cm) long

£180-220   **L&T**

A double-barrel 10-bore hammer gun, by Army & Navy, No. 5358, the barrels engraved "Army & Navy CSL', together with a double-barrel box lock ejector AYA Model

31in (79cm) long

£650-750 (pair)   **L&T**

A 12-bore side-by-side boxlock ejector, by Anson, No. 4620.

Barrel 28in (71cm) long

£220-280   **L&T**

A double-barrel 16-bore pinfire shotgun, slide thumb lever, by Westley Richards London, No. 10490, the barrels engraved "Westley Richards 170 New Bond Street, London".

c1864   Barrels 30in (76cm) l

£1,500-2,000   **L&T**

A double-barrel box lock ejector .400 big game rifle, by W.J. Jeffery, No 13111, the barrels engraved at breech "W. J. Jeffery 30 King Street, St. James's London", with Habich telescopic sight, sideplates signed "W. J. Jeffery & Co".

Barrel 24in (61cm) high

£4,500-5,500   **L&T**

A double-barrel 12-bore thumb-hole action hammer gun, No.8261 by James Purdey the barrels signed "J Purdey and Son Audley House, South Audley Street, London", the escutcheon engraved with "E" surmounted by a royal crown.

The makers confirm that they were built in 1870 as a pair for W. Rennie Esq.

£3,500-4,000   **L&T**

A 19thC British Cavalry sword.

£150-250   **CS**

A rare Continental basket hilted broad sword, the knuckle guard with cast coat of arms with two savages as supporters, the lower guard cast as Medusa's head with the wavy double-edge blade.

Blade 38in (96.5cm) long

£1,800-2,200   **L&T**

An English Pioneer hanger short sword.

£100-200   **CS**

A late 16thC Italian swept hilt rapier, with large ovoid pommel, straight cross quillian, the spiral grip bound with steel wire, plain double-edge blade.

c1590   *Blade 35in (89cm) l*

£500-600   **L&T**

An 18thC Indian tulwar, with slender curved single edge signed blade.

Blade 30in (76cm) long

£2,800-3,200   **L&T**

An 18thC Indian katar, with shaped fullers and thickened point, steel hilt with swollen handlebars, covered with silver foil damascene.

Blade 10in (25.5cm) long

£200-250   **W&W**

A CLOSER LOOK AT AN INDIAN KATAR

The tip of the blade is often reinforced, helping to pierce armour.

The blade is straight and double-edged.

Decorative examples are more desirable.

Katars were used exclusively by Hindus. There is no solid hilt like a dagger, but two crossbars which are held firmly by the fist, allow the weapon to be used with a punching action.

An 18thC Indian katar, with shaped fullers and thickened point, steel hilt with swollen handlebars, covered with silver foil damascene.

Blade 9.75in (25cm) long

£220-280   **W&W**

An 18thC Indian katar, the slender fullered blade with thickened point, hilt gold damascened overall with flowers and foliage, five slender grip bars, some moderate rust to hilt, damascene worn.

Blade 8.5in (21.5cm) long

£250-350   **W&W**

An 18thC Indian katar, the slender blade with deep fullers, thickened armour piercing tip, engraved number at forte, slender hilt bars and five-bar grip, in black leather sheath.

17.75in (45cm) long

£120-180   **W&W**

An 18thC Indian katar, sail-shaped steel guard with baluster finial, fluted grip bars, baluster handle bars.

Blade 12in (30.5cm)

£200-250   **W&W**

An early Malayan dagger Badek, with wavy pamor blade and one-piece hippo ivory hilt, in later wooden sheath.

Blade 11in (28cm) long

£150-200   **W&W**

A 19thC Spanish sailor's folding knife navaja, blade etched "Si persi que un la dron dabame en el coryzon".

Blade 10in (25.5cm) long

£280-320   **W&W**

An HM silver-mounted Skean dhu, for the Argyll & Sutherland Highlanders, Edinburgh, maker's stamp Marshall & Aitken, bog oak hilt carved with basket weave, glass pommel, in silver-mounted sheath with Celtic designs.

1918   *Blade 4in (10cm) long*

£250-350   **W&W**

A 19thC heavy military camp axe, deeply stamped "H Macneal Gordon Highlanders", on its original wooden haft.

Head 7in (18cm) wide

£300-350   **W&W**

An old Dyak head hunter's Mandau sword, with wire and rattan-bound carved bone hilt, human hair tuft issuing from pommel, in wooden scabbard.

Blade 19.5in (49.5cm) long

£280-320   **W&W**

BADGES

- Up to 1881, all regiments were known by a number. In 1881, the 'Cardwell System' was adopted and all regiments were named by their county. After World War II, many country regiments were amalgamated.
- Cap badges form a popular collecting area. Plastic cap badges were made after 1945 to cut costs and were unpopular with regiments and the collector. However, they are now increasingly being collected, as rarities are identified.
- Collectors should be beware of modern 'restrikes' which have extremely low values. Often used as 'gap fillers' by collectors, and of good quality, they are hard to recognise. Handle as many badges as possible to gain experience and always buy from a reputable source.

A Bengal unattached list officer's helmet plate.

£200-300   **CS**

A good other ranks white metal helmet plate of the 1st Glamorgan Rifle Volunteer Corps.

£160-200   **W&W**

A good Victorian other ranks brass helmet plate of The Royal Marines Light Infantry, one lug resoldered.

£150-200   **W&W**

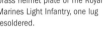

A 5th Volunteer Black Watch plaid brooch.

£100-200   **CS**

A Victorian other ranks white metal helmet plate of the 1st Volunteer Battalion Royal Berkshire Regiment.

£100-120   **W&W**

A good other ranks 1874-pattern glengarry badge of The 36th Herefordshire Regiment, 484, old copper lugs.

£120-180   **W&W**

A Victorian officer's silver-plated pouch belt badge of the 2nd Essex Rifle Volunteers.

£85-95   **W&W**

A scarce other ranks brass cap badge of the 3rd County of London Imperial Yeomanry, Sharp Shooters.

£180-220   **W&W**

A Victorian other ranks white metal helmet plate of the 1st Essex Artillery Volunteers.

£200-250   **W&W**

An NCO's silver arm badge of the Queen's Own Hussars, by LB & B Co, four prong and clip fasteners, Birmingham hallmarks.
1984

£45-55   **W&W**

MEDALS

- Medals for famous battles are highly desirable and valuable. Those awarded to higher ranks, such as a brigadier, are also more valuable.
- World War I groups are still inexpensive (although prices are rising) and form a good start to a collection.
- Medals were often worn every day with pride. Look for wear on 'highpoints', such as Queen Victoria's hair, that has been caused by frequent polishing. Too much reduces value. Dropped medals have dented edges, which also reduces value.
- Collectors should beware of re-engraved medals. If a man lost his medals, he bought others and had the name removed and his own engraved.

An Order of St Michael and St George companion's neck badge; OBE 2nd type Civil, BWM, Victory with MID emblem, Lieut C A Grossmith, Defence, EIIR Coronation; GMG EF; others; VF Caryll Archibald Grossmith; CMG 1953; OBE 1945

£500-600   **W&W**

Four medals, comprising MM George V first type; 1914-15 star; BWM; Victory (5571 Sjt W Barr 190/Bde RFA).

£220-280   **W&W**

Four medals, comprising MM George V first type; BWM; Victory; Defence; 242717 Pte J G Campbell 1/ E Lan R.

£400-450   **W&W**

Three medals, comprising George V first type;BWM; Victory; S 23004 Pte D Jolly 1/Cam'n Highrs.

£400-500   **W&W**

Three medals, comprising MM George V first type; BWM; Victory; M2 114160 Pte T C Shorrocks MT ASC.

£220-280   **W&W**

Three medals, comprising MM George V first type; BWM; Victory; 593508/6376 Pte L Phillips 1/18 Lond R.

£450-550   **W&W**

Three medals, comprising MM George V first type; BWM; Victory; 306452/ 4564 Pte-A Cpl F Y Bayliss 1/8 R War R TF.

£400-500   **W&W**

Three medals, comprising MM George V first type; BWM; Victory; 65683 Pte to A Cpl F C H Ellis, 202 Coy M.

£350-450   **W&W**

A South Africa 1877-79 clasp 1879 medal, engraved in upright capitals "943 Pte T Mellis 57th Foot".

£320-380   **W&W**

A Crimea one clasp Sebastopol medal, impressed in later QSA-style naming 3228 Pte W Gallagher 49th Foot, replacement clasp.

£220-280   **W&W**

A Hanoverian medal for Waterloo 1815, the obverse with Prince Regent, the reverse stand of arms above "Waterloo Jun XVIII", impressed "Soldat Michael Wedekind, Landwehr Bat Alfeld", some edge bruising.

£60-80   **W&W**

A copper powder flask, body with medallion of two dogs and hunter, common top stamped "Dixon & Sons Patent", twin hanging rings, retains much original finish overall, minor dents, one screw missing from top.

7.5in (19cm) long

£150-200   **W&W**

A copper powder flask, stamped "Sykes", common brass tip, fixed nozzle, retains some original finish overall.

3.75in (9.5cm) long

£150-200   **W&W**

A Continental brass-mounted powder horn, hinged charger, graduated nozzle, shaped retaining spring, brass border and four hanging rings, some age wear overall.

c1800   *6in (15cm) long*

£120-180   **W&W**

A late 18thC brass-mounted cowhorn powder flask, probably for Rifle Volunteers, common brass tip with sprung lever and adjustable nozzle, brass hanging band with suspension loop, concave brass base with suspension loop, original leather charger cover.

11in (28cm) long

£350-450   **W&W**

A Y-shaped Enfield rifle combination tool, comprising nipple key, oil bottle, turnscrew and pricker, stamped "T & CG", worm missing.

4.5in (11cm) long

£80-120   **W&W**

A late 17thC engraved flattened cow horn powder flask, engraved with a hunter, dogs, and animal in forest, reverse engraved with circles, branded "WL", later mounts.

9in (23cm) wide

£550-650   **W&W**

A T-shaped Enfield rifle combination tool, comprising nipple key, spring cramp, oil bottle, pricker, two turnscrews, ball spike, ball worm missing.

5.25in (13.5cm) long

£90-100   **W&W**

A nickel silver percussion cap dispenser, blued spring, cover plate stamped "M-Sykes".

2.75in (7cm) wide

£120-180   **W&W**

An "Air Raid Defences - NSDAP" steel helmet, without chinstrap, engraved "RL2 - 39/11".

£150-200   **TK**

An 1867-pattern Prussian pickelhaube, as worn during the Franco-Prussian war.

£500-600   **CS**

OIL LAMPS

OIL LAMPS

- Early oil lamps were fuelled by 'whale oil', which was highly flammable blend of alcohol and distilled turpentine. It was dangerous to use and expensive. By the late 1850s, kerosene had been introduced as a safer and more economical option.

- In 1878, Edison developed electric light which began to threaten oil lamp manufacturers. Partly to provide designs that fitted in with increasingly lavish rooms and later to compete with the revolution of electricity, late 19th century lamps became more decorative and attractive. Many glass manufacturers produced examples in a rainbow of colours and varied forms.

- Electricity eventually took over and the oil lamp industry died, but lamps were used up until the 1940s in rural areas without electricity supply and are still used by Amish communities today.

- Burners are also collected, partly to restore lamps that had been electrified and partly to gather parts for incomplete burners. Thousands of patents were taken out to protect new designs, so the variety of types is enormous.

- Condition is important. Lamps were functional objects that were the centre of many rooms. Chips, cracks and wear will affect value and desirability considerably. Replaced parts and electrification will also affect value, especially if the piece has been drilled to fit electrical parts.

- Reproductions are common, so use a good reference book to familiarise yourself with common styles and forms. Also look at levels of wear, particularly on the base of the lamp.

A pressed green satin glass mini lamp, square base with round shade, very good condition.

8in (20.5cm) high

£200-250　　　JDJ

A miniature red satin 'Gone with the Wind' or parlour lamp.

c1890　　8.5in (22cm) high

£320-380　　　RAA

A hand-painted 'Gone with the Wind' lamp, globes hand-painted with yellow and white flowers, flowers are highlighted with heavy white enamel, chip to fitter rim on top globe, lamp electrified, otherwise very good condition.

19in (48.5cm) high

£100-150　　　JDJ

A very large 'Gone with the Wind' lamp, with green shading to yellow background and hand-painted chrysanthemums, foot of lamp impressed with lion's faces at the feet and smiling cherub faces in between, lamp electrified, top globe appears to be a replacement painted to match and has a nine inch crack extending from the top opening, downward.

33in (84cm) high

£300-400　　　JDJ

An amber pressed satin glass mini lamp, amber exterior and white cased interior, small chip to inside top rim of shade.

9in (23cm) high

£200-250　　　JDJ

A Pairpoint painted lamp, painted with rust and green background and white and purple flowers, two flakes to top rim of shade, otherwise good condition.

11in (28cm) high

£200-300 **JDJ**

A decorated milk glass mini lamp, the shaded yellow background with red flowers, several chips to top of shade, roughness to bottom of shade, otherwise good condition.

8in (20.5cm) high

£80-120 **JDJ**

A hand-painted kerosene lamp with shade, light blue background with pink flowers and green leaves, original burner replaced with electric burner, metal foot has been painted gold, otherwise good condition.

15in (38cm) high overall

£150-200 **JDJ**

A blue swirl mini lamp base and shade, shade with several flakes to the fitter rim, two small flakes to the top rim, base in good condition, spider replaced.

7.75in (19.5cm) high

£420-480 **JDJ**

A honey-coloured reverse swirl mini lamp, two tiny fleabites to bottom fitter rim.

8.25in (21cm) high

£800-1,200 **JDJ**

A blue diamond quilted and 'mother-of-pearl' mini lamp, on eight petal-shaped frosted feet, shade has ruffled lip.

10.5in (26.5cm) high

£450-500 **JDJ**

An Amberina mini-lamp, melon-ribbed body with five applied amber glass feet extending in a feather-type design on the lamp base, burner marked "PAT FEBY 27 1877".

8in (20cm) high

£2,500-3,000 **JDJ**

A cranberry beaded swirl miniature lamp.

c1890 *8.5in (22cm) high*

£450-500 **RAA**

A mid-20thC pink satin glass diamond quilted and 'mother-of-pearl' mini lamp, with shade, shade cut down, bruise to shoulder of base.

10.25in (26cm) high

£150-200 **JDJ**

A cranberry mini lamp, tiny fleabites to fitter rim as well as top rim, otherwise good condition.

8.75in (22cm) high

£200-300 **JDJ**

A Thomas Webb & Son oil lamp and shade, double wick burner, bronze feet stamped "JD" and "71", signed "THOMAS WEBB & SONS", good condition.

20in (51cm) high

£1,500-2,000 **JDJ**

A Hinks No. 2 oil lamp, wth cranberry glass shade.

Hinks is considered to be the 'Rolls Royce' of the oil lamp.

c1860 *28in (71cm) high*

£200-250 **OACC**

A Victorian oil lamp, with green glass shade.

29.5in (75cm) high

£200-300   **OACC**

A cranberry glass oil lamp.

c1860   18.5in (57cm) high

£220-280   **OACC**

A cut overlay fluid lamp, several minor chips to marble base, otherwise good condition.

10in (25.5cm)

£220-280   **JDJ**

A EPNS oil lamp, with "Messenger" burner.

24.75in (63cm) high

£120-180   **OACC**

A cut overlay fluid lamp, small burst air bubble on the edge of one quatrefoil, otherwise good condition, lamp electrified, but not drilled.

14.25in (36 cm) high

£1,200-1,800   **JDJ**

A pair of Sandwich Glass Factory camphene lamps, blown glass, made in three parts, waterfall bases, engraved with grapes, vines and berries, original burners.

c1835   14in (35.5cm) high

£1,800-2,200   **RAA**

A cut overlay lamp, floral cutting on font is trimmed with gold, wear to gold trim on font, several open air bubbles on both font and stem, electrified but not drilled.

16.5in (42cm) high

£420-480   **JDJ**

A Sandwich Glass Factory whale oil lamp, with patterned glass.

c1830   9.5in (24cm) high

£550-650   **RAA**

A Victorian room heater, with ruby glass shade.

17.75in (45cm) high

£380-420   **OACC**

A pink melon ribbed hall light, with a white opalescent top to pink at the bottom, in brass pull-down frame, slight bend to filigree top collar, otherwise good condition.

10in (25.5cm) high

£120-180   **JDJ**

A rare hand-blown crystal lace maker's whale oil lamp, with applied handle, together with original lace maker's lens and wooden stool, lamp and lens are good condition, stool appears to have been top coated at some point.

Lens 11in (28cm) high

£1,200-1,800   **JDJ**

- Popular in the 19th century, opera glasses can be found in huge variety. The most desirable have ornately decorated tubes, with painted enamel patterns or scenes, guilloche enamel and inset metals. Ivory is a common material, which is well carved in the best examples. Opera glasses with plain cases will not be as desirable or valuable. Most are contained in soft-sided cases or small bags.

- Splits to ivory coverings or loss or damage to enamelling will reduce value. These items were made to be used which often led to them being damaged.

- Makers' names will add value. Look out for Lemaire, who used a small bee as his motif and Chevalier of Paris. Both were well-known French optical instrument makers. Opera glasses can be signed around the eyepiece lens or on the bridge between the tubes.

A pair of opera glasses, gilded brass enamel, mother-of-pearl eye pieces, by Chevalier, Paris.

c1880   4.25in (10.5cm) wide

£200-300   **OACC**

A pair of opera glasses, gilt enamel and mother-of-pearl.

3.5in (9cm) wide

£180-220   **OACC**

A pair of French enamelled opera glasses, in a suede bag with silver gilt base.

£120-180   **L&T**

A pair of opera glasses, mother-of-pearl, with case.

3.75in (9.5cm) wide

£40-50   **OACC**

A pair of Victorian mother-of-pearl and gilt brass opera glasses, in original leather bag.

c1870   4.25in (10.5cm) wide

£70-100   **MB**

A pair of late 19thC brass and tortoiseshell pique covered opera glasses.

4.75in (11cm) wide

£250-300   **DN**

A pair of opera glasses, engraved brass.

4.25in (10.5cm) wide

£50-70   **OACC**

A pair of opera glasses, ivory and gilded brass with tortoiseshell eye pieces, by Jumelle Duchesse, Paris.

c1890   4in (10cm) wide

£100-150   **OACC**

A velvet opera bag, designed with three compartments to hold opera glasses, make-up and a purse, by Chevalier, Paris.

4.75in (12cm) wide

£70-100   **OACC**

SPECTACLES

- Since their development in the 15th century, spectacles have always been viewed as lending the wearer an air of intelligence. 18th century gentlemen and aristocrats would often purchase spectacles to vainly create a certain studious and intellectual air about themselves.

- Early spectacles did not have arms and are sometimes wrongly called 'pince nez'. Some early models, such as 'Nuremburg types' are now less common and can command high prices. Other armless types, dating from the 19th century when the style regained popularity, are more affordable.

- Arms, which were developed in the 18th century, initially had loops at the ends which pressed against the temples to hold them in place. The loops could also be used to attach cords.

- These types can also be known as 'wig spectacles' as they were secured by poking the arms into a wig. They often had shorter arms for this purpose. Initially lens shape was round, with octagonal and square shapes being used in the late 18th and 19th centuries.

- Having been produced in quantity for many centuries, spectacles offer collectors a wide and varied collecting area. Look for notable makers, such as Benjamin Martin, McAllister and Sargeant.

A pair of silver-framed spectacles, with green lenses, made by M Boster.

1740s

£200-250 VE

A pair of solid gold-framed spectacles, made by the son of the founder of McAllister, Philadelphia.

1820s

£300-400 VE

A pair of steel-framed spectacles, dating from the American Revolution, dug up near Old Fort, Niagara, NY.

c1770

£150-200 VE

A maple haircomb and a pair of spectacles, dating from the Revolutionary War, found at Fort Campbell, Cherry Valley.

£150-200 RAA

A pair of double horseshoe silver-framed spectacles, made by McAllister, Philadelphia.

c1800

£700-1,000 VE

A pair of solid silver double-D spectacles, with original sun lenses, made by McAllister, Philadelphia.

Benjamin Franklin was a customer of McAllister.

c1800

£1,200-1,700 VE

A pair of French double-D spectacles, with K-bridge tortoiseshell frames with original sun lenses, sterling silver arms and a trim pin hinger.

1730s

£1,000-2,000 VE

A pair of tortoiseshell-framed 'Martin's Margin' spectacles.

c1840

£700-1,000 VE

Two pairs of marksmen's spectacles.

The lenses of marksmen's spectacles were designed to correct defective eyesight. Both the colour of the lenses and the depth of the border were believed to help the long-and short-sighted.

c1860

£70-100 each VE

Two pairs of English tortoiseshell-framed wig spectacles.

left c1750, right c1850

L £400-500, R £220-280 VE

Three pairs of spectacles, by unknown makers.

1840-60

£70-100 each VE

FIND OUT MORE...

Nancy N Schiffer, 'Eyeglass Retrospective: Where Fashion meets Science', published by Schiffer Publishing, 1999.

Three pairs of pince nez with coloured lenses.

1840-60

£70-100 each VE

A Chinese blue and white porcelain vase, Wanli, of lobed oval form, overall with floral and foliate decoration, Ming Dynasty.

7in (17.75cm) high

£1,000-1,500   **SI**

A pair of Chinese export porcelain sauceboats, , of silver shape with barbed rims and loop handles, painted with a bird above a peony and pine tree, on an oval foot decorated with lambrequins, some restoration, Qianlong period.

9.5in (24.5cm) wide

£280-320   **BonS**

A large Chinese export porcelain meat dish, painted in blue with pagodas in landscape within a cracked ice border, the rim painted with foliate scrolls, cell diaper panels and peony flowers, Qianlong period.

19.75in (50.5cm) wide

£420-480   **BonS**

A Chinese export deep meat plate, with an extensive river landscape within a cell diaper border, the rim decorated with foliate scroll lambrequins. Qianlong period, chip to rim.

14.75in (37.5cm) wide

£80-120   **BonS**

A Chinese export porcelain oval meat plate, decorated in blue with a river landscape within a cell diaper border, gilding worn, together with another similar plate, Qianlong period.

17.25in (44cm) wide

£350-450   **BonS**

A 19thC Chinese export platter, painted in underglaze blue with a koro in a flower garden, within Fitzhugh-style borders.

The Fitzhugh pattern, which contains peony blossoms, the auspicious objects and pomegranates, was a popular Chinese export pattern. It is unknown where the design originated, but it is thought that it is named after the family that originally commissioned it.

10.5in (26.5cm) wide

£70-80   **HamG**

A 19thC Chinese blue and white square-section vase, each face decorated with watery landscapes.

14.25in (36cm) high

£1,500-2,000   **WW**

A miniature Chinese blue and white vase, decorated with repeating figures, bearing Kang Hsi marks.

£90-100   **HamG**

An early 20thC Chinese blue and white vase.

16.5in (42cm) high

£250-300   **OG**

A pair of Chinese bowls, painted with bands of chrysanthemums and scrolling tendrils, within foliate borders, bearing Kang Hsi marks, small abrasion to one rim, one bowl damaged.

5.25in (13cm) wide

£60-100   **HamG**

A Chinese blue and white hotplate, octagonal and painted with a traditional riverscape in underglaze blue.

9.25in (23.5cm) high

£100-150   **GorL**

A Chinese blue and white vase, with sceptre handles and landscape decoration.

8in (20.5cm) high

£80-120   **GorL**

A Chinese export porcelain tureen and cover, of canted rectangular section, between foliate S-scroll handles, the cover with lotus blossom strap handle, the tureen painted with pagodas in extensive landscapes, the cover with foliate lambrequin design within diaper borders.

14.5in (37cm) wide

£800-900   **BonS**

FAMILLE ROSE

- The famille rose (pink family) palette was developed from famille verte (green family), which in turn was based on Wucai or five-coloured decoration.

- The name refers to a palette of enamel colours used in overglazed decoration and is typified by the use of mainly pink or purple. The pink colour was invented by Andreas Casssius of Leyden in the mid-17th century and is derived from gold chloride. It was introduced into China by a Jesuit priest in around 1720, where it was perfected.

- This new colour palette was of a very high quality and proved very popular in Europe where is was exported in huge quantities in the 18th, 19th and 20th centuries. As demand increased, quality was often sacrificed and as a result later pieces are not as collectable.

A Chinese famille rose plate, decorated with a cockerel and a bird amongst flowers on blue and green backed scrolls, all on a ruby ground with chrysanthemum flower heads, Yongzheng period, crack.

8.5in (22cm) diam

£320-380   **DN**

A pair of Chinese famille rose baluster vases, decorated with panels of flowers, figures, dragons and phoenix on a blue floral ground, six character Qianlong marks in iron red.

c1900   *16in (40.5cm) high*

£400-500 (pair)   **DN**

A Canton famille rose part dinner service, comprising a well and tree platter, a tureen, a covered vegetable dish, two sweatmeat dishes, five dinner plates, five dessert plates, four small side plates, one lobed saucer, two small sweatmeat dishes, two soup bowls, five plates, three cups, two square vegetable dish covers, an oval mazarin and an oval platter.

c1840   *Platter 16.5in (42cm) long*

£3,000-3,500   **SI**

A 19thC Chinese famille rose porcelain vase, of ovoid form, cylindrical neck, the shoulders applied with peach tree branches in high relief on a black ground, Qing Dynasty.

22.5in (57cm) high

£800-1,000   **SI**

A 19thC Chinese famille rose porcelain vase, of baluster form, with alternating cartouches enclosing figural and floral decoration, domed cover.

26in (66cm) high

£400-500   **SI**

A 19thC Chinese famille rose hu-shaped vase, with iron red side handles, each face painted with figures in various pursuits, unmarked.

10.75in (27cm) high

£500-600   **WW**

A 19thC famille rose baluster vase, decorated with phoenix perched amongst flowering peony and magnolia issuing from pierced rockwork, and pierced wood cover.

3.75in (35cm) high

£350-400   **DN**

A late 19thC Chinese export porcelain rose mandarin covered vegetable dish.

9.5in (24cm) long

£350-450   SI

A late 19thC Chinese rose mandarin gravy boat.

£220-280   SI

A late 19thC Chinese export porcelain rose mandarin platter.

18.5in (47cm) long

£1,000-1,500   SI

A late 19thC Chinese small rose mandarin teapot.

4.5in (11.5cm) high

£200-300   SI

Four late 19thC Chinese export porcelain rose medallion plates.

9.75in (24cm) diam

£100-150   SI

A 20thC Chinese export rose medallion porcelain umbrella stand.

24in (61.3cm) high

£700-800   SI

An early 19thC Canton dish, painted with a figure scene within a fret-pierced border.

£400-450   HamG

A large 19thC Chinese jar, decorated in underglaze blue in Transitional-style with figures, rocks and plantains.

15.5in (39cm) high

£1,000-1,500   DN

A China trade porcelain plate, painted to the centre with a bird-of-prey on an anchor, the rope forming the initials "J.H.", within an unusual blue enamel banded and gilt foliate scroll-decorated border.

The naval theme probably related to a London merchant who either traded or controlled ships to Canton.

c1800

7.75in (19.5cm) diam

£55-65   HamG

A Jiaqing coffee can, painted in famille verte enamel colours with a crest, probably for Radcliff or Walcott, between two five clawed dragons amidst scrolled clouds, against a café au lait ground.

c1815   2.5in (6.5cm) high

£100-150   HamG

A pair of Chinese porcelain baluster vases, with domed covers painted with prunus blossom against a dark blue ground.

11in (28cm) high

£220-280   GorL

A pair of Chinese green lead-glazed censers, raised on five legs issuing from dragon masks, paw feet, in Han-style, with wood covers and stands.

3.25in (8.5cm) high

£180-220   DN

Two Chinese wine cups, with green interiors, the exteriors decorated with dogs of Fo and dragons and a phoenix, with ormolu mounts.

2.5in (6.5cm) high

£35-45   DN

A pair of Chinese porcelain bowls and covers, decorated with lotus, with later gilt metal mounts and set up as censer and cover with vine knops and pierced border, some damage.

6.75in (17.5cm) high

£350-450   DN

A Japanese Satsuma earthenware vase, decorated with panels of warriors and domestic scenes with brocade panels, in polychrome enamels and gilding.

12in (30.5cm) high

£1,200-1,800   GorL

A 19thC Satsuma vase, cylindrical and painted with flowers in bright enamels.

10.5cm (26cm) high

£70-80   GorL

A Kutani earthenware bowl, the interior decorated with a square reserve depicting immortals surrounded by floral and bird reserves on a iron red ground with gilt scrolling foliage, the exterior with floral, figural and landscape reserves and a leaftip border, Meiji period.

8.75in (22.5cm) diam

£120-180   SI

A Japanese Satsuma earthenware bowl, with satsuma mon, figural and dragon decoration, signed, Meiji period.

12in (30.5cm) diam

£600-700   SI

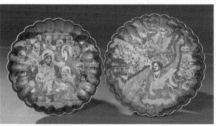

Two Japanese Satsuma earthenware chargers, of circular ribbed form, with scalloped rim, with dragon and figural decoration, Meiji period.

12.5in (32cm) diam

£600-700   SI

A Japanese Satsuma earthenware teapot, of flattened circular form, with a gilt dragon form handle and spout, floral decoration, Meiji period.

6in (15cm) diam

£180-220   SI

A late 19thC Satsuma ovoid vase, relief-moulded with male figures against an iron red and gilt ground, inscribed Hododa.

9.5in (24cm) high

£100-150   GorL

A late 19thC Japanese earthenware bottle vase, decorated with flowering branches of prunus and chrysanthemum within decorative border, with pierced and carved wood stand.

7.5in (19cm) high

£300-400   DN

A Satsuma pottery vase, of panelled baluster form, painted and gilded with immortals resting on clouds on a dotted ground, the shoulder decorated with fan and star-shaped motifs, seal mark to base, late Meiji period.

9.5in (24.5cm) high

£180-220   BonS

A Satsuma pottery vase, of baluster form, the shoulder and neck applied with pierced demi "mon" handles, decorated with Samurai warriors, birds amid peonies verso, probably late Meiji.

15.5in (39cm) high

£350-450   BonS

A Satsuma figure of bearded man, carrying a fan and bucket on back, clothed in a loose-fitting robe, brocaded with roundels.

12.5in (31.5cm) high

£180-220   **GorL**

A Japanese Kutani deep-footed bowl, decorated inside with a bird and clouds within iron red borders, the exterior with a continuous band of ducks and water plants, leaf band to the foot.

7.5in (19cm) diam

£180-220   **DN**

A Chinese agate snuff bottle, of pebble form, carved to depict a tree.

£200-250   **SI**

A 19thC Chinese agate snuff bottle, of flattened rectangular form with rounded shoulders, carved in high relief to depict a crane under a pine tree.

£350-450   **SI**

A Japanese earthenware U-shaped bowl, decorated with a band of fruiting branches.

4.75in (12cm) diam

£55-65   **DN**

A Japanese Raku-type bowl, the slightly conical body covered in a crackled glaze trailed in green and with stylized characters, seal mark.

5.25in (13.5cm) diam

£55-65   **DN**

A pair of Oriental slender baluster earthenware vases, each decorated with panels of figures on a brocade ground, both damaged.

6in (15cm) high

£60-80   **DN**

A Japanese Imari pail, with high-arched handle and decorated in underglaze blue with brocade panels over crashing waves.

15.5in (39.5cm) high

£800-900   **DN**

SNUFF BOTTLES

- Snuff is made from ground tobacco, often mixed with herbs or spices to improve its aroma. Tobacco originated in the Americas but had reached major European ports by the early 1600s. It was considered a more genteel way of consuming tobacco than smoking and reached the height of its vogue in Europe in the late 17th century.

- It is unclear how snuff and tobacco were first introduced to China, but it is possible that it came via Japan from Portuguese and Spanish traders. The first recorded mention is of a gift from the Jesuit missionary Father Enrico Ricci to the Qing Dynasty emperor in the late 17thC.

- As with Europe, smoking was unpopular with authorities in China and was banned during the Ming dynasty and into the Qing dynasty. As a result, with further influence from the West, snuff became the acceptable way of taking tobacco.

- As snuff became more popular, so the production of snuff bottles became more artistic and diverse. This was particularly so during the reign of emperor Chien Lung (1736-1796) under whose patronage the imperial workshops reached their peak. As well as practical vessels, these increasingly elaborate bottles became popular as gifts to dignitaries or court officials.

Two early 20thC Chinese snuff bottles, comprising one in agate of flattened ovoid form, carved to depict a bird perched on a rockery, the stone with russet and chocolate inclusions and one in celadon jade of flattened ovoid form, carved to depict a pagoda amongst flowering trees.

£150-200   SI

A fine Chinese shadow agate snuff bottle, of flattened rectangular form with rounded shoulders, carved to depict a large raptor standing on one talon and a smaller bird flying above, the stone of grey tone with café-au-lait and chocolate inclusions.

£450-550   SI

A 19thC Chinese moss agate snuff bottle, of flattened rectangular form, the stone a light grey tone suffused with moss-like green.

£180-220   SI

A 19thC Chinese shadow agate snuff bottle, Qing dynasty, of flattened rectangular form with rounded shoulders, carved through the brown skin to depict a cat. butterfly and flying magpie, the reverse a cicada, carved lion mask ring handles on the shoulders.

£400-600   SI

A Chinese cinnabar snuff bottle, of flattened ovoid form, carved to depict a dragon chasing the flaming pearl of wisdom.

£120-180   SI

A Chinese enamelled glass snuff bottle, Qianlong mark, of flattened rectangular form, with a bird and floral decoration.

£500-600   SI

A Chinese copper enamel European-subject snuff bottle, Qianlong mark, of flattened ovoid form, painted to depict a European lady in an orchard, enclosed within a medallion with blue foliate border, surrounded by a floral and foliate motif.

£1,000-1,500   SI

A Chinese blue glass overlay snowfleck snuff bottle, of flattened form, carved to depict scholars and attendants.

£200-300   SI

A 19thC Chinese inside-painted glass snuff bottle, Qing dynasty, of flattened ovoid form, painted on one side to depict a mountainous landscape, the reverse a praying mantis stalking two crickets on rockery, signed 'Yan Yutian', inscribed with red seal of Yutian.

£650-750   SI

A Chinese three-colour overlay on snowflake glass snuff bottle, of flattened rectangular form, carved in green, blue and pink overlay to depict fish, fans, chimes and lotus.

£400-600   SI

A Chinese ivory snuff bottle, of flattened ovoid form, carved in low relief to depict a man on horse back and boy, the reverse with calligraphy.

This is a commemorative snuff bottle, produced for one of the snuff bottle conventions.

£150-200   SI

A Chinese grey jade bottle, of pebble form.

£180-220 SI

A 19thC Chinese jade snuff bottle, of double-gourd form, carved in high relief through the darker skin to depict on one side opposing dragons; the other, fruiting gourd vine.

£150-200 SI

A 19thC Chinese celadon jade snuff bottle, of flattened rectangular form, carved to depict a frog overlooking fruiting gourds with vine and tendrils, the stone of celadon tone with apple green inclusions.

£650-750 SI

A 19thC Chinese celadon jade snuff bottle, carved to depict a goldfish, with carved details.

£150-200 SI

An unusual Chinese porcelain snuff bottle, modelled as a chilli pepper, with spinach jade stopper and overall red glaze. *c1800*

£900-1,100 SI

A 19thC Chinese rock crystal snuff bottle, Qing dynasty, of flattened rectangular form, undecorated body with bevelled corners.

£400-600 SI

A 19thC Chinese rock crystal coin snuff bottle, Qing dynasty, of flattened circular form, carved with a Spanish coin portrait design and inscription, the reverse with clock dial with Roman numerals.

£550-650 SI

A CLOSER LOOK AT A SNUFF BOTTLE

The technique of inside-painting was invented specifically for snuff bottles and is unique to China.

Legend has is that inside painting began after a court official scratched the inside of his glass bottle when he scraped out the snuff with a sharpened bamboo stick.

Artists used matchstick-sized bamboo sticks with a hooked end to paint the inside of the bottles.

A 20thC Chinese inside-painted rock crystal snuff bottle, of flattened ovoid form, painted to depict a river landscape amongst mountains, signed Wang.

£180-220 SI

Two Tibetan stone inlaid silver snuff bottles, one of rectangular form with turquoise and coral inlay and one of flattened ovoid form inlaid with stones on a filigree ground.

£120-180 SI

ORIENTAL

BRUSHPOTS

Japanese or Chinese brushpots were made as containers for artists' or calligraphers' brushes. The first ones were manufactured in the 16th century and were usually made from bamboo, porcelain or jade, and decorated with calligraphy or Oriental scenes. They are usually cylindrical in form. The use of polished hardwood was introduced from the 17th century. Today Oriental calligraphy is considered to be an elegant art form and brushpots have become highly sought after.

A white biscuit brushpot, intricately carved in low relief with figures in a landscape, mark of Chen Guozhi (1820-1860).

Chen Guozhi was a famous ceramic artist during the Qing Dynasty (1644-1911). He produced ceramic pieces that imitated the appearance of wood, bamboo and ivory.

5.75in (14.5cm) high

£500-600 DN

Two pale brown-glazed brushpots, one carved with two horses playing on a riverbank; the other a brown-glazed brush pot with prunus.

c1900   5in (12.56cm) high

£300-400 (pair) DN

A brown-glazed brushpot, carved in low relief with mountainscapes, mark of Zhang Maiyi.

5.25in (13.5cm) high

£350-450 DN

A pale-green glazed brushpot, carved in high relief with a Shou Lao and a boy beside a deer and five bats, mark of Tang Huxing.

6in (15.5cm) high

£550-650 DN

A tall green-glazed brushpot, by Li Yuchen, carved in high relief with cranes and deer under pine trees, wood stand.

11in (27.9cm) high

£800-1,000 DN

A green-glazed brushpot, carved with the eight horses of Mu Wang, mark of Li Yucheng.

6in (15cm) high

£850-950 DN

Two green-glazed brushpots, one carved in low relief with a landscape, the base with four character Guangxu mark, the other green-glazed and carved with cockerels.

c1900   5in (13cm) high

£300-350 (pair) DN

A pale yellow-glazed brushpot, by Li Yucheng, carved with monkeys playing in a landscape.

5.75in (14.5cm) high

£900-1,000 DN

A white biscuit brushpot, of lozenge section, carved in low relief with fishermen in a riverscape; and three further white biscuit brushpots, two carved with figures and one with rabbits.

6.75in (17.5cm) high

£220-280 DN

A Chinese light celadon jade brush washer, of cylindrical form, carved to depict a flowering prunus tree and calligraphy, late Qing/early Republic period,

4.7in (12cm) high

£320-380 SI

Three Yixing brushpots, each carved in imitation of a tree trunk, one with a 16-character inscription at the base.

Largest 5.75in (14.5cm) high

£180-220 DN

A 19thC Japanese ivory netsuke, of a boar with a monkey perched on his back, standing on an oval plinth carved with foliage on the border, Meiji period.

2in (5.2cm) long

£1,500-2,000 SI

A 19thC Japanese wood netsuke, of a cicada perched on a pine cone, Meiji period.

3.2in (8.2cm) long

£500-600 SI

A Japanese wood netsuke, of Tenaga and Ashinaga holding a fish, signed, Edo period.

£400-500 SI

A 19thC Japanese wood netsuke, of Okame seated holding his head with two hands, Meiji period

1.2in (4.5cm) high

£250-350 SI

Two Japanese ivory netsuke, one of Daikoku holding the rope of a performing rat upon two rice bales, signed 'Chokukazu', one of a hunter holding a rabbit by its ears and a pistol in the other hand, signed 'Masakazu', Meiji period.

Daikoku is the god of wealth and farmers and originates from India. He is usually depicted wearing a hood and standing on a bale of rice. He is also one of the Seven Lucky Gods of Japan.

Larger 1.7in (4.4cm) high

£1,200-1,500 SI

A Japanese ivory netsuke, of a nude mother and a child holding a bucket, Meiji period

£250-350 SI

Two Japanese Netsuke, one mask of Hyottoko in 'negoro' lacquer, one ivory mask of Hyottoko with a scarf around his head, signed.

£250-350 SI

A Japanese ivory kagamibuta netsuke, the plate inlaid in gilt with an oni holding a fish, Meiji period.

1.7in (4cm) diam

£180-220 SI

A 20thC Japanese horn netsuke, of a cat carved with C-form ears, a moustache and heavy tail, signed "Ken-Ji".

2in (5cm) long

£750-850 SI

A late 19thC Japanese cloisonne enamelled vase, of ovoid shape with bright orchids against a pale ground, Ando mark.

12in (30.5cm) high

£150-200   **GorL**

A Japanese silver wirework cloisonne vase, decorated with birds amongst prunus against a dark blue ground, Meiji period

12in (30.5cm) high

£450-550   **GorL**

A pair of Japanese dark blue ground cloisonné narrow neck vases, decorated with irises.

7.25in (18.5cm) high

£4,000-5,000   **GorL**

A Japanese cloisonné tray, enamelled with a view of Mount Fuji and pine trees in the foreground, the back with scattered flower heads and a seal, surface cracks.

9in (23cm) long

£4,000-5,000   **DN**

A Japanese cloisonné vase, of tall ovoid shape, enamelled with orchids against a pale ground.

9in (23cm) high

£200-250   **GorL**

A pair of Chinese inlaid bronze folding ship's candlesticks.

£45-55   **GorL**

A Japanese gilt bronze figure of an accountant, standing, fixed to a gilt brass inlaid rosewood stand, signed Miyau, Meiji period.

8in (20.5cm) high

£1,500-2,000   **GorL**

A fine Japanese gilt bronze figure of a fisherman, incised with gilt roundels and fixed to a gilt brass inlaid rosewood stand, signed "Miyao", Meiji period.

13in (33cm) high

£4,500-5,500   **GorL**

A Japanese gilt bronze figure of a carpenter, fixed to a gilt brass inlaid rosewood stand, signed "Maiyau", Meiji period.

8in (20.5cm) high

£1,500-2,000   **GorL**

A Japanese bronze round plaque, modelled in high relief with a lion's head, signed.

14.5in (37cm) diam

£700-800   **DN**

A mid-19thC Chinese ivory cricket cage, in the form of a gourd finely pierced with flowering branches on a pierced cell ground.

3.25in (8.5cm) high

£350-450   **DN**

A Chinese rock crystal figure of Pudai, the corpulent figure reclining on a cushion.

£100-150   **DN**

A Chinese white jade carving of a Ruji Scepter, Qing dynasty.

6.7in (17.2cm) long

£250-350   **SI**

A Chinese ivory cylindrical vase and cover, deeply carved with flowers and foliage, the cover with a knop carved as a farmer with an oxen, the knop damaged.

c1900   8.75in (22cm) high

£200-300   **WW**

A pair of yellow-glazed seals, each square column topped by a seated lion; and another yellow-glazed seal surmounted by an eagle perching on a pine tree.

Largest 4.25in (10.5cm) high

£400-450   **DN**

A Japanese iron and gilt tsuba, pierced and cast with five ducks in flight within a gilt diaper border, and a plain iron tsuba cast with three cranes.

3in (7.5cm) diam

£700-800   **DN**

A pair of 19thC Japanese iron tsuba, finely cast and pierced with scaly dragons, signed "Hiotsuyanagi Tomoyoshe at the age of 68".

3.5in (8.5cm) diam

£700-800   **DN**

A Japanese iron tsuba, probably 18thC finely pierced with stylised tendrils and droplets in gold.

3in (7.5cm) diam

£350-450   **DN**

A fine Japanese katana, with single-edged blade, the tang signed "Tsunemitsu", the grip covered with ray-skin, gilt copper tsuba and mounts with black lacquer scabbard with lacquer stand.

Blade 28in (71cm) long

£2,300-2,800   **L&T**

A 19thC Japanese red lacquer zushi, the doors with chased gilt metal mounts, the interior in gilt with the four armed Kannon seated on a pedestal.

9.75in (25cm) high

£450-550   **DN**

A Japanese black lacquer cabinet, of rectangular outline, with two doors opening to an interior with three small drawers, painted with feather decoration.

10in (25.4cm) wide

£120-180   **SI**

A 20thC Japanese carved ivory concentric ball on stand, having a naturalistic decorated shell containing approximately. ten pierced balls.

2in (5cm) high

£120-180   **GorB**

A carved ivory mystery ball, exterior carved with dragons and vines, the five interior balls pierced with holes around the exterior, ivory stand carved with an oriental gentleman holding a pillar on top of his head, which supports the ball, very minor loss to fins.

8.25in (21cm) high

£120-180   **JDJ**

Three views of a 19thC Japanese lacquer suzuribako and cover, the black ground decorated with a figure gazing at a rural landscape, the interior with figures pulling barges in a river landscape.

9in (23cm) high

£2,000-2,500   **DN**

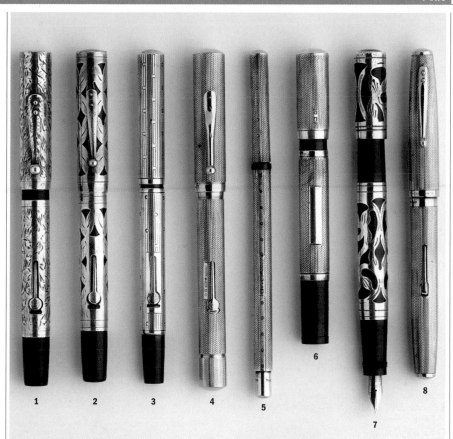

1 A 1920s Waterman's 452 'Hand Engraved Vine', marked "Sterling", with 2 nib, excellent, a lovely writer, engraved, replaced cap crown, recently overhauled.

£280-320   **CO**

2 A 1920s Waterman's 452 'Basketweave', marked 'Sterling', with 'Sterling' Clip Cap and 2 nib, lightly engraved name and initials, cap crown lip damaged.

£150-200   **CO**

3 A Waterman's silver overlaid 52, 'line and dot' overlaid lever-filler with Waterman's 2 medium nib, a rare pattern, slight oxidation on hard rubber, London hallmarks.
1933

£220-280   **CO**

4 A Waterman's 9ct gold 52, engine-turned overlaid lever-filler with 9ct gold clip and Waterman's 2 medium flexible nib, presentation inscription otherwise excellent/near mint, recently overhauled, London hallmark.
1939

£400-450   **CO**

5 A Waterman's silver [402] eyedropper, with alternating panels of barley and line-and-dot decoration, and Ideal 2 nib, quite rare, three dings in cap, 6mm split in barrel by section, London hallmarks.
1916

£120-180   **CO**

6 A Waterman's silver-overlaid 42, 'barleycorn' pattern overlaid black hard rubber retractable safety pen, with Waterman's 2 nib, in red Waterman's presentation box with papers, excellent/near inked mint, London hallmarks.
1920

£350-400   **CO**

7 A 1920s Waterman's 442V 'Filigree' safety pen, marked 'Sterling', with 2 nib, model number rubbed, two initials lightly scratched into the plate.

£180-220   **CO**

8 A Waterman's 9ct gold overlaid pen, 'barley' pattern engine-turned S.J. Rose overlaid lever-filler, with Waterman's 2 nib, excellent, London Coronation year hallmarks.
1953

£350-400   **CO**

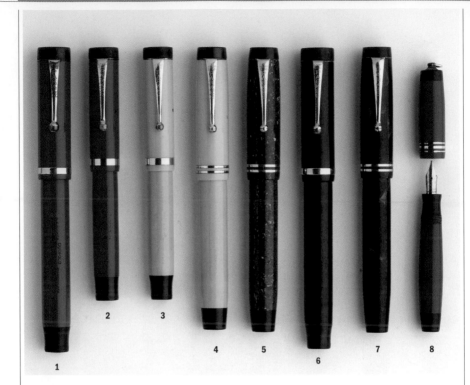

1 An American Parker Lucky Curve Duofold Senior, red Permanite, Canadian Duofold nib, very good but some brassing, clip screw chewed.

c1927

£120-180 CO

2 An American Parker Lucky Curve Duofold Junior, red Permanite, broad Duofold nib, ball on clip brassed, two scratches.

c1927

£40-50 CO

3 An American Parker Lucky Curve Duofold Junior, mandarin Permanite, Duofold nib, excellent, slight colour difference.

Yellow is one of the rarer colours for Duofolds. Collectors should examine the cap lip for cracks, which show up as grey lines.

c1927

£180-220 CO

4 An American Parker Duofold Senior, mandarin Permanite, Duofold nib, very good, band of colour difference beneath threads, light brassing.

1930s Duofolds can be told apart from 1920s versions by the streamlined shape of the ends. Compare those on this pen to No.1.

c1930

£400-450 CO

5 A Canadian Parker Duofold Senior, lapis Permanite, Canadian Duofold nib, near mint.

c1929

£500-600 CO

6 An American Parker Lucky Curve Senior, black Permanite button-filler with early Parker Lucky Curve medium nib, very good.

c1927

£120-180 CO

7 A Canadian Parker Duofold Senior, burgundy and black marble Permanite button-filler, nib split, otherwise excellent/near mint.

c1931

£150-200 CO

8 A Canadian Parker Vest Pocket Duofold Pen and Pencil, red Permanite button-filler with Parker Duofold pen nib, and matching rotary pencil, rare, especially in red, light brassing on cap bands.

Although red is one of the most common colours for other Duofolds, Vest Pocket Duofolds are rare in this colour.

c1932

£300-350 (set) CO

1   2   3   4   5   7   8

6

1 A Wahl Eversharp Oversize 'Deco Band' pen and pencil, black hard rubber lever-filler with Greek Key decoration and Gold Seal Manifold nib, with matching rotary pencil, minor brassing on pen, pencil near mint.

c1929

£300-350   **CO**

2 A Wahl Eversharp Oversize Gold Seal 'Deco Band', jade green plastic, with Gold Seal Manifold Post nib and roller clip, some discolouration.

c1929

£200-250   **CO**

3 A Wahl Eversharp Gold Seal Personal Point, coral Pyrolin, roller clip, and Gold Seal M Signature nib, excellent

c1929

£350-400   **CO**

4 A Wahl Eversharp Gold Seal Personal Point, black and pearl Pyrolin, roller clip, Gold Seal B Flexible nib, a difficult colour to find.

c1929

£150-200   **CO**

5 A mid-1920s Sheaffer Lifetime Senior, black lever-filler, with two bands and Lifetime 'number' nib, very good.

£50-80   **CO**

6 A Sheaffer's Lifetime Extended Balance Senior, pearl and black Radite, Lifetime nib, good, barrel pinched lightly in two places.

This plastic is often "browned" on the barrel due to sulphur in the ink sac. This is irreversible.

c1930

£80-120   **CO**

7 A Conklin Nozac, red, silver and black herringbone celluloid faceted Nozac-filler with Cushion Point medium nib, very good.

This is the most desirable colour Nozac.

c1932

£500-600   **CO**

8 A Carter's lever-filler, 'Pearl White' Pearltex, replaced 14K Warranted nib, together with a framed "Carter's, You Set the Pace" advert illustrating this pen, pen a rare colour in excellent condition.

c1931

£200-250   **CO**

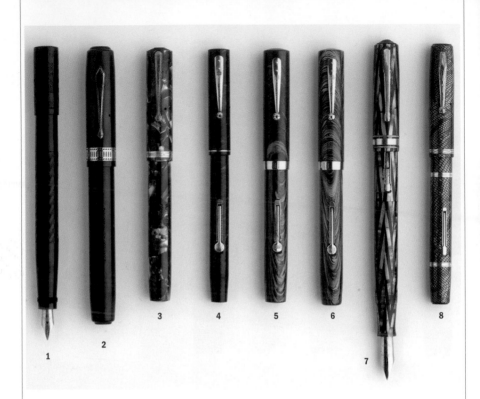

5 A Canadian Waterman's 94 ripple, blue ripple hard rubber lever-filler, with 9ct gold cap band and Ideal 4 fine nib, replaced lever, otherwise excellent.

Blue is one of the rarer ripple colours, the more common is the red/orange and black ripple which is worth less in a similar size.

1929

£200-250 CO

1 A 1920s American Waterman's 42, chased black hard rubber, with 2 nib, excellent.

This style of pen is known as a 'safety'. Twisting the bottom of the pen retracts the nib into the barrel. Safety pens were popular during the 1920s.

£35-45 CO

6 A rare Canadian Waterman's 94 ripple, olive ripple hard rubber, with 9ct gold cap band and Ideal 4 generous-medium nib, very good.

1928

£200-250 CO

2 A Canadian Waterman's Patrician pen and pencil, black hard rubber, Canadian Patrician medium nib, propelling pencil, lacks globe, light brassing and oxidation, clear imprints.

Black hard rubber Patricians are rare.

c1929

£280-320 (set) CO

7 A 1930s Canadian Waterman's Ink-Vue Deluxe, 'emerald ray' celluloid, keyhole 7 Canadian nib, fair to good.

This pen has a semi-transparent barrel allowing the user to see the ink supply.

£150-200 CO

3 A 1930s Canadian Waterman's 94, steel-quartz celluloid lever-filler with chrome trim and Waterman's medium nib, nib replaced, otherwise excellent.

£55-65 CO

8 A Canadian Waterman's 92, 'brown lizard' celluloid lever-filler, with slightly later English Waterman's 2 fine nib, very good, slight brassing on clip.

c1935

4 A 1930s Candian Waterman's 32?, red-flecked brown-black woodgrain celluloid, with Waterman's fine 2 nib, near mint, clip ball slightly brassed.

£80-120 CO **£180-220** CO

4 A 1930s-40s De La Rue 'The De La Rue Pen', un-numbered opaline pearl and black marble celluloid lever-filler, with bandless cap and unusual Onoto 14ct 5 nib, rare, hairlines in cap lip.

The cap on this pen is very prone to cracks due to the relative fragility of the plastic.

£80-120 CO

1 A De La Rue 9ct gold Onoto, barley design engine-turned fully-covered full-length plunger-filler with Onoto 3 nib, Onoto brown leather box, engraved "M.Y. Mary Rose 18-7-31" otherwise excellent / near mint, London hallmarks.
1919

£450-550 CO

5 A Burnham 'The Burnham', lapis blue and turquoise flecked caesin lever-filler, with Burnham 14ct gold fine nib, excellent.
c1927

£55-65 CO

2 A rare De La Ruc silver-overlaid Onoto, 'snail' overlaid cap and barrel marked "Sterling" with De la Rue nib, very good.
'Snail' refers to the ornate curling pattern on the overlay that resembles a snail's shell.
1915-20

£700-800 CO

6 A mid-1930s Ford's 'Large' Patent Pen, black hard rubber, phenomenally broad Ford 428 Mill 'spade' nib, with original instructions, inked mint.

£150-250 CO

3 A 1940s-50s De La Rue Onoto Magna 1703-35, chased black lever-filler with plain Onoto 7 medium nib, light marks on post.
Magna lever-fillers are rarer than the piston-filling mechanism that is usually found on Onoto pens.

£150-200 CO

7 A 1930s Dickinson 'The Croxley' Pen, lilac pearl marble lever-filler with juicy broad Dickinson nib, mear mint.

£35-45 CO

8 A scarce 1930s-40s Kingswood pen, rose herringbone celluloid button-filler, with correct Warranted nib, an attractive colour in excellent condition.

£50-60 CO

1 A Conway Stewart Duro, mottled red hard rubber, Conway Stewart nib with matching section and feed, near mint, noting minor brassing on clip and lever.

c1927

| **£350-400** | **CO** |

2 A 1920s Conway Stewart No. 200M, mottled red hard rubber, bandless cap, later Conway nib, excellent.

| **£80-100** | **CO** |

3 A rare Conway Stewart 1206, black celluloid lever-filler with two hallmarked 18ct gold bands and Duro nib, light posting wear, otherwise excellent.

1941

| **£55-65** | **CO** |

4 A Conway Stewart No. 266, blue pearl and black-veined marble celluloid button filler, with Conway Stewart medium nib, excellent, ball brassed, quite rare.

c1935

| **£120-180** | **CO** |

5 A 1950s Conway Stewart 60, blue and black-lined celluloid lever-filler, with firm fine Duro nib, excellent.

| **£100-150** | **CO** |

6 An extremely rare Conway Stewart 60, grey herringbone celluloid lever-filler, with broad cap band and 60 Duro nib, excellent/near mint.

The attractive grey herringbone Conway Stewart is far scarcer than well-publicised rarities such as the No.22 'Floral'. It was first brought to collectors' attention by Andreas Lambrou with the publication of "Fountain Pens of the World" in 1995, when the model 58 he illustrated was thought to be the only example. However, Conway Stewart also used the grey herringbone celluloid for their model 60 (essentially the same pen, but with different trim) and recent discussion among senior collectors has now identified a total of four or five known examples in these two versions. None has yet surfaced in any other size or model.

c1951

| **£700-800** | **CO** |

7 A 1950s Conway Stewart 60, 'cracked ice', silver pearl veined black celluloid, lever filler with Duro firm nib, excellent.

| **£150-200** | **CO** |

8 A Conway Stewart 22 'Floral', 'floral' celluloid laminated lever-filler with 5 nib, and box, very good, light darkening on barrel.

c1955

| **£250-300** | **CO** |

1 A 1920s Montblanc 2, octagonal black hard rubber safety pen, with Montblanc 2 nib, excellent, some wear to milled cap top.

£200-300 CO

2 A 1930s Danish Montblanc Masterpiece 25, coral push-knob filler, replaced Danish nib, good colour, engraved name on barrel.

£200-250 CO

3 A late 1930s/early 1940s Montblanc Meisterstück 136, black celluloid and hard rubber piston filler, with long ink window, unusual white cap star set within a metal ring, and metal 4810 nib, lacks tip, burn mark in threads.

The format of the cap star makes this an unusual pen.

£150-200 CO

4 A 1940s Danish Montblanc 244, green marbled celluloid piston-filler, with 4 nib, very good, one cap band slightly loose.

£100-150 CO

5 A 1950s Montblanc Meisterstück 144G, light silver-green striated celluloid piston-filler, with two colour 4810 nib, even discolouration.

£300-350 CO

6 A late 1950s Montblanc 254, black plastic piston-filler, with 'wing' nib, and original box and instructions, excellent/near mint.

£150-200 CO

7 A 1940s Pelikan 100, with grey and black striated celluloid sleeve, and Pelikan 14 K nib, fair, needs restoration.

£180-220 CO

8 A rare Pelikan 101N Weißgold, white rolled gold overlaid piston filler, with Pelikan .585 fine nib, cap top slightly brighter, otherwise excellent.

1938-39

£600-1000 CO

1 2 3 4 5 6 7 8

1 A Parker 51 'First Year' Blue Diamond Vacumatic, dove grey, with "Parker Made in USA" imprint around the blind cap, aluminium jewels, lined sterling silver cap and broad italic nib, good/very good.

Earlier Parker 51s from the 1940s used the 'vacumatic' system filling developed by Parker. To fill the pen, unscrew a small cap at the end of the barrel and press the small plastic or metal plunger.

1941

£280-320 CO

2 A 1950s English Parker 51 Insignia, teal blue aerometric-filler, with lustraloy cap and medium nib, a nice pen.

The 'aerometric' filler was used from the 1950s onwards and replaced the 'vacumatic' filling system on Parker 51s. To fill the pen, unscrew the barrel and squeeze the part of the metal cylinder that contains the latex ink sack.

£35-45 CO

3 A 1950s American Parker 51 Insignia, Midnight Blue aerometric-filler, with rolled gold cap and broad italic nib, juicy nib, pen worn.

£70-100 CO

4 A 1950s English Parker 51 Signet, with rolled gold cap and barrel and medium nib, a couple of small dings on barrel, light tool marks under clip.

£120-180 CO

5 A 1950s English Parker 51 Insignia, black aerometric-filler, with lustraloy cap and medium nib, excellent.

£45-55 CO

6 A 1970s Parker 61 Cirrus, finely-lined rolled gold 'cloud series' cartridge/convertor pen, with medium nib, tag and box, near mint, light scratch on barrel.

The delicately lined matt finish on this pen is very susceptible to wear. The 'Cirrus' is part of a series of pens with finishes that represented different cloud forms.

£70-100 CO

7 A Parker VP, red clean-filler, with transparent filler section, steel cap and broad oblique 75 'dial' nib, excellent.

This is a rare colour for a VP.

c1962

£80-120 CO

8 A Parker 'Royal Wedding' Pen, No 0491/1000, rolled gold bark-effect 'Royal Oak' 105, with medium nib, box, instructions, certificate and brown card outer, mint.

This pen was produced by Parker to celebrate the wedding of Prince Charles and Lady Diana Spencer.

1981

£550-650 CO

1 A Montblanc Agatha Christie No. 0116/4810, black Montblanc resin piston-filler, with vermeil snake clip marked "925", inlaid sapphire eyes and medium two-colour Agatha Christie 18k nib, with box, reply card, personal service card, card box and outer sleeve, mint.

The edition size of 4810 refers to the height of Mont Blanc in metres.

1993

£800-1,000 CO

2 A Montblanc Prince Regent No 4352/4810, gold-plated filigree-overlaid blue Montblanc resin piston-filler, with crown motif on cap and Prince Regent 18k medium nib, box, leaflet and card outer, mint.

1995

£1,000-1,500 CO

3 A mid-1990s Sheaffer Nostalgia 800, silver filigree cartridge/convertor pen, with import hallmark, two-colour Sheaffer medium nib, box and packaging dated 1997, mint.

£280-320 CO

4 A Conway Stewart Churchill 'The Writing Equipment Society 20th Anniversary' No 089/200, chased black hard rubber lever-filling pen, with Conway Stewart broad nib, box and packaging, mint.

2000

£150-200 CO

5 A Waterman Edson Signé Boucheron No 0622/3741, with 18ct gold filigree overlay by Boucheron on a blue Edson pen, with Waterman medium nib, with box.

1996

£600-700 CO

6 A Pelikan Souveran M850, green and black striped piston-filler, with vermeil cap marked "925", and two-colour 18k gold broad nib, mint and boxed.

c2000

£200-250 CO

7 A Henry Charles Simpole Snake pen No 250/250, hard-rubber button-filler with silver filigree overlay of two snakes each set with emerald eyes, mint and boxed.

This pen was inspired by the legendary Waterman and Parker snake pens of the 1900s-1910s.

2001

£450-550 CO

8 An Anthony Elson "Worshipful Company of Goldsmiths" pen, silver Montegrappa-style cartridge/convertor pen, with an engraved design showing the leopard's head, demi-maiden and motto "justitia virtutum regina" of the Worshipful Company of Goldsmiths with 18ct gold nib, mint, London millennium hallmark.

2000

£250-300 CO

A 1920s Wahl-Eversharp fountain pen desk set, onyx base decorated with a spelter dog (probably an English Setter), with two "Wahl-Eversharp Fountain Pen Desk Set" stickers, green/bronze marble celluloid tulip and matching Gold Seal desk pen with Wahl-Eversharp Signature nib, dog fatigued and lacks a paw.

£180-220 | **GorL**

A 1930s Dunhill Namiki maki-e lacquer bridge pencil, signed by Kosai and bearing the Namiki kanji, depicting three playing cards in takamaki-e on a roiro-nuri background.

3in (8cm) high

£200-300 | **PC**

An olive green blown three-mould diamond-pattern glass inkwell, made by Keene, New Hampshire.

c1830   2.25in (5.5cm) diam

£400-450 | **RAA**

A 1930s Dunhill Namiki urushi-e and maki-e lacquer deskbase, signed by Kosan and depicting a bird eating cherries from a basket, executed in takamaki-e and urushi-e on a roiro-nuri background.

Produced under the shortlived partnership of Namiki Manufacturing of Japan and Alfred Dunhill Ltd of London, this rare and unusual deskbase shows two types of lacquerwork, the more usual maki-e where the pigment is sprinkled onto the lacquer before it hardens and the scarcer urushi-e where lacquer and pigment are applied with a brush.

6in (15cm) wide

£300-400 | **PC**

An 1890s F. Soennecken Soennecken's Tintenfasser No. 276, shaped wooden base with grooved pen rest on three sides, ornate metal corner mounts, and ornate circular brass lift-up inkwell cover marked "SOENNECKEN'S PATENT" over a pale blue glass liner with graduated base, two chips to liner.

6in (15cm) wide

£100-150 | **GorL**

A 1930s marbled cast phenolic pen desk base, with hard rubber tulip.

4in (10cm) high

£30-40 | **JBC**

A European pewter writing set, probably Dutch, comprising three holders with long drawer on bottom, removable sander, covered ink box and open round box, possibly later.

11in (28cm) wide

£150-200 | **JDJ**

A Tiffany Studios 'Zodiac' pattern eight-piece desk set, comprising a pair of bookends, hexagonal inkwell, rolling blotter, calendar frame, pen tray and a pair of blotter ends.

1899-1928   19.5in (49.5cm) l

£1,500-2,000 | **SI**

A Tiffany Studios 'Zodiac' pattern seven-piece desk set, comprising two blotter ends, pin tray, inkwell, stamp box, covered pad holder and paper clip, signed on bottom "TIFFANY STUDIOS NEW YORK", some wear to finish.

£1,200-1,800 | **JDJ**

A Bradley & Hubbard seven-piece desk set, cast bronze with pattern of draped garlands, ribbons and shield centre, comprising letter rack, calendar, flat blotter and four blotter corners, signed "BRADLEY & HUBBARD".

£120-180 | **JDJ**

An American gilt-bronze seven-piece desk set, probably by Bradley & Hubbard, including inkwell, stamp box, pen tray, letter opener, calendar, envelope rack and blotter corners, each with pierced foliate design against mother-of-pearl, unmarked, hinge broken on stamp box, stand missing from calendar.

c1920

£300-350 | **FRE**

A George III oval silver inkstand, with gadrooned and pierced borders on four ball-and-claw feet, with a cut glass well and a pounce pot, by John Weldring or James Wiburd, London hallmarks.

1771   7in (18cm) high

£300-350   **DN**

A silver inkwell, by J.C.E. Dington, London.

1845

£1,000-1,500   **GS**

A silver inkstand, with two glass inkwells, by Charles and George Fox, London.

1848   7in (18.5cm) wide

£800-1,000   **JBS**

A Viennese bronze and crystal inkstand.

c1870   5in (13cm) wide

£200-250   **SS**

An unusual Victorian olive wood plough inkstand.

c1870   7.75 (20cm) wide

£200-250   **MB**

A brass lobster inkwell.

1860   13in (33cm) long

£550-650   **SS**

A Victorian papier-mâché rectangular inkstand, with two square-section cut glass wells, painted with landscapes, within gilt scroll borders.

10.5in (26.5cm) wide

£80-120   **LFA**

A French cut glass and silver inkwell, with miniature portrait of a lady in 19thC dress set in lid, by Tiffany and Co, Paris.

c1890   5.5in (14.5cm) high

£1,000-1,200   **JBS**

A mid-to late 19thC pottery phrenology head pen stand, the regions of the brain inscribed in gilding, on a scroll-moulded base, chip to tip of nose, light wear to gilding.

Phrenology was invented in the late 18th century by a Viennese doctor. It explained how the brain was the source for all human intellectual capacity and character traits, and that each part of the brain represented a different trait. According to this science the shape of the head reveals the character and intellect of a person. Hence, by measuring the shape of the head, practitioners could tell what type of a person they were. Unsurprisingly, phrenology had been dismissed as a 'quack science' by the mid-19th century. Collectors should beware of the great many modern reproductions on the market.

£250-300   **DN**

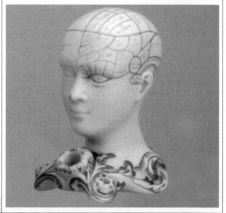

A CLOSER LOOK AT AN INKWELL

Very strong high Victorian styling and decoration with the entire design by John Huskinson, an in-house designer working in the 1880s at the Doulton factory.

Each piece is hand decorated and signed by the artist. This piece is signed 'ES' for Eliza Simmance, a famous woman artist in the Doulton factory.

The 'Isobath' was made for Thomas de la Rue who are better known for producing bank notes and also the 'Onoto' range of fountain pens.

Crimped edge acts as a pen rest, allowing pen to be laid down.

The inkwell is filled under this lid, where a swivel mechanism inside regulates inkflow to the well.

The writer would dip his nib here to replenish his pen.

This very rare inkwell is hard to find in complete condition as the base and lid chip easily and the interior mechanism is often lost. This inkwell is desirable as it crosses typical period styling with a mechanical and functional interest.

A rare Royal Doulton Lambeth 'isobath' inkwell.
c1888

6.5in (16.5cm) high

£400-600 **MHC**

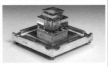

A silver inkstand, with two crystal inkwells, London hallmarks for 1903.
£800-1,000 **GS**

A late 19thC cast-iron inkwell, with sphinx to front and vertically-mounted thermometer to rear, with rose-glass inkwell, the whole mounted on a base with acanthus leaf motifs.

9in (23cm) high

£80-120 **MHC**

An Edwardian single inkstand, on a silver base, with London hallmarks and dated.
1911

£550-650 **GS**

A silver inkstand, of shaped outline, with two square glass and silver-mounted inkwells and inscribed with a presentation inscription, by Horace Woodward & Co Ltd, London hallmarks.

1906

10.75in (27.5cm) wide

£250-300 **DN**

A cut glass and silver inkwell, with desk calendar, by Mappin & Webb, Birmingham hallmarks.

1909 3.5in wide

£800-900 **Tag**

A silver double inkstand, with Birmingham hallmarks and dated.
1912

£750-850 **GS**

An oblong silver inkstand, with reed-and-ribbon border, a central oval sand box and two pen recesses, on ball-and-claw feet and with silver-mounted inkwells, by Horace Woodward & Co Ltd, London hallmarks.

1913   *10.25in (26cm) wide*

£250-300   **DN**

A 1920s carved wooden inkwell and pen rest, the head of a terrier forming the lid of the inkwell.

7.25in wide

£550-650   **Tag**

A cut glass inkwell, with silver watch set into the cap, Birmingham hallmark.

1917   *3.5in (9cm) high*

£1,500-2,000   **Tag**

FIND OUT MORE...

'Inkstands and Inkwells', by Ted & Betty Rivera, Crown Publishing, June 1973, ASIN: 0517504197.

'The Collector's Guide to Inkwells', by Veldon Badders, Collector Books, October 1997, ISBN: 1574320203.

Scrytion Museum, Spoorlaan 434a, 5038 CH Tilburg, The Netherlands. A museum housing over 1,200 inkwells and inkstands, amongst other exhibits relating to the evolution of script.

A silver inkstand, of concave oblong outline, by Asprey & Co Ltd, Birmingham hallmarks.

1935   *7.75in (19.5cm) wide*

£180-220   **DN**

A silver desk inkwell, of oblong shape with waisted and faceted well, with Birmingham hallmarks and dated.

£320-380   **GS**

A Continental Art Deco marble two-piece desk set, including a double inkwell and pen tray of heavily veined grey marble, with matching letter rack, one inkwell missing glass liner.

c1935

£100-150   **FRE**

PICNIC SETS

PICNIC SETS

- Although sets of accessories are known for use with carriages, the advent of the automobile saw the development of true picnic sets, with their 'golden age' beginning at the turn of the 20th century. Weekends out in the car had never been such fun!

- Early sets were very simple, catering for two people, but around 1910, as cars became increasingly lavish, so did picnic sets, which catered for up to six people. Some were integral parts of cars, fitting onto the running boards or boots/trunks.

- The earliest sets from the turn of the century are usually contained in wicker baskets, with leather and leather cloth covered boxes and wooden boxes being made from the 1920s onwards. Leathercloth was cheaper than leather, and became very popular during the 1930s. Black is the most common colour, with racing green appearing in the 1930s and other colours from the 1950s onwards.

- There are two standard types of set; those in suitcase form and those with fold down fronts, which tend to be the most sought after. The fold down front often has a metal panel on the interior, acting as a surface for the kettle and stand.

- Sets vary in their sophistication and variety of contents. Those with more accessories will fetch higher prices, with simple sets having lower values. Personal tastes and orders were catered for and many examples show complicated variations or a plethora of special implements. Sets containing original accessories made by noted manufacturers, such as plates by Minton or cutlery by Asprey, will also attract higher prices.

- Coracle is one of the most collected names, with sets usually being in a suitcase form covered in black leather cloth. Other renowned and collectable names to look for include Finnigan's (a central London luxury goods retailer), Drew, Vickery, Mappin & Webb and Louis Vuitton. Asprey sets from the mid 1930s were entirely made by Coracle.

- After the Second World War, the 'golden age' of picnic sets ended. Costs of manfacture rose, and those companies who only made picnic sets closed. Inexpensively produced, brightly coloured sets took over, made to match the cars of the time.

A wicker fold-fronted picnic set, by Drew, for four persons. *1910*

£3,000-4,000   FFA

A wicker fold-fronted picnic set, by Coracle, for four persons. *c1920*   *27.5in (70cm) wide*

£4,000-5,000   FFA

A wicker fold-front picnic set, by Coracle, for two persons. *c1908*   *11.75in (30cm) wide*

£2,000-2,500   FFA

A rare leather fold-fronted picnic set, by Coracle, for two persons, with suede interior and gilt Coracle stamp in lid. *c1908*

£2,500-3,000   FFA

A leather fold-fronted picnic set, by Mappin and Webb, for two persons, with grey interior. *c1906*   *14.25in (35cm) wide*

£2,500-3,000   FFA

A 1920s fold-fronted picnic set, by Coracle, for four persons.

£4,000-5,000   FFA

A leathercloth fold-fronted picnic set, by Coracle. for six persons. *c1909*   *23in (76cm) wide*

£4,000-5,000   FFA

A curved footrest picnic set, by Coracle, for four persons, with grey leathercloth interior. *c1906*   *21.5in (55cm) wide*

£7,000-9,000   FFA

A footrest picnic set, by Finnigans, for six persons, with black leathercloth interior. *c1909-1914*   *27in (69cm) wide*

£10,000-15,000   FFA

'STEP BOARD' AND 'FOOT REST' SETS

- 'Step board' and 'foot rest' sets were first introduced around 1904, and were made by all the major manufacturers, fitting onto the running board or into the foot-well behind the front seats.
- All classic cars of this period were different, and the range of styles and sizes varies with them. 'Step board' sets had flat surfaced cases and 'foot rest' sets had angular or curved cases, to match and fit their location.
- Both varieties were mainly fitted to Rolls Royce 'Ghosts' and 'Phantom' series cars. By 1925, production had largely ceased. Today, they are highly sought after, fetching high prices when found for sale.

An angled foot rest picnic set, by Coracle, for four persons.
c1909-14   *22.5in (57cm) wide*

£15,000-20,000   **FFA**

A flat stepboard picnic set, by Coracle, for four persons, specifically designed to fit on a running board of a Rolls Royce Ghost.
c1909-14   *35in (89cm) wide*

£8,000-10,000   **FFA**

A leather suitcase picnic set, by Asprey, for two persons.
c1906   27.5in (30cm) wide

£1,000-1,500   **FFA**

A leathercloth suitcase picnic set, by Coracle, for four persons.
c1925-36 23.5in (60cm) wide

£3,000-4,000   **FFA**

A leather suitcase picnic set, by Asprey, with honey stained mahogany lined interior, fawn leathercloth lined lid and Asprey stamping in the centre of the plate support straps.
c1908   18in (46cm) wide

£5,000-7,000   **FFA**

A curved foot rest picnic set, by Coracle, for two persons, with trade plaque in gilt.
c1905   14.25in (36cm) wide

£4,000-6,000   **FFA**

A leather suitcase picnic set, by Asprey, for four persons, with racing green leathercloth interior and four Minton saucer plates.
c1910   17.75in (45cm) wide

£6,000-8,000   **FFA**

A wicker suitcase picnic set, by Drew & Sons, for two persons, wicker-cased with wood and red leathercloth interior.
c1905   18in (46cm) wide

£8,000-10,000   **FFA**

A 1920s leathercloth suitcase picnic set, by Vickery, for six persons, with honey leather edged case.
31.5in (80cm) wide

£10,000-12,000   **FFA**

A running board picnic set, by Asprey, for four persons.
c1910

£6,000-8,000   **FFA**

BAKELITE

- Not all early plastics are 'Bakelite'. Real Bakelite can be identified by rubbing it for two minutes with your finger. If the item is Bakelite this will produce a strong carbolic smell.
- Tagged as 'the material of 1,000 uses', Bakelite was developed by the Belgian Dr Leo Baekeland in 1907. Bakelite is considered the first important truly synthetic plastic after the discovery of celluloid in the 19thC.
- The adaptability of Bakelite and related plastics allowed for cost-effective mass production of products, hence some pieces are common.
- Bakelite and early plastics were produced in a multitude of colours. It is commonly found in shades of brown and black, but also blue, red and green which are scarcer and more collectable. These coloured pieces broke away from the dull monotony of wood, ceramics and metal, ushering in a new age of style and were connected with new fashions such as Art Deco and Industrial styling.
- Many plastic objects were aimed at the domestic market, most notably the radio but also kitchenalia. Plastic also had office and even industrial uses, such as with switches and insulators.
- Fabulously coloured Bakelite jewellery is extremely collectable and can fetch high prices. Look for bright colours and deep-cut designs made from a single piece of plastic.
- Although it provided cheer during the Depression and World War II, the post war invention of cheaper injection moulded plastics saw the end of the golden age of plastics.

A brown Bakelite cigarette box for Teofani cigarettes.

1920s 6.25in (15.5cm) wide

£30-40 **MHC**

A selection of English celluloid simulated tortoiseshell dressing table items.

1920s

£3-5 each **JBC**

Two Bakelite Thermos flasks with chrome plated metal handles.

1920s 10.25in (26cm) high

£30-40 each **JBC**

A tabletop crumb sweeper in green and black Bakelite.

1920s 6in (15cm) wide

£20-30 **JBC**

A De La Rue Enduraware multi-coloured Bakelite inkwell.

1920s 2.5in (6.5cm) diam at base

£10-20 **JBC**

A brown mottled Bakelite lidded circular pot.

1920s 5in (12.5cm) diam

£10-15 **JBC**

A brown mottled Bakelite vase on a pewter base.

1920s 7.5in (19cm) high

£30-50 **JBC**

A maroon mottled Bakelite box by Stadium.

1920s 3.5in (9cm) square

£15-20 **JBC**

A tortoiseshell celluloid jewellery box in the form of a grand piano.

The legs and lid prop are extremely delicate and are often found damaged.

1920s 5in (13cm) long

£40-60 JBC

A brown mottled Bakelite Kodak Hawkette No.2 folding camera.

This camera was given away as a free gift with selected products such as Cadbury's chocolates and was designed by E.K. Cole.

1927 7in (18cm) high

£30-40 MHC

A French brown mottled Bakelite mantle clock, by Blangy.

The distinctive Art Deco styling of this clock makes it highly desirable.

1930s 5.25in (13cm) high

£100-150 MHC

A brown mottled Bakelite toast rack.

1930s 5.5in (14cm) wide

£10-15 MHC

A blue Bakelite wall mirror.

These popular mirrors were made in a variety of colours, brown was the most common.

1930s 9in (23cm) wide

£20-30 MHC

A Plastalite desk lamp, designed by Wells Coates and manufactured by E.K. Cole Ltd.

E.K.Cole Ltd is better known as manufacturer of the famous round 'EKCO' Bakelite radios.

1930s 14.5in (37cm) high

£150-250 MHC

A Dunlop promotional ashtray, by Roanoid Ltd.

These came in a variety of colours but cracks affect the value considerably. The three black cigarette rests fold inwards into the ball over the ashtray to complete the sphere.

c1930 5in (12cm) diam

£100-150 MHC

A marbled Bandalastaware plate, cup and saucer.

Bandalastaware was used extensively in 1930s picnic sets. Manufactured by Brookes & Adams, it was made from urea formaldehyde under the tradename 'Beatl'. In 1929 a shop called the Beatl shop opened in London's Regent Street.

1930s Saucer 5in (13cm) diam

£20-30 MHC

A orange catalin cruet set.

1930s 2.5in (6cm) high

£30-40 MHC

Three novelty animal-shaped cast-phenolic napkin rings.

These were made in a variety of animal shapes and bright colours, some being mounted on small wheels.

1930s Hen 3in (7.5cm) high

£15-20 MHC

Four novelty animal-shaped cast-phenolic napkin rings.

1930s squirrel 3in (7cm) h

£15-20 JBC

A blue urea formaldehyde lemon squeezer.

1930s 5.25in (13.5cm) diam

£20-30 JBC

An Art Deco cream and brown swirl urea formaldehyde Hurricane cigarette box, made by Nutt Products Ltd.
c.1930 *8.75 in (22cm) wide*

£50-70 **JBC**

A 1930s pale blue and copper marbled celluloid dressing table set, boxed.
comb 7.5in (19cm) long

£40-60 **JBC**

Two urea formaldehyde and Bakelite Thermos ice buckets.
1930s *8.75in (22cm) wide*

£40-60 (each) **JBC**

A multi-coloured urea formaldehyde six-person tea service.
1940s *plate 6in (15cm) diam*

£40-60 **JBC**

A Parker brown Bakelite "Baccy Flap" tobacco holder.
1930s *3.5in (9cm diam)*

£15-20 **JBC**

A brown Bakelite lidded pot with ribbed feet, marked 'Seaforth'.
1930s *4in (9.5cm) diam*

£10-15 **JBC**

A green and white mottled urea formaldehyde jelly mould.
1930s *2.75in (7cm) diam*

£3-5 **JBC**

An Art Deco carved blue acrylic horse brooch.
1930s *4.25in (10.5cm) long*

£20-30 **JBC**

A rare pale green urea formaldehyde chandelier.
1930s *21in (53cm) wide*

£80-120 **JBC**

A Lingalonga Ware muffin dish, in orange marbled urea formaldehyde.
1930s *6in (15cm) diam*

£40-60 **JBC**

A marbled Bandalasta tea cup and biscuit tray.
1930s cup 3.25in (8cm) diam

£30-40 **JBC**

A pale green and white marbled urea formaldehyde Thermos flask from a picnic set.
1930s *8.25in (21cm) high*

£20-30 **JBC**

A set of four egg cups, in marbled urea formaldehyde.
1930s *1.75in (4.5cm) diam*

£20-30 **JBC**

A salt and pepper set, in blue and white marbled urea formaldehyde.
1930s *2.75in (7cm) high*

£25-35 **JBC**

A brown Bakelite and cream urea formaldehyde bird cigarette dispenser.

1930s   7.5in (19cm) long

£50-70   **JBC**

A carved phenolic chess set, boxed, by Grays of Cambridge, one pawn missing.

1930s   pawns 1.5in (4cm) high

£40-60   **JBC**

A brown mottled Bakelite 'Eloware' desk stand and double inkwell manufactured by Birkby's of Liversedge, England.

This piece is very rare as it is usually found as a cigarette box rather than as a desk stand with two internal inkwells mounted on a pen rest. The lid design is typical of the Art Deco styling of the period.

c1936   9in (23cm) wide

£100-150   **MHC**

A green Carvacraft stamp sponge holder.

These holders were often used as ashtrays and burns inside the well reduce the value considerably.

1940s   3in (8cm) wide

£60-80   **MHC**

A rare green acrylic and black Bakelite ink stand.

1940s   6.5in (16.5cm) wide

£100-150   **MHC**

A Kodak Bullet camera, black Bakelite with box.

1940s   4.75in (12cm) wide

£5-10   **JBC**

A brown mottled Bakelite desk telephone directory.

1940s   8in (20cm) high

£10-15   **MHC**

A maroon mottled Bakelite torch.

1940s   4.75in (12cm) long

£10-15   **JBC**

A pink urea formaldehyde floral flask, marked 'The British Vacuum Flask Co Ltd.'

1940s   10.5in (27cm) high

£30-40   **JBC**

An red and yellow urea formaldehyde egg cup.

1940s   1.75in (4.5cm) diam

£3-5   **JBC**

PLASTICS

A set of four mottled Bakelite napkin rings.

1940s   1.75in (4.5cm) diam

£10-15 for set   **JBC**

A brown mottled Bakelite fruit bowl on a Celtic Plate plated base, English registration number for 1945.

8in (20.5cm) diam

£100-150   **MHC**

An amber Carvacraft double pen holder.

c1948   6.5in (16.5cm) wide

£60-80   **MHC**

A CLOSER LOOK AT BAKELITE

This ink stand features period Art Deco styling with stepped sides. Collectors should look for design features that exemplify the styles of a period.

The form is 'streamlined' following the popular designs of the period.

The colour of the plastic is bright and colourful, breaking away from the dull browns and blacks of the preceding years.

The item is well made and bears the maker's stamp depicting a hammer on the underside – for Dickinson Products.

This item is in amber, one of the three colours used for Carvacraft. Green is the rarest. The third colour used was yellow.

This item is typical of collectable plastics in that it was manufactured for use in the home and office.

An amber Carvacraft double ink stand.

Carvacraft objects were manufactured by the English company Dickinson in the late 1940s from a cast phenolic resin. The range included blotters, calendars and notepad holders. Collectors need to look for cracks, chips, inkstains and burns which reduce the value considerably.

c1948   10.5in (27cm) wide

£80-120   **MHC**

A yellow Carvacraft memo holder.

c1948   5.75in (14.5cm) wide

£40-60   **MHC**

A white urea formaldehyde 'Rototherm' desk thermometer.

Made in England, the styling is typical of the popular Industrial design of the period.

late 1940s   6.75in (9cm) high

£20-30   **MHC**

A Carvacraft amber blotter, with the rare original box.

c.1948   6in (15cm) wide

£40-60   **JBC**

An amber Carvacraft notepad holder, paper knife and stamp sponge holder.

The paper knife is a rare item.

c1948   *8in (20.5cm) long*

£100-150 (set)   **JBC**

A green marbled Halex dressing table set (part shown).

1950s   *Tray 10.75in (27.5cm) wide*

£10-15 (part set)   **MHC**

Two polythene duck-shaped clothes brushes and holders.

1950s   *11.25in (28.5cm) high*

Grey £10-15 Blue £15-20   **JBC**

A lacquered wooden tray with cast phenolic handles, by Belvane Ltd of Andover, England.

1950s   *14.5in (37cm) l*

£30-40   **JBC**

A Park Green 'The Peter Piper' pepperpot, in red urea formaldehyde.

1950s   *3.75in (9.5cm) high*

£20-30   **JBC**

A blue and cream celluloid child's dressing table set, boxed.

1950s   *comb 4.5in (11.5cm) long*

£20-30   **JBC**

Two urea formaldehyde electric clocks, marked 'Smiths English Clocks Ltd.'

1950s   *5in (12.5cm) high*

£10-15 each   **JBC**

A B C D E F G H I J K L M N O P Q R S T U V W XYZ

Film Posters

- Condition is vital when considering posters. Collectors should look for tears, water stains (although these can often be removed), fading and missing areas that extend into the design as these will have a detrimental effect on value. However, as posters were made to be used, made from easily damaged paper and often folded for storage (particularly before 1970), it is difficult to find a poster in mint condition. Creases and multiple folds, whilst affecting value, should be taken into mind when working out a price but can be corrected.

- Good restorers can be found who can correct many problems, so collectors should always ask about restoration. Many posters are backed onto linen to make them more robust and easier to display. This work should always be completed by a specialist, who will probably give the poster a 'full service' at this point.

- Posters from the country of a film's original release are usually the most desirable. Posters were produced for each country the film was released in, and although these are still collected, collectors should be aware of differences – for example Belgian posters tend to be smaller, are in an unusual language but often have visually stunning artwork, whilst Australian posters, whilst in English and being more impactful due to their larger size, tend to have artwork of a lesser quality.

- The artwork and artist of any poster will count towards value. Although you should always choose an image that you like, some artists and images will be very desirable and prices may be high.

- Collectors should look for posters for films that captured the public's imagination, are considered cult films or classics, and are thus still popular. Posters for unknown or unpopular films will not be as desirable.

- One sheet film posters are the most popular amongst collectors and are sized at 27in x 41in. British quads are also popular at 30in x 40in.

- The romance of travel has always appealed, and railway posters have commanded a premium for some time. Look for attractive scenes of the landscape or destination. Posters for the main British domestic railways, GWR, LMS, LNER and SR, are desirable and fetch high prices. Collectors are now looking for the later British Rail posters.

- Fakes and forgeries are comparatively rare and can usually be readily identified. Reproductions are common however: these are often photographic images of a design printed on poster paper. Seeing originals will enable you to spot these easily, so visit an auction or a reputable dealer. Do not confuse 're-issue' posters for reproductions as these were made when the film was re-released at a later date.

"1941", US one sheet poster, matted, with an autograph of John Belushi (Captain Wild Bill Kelso), in blue ink, mounted, framed and glazed.

1979 48in (122cm) high

£350-450 **CO**

"An American Werewolf in London", one-sheet video and DVD release promotional poster signed by director John Landis and Griffin Dune (Jack Goodman) in black marker pen, framed and glazed.

42in (100cm)

£180-220 **CO**

"Barbarella", US 'B' style one sheet poster, linen-backed.

1968 41in (104cm) high

£800-1,000 **ATM**

"Blade Runner", US one sheet poster, second printing, linen-backed.

1982 41in (104cm) high

£200-300 **ATM**

"The Blues Brothers", US one sheet poster.

1980 41in (104cm) high

£100-200 **ATM**

"James Bond - Dr. No", US one sheet poster, linen-backed.

This US version is scarce. 2002 also marks the 40th anniversary of the release of this film.

1962 41in (104cm) high

£1,200-1,600 **ATM**

"James Bond – From Russia with Love", US one sheet 'B' style poster, linen-backed.

1964   *40in (101cm) high*

£2,500-3,500   ATM

"James Bond - You Only Live Twice", US 'C' style one sheet poster, artwork by Robert McGinnis, linen-backed.

1967   *40in (101cm) high*

£800-1,200   ATM

"James Bond - Moonraker", US one sheet poster, linen-backed.

1979   *41in (104cm) high*

£100-200   ATM

"Breakfast At Tiffany's", US 40x60 poster, linen-backed, framed and glazed.

With its stylish and iconic image of Audrey Hepburn with her cigarette holder, this classic poster has enormous appeal to poster collectors, film fans and many others.

1961   *60in (152.5cm) high*

£10,000-15,000   ATM

"James Bond - Tomorrow Never Dies", UK quad poster.

This version was withdrawn from circulation as 'Tommorrow' is mis-spelt in the credits.

1997   *40in (101cm) wide*

£65-75   ATM

"James Bond – Die Another Day", advance US one sheet poster.

2002   *41in (104cm) high*

£35-45   ATM

"Triple-O-Seven", UK one sheet triple bill promotional poster, advertising "Three James Bond Adventures In One Action Packed Programme" Octopussy", "For Your Eyes Only", "Thunderball", together with a double bill poster for "The Spy Who Loved Me" and "Moonraker".

£200-250   CO

"Bullitt", US one sheet poster, linen-backed.

1969   *41in (104cm) high*

£650-750   **ATM**

"Bunny Lake Is Missing", Spanish one sheet poster.

1965   *39in (99cm) high*

£80-120   **CO**

"Cat on a Hot Tin Roof", US 'B' style half sheet poster, paper-backed, framed and glazed.

1958   *28in (71cm) wide*

£500-600   **ATM**

"Charade", US one sheet poster, paper-backed, framed and glazed.

1963   *41in (104cm) wide*

£520-580   **ATM**

"Chinatown", German language A1 poster, artwork by Amsel, framed and glazed.

1974   *33in (84cm) high*

£480-520   **ATM**

"Get Carter", international one sheet poster, lined-backed.

1971   *41in (104cm) high*

£320-380   **ATM**

"The Godfather: Part II", US one sheet poster.

1974   *41in (104cm) high*

£100-150   **ATM**

"The Godfather", UK one sheet poster.

1972   *41in (104cm) high*

£500-600   **ATM**

FIND OUT MORE...

The International Vintage Poster Dealer Association.
www.ivpda.com

R. Allen, 'Vintage Hollywood Posters' (Volumes I & II), published by Bruce Hershenson, 1998.

"The Graduate", US one sheet poster, first year release 'B' Style Academy Award poster, linen-backed.

1967   *41in (104cm) high*

£200-300   **ATM**

"Halloween", one sheet promotional poster, signed by Jamie Lee Curtis, in black ink, framed and glazed.

1978   *37in (94cm)*

£220-280   **CO**

"A Hard Day's Night", US one
sheet poster, linen-backed.

1964   41in (104cm) high

£750-850   ATM

"Jaws", US one sheet poster,
linen-backed.

1975   41in (104cm) high

£420-480   ATM

"The Magnificent Seven", US
one sheet poster.

1969   41in (104cm) high

£220-280   CO

"Manhattan", US one sheet 'B'
bridge style poster.

1979   41in (104cm) high

£300-400   ATM

"Magnum Force", UK quad poster, designed by Bill Gold.

1973   40in (101cm) wide

£480-520   ATM

"Colpo Grosso" (Ocean's
Eleven), Italian due foglio (two
sheet) poster.

1960   55in (140cm) high

£280-320   CO

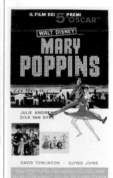

"Mary Poppins", Italian
locandina (insert) poster.

1964   28in (71cm) high

£80-120   CO

"The Party", US one sheet
poster, paper-backed, framed
and glazed.

*The artwork for this poster is by
Jack Davis, who is better known
as the artist for M.A.D. comics.*

1968   41in (104cm) high

£200-300   ATM

"Psycho", Italian language
photobusta, linen-backed,
framed and glazed.

1960

£350-450   ATM

"Raiders of the Lost Ark", UK
quad poster.

1981   40in (102cm) wide

£100-150   CO

"Raging Bull", advance US one
sheet poster, photography by
Kunio Hagio.

1980   41in (104cm) high

£250-350   ATM

"Raging Bull", US one sheet
poster.

1980   41in (104cm) high

£180-220   CO

"Return to Oz", design for promotional posters, comprising overlaid printed images, highlighted in paint and pen, by artist Michael Ploog, mounted, framed and glazed.

"Raiders of the Lost Ark", US one sheet poster.

1981   41in (104cm) high

£100-150   CO

"Return to Oz", design for promotional posters, highlighted in paint and pen, by artist Michael Ploog, mounted, framed and glazed.

1985   27in (68cm)

£450-500   CO

1985   27in (68cm)

£350-450   CO

"Blanche Neige et les Sept Nains (Disney's Snow White and the Seven Dwarfs)", Belgian language one sheet poster, paper-backed, framed and glazed.

1937   34in (86.5cm) high

£1,500-2,000   ATM

"Shaft", US one sheet poster, linen-backed.

1971   41in (104cm) high

£380-420   ATM

"Walt Disney's Sleeping Beauty", US window card.

1959   22in (56cm) high

£200-300   ATM

"The Sound of Music", US roadshow-style one sheet poster, linen-backed.

1965   41in (104cm) wide

£850-950   ATM

"The Sting", US one sheet poster.

1973   41in (104cm) high

£200-300   ATM

"Spider-Man", advance US one sheet double-sided poster.

This poster is extremely rare, it was re-called by Sony after the September 11th tragedy as it features the World Trade Center reflected in Spider-Man's eyes, making it a collector's item overnight.

2002   40in (101cm) high

£200-300   ATM

"Star Wars V: The Empire Strikes Back", 'Gone with the Wind'-style US one sheet poster, linen-backed.

1980   41in (104cm) high

£350-450   ATM

"The Terminator", UK quad poster.
1984   *40in (102cm)*

£200-250   **CO**

"The Thomas Crown Affair", UK quad poster, linen-backed.
1968   *40in (101cm) wide*

£200-300   **ATM**

"Thunderbirds Are Go", UK quad poster, framed, glazed.
1966   *41.5in (105cm)*

£450-550   **CO**

"Star Wars Episode I - The Phantom Menace", US 'B' style one sheet poster.

With artwork still remaining in the style of previous Star Wars film posters, despite being produced over 20 years later, this poster fits seamlessly into a Star Wars poster collection.

1999   *41in (104cm) high*

£200-300   **ATM**

Lobby cards

- Known as 'lobby cards' in the U.S. and 'front of house cards' in the U.K., these cards were made for advertising forthcoming films and placed in the foyer or entrance of cinemas.
- Lobby cards were usually produced in sets of eight (but sets of four and ten can also be found) with a title card accompanied by seven stills (single snapshots of scenes) from the movie. They are nearly always produced in colour and numbered.
- At 11in x 14in, American lobby cards are larger than front of house cards which are often only black and white stills from scenes in the film.
- Although it is most often preferable to have a complete set, single cards showing key scenes, lead characters or a visually appealing scene from the film are highly desirable. Value relates directly to the image depicted and its connection to the film.
- Pioneering and seminal genre films, such as science fiction or horror films, are highly popular amongst collectors, as are title cards.
- These cards can provide a way for collectors to collect contemporary visual imagery related to a film at a more affordable price than posters.

"2001 - A Space Odyssey", UK quad poster, re-release of the 1968 film.
2001   *40in (101cm) wide*

£50-80   **ATM**

"Titanic", US one sheet poster, signed by cast members including Kate Winslett (Rose De Witt Bukater), Leonardo DiCaprio (Jack Dawson), Billy Zane (Caledon 'Cal' Hockley) and Bill Paxton (Brock Lovett), framed and glazed.
1997   *42in (107cm) high*

£700-800   **CO**

"Black Christmas", set of eight UK front of house cards.
1974   *10in (25cm) wide*

£20-30   **CO**

"James Bond – Goldfinger", U.S. lobby card no. 1.
1964   *14in (35.5cm) wide*

£50-100   **ATM**

A B C D E F G H I J K L M N O P Q R S T U V W XYZ

"James Bond - The Man with the Golden Gun", US lobby card no. 1.
1974   14in (35.5cm) wide

£50-70   ATM

"James Bond - Octopussy", lobby card no. 8, mounted.
1983   14in (35.5cm) wide

£35-45   ATM

"Casablanca", Mexican lobby card, 1960s re-release of the 1946 film, mounted, central image replaced.
17in (43cm) wide

£100-150   ATM

"Casablanca", Mexican lobby card, 1960s re-release of the 1946 film, mounted, central image replaced.
17in (43m) wide

£100-150   ATM

"To Catch a Thief", US lobby card, mounted.
1955   14in (35.5cm) wide

£100-150   ATM

"Charade", lobby card no. 3, mounted.
14in (35.5cm) wide

£120-180   ATM

"The Hill", set of eight US lobby cards.
1965   11in (28cm) wide

£55-65   CO

"Let's Make Love", US lobby card no. 2, mounted.
1960   14in (35.5cm) wide

£100-150   ATM

"Marnie", US lobby card no. 4, mounted.
1964   14in (35.5cm) wide

£50-100   ATM

"Mary Poppins", set of twelve UK front of house stills.
1964   10in (25cm) wide

£100-150   CO

"The Nightmare Before Christmas", set of eight US lobby cards.
1993   14in (35cm) wide

£100-150   CO

"The Seven Year Itch", US lobby card no. 2, mounted.
1955   14in (35.5cm) wide

£200-250   ATM

Travel posters

"The Terminator", set of eight US lobby cards.

1984   *11in (28cm) wide*

£35-45   **CO**

"Vertigo", lobby card no. 3, mounted.

1958   *14in (35.5cm) wide*

£100-150   **ATM**

A Transaerienne, Paris lithograph poster, showing a dirigible balloon over the roofs of Paris, very colourful design, signed "Gatier", framed, some damage at edges.

This poster advertises airship flights above Paris and suburbs.

1915   *46.75in (119cm) long*

£1,200-1,800   **TK**

A KLM Airlines three-colour lithograph poster, depicting a single engine Focker airplane, signed, dated and framed.

1924   *33in (84cm) high*

£280-320   **TK**

A Beheer der Luchtvaart lithograph poster of the Belgian cargo airline, impressive illustration of several biplanes, background with "Hermes" and his winged helmet, signed "T.Michielsson", framed.

1925   *39.25in (99.5cm) long*

£1,300-1,500   **TK**

An early Imperial Airways lithograph poster, for the Baghdad-Basra air route, with illustration of a tri-motor biplane flying over the pyramids of Giza, signed "H. Cuther", framed and dated.

1927   *38.5in (98cm) long*

£1,500-2,000   **TK**

A Geneva Intercontinental Airport Switzerland poster.

    39in (99.5cm) high

£200-300   **DO**

A Koninklijke Luchtvaart lithograph poster, for the Dutch Airline airfreight company, showing the 'Flying Dutchman' with a pilot who explains the progress of aviation, framed.

1930   *41in (104cm) high*

£1,200-1,800   **TK**

A Hamburg-Amerika Linie five-colour lithograph poster of the airship 127 Graf Zeppelin, showing the air route from Hamburg, Germany to Rio de Janeiro, South America in three days, framed.

Due to their brief life as a reliable mode of mass transport, posters showing airships in this way are scarce. This example shows a very long distance route which seems incredible to us now.

1931

£1,500-2,000 TK

A British South American Airways 'A l'Amérique du sud' poster.

40in (101cm) high

£300-370 DO

A Deutsche Luftfahrt-Werbewoche 1932 five-colour lithograph poster, with two-seater aircraft, glider and hot-air balloon, framed.

1932 29in (48.5cm) long

£600-700 TK

A Lufthansa, Air France lithograph poster, showing the flight route Europe-South America, with an illustration of a Junker aircraft which goes around the world, with the German national emblem, showing all stopovers, framed.

1935 26.25in (66.5cm) long

£1,000-1,500 TK

A Soc. An. Aero Espresso Italiana lithograph poster, with an illustration of a single engine sea plane over the Aegean Sea, with the air routes, dated and signed "Keverta".

1932 39.25in (99.5cm) long

£800-900 TK

An American Overseas Airlines double Royal poster, designed by Jan Lewitt and George Him.

c1946 40in (101.5cm) high

£1,000-1,500 REN

An Air France three-colour lithograph poster, depicting an airplane flying over the jungle in Africa, signed "Guena", printed in France, framed and dated.

1946 39.25in (99.5cm) long

£800-1,200 TK

A British European Airways 'Meet the Spring - fly BEA' lithograph poster, with expressionistic depiction of an elegant lady on the runway signed, framed.

1948 41.25in (105cm) long

£500-600 TK

A Frederiksberg poster.

Frederiksberg is a popular beach in Denmark.

1938

£300-400   **DO**

A North Eastern Railways 'The Yorkshire Coast' quad royal poster, from the "Alice in Holidayland" advertising campaign, designed by Frank Mason.

c1910   *50in (127cm) wide*

£8,000-10,000   **REN**

A London & North Eastern Railways double royal woodcut-style 'Batchworth Heath' poster, unnamed artist.

c1924   *40in (101.5cm) high*

£1,000-1,500   **REN**

An L.M.S. railway poster, "Lowestoft", designed by Austin Cooper.

c1928   *50in (127cm) long*

£3,000-5,000   **REN**

A Southern Railways 'Canterbury' quad royal poster, designed by Leslie Carr.

c1928   *50in (127cm) wide*

£1,500-2,000   **REN**

A Great Western Railways 'Stratford Upon Avon' quad royal poster, from the series "This England of Ours", designed by Michael Reilly.

c1930   *50in (127cm) wide*

£3,500-4,500   **REN**

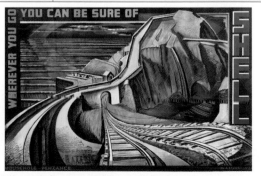

A Shell 'Mousehole, Penzance' poster from the "To Visit Britain's Landmarks" series, originally displayed on Shell lorries, designed by A. Stuart-Hill.

c1932   *45in (114.5cm) wide*

£4,000-6,000   **REN**

A London & North Eastern Railways 'Clyde Coast' quad royal poster, designed by Frank Mason.

1931   *50in (127cm) wide*

£2,000–2,500   REN

A Shell 'Folly Houses, Darley Abbey' poster from the "To Visit Britain's Landmarks" series, originally displayed on Shell lorries, designed by Rowland Suddaby.

c1935   *45in (114.5cm)*

£1,500–2,000   REN

A Shell Conchofile 'Explorers Prefer Shell' poster, designed by Edward McKnight Kauffer.

McKnight Kauffer is a celebrated poster artist. Born in Montana, he studied in Paris and San Francisco. After coming to London in 1914, he was commissioned by Frank Pick at London Transport to design posters. From there his popularity and commissions mushroomed. His work has been the subject of many retrospectives, including at the Museum of Modern Art, New York, and at the Victoria & Albert Museum, London.

1934   *45in (114.5cm) wide*

£4,000–6,000   REN

A London Transport 'Cut Travelling Time' double royal poster, designed by Tom Eckersley of Eckersley Studio.

c1968   *40in (101.5cm) high*

£600–800   REN

A London Transport 'Extension of the Piccadilly Line to Heathrow Airport' double royal poster, designed by Tom Eckersley, the foremost exponent of this "Swiss typographical" style.

1971   *40in (101.5cm) high*

£1,500–2,000   REN

Miscellaneous

A Bal du Moulin Rouge 'Femmes, Femmes, Femmes' poster.

24in (60.5cm) high

£80–120   DO

A Monis Cognac Fine Champagne poster.

17in (43cm) high

£120–180   DO

A Huntley & Palmers 'Dainty Afternoon Tea Biscuits' poster.

14.5in (36.5cm) wide

£40–60   DO

A Gibbs Cold Cream Soap poster.

14in (35.5cm) wide

£20–30   DO

A du Maurier 'The Most Widely Smoked Filter Cigarette in the World' poster.

30in (76cm) high

£100–150   DO

A Dunlop 'Fit Dunlop Tubes for Longer Life' poster.

30in (76cm) high

£200–250   DO

A Pneu Hutchinson 'Plus Solid que l'Acier' poster.

21.5in (55cm) high

£180-220 DO

A South African Oranges 'The Only Empire Summer Orange' poster.

20in (51cm) high

£180-220 DO

A Kodavox 'Pour Votre Magniphone, Produit Kodak' poster.

23.5in (60cm) high

£80-120 DO

A Daily Express 'A Help Your Neighbour...' poster.

23in (58cm) high

£60-80 DO

A Ministry of Food 'The Effects of Over-cooking and Keeping Hot' double crown poster, designed by Jan Lewitt and George Hlm.

c1941   30in (76cm) high

£600-800 REN

A Ministry of Food 'The Vegetabull' double crown poster, designed by Jan Lewitt and George Him.

c1941   30in (76cm) high

£600-800 REN

A Post Office Savings Bank 'War Production' quad crown poster, designed by Auben Cooper.

c1944   40in (101.5cm) long

£1,000–1,500 REN

A General Post Office 'Helps the Export Drive' quad crown poster, designed by Tom Eckersley of the Eckersley Studio.

1948   40in (101.5cm) wide

£1,500–2,000 REN

A 'Dick Whittington' David Allen & Sons poster.

27in (69cm) high

£200-300 DO

'A La Francaise Diamant' poster.

23.5in (60cm) high

£150-200 DO

An 'Exposition Internationale Mai-Novembre, Ministre du Commerce et de l'industrie' poster.

1937   12in (35.5cm) high

£120-180 DO

PRINTS

- Although not traditionally considered as 'collectables', modern prints are an accessible way of building a collection of works by usually unaffordable modern masters.

- There are three types of collectable prints: prints where production has been controlled by the artist; prints where the artist has full control but uses somebody else to assist; and finally prints where the artist has granted somebody else permission to make prints from an image. They are not poster prints where the image has been photomechanically reproduced on poster paper.

- Value is determined on the popularity of artist, the subject and visual appeal of the image, edition size and condition. The convention of numbering was introduced c1915. Look carefully at signatures, as some were 'in the block' meaning that the signature is part of the print (sometimes in reverse) and not signed by hand.

- Condition is vital, with scuffs and tears that affect the image reducing value. Although mint condition is best, it can be difficult to find older prints in such a condition. Crinkles, folds and even tears can be restored professionally.

- Prints should be handled with clean hands and should not be rolled for storage, but laid flat in acid free tissue paper. When framed, use acid free board and make sure the glass is not in contact with the print. Keep the image out of strong light, which can bleach the colours.

Peter Blake, (born 1932) 'Girl in a Poppy Field', screenprint, signed, from an edition of 125.
1974

£700-750   **WO**

Georges Braque, (1882-1963), 'Si Je Mourais La Bas', original colour wood engraving, signed in pencil and numbered X/X, edition of ten, and extra special edition of parchment.
18.25in (46.5cm) wide

£3,800-4,000   **WO**

Georges Braque, 'Le Tir a l'Arc', original colour lithograph, signed in pencil and numbered 16 from the edition of 20 on Japanese nacre paper.

This piece was inspired by 'Le Zen dans l'art chevalevesque du tir a l'arc' by T.D. Suzuki and E. Cahiers (1917-1952), published by Louis Broder, Paris.

1960

£2,000-2,500   **WO**

Georges Braque, 'Le Tir a l'Arc', original colour lithograph, from the edition of 20 on Japanese nacre paper, signed lower right in pencil and numbered "16/20".

Birds as shown here were a favourite motif for Braque. He also used them when painting a gallery ceiling in the Louvre in Paris.

1960   *6in (15cm)*

£2,200-2,600   **WO**

Georges Braque, 'Le Tir a l'Arc', original lithograph, signed in pencil, numbered 16 from an edition of 20.
1960

£1,800-2,000   **WO**

Max Ernst, (1891-1976) 'Oiseau Bleu', original etching with aquatint, signed in pencil and inscribed 'essai'.
16.25in (41.5cm)

£3,500-4,000   **WO**

Elizabeth Frink, (1930-1993), 'Nude', an original lithograph in two colours, signed in pencil from an edition of 85 plus 5 artist's proofs, printed by the Royal Academy.
25.5in (65cm) wide

£1,500-2,000   **WO**

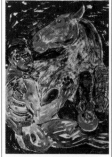

Elizabeth Frink, 'Man and Horse', original screenprint, signed in pencil, edition of 70.
1990   *27in (69cm) wide*

£2,600-3,200   **WO**

Elisabeth Frink, 'Viszla II', original etching and aquatint, signed in pencil, edition of 50.

36in (91.5cm)

£2,800-3,300   **WO**

Sir Terry Frost, (born 1915), 'Camberwell Green', original etching with aquatint and woodcut collage, signed, from an edition of 250.

19.75in (50cm) wide

£300-350   **WO**

Sir Terry Frost RA, 'Trewellard Sun', original linocut with hand-colouring, signed in pencil and numbered from the edition of 70 on Zerkall paper, published by the Paragon Press.

25.25in (64cm) wide

£450-500   **WO**

Sir Terry Frost RA, 'Green and Black Q'.

1997

£600-900   **WO**

Patrick Heron, (born 1920), 'Blue with Lime, Umber, Dull Red and Orange in Violet', original screenprint, signed in pencil from an edition of 50.

1978   *7in (18cm)*

£2,500-3,000   **WO**

David Hockney, (born 1937),'The Old Guitarist', hardground and aquatint, signed in pencil.

1977   *13.5in (34.5cm)*

£4,000-5,000   **WO**

David Hockney, 'What is this Picasso?', original etching in colours, signed in pencil, edition of 200.

1979   *20.75in (53cm) wide*

£3,000-4,000   **WO**

David Hockney, 'Red Square and the Forbidden City', original lithograph, signed in pencil, edition of 1000.

1982   *21.75in (55cm) wide*

£1,000-1,200   **WO**

Howard Hodgkin, (born 1932), 'David's Pool', original etching with hand-colouring, signed with initials in pencil, numbered from an edition of 100.

1979   *24.5in (62cm) wide*

£7,200-8,200   **WO**

A CLOSER LOOK AT A HODGKIN PRINT

This image is typical of Hodgkin, with the image consisting of overlapping broad brushstrokes in bright colours, which record his 'feelings' of an event.

Each print is hand coloured, meaning that individual prints within the edition are never identical, and signed by the artist with his initials. The edition number is 80, which is comparatively small.

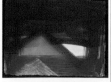

Howard Hodgkin, 'Snow', original carborundum etching with hand-colouring, signed in pencil, edition of 80.

1995   *14in (36cm) wide*

£2,000-2,500   **WO**

John Hoyland, (born 1934), 'Space Born', original screenprint with woodblock.

1993

£700-900   **WO**

Howard Hodgkin, 'Summer', original carborundum etching with hand-colouring signed with initials by the artist on pencil and numbered from the edition of 80.

1997   *14in (36.5cm) wide*

£2,000-2,500   **WO**

John Hoyland, 'Sanur Seal', original screenprint, signed in pencil, edition of 75.

1994 26.75in (68cm) wide

£600-700 **WO**

Henri Matisse, (1869-1954), 'Visages', original lithograph, edition of 250.

1946 10in (25.5cm) wide

£550-600 **WO**

Henri Matisse, 'Tête de Femme', original lithograph, signed in pencil, edition of 300.

1948

£3,600-3,800 **WO**

Henry Moore, (1898-1986), 'Reclining Nude I', original etching, inscribed 'Bon a Tirer HM', a unique proof in black aside from the edition of 50.

1978 7.75in (20cm) wide

£800-1,000 **WO**

A CLOSER LOOK AT A HENRY MOORE PRINT

The 'Mother and Child' is a typical and favourite theme for Moore, whose primitive forms are inspired by natural and landscape forms.

The 'Bon a Tirer' inscription means the artist approves the appearance of the print and the subsequent edition is compared to this visually.

Henry Moore, 'Mother and Child XXVIII', original etching with aquatint.

This print was inscribed 'Bon a tirer HM' in pencil on the lower right before being printed on Arches paper in an edition of 80.

1983 10.75in (27.5cm) wide

£3,000-3,400 **WO**

Henry Moore, 'Three forms in orange and yellow', original lithograph.

1967 11.5in (29cm) wide

£2,500-3,000 **WO**

Pablo Picasso, (1881-1973), 'Six Contes Fantasques', original drypoint.

1953

£900-1,400 **WO**

Pablo Picasso, 'Buste de Femme au Corsage Blanc', original lithograph, from an edition of 50, 17th December 1957.

19.75in (50cm) wide

£30,000-35,000 **WO**

Pablo Picasso, 'Minotaure Caressant Une Femme', etching from an edition of 250, plate 84 from 'La Suite Vollard'.

Named after the influential art dealer Ambroise Vollard, who launched many artists' careers and hosted Picasso's first exhibition in 1901, the Vollard Suite depicts the conflicts between Picasso's love affair with Marie-Therese Walter and his artistic drive. Dating from between 1930 and 1937, it is made up of 100 etchings and is considered an important part of Picasso's work.

1933 14.5in (37cm) wide

£16,000-20,000 **WO**

RAILWAYANA

- Railwayana is now a very active sector of the Collectables market, perhaps due to the nostalgia associated with steam trains and the closure of many coutry railway lines during the mid 20th century.
- Although steam locomotives and railways developed from the early 1800s (Stephenson's 'Rocket' was developed in 1814), memorabilia from this period is virtually non-existent. The 1820s saw many regional railway companies being set up, which either amalgamated or carried on independently. By the turn of the last century, there were 40 railways companies in existence .and memorabilia was very popular, but not always available to the collector.
- In 1921, the majority were amalgamated into four major groups; the 'London, Midland & Scottish' (LMS), 'London & North-Eastern Railways' (LNER), the 'Southern Railway' (SR) and the 'Great Western Railways' (GWR). It is from this period that most memorabilia available to the collector dates.
- The railways were amalgamated again just after the war, to form the nationalized 'British Railways'. Modernization and a rationalization, led by Dr Beeching, during the 1950s and 1960s saw many non-economical lines being closed. Again, much collectable memorabilia dating from this period can be found.

A Southern Railway cast brass nameplate.
1926

£18,000-22,000   **SRA**

NAMEPLATES

- Cast iron nameplates are often seen as the apex of railwayana. Many are in public collections and are very unlikely to come up for sale. Examples are available but prices are relatively high.
- Naming locomotives seems to have been a British peculiarity, with mainline locomotive plates being the most sought after and valuable. Nameplates from noted locomotives will fetch the highest prices. Plates made for industrial or commercial locomotives are less expensive.
- Reproductions do exist, but these are often marked as such. However, such markings may be removed and the signs sold as originals, so collectors should be careful.
- All locomotives also bore number plates, which are usually around half the size of nameplates. 'Cab side' plates are the largest and are the most valuable, the smaller 'smokebox' plates are less expensive.
- Restoration should be completed carefully, over restoration will have a dramatic effect on value.

A British Railways 'Britannia' class nameplate.
1952

£17,000-20,000   **SRA**

A London & North Eastern Railway cast brass nameplate.
1946

£12,000-15,000   **SRA**

A British Railways 'Western' class diesel nameplate.
1962

£8,000-12,000   **SRA**

A British Railways nameplate, from a Class 91 electric.
1991

£6,000-7,000   **SRA**

A British Railways (Scottish region) enamel 'totem' station sign.
1950

£4,500-5,500   **SRA**

A 1950s British Railways (North Eastern region) 'totem' station sign.
c1955

£1,500-2,000   **SRA**

A London & North Eastern Railway nameplate.
1929

£22,000-25,000   **SRA**

A Great Western Railways 'Grange' class nameplate.

1937

£13,000-15,000   **SRA**

A British Railways cast-iron smokebox numberplate, applied 1948 to the LMS locomotive 'Duchess of Sutherland' which had been built in 1938.

£6,000-7,000   **SRA**

DUNDALK NEWRY & GREENORE RAILWAY

CAUTION

PERSONS TRESPASSING UPON THE RAILWAYS BELONGING TO, OR LEASED OR WORKED BY, THE LONDON MIDLAND & SCOTTISH RAILWAY COMPANY, OR BY THAT COMPANY AND ANY OTHER COMPANY, AND ANY PERSONS TRESPASSING UPON THE STATIONS CONNECTED WITH SUCH RAILWAYS, ARE LIABLE TO A PENALTY OF **FORTY SHILLINGS**, UNDER THE LONDON AND NORTH WESTERN RAILWAY ADDITIONAL POWERS ACT, 1883, AND, IN ACCORDANCE WITH THE PROVISIONS OF THE SAID ACT PUBLIC WARNING IS HEREBY GIVEN TO ALL PERSONS, NOT TO TRESPASS UPON THE SAID RAILWAYS OR STATIONS.

EUSTON STATION LONDON   BY ORDER
DECEMBER 1945

A Dundalk, Newry & Greenore Railway, Ireland cast-iron trespass notice.

1945

£1,500-2,000   **SRA**

A Great Western Railway wooden jigsaw puzzle "Mountains of Killarney", after a painting by Warwick Goble, made by Chad Valley, approximately 150 pieces, very minor surface damage on lower edge, box with colour-printed black label to lid fair to good, complete with undated copy of "The Literature of Locomotion".

15in (38.5cm) wide

£30-40   **DN**

A Great Western Railway wooden jigsaw "Springtime in Devon - Fingle Bridge", after a painting by Edith Andrews, made by Chad Valley, approximately 150 pieces, good condition, box with colour-printed black label to lid fair to good.

17in (43cm) wide

£30-40   **DN**

A Southern Railway locomotive crest, from no. 34058 'Sir Frederick Pile'.

1947

£9,000-11,000   **SRA**

M G W R
NOTICE
ANY PERSON OPENING AND NEGLECTING TO SHUT THIS GATE INCURS A PENALTY OF 40 SHILLINGS

A Victorian Midland and Great Western Railway of Ireland cast-iron sign.

£500-600   **SRA**

Two railway hand-signalling oil lamps, one with flat front lens, outer case stamped "LMS B36891", three colour rotating inner with circular loop handle over tank, burner and reflector; the other with flat front lens, three colour rotating inner fixed fluted cowl with loop handle over, slide in burner, reflector and tank, both finished black, good condition overall, both lenses cracked.

4.5in (11.5cm) diam

£60-70   **W&W**

A Great Western Railway wooden jigsaw puzzle "A Cornish Fishing Village", after a painting by S. Clarke Hutton, made by Chad Valley, approximately 150 pieces, good condition, box with colour-printed black label to lid good.

15in (38.5cm)

£25-35   **DN**

W & T R
NOTICE
ANY PERSON OMITTING TO SHUT AND FASTEN THIS GATE IS LIABLE TO A PENALTY OF FORTY SHILLINGS

A Victorian Waterford & Tramore Railway cast-iron gate notice.

c1870

£3,000-4,000   **SRA**

A scarce Lancashire & York Railway Co., bulls eye lens, oil signalling lamp "5000 Saloon", three colour rotating liner with three section straight glass colour strips; loop handle over opening cowl top, fixed handle to rear of outer, original burner tank and reflector with replacement wick unit by Sherwoods, finished red overall and stamped "No 11758" to both major parts, good condition, minor wear overall, flaw to lens.

4.5in (11.5cm) diam

£180-220   **W&W**

ROCK & POP

- The general rule when collecting Rock & Pop memorabilia is 'the bigger the name, the bigger the price ticket'. As more people are interested in collecting a star's memorabilia, they will drive the prices up.
- A key rule to consider is provenance. Always buy from a reputable dealer or auction house and check that the item is what it purports to be. This may require the vendor showing adequate research, an unbroken history of the item's owners from the star, or a letter of provenance.
- Clothing is a popular area, with many stars defining the fashions of the period, such as The Beatles. 'Hallmark' clothing in a style that the star is known for, will usually be more popular, as will those used at key events and on album covers.
- Guitars are ever-popular, and cross value ranges. There are three types – those owned and played by a star at a major event, those owned and played by a star, and those simply signed, but not owned by a star. Values will be the highest for those in the first two categories, and considerably lower for the third.
- Signatures form one of the widest areas of collecting. Again, collectors should ensure that they are not forgeries or signatures by supporting staff. Ephemera connected to events is also popular, with those related to key events in an artist's career fetching higher prices.

Jerry Garcia's Hawaiian-style shirt, in faded blue and purple, worn by Jerry.

£1,500-2,000　　　　G

Jerry Garcia's Hawaiian-style shirt, in green, blue and white, worn by Jerry.

£1,500-2,000　　　　G

Jerry Garcia's Hawaiian-style shirt, in blue and white, worn by Jerry.

£1,500-2,000　　　　G

Jerry Garcia's black T-shirt, pictured wearing it while relaxing at the beach in Kona, Hawaii in 1992.

£1,500-2,000　　　　G

Ten Grateful Dead backstage passes, for different concerts between March 6 and June 24, 1994.

£1,500-2,000　　　　G

Ten Grateful Dead backstage passes, for different concerts between July 24 and December 18, 1994.

£1,500-2,000　　　　G

Jerry Garcia's Pacific Bell calling card, issued to 'J. Garcia'.

£200-250　　　　G

A set list handwritten by Jerry Garcia, for concerts of the Jerry Garcia Band in the 1980s; the list is written in pencil.

£1,000-1,500　　　　G

A signed cheque from the Grateful Dead's account, dated "10-4-1966" and signed by original band members Phil Lesh and Bill Kreutzman.

£400-500　　　　G

A Grateful Dead concert poster, featuring the Grateful Dead and the New Riders of the Purple Sage, fair condition with some fading, partially mounted.

This poster advertises the last concert that Ron McKernan, better known as "Pig Pen", played with the Grateful Dead. He was the original front man and a founding member.

22in (56cm) high

£1,000-1,500　　　　G

Ace Frehley's platform boots, worn during the Kiss Farewell Tour 2000-2001, custom-made six inch silver lamé-covered leather platform "space" boots which were worn onstage by Ace throughout the Farewell Tour.

£1,000-1,500   G

Peter Criss' platform boots, worn during the Kiss Farewell Tour 2000-2001, custom-made six inch silver and black snakeskin leather platform boots which were worn onstage by Peter throughout the Farewell Tour.

£1,000-1,500   G

Paul Stanley's platform boots, worn during the Kiss Farewell Tour 2000-2001, custom-made seven inch black and silver leather platform boots with rhinestone and studded "vein" designs which were worn onstage by Paul throughout the Farewell Tour.

£1,000-1,500   G

Gene Simmons' platform boots, worn during the Kiss Farewell Tour 2000-2001, worn onstage by Gene throughout the Farewell Tour.

£1,000-1,500   G

Vinnie Vincent's red shirt, Vinnie can be seen wearing this shirt on the back cover of his rare 1988 "Vinnie Vincent Invasion" compilation album and in worldwide media photographs in the same year.

£2,500-3,000   G

Handwritten lyrics for "Lick It Up", by Vinnie Vincent, this song appeared on the 1983 album of the same name.

£1,500-2,000   G

Vinnie Vincent's Indian jacket, Vinnie can be seen wearing this jacket on the cover of 1984 Guitar World magazine.

£4,000-5,000   G

An official Kiss/Sterling Marlin car banner, displayed at the NASCAR race at the Homestead-Miami Speedway on November 11, 2001 and featuring the band wearing the Kiss Farewell Tour "four faces" design above the No. 40 Sterling Marlin car with the classic Kiss logo.

96in (244cm) high

Vinnie Vincent's belt, decorated with Japanese symbols, he was given this belt by Gene Simmons for Christmas 1982 and can be seen wearing it on the cover of the 1983 Kiss album "Lick It Up" and in successive press and publicity photos.

£15,000-20,000   G

Handwritten lyrics for "A Million to One", by Vinnie Vincent, this album appears on the 1983 Kiss album "Lick It Up".

£700-1,000   G

An original employment contract between Vinnie Vincent and The KISS Company, dated July 18, 1984.

£1,500-2,000   G

£2,000-3,000   G

A set of Beatles' signatures, John, Paul and Ringo in green ballpoint pen on a clipped piece of paper, matted with a black and white photograph of the 'Fab Four.'

16in (40cm) high

£1,500-2,000 CO

"A Hard Day's Night", US half sheet poster signed by Paul, George and Ringo.

1964 22in (56cm) high

£1,500-2,000 G

A Beatles 'Sgt Pepper's Lonely Hearts Club Band' picture disc, on Parlophone Records (PHO 7027 Stereo), together with a promotional sampler, shrink-wrapped CD titled Paul McCartney's 'Standing Stone Celebration'.

£25-35 CO

A rare Beatles 'butchers' album cover for "Yesterday and Today", together with an original letter with post-marked envelope from Capitol Records, describing the recall of the cover, minor discoloration.

This original cover features the four Beatles dressed in butcher's overalls and surrounded by lumps of meat and dismembered dolls and was apparently a protest against the way Capitol Records had "butchered" their catalogue in the USA. Early copies shocked D.J.s, reviewers and store owners and the album was recalled, the cover being replaced with an innocuous picture of John, Ringo and George standing around a trunk with Paul sitting inside.

£1,200-1,800 DRA

"Help!", a set of eight original UK front of house stills.

1965 10in (25cm) wide

£250-350 CO

A printer's block for the Beatles movie "Help!", hand-crafted blocks photo-engraved on metal in reverse and used to produce the pressbook advertisements.

3in (7.5cm) wide

£100-200 G

Seven pieces of 1960s Beatles memorabilia, including two Beatles ads for dolls and posters.

£180-220 DRA

A Beatles merchandising talcum powder tin, by Margo of Mayfair (U.K.), printed with images of the band and their autographs.

c1964 7in (17.5cm) high

£120-180 CO

Five pieces of Beatles memorabilia, including a rare Yellow Submarine pop-out decoration book, and four Beatles buttons with mirror backs.

1968

£320-380 DRA

Six pieces of Beatles memorabilia, including a Beatles metal tray, four souvenir buttons, gold-coloured commemorative coin.

1964

£320-380 DRA

A 1960s George Harrison figure.

£40-50 Fra

A souvenir menu from the Summer Festival at the International Hotel, Las Vegas, signed Elvis Presley in black ballpoint pen, on the front cover.

11in (28cm)

£450-550 CO

A Summer Festival at the Las Vegas Hilton souvenir concert menu, signed by Elvis Presley, in black ballpoint pen on the front.

15in (38cm) high

£600-700 CO

A souvenir concert photo album, signed by Elvis Presley in blue ballpoint pen on the front cover.

14in (36cm) high

£350-450 CO

A Christmas card signed by Elvis Presley, the one-sided printed card signed and dedicated "To Mary from Elvis Presley" in blue ballpoint pen, with an image of Elvis and "Seasons Greetings Elvis and the Colonel 1966" on the front.

8.5in (16 cm) high

£420-480 CO

A Japanese Elvis Presley Panel Delux double album boxed set, on RCA RP-9201-2, both records unplayed.

This exotic album package has become the most coveted Elvis boxed set ever made.

c1970 *16in (40.5cm)*

£800-1,200 G

A 1964 Country and Western Gibson acoustic guitar, purportedly owned by Elvis Presley, together with case and accompanied by a letter of authenticity.

£8,000-9,000 CO

A typed letter from Elvis to Colonel Parker, dated March 23, 1971 and signed by Elvis in blue ink, includes Certificate of Authenticity.

£4,000-5,000 G

Elvis Presley's black leather briefcase, covered with various tour stickers from Elvis's shows and other music groups, including International Kenpo Karate Association sticker, slightly worn, includes an Elvis Presley Museum Certificate of Authenticity.

£7,000-8,000 G

A Graceland Security badge, marked "Cauley 5".

£550-650 G

Elvis Presley's Smith and Wesson Pistol, with 'TCB', and a lightening bolt on the black pearl handle.

On December 19, 1970, a captain of a Trans World Air flight was told that a V.I.P. on board was carrying a gun. At this point Elvis Presley was escorted into the cockpit where he explained that he had just met President Nixon, and showed the captain a letter stating that he was an agent for the D.E.A., allowing him to carry a concealed weapon. The captain agreed to let Elvis carry the gun on board. After landing, the captain gave Elvis a behind-the-scenes tour and helped Elvis out with the captain of his next flight. Elvis was so impressed with this man that he insisted he accept his Smith & Wesson pistol as a gift. Presley's fascination with guns is well-documented and forms a popular area of interest to collectors.

T.C.B. stood for 'Taking Care of Business' and was a favoured motto used by Elvis Presley.

£27,000-30,000 G

A Carlo Robelli acoustic guitar, signed by Cat Stevens in black marker "Peace Train/Holy Roller, Yusuf Islam", sold with a photo of him posed with the guitar after signing.

£600-700   G

A red Fender Squier Telecaster guitar, signed by the Rolling Stones, signed on the body by Mick Jagger, Keith Richards, and Ron Wood and on the pickguard by Charlie Watts, Bill Wyman, and Mick Taylor.

Guitars signed by all six members of The Rolling Stones are very rare. With a five-page handwritten letter of provenance from the collector who obtained five of the autographs, detailing where and when each member signed it.

£3,500-4,000   G

A black E-ROS 12 string acoustic guitar, signed by the Rolling Stones in silver marker pen by Mick Jagger, Charlie Watts, Keith Richards and Bill Wyman and on the scratchplate in gold marker pen by Mick Taylor.

£850-950   CO

A white Fender Squier Telecaster guitar, signed by The Who, signed boldly on the body by bassist John Entwistle and on the pickguard by Pete Townsend and Roger Daltrey.

£1,000-1,500   G

An autographed Cher CD cover, issued as a promotional item.

£50-80   MSC

A 1973 Beach Boys In Concert signed album sleeve, on Reprise Records, signed by Brian Wilson, Carl Wilson, Dennis Wilson, Al Jardine and Mike Love, each in black marker pen.

12in (31cm) wide

£180-220   CO

A signed contract between The Doors and the Kaleidoscope club, Los Angeles, dated 30th March, 1967 and signed by Robbie Krieger of the Doors.

£2,000-3,000   G

A handwritten poem "Explosion" by Jim Morrison, unsigned, 'instant of creation (fertilization), not an instant seperate from breakfast, it all flows down & out, flowing, ...'.

12in (31cm)

£6,500-7,500   CO

Elton John's red stage platform shoes, owned and worn by Elton John.

£4,500-5,500   G

A miniature Colt 45 pistol charm, removed from Sid Vicious' jacket and given to the late Helen Wheels, attached to a note signed and dedicated by Vicious: "CBGB For Helen SID" with his bloody thumb print, together with a Helen Wheels and the Skeleton Crew concert flyer, one of her business cards and a letter of provenance from the vendor.

7in (18cm) wide

£850-950   CO

A Cher poster, signed "To Mark all my love Cher".

£50-80   MSC

A handmade brown suede vest worn by Jimi Hendrix, possibly made by Omar's of the Village, NYC, and given to Hendrix by Steve Paul, a club owner and manager, subsequently signed inside by James "Booty" Neil, Noel Redding and Eugene McFadden, in silver pen, accompanied by a letter from the vendor explaining the vest's history.

c1968

£1,200-1,800   CO

A giclee print of Aerosmith, performing at Madison Square Garden, by Roberto Rabanne.

A giclee is a faithful reproduction of a fine art archival print using state-of-the-art printing technology.

19in (48cm) wide

£800-1,000   G

A giclee print of James Brown, performing at John Harms Theater, N.J., 2000, by Roberto Rabanne.

19in (48cm) high

£1,000-1,200   G

A giclee print of L.L. Cool J., by Roberto Rabanne.

19in (48cm) high

£1,000-1,200   G

A giclee print of Sheryl Crow and Keith Richards, performing at Central Park, NYC, 2000, by Roberto Rabanne.

19in (48cm) high

£1,000-1,200   G

A giclee print of Miles Davis, performing at Montreaux, Switzerland, late 1980s, by Roberto Rabanne.

19in (48cm) high

£800-1,000   G

A giclee print of Bob Dylan, performing at U.C. Berkley Greek Theatre in the 1970s, by Roberto Rabanne.

19in (48cm) high

£1,000-1,200   G

A giclee print of Bob Dylan and Eric Clapton, performing at the Crossroads Benefit at Madison Square Garden, 2001, by Roberto Rabanne.

19in (48cm) wide

£1,000-1,200   G

A giclee print of Ray Charles, performing at the Great American Music Hall, 1976, by Roberto Rabanne.

19in (48cm) high

£1,200-1,500   G

A giclee print of Dizzy Gillespie, backstage at the Great American Music Hall, 1975, by Roberto Rabanne.

19in (48cm) high

£1,000-1,200   G

A giclee print of Dizzy Gillespie and Carmen Miranda, by Roberto Rabanne.

19in (48cm) high

£1,000-1,200   G

A giclee print of Debbie Harry, performing at Berkley, 1977, by Roberto Rabanne.

19in (48cm) high

£800-1,000   G

A giclee print of Hole, Los Angeles, mid 1990s, by Roberto Rabanne.

19in (48cm) wide

£1,000-1,500   G

A giclee print of John Lee Hooker, performing at Keystone, Berkley, 1975, by Roberto Rabanne.

19in (48cm) wide

£800-1,000   G

A giclee print of Mick Jagger, by Roberto Rabanne.

19in (48cm) high

£1,000-1,500   G

A giclee print of Dr. John, at Keystone, Berkley, 1975, by Roberto Rabanne.

19in (48cm) high

£1,000-1,200   G

A giclee print of Grace Jones, performing in San Francisco, 1973, by Roberto Rabanne.

19in (48cm) high

£1,000-1,500   G

A giclee print of Janis Joplin, performing in San Francisco, 1967, by Roberto Rabanne.

19in (48cm) high

£1,400-1,600   G

A giclee print of B.B. King, performing at the Apollo Theater, NYC, 1993, by Roberto Rabanne.

19in (48cm) high

£1,000-1,500   G

A giclee print of Lenny Kravitz, performing in NYC, late 1990s, by Roberto Rabanne.

19in (48cm) high

£1,000-1,200   G

A giclee print of Madonna, by Roberto Rabanne.

19in (48cm) high

£1,400-1,600   G

A giclee print of Madonna, by Roberto Rabanne.

19in (48cm) high

£1,400-1,600 G

A C-print of Bob Marley, by Roberto Rabanne.

60in (152.5cm) wide

£1,500-2,000 G

A giclee print of Bob Marley, performing at the Boarding House, San Francisco, by Roberto Rabanne.

20in (51cm) high

£1,400-,1600 G

A giclee print of Slick Rick, NYC, early 1990s, by Roberto Rabanne.

19in (48cm) high

£800-1,000 G

A giclee print of the Sex Pistols, performing at the Winterland, San Francisco, by Roberto Rabanne.

This was the last perfomance by the group.

19in (48cm) wide

£1,000-1,200 G

A giclee print of Rod Stewart, in Frankfurt, Germany, 1989, by Roberto Rabanne.

19in (48cm) high

£800-1,000 G

A giclee print of Bruce Springsteen, performing at the Amnesty International Benefit, Paris, 1989, by Roberto Rabanne.

19in (48cm) high

£1,000-1,500 G

A giclee print of Bruce Springsteen and Patti, Amnesty International Benefit in Paris, 1989, by Roberto Rabanne.

19in (48cm) high

£1,000-1,500 G

A giclee print of Tricky, NYC, 1999, by Roberto Rabanne.

19in (48cm) high

£800-1,000 G

A giclee print of Stevie Wonder, by Roberto Rabanne.

19in (48cm) high

£1,000-1,500 G

An English clear cut-glass double-ended scent bottle, with silver stoppers.

£100-200   Trio

An English ruby glass double-ended scent bottle, with silver-gilt stoppers.

£180-220   Trio

A pair of early 20thC Baccarat crystal scent bottles, each of geometric form with lobed stopper and acid-stamped signature.

3.75in (35.5cm) high

£80-120   FRE

A set of three Art Deco cut glass sunburst perfume bottles.

c1935   *Tallest 12.5cm (5in) high*

£60-70   OACC

A 1930s Czechoslovakian carved glass atomizer.

4.5in (11.5cm) high

£150-200   LB

A Steuben gold Aurene perfume bottle, unsigned.

6in (15cm) high

£450-550   JDJ

A Victorian ruby glass scent bottle.

£180-220   Trio

A clear cut-glass scent bottle, with silver top.

1897

£100-150   Trio

A Venetian latticino glass scent bottle.

The name 'latticino' refers to the milk-coloured thread-like design incorporated into the glass. It was a technique typically used by Venetian glass manufacturers.

£150-200   Trio

A Sandwich Glass Factory panelled paperweight perfume bottle, smokey canary colour.

c1840   *7.5in (17.5cm) high*

£900-1,000   RAA

A clear cut-glass scent bottle, with silver top.

1919

£80-120   Trio

An Art Nouveau silver overlaid iridescent blue glass perfume bottle, overlaid with scrolling foliage, the stopper of clear glass with silver overlay, marked "Sterling", monogrammed "JRB".

c1900   *6.5in (16.5cm) high*

£350-450   SI

A Daum-covered perfume bottle, with purple ground and acid-cut thistles, stems and leaves, and enamel and gilt decoration, signed, some minor wear to gilt.

3in (7.5cm) high

£800-1,000   **JDJ**

A Daum 'Nancy' cameo scent bottle, green over clear glass, acid-etched with gold highlighting, signed on base in gold script "Daum Nancy", some wear to the gold enamelling.

6.25in (16cm) long

£450-550   **JDJ**

An English cameo scent bottle, white over yellow glass with a wheel-cut decoration of branches and leaves with a silver top.

2.5in (6.5cm) high

£350-450   **JDJ**

A Galle cameo perfume bottle, purple flowers and leaves against a white background, signed "GALLE" in one of the cameo leaves.

3.5in (9cm) high

£450-550   **JDJ**

A Lalique atomizer, opalescent glass with ten moulded nudes, brass metal hardware, signed on base "R. LALIQUE FRANCE J6 2687".

9in (23cm) high

£650-750   **JDJ**

A Webb Burmese scent bottle, pink shading to yellow glass with enamel decoration of leaves, berries and branches, original silver top.

4.75in (11cm) high

£700-800   **JDJ**

A French blue opaline scent bottle.

£120-180   **Trio**

A clear glass scent bottle, painted with flowers, with pinchbeck stopper.

£120-180   **Trio**

Two scent bottles, one heart-shaped, the outer sleeve decorated with putto, C-scrolls and roses, London 1898, William Comyns, the other drop-shaped with screw-off cap, the body with stippled ground, floral and bird decoration, Birmingham, 1884.

Largest 4in (10cm) high

£450-550   **L&T**

A clear glass scent bottle, decorated with filigree set with pearls and a garnet, with pinchbeck stopper.

£120-180   **Trio**

A late 19th/early 20thC French gilt metal-mounted glass perfume atomizer, of square chamfered section, overlaid with an eagle, oak branches and laurel garlands.

7in (18cm) high

£200-300   **SI**

A 1960s Avon black cat perfume bottle.

4.5in (11.5cm) long

£25-35   **LB**

A small porcelain scent bottle.

£70-100 **Trio**

A Caron "Les Pois de Senteur de Chez Moi" perfume bottle.

1927 *4.5in (11.5cm) high*

£100-130 **LB**

A Christian Dior "Miss Dior" perfume bottle, with box.

c1947 *5.5in (14cm) high*

£150-200 **LB**

A 1920s Richard Hudnut "Dubarry" perfume bottle, compact and lipstick.

Perfume 2.75in (7cm) high

£120-180 **LB**

A Guerlain "Parure" glass perfume bottle.

1974 *6.75in (17cm) high*

£70-90 **LB**

A Gabilla "La Rose de Gabilla" perfume bottle, by Baccarat, in box.

c1912 *3in (7.5cm) high*

£250-350 **LB**

A 1950s Guerlain "Shalimar" perfume bottle, by Baccarat.

6in (15cm) high

£100-130 **LB**

A Charles Kaziun paperweight perfume bottle, decorated with a spider lily on a white ground, signed with gold "K" on base and stopper.

3.25in (8.5cm) high

£650-750 **JDJ**

A 1950s Max Factor perfume bottle.

6in (15cm) high

£35-45 **LB**

A 1960s/70s Nina Ricci "L'Air Du Temps" perfume bottle, by Lalique.

4in (10cm) high

£100-200 **LB**

A 1930s "Saturday Night Lotion" bottle.

5in (12.5cm) high

£25-35 **LB**

A
B
C
D
E
F
G
H
I
J
K
L
M
N
O
P
Q
R
S
T
U
V
W
XYZ

SCIENCE & TECHNOLOGY

- Instruments from the 18th century can be found but these will most often command high prices. Earlier instruments from the 1600s and 1500s are generally unavailable to private collectors, unless common or of basic construction.
- The majority of scienctific and technological instruments available to collectors today date from the 19th century, which was a period of prolific production and many new inventions and ingenious innovations. Many are stored in fitted wooden boxes, often made from mahogany.
- The quality of production in the 19th century was high; bodies are usually finely made in brass with precise optical components.
- Instruments fall into a number of categories which include those for navigation, surveying, scientific purposes, optical instruments and functional mechanical and technical instruments, such as the telephone and typewriter.
- Look for good workmanship when examining a piece. Pieces should be well-engineered and 'fit' and function together. If an instrument came with a range of accessories, they should be as complete as possible as this helps increase value and desirability.
- Collectors favour pieces in good condition or bearing a maker's mark. If a piece was made by a renowned maker this can increase its value considerably.
- Makers' addresses can help identify a period of manufacture. From 1767, street numbers replaced signs and makers often moved. Specialist reference works allot dates ranges to specific addresses.
- Beware of cleaning brass instruments, abrasive cleaners can remove the surface of lacquer on brass.

A black lacquered brass three drawer pocket telescope, with leather-covered tube, signed "Parascope W. Watson & Son Ltd, 313 High Holborn, London".

Extended 16.75in (42.5cm) long

£50-70 BA

A 19thC four drawer lacquered brass and mahogany telescope, marked "Thos. Harris & Son, Opticians to the Royal Family, Oppos. the British Museum London".

Extended 43.5in (110.5cm) long

£200-300 BA

A six drawer lacquered brass pocket telescope, with black ribbed grip and screw-in mount, in velvet-lined fitted mahogany case, signed "Edwd Davis, 65 Bold St, Liverpool".

Extended 5in (12.5cm) long

£400-500 BA

A five drawer brass telescope, with tripod and fitted mahogany case, signed "Ramsden, London".

Extended 40.5in (103cm) long

£500-600 BA

A Victorian tortoiseshell and brass two drawer spy glass.

Extended 5.5in (14cm) long

£100-200 BA

A pair of military regulation field glasses.

4.5in (11.5cm) wide

£18-22 OACC

A pair of racing binoculars, marked "Le Jockey Club, Paris".

4.75in (12cm) wide

£70-90 OACC

A pair of Leitz Fernglass 08 field glasses, marked, with leather case.

c1916

£80-120 TK

A pair of early 20thC Baker binoculars.

£40-60 OACC

An early Zeiss monocular field glass, marked "Carl Zeiss, Jena", with old Zeiss company logo, with maker's case.

c1896

£200-250 TK

A pair of Carl Zeiss 6 x 30 binoculars, No. 2021729, in hard black plastic case, well worn.

£25-35 W&W

A late 19thC mahogany and black painted tin magic lantern.

The magic lantern has existed since the 17thC and used a light source behind a glass plate with an image painted or printed onto it. A magnifying lens at the front of the lantern projected an enlarged image onto a surface for viewing.

24in (61cm) long

£400-500 BA

A Skioptikon magic lantern, with original electrical lighting mechanism.

c1920   18.5in (47cm) wide

£60-100　　　　　　　　**TK**

An Ernst Plank magic lantern, with original box and 13 glass slides, no burner, reflector loose.

c1910

£100-150　　　　　　　　**TK**

An 1860s Pestalozzi handheld stereo viewer, with stereocards.

Stereographic images have two seemingly identical images of the same scene beside each other on a card or on a glass plate. They are taken using a special camera with two lenses mounted side by side which capture the same scene but from a slightly different viewpoint. When viewed through a stereographic viewer, the eyes are tricked into merging the images to create an almost 'three-dimensional' image.

Established as a principle by Sir Charles Wheatstone in 1832, stereography reached the height of popularity during the third quarter of the 19th century. Popularity declined after the 1860s, but it was still popular around 1900 when cards mounted with photographic images were being mass produced.

These cards typically show tourist scenes of popular venues such as the Alps, Rome, the Holy Land and Chicago. Rarer subjects include historical events or scenes.

A large mahogany and japanned tinplate magic lantern, with tilt facility and brass knob adjustments for front bellows and rear light, with early electric fitting.

23in (58.5cm) long

£70-100　　　　　　　　**DN**

A wooden Graphoscope viewer.

The Graphoscope was used for viewing photographs easily and comfortably. The image would be placed on the rest behind the magnifying lens which was angled to allow viewing.

5.5in (14cm) high

£80-120　　　　　　　　**TK**

3in (33cm) long

£50-70　　　　　　　　**MHC**

MICROSCOPES

- There are two different types of microscope, the simple with one lens and the compound with more than one, usually mounted apart in a tube. Tubes can be made from card, brass or wood. The invention of the microscope in 1608 is credited to Sacharias Janssen, a spectacle maker in the Netherlands.

- Earlier microscopes are usually very valuable and fetch high prices when offered. 19th century microscopes are more readily available. They are typically made from brass and are often contained in wooden boxes that also contain accessories.

- Makers' names are very important and can give an indication of date. Unmarked versions, unless in a rare type or from an early period, will generally not be as desirable. Some names, such as George Adams and Benjamin Martin attract great attention and high prices. Others have lent their names to types of design, such as the 'Cuff' type and the 'Culpeper' type with its three distinctive curving legs and centrally placed tube. Twentieth century microscopes with blackened metal stands by makers such as Leitz are usually less valuable and desirable.

- Accessories are also important, with those having a complete or near complete set of accessories being more valuable than those without.

A lacquered brass binocular microscope, with fitted mahogany case containing different objectives, eyepieces and other accessories, signed "R. & J. Beck, 31 Cornhill, London".

Closed 15.25in (39cm) high

£1,000-1,500　　　　　　**BA**

A large lacquered brass monocular microscope, in brass bound mahogany case.

£800-1,100　　　　　　　**BA**

A lacquered brass compound drum microscope, in a fitted wooden box, unmarked.

10in (25.5cm) high

£350-450　　　　　　　　**BA**

A lacquered brass microscope, in fitted wooden case, marked "Gardner & Co., 21 Buchanan Street, Glasgow".

The opticians and mathematical instrument makers Gardner & Co are recorded as being at 21 Buchanan St, Glasgow from 1839-1859, and then at 53 Buchanan Street from 1860-1882. They were active and working between 1837 and 1883. With this microscope, the stand and tube are separate and are screwed together after removing them from the case, which also contains an array of eyepieces, objectives and accessories.

Case 11.5in (29cm) high

£1,200-1,700   **BA**

A lacquered brass microscope, in fitted mahogany case, marked "Watson & Son, 313 High Holborn, London".

Watson & Son are recorded as being active and working at 313A High Holborn, London between 1869 and 1872.

16in (40.5cm) high

£600-700   **BA**

A painted and lacquered brass microscope, in fitted wooden case, marked " Henry Crouch, London, 4085".

11in (28cm) high

£200-250   **BA**

A brass microscope, by Bausch & Lomb, in locking walnut case, includes instruction manual, cover glasses, slides and extra lens.

Case 14in (35.5cm) high

£120-180   **TWC**

A lacquered brass pocket microscope, with fitted mahogany box and ivory slides.

This microscope is taken to pieces and the stand folded away to fit into the mahogany box, which also has fitted areas to hold accessories.

10.5in (26.5cm) high

£450-550   **BA**

An early brass microscope, by Carl Zeiss, No. 11890, with three lenses, one later and two different oculars, in original mahogany box, with key.

£400-500   **TK**

A black microscope, by Ernst Leitz, No. 367.690.

Ernst Leitz are a famous optical manufacturer based in Wetzlar, Germany. They also developed and manufactured the famous 'Leica' cameras.

£120-180   **TK**

A lacquered brass microscope, by R. & J. Beck, No. 8.212.

c1860   *15.25in (39cm) high*

£800-1,200   **TK**

A brass mounted bullseye, on ball-jointed arm.

A bullseye lens was used for focusing light to allow use of a microscope. These lenses have a flat and a bulbous side, the latter giving them their characteristic name.

1.75in (4.5cm) diam

£70-100   **BA**

A lacquered brass transit theodolite, in fitted wooden case, signed "T. Cooke & Sons, York, England No. 5115", the case with printed label dated December 1932.

11in (28cm) wide

£550-650 BA

A brass theodolite, signed "Fraget A Paris".

11in (28cm) high

£600-700 BA

A black lacquered brass Starke & Kammerer theodolite, No. 8.705.

c1890   11.75in (30cm) high

£450-550 TK

A brass French cross staff, by Radiguet, Paris, silver nonius scale.

c1860   6.25in (16cm) high

£70-100 TK

A lacquered brass octagonal cross staff, the top set with a compass, in a wooden box.

5in (12.5cm) long

£100-150 BA

Two early French brass cross staffs, with original boxes.

c1860

£160-200 TK

A lacquered brass "Director No. 5 Mark I" level, in fitted wooden case, marked "E. R. Watts & Son, 1916, No. 3397".

14.75in (37.5cm) long

£250-350 BA

A lacquered brass Abney level, marked "F.B. & Son Ltd 2904".

5.75in (14.5cm) long

£80-100 BA

A lacquered brass dial, in fitted wooden case, signed "Pyefinch, London".

£1,000-1,600 BA

A lacquered brass miners dial, on wooden base, signed "John King, Bristol".

Dial 5.5in (14cm) diam

£400-500 BA

A lacquered brass protractor, in fitted mahogany case, signed "Troughton & Simms, London".

Case 13in (33cm) wide

£200-300 BA

A pocket sextant, with leather case, marked "Liddon & Co. London B818 1916".

The pocket sextant was invented by Edward Troughton around 1800 and was one of the most useful surveying instruments available, particularly for trigonometric purposes. The tiny scales are read with a magnifier.

2.5in (6.5cm) diam

£200-250 BA

A lacquered brass octant, signed "H.C. Coles, London", with later conservation varnish, complete.

£250-350 TK

A lacquered brass octant, in fitted mahogany case, case marked "J. Sewill, Chronometer Manufacturer, 30 Cornhill, Royal Exchange".

9.5in (24cm) long

£600-700 BA

A wood and brass octant, with ivory label "Browning maker, Boston".

Octants were used to measure angles in navigation from c1750 to c1900. As the name suggests, they take the form of an eighth of a full circle.

Its invention is credited to John Hadley, who modified and adapted another navigational instrument, the back staff, into the octant in the early 1730s.

The earliest frames, dating from before 1800, were made of mahogany, but octants are usually found in ebony in styles identical to this example.

Browning, based in Boston MA, is a known maker and his name is found on a small inset ivory plaque on the cross bar.

13in (33cm) high

A black lacquered brass sextant on stand, marked "Bottomley, 11 Billiter Street, London".

20in (51cm) high

£1,500-2,000 BA

A lacquered brass flying boat sextant, with fitted wooden box and printed paper label "for Henry Hughes & Son Ltd, London", dated 10/6/44.

1944 8in (20.5cm) wide

£250-350 BA

£400-500 BA

A marine chronometer, in fitted, gimballed case, marked "Kelvin, White & Hutton, 11 Billiter Street, London", case marked "Kelvin, White & Hutton 5464" and with paper label "J. Sewill Ltd, makers to the Royal Navy, 36 Exchange Street, East Liverpool, L2 3PT, Date: May 1982".

Marine chronometers are mounted on a series of moving mounts, known as 'gimbals'. Accurate chronometers were essential for discerning longitude to enable correct navigation at sea and a competition was held in the early 18thC to devise the most accurate timepiece. John Harrison, a talented British clockmaker, developed the first reliable marine chronometer that was not affected by the movement of the sea or the varying temperature – it was tested successfully in 1736.

Dial 4.75in (12cm) diam

£1,000-1,600 BA

A brass compass, signed "Dent & Co Ltd" and "No. 3039 Patt 20".

12in (30.5cm) high

£1,500-2,000 BA

A near pair of brass and copper ship lanterns, marked "Port" and "Starboard".

12in (30.5cm) high

£150-200 BA

A lacquered brass ship's log, with painted enamel dial, marked "T. Walker's Patent Harpoon Ship Log A1, London".

19.25in (49cm) long

£400-500 BA

A ships flare gun, with brass and wood grip and painted metal barrel, marked "SFRA".

19.5in (49.5cm) long

£220-280 BA

An American 'The Fox' typewriter.

c1902

£400-450 TK

A Hammond No. 12 typewriter, with wooden case and ten part documentation, three type sleeves in original boxes and three box ribbons.

c1893

£280-320 TK

A very rare Imperial Visible typewriter, with sloping type bar by Triumph Visible Co., Kenosha, Wisconsin, USA.

This typewriter is the forerunner of the rare Burnett model, but even scarcer. Only three examples are known worldwide, and this one bears the low serial number of 304, adding to its desirability.

c1907

£7,200-8,000 TK

A Mignon Model 2 typewriter.

c1905

£400-500 TK

A Royal Bar-Lock typewriter, with original wooden hood.

c1902

£250-300 TK

A CLOSER LOOK AT A VIROTYP MACHINE

The circular plate had a series of letters printed on it. Below this was a series of letter stamps and under that, rollers to hold the paper.

The knob was turned to point at a letter the printing key pressed and letter stamped onto the paper.

A French 'Virotyp' index machine, in good working condition.

The Virotyp, invented by the Frenchman H. Viry in 1914, was a comparatively small machine primarily made for use during the First World War.

It had a strap and series of hooks that meant it could be cradled between both hands and operated without needing a hard surface to rest it on.

Combined with its small size and lightness of weight, it became popular for people who had to type whilst on the move. A further strap allowed it to be attached to a forearm enabling it to be used even on horseback!

c1914

£350-450 TK

An American Odell 'Type Writer' index typewriter, wooden case replaced.

This model was one of Chicago-based Odell Type Writer Co's most popular machines and used a sliding linear index fixed at a 90 degree angle to the paper. A patent was issued in 1889 and versions with upper and lower case as well as upper case only (as with this example) were sold. The user would select the letter with the slide and rock the slide to print the letter.

1890

£700-800 TK

A rare Urania-Piccola portable typewriter, with scarce German Gothic type, the successor of Perkeo.

c1925

£160-200 TK

FIND OUT MORE...

Scryption Museum, Spoorlaan 434a, 5053 CH Tilburg, The Netherlands. www.tref.nl, This 'museum of writing' contains an incredible and diverse collection of typewriters.

Michael Adler, 'The Writing Machine – A History of the Typewriter', published by George, Allen & Unwin, 1973.

A rare Swedish table telephone, by L. M. Ericsson, for 10 lines.
c1905

£1,000-1,500   TK

A French table telephone, with wooden case, and coil, minimal damage on edge of case.

c1910

£200-300   TK

A telephone, by Grammont, Paris, wooden case with marble effect socket.

c1900

£700-800   TK

L. M. ERICSSON

- L.M. Ericsson, well known for their mobile telephones today, were founded in Stockholm in 1876 by Lars Magnus Ericsson as a telephone repair company.
- They began to manufacture their own telephones in 1878 and began selling in America in the 1890s. By 1905, when a factory was set up in Buffalo, New York, a sales office had been in existence for three years.
- Their candlestick telephones are sought after by collectors, as is the highly decorative skeleton model, which is also sometimes known as the 'Eiffel Tower' telephone. It shows many of the internal workings as decorative features.
- Condition is important, as the black finish is prone to wear and scratches. The gilt transfers on the legs can also be scratched and show signs of wear.

An L. M. Ericsson telephone.
c1910   *13in (33cm) high*

£80-120   OACC

An L.M. Ericsson skeleton telephone.
c1900

£750-850   TK

A rare Swiss wall telephone, by G. Hasler, Bern, with original receiver, fixed microphone.
c1925

£350-450   TK

A white painted candlestick telephone.

£100-150   BA

A wall telephone, by L.M. Ericsson, Stockholm, with turnable microphone protectors for use during a thunderstorm, no receiver.
c1900

£2,000-2,500   TK

An early 20thC Western Electric oak wall telephone.

19in (48.5cm) high

£100-150 **TWC**

A pocket barometer, with silvered dial, marked "W. H. Blackler Bulawayo".

2.75in (7cm) diam

£100-150 **BA**

A brass pocket barometer, with silvered dial, signed "P. H. Steward, 457 West Strand, 406 Strand & 7 Greenchurch Street, London 3520".

2in (5cm) diam

£70-100 **BA**

A brass holosteric pocket barometer, signed "H A Reens, Opticien Rotterdam".

2in (5cm) diam

£70-100 **BA**

A cased barograph, with pull-out drawer.

12in (30.5cm) wide

£600-700 **BA**

A German barometer, by G.Müller, Braunschweig.

c1900

£100-150 **TK**

A marine barograph.

12in (30.5cm) wide

£500-600 **BA**

A Sestral clock and barometer, mounted on a wooden board, signed "The Seaway Co."

13.5in (34.5cm) wide

£200-300 **BA**

A compass, in carved wooden case, with printed paper dial and carved wooden meridian ring, signed "Thomas Heath".

1720-33 *Case 6in (15cm) wide*

£650-750 **BA**

A pocket compass, in fitted wooden case, with printed paper dial and yellow paper label "Hudson, Optician, Greenwich".

2in (5cm) wide

£60-80 **BA**

A compass, in carved wooden case, with engraved brass dial, marked "I. Coggs, Fleet Street, London".

Case 6in (15cm) wide

£800-1,100 BA

A brass equinoctial dial, in a fitted case, marked "KOHN Onmukb".

4.5in (11.5cm) diam

£1,000-1,500 BA

A pocket compass, with silvered dial and wooden case.

3in (7.5cm) wide

£55-65 BA

A brass compass, in fitted wooden case, signed "J. Wardale & Co., London No. 7906 1918".

3.25in (8cm) wide

£55-65 BA

A pocket compass, with printed paper dial and brass case.

3.5in (9cm) wide

£100-140 BA

A silvered brass pocket sundial, signed "Lynch, Dublin".

3.5in (9cm) wide

£600-700 BA

A "Willis World Time Clock", in seven-sided wooden case, with printed dial, lacks hands.

13in (33cm) diam

£700-800 BA

A CLOSER LOOK AT AN ORRERY

The oil lamp on the main body of the instrument represents the sun, with the globe at the end of the arm being the Earth, mounted at the correct angle. The small sphere held near it on another arm is the moon.

By turning the handle, the whole revolves including the Earth and the moon and the Earth's orbit around the sun associated with the moon's placement can be seen.

A German painted metal orrery, with hand-cranked mechanism, the globe marked "ZEMÉKOULE VYDAU J. FELKLASYN ROZTOKYAPRAHY".

Through use of winding, gears and revolving spheres, orreries illustrate the movement of planets and solar system. They are found in various degrees of sophistication with one or numerous planets. They are a good example of demonstration instruments and are popular with collectors of globes.

20in (51cm) wide

£1,500-2,000   BA

A 17thC Continental set of bronze weights, the hinged case with punchwork decoration and hallmarks fitted with eight stacking weights.

3.5in (9cm) wide

£800-1,200   SI

A minimum-maximum thermometer, cased.

8.5in (21.5cm) wide

£80-120   BA

A set of 18thC monetary beam scales.

7.25in (18.5cm) wide

£300-400   OACC

A minimum-maximum thermometer, cased.

8.5in (21.5cm) wide

£80-120   BA

A Curta Type 1 calculator, input imperfect, with original metal box.

c1948

£300-400   TK

An ivory and brass hydrometer, in fitted mahogany case, marked "Buss, 48 Hatton Garden, London".

Hydrometers were used by brewers and excise officers to measure the gravity of liquids, from which the alcohol content could be discerned. A common maker of hydrometers is 'Sikes', whose highly accurate patent was introduced in 1817. The small disc weights are often missing from sets, so collectors should examine boxes closely.

Case 8in (20.5cm) wide

£70-100   BA

A lacquered brass pantograph, in fitted wooden case, signed "Allen, London".

A pantograph was used for copying and enlarging or reducing the size of maps and diagrams.

15.25in (39cm) wide

£220-280   BA

A mahogany and brass Cuthbert electricity generating machine, with large glass disc rotating between to sets of leather pads.

19in (48.5cm) high

£500-600   BA

A George III caddy spoon, by Duncan Urquhart and Napthali Hart, with wriggle-engraved round bowl and bright-cut engraved handle with monogram, London hallmarks.

1799   3in (7.5cm) long

£120-180   **DN**

Two George III shell bowl caddy spoons, one by S. Godbehere & Co., with an old 'English' pattern handle and London hallmarks, the other with a short handle, London hallmarks rubbed.

1801 & 1809 3.5in (9cm) long

£150-200   **DN**

CADDY SPOONS

- Caddy spoons were used for transferring tea from a tea caddy to a teapot.
- They are often fancifully shaped and highly decorative and were made from the 1770s until the decline in use of tea caddies in the late 19th century.
- They are made from a single sheet of silver which is stamped into the form, and stamped with the design and pattern, so they are often fragile. Collectors should look for repaired bends, which reduce value if serious, and splits.
- Handles are often made from bone, ivory or mother-of-pearl. Popular motifs include shells, jockey's caps, hands and an eagle's wing.

A Victorian caddy spoon, by Hilliard and Thomason, the lobed bowl embossed with shells and leaves, the handle in the form of a lily, London hallmarks.

1852   3.5in (9cm) long

£420-480   **DN**

A Liberty & Co silver caddy spoon, the oval-shaped bowl decorated with a panel resembling basket weave, the handle with scrollwork and a further panel of basket weave, marked "L&Co" for Birmingham.

1924   3.3in (8.5cm)

£250-300   **DN**

A silver spoon, by Sibyl Dunlop, the almost heart-shaped bowl with the handle terminating in a pointed oval, with overall planached surface, marked "SD" and stamped "S. Dunlop", with London hallmarks.

1969   6in (15cm) long

£150-200   **DN**

A set of six enamelled silver coffee spoons, by W. H. Haseler, each with an oval bowl and a slender handle with foliate terminal, the detail heightened with coloured enamels, each marked with "W.H.H.", Birmingham hallmarks, fitted case.

1906   4.5in (11.5cm) each

£450-500 (set)   **DN**

A silver gravy ladle, by Georg Jensen, the curved handle terminating in a stylized blossom.

1933-44   8in (20.5cm) long

£300-400   **SI**

A silver sauce ladle, by Georg Jensen, with deep elliptical bowl, the handle with central slender beaded knop and bud finial, stamped with maker's marks, Copenhagen date mark and London import marks.

1927   5.5in (14cm) long

£220-280   **DN**

Two pairs of 20thC silver serving pieces, comprising a serving fork and spoon cast with rosebud decoration on handles and terminals, and a serving fork and spoon cast and pierced with scrolls and shells.

£200-250   **SI**

50 pieces of 19thC coin silver and plated flatware, including 30 engraved "Oregon" bearing maker's mark of Salisbury, 212 Broadway, New York, NY, together with flatware similarly designed by E.W. Moir, and coin silver serving spoons bearing the maker's mark of Griffen.

The ship "Oregon" sunk in Boston Harbour in 1863. The engraved flatware was salvaged and used by the family of Phillip White of Boston as their family silver. All pieces bear the White family monograms.

£280-320   **SI**

A 156-piece silver flatware service, by Georg Jensen, 'Acanthus' pattern, comprising 18 dinner forks, luncheon forks, salad forks, dinner knives, coffee spoons, dessert spoons and table serving spoons, twelve teaspoons and bouillon spoons, one cake server, three cold meat forks, a pie server and salad spoon.

£5,000-6,000   **SI**

A George V silver circular tray, by Mappin & Webb, Sheffield, the centre engraved with C-scrolls, flowers and foliage, the rim chased with conforming decoration and the scalloped rim applied with foliage.

1913   *14in (35.5cm) diam*

£420-480   **SI**

A silver circular tray, by Frank M. Whiting Co., North Attleboro, MA, chased with floral and foliate swags, applied with a fruit and leaf rim.

12.25in (31cm) diam

£100-150   **SI**

A silver circular platter, by Tiffany & Co., moulded with a laurel chain border and a central reserve within a radiating petal surround, monogrammed "HAF".

1907-38   *15in (38cm) diam*

£800-1,200   **SI**

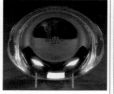

A silver two-handled oval dish, by Tiffany & Co., with cut-out shaped handles, bright cut with triangular panels of bellflowers, monogrammed "MMC".

1907-38 9.25in (23.5cm) wide

£280-320   **SI**

A silver-plated salver, by G. Forbes, New York, NY, of oblong form with gadrooned edge with the initials "M.O." at the centre, on paw feet.

c1810   *10in (25.5cm) long*

£220-280   **SI**

One of a pair of Austro-Hungarian Art Nouveau silver trays, possibly used as wine coasters, each with a wavy everted rim embossed with lilies-of-the-valley with sinuous foliage, marked with Diana head standard mark and maker's mark "FR".

4.5in (16.5cm) diam

£100-150 (pair)   **DN**

A silver and enamel small dish, by Omar Ramsden, with planished surface and a notched rim, centred with a pierced rose motif revealing a red enamelled panel beneath, marked "OR" with London hallmarks for 19.. and signed "Omar Ramsden Me Fecit".

4.25in (10.5cm)

£520-580   **DN**

A Taxco Mexican silver and copper bird dish, modelled as a stylized bird with silver wings, brass beak and inlaid silver and malachite eye, stamped "METALES [____] HANDWROUGHT LOS CASTILLO TAXCO".

12in (30.5cm) high

£180-220   **FRE**

A silver centrepiece dish, by Tiffany & Co., the circular bowl with everted wide rim applied with leaf tip edge, rosettes and scallop shells, engraved with scrolling foliage and monogrammed "MFG".

1907-38 13.5in (34.5cm) diam

£1,000-2,000 SI

A silver bowl, designed by Harald Nielsen for Georg Jensen, of half-spherical form with hammered texture and simple ring base, date mark for 1933-44, "HN" initials, "580A" and other markings.

4.75in (12cm) diam

£700-800 FRE

A late 19thC/early 20thC German silver vase, of tapering lobed ovoid form, applied with two lions' mask and ring handles and with leaf tip borders.

7in (18cm) high

£300-400 SI

A silver vase, by Tiffany & Co, waisted vessel chased in high relief with flowers.

7in (17.7cm)

£900-1,000 SI

A George III silver creamer, of baluster form, engraved with bands of foliage, ovolus and serpentine lines and a vacant shield-form cartouche, London hallmarks.

1799   4.25in (10.5cm) high

£250-300 SI

A late 19thC Continental silver small ewer, of pear form, chased with Biblical scenes, the hinged cover surmounted by a phoenix with chicks.

9in (23cm) high

£420-480 SI

A Danish-style silver coffee pot, probably American, lobed body with hammered texture and floral bulb to lid, applied spout and carved ivory handle on three "webbed" feet, stamped "STERLING".

c1930   7.5in (19cm) high

£600-700 FRE

A modern English silver creamer, modelled as a cow wearing a garland of flowers and with a bumble bee on her back.

6in (15cm) long

£550-650 SI

A contemporary Italian silver five-piece tea service, by Miniati, Florence, comprising teapot, coffee pot, creamer, sugar and two-handled tray, each of angular pentagonal section with hinged cover and angular handle mounted with square lapis lazuli tiles.

20in (51cm) wide

£3,000-4,000 SI

A Continental silver and glass liqueur set, comprising two bottles and eight glasses on a stand.

c1900   9.5in (24cm) wide

£200-300 JBS

A Victorian pepper pot, by Hukin & Heath, naturalistically modelled as a toadstool, the domed cover unscrewing from the shaped stem, London hallmarks.

1889   2in (5cm) diam

£400-500 DN

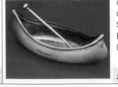

A pair of cased silver beakers, by Elfin, of cylindrical form, with inset discs inscribed "ELFIN".

c1850   2.75in (7cm) diam

£150-200 DN

A salt cellar in the form of a canoe, by Saunders and Shepherd, the canoe Birmingham 1904, the spoon London 1903.

3.25in (8.5cm)

£150-200 DN

A Japanese silver-mounted and enamelled ostrich egg cup, the egg painted brown and enamelled in gilt and red with insects and plants, the mixed metal base in the form of a flower stem on a mound applied with a cricket and cover.

Ostrich egg cups were made from a cleaned-out shell that was mounted onto a silver or gold stem and foot which is usually highly and intricately decorated. Although this example is certainly 19th century due to its form and country of manufacture, they were popular during the 16th and 17th centuries, having originated in Europe as an exotic curiosity during the 15th century.

7.5in (19cm) high

£420-480 **SI**

A late 19thC Derby crumb scoop, the handle painted in the Imari palette with stylized flowers, the electroplated scoop engraved with scrolling foliage.

12.5in (31.5cm) long

£40-60 **Chef**

A pair of silver sugar tongs, by George Jensen, marked "925".

1910

£150-200 **SSp**

A silver toast rack, by H.G. Murphy, marked for the Falcon works, "HGM" and London hallmarks.

1934   3.5in (9cm) high

£1,200-1,500 **DN**

Two pairs of contemporary American silver salt and pepper shakers, by Pampaloni, of asymmetric pyramidal form.

Largest 4.25in (10.5cm) high

£650-750 **SI**

A pair of silver wine glass coasters, by Georg Jensen, of circular shape with beaded rims and embossed in the centre with buds and foliage, stamped "GI", "925", and numbered "41", with London import marks.

1930   3.3in (8.5cm)

£120-180 **DN**

A set of six George III wine labels, 'Port' and 'Madeira', London 1805 by John Rich; 'Brandy', 1800 by Mary Hyde and John Reily; 'Sherry', 1803 by Phipps and Robinson; and two 'Sherry', canted rectangular with reeded borders, 1794 by Phipps and Robinson, 1820 by George Knight.

£200-300 **DN**

A silver box, by John Linnit, with lid depicting scene from 'The Pickwick Papers'.

£1,000-1,500 **GS**

A pair of Victorian bath-shaped silver spoon stands, by Edward Smith, each engine-turned with a cartouche, one lacking a small section of border, Birmingham hallmarks.

1864   4in (11.5cm) long

£300-400 **DN**

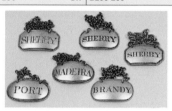

A pair of silver shaped rectangular menu stands, by Samuel Jacob, cast, pierced and chased with winged putti amid foliate scrolls, London hallmarks.

1899   2.75in (7cm) wide

£150-200 **DN**

A late 19th/early 20thC Continental silver box, rectangular with hinged cover, repousse with floral baskets, floral sprays, foliage and scrolls and with a vacant cartouche, lined with purple velvet, partial hallmark and marked "925".

5in (12.5 cm) wide

£250-350   **SI**

A 20thC Continental silver-mounted glass box, of casket form, mounted with ribbon-tied bellflower garlands, ovolo and beaded edges, the domed cover engraved with laurel branches, ribbons and flowerheads.

5in (12.5 cm) long

£280-320   **SI**

A Dutch silver cabinet-shaped tea caddy, embossed with figured and foliate scrolls, the cover with an animal finial, date letter.

1912   5.5in (14cm) high

£350-400   **DN**

A silver repousse tea caddy, by S. Kirk & Son, Baltimore, the ovoid vessel and cylindrical cover chased with flowers and foliage on a stippled ground, the base monogrammed "GPG".

1868-1896   3.5in (9cm) high

£500-550   **SI**

Two silver vinaigrettes, by John and Joseph Wilmore, both with cast border, engine-turned panels and pierced grill, Birmingham hallmarks.

1827 and 1836   1.5in (3.5cm) wide

£350-450   **L&T**

A silver embossed pot, with foliate and floral decoration, Birmingham hallmarks.

1890   2in (5cm) diam

£80-120   **PSA**

A Dutch silver trinket box, the top with pastoral scene with pierced mother-of-pearl behind.

2.25in (5.5cm) wide

£70-90   **PSA**

A single sovereign holder, by Mordan and Storr, Birmingham.

£100-200   **GS**

A silver double sovereign holder, engraved with initials "W.W.", Birmingham.

1912

£100-200   **GS**

A silver compact, by Georg Jensen.

c1925

£600-700   **PC**

A silver vesta, engraved with initials "E.H.", Birmingham.

£40-60   **GS**

A silver hip flask, with pull off lid, Edinburgh hallmarks.

1924   6in (15cm) high

£700-1,000   **Tag**

A plain silver playing card case, Birmingham hallmarks.

1909

£120-180   **L&T**

A silver stamp box, by A. & J. Zimmerman, in the form of a serpentine side table, with a hinged lid, one dummy drawer on square legs, Birmingham hallmarks.

1910   2.25in (6cm) wide

£250-300   **DN**

A silver vesta/match case, by William Hornby, in the form of a dog kennel with a hinged roof and a nephrite bulldog at the door, a chip to one ear and leg, London hallmarks.

1907   2.25in (5.75cm)

£850-950   **DN**

A silver and enamel five-piece toilet set, the grey enamel backs mounted with Art Deco influenced mounts, Birmingham hallmarks, some damage.

1936

£40-60   **LFA**

A silver-backed clothes brush, by William Hutton & Sons, embossed with the profile of a girl wearing a cap, flanked by stems of lilies, from a design by Kate Harris, maker's mark for London.

1902   7in (18.5cm)

£50-70   **DN**

A late 19thC/early 20thC American enamelled silver travelling set, comprising of hand mirror, hair brush, clothes brush, comb, two canisters, two bottles, jar, pill box, button hook, two fingernail files, fingernail scissors and fingernail buffer, all in a fitted case.

Dressing sets need to be complete to fetch the highest prices. Damage to the enamelling will affect value. These were functional pieces and were used frequently, so were easily damaged. Where possible, bottles should have original stoppers. Many such sets were contained in fitted boxes with a myriad of accessories, as well as being loose and displayed on a dressing table. Incomplete sets still have a value as collectors may buy incomplete sets to 'make up' complete sets.

£320-380   **SI**

A silver pin cushion, by Levi and Salaman, in the form of the coronation throne, Birmingham hallmarks.

1901   2.75in (7cm) high

£120-180   **DN**

A silver pin cushion, by Levi and Salaman, in the form of an ostrich, standing on a round composition base, Birmingham hallmarks.

1911   2.5in (6.5cm) high

£400-450   **DN**

A George IV 'King's Husk' pattern silver-gilt grape scissors, engraved with a crest, London hallmarks.

1822

£400-500   **DN**

A 20thC enamelled silver and engraved glass dresser set, decorated with blue, pink, yellow and green birds, ribbons and flowers on a green engine-turned ground, with an engraved glass pin.

Mirror 13.5in (34cm) long

£1,800-2,200   **SI**

A five-piece silver dressing table set, Birmingham hallmarks.

1924 Brush 11in (28cm) long

£100-140   **OACC**

A Dutch silver shoe-shaped basket, embossed with pastoral scenes, lacking the swing handle, date letter for 1902.

6in (15cm) long

£250-300   **DN**

An 18thC silver scissors case, the rounded oval top with simple acanthus engraving and "Eliz Mills Bristol", plain lower section, ball end finial, unmarked.

4in (10cm) long

£550-650   **L&T**

SILVER

A Victorian silver pocket knife, with integral scissors, corkscrew, hook, knife and more, engraved monogram, London hallmarks.

1870   3in (7.5cm) wide

£350-450   **Tag**

A Victorian miniature watering can, by Henry Wilkinson & Co, engraved with initials, handle to the lid detached, Sheffield hallmarks.

1888   1.75in (4.5cm) high

£200-250   **DN**

A silver rattle, Birmingham hallmarks.

1915   4.75in (12cm) long

£200-250   **OACC**

An early 20thC silver-plated and horn trophy, on ball feet, inscribed 'HOGMANAY/ 1914'.

6in (15cm) high

£150-200   **SI**

A silver rattle, by Crisford & Norris, compressed round form, pierced with a pig, suspended from a plastic teether, Birmingham hallmarks.

1920   2in (5.5 cm) diam

£70-90   **DN**

An Edwardian silver-mounted horse's hoof, by George Neal & George Neal, London, the interior fitted with an inkwell, the cover inscribed 'In memory of Brigand / died February 26th 1918 / a favourite and the last Hunter of W.H.P. Jenkins, Frenchay Park, Bristol.'

Desk accessories made from horses' hooves were popular Victorian and Edwardian items and were often finely made by noted silversmiths. Intensely personal, they were made from the hooves of favourite horses, or local horses who achieved success with their rider. They are often engraved with an inscription and dated, commemorating the horse's life or the event.

1918   6.5in (16.5cm) long

£600-700   **SI**

An early 20thC silver Torah breast plate, chased with foliate scrolls, mounted with a crown with bird finial, flanked by lions and columns hung with bells, centring a small door enclosing a model of the Torah within a bird and foliate pierced surround, inscribed in Hebrew and dated "5711".

13.5in (34.5cm) high

£800-1,200   **SI**

A silver and green marble postal scale, with ivory scale, Birmingham hallmarks.

1922   3.75in (9.5cm) high

£150-250   **Tag**

A cast silver model of a pig, maker S.C., retailed by A. Barrett & Sons, inscribed "Ye Ancient Lucky Pig" on the back ridge, London hallmarks.

1902

£350-450   **L&T**

A leather clay pipe wallet, dated 1761, and an 18thC facsimile packet from Willsons Snuff Shop, 27 St John Street, West Smithfield, also labelled Wills, Bristol.

£350-450 | **BAR**

A collection of five 19thC European black clay character pipe bowls.

£40-60 | **BAR**

CLAY PIPES

- Clay pipes are the most common and inexpensive type of pipe found due to the huge volume made.
- Made from kaolin (china clay), they were produced in vast quantities from the 17thC to the 19thC.
- The shape of clay pipes has changed over the centuries – either due to fashion or to the falling price of tobacco. The earliest pipes from the 17thC are very small. After c1700, pipe bowls became larger and stems longer. The 1800s saw bowls becoming shorter and fatter, allowing for more decoration. Stems became shorter.
- Collectors should look for clay pipes bearing arms or crests, maker's names, initials or trademarks. 'Churchwardens' – pipes with elongated stems up to 24in (60cm) long – are very desirable. There is little interest in clay pipes produced after 1900.

A collection of five French polychrome clay pipes: two with character bowls, three with flower motifs.

Longest 8in (20cm) long

£200-250 | **BAR**

A collection of five 19thC French clay pipes and bowls, representing hands, feet and a leg.

Longest 6in (15cm) long

£120-180 | **BAR**

A pair of 19thC large clay pipes, one carved in full relief as a Christ-like character, the other bas relief moulded with a football game.

8in (20cm) long

£70-100 | **BAR**

A collection of four 19thC European clay pipes, of various animals including an unusual full relief fish pipe.

Longest 6in (14cm) long

£100-150 | **BAR**

A collection of four 19thC French red clay pipes, named Negresse, Le Tzar, Un Maroc and another of a lady's head.

£180-220 | **BAR**

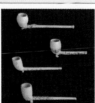

A collection of four French polychrome clay pipes, three with a floral motif and one with a French Navy anchor.

2in (5cm) long

£100-150 | **BAR**

A collection of four 19thC European clay pipes, one with large bowl with Crystal Palace motif and amber mouthpiece, one double-bowl pipe, one in full relief of an owl, the other as Atlas holding up the world.

Longest 8in (20cm) long

£70-100 | **BAR**

A collection of five 19thC French polychrome clay pipes, representing a horse, cat, monkey, dog and bull.

Longest 6in (15cm) long

£350-450 | **BAR**

A collection of six English clay pipe bowls, in full relief, of Disraeli, Edward VII, George V and others.

£100-150 | **BAR**

SMOKING ACCESSORIES

A well-carved 19thC meerschaum pipe, carved in bas relief with the head of Prince Albert flanked by pair of angels, the silver coloured metal mounts and cover with a Royal Crown surrounded by medallions and turquoise stones.

Albert, Queen Victoria's beloved Prince Consort, died in 1861.

21.5in (55cm) long

£800-1,000 BAR

A collection of four 19thC meerschaum cheroot holders, one full relief carved a boy (some damage), one carved as a bearded head, one full relief carved as two stallions, and a suave gentleman with monocle and top hat (damage to hat brim).

£50-80 BAR

An unusual 19thC meerschaum cigar holder on stand, carved with two Saxon figures, silver-coloured metal mount and lion claw feet to base, Wills Collection label No. M92.

7in (18cm) high

£3,500-4,500 BAR

A 19thC meerschaum pipe, finely carved as a young lady's head, with coiffured hair and a flower-and-ribbon bedecked bonnet perched above her forehead, silver coloured mount and amber stem.

Bowl 3in (8cm) high

£250-300 BAR

A collection of three 19thC meerschaum pipe bowls, one full relief carved as a bearded man with Wills Collection label No. M225, one two-tone coloured plain bowl, the top off white, the rest biscuit, the last with engraved floral motif and silver-coloured metal mount.

Max 4.75in (12cm) long

£30-40 BAR

MEERSCHAUM PIPES

- The name 'meerschaum' is taken from the German words for 'sea scum' alluding to the colour of sea foam. It is made from a form of magnesium silicate found in rock veins.
- Meerschaum was first used by the Hungarians in the 18thC after they discovered that it sweetened tobacco, was largely resistant to heat and was easily carved to great decorative effect.
- As meerschaum pipes are smoked, they turn from a pale creamy beige colour to a much stronger yellowy amber colour.
- Many fantastic and intricate shapes were produced and the most unusual and deeply carved, or those with precious metal parts, are highly sought after and fetch high prices. Bowls decorated with or in the form of an old man's face are relatively common.

A 19thC meerschaum pipe, finely full relief carved as a cuffed hand holding an egg, with silver-coloured metal band on two-piece amber stem.

9.5in (24cm) long

£250-300 BAR

A good 19thC meerschaum bird claw pipe, the claw holding a pipe bowl, with an amber stem.

7in (18cm) long

£70-100 BAR

A hand-carved meerschaum pipe, in the form of a Turk's head, with an amber stem.

c1900 *6in (15cm) long*

£3-5 TWC

A 19thC Persian Nargileh, decorative pink flash glass bowl, decorative brass stand, fitments and flexible stem.

£60-80 **BAR**

A Qajar period decorative Persian Nargileh water pipe, coloured enamel, matching base.

£1,500-2,000 **BAR**

A 19thC Persian Nargileh, inlaid bi-metal ovoid body, scroll tripod base.

£450-500 **BAR**

A 20thC leather and metal water pipe, probably Middle Eastern.

£50-60 **BAR**

WATER PIPES

- Water pipes were used in Asia, Africa and Persia (the Middle East). It is believed they spread from Africa to Arab countries, India and China from the 17th century onwards. Styles became more elaborate according to fashion and as they grew in popularity.
- They are also known as 'nargileh' pipes, an Indian word meaning 'coconut', which echoes the shape, and also the original material, of the water container.
- The container holds water through which the smoke is passed, which cools and cleanses the smoke.
- Smaller ornate and handheld water pipes are generally Chinese in origin. Larger, floor or table mounted water pipes are usually Middle Eastern or Indian in origin. To use them, smokers reclined on cushions or a low divan, or sat cross-legged on the floor.

A 19thC Persian water pipe, inlaid with various metals in a geometric design, on a circular base with feet.

£50-70 **BAR**

A 19thC Persian Nargileh, the bowl formed from a gourd, decorative brass finish.

£450-500 **BAR**

A 19thC Turkish water pipe, with plain glass bowl.

£40-60 **BAR**

A 19thC decorative Turkish water pipe, European cut glass ovoid bowl, metal arrow-decorated mount.

£80-120 **BAR**

A 19thC decorative glass water pipe, frosted and white enamel, embossed brass top.

£70-100 **BAR**

A 19thC Bohemian decorative water pipe, square cut glass foot, the pear-shaped body pink stained and with brass fittings, fabric stem and mouthpiece.

£80-120 **BAR**

An unusual 18thC root wood pipe in the Kalamasch style, inlaid with green and red cut glass and brass, with decorative silver-coloured metal mounts and horn stem.

2in (30cm) long

£300-350 BAR

An unusually painted early 19thC long bowl porcelain pipe, handpainted with figures in military uniforms, with wood and horn stem and brass mounts.

Bowl 4in (10cm) long

£200-250 BAR

An early 19thC Prattware puzzle pipe, with pot bellied bowl, three outer rings and looped coils to centre, restored and missing a small section.

8.5in (21.5cm) long

£450-550 BAR

An Austro Hungarian pipe, with finely relief carved portrait of Napoleon, the plain bowl with silver-coloured metal hallmarked mounts and lid.

c1830   *6in (15cm) long*

£400-500 BAR

An unusual painted 19thC porcelain pipe, formed as a rabbit in full dress, the lid being its head, with wood and horn stem.

Bowl 6in (15cm) long

£250-300 BAR

A 19thC German porcelain pipe, with mountain goat scene, white metal lid, wood and horn stem.

14.5in (37cm) long

A polychrome porcelain pipe bowl, with a man in a green hat in bas relief.

4.75in (12cm) high

A porcelain pipe bowl, painted with a running deer.

4in (10cm) high

£60-80 BAR

A scarce 19thC carved amber pipe, the bowl formed as a tower with bear in full relief, plain silver ferrule and amber stem, slight damage.

6.25in (16cm) long

£170-220 BAR

A large English pottery Codgers pipe, with transfer print entitled 'The Pig Race' to bowl, black and white glaze, damaged stem.

c1860   *12in (30cm) long*

A brown glazed Codgers clay pipe with a football game in bas relief.

c1860   *9in (23cm) long*

£130-180 BAR

A 19thC Japanese wood opium pipe holder, of an elongated man with a well-carved bamboo pouch in full relief of a man hanging by a cord, a carved wood bowl and a copper and brass long decorative pipe, possibly Burmese.

£130-180 BAR

A 19thC Chinese embroidered pipe holder, with tassel and two porcelain balls, containing a white metal and black wood pipe, a 19thC silver-coloured metal miniature Chinese water opium pipe, and a Persian water pipe bowl, silver-coloured metal on brass.

Pipeholder 14.5in (37cm) long

£700-1,000 BAR

A 19thC Chinese porcelain famille rose dry opium pipe with porcelain bowl.

21.25in (54cm) long

£1,500-2,000 BAR

A large 19thC English decorative clear glass pipe, with tulip-shaped bowl and knopped stem.

19in (48cm) long

£70-100 **BAR**

A 19thC Bristol blue glass pipe.

25.5in (65cm) long

£220-280 **BAR**

A 19thC moulded blue glass pipe, cut glass pipe and blue twist glass cheroot holder.

Max 6.25in (16cm) long

£200-250 **BAR**

A Matsikolumbwe zoomorphic black clay pipe, bowl shaped as an antelope, and two Botswan engraved stone pipe bowls.

Pipe 5.5in (14cm) long

£250-300 **BAR**

FIND OUT MORE...

'The Pipe Book' by Alfred Dunhill, published by Arthur Barker Ltd, London, 1969. Out of print, but an excellent book.

'The Intriguing Design of Tobacco Pipes' by Benedict Goes, published by Uniepers b.v., Leiden, 1993.

A Wedgwood blue jasper pipe bowl, applied with a cherub scalding an insect with a torch, another with a flower garland, upper case mark.

2.5in (6.5cm) long

£300-350 **BAR**

A Wedgwood blue jasper pipe bowl, applied with anthemion leaves, four paterae to bowl edge, impressed SIAITE S PATENT and WEDGWOOD.

2.75in (7cm) long

£180-220 **BAR**

Two 19thC German porcelain pipes, one bowl with a transfer print of a horse, abalone inlaid wood, horn and woven stem, the other with two-piece bowl handpainted with blue cornflowers, wood and horn stem; plus a white porcelain bowl, naively painted with a lady.

Max 13in (33cm) long

£40-60 **BAR**

A collection of three 19thC pipes: a silver-coloured metal studded Hungarian pipe, part of stem missing; a wood pipe, full relief carved as a man's head, with horn mouthpiece; and a meerschaum pipe, in full relief as a head held by a hand, bone stem.

Max 15in (38cm) long

£50-80 **BAR**

A German porcelain pipe, with bas relief of a sailor boy on a dock, the silver lid marked London 1881, with light wood and horn stem.

4.25in (11cm) long

£80-120 **BAR**

A 19thC memento mori porcelain pipe of a skull, a pottery pipe in full relief of man with large nose, metal hat as lid, and a large 19thC Negro head pottery pipe.

Max 4in (10cm) long

£220-250 **BAR**

A 19thC African Mahsikulumbwe pipe, the black pottery bowl in the form of an antelope, the stem of wood and ivory inlaid with abalone.

21.25in (54cm) long

£400-500 **BAR**

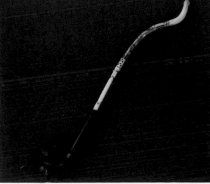

DUNHILL LIGHTERS

- Alfred Dunhill opened his first shop in 1907 in Duke St., London and retailed lighters from the 1920s. These lighters are amongst the most desirable and collectable today, with many fetching the highest prices.

- Their popular proprietary lighters were developed by Willey Greenwood and Frederick Wise. They patented a new design in 1919 that placed the flint horizontally and allowed the lighter to be triggered with one hand. Dunhill built a prototype using a mustard can that directly led to their new lighter, the 'Unique', which was released in 1922-1923.

- The Unique came in many different sizes and designs, including the tiny 'bijou' and novelty designs including a desk ruler lighter.

- Precious metal lighters are very desirable as are those with 'maki-e' lacquered decoration. The most desirable and valuable versions include extra or concealed features such as a lady's compact or, more commonly, a watch.

- Some wear is expected as these lighters were used, with entirely mint examples being extremely scarce. Dents, splits and missing or non-original replaced parts will devalue a piece. Prices have risen steeply in recently years for top quality pieces in fine condition.

A late 1940s French Dunhill Salaam manual petrol pocket lighter, with lacquer-over-aluminium decoration.

Thanks to the aluminium case, this lighter is very light in weight. The Salaam was introduced in 1946.

2.25in (5.5cm) high

£120-150 RBL

A Swiss Dunhill Unique Sport manual petrol pocket lighter, brass and leather with lift-arm.

Early Unique lighters have a single wheel for the user to trigger the lighter, after 1932 they consistently have two – a wheel for the user to turn which is below the wheel that strikes.

1926   2.25in (5.5cm) high

£180-200 RBL

A CLOSER LOOK AT A DUNHILL LIGHTER

Parts can often be replaced. Check for consistent markings such as a serial number.

The integral watch first appeared as a special commission for a wealthy South American in 1926 and went into production in 1927.

The body is made from solid silver, gold versions are also known. Larger table sizes, some with eight day inset watches were also made.

The Sports' model with raised flame guard was introduced in 1926. It protected the flame from wind when used outside.

A Swiss Dunhill Unique Sports manual petrol pocket watch lighter, silver with lift-arm.

1927   2.25in (5.5cm) high

£2,200-2,600 RBL

A 1940s English Dunhill Unique manual petrol table lighter, silver-plated and shagreen decoration with lift-arm.

3.75in (9.5cm) high

£250-300 RBL

A Swiss Dunhill Unique manual petrol pocket lighter, silver with lift arm and engine-turned decoration.

c1926   2.25in (5.5cm) high

£400-500 RBL

A 1940s French silver Dunhill Handy manual petrol pocket lighter.

Earlier versions of this model were called the Savory.

2in (5cm) high

£120-180 RBL

A 1940s Dunhill Squareboy manual petrol pocket lighter, silver-plated with engine-turned decoration.

The Squareboy was introduced by Dunhill in 1937.

1.5in (4cm) high

£90-100 RBL

FIND OUT MORE...

The Dunhill Museum, 48 Jermyn Street, London, SW1Y 6DL, England. www.dunhill.com

A late 1920s Swiss Dunhill Unique Club manual desk lighter, silver-plated with single wheel.

5.5in (14cm) high

£200-250 RBL

A 1930s French Parker manual petrol pocket lighter, silver-plated with ribbed decoration and lift-arm.

Parker was a sub-brand of Dunhill, founded in 1923.

2in (5cm) high

£80-100 RBL

A 1930s German Everest manual petrol pocket lighter, silver with engine-turned decoration.

These lighters were imported into the UK marked with other manufacturers' names.

1.75in (4.5cm) high

£100-120 RBL

A 1940s French Dupont Jerobaum manual petrol table lighter, silver-plated with engine-turned decoration, lift-arm and pipe wand.

3.75in (9.5cm) high

£500-600 RBL

OTHER LIGHTERS

- Cigarette lighters began to be developed as the cigarette grew in popularity at the beginning of the 20th century. The field of lighter collecting has developed in the past five to ten years and is now supported globally. As the field has widened, more collectors and further research has led to a growing interest and higher prices.

- Collectors should look for innovative design, precious materials and notable names such as Dunhill, Ronson, Zippo, Thorens and Colibri as well as those by well-known jewellers such as Van Cleef & Arpels and Cartier.

- Although modern and generally similar in form and materials, Zippo lighters (founded 1933) are hotly collected, with a multitude of patterns and decoration available to the collector at comparatively inexpensive prices.

- Most collectable lighters used fluid or 'petrol' with gas being introduced and superseding fluid in the 1950s. There are three main categories – smaller pocket lighters, larger table or desk lighters and finally lighters that are part of something, such as a ladys' compact. Novelty shapes such as aeroplanes and figures are popular.

- Trench Art lighters are commonly found. They were made by civilians and soldiers during the World Wars from materials they found, such as bullet shells and coins. They are generally of comparatively low value but due to the variety on offer make a superb collection.

- Lighters are devalued by bad wear to plating, damage to lacquered decoration, missing or non-original replaced parts.

A Swiss Thorens manual petrol pocket lighter, chrome-plated Christmas edition given to German soldiers.

Thorens (founded in 1883) were based in Sainte-Croix, Switzerland and were well known for their production of fine quality musical boxes. Production of lighters began during the First World War and continued until c1964.

1944 *2in (5cm) high*

£80-100 RBL

A 1960s chrome-plated advertising Zippo manual petrol pocket lighter.

2.25in (5.5cm) high

£25-35 RBL

A late 1940s Polish Duplex or Tandem manual petrol pocket lighter, aluminium with two gas tanks.

2in (5cm) high

£70-90 RBL

An early 1930s Austrian Princess advertising semi-automatic petrol pocket lighter, chrome-plated with removable fuel tank.

2.25in (5.5cm) high

£20-30 RBL

A 1930s Swiss Pall Mall manual petrol pocket lighter, gold-plated and simulated snake skin, the flint wheel with horizontal striking surface.

2.25in (5.5cm) high

£150-180 RBL

A no-name 1940s simple manual petrol pocket lighter, chrome-plated the lift-arm with cigar-cutter.

2in (5cm) high

£150-200 RBL

A 1940s French no-name manual petrol pocket lighter, with celluloid wrap and lift-arm.

1.75in (4.5cm) high

£10-30 RBL

A 1940s German no-name manual petrol pocket lighter, with mother-of-pearl wrap and lift-arm, marked "Foreign".

1.75in (4.5cm) high

£50-60 RBL

A 1930s American Pollak ladies' manual petrol pocket lighter, chrome-plated with lift-arm, rouge and compact.

2in (5cm) high

£300-350 RBL

A late 1940s Ronson Banker automatic petrol pocket lighter, 14ct gold with engine-turned decoration.

2.25in (5.5cm) high

£250-300 RBL

A 1930s American Ronson Standard automatic petrol pocket lighter, with wind shield, leather wrap and monogram shield.

2in (5cm) high

£120-180 RBL

A 1940s French Atomy manual petrol pocket lighter, aluminium with interesting fuel and flint access system.

2in (5cm) high

£70-100 RBL

A 1940s German Myflan Strato semi-automatic petrol pocket lighter, nickel-plated.

2.75in (7cm) high

£40-60 RBL

A 1930s ladies' semi-automatic petrol pocket lighter, chrome-plated, unknown maker, probably German.

1.75in (4.5cm) wide

£50-60 RBL

A WWII hand-made Trench manual petrol pocket lighter, the body formed from two penny.

2in (5cm) high

£80-90 RBL

A WWII Trench miniature manual petrol pocket lighter, with engraved initials.

1.5in (4cm) high

£25-35 RBL

An artisan's netsuke miniature tinder pistol, in the form of a walnut, decorated with silver and copper on brass with florettes on a hammered surface.

The flint produces a spark which ignites charred silk floss in the base, creating a flame.

c1880 *1.75in (4.5cm) high*

£1,400-1,800 RBL

A French Sarhon "spinner" manual petrol pocket lighter, with clockwork mechanism and niello-style and engraved decoration.

c1880 2in (5cm) high

£250-300 RBL

A French Cito bijoux manual petrol pocket lighter, probably 1920s, silver, with special mechanism.

2.75in (7cm) high

£150-200 RBL

An early 1960s Zippo Coca-Cola advertising manual petrol pocket lighter, with lanyard, mint and boxed.

2.25in (5.5cm) high

£250-350 RBL

An Austrian TCW Pretty manual petrol pocket lighter, chrome-plated in fitted leather case.

c1920 2.25in (5.5cm) high

£80-100 RBL

A Carlton Ware 'Rouge Royale' table lighter.

8.5in (22cm) long

£60-70 OACC

Six late 1950s to mid-1990s loss-proof Zippo manual petrol pocket lighters, all mint and boxed.

'Loss Proof' Zippo lighters have small loops or 'lanyards' that can be attached to objects or a belt to prevent loss.

2.25in (5.5cm) high

£500-600 RBL

A 1930s American Ronson automatic petrol table lighter.

The standard model, without feet, is worth about £5.

4.25in (7cm) high

£175-225 RBL

A Dorset Light Industries petrol table lighter, Bakelite with electronic ignition, special Coronation edition.

1953 4.5in (11.5cm) high

£100-120 RBL

A 1930s Thorens bar fuel dispenser, nickle-plated.

5.75in (14.5cm) high

£80-120 RBL

An American Ronson Beauticase combination cigarette case and automatic petrol lighter, chrome-plated with lacquer decoration.

c1930 4.5in (11.5cm) high

£150-200 RBL

An early 1920s Austrian Juwel silver semi-automatic petrol ring lighter.

These ring pocket lighters were also made in brass, which is more common.

Face 0.75in (2cm) high

£700-900 RBL

FIND OUT MORE...

Stefano Bisconcini, 'Lighters', Edizioni San Gottardo, 1984.

A.M.W. van Weert, 'The Legend of the Lighter', published by Abbeville Press, 1995.

Ira Pilossof & Stuart Schneider, 'Handbook of Lighters', published by Schiffer Publishing, 1999.

National Lighter Museum, 107 South 2nd Street, Guthrie, OK 73044 USA.

A Scottish ivory and silver-mounted table snuffbox.

c1770   3.25in (8cm) long

£550-575   **MB**

A George III tortoiseshell and silver snuffbox.

c1780   13.25in (8.5cm) wide

£300-350   **MB**

SNUFFBOXES

- Snuff-taking became popular at the French court during the late 1500s, spreading and becoming generally fashionable by the late 1600s, but did not spread to Britain until the early 1700s. Snuffboxes tend to be hinged, rather than having lift-off lids.

- Snuff was originally made by grating tightly rolled blocks of tobacco leaves with a snuff rasp or grater. Use of rasps ended by the mid 1700s with the proliferation of ready-ground snuff.

- The Scots continued taking snuff into the late 19th century, long after the habit had become less fashionable elsewhere in Europe.

- Enamelled copper snuffboxes were mass-produced in Staffordshire and Birmingham during the late 18th and early 19th centuries. These snuffboxes are highly decorative, with brightly coloured, transfer-printed scenes.

- Thanks to new mechanical die-stamping and rolled silver sheet techniques, silver snuffboxes from the early to mid-19th century could be mass-produced to meet demand. Such Victorian examples are more flamboyantly engraved and decorated than simpler and plainer 18th century boxes.

- Silver boxes by the maker Nathaniel Mills are highly sought after and will usually command a premium over similar boxes by other makers.

- Silver boxes with lids showing cast scenes such as battle scenes or castles are particularly desirable. Cast pieces are heavier than die-stamped examples, which use a thinner grade of silver sheet.

- Collectors should look carefully for damage to hinges and splits or dents which will affect value. Beware of lids that do not fit tightly and of worn engraved decoration that lacks precision.

A yo-yo snuffbox, in partridge wood.

c1790   3.5in (9cm) diam

£50-100   **MB**

A late 18thC French tortoiseshell snuffbox, the hinged cover inset a miniature painting of a young couple in landscape under glass and with gold banding and initials to tablet "JP to JR".

3.5in (8.5cm) long

£200-300   **BAR**

A late 18thC octagonal snuffbox, in silver-mounted mother-of-pearl, engraved with flower borders and dotted lines.

3.25in (6cm) wide

£120-180   **BAR**

A late 18thC English oval enamel snuffbox, the cover polychrome-painted with a stag hunt, the front with a bear and back with stag on a white ground.

2.25in (6cm) wide

£280-320   **BAR**

A brass one dial puzzle snuffbox.

c1880   2.75in (7cm) long

£80-125   **MB**

A papier-mâché circular snuffbox, the cover painted with a view titled "Lindau am Bodensee" in red inside and incised indistinctly "...1833, Brunsvig".

1833   3.5in (9cm) diam

£400-500   **BAR**

A mid-19thC Austro Hungarian tortoiseshell snuffbox, with silver mounts and massed flowers thumbpiece, 13 lothige, maker's mark "F.V.".

3in (7.5cm) diam

£250-300   **BAR**

A Victorian silver snuffbox, of serpentine outline, engraved acanthus scrolls and presentation inscription, Birmingham hallmarks for Nathaniel Mills.

1846   *3in (7.5cm) wide*

£260-280   **L&T**

A mid-19thC circular papier-mâché snuffbox, the cover printed and painted, showing an itinerant violinist with daughter, cracking.

3.25in (8.5cm) diam

£150-200   **BAR**

An English, black papier-mâché rectangular snuffbox, the hinged cover with a printed and painted scene of three card players.

3.5in (8.5cm) wide

£160-180   **BAR**

A 19thC Bavarian wood snuffbox, carved as a hound's head, with glass eyes and open mouth displaying its bone teeth, painted tongue, and hinged fox mask cover.

4.25in (11cm) long

£500-600   **BonS**

A tortoiseshell banjo snuffbox, inlaid with mother-of-pearl with ivory pegs.

c1870   *4in (10cm) long*

£200-250   **RdeR**

A late 17thC Netherlandish ivory snuff rasp, carved as a figure of a man with full wig wearing long robes with arms together, worn features, cracked, lacking iron rasp.

From the Redfern Collection, no.32.

7in (18cm) long

£1,500-2,000   **BAR**

A 19thC Scottish rootwood snuff mull, of asymmetric form, the hinged split lid also with applied root.

8.5in (22cm) long

£1,000-1,500   **L&T**

A 19thC Scottish burr-boxwood snuff mull, of carved asymmetric form, the corresponding lid with chased brass hinge.

2.75in (7cm) long

£250-300   **L&T**

An 18thC French ivory snuff rasp, well-carved with a Classical maiden in diaphanous robes holding a tablet and resting on a pillar, with fruit and leaves above and shell terminal, chipped to one side, lacking iron rasp.

From the Redfern Collection, no.28.

7.25in (18.5cm) long

£1,600-1,800   **BAR**

An 18thC French ivory snuff rasp, carved with a woman representing Summer with sickle and cornucopia between scrolls, a crowned coat of arms and shell above, with iron rasp.

7.5in (19.5cm) long

£2,000-2,500   **BAR**

A silver Mappin & Webb cigarette box, on four plain feet, cedar-lined with engine-turned decoration, in original Garrards cardboard box, Birmingham or London hallmarks.

1947

£100-150 | **BAR**

A Victorian silver cigar box, with two compartments with lift-up lids, two cigar cutters and a lighter, London hallmark.

1893 | *10.25in (26cm) wide*

£1,500-2,500 | **Tag**

An enamelled cigarette case, painted with the head of a black horse.

3.25in (8.5cm) high

£700-800 | **Tag**

A Victorian lacquer cigar box.

5in (13cm) long

£40-50 | **OACC**

An early 20thC pietra dura and ebonised wood matchbox with striker, probably Florentine.

2in (5cm) wide

£30-40 | **MHC**

A decorated Handel tobacco jar, with a hunting dog on point in a field, the reverse with lightly painted Bavarian pipe, the silver-plated lid with pipe mounted on top, plated top shows pitting and loss of plating, some wear.

7in (18cm) high

£550-650 | **JDJ**

A late 19thC walnut table top smoker's companion, with central two-handled jar with domed cover, apertures for ten pipes with match holder, striker and ashtray on a circular base.

9.5in (24cm) high

£120-180 | **Clv**

An Australian WWII commemorative ashtray.

6.25in (16cm) wide

£80-100 | **OACC**

A 1930s clown ashtray, unmarked.

£320-380 | **BAC**

A novelty dog ashtray.

3.5in (8.5cm) high

£30-40 | **RH**

A tobacco cutter, NY State, butternut board, cutting blade has whirling decorative centre, used to cut tobacco plugs for smoking / chewing.

c1830 | *19in (48.5cm) long*

£900-1,000 | **RAA**

A kitsch clockwork cigarette dispenser, with devil's feet and angel finial, Italian with Swiss mechanism.

13.5in (34cm) high

£220-280 | **V**

SPACE MEMORABILIA

- Space memorabilia has become increasingly popular over the past 10 years. A realisation of the historical importance of these items twinned with increased visibility and availability at auctions has led to growing interest and thus rapidly rising values.
- Space memorabilia can be divided into categories: items carried to the moon; items carried in space; items used by astronauts in training; items used in training but not flown; space agency documents; astronauts' autographs; and commemorative items.
- Although lunar and space used items, such as clothing, fetch high prices, the vast majority of items are affordable. Collections of non-unique items such as autographs, small pieces of craft, training items, associated documents and commemorative pieces can be bought comparatively inexpensively.
- Condition is important, but as much was stored (often improperly) by ex-employees, wear is common. Many items are unique, so rarity takes precedence over condition.
- Russian pieces are more common than American pieces as Russian cosmonauts were allowed to take pieces home after flights, whilst American astronauts were only allowed limited 'souvenirs'. Collectors are usually unfamiliar with Russian programmes and language so it can be difficult to tell how a piece relates to a mission. American memorabilia is therefore more valuable, particularly as the Americans landed on the moon.

An extremely rare flown two-piece white Beta cloth flight suit, worn by Command Module pilot Dick Gordon, onboard the Command Module "Yankee Clipper", with correct NASA and Apollo XII tags and badges.

This important suit was worn by Gordon onboard the orbiting Command Module for over 10 days whilst in earth and lunar orbits. The seams contain moon dust that was picked up from contact with Gordon's crew members (Charles Conrad and Alan Bean) after their mission on the moon's surface. Provenance: Ex Dick Gordon Collection.

£60,000-70,000   **AGI**

A blue flight coverall, worn by Dick Gordon during the Gemini Program training, with "R. F. Gordon / M.S.C. N.A.S.A." nametag and NASA meatball patch on the chest.

£3,000-4,000   **AGI**

A flown component threaded screw, recovered from the Liberty Bell 7 from a depth of 16,043 feet on July 20, 1999.

'The Kansas Cosmosphere', sponsors of the recovery and restoration of the capsule from the sea, encased certain parts that could not be reinstalled due to corrosion, in Lucite blocks and sold them as fundraisers to help offset costs of restoration and exhibition of the spacecraft.

£320-380   **AGI**

A training/prototype white Beta cloth right handed glove, for Gordon Cooper, with red wrist ring, battery pack and light on one finger, interior ID label "Glove, Space Suit; NASA designation GC-4C-10; Mfg. David Clark Company, Inc.; P/N A-1715D Serial No. 410-A; Size Cooper August 1965."

£1,200-1,800   **AGI**

A flown US silk flag, carried by David Scott to the lunar surface, unmounted and marked "DRS Aug 71" in blue ink in the lower right hand corner.

6in (15cm) wide

£2,500-3,000   **AGI**

A flown Russian silk flag, carried by STS-105 crew member Vladimir Dezhurov to the International Space Station.

6in (15cm) wide

£280-320   **AGI**

A tan cloth communications flight cap, by David Clark Co., worn by Robert Overmyer, with openings for a pair of earphones and an open-ended pocket with three snaps across the top, together with a white cloth cap designed to be worn under a hard flight helmet.

£120-180   **AGI**

A flown piece of shuttle tile, encased in clear Lucite block, with descriptive sheet enclosed.

£300-350   **AGI**

A presentation plaque, given to George R. Faenza upon his retirement from McDonnell Douglas at KSC in 1996, reading "This piece of Orbiter Columbia (OV-102) Thermal Protection System (TPS) tile has successfully flown all twenty Columbia missions, including the first STS-1 on 12 April 1981. The tile was removed after the LMS STS-78 mission, launched 20 June 1996", together with a piece of "Multilayer Insulation (MLI)" that was successfully flown on four Spacelab Module missions, including the Spacelab-MIR rendezvous docking mission (STS-71, the 100th United States Manned Space Flight".

£280-320	AGI

Two Challenger Shuttle tiles.
6in (15cm) wide

£200-250	AGI

A flown parachute line cutter, from the Space Shuttle.

This was flown as part of the Shuttle's solid rocket booster assembly. When the boosters are jettisoned from the shuttle, at T+2 minutes and 7 seconds, they drop from an altitude of about 30 miles into the Atlantic for recovery. Their descent is controlled by a series of parachutes. This device is part of the system. At specified time delays, the cutters use an explosive charge applied to a metal guillotine blade to sever the main chute's reefing lines, allowing the chutes to inflate to their second reefed and then full open positions. A "Clarkson" photo certificate of authenticity for this unit is included.

£45-55	AGI

A piece of flown gold foil, mounted on a green "Slezak" certificate of authenticity that reads: "This is to certify that the attached material was part of the outer reflective skin of the Apollo spacecraft CM-107, that carried astronauts Armstrong, Aldrin and Collins on their historic flight to the moon, 16-21 July 1969".

£180-220	AGI

A flown titanium film canister, with Federal Scientific-Research and Industrial Center "Priroda" certificate of authenticity and with a colour back-up film "Kodak-Rollfilm-120-EPR", numbered "6".

The film was used for interior photo shoots aboard the space crafts during the mutual experimental "Apollo-Soyuz" flight as part of the "EPAS" programme. The shoot used a Hasselblad camera by the crew of the space craft "Soyuz-19" with cosmonauts A. Leonov and V. Kubasov from July 15 to 21 1975.

£150-200	AGI

A flown Soyuz mission clock, No. 653b/1081 from the main control panel, in wooden carry case and with instruction manual indicating the unit was flown, but not which flight.

£450-500	AGI

A red "Remove Before Flight" tag.

This tag is used to ensure that key connectors are not pulled prior to launch and as a safety check to ensure that those that should be disconnected prior to launch are pulled.

£22-28	AGI

A flown mission summary card, signed by Rominger, Ashby, Parazynski, Phillips, Hadfield, Guidoni and Lonchakov and annotated by Lonchakov "Flown on STS-100 to ISS".

£180-220	AGI

Two similar food cubes, each wrapped in rice paper, and designed to have been eaten by the astronauts without having to be unwrapped.

£120-180	AGI

A flown miniature lunar rover licence plate, carried by David Scott aboard the first manned lunar rover vehicle during the entire exploration of the Hadley-Apennine from July 30 to August 2, 1971.

£10,000-15,000	AGI

A NASA publicity photo of Neil Armstrong, wearing his white spacesuit, uninscribed.

10in (25.5cm) high

£550-650 AGI

Four NASA publicity photos of Fred Haise, wearing his white spacesuit, each signed by Haise.

10in (5.5cm) high

£55-65 (set) AGI

A NASA publicity photograph of Vladimir N. Dezhurov, wearing his orange NASA spacesuit, signed.

10in (25.5cm) high

£25-35 AGI

An NASA publicity photo of James McDivitt and Ed White, signed by both.

10in (25.5cm) high

£450-500 AGI

A NASA publicity photo of John Young, wearing his Gemini spacesuit as taken during training, signed.

Informal signed photos such as this are scarce today.

10in (25.5cm) high

£450-500 AGI

A publicity photo, signed by Shepard, Krikalev and Gidzenko, plus back-up crew Bowersox, Dezhurov and Tyurin.

10in (25.5cm) high

£280-320 AGI

A set of 15 NASA publicity photos and lithographs.

£120-180 AGI

A NASA publicity lithograph, signed by Neil Armstrong and Buzz Aldrin, trimmed.

3.5in (9cm) high

£350-400 AGI

A McDonnell Douglas photo, taken in space and signed by James Lovell and Buzz Aldrin, together with a NASA montage lithograph inscribed and signed by Buzz.

£150-200 AGI

A colour lithograph of the International Space Station, signed by Shepard, Gidzenko and Krikalev.

£55-65 AGI

A NASA lithograph of the first seven Mercury astronauts, signed by Scott Carpenter, Gordon Cooper, John Glenn, Virgil Grissom, Wally Schirra, Deke Slayton and Alan Shepard.

10in (25.5cm) wide

£4,000-4,500 AGI

A WonderWorks replica Apollo capsule, used as back-up model to that used in the movie "Apollo 13", with highly detailed interior.

£10,000-12,000 AGI

Worden, Alfred M., "Hello Earth – Greetings from Endeavor", first edition signed on the front page by the author.

Al Worden was the pilot during the 67 hours his fellow astronauts Scott and Irwin were on the Moon. He was in complete solitude, floating in space. The overwhelming experience of being completely alone in the universe gave him a profound feeling of rejuvenation. That experience changed his life.

1974

£60-80 AGI

A full-scale WonderWorks Mercury capsule replica, used in the films "Rocket's Red Glare" (2000) and "Race to Space" (2002), with highly detailed interior.

£6,000-7,000 AGI

A Robbins silver commemorative medallion, no. 91.

This mission patch commemorates the third Space Shuttle flight supporting the assembly of the ISS. The flights' primary tasks are to outfit the ISS, extend its lifetime and to conduct a spacewalk to install external components in preparation for docking of the Russian Service Module "Zvezda" and the arrival of the first ISS crew. The Space Shuttle Is depicted on the medallion in an orbit configuration prior to docking with the ISS. Only 114 silver medallions were produced for this mission, of which 24 were flown and 90 were not. This medallion was not flown. A Weinberger certificate of authenticity is included.

2in (5cm) wide

£200-250 AGI

NASA

Space Shuttle Mission 51-L

Press Kit   January 1986

A Challenger STS-51L press kit, dated January 1986, detailing general information, mission statements, timetables and diagrams of the ill-fated Space Shuttle, together with a biography and training history of teacher astronaut Christa McAuliffe and others and a certificate of authenticity.

£180-220 AGI

Eight unopened sets of Mission Space trading cards, comprising STS-81 to -87, and STS-94.

3.25in 98.5cm) high

£60-80 AGI

A Wonderworks replica Saturn V launch vehicle rocket, configured for the Apollo 11 launch and includes the engines, piping, Apollo capsule, escape tower, graphics and paint.

144in (366cm) high

£14,000-16,000 AGI

A silver "Snoopy" lapel pin, wearing a space helmet and space suit, together with a photo of Fred Haise presenting the pin to Ossie Reid, with original issue plastic box.

1in (2.25cm) high

£280-320 AGI

A presentation brass ashtray, with 12 raised images around the edges, a cloisonné inset in the centre with the inscription "For your contribution to the First Manned Lunar Landing, 1969, NASA-MSC".

5.75in (14.5cm) diam

£120-180 AGI

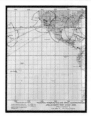

An Apollo 16 earth orbit chart, displaying the proposed earth orbit, revolution 2.

41.5in (105.5cm) high

£60-80 AGI

A John Glenn Orbit Globe, showing the three orbits made by MA-6.

8in (20cm) high

£60-80 AGI

- With its origins dating back to at least 2000BC, the sport of fishing has built up a huge range of associated objects over the centuries, many of which are now collected.

- Of the vintage equipment available, reels can form fascinating collections. Early reels are very simple, but during the 19th century designers and anglers experimented with different types that enabled anglers to handle their more easily and efficiently. Rarity is as important as condition and a huge variety of different types of reel mechanism and design were made during the 19th and 20th centuries, including 'multiplying', 'half-crank', 'cage' and 'freespool clutch' reels.

- Bakelite reels dating from the 1920s-1930s and basic reels made from wood with no markings are often of low value. collectors should familiarise themselves with the different types made, using reference books. Some reels are desirable to collectors due to their mechanisms and design. However, generally speaking, reels marked with the maker's name, such as Hardy Bros of England, will be more desirable.

- Restoration is easy to spot as the original patina is often removed and is impossible to replace. When considering cleaning a reel, be aware of its construction and take care not to break screw heads. Record where particular screws fit as some will not be interchangeable.

- Over the years many different tools were made. The 19th century fly fisherman would have had a vast range of gadgets to help him. Developing technology outmoded certain gadgets only for them to be replaced by others – such 'vest pocket' gadgets form a collecting area of their own.

- Like most sports, fishing has ephemera associated with it and pre 1930s catalogues are much sought after. Hardy Bros is a popular and collected name and produced annual catalogues. Items celebrating and commemorating the sport are also popular and include prize catches stuffed and mounted, pictures and ceramics.

Fishing Reels

A rare 4in Allcock "Aerial" alloy centrepin reel, the drum having 12 large and 12 small perforations to both front and rear flanges, with spoke tension regulator, drum removal fork, twin white xylonite handles, brass optional check button and brass foot, backplate stamped with bordered circular logo and registered design details.

c1930   *4in (10cm) diam*

£1,200-1,800   **MM**

A rare 3in Allcock "Aerial" alloy centrepin reel, the drum having 12 perforations to both front and rear flanges, with drum removal fork and spoke tension regulator, twin white xylonite handles, brass optional check button and brass foot, backplate stamped with bordered circular logo and reg. design details.

c1930   *3in (7.5cm) diam*

£1,000-1,500   **MM**

A rare Allcock "The Aerial Match" 4in alloy centrepin reel, listed for one season only in the 1939/40 catalogue, the moulds for the reel being destroyed during the bombing of World War II, the reel with bright finish perforated drum measuring 9/16in between the plates, spoke tension regulator and drum removal fork, backplate with integrally cast line guard mounts with alloy line guard supported by twin brass pillars, brass foot secured by two screws, backplate with brass optional check button and stamped with "Stag" registered trademark and "The Aerial Match", a superb example retaining nearly all the original finish.

c1939   *4in (10cm) diam*

£2,500-3,000   **MM**

An unnamed 4.5in Allcock "Aerial" alloy centrepin reel, drum stamped "Patent", with ventilated front flange, drum removal fork and spoke tension regulator, twin white xylonite handles, "B.P." aluminium line guard, brass optional check button and brass foot, retaining much of original lead finish.

c1920   *4.5in (11.5cm) diam*

£550-650   **MM**

An Allcock-made 4in brass "Hercules" style platewind reel, retailed by G. Little, with raised constant check housing to frontplate, tapered horn handle, quadruple pillared cage and pierced and waisted brass foot, handleplate stamped with 'Stag' regd. trademark and "S. Allcock & Co. Makers" in shield logo and scroll engraved "G. Little & Co., 63 Haymarket, London SW".

c1890   4in (10cm) diam

£120-180   MM

An unused Allcock "Match Aerial" 4.5in alloy centrepin reel in original box, with drum removal fork and spoke tension regulator, optional check and chromed foot, in mint unused condition and complete in original maker's red card box.

c1970   4.5in (11.5cm)

£180-220   MM

A J. Atherton & Son 3.75in Nottingham centrepin reel, with wide tapering brass spineback stamped "J. Atherton & Son, Sheffield", alloy foot, twin waisted rosewood handles to elliptical brass receivers and mahogany drum with large deep well with steel securing nut, together with a 41/4" Nottingham with 'fishtail' brass starback foot, twin light bone handles to square brass receivers and sliding drum latch to three screw plate, together with a 3.5in Nottingham with brass spineback feet and optional check.

3.75in (9.5cm) diam

£200-250   MM

A Carter & Co. 4.5in brass and ebonite "Hercules" style platewind reel, with tapered and waisted dark horn handle to raised brass handleplate stamped "Carter & Co. Makers, London", raised ebonite constant check housing to backplate, cupra brass frame and quadruple pillared cage, retaining near all original bronzing to handleplate and complete in a Farlow block leather reel case.

4.5in (11.5cm) diam

£280-320   MM

A "Cone" Patent 4.5in centrepin reel, the reel with mahogany drum revolving on brass spindle with cone-shaped milled wheel tensioner and brass locking nut, brass backplate sitting in countersunk recess on the drum rear face, brass starback foot stamped "Cone Patent No. 24776", brass optional check button, brass Bickerdyke line guard and twin tapered wood handles mounted to elliptical brass receivers.

R.L. Kenton's 1903 patent refers to the use of cones to eliminate drum shake. This is one of only a very few known examples.

c1903   4.5in (11.5cm) diam

£450-550   MM

A Chevalier Bownefs & Son 3.5in brass anti-foul handle crankwind winch, with tapered dark horn handle to anti-foul crank arm, triple pillared cage, raised constant check housing to backplate, faceplate scroll engraved "Chevalier Bownefs & Son, 12 Bell Yard, Temple Bar, London".

c1866-1882 3.5in (9cm) diam

£100-200   MM

A J.A. Coxe big game multiplying reel, probably 9/0 with 5.5in black hard rubber plates, stainless steel rims and fittings, offset non-reversing and counter balanced crank, five point capstan wheel drag, twin harness lugs to pillars, stamped to winding arm "Genuine J.A. Coxe Reel, U.S. Pat. 1495676, others pend." and "Made by Bronson Reel Co. Bronson Mich."

c1940

£400-450   MM

A Chas. Farlow 4in walnut and brass Perth reel, with constant check, quadruple pillared cage, brass bound rims and brass handle plate scroll engraved "Chas. Farlow Maker, 191 Strand, London".

1852-1884 4in (10cm) diam

£300-400   MM

FIND OUT MORE...

Harold Jellison & Daniel Homel, 'Antique & Collectible Fishing Reels: Identification, Evaluation and Maintenance', published by Forrest Park Publishing, July 1998.

Karl T. White, 'Fishing Tackle – Antiques & Collectables: Reference & Evaluation', published by Holli Enterprises, 1995.

The International Fly Fishing Centre and Fly Fishing Museum, 215 East Lewis Street, Livingston, Montana 59047, U.S.A.. www.fedflyfishers.org

The Flyfisher's Club, 69 Brook Street, London W1Y 2ER.

A first model Hardy "The Elarex" freshwater multiplying reel, drum with raised boss to centre, level line mechanism with tubular guard fitted over the distributor shaft, optional check button, graduated tension adjuster and twin reverse tapered ebonite handles to serpentine cross-bar.

c1939

£100-150 MM

A Hardy "The Jock Scott" freshwater multiplier and line winder in Box, 4:1 gear ratio, 2 1/8in frame with rim mounted free spool lever, the gears engaged automatically upon retrieve, agate centred adjustable bearing cap, four point capstan drag, rim mounted casting control, reverse tapered ebonite handle to curved winding arm, thumb bar and grooved alloy foot, together with a Hardy "The Jock Scott" brass line drier and cork arbour in fitted hardwood box, lacks oil bottle.

£850-950 MM

A "Spitfire" finish Hardy "The Uniqua" 2 7/8in alloy trout fly reel, with Mark I check, rim regulator, nickel silver telephone drum latch, ebonite handle and smooth brass foot.

c1940

£250-300 MM

A 1930s Hardy "The Fortuna" 7in Duralumin big game centrepin reel, fixed check with Andreas slipping cutch allowing the handles to remain stationary whilst line is being stripped off the drum, twin reverse tapered ebonite handles mounted to brass cross bar with later nickel plating, six point capstan wheel drag control, backplate with free spool lever and stamped with "The Fortuna Reel, Hardy", size and Andreas patent details, repair to front rim.

7in (18cm) diam

£180-220 MM

A rare 1921 pattern Hardy "The Longstone" 4in sea centrepin reel, with brass lever action rim check, ebonised wooden drum with alloy rear drum flange, knurled nickel silver drum screw with slotted locking nut, ebonite handle to elliptical brass receivers, one handle lacking, alloy backplate, Bickerdyke wire line guard and smooth alloy foot, retaining near all original finish.

c1921 *4in (10cm) diam*

£300-500 MM

A Holbrow & Co. 3.75in brass and ebonite Perth-style reel, with constant check, tapered dark horn handle and quadruple pillared cage.

c1879-1883 *3.75in (9.5cm) diam*

£150-200 MM

A rare 1920s variant Hardy "The St George" 3 3/8in alloy trout fly reel, the reel with milled on/off check lever to backplate, this bringing an additional floating pawl into use, the reel with Mark I check, rim regulator, grey agate line guard, three screw latch, ebonite handle and ribbed brass foot, backplate stamped with "on" and "off" positions, stamped to interior "D.W." (Denys Ward).

£750-850 MM

A 1920s Hardy "The Sea Silex" 5in aluminium alloy sea centrepin reel, early model, drum faceplate with two rows of perforations and twin reverse tapered ebonite handles, large ivorine rim brake lever, rim mounted brass optional check lever and further rim mounted brass brake lever, this operating compression brake and stamped "Pat. No. 7893", brass foot and nickel silver drum latch.

5in (12cm) diam

£350-400 MM

A rare 4in Malloch Patent multiplying alloy sidecasting reel, with tapered ivorine handle to offset waisted brass crank arm.

c1920 *4in (10cm) diam*

£1,200-1,500 MM

A rare early pattern Hardy "The St George" 3 3/8in alloy multiplying fly reel, 2:1 ratio, with handle plate casing high up on the reel near the foot, rim regulator, grey agate line guard, smooth brass foot, three screw drum latch and ebonite handle, stamped to interior "J.A.J." (Joe Johnson).

c1927

£900-1,000 MM

A 1930s Hardy "The Hardy Zane-Grey" 6in Monel Big Game multiplying reel, 2.5:1.5 gear ratio, large rosewood handle to offset shaped winding arm mounted above five point capstan wheel drag adjuster, four rim mounted harness lugs, large auxiliary leather brake pad, backplate with milled on/off check lever and stamped with two circular medallions, one with "Made by Hardy Bros. Ltd., Alnwick, England 491", the other with "The 'Hardy Zane-Grey' Size 6", to hold 600 yds 39 thread", faceplate with two Royal appointment medallions, handle replaced.

6in (15.5cm) diam

£4,000-5,000 MM

A Milwards 5in "Frogback" Nottingham sea centrepin reel, walnut with brass rear drum flange, brass lined backplate, optional check button, twin bulbous wood handles, wing nut drum tensioner and brass Bickerdyke line guard, brass frogback foot stamped "Milwards".

5in (12.5cm) diam

£250-300 MM

A 4in brass Moscrops "Manchester" reel, with half-coin type drag control to drum faceplate, pillared drum core, drum latch of two spring wires, tapered horn handle and backplate with inset central brass medal with "J.B. Moscrops Patent, Manchester", retaining much original finish.

c1900 4in (10cm)

£60-80 MM

A Sherriff 4.25in brass and rosewood Perth reel, with constant check, tapered rosewood handle, quadruple pillared cage and handleplate stamped "Sherriff, Glasgow".

c1900 4.25in (11cm) diam

£350-400 MM

A rare 5in all-brass sea centrepin reel, probably by David Slater of Newark, with highly perforated drum plates and backplate.

c1890 5in (12.5cm) diam

£180-220 MM

An unnamed 3.5in Allcock "Aerial" alloy Centrepin Reel, six spoke drum with ventilated alloy front flange and ebonite rear flange.

c1915 3.5in (9cm) diam

£520-580 MM

A 4.5in "Coxon Aerial" style centrepin reel, six spoke ebonite drum with twin horn handles, spoke tension regulator and drum removal fork, walnut backplate with brass starback foot.

4.5in (11.5cm) diam

£250-300 MM

An unnamed 6in "Future" sea centrepin reel, attributed to Slater, the mahogany drum with six large perforations and central dished well, large dark horn handles mounted to elliptical brass receivers, brass rear flange, fully brass-lined mahogany backplate with four large circular decorative cut outs.

c1910 6in (15.5cm) diam

£220-280 MM

A rare unnamed Irish pattern brass spike winch, with constant check, fine turned ivory handle to curved winding arm, quadruple pillared cage and brass block foot with square threaded spike, replaced.

c1840 3in (7.5cm) diam

£350-400 MM

An unnamed George Moore 4in centrepin reel, with twin pear-shaped wood handles mounted to brass lozenge-shaped receivers, drum ventilated to both flanges and revolving on spindle, brass stanchion and foot.

c1905 4in (10cm) diam

£200-300 MM

An unnamed 3in rosewood and brass Perth reel, with constant check, brass bound rims, triple pillared cage and waisted wood handle to brass winding plate.

c1880 3in (7.5cm) diam

£200-250 MM

An unnamed 5in Slater wooden combination reel, walnut with alloy rear drum flange and backplate fully lined in alloy, brass Annular line guard, twin tapered ebonite handles.

c1890 5in (12.5cm) diam

£250-300 MM

An unnamed 4in Slater wood and ebonite combination reel, with walnut drum face, and alloy rear flange, nickel silver bound ebonite backplate, brass starback foot with optional check button.

c1890 4in (10cm) diam

£350-400 MM

A brass fishing reel, with shanked handle.

2.75in (7cm) wide

£70-90 BS

A 1920s brass fishing reel.

2.75in (7cm) wide

£70-90 BS

Fishing Equipment

An unnamed Allcock glass-eyed "Gilt and Plated" Bait, No 732, the hollow fish-shaped lure with twin swimming vanes and fish scale decoration, retaining much of original gilt, lacking one of its yellow glass eyes.

c1882   2.25in (6cm) long

£380-420   **MM**

A early Edward Vom Hofe "Sams" spoon complete with original swivel, with large single hook mounted to bar protruding through centre of spoon, stamped "Edward Vom Hofe, New York, Patd. May 26.08", "5" and "Sams", this last in italic type script.

c1910

£100-150   **MM**

A Livesey "Swiveltail" bait, the hollow nickel-plated brass bait with integrally cast eye, fin and mouth detail, stamped "H. Livesey's Patent" to tail and revolving on internal swivel.

c1890   3.25in (8.5cm) long

£350-400   **MM**

An unnamed "Paragon" bait, attributed to Gregory, the hollow nickel silver fish-shaped main lure body with twin spinning vanes and fish scale patterning, with orange glass eyes,

c1900   3in (7.5cm)

£150-200   **MM**

A "Nickel Plated" bait, attributed to Gregory, retailed by Allcock as the No.930 bait, the hollow nickel-plated fish-shaped body with twin swimming vanes.

c1900   3in (7.5cm) long

£280-320   **MM**

An Allcock "Aquatic Spider", mounted to original green and yellow printed card with directions to verso and complete in original Allcocks waistcoat pocket size tin box with trade label to lid.

£90-100   **MM**

A J. Bernard & Son hickory and steel folding gaff, the gently tapering turned wood handle with banded hand grip, 22" steel hinged gaff point with brass sliding collar locking joint, this engraved "J. Bernard & Son Makers, 45 Jermyn St., St James's S.W.", the sprung sliding collar with milled and incised decorative banding, the gaff point folding into recess in handle with further sliding brass securing collar to keep closed.

c1870   46in (117cm) long

£480-520   **MM**

A Hardy brass gaff, two drawer with turned rosewood handle, brass hook guard and copper belt clip, stamped with bordered oval logo.

c1900

£200-300   **MM**

A zinc angler's tackle box.

c1900   6in (15cm) wide

£50-70   **BS**

A brass angler's telescopic gaff, manufactured by Hardy.

c1900   29.5in (75cm) long

£200-300   **BS**

A Hardy "The Pocket Gaff", the hinged gaff head folding neatly into the shaped alloy handle, stamped "Hardy Bros. Ltd." and details.

c1962 Extended 7.5in (19cm) l

£220-280   **MM**

A Hardy "The Salmon Spintac" oak tackle box, with compartmented base for spinning lures, lid interior with fold-down door revealing trace compartments, Hardy's oval nickel silver plaquette, and containing assorted Hardy lures and traces, in good condition.

These boxes are scarce as they were only made for a few years.

1956/57

£120-180   **MM**

An Allcock & Co. combination pike gag/scissors, steel with notched locking bar and stamped "Allcock & Co." to arm.

c1890

£120-180   **MM**

An Edward Vom Hofe "The Van Vleck Tarpon Trolling Hook", hook stamped to shank "Van Vleck" and "E. Vom Hofe N.Y.", together with original linked chain and wire trace and in maker's paper packaging printed with hook and Vom Hofe address details.

£70-100 MM

A fine Wadham's "The X-Ray" celluloid live May fly box, transparent celluloid with corrugated and highly perforated side and pivoted circular lid, the top with solid rim forming a trap to keep live insects inside and twin locking catches, lid stamped "Dreadnought Casting Reel Co. Ltd., Newport, I.W.".

1920s   *3in (7.5cm) diam*

£650-750 MM

A 1930s Hardy "The Fisherman's" rustless steel gauge, the combined hook/gut gauge stamped "Chesterman, Sheffield, England" and Hardy Bros. Ltd. and details, the steel plates with finely engineered tapering slot for measuring gut size and line thickness, stamped with salmon hook gauge and inch scale to one side and with fine scale in one thousands of an inch to the other.

4in (10cm) long

£280-320 MM

A scarce Allcock's "The Otter" wading net, with iron knuckle joint, brass tube ferrule to either end, oval bentwood frame, brass belt clip and whole cane handle, brass butt cap stamped with maker's bordered oval logo.

c1915

£180-220 MM

A Hardy The No. 2 "Alma" rustless swivel, the larger of the two sizes made at the request of Mr H. White-Wickham to lift a deadweight of 750lbs, made from "Sildur" non-corrosive metal and nickel silver, together with the smaller No. 1 size "Alma" Swivel, both stamped "Hardy's England".

c1935

£80-120 MM

A spool of 1930s Hardy "Atlas" flax line, the black-painted softwood spool with black-on-white circular trade label "Hardy's 'Atlas' Square Plaited Flax Line No. 4, 100yd", with line and in a Hardy card box.

3in (7.5cm) diam

£70-80 MM

An unusual combination priest and knife, the tapering alloy priest with weighted head and integrally cast ridge, threaded to screw onto handle section, this with knife that fits into hollow priest head, together with an unnamed alloy priest of tapering form with brass head and a Hardy the "Driflydresser", this lacking felt and amadou pads.

First 8in (20.5cm) long

£180-220 MM

A leather bound reedwork creel, probably American, sides and lid woven into traditional corrugated patterning, with hole in lid for putting in the trout, leather bound rims with attractive strap work decoration, lacks carry strap.

15in (38cm) wide

£250-350 MM

An Allcock's No.34 trade catalogue, large 8vo.

1937

£70-100 MM

A DAM catalogue No.25, with illustrations in both colour and black and white.

c1954

£80-120 MM

A C. Farlow & Co. Ltd. fishing tackle catalogue, 75th edition.

c1916

£150-200 MM

A Wadham's catalogue, spine detached, cover rubbed, tears.

1920

£150-200   MM

A 1930s anonymous fishing tackle catalogue, 90 pages featuring Allcocks tackle and entitled "Illustrated Price List of High-Class Fishing Rods and Tackle".

£120-180   MM

Buller, Fred, "Pike", first edition, Macdonald, 4to, photos, dust wrapper.

1971

£220-280   MM

A Hardy Angler's Guide, 39th edition.

1912

£380-420   MM

Martin J.W. (The Trent Otter), "My Fishing Days and Fishing Ways", first edition, W. Brendon & Son Limited, photos, green cloth with gilt spine, signed copy.

1906

£400-500   MM

Wheat, Peter, "The Fighting Barbel", first edition, Ernest Ben Limited, illustrations, photos, dust wrapper, signed.

1967

£180-220   MM

A pair of perch by J. Cooper & Sons, mounted in a setting of reeds and grasses against a turquoise background in a gilt-lined bow front case with gold on black plaquette reading "Perch. Caught by S.F. Maybrick, Warminster, July 14th 1934" and with J. Cooper & Sons label to case interior, restorations.

Case 27.75in (70.5cm) wide

£700-900   MM

A fine perch by F.W. Anstiss, the fish mounted in a setting of reeds and grasses against a blue background in a rare gilt-lined wrap-around case with gilt inscription "Perch 21/2lbs. Caught by Mr H. Webb in the Avon. March 21st 1918" and with F.W. Anstiss label to case interior.

Case 18.5in (47cm) wide

£2,200-2,800   MM

A fine pike attributed to W.F. Homer, mounted in a setting of reeds and grasses against a typical reed painted green background in a gilt-lined bow front case with gilt inscription "The Fenton & District Angling Society. Pike 10lbs. Caught by Mr J. Wilkes. Jany. 1928.

Case 38.75in (98.5cm) wide

£1,000-1,500   MM

A fine carved pike by Brian Mills, the half-block fish with scale and fin ray detail and stained wood backboard to match the pike's distinctive markings, mounted against a stained weed backboard and set within a frame, inscribed "Pike. 15 lbs. Hand carved by" and signed "B.W. Mills".

42.5in (108cm) wide

£300-400 MM

A fine and very rare Jack pike in a picture frame case attributed to J. Cooper & Sons, the fish mounted to graduated green background with ivorine label "4lbs 8oz. Length 24ins. Caught by John P. Ashcroft. 30.8.53".

Backboard 30in (76cm) wide

£4,500-5,500 MM

An exceptionally fine Fochabers Studio carved wooden salmon, the half block fish naturalistically painted and with characteristic finely carved fin detail, mounted to oak backboard with the lure that caught the fish and painted with details "44lbs. Killed by Barbara Williams in the Wye, Aramstone, 17th April 1930, on a 2" wood minnow. Length 48" Girth 26 1/2", with a facsimile of the fishing register recording details of the capture and an article appearing in the "Field" June 1930.

Backboard 56in (142cm) wide

£7,000-8,000 MM

A carved and painted wooden rainbow trout by Brian Mills, mounted to painted wooden backboard within frame, signed, dated Sept. '82.

17in (43cm) wide

£120-180 MM

R.A. Johnson "Common Carp", 20thC, signed, oil on board.

24in (61cm)

£350-400 MM

R.A. Johnson "Mirror Carp", 20thC, signed, oil on board.

24in (61cm) wide

£350-400 MM

Esther Blaikie Mackinnon, 'The Young Fisherman', signed, oil on canvas.

£2,500-3,500 L&T

John Russell, British 1820-1893, "A Day's Catch", oil on canvas.

36in (91.5cm) wide

£1,000-£1,500 MM

English School, 20thC, "Loch Katrina", still life of salmon, trout and fishing tackle in a highland landscape, oil on board.

12.25in (31cm) wide

£320-380 MM

A mid-19thC Dutch tile, a blue-on-white glazed earthenware tile, depicting two anglers.

£70-100 MM

A Royal Doulton Isaac Walton ware series plate, the central reserve with two 17thC gentlemen anglers, within tree-decorated rim and with verse, signed "Noke" printed factory mark.

1901-38 *10.75in (27.5cm) diam*

£80-120 MM

A Staffordshire porcelain cabinet plate, with moulded celadon border, the central reserve hand-painted with Gregory "Bug-eyed Stoker" lure and inscribed "Gregory (Maker) Birmingham, England c1885", signed "L. Woodhouse", in original box.

c1885 9.25in (23.5cm) diam

£100-150 MM

A Beswick porcelain model of a trout, impressed and printed factory marks and impressed "1032 Trout".

6.5in (12.5cm) high

£100-150 MM

- Golf developed during the 15th to 17th centuries on the scrubby grassland between farmland and the Scottish coasts, but has its origins in the ancient Roman game 'Paganica', and in the Middle Ages in France ('jeu de mail') and Holland ('ket holven').

- Clubs and balls usually form the basis of many collections. Clubs and balls from the 18th century and earlier are not commonly found and are usually museum pieces, the 19th century is a good hunting ground for collectors – look for age, condition and maker.

- Most desirable are the rare 'long nosed' clubs of the early 1800s to the 1880s which were made with long whippy shafts which were spliced, glued and bound to a long nosed wooden head. Notable makers include Thomas Dunn, Charlie Hunter, Douglas McEwan, Tom Morris, and Robert Forgan.

- More affordable are 'transitional' wooden clubs used for playing with 'gutta percha' balls, which have thicker necks and shorter heads. Those that have a rounded bulge on the face are known as 'bulgers', whilst 'brassies' have a brass sole plate. Makers' marks are important – look out for Robert Simpson, Dunn & Son, Peter Paxton or Tom Morris, or renowned or champion player's names such as Harry Vardon (1870-1937) or the player and course designer James Braid (1870-1950).

- The third type collected are the 'socket clubs', the forerunners of today's clubs, where the (often hickory) wooden shafts were inserted into the heads, not spliced. Metal shafted clubs usually date from the 1920s and 30s and are less valuable. Notable makers include Robert Simpson, Anderson & Blyth, McGregor and Spalding.

- Although clubs now come in sets, metal-headed sets, known as irons, used to be named individually – such as mashies, niblicks, cleeks and putters. A huge variety of metal-headed putters were made from the late 19th century onwards, allowing for diverse collections. Look for Slazenger, William Gibson, George Nicoll and Alex Anderson.

Golf Clubs

A Spalding Cran cleek, stamped patent "June 8. 97 Pryor".

£450-550 | **L&T**

A Stewart cleek, the shaft stamped "T. Morris, St. Andrews", the head also with pipe mark, patent "3059".

£2,250-2,750 | **L&T**

A Jackson play club, with horn insert and lead back weight, head stamped.

£8,000-9,000 | **L&T**

A McEwan play club, with leather face insert and pegged horn sole plate, lead back weight, head stamped "McEwan and Todd".

£4,000-5,000 | **L&T**

An R. Forgan scared head long nosed grassed driver, the head stamped "R. Forgan" with Prince of Wales feathers.

£1,250-1,500 | **L&T**

A W. M. Park long-nosed driver.

£600-800 | **L&T**

A Tom Morris long-nosed play club, with old replacement grip.

£2,500-3,500 | **L&T**

A T. Morris play club, with replacement grip.

£2,500-3,000 | **L&T**

A T. Morris semi long-nosed club, with brass sole plate and lead back weight.

£700-800 | **L&T**

An Anderson of Anstruther rut iron.

£700-800   **L&T**

A Glover patent adjustable iron, with frilled neck 1-8.

£400-500   **L&T**

A rut iron, with leather grip.

c1890

£800-1,000   **L&T**

A Spalding Gold Medal #1 iron, with pierced hexagonal shaft and original leather grip.

£1,400-1,600   **L&T**

A Hutchison, North Berwick, smooth-faced mussel back lofter.

£650-750   **L&T**

A D. Anderson & Son, St Andrews, ball back smooth faced mashie.

£900-1,000   **L&T**

A Mammoth Niblick, by Cochrane for Fort Mason, Piccadilly, London.

£1,000-1,500   **L&T**

A Hendry & Bishop Ltd The Giant 'Cardinal Niblick'.

£600-700   **L&T**

A Mammoth Niblick, stamped "Harrods, Sparton, London".

£550-650   **MM**

A T. Morris putter, the sole with horn insert, lead back weight.

£1,400-1,800   **L&T**

A Gibson putter, with perforated face.

£600-800   **L&T**

A Gossiat-type putter, with mallet head, reduced.

£400-500   **L&T**

An Otto Hackbarth aluminium putter, with bridge hosel and lead weight, patent "687580".

£450-500   **L&T**

An Arthur S. Hardingham's patent putter.

According to Hardingham's patent, he proposed to form a putter head with a rear projection or bar at right angles to the striking face and of sufficient length to form a straight line to assist the aim of the player.

£8,000-10,000   **L&T**

A C. Hunter putter, the head stamped.

£1,000-1,200   L&T

A T. Morris putter, the head stamped.

£1,500-2,000   L&T

A T. Morris Juvenile putter, head stamped.

£1,000-1,200   L&T

A Schnectady putter, with patent "March 24 1903".

£150-200   L&T

A Slazenger 'Emperor' gooseneck putter, the face insert with brass plate and five screws.

£650-750   L&T

A putter, the shaft stamped "R.R. Wilson, St. Andrews", patent "1000".

£1,200-1,700   L&T

A Roller golf club, the back of the head stamped "M.N.7", the shaft stamped "Moodie".

£700-800   L&T

A Mills brassie spoon, with patent "142038".

£250-300   L&T

An R. Simpson short spoon, with three additional lead weights to sole, indistinctly stamped.

£1,000-1,500   L&T

A presentation golf club, with silver blade and fittings and leather wrapped shaft, engraved "Putting Competition", London hallmarks.
1895   *36in (91.5cm) long*

£1,500-2,000   Tag

An Osmond's patent "The Automaton Caddie", the canvas pencil bag and conforming ball and tee pouch with brass mounted wood frame and leather strap handles.

£800-900   L&T

Two "Special Argus" Bramble rubber core balls, both unused with added owners' early identification numbers.

£220-260   MM

GOLF BALLS

- Prior to the mid 19th century, golf was played with leather covered, feather stuffed balls called 'featheries'. Easily damaged, these are now highly sought after and fetch thousands of pounds at auction.
- Around 1848, 'gutta percha' balls began to take over from 'featheries'. These were made from moulded strips of a hard rubber-like material from India and Malaysia. Smooth surface 'gutties' are highly desirable, the usual design being 'meshed'. Good makers include Robert Fogan, Archie Simpson and Alex Patrick.
- From c1898, rubber core balls superseded the 'gutty'. These had a gutta percha core and a centre of elastic rubber thread wound around itself. They travelled further than 'gutties' but were still hard to control until the superior bramble pattern balls were introduced. Top makers include Cheals, Spalding, JB Halley, Slazenger and Michelin.

Top left: A feather ball, indistinctly stamped "W.M. Gourlay", good patina, slightly worn from usage.

£7,000-8,000 **L&T**

Bottom left: A Scoto mesh ball, marked at poles, some paint lacking.

£180-220 **L&T**

Top right: A mesh marked gutty, unnamed but perfect.

£250-300 **L&T**

A North Berwick square mesh rubber core ball.

£70-90 **MM**

A Gray & Sons Ltd square mesh rubber core, unused.

£75-95 **MM**

Bottom right: An Allan Robertson featherball, size 30, indistinctly stamped with some hack marks.

£6,000-7,000 **L&T**

A rare 'The Standard' advertising ball in painted brass.

6.5in (16.5cm) diam

£300-350 **BG**

A rare double gutty ball press, iron bound with shaped stout oak base and a double tongued compression plate below the screw, together with two brass smooth gutty moulds, one stamped "+1/2" the other stamped "worn" and with dagger stamp resembling the printer's sign for "take note".

12in (31cm) high

£100-150 **BG**

Golf Memorabilia

An early 19thC portrait of a boy from the Scottish School, half length, wearing a blue jacket with white silk collar, a hickory-shafted long nose club held in his left hand and slung over his left shoulder, oil on canvas.

c1810   76 x 63cm

£2,000-3,000 **L&T**

A C. Jacobs watercolour, entitled 'A golfing portrait of a member of the Royal Family', signed and dated '99, framed.

20in (51cm) high

£850-950 **L&T**

GOLFING MEMORABILIA

- Memorabilia showing golf or golfers generally dates from the 1890s onwards. Ceramics celebrating the game were made by a great many factories including Doulton, Shelley and Staffordshire factories. Useable memorabilia is very popular as it has a functional use, making otherwise static collections more interactive and useable.

- Golfing prints and images can form a collecting area of their own and particularly interesting are early photographs which are an important record of clothing, equipment, well-known courses and famous golfers.

- Most golfing collectors focus on the history of the game and golfing books offer a good way of learning more whilst building a collection.

A Norman Orr watercolour, entitled 'A delicate touch', signed and inscribed.

£700-800　　　　**L&T**

A Lance Thackery pastel illustration, entitled 'The Link Man', signed, inscribed and dated on an accompanying note.

c1911　　12.25in (31cm) wide

£2,200-2,800　　　　**L&T**

A Louis Wain pen-and-ink study of a cat, entitled 'Missed', the cat taking a wild swing at a ball, signed and framed.

The artist Louis Wain (1860-1939) is famous for his character drawings of cats. Highly popular at the turn of the century, he was obsessed with his work and when his popularity fell and demand for his work evaporated he was admitted to a mental hospital. His work is becoming highly sought after again, particularly since the late 1960s when a book was written about his life.

20.75in (53.5cm) high

£650-750　　　　**L&T**

One of a set of six Cecil Aldin prints, entitled 'Sunningdale, 4th Green'.

Cecil Aldin (1870-1935) was one of the most popular and successful British sporting artists. He is best known for his large chromolithographs of hunts, golfing and racing. His compositions are charming with bright colours and quality production. He worked from the late 19th century onwards at a time when sporting art had become immensely popular.

20in (51cm) wide

£3,500-4,500 set　　　　**L&T**

A Thomas B. Allen oil portrait of Arnold Palmer, commissioned by Sports Illustrated Magazine when he was named Sportsman of the Year 1960, together with a limited edition autographed replica cover of the January 9th 1961 edition depicting the painting, press release and photograph.

£55,000-65,000　　**L&T**

One of a set of six Cecil Aldin prints, entitled 'St. Andrews, The 5th and 13th Greens'.

20in (51cm) wide

£3,500-4,500 set　　**L&T**

A Charles Whymper watercolour, entitled 'Farewell Old Friend', an extensive panorama over the Old Course, with Tom Morris lower centre field with the town beyond and a railway engine in full steam passing the sheds by the 17th, signed and dated lower right and inscribed lower left.

c1909　　38in (96.5cm) wide

£12,000-15,000　　　　**BG**

A Michael Brown Life Association of Scotland original colour Lithograph Print insert, entitled "Prestwick - Himalayan Hole", featuring George Duncan, J.H. Taylor, James Braid and Harry Vardon, with gilt border.

19in (48.25cm)

£150-180　　　　**MM**

A framed copper plaque, relief-decorated with a scene of Charles I on Leith Links receiving news of the Irish Rebellion, with floral outer border and ebonized frame.

9.75in (25cm) wide

£200-250   **L&T**

A half-plate glass negative, depicting an unidentified golfing scene as two golfers on a links course, one playing a fairway shot, a caddie looking on.

c1870   8.5in (21.5cm) wide

£650-750   **L&T**

A half-plate glass negative, believed to depict members of the Bruntsfield links Golfing Society, Edinburgh.

c1890   8.5in (21.5cm)

£350-450   **L&T**

A half-plate glass negative, depicting a studio portrait of the renowned Musselburgh caddie John Carey (known as Fiery), standing against a white cloth and holding a bag of clubs under his left arm, inscribed to the upper border, "Photo of 'Fiery' for J.F. McClymont, Sandwick Pl.48, 24/8/98".

c1898   8.25in (21cm) high

£1,200-1,600   **L&T**

A half-plate glass negative, depicting an unidentified golf scene, one golfer holing out at the 11th and ladies looking on.

c1900   8.5in (21.5cm) wide

£400-500   **L&T**

A half-plate glass negative, depicting a double portrait of Harry Vardon and James Braid at Murrayfield Golf Club, Edinburgh.

£1,500-2,000   **MM**

A half plate glass negative of Harry Vardon and James Braid in competition, Vardon teeing off, the border inscribed "Murrayfield".

8.5in (21.5cm)

£750-850   **L&T**

A Royal Doulton biscuit barrel, with swing handle, the circular white metal lid surmounted by a mesh gutty ball, the circular tapering body with a scene of golfers with mountains behind.

6in (15cm) high

£750-1,250   **L&T**

A Lenox pottery tyg, hand-painted by W. Clayton with a wraparound scene of a lady golfer putting, watched by her caddy with the clubhouse in the background.

7in (18cm) high

£10,000-15,000   **L&T**

A Staffordshire baluster tobacco jar and cover, decorated with a cartoon golfing scene and golfing trophies, the reverse with a humorous eight line verse.

5in (12.5cm) diam

£180-220   **BG**

A glass tankard, with hinged pewter lid and hand-enamelled decoration of a lady golfer at the top of her swing.

7.5in (20cm) high

£400-500   **L&T**

A golf trophy, with multi-sport decoration and three-handle footed cup, the lid with figural golfer hitting a ball, the base painted metal with an engraved silver plated band featuring various sports scenes, trophy winners engraved on side from 1929-1935, replaced golf club.

22in (55.5cm) high

£250-350 HA

An impressive golfing medal, with a thistle and oak leaves emblem and crossed long nosed club behind, enclosed in a wired ribbon band above a pennant, bears the motto "never up, never in", for Edinburgh Burgess Golfing Society, instituted 1735, the centre with crossed clubs and three balls amidst thistles, the back engraved "won by Mr John Cruickshank with 52 strokes", Edinburgh, makers mark "J. B", cased.

c1873 *3in (8cm) high*

£3,000-4,000 L&T

A golfing prize medal, cast to the obverse with a scene of a golfer in the follow-through, with traces of gilding, made by Walker & Hall and inscribed "XVIth Golf Club", and another, the obverse cast with a scene of golfers and caddies, one figure in the foreground at the top of his swing, the obverse with a vacant scroll and a figure emblematic of victory, made by J. & F. Anderson, Birmingham, cased.

c1905 *3in (7.5cm) diam*

£250-300 L&T

An early Open Championship Memorabilia Victorian snuffbox, by George Unite, with shaped sides, cast scroll thumb piece, gilt interior, the oval cartouche to the cover engraved in various Victorian scripts "A gift to W. (Willie) Park on his achievement on winning the championship at the Prestwick Golf Club, presented by his friends and colleagues as a testimony of their esteem, 1867", Birmingham.

4in (10cm) wide

£5,000-6,000 BG

An Honorary Life Membership Gold Card, presented to Robert Tyre Jones Jnr. by the Board of Directors, Detroit Golf Club for his distinguished service, William G. Burton Secretary, William A. Sells President, Sept 22 1941.

c1941

£6,000-8,000 L&T

A silver and niello cigarette case, decorated in silhouette with a golfer at the top of his swing, with caddy on a fairway, possibly Japanese, stamped "950" and three characters mark to the interior.

c1930 *3.25in (8.5cm) wide*

£200-300 L&T

A white metal cigarette case, chased and engraved, with a wraparound scene of a golfer teeing off, with attendant caddy, the gilt interior with clip, reverse engraved with cursive initials "INS", stamped "Sterling-B9".

3in (8cm) wide

£100-150 L&T

A glass humidor, with white metal lid depicting a Victorian golfer at the top of his swing.

6.75in (17cm) high

£250-300 L&T

A glass decanter and two matching glasses, overlaid with sterling silver bands depicting golfers.

Tallest 12.25in (31cm)

£500-550 **L&T**

A pair of silver-plated "golfing" candle sticks, with three golf clubs forming the stem and a golf ball in the middle.

7in (18cm) high

£500-600 **Tag**

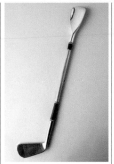

A Scottish silver and enamel Trushot "golfing" shoe horn, in the shape of a golf club.

7in (17.75cm) long

£900-1,000 **Tag**

A propelling pencil, in the form of a golf club.

£70-90 **LFA**

A pair of bronze bookends, depicting a golf player and golf caddy, the golfer in plus fours, his diminutive caddy in similar attire, on marble bases.

Tallest 9.5in (24cm) high

£400-500 **L&T**

A painted plaster Dunlop advertising figure, depicting the familiar golf ball headed man, in golfing attire and carrying a bag of clubs on a naturalistic shaped square base, inscribed twice "We Play Dunlop".

16in (40.5cm) high

£300-400 **L&T**

A Golf Calendar by Edward Penfield, with twelve calendar months to ten pages, published by R.H. Russell.

c1900

£3,500-4,500 **L&T**

A brass golf inkwell, with crossed clubs in front of a ball.

c1900

£200-300 **PC**

A small silver-mounted pottery vesta holder, modelled as a gutty ball, marked "Chester 1894"

£180-220 **L&T**

FIND OUT MORE...

The British Golf Museum, Bruce Embankment, St Andrews, Fife, Scotland. www.britishgolfmuseum.co.uk

The Heritage of Golf, West Links Road, Gullane Golf Club, East Lothian, Scotland. The private collection of Archie Baird, a long time avid collector.

James River Country Club Museum, 1500 Country Club Road, Newport News, Virginia, 23606, USA. www.ouimet.org. Founded in 1932 by Archer M. Huntington a keen golf collector who never actually played, this claims to be the first golf museum in the world.

Ouimet Museum, The Golf House, 190 Park Road, Weston, Massachusetts, USA. Frances Ouimet rose from being a caddie to make golfing history, winning against champions Harry Vardon and Ted Ray in 1913. He went on to win the US Amateur twice. His life is now celebrated in this museum and also by a caddie scholarship fund.

FOOTBALL

- Collecting football programmes became popular during the 1960s. Football programmes form the spine of many collections, and vary enormously in price depending on the popularity of the match and scarcity of the programme.

- Caps are also popular. Those dating from before the Second World War are traditionally made from a velvet-like material, bear the date of the match on the narrow peak and often the location, tour or organisation. After the war, they have both teams' names and the date embroidered onto them.

- The most desirable medals were those awarded to F.A. Cup winners. Medal design has barely changed, and medals of the 20th century are still in similar designs to those from the late 19th century.

- As with most sports, memorabilia or items associated with either important players or key events are likely to hold the highest values. Kit and signed balls from globally renowned players such as Stanley Matthews, Bobby Moore and Pelé are highly desirable, and this interest and value structure is now being extended to today's top players, including David Beckham and Michael Owen.

A Scottish Schools National Football Association silver hallmarked medal, produced by Fattorini & Sons, inscribed on reverse "W. Stevenson 1954" with suspension ring.

£120-180   **MM**

A 9ct gold and enamel Scottish Football League Championship medal, the reverse inscribed "First Division Season 1958-59 Rangers FC W. Stevenson", with suspension ring.

£1,800-2,200   **MM**

A 9ct gold The Football League Champions Division 1 medal, the reverse inscribed "Season 1963-64 W. Stevenson", with suspension ring.

£4,000-5,000   **MM**

Two oblong Football Association Stewards badges, one with scroll design, and a second small circular badge, with red and gold lettering.

1952

£70-100   **MM**

A fine 9ct gold and enamel medal, reads "Scottish Football League", the reverse inscribed "Reserve League Championship 1961-62 Rangers FC W. Stevenson", with suspension ring.

£450-550   **MM**

Two Football Association Stewards' badges, one shield design in red and black enamel, the other circular design in blue and white enamel.

1954

£70-100   **MM**

A collection of 19 Manchester United football supporters' badges, mostly enamel, including one for 1967 League Champions and 1968 European Cup Winners, two in the shape of letters "OK", one boot, one red devil, one pint of beer, and various others.

£180-220   **DN**

A bound volume of 21 Chester Programmes 1908/09 season, including matches against Wrexham, Tranmere and Crewe, bound with green boards and gilt lettering, signed by J.R. Lipsham to the inside front page.

£3,500-4,000   **MM**

FIND OUT MORE...

The National Football Stadium, Deepdale, Preston, Lancashire PR1 6RU. www.nationalfootballmuseum.com

F.A. Premier League Hall of Fame, County Hall, Riverside Building, Westminster Bridge, London SE1 7PB. www.hall-of-fame.co.uk

An official World Cup Final Programme Sweden vs Brazil, played at the Solna Stadium 29th June 1958, 88 pages, some foxing to cover, internally very good.

£280-320   **MM**

A Millwall Football Club 1912/13 season bound volume of Southern League Programmes, including an FA Cup match vs Middlesbrough, London Senior Cup Semi Final and Final, Inter League London vs Paris, Irish League vs Southern League and Southern Charity Cup Final, bound with blue boards.

£3,500-4,000   **MM**

A red England International cap, with embroidered rose and date "1902" to peak, with maker's label Young & Co. inside.

£220-280   **MM**

A purple and cream eight-panelled England Trial cap, embroidered initials "F.A." to front and "1906-7" to peak, with maker's label A.W. Gamage Ltd. inside.

£500-600   **MM**

A unique collection of 14 Manchester United signatures, including all 11 players from the 1968 European Cup winning team, including Matt Busby and Dennis Law, in red pen signed on hexagonal sections arranged in football design with club crest to centre.

£280-320   **MM**

A black and white Manchester United squad photograph, depicting 16 players in full kit, trainer and manager, titled "League Champions 1964-65" with the championship trophy and charity shield to either side, autographed below by nine players including Styles, Foulkes, Brennan, Law, Charlton, etc.

£120-180   **MM**

A limited edition Manchester United FC European Cup Winners 25th Anniversary football, signed by 11 players and Matt Busby, mounted on Perspex stand with full legend engraved, wooden base with brass plaque, No. 0216/1968, in glass dome.

£400-500   **MM**

An enamelled silver cigarette case, painted with a footballing scene.

3.5in (9cm) high

£800-1,000   **Tag**

A complete set of 512 Murillo cigar bands, depicting all major European teams, all in very good condition.

£280-320   **MM**

A Henry Armstrong autographed photo, full body pose of this boxing Hall of Fame member who held three World Championships at the same time, personalized in black ink, signature is strong.

10in (25.5cm) long

£100-150 HA

A Jack Dempsey signed photo, personalized in bold black ink, classic full body shot.

10in (25.5cm) long

£100-150 HA

A Benny Leonard autographed photograph, classic bust shot of this boxing great, autographed in bold black ink, personalized.

1947 *10in (25.5cm) long*

£450-550 HA

An autographed colour press photograph of Cassius Clay, standing over Sony Liston, signed in felt-tip pen "Muhammed Ali aka Cassius Clay", mounted with engraved plaque, which reads "Phantom Punch", framed and glazed.

21.5in (54.5cm) high

£150-200 MM

An autographed colour press action photograph of Muhammad Ali and Frazier, signed by both in silver pen, mounted with engraved plaque "The Thriller in Manila", framed and glazed.

21.5in (54.5cm) high

£180-220 MM

An autographed colour press photograph of Muhammed Ali, standing over a floored Ken Norton signed by both fighters in blue felt-tip ink, engraved plaque "The Rumble in the Jungle", matching frame.

21.5in (54.5cm) high

£180-220 MM

An autographed colour press photograph, signed in gold felt-tip pen by Ali, Joe Frazier, Ken Norton, George Foreman and Larry Holmes, plaque "Champions Forever", in matching frame.

£250-350 MM

An autographed display, comprising scorecard detailing each fight including World Heavyweight Championship bout between Rocky Marciano v Don Cockell, 15 rounds; black and white magazine action photograph mounted with brass plate engraved with fight details which Rocky won by T.K.O. in 9th round.

1955 *21.5in (54.5cm) high*

£450-550 MM

A signed boxing glove, mounted on mahogany based display case with engraved brass name plate "Ali, Foreman, Frazier, Norton, Lennox Lewis, Holmes, Tyson, Holyfield and Riddick Bowe".

16.5in (42cm) wide

£600-700 MM

A Joe Louis funeral service programme, dated April 12, 1981.

£40-60 SI

A Joe Louis World's Heavyweight Champion pinback button, featuring Joe in classic white training tanktop.

1.25in (3cm) diam

£40-50 HA

CRICKET

- The basic design of cricket equipment has remained the same for over a century, so unlike golf and tennis, pieces need to have other features in order to add value. These usually comprise signatures, personal associations or the fact that they were used at a certain important event.

- A large amount of literature has been published about cricket and it gives excellent accounts of key events and players, such as W.G. Grace. 'Wisden's Cricketer's Almanac' is perhaps the best-known publication, and has been published annually since 1864. Some collectors just collect these annual editions, with some early examples commanding a premium due to their rarity.

- As with most other sports, a range of associated memorabilia has surrounded cricket for some time, including ceramic figures inspired by those made in Staffordshire. Images and early photographs help to add decorative variety to a collection as well as illustrating the key characters and events.

An official Prudential Trophy 1975 team sheet, signed by 15/15 players including Asif Iqbal (Captain), Wasim Bari, Masood and Imran Khan, framed and glazed.

12.5in (31.5cm) high

£50-70   **MM**

Three cricket programmes for The Invincibles, comprising a scarce Scotland vs Australians at Edinburgh September 13 and 14, 1948.

£120-180   **MM**

A John Wisden's Cricketers' Almanac for 1887, edited by Charles F. Pardon, 24th edition, with original wrappers, recently bound volume with gilt spine, although a small stain patch to the last two pages.

1887

£280-320   **MM**

A scarce original Frank Sugg Ltd, Lord Street, Liverpool, colour cricketing poster featuring batsman with G.L. Jessop bat and bowler, using Special Frank Sugg Ltd County Cricket ball, framed and glazed.

21in (53.5cm)

£220-280   **MM**

An autographed sepia photograph of John Tunnicliffe, in batting pose at the wicket, signed in ink "Faithfully Yours – John Tunnicliffe 1905", framed and glazed with gilt slips (John Tunnicliffe Yorkshire CC 1891-1907).

13in (33cm) wide

£150-200   **MM**

A set of three H.J. Wood cricket character jugs, comprising bowler, batsman and wicket keeper.

7in (18cm) high

£150-200   **MM**

A pair of cricketing figures, representing Julius Caesar and George Parr, both standing next to the wicket.

10in (25.5cm) high

£120-180   **MM**

A pair of late 19thC continental bisque figures, comprising a young boy holding a cricket ball in both hands and a young girl holding a cricket bat.

9.5in (24cm) high

£80-120   **MM**

A pair of Victorian skeleton cricket pads.

£100-150   **MM**

A New Zealand, Pakistan and Northamptonshire autographed cricket bat, a Gray-Nicholls five-star steel sprung bat with the face signed by members of the New Zealand 1978 team and the back with signatures of Pakistan and Northamptonshire, rubber handle sheath missing.

1978

£30-40   **DN**

A full-size replica Grand Prix racing helmet, signed on visor in silver marker pen by Michael Schumacher, World Champion, with Ferrari, Marlboro and Asprey sponsors' logos.

£1,800-2,200   MM

A large signed colour photograph of Ayrton Senna, on the winners' podium, signed in black felt-tip pen, mounted, framed and glazed.

16in (40.5cm) long

£550-650   MM

A signed limited edition print of Ayrton Senna, fighting off Nigel Mansel's challenge in the closing laps of the Monaco Grand Prix on 31st May 1992 where he clinched victory driving Marlboro McLaren, the border signed in pencil by Ayrton Senna and artist Alan Fearnley, No. 14/850.

£2,500-3,500   MM

Three Winter Olympic Programmes in Oslo 1952, covering ice hockey, skiing and Nordic events on 5th, 6th and 11th day of the Games held during the month of February.

£50-70   MM

Four pieces of Olympic ephemera, including two tickets for 1936 Games in Berlin; 1974 Munich Games Athletic Ticket; and programme for the Closing Ceremony in Helsinki 1952.

£100-150   MM

A rare late Victorian/early Edwardian table billiards game, with one original red and one white ball, plus a set of later snooker balls.

19in (48.5cm) long overall

£150-200   MM

Mannock, J.P., 'Billiards Expounded – to all Degrees of Amateur Players', two early first editions, red cloth and gilt boards, some wear and dust staining.

c1920

£50-70   MM

An interesting silver-plated and enamel Albion Auto Racers winged motif, mounted on silver hallmarked plate, with three matching silver hallmarked name plates, each decorated with rose motifs including enamel red rose.

A scarce signed sepia photograph of national champion H.W. Payne, on his racing cycle, signed in ink "Yours sincerely H.W. Payne 1899".

£45-55   MM

A D&M hockey puck, embossed with the Lucky Dog logo, this practice puck shows use but logo remains strong.

£60-100   HA

£45-55   MM

A brass sculpture of single rower, mounted on black marble base in the shape of a rowing boat, with brass plaque engraved "M.C.R.C. – Singles – 1922", possibly of U.S. origin.

£180-220   MM

A good R. Wylie Hill & Co, Glasgow boxed table tennis set, including accessory price guide and Thos. de la Rue Illustrated Retail Price List Guide.

£150-200   MM

A white metal ashtray, with two matchbox holders, one embossed with laurel wreath and monogram "GBO", and decorative sides with embossed sporting accessories including tennis, golf, cricket and croquet.

7in (18cm) diam

£90-100   MM

An Azzedine Alaïa black taffeta gored dress.

51.5in (131cm) long

£300-350 S&T

A Balenciaga two-piece red skirt and top.

35in (89cm) long

£80-120 S&T

A 1960s Balmain yellow and black silk dress.

36.5in (93cm) long

£120-180 S&T

A 1970s Liz Berg for Bernie Bee Pucci-style gown.

£70-80 S&T

A 1960s Biba plaid dress.

54.25in (138cm) long

£80-100 S&T

A Biba vintage floral gown.

52.75in (134cm) long

£180-220 S&T

BIBA

- Set up by Barbara Hulanicki in 1964 in Kensington, London, the Biba boutiques defined the 'Swinging London' of the 1960s and early 1970s with a softer, more romantic feel than her contemporaries. Her 'slinky' figure-flattering look was particularly successful.

- Offering a complete look, including bags, hats and clothing at very inexpensive prices, Biba attracted a cult following until its closure in 1975. Its clothes are now highly sought after.

A Byblos iridescent pink rain jacket.

23.75in (60cm) long

£80-120 S&T

A 1960s futuristic dress, possibly by Cardin.

57.5in (146cm) long

£800-1,000 S&T

An Ossie Clark elegant black dress, in crêpe tie with satin trim.

50in (127cm) long

£320-380 S&T

A rare 1960s Pierre Cardin couture space age green and black block dress.

Like André Courrèges, Pierre Cardin is renowned for his outer space inspired designs during the 1960s.

41.25in (105cm) long

£650-700 S&T

A B C D E F G H I J K L M N O P Q R S T U V W XYZ

An Ossie Clark black crêpe dress, with green trim.

£400-500   **S&T**

A rare Ossie Clark three-piece strawberry trouser suit, exhibited at the Ossie Clark Retrospective.

Jacket 17.25in (44cm) long

£700-1,200   **S&T**

A 1960s Ossie Clark cream floral dress, with Birtwell print.

57in (145cm) long

£430-480   **S&T**

An Ossie Clark romantic black and tan chiffon top.

22.5in (57cm) long

£250-300   **S&T**

OSSIE CLARK

- Born Raymond Clark in 1942 in Lancashire, England, Clark first studied building and art before moving on to the Royal College of Art, London, to study fashion. His first pieces, in partnership with Alice Pollack, hinted at accentuating female curves, which was to become his hallmark later in his career.

- In 1969 he married the fabric designer Celia Birtwell whose designs for beautiful dress fabrics included Art Deco and heavy floral motifs in a range of unusual colours, such as saffron, blues, prune and antique rose. Choice of fabric was also important, with chiffons, moss crêpes and satins being common.

- Clark and Birtwell's marriage was immortalised by David Hockney in the famous painting 'Mr & Mrs Clark with Percy', now in the Tate Modern, London.

- His wife's innovative fabric designs combined perfectly with his famed cutting skills and his style completely broke away from the square cut, mini shift dresses of the period to a more sensual and sinuous shapeliness that accentuated female curves. His popularity reached its height from 1964-1976. Ossie Clark pieces with prints by Birtwell are very desirable.

- In 1964, Clark travelled to the USA and met Bette Davis, Jimi Hendrix and Andy Warhol. He was inspired by the Op Art he saw there.

- From his boutique in London called 'Quorum', he dressed Elizabeth Taylor, Twiggy, Raquel Welch and Bianca Jagger on her wedding day to Mick Jagger.

- Never a skilled businessman, he went through divorce, depression and bankruptcy in quick succession in 1981 and during the 1980s and 1990s, he struggled in vain to relaunch himself. He was murdered by a former lover in 1996.

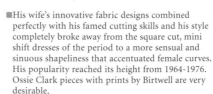

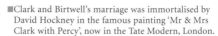

A very rare late 1960s Ossie Clark velvet floral maxi skirt.

£350-450   **S&T**

A rare Ossie Clark Art Deco floral blouse, rust and cream.

32.5in (83cm) long

£650-750   **S&T**

An early 1970s Ossie Clark Oriental-style wrap.

39.25in (100cm) long

£50-100   **S&T**

A very rare Ossie Clark sample jacket, in green and black printed cotton.

8.75in (73cm) long

£550-650   **S&T**

COURRÈGES

A Courrèges ivory knit dress.

40.5in (103cm) long

£180-230   **S&T**

A Courrèges size 10 skirt and blouse, with cream and beige stripes.

£225-275   **S&T**

- André Courrèges was born in Pau, France in 1923. He studied fashion design before going on to work as an assistant to Cristobal Balenciaga from 1960-1961.
- His fashion house, the 'White' salon, was opened in 1961 and 1965 saw his 'Space' collection being shown. In 1967, he introduced three lines: 'Prototype' (made to measure), 'Couture Future' (expensive prêt a porter) and 'Hyperbole' (inexpensive prêt a porter).
- Outer space was a popular theme during the entire 1960s, culminating with Neil Armstrong landing on the moon in 1969. This was expressed in clothes of the time through ultra modern, non gender-specific futuristic uniforms. Today, this look is highly popular amongst collectors.
- Courrèges' style was based around mini-dresses, catsuits and two piece suits in a stiff and wrinkle free fabric that gave the wearer a clean and linear profile.
- In 1985, his business became part of the Japanese group 'Itokin'.

A Courrèges black and white dress and belt.

34.5in (88cm) long

£300-350   **S&T**

A Courrèges museum quality couture maxi skirt, with appliqué daisies.

40in (102cm) long

£1,200-1,800   **S&T**

A Courrèges couture green dress, unlabelled.

35in (89cm) long

£500-600   **S&T**

A Courrèges couture two-piece red trouser suit.

22.5in (57cm) long

£1,150-1,650   **S&T**

A Courrèges couture two-piece tan and white suit.

c1960

£900-950   **S&T**

A Courrèges white and blue dress.

2.5in (108cm) long

£325-375   **S&T**

A Courrèges couture green wool coat.

37in (94cm) long

£1,800-2,300   **S&T**

A Courrèges two-piece rust and cream tweed suit.

27.5in (70cm) long

£250-300   **S&T**

A Courrèges brown jacket.

28.75in (73cm) long

£200-250 **S&T**

A Courrèges fuchsia jacket.

26in (66cm) long

£75-135 **S&T**

A Courrèges pink jacket.

31.5in (80cm) long

£150-200 **S&T**

A Courrèges pink and white silk blouse.

£100-130 **S&T**

A Courrèges 1980s re-issue wet-look pink waistcoat.

21.5in (55cm) long

£250-300 **S&T**

A Courrèges wet-look turquoise jacket.

Although this futuristic material may look robust like other fabrics used by Courrèges, it is quite fragile and is easily damaged. Damage to these pieces will affect value and desirability.

21.5in (55cm) long

£270-430 **S&T**

A Christian Dior fuchsia suit.

Jacket 24.5in (62cm) long

£80-120 **S&T**

A Christian Dior Puc dress.

46.5in (118cm) long

£100-150 **S&T**

A Gina Fratini dress, some damage.

60in (152cm) long

£80-100 **S&T**

A Bill Gibb print turtleneck top.

28.25in (72cm) long

£80-110 **S&T**

BILL GIBB

A Bill Gibb black striped top.

£40-50   **S&T**

- Gibb was born in Scotland in 1943 and studied at the St Martin's School of Art from 1962-1968.

- Opening his first shop in 1975, he was inspired by the rich diversity of ethnic patterns from other cultures as well as by Scottish dress. His style is typified by layered clothing to fit and flatter the body, using contrasting materials, colours and patterns.

- He worked with Kaffe Fassett on knitted garments and used the 'bee' logo as a signature.

- Interest in his work declined during the recession of the 1970s, but he continued to work for a small group of private clients up until his death in 1988.

A Bill Gibb multi-print dress.

60in (150cm) long

£80-100   **S&T**

A 1960s Givenchy two-piece suit.
Jacket 23.5in (59cm) long

£100-150   **S&T**

A 1970s Fiorucci silk and tartan dress.

£280-320   **S&T**

A Hartnell aqua and pink sequin dress and jacket.
23.25in (59cm) long

£350-450   **S&T**

A Christian Lacroix yellow prêt-à-porter jacket and skirt.
17.75in (45cm) long

£150-200   **S&T**

A Liberty flow gown.
55in (140cm) long

£150-200   **S&T**

A Missoni two-piece print skirt and top.
Top 23.25in (59cm) long

£50-100   **S&T**

A rare Missoni dress, in blue, orange and white.

Milan-based Missoni is also well-known for knitted designs, including vertically striped sweaters.

£600-700   **S&T**

A Missoni orange and red dress with belt.
46in (117cm) long

£400-450   **S&T**

A Hanae Mori gown.

53in (135cm) long

£400-450   **S&T**

A rare Benny Ong blue and yellow two-piece crêpe suit.

26.25in (67cm) long

£250-300   **S&T**

A rare Jean Patou blue, leather trim coat and matching dress, (dress not shown).

Jean Patou (1880-1936) saw his heyday during the 1920s and is notable for being the first European designer to present his designs on American models. Designers including Marc Bohan, Karl Lagerfeld and Christian Lacroix continued his business and name.

43.25in (110cm) long

£800-1,200 (set)   **S&T**

A rare 1960s Alice Pollock two-piece grey trouser suit.

£80-220   **S&T**

An early Pucci size 10 dress and belt, printed with blue and green flowers.

43.75in (111cm) long

£350-400   **S&T**

A 1960s Emilio Pucci blouse and skirt.

skirt 21.5in (55cm) long

£350-400   **S&T**

A late 1960s Emilio Pucci size 10 pink dress.

39in (99cm) long

£310-360   **S&T**

A 1960s Pucci Saks 5th Avenue size 12 dress and belt.

47.25in (120cm) long

£320-360   **S&T**

An Emilio Pucci turquoise dress.

52.75in (134cm) long

£80-120   **S&T**

A CLOSER LOOK AT A PUCCI DRESS

This instantly recognisable use of complicated geometric design and bright colours are Pucci hallmarks. Pieces in this style are the most sought-after as they exemplify his style.

The 'T-shirt' or 'chemise' dress with a thin belt is one of his most used, and most popular, designs.

Genuine pieces bear the name 'Emilio' as part of the design. The word is very small, so look closely to ensure the piece is not one copy.

This dress was owned and worn by Marilyn Monroe which adds value.

EMILIO PUCCI

- Born the Marchese Emilio Pucci di Barsento in 1914, he studied political science and shone as a First World War pilot.
- In 1947, he was discovered skiing in a suit of his own creation by a 'Harper's Bazaar' photographer. This tapered pant ski suit was soon introduced in America. His first women's wear collection was shown in 1949, and he opened a studio in Florence in the same year.
- His earliest pieces are characterised by solid colours or simple figural motifs, some typical of the 1950s. However, during the late 1950s and 1960s, his style changed and pieces were made in highly recognisable bright, psychedelic colours, most famously with sophisticated freeform or geometrical psychedelic designs that covered the entire body.
- Fabric is typically silk or silk jersey, but during the late 1950s he worked on improving a figure-hugging stretch material. This became known as 'Emilioform' and was heavily used during the 1960s and 70s.
- His designs soon covered a wider range of items including dinner sets, ties, scarves, lingerie and towels. During the 1980s he enjoyed a revival of his style. After his death in 1992, his daughter carried on his name and work.
- During the 1990s his clothing was revisited again and is now fixed as being highly popular amongst collectors. In the late 1990s, Christie's and Sotheby's held fashion and costume auctions containing pieces by Pucci.

An Emilio Pucci long-sleeved mini dress, in silk with geometric abstract design in shades of blue and turquoise, with stitched "Emilio Pucci made in Italy" label to neck, separate cord tie belt and clear bead ends, owned and worn by Marilyn Monroe, with a letter of authenticity, dated April 23, 1998, from Eleanor "Bebe" Goddard.

£2,000-2,500 **CO**

A Pucci blue silk blouse.
27in (69cm) long
£75-125 **S&T**

A Pucci fuchsia shirt.
30in (77cm) long
£200-250 **S&T**

A Pucci red sweater.
25.5in (65cm) long
£125-185 **S&T**

A Pucci peach halter top.
9in (22cm) long
£25-50 **S&T**

A pair of 1960s Pucci trousers, with red and purple designs on yellow.

41in (105cm) long

£220-280   **S&T**

A 1960s Pucci pink nylon long skirt.

37in (94cm) long

£200-250   **S&T**

A pair of Mary Quant red and white striped slacks and top.

46.75in (119cm) long

£150-200   **S&T**

A 1960s rare Mary Quant two-piece black and white striped slacks and top.

49.5in (126cm) long

£180-220   **S&T**

A 1950s Ric Roc red and white dress.

£50-70   **S&T**

A Sonia Rykel red and black knit dress.

41.25in (105cm) long

£120-180   **S&T**

An early 1970s three-piece Yves Saint Laurent outfit, including jersey, trousers and necklace.

£800-900   **S&T**

A rare Yves Saint Laurent couture crème satin evening coat.

£800-1,200   **S&T**

A Diane Von Furstenberg black and white gown and jacket.

Jacket 28in (71cm) long

£80-120   **S&T**

A jacket from a Valentino two-piece print suit.

19in (48cm) long

£50-100 (suit)   **S&T**

A Versace two-piece black, yellow and purple trousers and top.

Top 17.75in (45cm) long

£220-280   **S&T**

A Vivienne Westwood Gold Label primrose angora bow dress, from 'Vive la cocotte', from Westwood's own archive.

97cm long

£320-380 S&T

A Vivienne Westwood tulip bow dress, from Pagan I collection, also from Westwood's own archive.

36.25in (92cm) long

£400-450 S&T

A Vivienne Westwood Sèvres porcelain print rain cape, from the Pagan V collection, also from Westwood's own archive.

42in (107cm) long

£300-350 S&T

A Vivienne Westwood two-piece suit.

Jacket 22.5in (57cm) long

£200-250 S&T

VIVIENNE WESTWOOD

- Westwood was born Vivienne Isabel Swire in 1941. She opened 'Let It Rock', her first boutique selling second hand clothes with her partner Malcolm McLaren in 1971 on the King's Road, London.

- The 1970s saw Westwood making headline news with the aggressive S&M, bondage and punk themed clothes, which were worn by The Sex Pistols.

- After the punk look had become too commercial, they released their first collection, 'Pirates', in 1981. This was followed by the 'Buffalo Girls' collection of 1982 which foresaw the 'grunge' look of the 1990s with its dirty colours and camouflage.

- Her solo career began in 1983 with her 'Witches' collection. Since then her hallmarks of unconventionality, theatricality and sexuality that allow her to shock, combined with an understanding of historical dress, have made her a global name in fashion design.

A Vivienne Westwood nautical jacket.

31in (79cm) long

£150-200 S&T

A pair of Vivienne Westwood purple trousers.

39.35in (100cm) long

£50-100 S&T

A pair of Vivienne Westwood silver leather trousers, slight tear to rear.

43in (109cm) long

£100-150 S&T

A 1960s collectable pair of Vivienne Westwood shorts.

12.5in (32cm) long

£50-100 S&T

A Vivienne Westwood brown fuzzy skirt.

20in (51cm) long

£180-220 S&T

A Vivienne Westwood body.

Westwood began using the now familiar orb motif for her clothing in 1987.

28in (71cm) long

£100-150   **S&T**

A 1920s Art Deco beaded dress, probably French.

£1,000-1,400   **S&T**

A 1970s pink lamé dress.

£40-45   **S&T**

A 1920s devoré velvet dress, with maribou trim.

£500-550   **S&T**

A 1920s pink and grey beaded flapper dress.

£250-300   **S&T**

A 1930s brown and orange dress.

£80-90   **S&T**

A 1950s black and white floral dress, with swagged waist.

£70-80   **S&T**

A 1950s black and white spotted prom dress, with crinoline.

£220-260   **S&T**

A 1950s cream and wool dress, with blue robe swirls.

£120-160   **S&T**

A 1950s blue and white puffball dress.

£180-220   **S&T**

A 1960s pink floral print dress.

£60-80   **S&T**

A 1960s flower print coat.

£60-70   **S&T**

A 1950s pink dress, with appliqué flower motif.

£80-90   **S&T**

A 1960s dress, with belt.

£60-80   **S&T**

A 1970s patterned dress.

£40-50   **S&T**

A very rare and touchingly handmade tunic, with pink embroidery, buttons, metal bits, and coins, possibly Afghan.

£850-950   **S&T**

A vintage Chinese robe, with black appliqué embroidered grape vines.

£385-425   **S&T**

A B C D E F G H I J K L M N O P Q R S T U V W XYZ

A 1960s silk scarf, with figural pattern, produced for the "21 Club" New York, maker unknown.

66in (167.5cm) long

£60-80 REN

A 1950s Hermes 'La Clé des Champs' pattern scarf, Jacquard silk with hand-rolled edges, designed and signed by F.R. Façonnet.

35in (89cm) wide

£100-150 REN

A Hermes 'Brides de Gala' pattern scarf, silk twill with hand-rolled edges, designed by the Hermes Studio (unsigned).

c1960   35in (89cm) wide

£80-120 REN

A 1970s Hermes 'Les Bécanes' pattern scarf, silk twill with hand-rolled edges, designed by the Hermes Studio (unsigned).

35in (89cm) wide

£100-130 REN

A 1970s Hermes 'Grand Apparat' pattern scarf, silk twill with hand-rolled edges, designed and signed by Jacques Eudel.

35in (89cm) wide

£80-100 REN

A 1950s Hermes 'Chiens et Valets' pattern scarf, silk twill with hand-rolled edges, designed and signed by C.H. Hello.

35in (89cm) wide

£80-120 REN

A 1980s Hermes 'Grands Fonds' pattern scarf, silk twill with hand-rolled edges, designed by the Hermes Studio (unsigned).

35in (89cm) wide

£100-140 REN

A 1970s Hermes 'Harnais des Presidents' pattern scarf, silk twill with hand-rolled edges, designed by the Hermes Studio (unsigned).

35in (89cm) wide

£80-120 REN

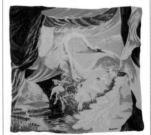

A 1940s Jacqmar 'Swan Lake' pattern parachute silk scarf.

33in (84cm) wide

£60-80 REN

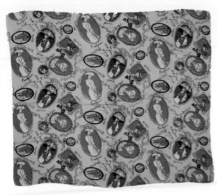

A 1940s Jacqmar 'Les Belles Dames' pattern rayon scarf.

34in (86.5cm) wide

£60–90   **REN**

A 1940s Kaystyle 'Wartime' pattern rayon scarf, signed "London by Kaystyle".

33in (84cm) wide

£200–250   **REN**

A 1970s Liberty's of London 'Paisley pattern' silk scarf.

26.5in (67.5cm) wide

£15–30   **REN**

A 1940s synthetic fabric 'Sporting' pattern scarf, designed by Thirkell.

32in (81.5cm) wide

£20–40   **REN**

A 1950s Jacqmar 'Geese' pattern silk scarf, designed by Peter Scott.

29in (73.5cm) wide

£30–50   **REN**

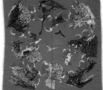

An Yves St. Laurent silk scarf.

c1970   *35in (14cm) wide*

£60-80   **REN**

A 'Winston Churchill 80th Birthday' pattern silk scarf, designer's signature illegible.

1954   *27in (68.5cm) wide*

£50–70   **REN**

A 1950s 'Letters' pattern silk scarf, maker unknown.

35.5in (90cm) wide

£30–50   **REN**

A 1940s Jacqmar 'The Flower Seller' pattern rayon scarf.

1940s   *29in (73.5cm) wide*

£60–80   **REN**

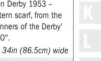

A Welsh Margetson & Co. Ltd 'Coronation Derby 1953 – Pinza' pattern scarf, from the series "Winners of the Derby' since 1780".

1953   *34in (86.5cm) wide*

£150–200   **REN**

An 'Empire Games 1958' pattern synthetic fabric scarf, maker unknown.

1958   *25.5in (64.5cm) wide*

£15–20   **REN**

HANDBAGS

■ The 'retro' trend of the past decade has seen a revival in use of handbags from previous decades. Collectors and specialist dealers have sprung up all over the world to service celebrities, fashion stylists, 'fashionistas' and collectors with uniquely stylish and highly individual handbags.

■ The increase in informal occasions during the 1950s saw an explosion in 'light hearted', highly decorative handbags that used different materials such as plastic, brocade, straw, metal and raffia, embellished with sequins, hand-painted scenes and ribbons.

■ Bags by named and notable designers are hotly sought after, as are early plastic bags from the 1930s-1950s. These are generally made in bright colours, from 'Catalin', a brightly coloured form of Bakelite, or 'Lucite' a largely transparent plastic that is also often coloured brightly or made to look like tortoiseshell. These bags are rigid, generally in the form of shaped boxes and can be decorated with metal strips, jewels or carved patterns.

■ Before you buy a Lucite or early plastic bag, smell the interior – if it exudes a chemical smell, do not buy it as this marks the beginning of the material degrading resulting in a bag covered with tiny cracks. Look for names such as 'Rialto' or 'Willardy' and keep them away from heat or strong sunlight which will bring on disintegration.

An early 19thC figural beaded bag.
4in (10cm) wide

£80-130 **S&T**

A late 19thC beadwork bag.
4.75in (12cm) wide

£50-100 **Men**

A beadwork purse, hand-worked on black velvet with flowers and the name Emily M. Hollister, back and front detail.
c1810 *9in (23cm) long*

£450-550 **RAA**

BEADWORK

■ Beadwork is a form of embroidery where small glass beads are threaded onto silk thread and stitched to a fabric ground, or threaded onto wire, which is then shaped.

■ It was popular during the 19th and 20th centuries for handbags and purses, but was first used in the 17th century for picture or mirror frames and small cabinets.

■ The intricate nature of beadwork allows for sophisticated designs, some of which recorded specific dates or events.

■ As coloured glass beads are used, the colour tends not to fade, meaning that bags most often retain their brilliance even after a century or more.

■ Condition is important as it is difficult to repair beaded bags through replacing torn silk linings or sewing the tiny beads back on.

A Victorian beaded bag.
6in (15cm) wide

£120-160 **S&T**

A late 19thC beadwork bag, with blue and gold beads.
3.25in (8.5cm) wide

£50-75 **Men**

An antique beaded bag, with faux tortoiseshell clasp.
6in (15cm) wide

£70-90 **S&T**

A late 19th/early 20thC metal and beadwork bag.
c1900 *6in (15cm) wide*

£100-200 **Men**

A late 19thC beadwork bag.
5.5in (14cm) wide

£50-100 **Men**

An extremely rare French beaded black and floral vanity bag, with lipstick, powder and cigarette compartments inside.

£425-475 **S&T**

A 1940s black beaded bag, with flowers.

10.25in (26cm) wide

£150-200　　　　　　**S&T**

A 1940s black beaded figural bag.

10in (25.5cm) wide

£350-450　　　　　　**Rox**

A beaded moth purse.

9in (23cm) long

£1,500-2,000　　　　　**Rox**

A 1940s black beaded purse with rose design.

11in (28cm) wide

£200-250　　　　　　**Rox**

A 1950s black beaded and jewelled bag, with poodle motif.

14.5in (37cm) wide

£140-170　　　　　　**SM**

A 1950s black jersey jewelled and beaded tapestry handbag.

7.5in (19cm) wide

£80-100　　　　　　**SM**

A 1940s white beaded figural bag.

9in (23cm) wide

£300-400　　　　　　**Rox**

A late 1950s Enid Collins beaded bucket bag, with butterfly motif.

13in (33cm) wide

£80-100　　　　　　**SM**

A 1940s white beaded box purse.

7in (17.5cm) wide

£200-300　　　　　　**Rox**

A 1950s black Lucite compartment purse.

£400-500　　　　　　**Rox**

A 1950s red Lucite purse.

8.5in (21.5cm) wide

£1,200-1,800　　　　　**Rox**

A 1950s black purse with goldfish, wood, straw and Lucite.

11.5in (29cm) wide

£150-200 Rox

A 1950s yellow Lucite bag, with clear Lucite top.

9.5in (23.5cm) wide

£150-200 SM

A 1950s wooden box bag, with purple velvet grapes and Lucite handle, lined with brocade and ribbon, specially handmade by "Susan".

9.25in (23.5cm) wide

£80-100 SM

A strawberry wooden box bag, with hand-painted motif.

12.25in (31cm) wide

£50-60 S&T

A 1950s wooden octagonal handbag, with butterfly découpage and Lucite handle.

7in (18cm) wide

£80-100 SM

A metal box bag.

8.75in (22cm) wide

£60-80 S&T

A 1950s white woven basket, with felt fruit baskets.

8.5in (22cm) wide

£80-100 SM

A 1950s handmade wooden happy-house handbag.

10.5in (26.5cm) wide

£130-150 SM

A 1930s Bakelite purse.

5.5in (14cm) wide

£500-600 Rox

A 1920s brocade bag with white metal clasp.

6.75in (17cm) wide

£100-150 Men

A 1920s tapestry petit point bag, with enamel clasp.

9.5in (24cm) wide

£100-150 Men

A 1920s tapestry petit point bag.

7in (18cm) wide

£100-150 Men

A 19th/20thC Native American bag.

6in (15cm) wide

£200-300 Rox

A beautiful 19thC petit point bag, with gilt frame.

8in (21cm) wide

£150-200   **S&T**

A 19thC satin Turkish bag, made for the European market.

5in (12.5cm) wide

£100-150   **Men**

A 1930s tapestry bag, probably French.

9in (23cm) wide

£180-230   **S&T**

A 1950s Souré black leather bag, with 3D scenic tapestry work, New York.

15.25in (38.5cm) wide

£120-150   **SM**

An incredibly detailed Art Nouveau bag, with celluloid clasp.

c1900   *8.25in (21cm) wide*

£425-475   **S&T**

A 1950s tapestry bag.

10.75in (27cm) wide

£80-120   **S&T**

A rare vintage 'Fragonard' girl on swing vanity case.

4in (10cm) wide

£180-220   **S&T**

A 1950s poet bag, with 'La Maison du Poet' on the front.

11.5in (29cm) wide

£80-120   **S&T**

A 1950s Rialto purse.

Bags from the 1950s are characterised by having shorter handles.

£100-150   **Rox**

A needlepoint clutch bag, with ladies' legs motif.

16.5in (42cm) wide

£60-80   **S&T**

A highly collectable 1940s felt bag, with appliqué fruit.

13.25in (34cm) wide

£80-100   **S&T**

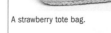

A strawberry tote bag.

11.75in (30cm) wide

£40-50   **S&T**

A B C D E F G H I J K L M N O P Q R S T U V W XYZ

A 1930s silk and celluloid rose purse.
9in (23cm) wide

£500-800   **Rox**

A vintage purse, with gold lace.
6.75in (17cm) wide

£80-100   **S&T**

A vintage Gucci blue leather clutch bag, probably 1950s.
11in (28cm) wide

£80-120   **S&T**

A Judith Lieber bird bag, with two small birds inside.
6.75(17cm) wide

£800-900   **S&T**

JUDITH LIEBER

- Judith Lieber was born in 1921 to a Jewish family in Budapest. After escaping capture during the Second World War, she met Gertson Lieber, an American GI in 1945 and married him a year later, moving to New York.
- She initially worked for other handbag manufacturers and started her own business in 1963.
- Although she does make day bags, she is most renowned for her glittering and highly individual evening bags, many of which are covered in rhinestones or diamanté. These are known as 'minaudières', and her style is often imitated.
- All her bags are hand decorated and can take many weeks to create. They are popular with stars and First Ladies of America, with Jackie Kennedy, Hillary Clinton, Nancy Reagan and Joan Collins being amongst the illustrious owners.
- Her work is now highly sought after by collectors and the glamorous who use them. In 1997, the Victoria & Albert Museum in London added one of her bags to its collection and an exhibition of one lady's collection of 300 Lieber bags in New Orleans was visited by over 10,000 people.

A Judith Lieber-style penguin minaudière bag, with diamanté.
6.25in (16cm) high

£700-800   **S&T**

A Christian Dior hat, with appliqué daisies.
8.75in (22cm) wide

£50-80   **S&T**

A Norman Edwin hat, with blue, yellow and pink print.

£30-40   **S&T**

An Original Louise's Showcase pink hat.

8.75in (22cm) diam

£40-50 S&T

A Ranleigh green feather hat.

8.75in (22cm) wide

£50-60 S&T

A Schiaparelli fake fur hat, with diamanté trim.

11.75in (30cm) wide

£150-180 S&T

A Schiaparelli black fuzzy hat.

11.75in (30cm) wide

£150-200 S&T

A Schiaparelli blue-jewelled hat.

8.25in (21cm) wide

£200-250 S&T

ELSA SCHIAPARELLI

- Elsa Schiaparelli (1890-1973) is considered one of the most influential designers of the 20th century and her inventive clothes, costume jewellery and hats are highly desirable amongst collectors.
- Her name is also synonymous with a stunning shade of pink. Many of her designs were inspired by the Surrealist art movement, such as her famous 1937 shoe-shaped hat which was suggested by Salvador Dali.

An Eddi Stix and Fuller cherry hat.

7in (18cm) wide

£60-70 S&T

An Italian grey feather trim hat, handmade by Shirley Sverett.

7.75in (20cm) wide

£60-70 S&T

A pink hat, with woven ribbon.

11in (28cm) wide

£10-20 S&T

A 1960s orange fake fur hat.

9.75in (25cm) diam

£25-35 S&T

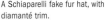

A blue and white striped hat, with orange trim.

11in (28cm) wide

£30-40 S&T

An Oriental cat hat.

8.25in (21cm) wide

£100-130 S&T

A 1950s Coty brushed gold compact and lipstick, with original cream powder instructions.

3.25in (8.5cm) wide

£40-50 SM

A 1920s enamelled compact and cigarette case, by Chelsea Cigarettes.

Larger 3.25in (8.5cm) wide

£125-155 SM

A 1950s jewelled pocket lipstick and mirror.

2.5in (6.5cm) wide

£20-30 SM

A 1950s Mop compact, by Ansico.

2in (5cm) wide

£20-30 SM

A 1950s Kissing Couples musical compact and lipstick by Thorens, plays 'The Night They Invented Champagne', original box.

4in (10cm) wide

£130-150 SM

A 1950s Dorset Fifth Avenue compact, lipstick and leather case.

6.75in (17cm) wide

£40-50 SM

A 1950s mirrored musical compact, with carved glass oriental scene, in the original box.

3in (7.5cm) wide

£70-90 SM

A pair of Balenciaga gold shoes.

9.75in (25cm) long

£65-75 S&T

A pair of Dolce and Gabbana green velvet shoes, with floral decoration.

12.25in (31cm) long

£225-275 S&T

A 1950s Johansen patterned shoe.

£50-70 S&T

A 1950s pair of Kitty Kelly leather and Lucite shoes, with yellow squiggles in the heel.

8in (22cm) long

£80-100 SM

A 1950s pair of blue leather stilettos, with a springalator, created for Kims.

The stiletto arrived on the fashion scene in 1952, although it is not clear who was responsible for its design.

Despite the fact that stilettos were often uncomfortable and dangerous to wear, and sometimes caused damage to floors, by the late 1950s they were highly fashionable, with Jayne Mansfield owning some 200 pairs.

Often seen as a sign of playful female aggression and sexuality, their popularity waned in the 1960s before returning in the late 1970s.

9.5in (24cm) long

£55-65 SM

A pair of La Rose Jacksonville clear Lucite wedges made in USA.

This shoe uses Lucite, a plastic commonly used during the 1950s for decorative and fashionable handbags.

8.75in (22cm) long

£80-100 SM

A pair of Anne Klein pumps.

10.5in (27cm) long

£50-60 S&T

A pair of Herbert Levine asymmetrical blue suede stilettos.

11in (28cm) long

£50-60 SM

A pair of 1950s Nina flower pumps.

10.25in (26cm) long

£70-90 S&T

A pair of 1950s Pandora Footwear lilac devoré shoes.

9.75in (25cm) long

£70-90 SM

A pair of Randalls brown croc shoes.

11in (28cm) long

£100-150 S&T

A pair of Safinia Saks 5th Avenue shoes, in brown leather.

10.5in (27cm) long

£70-90 S&T

A pair of Saks 5th Avenue gold shoes.

£40-50 S&T

A pair of 1940s grey cut-out platforms.

9.5in (24cm) long

£15-20 S&T

A 1940s pair of snakeskin ankle strap platforms, with utility mark.

9in (23cm) long

£80-100   **SM**

A pair of early 1950s black leather and suede pumps.

11in (28cm) long

£70-80   **S&T**

A pair of 1950s pumps.

11in (28cm) long

£45-55   **S&T**

A pair of 1950s beige lace pumps.

10.25in (26cm) long

£35-45   **S&T**

A pair of 1940s pink Lucite sunglasses.

5.25in (13.5cm) wide

£30-40   **SM**

A pair of 1950s Verres Filtrants cat's-eye and Lucite sunglasses, made in France.

5.5in (14cm) wide

£45-55   **SM**

A rare pair of 1960s Biba boots.

22.75in (58cm) high

£280-320   **S&T**

A pair of gold metallic boots.

7in (18cm) high

£65-75   **S&T**

A pair of 1950s blue tinted sunglasses, made in France.

5.5in (14cm) wide

£30-40   **SM**

A 1950s pair of plastic sunglasses, with stiffened cotton daisy trim.

5in (12.5cm) wide

£60-70   **SM**

A pair of original 1950s Ray-Bans sunglasses, with blue fleck colouring, made in USA.

5.5in (14cm) wide

£80-100   **SM**

A pair of early 1960s black sunglasses.

5.75in (14.5cm) wide

£35-45   **SM**

A pair of 1950s Doscar cat's-eye and diamanté sunglasses, with original tag, made in Italy.

6in (15cm) wide

£70-80   **SM**

A pair of late 1950s tortoiseshell plastic men's sunglasses, made in Italy.

5.75in (14.5cm) wide

£35-45   **CVS**

A 1940s hand-painted red palm tree tie.

£75-85   **CVS**

A 1940s hand-painted silk screened 3D 'Booby' tie.

Images of buxom or skimpily dressed ladies were favourite motifs during the late 1940s and 1950s and can be found on a wide range of objects.

1940s

£150-200   **CVS**

A late 1940s Salvador Dali tie, with candelabra motif.

£250-300   **CVS**

A 1950s hand-painted 'butterfly' tie.

£35-45 CVS

A 1940s National Shirt Tops heart design silk tie.

£55-65 CVS

A King Kong tie, by Wembley.

£15-20 S&T

A Mickey Mouse tie.

£15-20 S&T

A Peanuts cartoon graphic tie, showing Charlie Brown and Snoopy.

£15-25 S&T

A musical jazz tie.

£15-20 S&T

A spaceship tie.

£15-20 S&T

A striped tie, with street scenes, made in Italy.

£15-20 S&T

A cartoon graphic tie, showing Disney characters including Bugs Bunny, Daffy Duck and Sylvester the Cat playing snooker.

'Humorous' ties depicting cartoon characters, were popular during the late 1980s and the early 1990s.

£18-22 S&T

A 1940s Swank sword tie-bar, with mother-of-pearl.

3.5in (9in) long

£15-25 CVS

A pair of Spotlight Sheers stockings, in off-black glamour sheer with a dark seam.

£20-30 SM

A pair of 1950s Missouri full-fashioned nylons, with a dark seam.

£35-45 SM

A 1930s packet of black rayon stockings, by Bluebird.

6.5in (16.5cm) wide

£15-20 SM

Three 1950s pin-up girl match boxes, made by the Superior Match Company, by the artist Petty.

2in (5cm) high

£8-10 each SM

A 1950s Gossard black lace and stretch all-in-one.

£65-75 SM

A 1950s Lady Marlene white all-in-one.

£45-55 SM

A 1950s Extasy matching blue lace-trimmed, suspender belt and bra, the bra with scalloped trimmed push-up cups, made in France.

£45-55 SM

FANS

- Fans date back some 3,000 years and were used as ceremonial tools, status symbols and fashion accessories. During the mid-18th century, they became popular amongst the upper classes but went into decline during the 1930s.

- Folding fans are the most common type and have a folding screen, known as a 'leaf', mounted on a series of folding 'sticks'. The front and back sticks are known as 'guard sticks' and are can be exquisitely decorated, being carved or beautifully inlaid with precious materials. Sticks can be made from wood, ivory, tortoiseshell, precious metals or Bakelite.

- Oriental fans often bear Eastern imagery such as pagodas and rustic scenes with and without figures and were made for export during the 18th and 19th centuries. Although they are not of as fine quality as the fans that the Chinese made for themselves, many are of excellent quality and are highly collectable.

- Look out for hand-painted fans from the 18th and 19th centuries, which are very desirable, particularly fans bearing unusual motifs such as hot air balloons, or specific scenes or famous events. Less expensive are advertising fans produced from the mid-19th century.

- Condition is important and splits to the leaf, broken sticks and staining affect value. Always take care when opening a fan, handle them as little as possible and avoid having them framed for display as light and heat will damage them.

A late 18thC fan, with decorated ivory sticks, the guards carved as figures.

11.75in (30cm) wide

£100-200   **Men**

A late 18thC fan, with painted scene entitled 'Rebecca at the well'.

11in (28cm) wide

£200-300   **Men**

A 19thC mother-of-pearl fan, painted on satin with romantic lady motif.

12.5in (31.5cm) wide

£200-250   **Men**

A 19thC gauze leaf fan, decorated with mischievous cherubs, with mother-of-pearl sticks, signed "L. S. Toudes".

12.5in (31.5cm) wide

£200-250   **Men**

A Victorian printed fan, decorated with scene of a gathering of ladies, with bone sticks.

10.5in (26.5cm) wide

£50-100   **Men**

A late 19th/early 20thC Japanese fan, the ivory guard sticks decorated with Shibayama, the semi-precious stones in the form of insects.

10.75in (27cm) wide

£200-250   **Men**

A late 19thC Cantonese lace fan, the leaf decorated with people wearing painted garments, with carved ivory sticks.

11in (28cm) wide

£200-300 **Men**

A 19thC black lace fan, decorated with birds and blossom, with mother-of-pearl sticks.

12.5in (31.5cm) wide

£200-250 **Men**

A 19thC black ebony fan, decorated with flowers.

12.75in (32.5cm) wide

£50-100 **Men**

A 1920s tortoiseshell and feather fan.

12.75in (32cm) wide

£50-100 **Men**

FIND OUT MORE...

The Fan Museum, 12 Crooms Hill, Greenwich, London SE10 8ER, England. www.fan-museum.org.

Helene Alexander, 'Fans', published by Shire Books, 1995.

Susan Mayor, 'The Letts Guide to Collecting Fans', Letts, 1991.

A 19thC mother-of-pearl fan, with Carrickmacross lace, the sticks in silver and gilt.

A 1920s ivory and red feather fan, with ivory sticks.

16in (41cm) wide

£50-100 **Men**

Lace fans were popular in Europe and the United States from the early 18th century until the early 20th century and are now a collectable field in their own right. Before the 18th century, all lace fans were produced from hand-woven lace, either 'needlelace' or 'bobbin' lace, with the finest examples being woven from silk. The high cost of manufacture made them the preserve of the wealthy and powerful. Machine-woven lace, such as 'Nottingham' or 'Swiss' lace, manufactured from the late 18th century onwards, made lace fans less costly. More of these fans survive than the delicate early versions which fetch high prices when found in good condition.

A 19thC black lace and mother-of-pearl fan.

11in (28cm) wide

12.5in (31.5cm) wide

£200-250 **Men**

£50-100 **Men**

TEXTILES

LACE

- Prior to the late 18th century, lace was hand made from flaxen thread, silk, wool or cotton yarn. It was either stitched with a needle and thread (needlelace) or by twisting bobbins around pins that had been stuck into a stuffed pillow to outline the pattern (bobbin lace).
- Patterns included stylized animals, birds, foliate designs, floral patterns linked with scrolling designs and more. Needlelace patterns differ and there are many techniques – it is best to refer to an illustrated book to learn about them. 17th and 18th century lace is usually very expensive.
- During the 16th century, production centres sprang up in Italy (at Venice, Genoa and Milan), in Belgium (Brussels, Mechelen and Antwerp), in Spain and Portugal. France (Alençon, Argenton, Paris and Chantilly) and England (Honiton) developed centres during the 17th century. Most centres have carried on production to the present.
- Early lace was deemed a commodity and also displayed the wealth and influence of the wearer. This can be seen particularly in 16th and 17th century Dutch paintings.
- Machine-made lace, invented in the late 18th century, took off during the 19th century. It is much more affordable and can form excellent collections. Stitching is much more regular than hand-stitched lace.
- Check that modern lace has not been artificially aged in tea. Cleaning lace is best left to professionals, but can be achieved by washing gently in distilled water.

A mid-17thC Flemish lace, one of earliest and rarest laces.
56in (142cm) long

£500-700 — Men

A pair of late 17thC point de France lace lappets.
53.5in (136cm) long

£300-400 — Men

A pair of Brussels bobbin lace lappets. c1725

£750-800 — Men

An early to mid-18thC length of Milan bobbin lace.
143.75in (365cm) long

£300-400 — Men

An 18thC length of Flemish bobbin lace.
151in (384cm) long

£700-800 — Men

An 18thC point de Venise needlepoint.
50in (127cm) long

£400-500 — Men

A length of Alençon needle point lace. c1750 *69.25in (176cm) long*

£200-300 — Men

A piece of 18thC lace.
48.75in (124cm) long

£200-300 — Men

An very fine 18thC length of Binche bobbin lace.
76in (193cm) long

£300-400 — Men

A 19thC length of Brussels duchesse lace.
63in (160cm) long

£100-150 — Men

A piece of blonde silk lace. c1800

£100-200 — Men

A length of Binche lace.
55in (140cm) long

£200-300 — Men

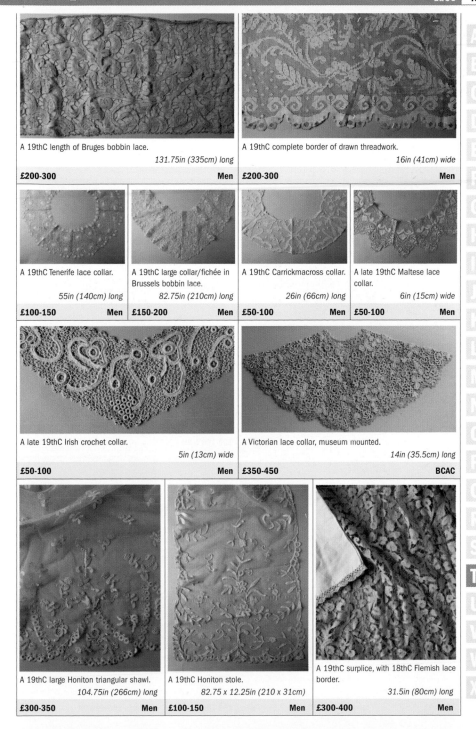

A 19thC length of Bruges bobbin lace.

131.75in (335cm) long

£200-300   **Men**

A 19thC complete border of drawn threadwork.

16in (41cm) wide

£200-300   **Men**

A 19thC Tenerife lace collar.

55in (140cm) long

£100-150   **Men**

A 19thC large collar/fichée in Brussels bobbin lace.

82.75in (210cm) long

£150-200   **Men**

A 19thC Carrickmacross collar.

26in (66cm) long

£50-100   **Men**

A late 19thC Maltese lace collar.

6in (15cm) wide

£50-100   **Men**

A late 19thC Irish crochet collar.

5in (13cm) wide

£50-100   **Men**

A Victorian lace collar, museum mounted.

14in (35.5cm) long

£350-450   **BCAC**

A 19thC large Honiton triangular shawl.

104.75in (266cm) long

£300-350   **Men**

A 19thC Honiton stole.

82.75 x 12.25in (210 x 31cm)

£100-150   **Men**

A 19thC surplice, with 18thC Flemish lace border.

31.5in (80cm) long

£300-400   **Men**

A 19thC lady's lace dressing jacket.

18.5in (47cm) long

£80-150 Men

A late 19thC pair of Irish crochet lace cuffs.

10.5 x 4.75in (27 x 12cm) wide

£40-80 Men

A 19thC needlepoint cushion cover, with musicians and dancing figures.

40.25in (62cm) long

£200-300 Men

A 19thC decorative needlepoint panel, possibly for a cushion.

17.5in (44cm) diam

£100-150 Men

One of a set of six 19thC Normandy lace mats.

These mats encompass a mixture of embroidered and other lace with a needlepoint centre, and as such they show a fine display of various techniques.

9in (23cm) diam

£50-100 (set) Men

An early 19thC large lawn handkerchief, with whitework, drawn threadwork and lace surrounding.

26.25in (67cm) wide

£100-200 Men

A 19thC handkerchief, with Valenciennes lace and drawn threadwork.

16.5in (42cm) wide

£50-100 Men

A late 19thC lawn handkerchief, with needlework border.

17in (43cm) wide

£50-100 Men

A late 18thC handkerchief, edged with lace.

17in (43cm) wide

£100-150 Men

A 19thC handkerchief, edged with fine Irish crochet.

13.25in (34cm) wide

£50-100 Men

A late 18thC lace handkerchief, embroidered with whitework.

26in (66cm) wide

£150-200 Men

A late 19thC lawn handkerchief, with border and insertion in Valenciennes lace.

13in (33cm) wide

£50-100 Men

An early 19thC lawn handkerchief, with drawn threadwork and lace border.

22.5in (57cm) wide

£50-100 Men

A 19thC lawn handkerchief, with whitework and surrendered Valenciennes lace.

15.25in (39cm) wide

£30-50 Men

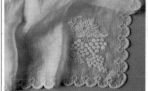

A late 18thC handkerchief, with whitework.

15.75 (40cm) wide

£100-200 Men

A 19thC handkerchief, with lawn Valenciennes lace.

14in (36cm) wide

£30-50 Men

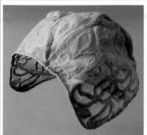

A late 18thC baby's bonnet.

9.5in (24cm) wide

£150-200 Men

A late 18thC baby's bonnet.

11in (28cm) wide

£150-250 Men

A bonnet edged with lace and with a lace insert.

c1800 *12.25in (31cm) wide*

£75-100 Men

A late 18thC baby's bonnet.

11in (28cm) wide

£40-50 Men

A lawn and Valenciennes lace baby gown.

c1880 *18.5in (47cm) long*

£60-80 Men

A 19thC broderie anglaise baby gown.

21.25in (54cm) long

£40-60 Men

A 19thC embroidered lawn baby coat, with large collar.

A coat is more desirable and unusual than a gown.

19.75in (50cm) long

£80-100   **Men**

A 19thC embroidered lawn child's pinafore, with lace and ribbon, opening at back.

20.5in (52cm) long

£80-100   **Men**

A 19thC baby's christening gown, with whitework.

43.7in (111cm) long

£100-150   **Men**

An infant's chemise, with lawn ruffles.

c1800   12.5in (32cm) long

£100-150   **Men**

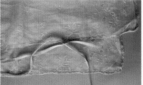

An 18thC apron, with whitework embroidery.

41.25in (105cm) long

£100-200   **Men**

A Regency lace stole.

35in (89cm) wide

£150-200   **Men**

A George III linen sampler, worked in crosstitch with coloured silks, with a central verse "Favour is deceitful and beauty is vain, but a woman that search the Lord, she shall be praised....", surrounded by motifs including a three mast ship, stylized flowers and trees, a gentleman with a walking stick and a lady with a basket, enclosed with a border of stylised flowers.

9.75in (25cm) high

£250-350   **DN**

A George III needlework map of the British Isles, worked in coloured silks and wools on canvas.

22.5in (57cm) high

£200-300   **DN**

A 19thC linen sampler, by Ann Crook of Bucklebury, worked in crosstitch with silks and wools, with alphabets above a central verse "Beauty; There is beauty in the flower, Though it fades within the hour...", surrounded by stylized flower trees, flowers, animals and birds, dated 1857.

12.5in (31.5cm) high

£200-300 **DN**

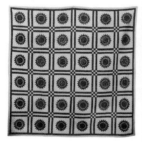

An American hand-sewn summer quilt, with cotton backing and pinwheel design, some deterioration.

6in (193cm) long

£50-80 **TWC**

An American hand-sewn summer quilt, with a large and colourful starbust centre, some stitches visible.

c1920 *70in (178cm) wide*

£70-120 **TWC**

An American quilt.

1841

£200-300 **Men**

A CLOSER LOOK AT A WOVEN PANEL

17th century woven silk panels such as these are highly desirable and fetch high prices at auction.

Usually referring to Biblical stories, they have an allegorical meaning and were often meant to educate. Additionally, some of the motifs used within the picture, such as the animals, have meanings in themselves that are related to the story.

Condition is vitally important with damage affecting value. Fading is common, with undamaged examples with the brightest colours fetching the highest prices. These panels were highly coloured when made.

This panel tells the Biblical story of Abraham, Hagar and Ishmael. Abraham was married to Sara, but she bore him no children, so Sara gave her maid, Hagar, to Abraham so she could bear children for them. Hagar gave birth to Ishmael. God (usually represented by the sun) then made Sara pregnant and she bore Isaac. Ishmael mocked Isaac which displeased Sara who took her son away (right-hand scene) ordering her husband to banish Hagar and Ishmael, which he did (central scene), giving them a vase of water as they went into the desert. When the water was gone, Hagar cast Ishmael under bush (the left-hand scene) in despair. An angel appeared and provided a well of water so that they were saved. This scene is also found in 17th century paintings.

A 17thC English linen and silk embroidered panel, depicting the story of Abraham, Hagar and Ishmael, executed in bold colours, in a tortoiseshell frame.

19.7in (50cm) high

£11,500-12,500 **FRE**

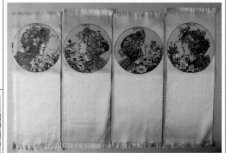

An 1920s double shawl, with two different patterns.

63in (160cm) wide

£200-300 **Men**

Four Art Nouveau Arpad Basch silk panels, representing the four seasons.

15.5in (39cm) long

£200-300 **Men**

An American Shelton & Osborn, Birmingham, CT, rosewood coffin plane, with ivory and ebony inlay, very nice original as found condition with minor dents.

7.75in (19.5cm) long

£300-400 TWC

An American fine small cabinet maker's plane, maker unknown, probably made by "J.F.Helm" as marked by original owner and tool maker, with rosewood knob, excellent condition.

6in (15cm) long

£60-100 TWC

A mixed set of beech woodworking planes, by A. Mathieson & Son of Glasgow, Alex Marshall of Glasgow, Malloch of Perth, D Menzies and others; and various other woodworking tools.

£480-520 L&T

An American adjustable steel and iron woodwoker's plane, marked "R.H. Mitchell & Co. Hudson, N.Y.", marked "Evans, pat. Jan 28 1862 - Mar. 22 1864", some paint loss, surface rust.

1862   10.5in (26.5cm) long

£80-120 TWC

An American early expandable ruler, marked "Charles B. Long Worcester Mass", with pattern "Apr. 25/26", brass trim, very good condition, specific use unknown.

24in (61cm) long

£600-700 TWC

An American "L.S. Starret" rule, with "C.S.Grannis" mounts with level, nice condition.

12in (30.5cm) long

£8-12 TWC

An American "Jordon" steel measure, marked "Germany", in millimetres and inches.

6.5in (16.5cm) long

£8-12 TWC

An American maple scraper, used by cabinet makers to smooth wood.

c1830   10in (25.5cm) long

£120-180 RAA

An American steel compass, marked "P. Lowentraut - Newark, N.J." and stamped "J.F. Helm", minor surface rust.

8.5in (22cm) long

£12-18 TWC

An American 19thC brass decorative beam trammel, set with steel points on mahogany bar.

6.5in (16.5cm) high

£220-280 TWC

An American turned wood device, with six wheels covered in black rubber.

8in (21cm) diam

£20-25 TWC

An American rosewood and brass gauge, marked "R. Helm", maker unknown, possibly made by owner, good condition.

7.5in (19cm) long

£25-30 TWC

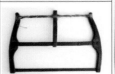

An American primitive early bow saw, as found, worn condition.

c1850   18in (45.5cm) long

£10-20 TWC

An American ash cabinet maker's mallet.

9in (23cm) long

£4-8 TWC

LEAD FIGURES

- Solid cast figures were popular during the 19thC. Look around the base of a figure as many manufacturers place their marks and names there.
- Repainting affects value considerably – undamaged pieces in original colours have higher values. Modern paints are usually more opaque and have a different finish and touch. Never repaint a figure if the original paint shows wear as this will reduce the value.
- Repairs or conversions (where pieces, such as heads are replaced making a rare figure) usually cause lumps and require repainting so, with close inspection, can usually be spotted.
- New collectors should handle and see as many figures as possible to see original condition, colours, forms and which pieces comprise a correct set. Some collectors 'customised' figures with extra detail. This is also detrimental to value.
- Original boxes can almost double a value, especially if the box is in good condition with labels intact and little or no damage. If the box was inexpensively made or by a smaller maker, these are usually rarer as they were generally thrown away. Britains' boxes are more common.
- After World War I, the 1920s saw non-military subjects and characters being produced, such as Britains' famous 'Home Farm' series, zoo animals and footballers.
- Don't store lead figures in oak cases as the oak can secrete an acid which degrades lead. Damp also causes 'lead rot', which is irreversible.
- The 1950s, with the Coronation and the introduction of children's television, saw a massive resurgence of interest in lead figures, but plastic was becoming popular as it was inexpensive. Most companies moved to plastic from the mid-1950s onwards.

A boxed Britains' 1470 State Coach, comprising gold coronation coach containing the figures of King George VI holding the sceptre with Queen Elizabeth beside him, drawn by eight horses (four with riders) and with associated harness pieces, box good except for split corners at one end.

Horseman 3in (8cm) high

£100-150　　　　　　　　　　　　　**DN**

A selection of Britains' farm vehicles, comprising a farmer's gig with grey horse, a dairy cart with walking milkman and assorted churns (no horse), a roller with brown horse, and three four-furrow ploughs, unboxed.

£180-220　　　　　　　　　　　　　**DN**

A farm collection, mostly more-modern Britains', including Land Rover and horsebox, horse-drawn farm cart, two tractors and various items of machinery, and approximately 20 plastic horses, cows etc, unboxed.

£140-180　　　　　　　**DN**

A Britains' 44F Country Cottage, with a collection of lead garden items, the cottage of moulded composition cardboard, the garden items including a sundial, gate, walling and pillars, paving, lawn, flowerbeds and a quantity of flowers.

£550-650　　　　　　　**DN**

Three rare Britains' Mickey Mouse figures, from set 1645, comprising Minnie Mouse and Goofy and Pluto, some damage, all unboxed, and a small tinplate flat figure of Mickey Mouse playing the concertina.

£220-280　　　　　　　　　　　　　**DN**

A Richard Courtenay figure of Sir Walter Raleigh, good, nose chipped, sword bent, paint chips.

£60-80　　　　　　　　**SI**

A Richard Courtenay figure of Charles I, circular red base, signed "Made in England".

£50-70　　　　　**SI**

A Richard Courtenay figure of Nell Gwynne.

£60-80　　　　**SI**

A Britains' set #1474 gilt Coronation Chair, two pieces with cushion.

1937

£50-80　　SI

An early 20thC collection of 17 rare Heyde Arabs and Bedouins, including three seated smoking, three seated playing instruments and others, some flaking paint.

£250-300　　SI

A set of 12 unusual Heyde tribesmen, each walking with circular and elongated shield, wearing striped loin cloths and carrying pole spears, some flaking paint.

£100-150　　SI

A C.B.G. Mignot figure of a lady in waiting, wearing blue dress, in original box, box good.

£50-70　　SI

A boxed set of Hornby engineering staff.

1.5in (4cm) high

£50-70　　WHP

A John Hill & Co stagecoach, with driver and shotgun, together with two Britains' Indians, coach and horses.

John Hill & Co, often known as 'Johillco', produced figures in England from 1898-1959. Their figures often show less rigidity in pose and style than those by Britains'.

Coach and horses 6.75in (17cm) long

£40-50　　WHP

A C.B.G. Mignot figure of George Washington, with sword, in original box, chip to slightly bent sword.

£70-100　　SI

A C. B. G. Mignot figure of Saladin, with wrong box, chips to hand and legs.

£70-100　　SI

A collection of eight assorted Mignot, German and other horses, comprising three Mignot, one Lucotte and four German horses, chips.

£60-100　　SI

Two C.B.G. Mignot figures of Louis XVI, one as a boy, the other as an adult wearing a blue coat, both in original boxes.

£120-150　　SI

A C.B.G. Mignot figure of Cardinal Richelieu on horseback, in original box, chips, box poor.

£100-150　　SI

A Vertunni figure of Queen Elizabeth I.

£40-60 SI

A Vertunni figure of Catherine De Medicis #A-12, chip to head.

£30-50 SI

A Vertunni figure of Madame Du Barry #A-16.

£130-180 SI

A Vertunni figure of Empress Josephine, in Coronation robes.

£70-100 SI

A Vertunni figure of Marie Leczinka, with two ladies of the court, chips to pink robe.

£150-200 SI

A collection of four Vertunni figures, including Louis XIII, Francis I and others, bases repainted.

£100-150 SI

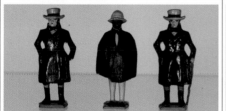

A collection of three Vertunni figures of personalities, including Heleise Selessi and two gentlemen in 19thC dress.

£250-300 SI

A collection of five Vertunni personality figures, including Conde, Henry II, Louis XI and Henry VIII, chips, the bases repainted.

£200-300 SI

A Vertunni figure of Charles VI, set #7, chipped nose.

£40-60 SI

A Vertunni figure of Louis XVI.

£80-120 SI

A Vertunni figure of Marie De Valois, wife of Henry IV.

£80-120 SI

A Vertunni figure of Catherine Parr, set #284, chips to face.

£50-80 SI

A B C D E F G H I J K L M N O P Q R S T U V W XYZ

A Vertunni figure of Marie D'Anjou, wife of Charles VII, set #43, chip to hat.

£40-60 | | **SI**

A Vertunni figure of Eleanor D'Aquitaine, chips to nose.

£80-120 | | **SI**

A large scale figure of George Washington, unknown maker, on a Heyde horse, some chips and scratches.

c1900-1912   4in (10cm) high

£100-150 | | **SI**

A Vertunni figure of Louise De Lorraine, excellent condition except for chips to hand.

£50-80 | | **SI**

A 29-piece part circus/zoo set, comprising three clowns, a ringmaster, a lion tamer and others, various factory marks.

Largest 4.75in (12cm) high

£120-160 | | **WHP**

An unusual set of 23 English Robin Hood figures, unknown maker, with thick bases stamped, "England" and "M" numbers in pencil, together with two foot knights, three civilians and six knights, some off bases.

£200-300 | | **SI**

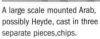

A large scale mounted Arab, possibly Heyde, cast in three separate pieces, chips.

3.75in (9.5cm) high

£100-150 | | **SI**

A collection of six assorted Ballada Napoleonic infantry figures, including a flag fearer, a grenadier, a drummer, a light infantry soldier and others.

£200-300 **SI**

A Britains' part set #241 Chinese infantry, including two red jackets, one blue and green jacket, one figure repainted.

£120-180 **SI**

A pair of Britains' Collector's Series individual mounted figures, #8878 General Grant and #8877 General Lee in original boxes, boxes mint.

£40-80 **SI**

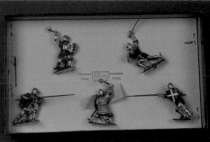

Five Britains' Historical Series set #1664 Knights of Agincourt, comprising foot knights, in original box.

£200-300 **SI**

A Britains' set #5872 Valley Forge, in original box.

£15-25 **SI**

A Britains' set #276 US Cavalry, third version, three mounted on black horses and two mounted on brown, one leg broken, no box. *c1930*

£120-180 **SI**

A Britains' part set band of 2nd Dragoons (Royal Scots Greys), six instrumentalists, in original box, chips to legs, lacks kettle drummer, box poor.

£130-180 SI

A collection of ten Britains' soldiers, including two fire fighters, two aviators, three 1930 bandsmen, one gunner set #28, two repainted squires, one figure has broken drumstick.

£100-150 SI

A collection of 12 Britains' Royal Air Force figures, comprising six set #2011 infantrymen, one WAAF in blue and five Infantry from set #1518, a few chips.

£100-150 SI

A Britains' Special Premier series set #8926 Thornycroft A.A.truck, created by Charles Briggs, with service detachment, the truck marked W.D., four personnel with paper labels, in original box, truck with two weak/bent supports, box good, one tear.

£100-150 SI

A Britains' set #9740 mobile 18in (46cm) heavy Howitzer, mounted for field service, in original box, some ammunition.

£150-250 SI

A Britains' set #2150 Centurian tank, a dark green model with aerials, tracks and revolving turret, with white United Nations Korean Conflict Star and chassis, in original box, a few chips.

c1957-1963

£350-450 SI

A rare early Britains' Ltd set#1643 Heavy Duty Underslung Lorry, with driver, anti-aircraft, gun #1522, and kneeling gunners, #1643 18 white wheels, with original illustrated box, a few chips.

£1,000-1,500 SI

A Britains' set #1725 Howitzer.

£120-180 SI

A Britains' set #1716 A.A. gun, together with a Saledo metal tank.

£20-30 SI

A large R. Cameron French Grenadier, by Ray Rubin, 1810 era, metal base, signed.

3.5in (9cm) high

£100-150 SI

A Richard Courtenay archer, the base signed "Made in England by R. Courtenay".

£350-400 SI

A Richard Courtenay Sieur William De Liniers, position XI, the base signed in black "Made in England by R. Courtenay".

£800-1,000 SI

An early Richard Courtenay Guy Sieur de Rochefort, position Z-8.

£800-1,200 SI

A Richard Courtenay Sieur W.M. de Courtenay, position Z5, moveable visor, signed, "Made in England by R. Courtenay".

£400-600 SI

A Richard Courtenay fallen knight, wounded by arrow, chips to left thigh and left shoulder.

£400-600 SI

A Richard Courtenay Sir Robert Holland, position H-2, the base signed, "Made in England by R. Courtenay", chip to nose.

£700-1,000 SI

A Richard Courtenay mounted Earl of Warwick, position H12, the base with hairline crack under right leg due to weight of figure.

£800-1,000   **SI**

A collection of four Richard Courtenay figures, including the Earl of Suffolk, K.G., position 19, base badly scratched, Prince Valiant, chips, Sir Miles Stapleton K.G., position 17, moveable sword, base chipped.

£350-550   **SI**

A collection of nine mounted Heyde American Revolution continental regulars, with black vests and blue neck facing.

£150-200   **SI**

A rare large-scale Richard Courtenay figure of Edward the Black Prince, the base signed "Made in England by R. Courtenay", chips to base and right elbow.

4.25in (10.5cm) high

£500-800   **SI**

A collection of 52 Heyde foot and mounted knights, including 21 foot knights with green bases, two knights on single green base in combat, nine knights running and charging with brown bases, six standing with arms overhead with brown bases, five mounted knights on galloping horses, one bugler, one standard bearer, seven banners on poles, some slightly damaged.

£350-450   **SI**

A collection of ten Heyde knights, with shields and spears, chips and some slightly damaged.

£60-100 SI

A Mignot Roman chariot and rider, the red chariot box ornamented with gilding, the horses at full gallop, with box, scratch to harness, box fair.

C.B.G. Mignot were founded in France in 1825 after taking over the historic Lucotte name and expanding the range enormously. Lucotte are recognised as being the first company to commercially produce three dimensional toy figures. Mignot are still producing solid cast toy soldiers today, and their past ranges are highly sought after.

£120-180 SI

A Mignot set #361/12 French Dragoons, nine marching at the slope, one drummer, one officer, retied in original box, box poor.

£170-220 SI

An Imrie/Risley French 5th Hussar, with Highland feather bonnet in hand, on wood base.

£40-80 SI

A Mignot Regiment of the Dauphine standard-bearer (1747), mounted on wood base in original box, re-glued to base, box poor.

£80-120 SI

An Imrie/Risley British Grenadier c1750, by Peter Blum, special figure made for a diorama at Trenton Barracks Museum, on wood base.

£100-150 SI

A Mignot General Lee figure, mounted, in original box, box fair.

£50-80 SI

A Minikin Norman Knight, after Richard Courtenay, in red, in original box, chip to leg.

£25-35 SI

A collection of eight assorted Mignot Standard bearers, including two Greeks (1917), two English Colonials, one Russian First Empire and others, a few chips, one repainted base.

£100-150 SI

A collection of eight assorted Mignot flag bearers, Armies of the World, all on foot, various regiments, one repainted base, chips.

£100-150   **SI**

A collection of five The Soldier Shop War of 1812 British Line Infantry, together with three additional flagbearers, three mismatched bases.

1988

£100-150   **SI**

A rare early Charles Stadden plaster mould British Scot Officer/Seaforth (1890-1900), sculpted and painted by Charles Stadden, on wood base, signed "Charles Stadden" on base in silver, some chips to legs and belt.

Figure 2.5in (6.5cm) high

£180-220   **SI**

A rare Charles Stadden 54mm super figure, 1914 British 11th Hussar Officer, the base with Charles Stadden stamp.

£400-500   **SI**

A Charles Stadden by Keith Whippler figure, Virginia Provincial Infantry Private 1755, on diorama base, signed "by Keith Whippler".

£35-55   **SI**

A Charles Stadden 1750 British Officer, on diorama base.

£100-150   **SI**

A large scale Stadden 1968 Drummer of the Coldstream Guards, on high oval base.

4in (10cm) high

£70-100   **SI**

A rare Warren set #41 U.S. Army scout car, with machine gunner, driver and seated soldier with rifle, white wheels, chips.

£1,000-1,500   **SI**

A group of Warren U.S. infantry figures, one U.S. standard bearer, one trumpeter, one flag bearer, one officer with sword raised and four marching troops, a few chips.

£800-1,200   **SI**

A World War II Recognition model 105 mm Howitzer, cast metal tank.

£80-120   **SI**

TOYS, GAMES, DOLLS & TEDDY BEARS

OTHER TOY FIGURES

- Elastolin was the name for a composition material used for toy figures by the German company Hausser between 1920 and the 1950s, when they converted to plastic. Elastolin products can be discerned from similar versions by their oval bases.
- 'Plastic' figures should not be considered unbreakable. Both age and the fact that the material was often mixed with chalk or kaolin to help the paint adhere can make them brittle and easy to damage.
- 1954 saw the introduction of Britains' first plastic figures – their 'Herald' range – which are considered to be the best moulded figures ever.

A Herald Set #790 Horse Guards Unbreakable models, comprising three mounted and three foot, tied in original illustrated box, one flag broken, box good.

c1950

£120-180 SI

A Herald Set #H7601 Cowboys and Indians Unbreakable models, comprising four cowboys and four Indians in active foot positions, tied in original box, box good to fair, age wear.

c1950

£120-180 SI

Four Elastolin, John Niblett & Co. and other figures, including three plastic figures including a 2.75in (7cm) Elastolin Norman knight on rearing horse, a mounted knight in Gothic armour and a foot knight (540 by Niblett), together with a silver figure of a Man-at-Arms by Plata De Ley.

£50-80 SI

A set of three Elastolin American Revolutionary band figures, including two drummers and another, chips.

1930s   *2.75in (7cm) high*

£60-80 SI

A large scale Elastolin American Flag Bearer.

7.25in (18.5cm) high

£100-150 SI

A set of three Elastolin totem poles , a few hairline cracks.

£250-350 (set) SI

A rare Elastolin figure of a condor, together with a turkey figure, wrong Elastolin box.

£100-150 SI

A rare composition Elastolin turtle.

£80-100 SI

A rare Elastolin figure of a bison, together with a small snail figure.

£80-120 SI

TOY TRAINS

- The first model trains were produced in the 1850s but were simple, heavy designs and not very realistic. It was not until the late 19thC that trains became more life-like and internal clockwork or steam-driven mechanisms were used.

- The German companies Marklin, Bing and Carette dominated the early years with good quality tinplate trains which were exported until World War I temporarily halted sales. Bing trains are lighter and have more realistic modelling than Marklin. Top quality pieces were hand painted but the majority had lithographed livery and decoration.

- Marklin introduced the concept of 'gauges' in 1891 at the Leipzig Toy Fair. The larger gauges of I, II and III were gradually replaced around 1910, due to a demand for smaller trains, by the smaller 0 gauge which itself was phased out in 1954. The even smaller 00 gauge was introduced in 1935. In 1948 the H0 gauge with better designed trains was introduced.

- By 1923 most British train companies had started to merge into four companies (LNER, GWR, SR and LMS) and manufacturers had to redesign liveries to match.

- Couplings between the locomotive and carriages help to date trains. Tin loops were used before 1904, hook couplings were used from c1904-c1913 and sliding drop link couplings thereafter.

- Plastic trains were introduced in the 1960s.

- Condition is important, with lost pieces and damage such as dents and wear on paintwork on early tinplate models seriously affecting value. Later examples should be in as fine condition as possible and sets or components with their original boxes will command a premium.

A Bing 0-gauge clockwork George the Fifth RN 2663, 4-4-0 and tender, well refinished with two-colour lining, three control levers to cab, central handle missing, minor wear to finish, distortion to cab roof.

£65-75   **W&W**

A Carette for Bassett Lowke clockwork 4-4-0 George the Fifth locomotive RN 2663, and six wheel tender finished overall in black with two-colour fine lining, with two-control rods to cab, minor wear to finish, some damage to cab.

Many of the trains sold by British company Bassett-Lowke (1899-1969) between 1900 and 1933 were supplied by the German companies Gebruder Bing and Carette. They also had their own factory, called George Winteringham, which they relied on after their relationships ended with Carette c1917 and Bing in 1933.

£150-180   **W&W**

A Hornby 0-gauge clockwork 4-4-0 no. two special tender locomotive, Yorkshire, RN 234, in LNER green livery with black running plate, LNER to tender sides, some repainting, tender reworked and refinished.

£130-150   **W&W**

A Bassett Lowke 'Duke of York' green clockwork 0-gauge train. *c1927*

£225-265   **WoS**

A Bing 0-gauge 4-4-0 electric motored green RN 3422 locomotive, with litho-finish, some age wear to finish.

£100-120   **W&W**

A Hornby 0-gauge clockwork no. two tender locomotive, 4-4-0 with six wheel tender, refinished in green, with brass plate no. 2711 to cab sides, bolt together construction, minor wear, rust through to corner of tender, one driving wheel loose.

£200-240   **W&W**

A Hornby 0-gauge clockwork 2-6-0 Mogul and six wheel tender, based on Bassett Lowke mechanism with adapted body, valve gear, finished black with RN2867 to cab side, and associated six wheel tender finished LMS maroon, loco cab's coupling missing.

£180-220   **W&W**

A Leeds Model Co. 0-6-2 tank locomotive in LNER green livery, with black and white lining, LNER and RN 9356 to side tanks, applied Leeds label on underside of cab roof, electric motor good condition, overall minor wear and retouching.

£230-260   **W&W**

A Leeds Model Co 0-gauge 2-4-2 tank locomotive, refinished in LMS overall black with RN 10952, ex L&Y Railway Company, electric motored, minor wear.

£180-220   **W&W**

A Leeds Model Co 0-gauge 0-6-0 electric motored tank locomotive, in Southern green livery, RN 258, few minor chips.

£900-1,000   **W&W**

An 0-gauge assembled locomotive 4-4-2, in LNER green with RN 246 to tank, main body possibly Leeds, but with two-part chassis plate, minor wear overall.

£100-150   **W&W**

A GWR-style 0-gauge clockwork scratch-built tinplate 4-4-2 sloping boiler tank locomotive, finished in dark green, with no lining or transfers, handrails, brakepipes, with two control rods to cab, some overall wear.

£100-150   **W&W**

A Bing 0-gauge short precursor tank 4-4-0, in mid-brown LMS livery, RN 420, clockwork version, retouching to paintwork.

£120-150   **W&W**

HORNBY

■ Frank Hornby began manufacturing 0-gauge trains in 1920 as German imports became unpopular. Early trains were crude and sturdy, with clockwork mechanisms. By 1923 and particularly during the 1930s, they became more realistically modelled.

■ Hornby Dublo was introduced in 1938 to compete with Marklin's 00 gauge. Inexpensive clockwork Dublo version were produced until 1940 and are comparatively scarce and highly desirable today.

■ Lingering effects from World War II and the success of Dublo led to a serious decline in quality of 0-gauge trains. The range was redesigned in 1946 and was discontinued in 1969.

■ From 1953, trains displayed nationalised British Rail liveries, but these were dull. In 1957, the range was upgraded with great success. The introduction of plastic trains in 1960 proved to be too costly for Hornby who were taken over by Triang in 1964.

■ After 1964, production of Dublo passed to G&R Wrenn of Basildon, Essex, England. Triang saw its demise in 1971, but the Hornby name continued with the popular 'Hornby Railways', which has dominated 00 gauge ever since.

■ Increasing demand and nostalgia has extended collecting to later Triang pieces and 1970s and 80s 'Hornby Railways' sets. When assessing value look for complete sets, boxed and in excellent condition.

An 0-gauge clockwork scratch-built 4-4-2 LMS tank locomotive, finished in maroon, with lettering to side tanks, RN 701 to bunker sides, a metal chassis with mainly wood body and two control rods from rear of bunker, minor wear overall.

£120-160   **W&W**

A 1930s Hornby LMS train Tank locomotive, red clockwork, 0-gauge.

£45-55   **WoS**

A Trix Twin Railway 0.4.0 tender electric green loco, OO-gauge.

Until 1958, Trix Twin trains were produced by George Winteringham, the manufacturing arm of Bassett Lowke.

c1955

£45-55   **WoS**

A Hornby Dublo 'Duchess of Montrose' electric OO-gauge green locomotive.

c1956

£55-65   WoS

An East German Rokal loco and two timber wagons, electric and T-gauge.

c1955

£55-65   WoS

A Lionel 1668E grey electric train and tender, 20V, O-gauge.

c1930

£125-165   WoS

A Hornby Dublo 'Creppello' electric green diesel, OO-gauge.

c1962

£55-65   WoS

A Märklin S.B.B. electric RET 800 green locomotive, HO-gauge, with box.

c1956

£180-220   WoS

A Lionel O-Gauge locomotive, 'Santa Fe', no.2333-20, in silver and red with yellow trim, mint condition, with box.

1949   *13.25in (34cm) long*

£400-500   CR

A Lionel 027-Gauge loco and tender, the locomotive no. 2055 with smoke chamber and pellets, the tender no. 6026W with whistle, in original boxes, missing red jewel running light.

1953

£150-200   CR

An early Lionel O-Gauge tin green locomotive, no. 252 and observation car no. 604, enamel loss and pitting.

The US market was dominated by Lionel (1901-1969), New York, who bought the popular Ives company in 1928. Trains after World War I were mostly O-gauge, but Lionel introduced its own size called 'American Standard Gauge'. Other popular American companies included American Flyer (1907-1960s) and Carlisle & Finch (1896-1915).

£80-100   CR

An assembled Lionel O27-Gauge locomotive, 'Picatinny Arsenal', no. 42, along with box car no. 6454, cattle car no. 6656, double-dome tanker no. 6465, gondola car no. 6462, and caboose no. 6452, crack to one side.

1950s

£250-350   CR

A Märklin steam locomotive, no. 5747, 1-gauge with sound effects and three passenger wagons, two with serial no. 5.804, the other no. 5.805.

£750-800   TK

A Tri-Ang transcontinental blue electric train set, OO-gauge. *c1960*

£65-75 **WoS**

An O-gauge fine scale electric 4-4-0 and six wheel tender, entitled 'The Boat Train', of the SE & CR RN 740, finished in green lined livery with brass dome, heavy mainly brass construction, together with three built-up South Eastern Railway fine scale bogie coaches, cast compensating bogies and steel wheel sets, the whole train to represent a period boat train, minor wear.

£1,000-1,500 **W&W**

Two O-gauge LNER kit built coaches, the bodies varnished with teak finish, fully-glazed and with interior detail, cream wood roof to one and tinplate to the other, on cast bogies with metal wheels, minor wear.

17in (43cm) long

£70-100 **W&W**

A Bing O-gauge LNER saloon coach, in litho-print teak woodgrain effect with red and cream lining, with recessed vestibules with opening doors, white opening roof to reveal interior table and chair details, minor wear, roof refinished and coupling missing.

£100-130 **W&W**

A rare Leeds Model Co. O-gauge Nettle Sentinel Scammell Rail Car LNER, with all-wood construction with litho print paper detail overlays, electric motor bogie, die-cast Mansell-type wheels, minor wear over all.

£100-140 **W&W**

A Hornby Dublo 2-rail 'Start Set', OO-gauge, boxed. *c1964*

£100-140 **WoS**

Three O-gauge Hornby Metropolitan coaches, with litho tinplate wood grain finish, grey roofs, nut and bolt fixings to sole plates and bogies all finished in black, with tinplate and plastic wheels, one has "Fabrique en Angleterre" oval transfer to base, wear to finish.

£100-150 **W&W**

A rare Leeds Model Co. O-gauge SR Brighton Belle Pullman car 'Doris', in brown and cream livery with full lining and detailing on litho-print paper overlay on wood core, with two late-style bogies with plastic wheel sets, corridor connections and replacement brass buffers, minor wear.

£150-180 **W&W**

A Hornby Dublo Pullman coach, with OO-gauge, boxed.

c1962

£25-35 **WoS**

A Lionel Lines O-Gauge Pullman car, 'Madison' no.2627, in maroon, mint condition, with box.

1948-1949 15in (38cm) long

£350-450 **CR**

A Lionel Lines O-Gauge Pullman car, 'Manhattan' no.2628, in maroon, mint condition, with box.
1948-49   14.5in (37cm) long

£300-400   **CR**

Three O-gauge Leeds Model Co. articulated LNER coaches, the rake made up of three 1st/3rd composite non-corridor bodies finished in teak litho-print details with white tinplate roofs, standard bogies with die-cast wheels, some wear and repainting.

£80-100   **W&W**

A OO-gauge rake of three articulated coaches, in LNER livery, with litho-print teak paper detailing over wood with cream finished roofs in the style of LMC, all 3rd RN86703, 1st/3rd RN86701 and 3rd/Brake RN 86705, cast bogies with nickel silver wheels, minor wear.

£80-120   **W&W**

An American Flyer O-gauge 20V rolling stock, with two coaches, roofs repainted.
c1935

£200-240   **WoS**

A Bassett-Lowke catalogue.

£15-20   **WoS**

A Hornby Dublo catalogue.

£15-20   **WoS**

A Tri-Ang catalogue.

£15-20   **WoS**

A Tri-Ang catalogue.

£15-20   **WoS**

A Wrenn Railways catalogue.

£15-20   **WoS**

A 1920s clockwork turntable, rare gauge 2 size, possibly Bing.

£35-45   **WoS**

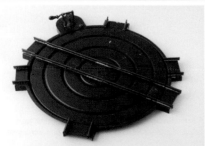

Two Lionel train accessories, including Trestle Bridge no. 317 and 'The Whistling Station' no. 125, with original boxes.

£70-100   **CR**

TINPLATE

- The early 19th century saw toy makers turn away from wood and on to tinplate. New production methods meant it was cheaper and faster to produce.

- Tinplate toys are made from a stamped sheet of steel, plated with tin and then brightly coloured. Toys made before 1895 were hand decorated and can show a very fine degree of detail, later ones were lithographed in colour and are of comparatively lesser quality, but are still highly collectable.

- The second half of the 19th century saw many successful and prolific companies being set up, primarily in Germany, such as Marklin (1856), Gebruder Bing (1863) Ernst Planck (1866) and E.P. Lehmann (1881).

- Tinplate toys were made in the USA from the 1830s onwards, but not to the same extent as in Europe. The industry grew in the early 20th century, with prolific makers such as Louis Marx, who even opened a factory in England. Today, 19th century American tinplate toys are rare and much sought after.

- Many toys from the 1850s onwards were die-stamped 'penny toys', which were very simple cars, aircraft or boats with a simple flywheel or a push-along action. Their popularity peaked around 1905.

- German toys were not exported during wartime.

- Tinplate toys continued to be very popular until the 1930s, when die-cast toys superseded them, only to be followed in the mid 20th century by mass-produced, inexpensive plastic toys. Japan produced tinplate toys from the 1920s onwards and their battery operated robots from the 1960s are very popular.

- Cars, trucks (including fire trucks) wind up or mechanical models, airplanes and particularly boats are very popular amongst collectors. As well as date, sophistication of design and any mechanical features, large sizes, bright colours and noted makers are all important factors to look for when collecting.

- Condition is imperative as when damaged, the surface is difficult to restore and poor restoration brings values down. Dents, splits and missing pieces will also affect value detrimentally. Packaging, especially from early toys, is hard to find and will augment values.

A clockwork Schuco streamlined car, orange and black body, missing key, excellent condition.

c1950

£180-220 TK

A clockwork Schuco 1010 Maybach streamlined car, working, missing key.

.

c1950

£180-220 TK

A clockwork Schuco streamlined toy car, missing key.

c1950

£150-200 TK

A clockwork Schuco Freilaufrrenner 1250, steering front wheels, with automatic clutch, no key.

c1950

£100-150 TK

A clockwork red Schuco Fex 1111 toy car, distressed, with instruction leaflet.

c1950

£180-220 TK

A clockwork "Tipp & Co." toy car, rubber tyres, steering front wheels.

c1950　　　*9in (23cm) long*

£70-100 TK

A Schuco Examinco 4001 driving school toy car, five gears, front wheel steering, no windscreen, steering wheel and key.

c1950

£220-280 TK

A Spanish Schuco Commando Auto 2000 streamlined toy car, with nickel parts, steering front wheels, with instructions and original box, no key.

c1950

£250-300 TK

SCHUCO

- Schuco was the trademark for the German company Schreyer & Co.. who were founded in 1912.
- They are well known for their soft toys such as monkeys and teddy bears as well as for their clockwork toys.
- By comparison, their cars are often less expensive, with mechanical versions and well-known cars such as Donald Campbell's 'Bluebird' sitting at the top of the desirability stakes.
- The Schuco 'Akustico-Auto' was capable of making noises, using two separate clockwork mechanisms. It also could be fitted with a driver, 'Schuco Fritz', who had moveable arms and legs.

A Schuco Akustico 2002 toy car, with horn, two different clockworks, one distressed, steering front wheels, missing windshield and key, with instruction leaflet.

c1950

£180-220 TK

Three wind-up Schuco Micro Racers toy cars, one Mercedes 220, one VW-Käfer and one Porsche, made with original Schuco tools by Nutz, Germany, mint condition with original boxes.

1987

£150-200 TK

A Japanese Isetta tinplate clockwork bubble car.

7.5in (19cm) long

£150-200 CB

A Japanese Yonezowa tinplate MG car, friction-driven.

4.75in (12cm)

£25-35 CB

A 1930s Japanese tinplate clockwork tank.

4in (10cm)

£40-50 CB

An early tinplate lithographed racing car, with fly wheel propulsion, maker unknown, probably German, original finish with scratches.

c1910   4.75in (12cm) long

£200-300 TWC

A French Meccano Constructor motor car, with green body and wheels, yellow roof and wings, and white tyres, marked "Meccano / France" at base of driver's side bonnet; no windscreen glass but generally fair condition, unboxed.

£200-250 DN

A post war Tri-Ang Minic Toys tinplate streamlined saloon.

5in (12.5cm)

£100-140 CB

A JEP ladder truck.

£600-800 BCAC

A TP fire engine.

£800-1,000 BCAC

A Burnett ladder truck.

£300-400 BCAC

An MMN fire truck.

£1,000-1,300 BCAC

A rare clockwork Baukastenauto Märklin truck, opening door, rubber tires, steered from driver's seat, original condition.

c1930   16.5in (42cm) long

£1,000-1,500 TK

A tinplate Sutcliffe Racer 1 speedboat.

9.5in (24cm) long

£60-70 CB

A tinplate "United States" cruise liner.

15.5in (39.5cm) long

£400-500 CB

A scarce Japanese Hadson tinplate friction-driven Greyhound bus.

13in (33cm) long

£320-380 CB

A rare musician clown, probably made by Distler, with a small musical box in the base, spring-operated, lithographed tin, in very good working condition.

Distler, of Nuremburg, Germany, is very well known for its tinplate cars, produced primarily during the 1920s and 1930s. The company was active between c.1900 and 1962.

c1950

£400-500 TK

A Japanese tinplate San Francisco cable car, friction driven, boxed.

5in (19cm) long

£50-60 CB

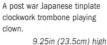

A post war Japanese tinplate clockwork trombone playing clown.

9.25in (23.5cm) high

£200-300 CB

A Calypso Joe the Drummer tinplate wind-up toy, complete with original box, good condition.

4in (10cm) high

£120-180 CR

A West German tinplate part train set and terminal.

£25-35 WHP

A J Chein wind-up duck, in working order.

c1920-1930

£100-150   BCAC

A 1920s French tinplate clockwork frog.

4.25in (10.5cm) high

£320-380   CB

A very rare early version of a toy zeppelin, with two passenger cabins mounted directly under the airship.

c1912

£300-400   TK

A Lehmann tin toy, 'The Performing Sea Lion'.

c1899

£200-300   TK

A tinplate clockwork crocodile.

15in (38cm) long

£70-90   CB

A CLOSER LOOK AT A TIN MERRY-GO-ROUND

This complicated and attractive tin toy is highly unusual, and very well made. By winding up the mechanism, the airships revolve at speed and lift slightly, with their propellers twirling as they move through the air.

It has many protruding parts which could have become damaged or broken off, but on this example all parts are still in very good condition with bright colours.

Airships, or 'zeppelins', are an unusual vehicle to be used on a toy as they were only generally used as a mode of transport during the first few decades of the 20th century. Today, pieces and memorabilia related to airships are highly collectable.

Despite lacking a maker's name, it dates from before the First World War. This fact, the condition and the combination of hand-painted and lithographed parts makes it a desirable piece for collectors.

FIND OUT MORE...

David Pressland, 'The Art of the Tin Toy', published by Schiffer Publishing, 1992.

Jurgen Franzke, 'Tinplate Toys: From Schuco, Bing & Other Companies', published by Schiffer Publishing, 1997.

A rare Arnold Mac 700 tinplate clockwork motorcycle, black with green, cream and silver detailing, rider in period clothing will mechanically mount and dismount in between riding his machine, produced in the immediate post WWII period, very good condition for age and type, minor wear, complete with key and original instruction sheet.

£220-280   W&W

A wind-up tin merry-go-round toy, with zeppelin-type air ships, French flag on top, unknown manufacturer, hand painted tin socket and lithographed airships, good working condition, extremely rare.

1910   *15.75in (40cm) high*

£800-1,000   TK

DINKY TOYS

- Dinky Toys were manufactured by Meccano. The first toys were released in 1931 as accessories to Hornby train sets with the first cars (set 22) being released in 1934, both under the name 'Meccano's Model Miniatures'. Both ranges were very successful and by late 1934, the name had changed to 'Dinky Toys' and over 100 models were available.

- The earliest models were made of lead, but this soon changed to aluminium zinc which can be die cast better, with greater detail. The years from 1931 until 1941 are considered the 'golden age' of Dinky.

- The Second World War led to a decline and pause in production. Many pre-war toys did not survive in good condition. As such, pre-war Dinky toys in excellent condition are very highly sought after. Series 28 delivery vans and 25 series lorries are particularly desirable.

- After the war, Dinky reintroduced pre-war models, but there are differences. These include fatter wheels, drab colours and black finished base plates.

- The larger range of 'Dinky Supertoys' was introduced in 1947. In 1954, Dinky changed their numbering system from numbers with a letter suffix to a three digit code from 001-999. Models using this new numbering system sell for less.

- By 1963, the company was in financial trouble and in 1964 was bought out by Lines Bros, who made Triang products, in 1964. In late 1979, the Liverpool factory closed.

- Scratches, repainting and other damage seriously affects value.

A No. 501 Foden Dinky Diesel eight-wheeled wagon, with first-type brown cab and back, black chassis, silver side flash, brown ridged wheels, herringbone tyres, no hook, back with some corrosion, in buff box, split at one end.

£150-200   **Vec**

A rare US export No. 501 Dinky Foden eight-wheeled wagon, with first-type red cab and back, silver cab flash and black chassis, in early Supertoy box with red spot on end label.

The Dinky Foden 501 Diesel 8-Wheel Wagon, with the first type cab, was issued in various colours, but the rare US export only issue had a red cab and back, silver cab flash and black chassis. In mint condition it can be worth up to £4,000. The common UK version (above) is in mid-brown with silver flash and black chassis and in mint condition is worth up to £350.

£800-1,000   **Vec**

A Dinky Toys 504 Foden 14-ton tanker, first type cab and chassis, in red with silver flash to cab, fawn tank, red wheel hubs, boxed, some wear, vehicle in good condition, minor chipping, rusting to tank.

£250-300   **W&W**

A Dinky Toys 942 Foden 14-ton tanker "Regent", with red hubs, fair condition with paint chipping and wear, blue-stripped box.

£55-65   **DN**

A Dinky Toys 905 Foden flat bed truck with chains, boxed.

7.25in (18.5cm) long

£150-200   **CB**

A Dinky Toys 903 Foden flatbed truck with tailboard, dark blue cab and chassis, orange flatbed and light blue hubs, unboxed.

£80-120   **DN**

A Dinky Toys 959 Foden dump truck, red with silver chassis and yellow wheel hubs, complete with plough blade to front, boxed, minor wear, minor chips.

£300-350   **W&W**

Two Dinky Toys commercial vehicles, a 533 Leyland Comet Cement Wagon "Ferrocrete", unboxed and a 922 Big Bedford Lorry with maroon cab and chassis and fawn truck body.

£55-65   **DN**

A Dinky Toys 917 "Spratts" Guy van 917, with box.

5.25in (13.5cm)

£300-400 CB

A Dinky Toys 945 AEC Fuel tanker in Lucas Oil livery, green cab and tank with white decals, promotional model for Lucas Services in original Lucas bubble pack, age wear to pack.

£120-180 W&W

Five Dublo Dinky small vehicles: an 061 Ford Prefect in fawn with smooth grey wheels, box good; an 064 Austin Lorry in green with smooth grey wheels, box fair to good; an 068 Royal Mail Van with treaded grey wheels, box poor; an 062 Singer Roadster in orange with smooth grey wheels, unboxed; and another 064 Austin Lorry in green with treaded grey wheels, paint faded, unboxed.

£80-120 DN

Three Dublo Dinky commercial vehicles: an 066 Bedford Flat Truck in grey, no hook, unboxed, an 072 Bedford Articulated Flat Truck in yellow and red with grey wheels, small paint blemish on trailer, box fair and an 070 AEC Mercury Tanker in Shell/BP livery with green cab, red tank and grey wheels, box fair.

£100-150 DN

A Dinky Toys 987 ABC TV mobile control room, in light blue and grey, with red flash, complete with camera and camera man, boxed, minor wear.

£120-180 W&W

A Dinky Toys 986 BBC TV roving eye vehicle, in standard green-grey livery, complete with cameraman, camera and aerial, boxed.

£80-120 W&W

A Dinky Toys Ambulance "ID19" Citroen, produced by the French factory, with box.

4.5in (11cm) long

£120-180 CB

A Dublo Dinky Toys 073 Land Rover and Horse Trailer, with green vehicle fitted with black ramp, complete with horse, box good.

£100-150 DN

Four assorted Dinky Toys cars, comprising a 38d Alvis in maroon with grey seats and black hubs, a 23d Auto-Union in silver with racing number 2 and no driver, a 230 (205) Talbot Lago in blue with yellow racing number 4 and uncommon yellow plastic hubs, and a similar but smaller French Dinky 23h Talbot Lago unboxed.

£90-100 (four) DN

Four early post-war Dinky Toys cars, including a 30b Rolls-Royce in fawn with black chassis, a 36f British Salmson Four Seater Sports in green with black chassis, and a 39a Packard Sedan in brown, unboxed.

£160-200 DN

A Dinky Toys 255 Mersey Tunnel Police van, with box, one end missing flap.

2.75in (7cm) long

£35-45 CB

A pre-war French-made Dinky Super Streamline Saloon, of 24e type but with no side window framing, possible repaint, unboxed.

£150-200 DN

Three Dinky toys, comprising: a 23e/221 Speed of the Wind racing car, playworn, unboxed; a 163 Bristol 450 Sports Coupé in green with racing number 27, box good; and a 481 Bedford van "Ovaltine", unboxed.

£80-120   DN

A Dinky Toys Observation Coach.

4.5in (11cm) long

£25-35   CB

A Dinky Toys prototype model in diecast of the Phantom II F-4K, painted in light grey, with hand-applied dark green camouflate, minor wear.

£150-200   W&W

A Dinky Toys prototype wooden model 671 Mk 1 Corvette high speed warship, painted in grey, cream and white with simple detailing but includes diecast metal rocket launcher to aft deck, some marking.

£120-180   W&W

A Dinky Toys die-cast Lady Penelope FAB1 Rolls Royce and Thunderbird 2.

5.75in (14.5cm) long

£50-70   WHP

A Dinky Toys 289 Routemaster bus, with box.

4.75in (12cm)

£40-60   CB

A rare pre-war Dinkie Toys RML bus.

4in (10cm) long

£300-400   CB

A rare Dinky Toys 749 Avro Vulcan, cast in aluminium; some roundel deterioration, unboxed.

Only 500 of these Vulcans were made, for export to Canada, the models being numbered 749 under the wing whereas 992 was used in the catalogue and on the box.

£1,000-1,400   DN

FIND OUT MORE...

John Ramsay, 'Ramsay's British Die-Cast Model Toys Catalogue', 9th edition, published by Swapmeet Publications, 2001.

Mike Richardson & Sue Richardson, 'The Great Book of Dinky Toys', published by New Cavendish Books, 2000.

A Dinky Toys Joe 90's car, together with two Sam's cars from the same TV series.

4in (10cm) long

£30-40   WHP

A Dinkie Toys 698 Gift Set Tank Transporter with tank, boxed, one corner frayed.

12in (30.5cm) long

£100-150   CB

A Dinky Supertoys Ruston Bucyrus Excavator, 975 red chassis, yellow cab and green jib. In original box with inner packaging and instructions, minor wear.

£80-120   W&W

CORGI TOYS

■ Corgi Toys were made by Mettoy Limited, based in Swansea, Wales. Although Mettoy has its origins in the 1930s, Corgi toys were not introduced until the 1950s, and are still in production today.

■ In 1950, Mettoy released a range of 'Entirely New Miniatures' as a forerunner to Corgi. In 1954 Marcel van Cleemput produced the first Corgi designs. The range was launched in July 1956.

■ Corgi aimed to compete with Dinky's 'Supertoys' range, and its innovation over Dinky was that each toy had windows, a fact that was used in advertising slogans of the period.

■ 1957 saw the first catalogue and 1959 saw other popular innovations such as suspension (known as 'Glidamatic') and boots and doors that opened.

■ Corgi produced highly successful models from many TV programmes and films, primarily from the 1960s onwards, including cars from 'Batman', 'The Man from U.N.C.L.E.', James Bond films, 'Chitty Chitty Bang Bang' and 'Superman'.

■ Versions are a key area for collectors. Some models were re-released and values differ depending on the version you own. A good example is the 1964 range of 'Corgi Classics' which ceased in 1969 after a factory fire and was re-released in 1985. Here, as with many variations, the later base plate has a different name, reading 'Special Edition'. Wheels are also important with some having flat 'WhizzWheels' rather than cast wheels.

■ Variations are another key area to understand. Many models were produced in limited production runs, finished in different colours to the standard model, or with different elements such as differently coloured components.

■ Condition is vital, with scratches and repainting reducing the value seriously. The original box will always make a model more desirable, but the box must be in good condition too. If it is crushed, faded or has damaged cellophane, the value will be affected.

A Corgi Toys Mini-Cooper 249, black with deluxe wickerwork, with box.

2.75in (7cm) wide

£70-90 | CB

A scarce Corgi Austin Mini van 450, metallic mid-green with red interior and silver grille, boxed, vehicle mint.

£55-65 | W&W

A Corgi BMC Mini Cooper S 1967 Monte Carlo winner 339, red with white roof, RN 177, LBL 6D numberplates, complete with roof rack and spare wheels, in special box with paperwork, minor wear to label, car mint.

£45-55 | W&W

A pale blue Corgi Toys Morris Mini-Minor.

2.75in (7cm) long

£20-25 | CB

A scarce Corgi Toys Mercedes Benz 220 SE Coupé 230, black, with box.

4in (10cm) long

£70-90 | CB

A Corgi Toys BMC Mini police van with tracker dog 448, with box, box missing one flap.

It is hard to find this car complete with the policeman and dog as they were often lost when played with due to their size.

Car 3in (7.5cm) long

£80-120 | CB

A Corgi Toys Bentley Continental Sports Saloon 224, by H. J. Mulliner, black, some minor chips, tears along folds in box.

4.25in (11cm) long

£50-60 | CB

A Corgi Toys Ford Mustang Fastback 2+2 competition model 325, with box.

3.75in (9.5cm) long

£55-65 | CB

A Corgi Toys Le Dandy Coupé Henri Chapron body on Citroën D.S. chassis, burgundy, doors and boot open.

4in (10cm) long

£45-55 | CB

An aqua blue Corgi Toys Citroën D.S., Monte Carlo Rally No. 75.

4in (10cm) long

£60-80 CB

A racing green Torgi Toys Bentley Le Mans 1927, soft top lifts up.

3.75in (9.5cm)

£20-25 CB

A Corgi Toys T.S. 9B Whizzwheels 153, with Italian finish, mint and boxed.

Box 6.5in (16.5cm) wide

£20-30 CB

A scarce Corgi Toys London Route Master bus 469, mint with box.

Box 6in (15cm) wide

£25-35 CB

A Corgi Toys Circus Giraffe Transporter with giraffes 503, with box, flap torn, one taped.

3.75in (9.5cm) long

£80-100 CB

A Corgi London Transport Routemaster double-decker bus, in the colours of the New South Wales Govt. Transport Dept., green, cream and dark brown, with Naturally Corgi Toys Corgi Classics adverts, boxed, with small paper slip.

£45-55 W&W

A Corgi Toys Chipperfields Circus Crane Truck 1121, with box, box taped at one corner,

5.5in (14cm) long

£100-130 CB

A Corgi Chipperfields Performing Poodles set 511, comprising a light blue and red Chevrolet Impala with bodywork conversion to carry dogs, complete with poodles and female figure on green stand, boxed, contents mint.

The diverse Chipperfield's Circus range was first released in 1960. Today, complete sets in boxes in excellent condition are highly sought after.

£80-120 W&W

A Corgi Prototype Tarzan gift set 36, a manufacturer's pre-production die-cast metal mock-up containing a green and white striped Land Rover and trailer with opening roof hatch, diorama background, with made-up box illustrated with stick-on lettering and decals, some age wear.

£150-200 W&W

A pre-production white metal Corgi Supermobile, finished in blue with decals.

This rare model was produced by the factory before the release of the toy. It has a small factory fault on the left hand arm, but is otherwise in near mint condition. Constructed from a white metal, it has silver-coloured arms rather than red plastic arms as on the standard model. These facts make this a desirable model with a higher value standard models.

£250-300 | **W&W**

A Corgi Toys "Man From Uncle" Oldsmobile Super 88.

4.25in (10.5cm) wide

£40-50 | **CB**

A Corgi Magic Roundabout Citroën Dyane, with Dougal, Dylan and Bryan.

4.75in (12cm) long

£30-50 | **WHP**

A Corgi Toys Chitty Chitty Bang Bang.

6in (15cm) long

£45-55 | **WHP**

A Corgi Toys Batmobile with Batman and Robin 267, first issue with box.

Corgi has always enjoyed great success with its models produced from popular TV programmes and films. The TV programme 'Batman' starring Adam West is a good example.

The Batmobile was the first Batman model and was released in 1966. It came in a gloss or matt finish, with a red 'Batman' decal on the doors and an array of accessories including rockets.

Box 6in (15cm) wide

£400-450 | **CB**

ROBOTS

■ The 1960s saw a deep fascination with outer space, reinforcing the popularity of robots. Collectors should look for battery powered robots from this period made from tin plate, particularly those by Japanese manufacturers. 'Remote control' robots from the 1980s are now also becoming popular amongst a new breed of collectors, but it will be some time before they begin to fetch the high prices commanded by those from the 1960s.

A battery-powered toy robot, with plastic body.

12.25in (31cm) high

£35-45 | **TK**

A 1960s battery-powered toy robot.

11in (28cm) high

£150-200 | **DH**

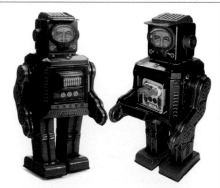

A rare Secret Weapon Space Scout toy robot, by SH Horikawa Toys, Japan, battery-operated.

c1960   *8.75in (22cm) high*

£600-700 | **TK**

A Tomy Omnibot programmable or remote control robot.

c1984   *14.in (36cm) long*

£80-120 | **HLJ**

A Tomy Omnibot Jr. remote control robot.

c1984   *10.25in (26cm) long*

£40-60 | **HLJ**

An American cast-iron trolley bank, unmarked, with rolling wheels painted gold and embossed "Main Street", minor paint losses.

6.5in (16.5cm) wide

£180-220 CRA

A 1940s Pearson Page Jewsbury & Co. Lloyds Bank money box, in the shape of a book.

4.5in (11.5cm) high

£15-18 DH

A clock-work driven 'Santa', by Alps, Japan, with original box, moves arms, rocks from left to right and rings the bell.

10in (25.5cm) high

£200-250 TK

A 1930s Celluloid 'Happy' dwarf skittle, unmarked.

9in (23cm) high

£60-80 BEJ

An American composition 'Felix the Cat' figure.

c1930

£220-280 Fra

A battery-powered animated bear, by Alps, Japan, Cragstan Toy No.714, excellent working condition.

c1958   8.25in (18.5cm) high

£200-250 TK

A post-war English plastic clockwork Bo Peep and sheep.

£75-85 CB

A 'Jabba the Hutt' boxed action playset, from the Star Wars series.

£10-15 WHP

A Product Enterprises 'Talking Dalek', in white and gold plastic, designed by Stephen J. Walker.

c2001   6.25in (16cm) high

£20-40 FFM

A B C D E F G H I J K L M N O P Q R S T U V W XYZ

A Product Enterprises 'Dalek Rolykin', designed by Stephen J. Walker.

From the 'Dr Who' TV series originally conceived by Terry Nation.

2000-02   1.75in (4.5cm) high

£4-6   **FFM**

A rare 1940s vintage hollow-hull schooner pond sailboat, of mahogany and other woods with painted hull, two tall masts, two sails and full spinnaker, brass fittings and movable rigging, tiller and rudder, complete with 48-star miniature American flag, in wooden table stand, some solder to tiller, rigging loose.

72in (183cm) high

£600-700   **CRA**

A model ship #29 "Falcon", in original box, box fair.

£50-60   **SI**

A 1940s Wilesco working steam engine, with horizontal cast-metal boiler, flywheel, and seven experiment accessories including electro-magnet, light, bell, battery unit, belt and pulley and more, the main unit mounted on metal base and attached to plywood, metal tag and "Made in England".

16in (40.5cm) wide

£350-450   **CRA**

Two 20thC painted cast-iron 'Overland Circus' Wagons, one with six musicians dressed in white, two outriders and driver, pulled by four white horses, a red Polar Bear Wagon with driver and two outriders, white horses, some new paint, missing bear, unmarked.

Larger 16in (40.5cm) wide

£150-200   **CRA**

A 1960s friction-powered 'X-Ray Space Pilot' toy gun, 'With Sparkling Barrel & Explosive Firing Noise', made in Japan.

Box 8.25in (21cm) wide

£80-125   **DH**

A 1950s friction-powered toy Rocket Racer.

6.75in (17cm) wide

£70-90   **DH**

A 'Captain Marvel Club Kit', by Fawcett, including envelope, induction letter, membership card, with pin, a secret message, an ad for various goodies and a secret message clipped from a comic book.

c1946

£180-220   **HC**

A Dubreq 'Rolf Harris Stylophone', signed by Rolf Harris.

c1971   Box 13in (33cm) wide

£45-65   **HLJ**

An MB 'Big Trak and Transport' programmable tank.

c1979   23.5ins (60cm) long

£80-120   **HLJ**

CHESS

■ Most chess sets date from the 18th, 19th and 20thC. Sets from the 17thC do exist but these are extremely rare and very valuable. Most sets were made in India and China and exported to England.

■ The 19thC saw the largest growth in chess set manufacture as the Industrial Revolution improved distribution and the growing middle class began to play this formerly 'aristocratic' game.

■ Look for complete and original sets as missing or replaced pieces devalue a set. The exceptions are very rare incomplete sets which will retain a value as collectors often buy several incomplete examples of the same set to assemble a complete set.

■ Cracked pieces devalue a set considerably, so examine all the pieces carefully. Pay special attention to ivory sets with stained or coloured pieces, especially those in green or red, as the precise colour is very difficult to match exactly when effecting a repair.

■ 'Staunton' sets by Jaques of England are highly desirable and represent a collecting field of their own. Staunton sets were made in materials including wood and ivory from the 1840s and are still produced today. Most pieces are marked 'Jaques of London' but marks do vary depending on period. Boxes for Jaques sets usually have green labels, but yellow and red are also known.

■ Chess boards are comparatively good value for money as, unlike today, sets were originally sold without boards. Demand amongst collectors is low as they usually focus on sets rather than boards.

An 18thC Burmese carved ivory figural set, one side stained dark red, the other side left natural, kings and queens as crouching deities, bishops as towers, knights on horseback, rooks as figures on elephants, pawns as crouching monkeys.

King 3.2in (8cm) high

£8,000-10,000 **FRE**

An early 19thC Russian carved mammoth ivory figural set, one side stained red, the other side left natural, kings wearing crowns, cloaks and holding orb and sceptre, queens in Empire period dress and wearing tiaras, bishops with beards and wearing cross-surmounted caps, knights as Roman cavalry with shields, rooks as elephants bearing turrets and flags, the pawns as footsoldiers wearing Roman-style helmets, holding spears in their left hands and swords in their right.

King 4.2in (10.6cm) high

£7,500-8,500 **FRE**

A late 18thC Russian walrus ivory Kholmogory set, the Christians versus the Turks, the Christians dressed as Roman soldiers, the Turks in national dress, kings seated on thrones, queens as viziers, bishops as elephants, knights as rearing horsemen, rooks as double-masted sailing ships, pawns as footsoldiers, the chessmen mounted on circular elephant ivory bases, one rook missing half a mast.

The set reflects Eastern influences with the use of viziers as queens and the use of elephants as bishops. As is usual with Russian sets, rooks are depicted as ships. Kholmogory sets are carved typically from walrus ivory.

King 3.5in (8.8cm) high

£6,500-7,500 **FRE**

An early 19thC Nepalese carved ivory figural set, one side stained red, the other side left natural, kings as deities seated on thrones, queens as viziers, bishops on elephants, knights as horsemen, rooks as pagodas, pawns as squatting soldiers.

King 3.2in (8cm) high

£7,000-8,000 **FRE**

An Indian Vizagapatam ivory playing set, one side stained a nut brown colour, the other side left natural, kings with open galleried crowns incorporating a seated prince of alternate colour, queens with foliate decoration and mounted kneeling viziers, bishops with curved foliate mitres, knights as rearing horses, rooks as turrets mounted with standard bearers, again in an alternate colour.

c1840 *King 5in (12.7cm) high*

£1,800-2,200 **FRE**

A Berhempore ivory 'East India (John) Company' figural set, the British East India Company versus native troops, one side with black-stained bases, the other side left natural, kings as elephants with howdahs, queens as elephants with open howdahs and parasols, bishops as camels, knights as horsemen, rooks as turrets with standard bearers, pawns as sepoys wearing pearls, and native troops, together with a framed certificate from Maskett-Beeson explaining the historical background to the set.

These sets reflect the extent of British colonialism, before the Indian Mutiny of 1857 led to the imposition of direct rule from the United Kingdom. One side represents the East India Company, while the other side are Indian native troops. The East Indian pawns are Indian-born sepoys in the uniform of the East India Company. Sets such as these were intended for display, rather than play.

c1840   *King 4in (10cm) high*

£10,000-12,000   **FRE**

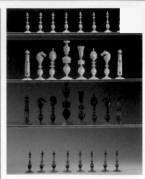

An Indian Vizagapatam ivory playing set, one side stained dark brown, the other side left natural, kings with pierced galleries and foliate knops, queens with split feathered open crowns, bishops as pierced mitres, knights as horses' heads, rooks as slender turrets raised on circular bases, pawns with decorated bulbous knops.

c1840   *King 5in (12.7cm) high*

£1,500-2,000   **FRE**

A 19thC ivory chess set, of turned form, half stained in red, some damage.

King 4in (10cm) high

£1,000-1,500   **DN**

A Northern Chinese ivory figural set, the pieces in traditional dress, kings with swords, queens with robes, bishops with horsewhips, knights as warriors on horses, rooks as elephants, pawns as footsoldiers.

King 3.5in (8.8cm) high

£1,500-2,000   **FRE**

A 19thC Indian ivory chess set, the castle with flags, half stained in red, some damage.

King 4.7in (12cm) high

£800-1,000   **DN**

A 19thC Chinese carved ivory chess set, the castles with Union Jack flags, stained in red and green, some damage, lacking one pawn.

King 3.5in (9cm) high

£800-1,000   **DN**

A 19thC Cantonese export ivory 'Puzzleball' set, stained red and left natural, the pieces in traditional Chinese dress, kings and queens as Emperor and Empress, bishops as mandarins, knights as warriors on horseback, rooks as elephants, pawns as footsoldiers, together with a 19thC Cantonese Export japanned gilt-decorated chess board/box, the interior for backgammon.

King 5.2in (13.2cm) high

£650-750   **FRE**

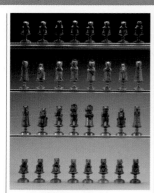

A 19thC Swiss pearwood 'Bear of Berne' figural set, one side in a darker wood, kings and queens wearing crowns and holding sceptres, bishops with staffs, knights as bears carrying smaller bears on their backs, rooks as turrets with bears' heads looking out, pawns as squatting bears.

'Bear of Berne' sets appear to be scarce. The centre for carving of this type was the area around Brienz in the Bernese, Switzerland.

King 3.5in (8cm) high

£3,000-4,000 FRE

A 19thC English ivory playing set, one side stained red, the other side left natural, the king and queen with multi-knopped stem, the bishops with bulbous split mitres, knights as horses' heads, rooks as stepped turrets with carved brickwork decoration.

King 2.5in (64.5cm) high

£800-1,000 FRE

A 19thC Cantonese export ivory 'Puzzleball' set, stained dark red and left natural, the pieces in traditional Chinese dress, the king and queen as Emperor and Empress, bishops as mandarins, knights as warriors on horseback, rooks as elephants with flags, pawns as warriors on horseback.

King 5.5in (13.9cm) high

£1,500-2,000 FRE

A 19thC Cantonese export ivory figural set, one side stained red, the other side left natural, the white king as King George III, the white queen as Queen Charlotte, bishops as mandarins, knights as warriors on horses with bows, rooks as elephants, pawns as footsoldiers with triangular shields.

King 4in (10.5cm) high

£1,000-1,500 FRE

A 19thC Cantonese export ivory chess count set, one side stained red, the other side left natural, the pieces with chess symbols against a pierced and carved florally-decorated ground.

1.5in (3.8cm) diam

£800-1,000 FRE

A 19thC English bone barleycorn playing set, stained red and left natural, kings and queens with petalled knops, bishops with split mitres, knights as horses' heads, rooks as turrets with flags, some damage to stems.

King 4in (10cm) high

£350-450 FRE

A 19thC English ivory playing set, stained red and left natural, the pieces with multi-knopped stems, bishops with split mitres, knights as horses' heads, rooks as turrets with flags.

King 3.5in (9cm) high

£350-450 FRE

A 19thC French bone Lyon set, one side stained black, the other side left natural.

King 3.75in (9.5cm) high

£1,000-1,500 FRE

A 19thC Jaques Staunton boxwood and ebony set, the white king stamped "Jaques London", in a wooden box with a sliding lid and a green label marked "Jaques & Son, London".

King 3.5in (9cm) high

£400-600 FRE

A 19thC Jaques Staunton ivory set, one side stained red, the other side left natural, the white king signed "Jaques London", in a Jaques Cartonpierre paper-mâché box, the underside with red label marked "Jaques London", together with a 19thC leather mounted folding board by Leuchars of London, the board with alternate tan and red squares, gilt-tooled borders, and signed "Leuchars...Piccadilly".

King 3.5in (9cm) high

£1,800-2,200 | **FRE**

A late 19thC Chinese ivory chess set, each piece carved with concentric balls, the bishops carved with masks, and two dice shakers half stained in red, some damage, lacking a bishop.

King 4in (11cm) high

£450-550 | **DN**

A late 19thC German cast iron figural set, in the Zimmerman style, Romans versus Gauls, the Roman side with black stained bases, the Gaulish side with brown coloured patinated bases, kings and queens as generals and their consorts, bishops as standard bearers, knights as cavalry, rooks as campaign tents, pawns as footsoldiers, one pawn with damaged base.

King 2.5in (6.5cm) high

£400-500 | **FRE**

A late 19thC Ceylonese ivory and ebony figural set, the king and queen in the lotus position, the queen praying, bishops as turrets, knights as rearing horses wearing crowns, rooks as elephants heads, pawns as flower buds.

King 5.5in (14cm) high

£6,000-7,000 | **FRE**

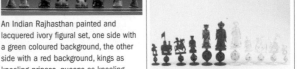

An Indian Rajhasthan painted and lacquered ivory figural set, one side with a green coloured background, the other side with a red background, kings as kneeling princes, queens as kneeling viziers, bishops as camel heads, knights as horses' heads, rooks as elephants' heads, pawns as seated footsoldiers, all the pieces with gilt decoration.

King 4.5in (11.5cm) high

£3,000-4,000 | **FRE**

A Chinese carved ivory chess set, each mounted on a concentric ball and round base, half stained in red, some damage, lacking a pawn.

King 5.5in (13.5cm) high

£180-220 | **DN**

A Jaques Staunton boxwood and ebony weighted set, both kings stamped "Jaques London", in a box with a green label marked "J. Jaques & Son Ltd, London, England", the box stamped "Made in England".

King 4in (10cm) high

£400-600 | **FRE**

An Indian ivory and sandalwood playing set, the pieces with circular foliate carved bases, kings and queens with open crowns, bishops with closed mitres, knights as horses' heads, rooks as pagodas.

King 4in (10.5cm) high

£500-600 | **FRE**

A Mexican bone and wood mounted playing set, one side stained purple-brown, the other side in a lighter colour.

King 5.5in (14cm) high

£170-220 | **FRE**

A hardstone bust set, one side an amber colour, the other side opaque white, with an onyx board.

King 3.5in (9cm) high

£100-150   **FRE**

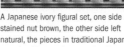

A Japanese ivory figural set, one side stained nut brown, the other side left natural, the pieces in traditional Japanese costume, kings and queens in robes, bishops holding scrolls, knights as warriors on horseback, rooks as pagodas, pawns as Japanese footsoldiers holding staffs, in a fitted board/box.

c1950   *King 2.5in (6.5cm) high*

£700-1,000   **FRE**

A 20thC Spanish Pulpit-style wooden set, one side in a lighter coloured wood, the other side in a darker coloured hardwood.

This set is a modern copy of the 18thC bone Spanish Pulpit sets. Debate continues as to the origin of these sets.

King 5in (13cm) high

£100-150   **FRE**

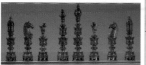

A 20thC Indian bone playing set, one side stained dark red, the other side left natural, kings with pierced crowns, queens with petalled knops and multi-faceted stems, bishops with tri-form knops, knights as horses' heads, rooks as castellated turrets on multi-faceted stems, pawns with multi-faceted knops.

King 6in (15cm) high

£250-350   **FRE**

A 20thC Indian bone set one side stained brown, the other side left natural, kings and queens with alternate coloured knops, the bishops similar, knights as double-headed horses, pawns with alternate coloured knops.

King 5.5in (14cm) high

£200-300   **FRE**

A 20thC Peruvian pottery figural set, one side predominantly red/brown, the other side a cream colour, kings wearing helmets, queens with plaits, bishops as stags, knights as llamas, rooks as rusticated towers, pawns with pipes, with wooden board/box.

King 2.5in (6.5cm) high

£70-100   **FRE**

A Soviet Olympiad plastic set, collector's edition, one side black, the other side white, the pieces with gilt bands around the stems, in a fitted plastic and velveteen lined board/box.

King 4in (10cm) high

£150-200   **FRE**

A Russian wooden doll Star Wars set, one side painted predominantly blue, the other side red, the pieces depicting the various Star Wars characters.

King 3.75in (9.5cm) high

£120-160   **FRE**

A 20thC American stained glass set, one side with white opaque glass, the other side with pale green glass, the pieces of abstract form and metal-mounted, kings and queens with copper 'crown' finials.

King 4.5in (11.5cm) high

£450-500   **FRE**

A Venetian Murano decorative glass figural set, one side predominantly white, the other side predominantly black, kings and queens wearing crowns, bishops wearing caps, knights as horses' heads, rooks as turrets, pawns with striped bases and stems.

King 7.5in (19cm) high

£1,200-1,500   **FRE**

An Indian camel bone Americans versus Taliban figural set, the Taliban side stained black, the American side left natural, Americans with carved eagle motif, Taliban with crescent moon and star motif, knights as rearing horses, rooks as turrets.

King 4.5in (11.5cm) high

£200-300   **FRE**

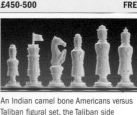

A resin The Lord of the Rings figural set, by Dennis Fairweather, representing good versus evil, kings as Aragon and Sauron, queens as Lady Galadriel and Shelob, bishops as Treebeard, Gollum, Gandalf and Sarmuran the White, knights as Bilbo, Frodo and the Ring-Wraiths, rooks as Hobbit holes, Rivendell, the Dark Tower and the Mines of Moria, pawns as Hobbits and Orcs, together with an accompanying leaflet describing the characters in The Lord of the Rings.

King 7in (18cm) high

£350-450 **FRE**

A Chess Teacher of the Century board in honour of John Collins, from the players of the U S Amateur Chess Team Championship, February 1991, the wooden board has several plaques inscribed with the names of chess champions including: Robert Fischer, Robert Byrne, Donald Byrne and William Lombardy.

30in (75cm) wide

£200-300 **FRE**

Chess Memorabilia

A Dresden Meissen-style porcelain group depicting a lady and gentleman in 18thC dress playing chess.

5.5in (13.9cm) wide

£200-250 **FRE**

A 20thC Japanese ceramic group, depicting two gentleman in 18thC dress playing chess, one smoking a pipe.

7in (17.7cm) high

£60-80 **FRE**

A 20thC cold-painted bronze group, in the Vienna style and after Bergman, depicting two Arabs playing chess, seated on a carpet.

3.5in (8.8cm) wide

£250-350 **FRE**

Bill Jacklin (American, b. 1943), "The Chess Players" screenprint, signed, inscribed A/P and dated.

This print shows chess players in Washington Park Square, New York.

1987 *29in (73.6cm) wide*

£350-450 **FRE**

A collection of international chess tournament flags, including the Reykjavik International Chess Tournament 1986, Stofnad 1954, the Iceland Chess Safari 1985, and the Ethel B. Collins Memorial Chess Festival.

1995-1996.

£40-60 **FRE**

A chess tournament clock, by Linden, the twin dials mounted on a wooden block, with a push rod mechanism, together with an American chess clock, 'The Blitzer' and a hand-built ten-second chess timer by Edward Lasker, the timer in a wooden case.

8in (20.3cm) wide

£200-300 **FRE**

A Tomy Blip hand-held analogue game.
c1977 *6.76in (17.5cm) wide*

£20-30 HLJ

A Prinztronic Tournament 1V games system.
c1978 *11.75in (30cm) wide*

£30-50 HLJ

An Atari 2600 Video Computer System game console.

c1978 *13.5in (34cm) wide*

£40-70 HLJ

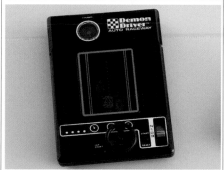

A Tomy Demon Driver hand-held analogue game.
c1978 *5.5in (14cm) wide*

£20-30 HLJ

COMPUTER GAMES

- Computer games first arrived on the mass market around 1979 and grew rapidly in popularity during the 1980s. Early games can be characterised by the simple – but addictive – game 'Pong'.

- Japan is considered to be the 'home' of the computer game. Many games were produced solely for the Japanese market and these are desirable as comparatively few are found outside Japan. However, it is important that these games contain little Japanese text so that it is easy to work out how to play them.

- Collectors look for 'shoot 'em up' and 'beat 'em up' games. These are highly sought after by dedicated collectors as they tend to be the most popular types of game format.

- Collectors should look out for highly sought after names including 'Neo-Geo', 'PC Engine' and 'Vectrex', all produced during the 1980s and 1990s. Sinclair products are also popular and constitute a collecting field of their own due to the wide range of models made and their innovative nature.

- Games must be complete and in working order. The box and instructions add further value, especially with handheld models.

An Atari, Ultra Pong 4-player game system.
c1978 *10in (25.5cm) wide*

£50-60 HLJ

A Tomy Stunt Bike hand-held analogue game.
c1978 *8.75in (22.5cm) wide*

£20-30 HLJ

A Kenner Star Wars Electronic Battle Command tabletop game.
c1979 *8.25in (21cm) wide*

£60-80 HLJ

A Videomaster Superscore game, with spy briefcase-style box.
c1978 *13.5in (34cm) wide*

£40-60 HLJ

A Grandstand Kevin Keegan's Match of the Day tabletop game.
c1979 *4in (10.5cm) wide*

£40-50 HLJ

A Tomy Desert Race hand-held clockwork game.
c1979   *5.75in (14.5cm) wide*

£10-15   HLJ

A Bambino Basketball tabletop game.
c1979   7.5in (19.5cm) wide

£25-35   HLJ

A Bambino Football tabletop game.
c1979   7.5in (19.5cm) wide

£25-35   HLJ

A Toytronic Racetrack hand-held game.
c1980   3.5in (9cm) wide

£20-30   HLJ

A Bambino Safari tabletop game.
c1980   9.5in (24cm) wide

£30-40   HLJ

A Sinclair ZX 81 home computer.
c1981   6.25in (16cm) wide

£50-60   HLJ

A CGL Grand Prix hand-held game.
c1981   5in (13cm) wide

£30-40   HLJ

A CGL Galaxy Twinvader tabletop game.
c1981   6.5in (17cm) wide

£20-30   HLJ

A Grandstand Astro Wars tabletop game.
c1981   5.7in (14.5cm) wide

£30-40   HLJ

A Tomy Lupin tabletop game.
c1981   6in (15cm) wide

£30-40   HLJ

A Grandstand Crazy Kong hand-held game.
c1981   4in (10.5cm) wide

£30-35   HLJ

A Grandstand Mini-Munchman hand-held game.
c1981   4in (10.5cm) wide

£25-30   HLJ

A Nintendo Fre FR-27 wide screen game and watch.
c1981   4.25in (11.5cm) wide

£30-60   HLJ

A Nintendo Popeye PP-23 wide screen game and watch.
c1981   *4.25in (11cm) wide*

£50-70   **HLJ**

A Sinclair ZX Spectrum Personal Computer, with rubber keys.
c1982   *8.75in (22.5cm) wide*

£60-80   **HLJ**

A Grandstand BMX Flyer hand-held game.
c1982   *6in (15cm) wide*

£30-40   **HLJ**

A Tomy Caveman tabletop game.
c1982

£20-30   **HLJ**

A Tomy Thundering Turbo 3-D hand-held game.
c1983   *5.5in (14cm) wide*

£20-30   **HLJ**

A Tomy Tron tabletop game, based on the 1982 Walt Disney movie.
c1982   *6in (15cm) wide*

£50-70   **HLJ**

A Nintendo Donkey Kong DK-52 multiscreen game and watch.
c1982   *4.25in (11.5cm) wide*

£25-40   **HLJ**

A silver Nintendo Fireman RC-04 game and watch.
c1980   *3.75in (9.5cm) wide*

£100-200   **HLJ**

A Nintendo Snoopy Tennis SP-30 wide screen game and watch.
c1982   *4.25in (11cm) wide*

£25-40   **HLJ**

A Nintendo Greenhouse GH-54 multiscreen game and watch.
c1982   *4.25in (11.5cm) wide*

£35-60   **HLJ**

A Nintendo Mickey & Donald DM-53 multiscreen game and watch.
c1982   *4.25in (11.5cm) wide*

£35-60   **HLJ**

A Nintendo Donkey Kong Jr. DJ-101 new wide screen game and watch.
c1982   *4.25in (11cm) wide*

£25-40   **HLJ**

A Nintendo Oil Panic OP-51 multiscreen game and watch.
c1982   *4.25in (11.5cm) wide*

£25-45   **HLJ**

A B C D E F G H I J K L M N O P Q R S T U V W XYZ

An ORIC-1 home computer.

c1983   *10.75in (27.5cm) wide*

£40-70   **HLJ**

A CBSD Electronics Colecovision game console.

c1983   *14.5in (37cm) wide*

£80-100   **HLJ**

An Atari 800 XL home computer.

c1983   *15in (38cm) wide*

£50-80   **HLJ**

A Grandstand Pocket Scrambler hand-held game.

c1983   *6.7in (17cm) wide*

£30-35   **HLJ**

An MB Vectrex game system, with built in TV screen.

c1983   *9.5in (24cm) wide*

£150-200   **HLJ**

A CGL Junglar tabletop game, with pop up screen.

c1983   *6.5in (16.5cm) wide*

£40-50   **HLJ**

FIND OUT MORE...

'Electronic Plastic' edited by Jaro Gielens, Die Gestalte Verlag, 2001 ISBN: 3931126447, which covers handheld games only.

'The Ultimate History of Video Games: From Pong to Pokemon – The Story Behind the Craze That Touched Our Lives and Changed the World' by Steve L. Kent, Prima Publishing, 2001. ISBN: 0761536434

eBay (www.ebay.com) is recognised as being one of the best venues to buy and sell games, but also try www.gamesradar.com who have a special section for 'retro games'.

A Rosy Astro Attack tabletop game.

c1983   *7.5in (19cm) wide*

£30-40   **HLJ**

A Grandstand Firefox F-7 tabletop game.

c1983   *7.5in (19cm) wide*

£30-40   **HLJ**

A Nintendo Mario Cement Factory ML-102 new wide screen game and watch.

c1983   *4.25in (11cm) wide*

£25-50   **HLJ**

A Grandstand Pocket Scramble hand-held game.

c1983   *3.75in (9cm) wide*

£30-35   **HLJ**

A Nintendo Donkey Kong II JR-55 multiscreen game and watch.

c1983   *4.25in (11.5cm) wide*

£25-40   **HLJ**

HUGO LEE-JONES
ELECTRONIC COLLECTABLES

telephone: 01227 375375
mobile: 0794 118 72027
e.mail: electroniccollectables@hotmail.com

A
B
C
D
E
F
G
H
I
J
K
L
M
N
O
P
Q
R
S
T
U
V
W
XYZ

A Nintendo Rain Shower LP-57 multiscreen game and watch.
c1983   *3.25in (8.5cm) wide*

£45-90   **HLJ**

A Nintendo Mario's Bomb's Away TB-94 panorama screen game and watch.
c1983   *3.75in (9.5cm) wide*

£80-120   **HLJ**

A Nintendo Donkey Kong Jr. CJ-93 panorama screen game and watch.
c1983   *3.75in (9.5cm) wide*

£80-120   **HLJ**

A Nintendo Mario Cement Factory CM-72 tabletop game and watch.
c1983   *5in (13cm) wide*

£70-90   **HLJ**

A CLOSER LOOK AT A COMPUTER GAME

Nintendo is a renowned name still producing highly popular and innovative games and gaming systems today.

Hand-held games often had detachable battery covers - it is essential that they are present.

This 'Game & Watch' game is rare, complete and in excellent condition which means that the price is comparatively high.

The 'Game & watch' range is highly desirable for three reasons: the size of the games; the reputation of the manufacturer; and the size of the range.
Around 65 different versions were produced and rarer games can fetch comparatively high prices as collectors need them to complete the set.

A Nintendo Donkey Kong Circus MK-96 panorama screen game and watch.
c1984   *3.75in (9.5cm) wide*

£200-300   **HLJ**

A Sinclair ZX Spectrum+ personal computer.

c1984   *12.5in (31.5cm) wide*

£50-60   **HLJ**

A Systema Pac-Land hand-held game.

c1984   *5.25in (13.5cm) wide*

£20-30   **HLJ**

A Nintendo Entertainment System Deluxe set, including R.O.B. (Remote Operating Buddy).
c1985
£80-120 HLJ

An Atari 2600 game console.
This is a smaller version of the more common woodgrain model.
c1986 *15in (26.5cm) wide*
£40-60 HLJ

An Atari 7800 game console.
c1988 *11.5in (29cm) wide*
£40-60 HLJ

A Ninetendo Climber DR-106 new wide screen game and watch.
c1988 *4.25in (11cm) wide*
£35-55 HLJ

A Ninetendo Super Mario Bros. YM-105 new wide screen game and watch.
c1988 *4.25in (11cm) wide*
£25-40 HLJ

A PC Engine game console.
c1987 *5.5in (14cm) wide*
£100-150 HLJ

A Ninetendo Balloon Fight BF-107 new wide screen game and watch.
c1988 *4.25in (11cm) wide*
£50-100 HLJ

A PC Engine GT hand-held portable game system.
c1990 *4in (10cm) wide*
£120-175 HLJ

A SNK Neo-Geo CD top-loader console.
c1994 *10.5in (27cm) wide*
£140-170 HLJ

A Sega Multi-Mega (combined Mega Drive-Mega CD) game console.
c1994 *5in (12.5cm) wide*
£100-120 HLJ

An SNK Neo-Geo Pocket Color portable game system.
c1999 *5in (13cm) wide*
£40-60 HLJ

An MB 'Pac Man' board-game.

c1982   *Box 19in (48.5cm) wide*

£10-15   **HLJ**

An MB 'Defender' board-game.

c1983   *Box 19in (48.5cm) wide*

£15-20   **HLJ**

An MB 'Donkey Kong' board-game.

c1983   *Box 19in (48.5cm) wide*

£15-20   **HLJ**

An MB 'Frogger' board-game.

c1983   *Box 19in (48.5cm) wide*

£10-15   **HLJ**

An MB 'ZAXXON' board-game.

c1983   *Box 19in (48.5cm) wide*

£15-20   **HLJ**

A Waddingtons 'Super Mario Bros' board-game

c1992   *Box 15in (38cm) wide*

£10-15   **HLJ**

An Astronauts jigsaw puzzle, containing 20 pieces.

c1968   *4.5in (11.5cm) high*

£4-5   **DH**

An electronic 'American Flipper Coney Island' pinball game, coin-operated for four players.

Coney Island, Brooklyn, New York was considered to be the world's largest and foremost amusement area during the first half of the 20th Century. As well as a beach resort, it contained three large amusement parks; Luna Park, Steeplechase and Dreamland, all for the amusement of New Yorkers.

63in (160cm) long

£120-180   **TK**

A pair of Regency lacquer card trays, one decorated with a king and queen, the other with the word "GAME".

4.5in (11.5cm) long

£100-150   **PSA**

A 'Centennial Presidential Game' board-game, by McLoughlin Bros., New York, covering the first 100 years of American Presidency, with a deck of 54 cards, wood block spinner and instructions, boxed.

1876

£800-1,000   **TK**

A rare 1930s Alfred Dunhill bridge set, comprising four Royal Doulton ashtrays and a Dunhill Namiki maki-e lacquer bridge pencil in a fitted case.

This set is extremely rare and typical of the high quality items retailed by Alfred Dunhill in the 1920s and 1930s.

Pencil 3in (8cm) high

£400-600   **PC**

PELHAM PUPPETS

- Robert Pelham (1919-1980) founded 'Wonkey Toys Ltd' based in Marlborough, England in 1947. It was renamed 'Pelham Puppets Limited' a year later and underwent a number of name changes in subsequent years before being dissolved in 1997.

- An architect who enjoyed making toys during World War II, Pelham's first designs included a black girl called Chloe, Sandy McBoozle and Wonky Cowboy.

- In 1953, Pelham Puppets acquired the rights to manufacture Walt Disney characters. Pinocchio is one of the most produced characters ever, but the factory also made Mickey and Minnie Mouse, Donald Duck, Snow White and the Seven Dwarfs and Cinderella. Some characters, such as Mickey Mouse, were made in different variations over the years.

- Other well-known characters to have had their own Pelham Puppet include Andy Pandy, the Muppets, Peanuts, Thunderbirds, the Pink Panther and Muffin the Mule.

- Condition is very important as in its peak the company produced thousands of each character and many people have kept their puppets since childhood. Puppets that were not played with and do not have blemishes, scratches or worn clothes and retain their strings intact will be more desirable.

- As a general rule early puppets are more valuable than later ones. However, some of the rarest puppets are the later ones as relatively few of them were made.

- If the puppet has its original box, this will make it more desirable. It is possible to date a Pelham puppet from its box (if correctly matched):
  - 1947-1956 A brown box with a blue label followed by yellow box with a blue and red label.
  - 1956-1968 A yellow-lidded box for the first six years featuring the Mad Hatter from Alice in Wonderland. He was then replaced by a snake charmer character.
  - 1968-c.1970 A yellow box with a clear acetate window.
  - 1970-1986 A band of card was added across the acetate window.
  - Late 1980s A red and yellow candy striped box.
  - Note: Some late production special collectors' characters had differently designed boxes.

A boxed Pelham puppet type SL "Ballet Girl", with original control bar and coloured strings, generally good condition in good original first type yellow box with lid.

12.5in (32cm) high

£50-80   **DN**

A boxed Pelham puppet "Big Ears", early version with large wooden head, with black strings and original control bar, minor damage but generally good condition in good period but incorrect card box with red and blue label to the lid, marked Type LS "Gypsy".

11in (28cm) high

£420-480   **DN**

A boxed Pelham puppet type SL "Bom", Enid Blyton's toy soldier character with original control bar fitted with coloured strings, moth hole in cap otherwise generally good condition, in poor type yellow box with lid, colours faded, lid split and torn.

13.5in (34cm) high

£200-250   **DN**

A boxed Pelham Puppet type SM "Chef", with original control bar, in need of restringing, some signs of age and one half of moustache missing but otherwise in good collectable condition in poor original card box with blue label to lid.

13.5in (34cm) high

£900-1,000   **DN**

A boxed Pelham puppet type SL "Cinderella", with original control bar and coloured strings, and complete with instruction sheet, very good condition in very good original second type yellow box with lid.

11.5in (29cm) high

£35-45 DN

A boxed Pelham puppet type SM "Clown", with original control bar and coloured strings, good condition in good original yellow window box.

13.5in (34cm) high

£40-60 DN

A boxed Pelham puppet type SS "Clown", dressed in red jump suit with white spots and red felt hat, with original control bar and coloured strings, complete with instruction sheet, good condition in good original card box with red and blue label to the lid.

£70-100 DN

A boxed Pelham puppet "Baby Dragon", with 1963 tag beneath left wing, original control bar and coloured strings, complete with instruction sheet, good condition second type yellow box, minor graffiti to lid.

£250-300 DN

A boxed Pelham puppet type SS "Dutch Girl", with original control bar and coloured strings, very good condition in very good original first type yellow box with lid.

12.25in (31cm) high

£30-50 DN

A boxed Pelham puppet A5 "Foal", with original crossbar and coloured strings, yellow box with lid also good except for one part-split corner and graffiti to underside of base.

7.75in (20cm) high

£30-40 DN

A boxed Pelham puppet type SL19 "Giant", with original control bar and coloured strings, very good condition in good larger-size yellow box with lid.

13in (33cm) high

£50-80 DN

A boxed Pelham puppet Jumpette "Girl", with original control bar and strings, very good condition in good small-size yellow box with lid.

9in (23cm) high

£30-40 DN

A boxed Pelham puppet type SS "Golliwog", dressed in red trousers and green and white striped shirt, with original control bar and coloured strings, complete with instruction sheet and untangling chart; good condition in good original card box with red and blue label to the lid.

£250-350 DN

A boxed Pelham puppet type SL "Gretel", with original control bar and coloured strings, and complete with instruction sheet and 1966 club slip, very good condition in very good second type yellow box with lid.

12.5in (32cm) high

£35-45   **DN**

A boxed Pelham puppet type SS "Gypsy", with original control bar, coloured strings and additional clothing, very good condition in very good original second type yellow box with lid.

11.75in (30cm) high

£30-40   **DN**

A boxed Pelham puppet type SS "Gypsy", with original control bar and coloured strings, good condition in good original second type yellow box with lid.

12.25in (31cm) high

£25-35   **DN**

A boxed Pelham puppet type LL "Lulabelle", with coloured strings, early version with bamboo limbs and rubber-ring lips, some paint loss but generally very good condition in fair to good original card box with blue label to the lid.

23.5in (60cm) high

£150-200   **DN**

A boxed Pelham puppet type SM "Macboozle", with original control bar and coloured strings, good condition in fair to good original card box with red and blue label to the lid.

13.5in (34cm) high

£40-50   **DN**

A boxed Pelham puppet "Muffin the Mule", early example with original control bar, good condition in fair to good original yellow-striped box.

6.75in (17cm) long

£220-280   **DN**

A boxed Pelham puppet type SL "Merlin", dressed in blue robes and hat with original coloured strings, complete with instruction sheet; moth damage to robes but in good condition in good original second type yellow box.

£200-250   **DN**

A boxed Pelham puppet type SL "Mickey Mouse", with original control bar and coloured strings and complete with instruction sheet, excellent condition in good original second type yellow box with lid.

10.25in (26cm) high

£80-100   **DN**

A boxed Pelham puppet type SL "Pinocchio", version with plastic legs, with original control bar and coloured strings and complete with instruction sheet, excellent condition in good but incorrect second type yellow box with lid, marked for "Tyrolean Boy".

11.75in (30cm) high

£40-60   **DN**

A boxed Pelham puppet type SS "Pirate", with black strings and original control bar, minor moth damage but generally in good condition in good period but incorrect card box with blue label to the lid, marked type SS "Pinocchio".

12.25in (31cm) high

£180-220 | **DN**

A boxed Pelham Puppet 'White Poodle', with black strings and original control bar, fair condition in good original card box with red and blue label to the lid.

8.5in (22cm) high

£30-40 | **DN**

A boxed Pelham puppet type SL "Gretel", with original control bar and coloured strings, and complete with instruction sheet and 1966 club slip, very good condition in very good second-type yellow box with lid.

12.5in (32cm) high

£35-45 | **DN**

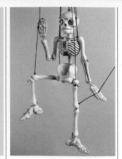

A boxed Pelham puppet "Skeleton", with disjointing action and original special control bar and complete with instruction sheet, good condition in good original card box with red and blue label to the lid.

14.5in (37cm) high

£70-100 | **DN**

A Pelham puppet 'Vent Boy', with striped trousers, check jacket, green tie and black sheepskin hair, good condition, unboxed.

26.75in (68cm) high

£50-70 | **DN**

An unboxed Pelham puppet type LA "Wags", an early dog with brown-spotted yellow body and leather ears, small amount of paint loss but generally good condition, unboxed.

8.5in (22cm) high

£50-80 | **DN**

A boxed Pelham puppet type SL "Wicked Witch", with 1963 tag, original control bar and coloured strings, and complete with instruction sheet and 1966 club slip, good condition in good original second type yellow box with lid.

13in (33cm) high

£80-100 | **DN**

A boxed Pelham puppet type SM "Witch", with black strings and original control bar, good condition in good original card box with red and blue label to the lid.

12.5in (32cm) high

£40-50 | **DN**

A boxed Pelham puppet type SM "Witch" with original control bar and coloured strings, generally very good condition in fair to good original first type yellow box with lid.

13in (33cm) high

£30-40 | **DN**

A boxed Pelham puppet de-luxe type SL21 "Wolf", with original control bar and coloured strings, very good condition in fair larger-size yellow window box, acetate missing from sliding cover and some tearing.

13.75in (35cm) high

£40-60 | **DN**

AUTOMATA

- The production of automata originates in the 18th century with clocks mounted with complicated mechanical figures. Commercial production began in the early 19th century and reached its apex between c1880-c1920.
- Value is dependant on the originality and complexity of the mechanism and the condition of the head and costume, which should be original. Replacements and repair will reduce value, less so if done appropriately.
- Makers from around Paris such as Roullet & Descamps (1832-1972), Vichy (1862-1905), Bontems (1840-1905) and Phalibois (c1850-c1910) are the most desirable names.

A papier-mâché musical bust of a black banjo player, by G. Vichy, on a wooden base, plays two tunes strumming his banjo and pauses to thumb his nose and stick out his tongue, re-dressed.

This example has dancing eyelids, which are a trademark of Vichy.

c1880   21.75in (55cm) high

£10,500-12,500   **AMM**

A papier-mâché 'The Acrobat' automaton, by G. Vichy, Paris, with clockwork mechanism, performs handstand and then lifts one hand off to two-air musical movement, all original.

It is rare to find a piece with all its original clothing.

c1880   31.5in (80cm) high

£26,000-28,000   **AMM**

An original German wind-up bisque doll, attributed to Porzellanfabrik Rauenstein.

£850-950   **DE**

A fur-covered papier-mâché tiger automaton, by Roullet & Decamps, with later harness and inset glass eyes, the tiger crouches, roars and leaps with movement of the jaw and head.

c1875   20.75in (53cm) long

£1,600-1,800   **AMM**

A life-size flock-covered papier-mâché French bulldog automaton, with nodding head and bark and inset glass eyes, on wheels.

c1900   15in (38cm) high

£1,200-1,600   **AMM**

A Japanese Kobi hand-operated automaton, made of carved and stained fruitwood.

Kobi toys are named after the Japanese port and were made as souvenir pieces for tourists. They are based on Japanese folktales and always have a grotesque element.

c1880   4in (10cm) high

£250-300   **AMM**

BISQUE DOLLS

- Look on the back of the bisque head above the nape of the neck to see the incised marking which shows the mould number, which helps identify the maker and period. Unmarked dolls can often be identified by their facial characteristics and form.

- The body should be original. Dolls made from different pieces have lesser values – a head is generally worth around 50% of the complete doll. Size is important with larger sizes being more valuable.

- Condition is important, with damage reducing value. Some factory defects or flaws are acceptable if not too conspicuous – bisque should be smooth and clean. Cracks decrease value – shining a strong light into a bisque head will reveal cracks, but always ask before carefully removing the wig to do this.

- Look for dolls with original clothing as these command a premium over redressed examples. However, dolls in original clothing are not common and appropriate clothing is acceptable as standard.

- As well as condition, the visual appeal and attractiveness of the doll affects the price. Dolls with the same mould number can even vary in price, with finer quality and more attractive painting being more valuable. Experience will generate an ability to spot a fine doll.

An Armand Marseille bisque-head doll, with sleeping blue glass eyes, four upper teeth, jointed composite body and woven wig, some original clothing, model number 390 61/2.

The 390 series, made from 1900 onwards, is the most commonly found doll by Armand Marseille. Collectors should look for examples with finer, less simplistic features.

3.5in (60cm) high

£120-160 **WHP**

An Armand Marseille baby, with five-piece body, mould 971.
c1915 *17in (43cm) high*
£400-500 **BEJ**

An Armand Marseille German child doll, mould 390.
c1890 *20in (50cm) high*
£500-550 **BEJ**

A marotte bisque shoulder-head doll, with inset blue glass eyes, open mouth, music box plays when doll is turned, wig missing, marked "370 A.M 10/0X. DEP".
c1920 *15in (38cm) high*
£250-300 **TK**

An Armand Marseille bisque socket-head baby, human hair wig and bent limb composition body, for George Borgfeldt, marked "G.327.B Germany A.12.M".
c1913 *19in (48cm) high*
£350-400 **TK**

An Armand Marseille Oriental bisque-head doll, with composition body, all original.
12in (30.5cm) high
£500-550 **DE**

An Armand Marseille black child doll, with three outfits, mould 390.
c1890 *11in (28cm) high*
£300-400 **BEJ**

ARMAND MARSEILLE

- Armand Marseille, based in Thuringia, Germany is one of the most prolific doll makers.
- They made bisque dolls from 1885 onwards after Armand Marseille and his son took over a porcelain factory. Production peaked from around 1900 to 1930.
- Their dolls are marked with 'A M' lettering amongst the German marks.

An Armand Marseille googly doll, all original, no. 323.

c1915 *10in (25.5cm) high*
£1,750-1,850 **BEJ**

SIMON & HALBIG

- Simon & Halbig, based in Grafenheim in Thuringia, Germany, were active from c1869 until c1930 and made many dolls heads for other companies including Kammer & Reinhardt and the French company, Jumeau.
- Their early dolls had fixed glass eyes, solid domed heads and closed mouths. Later dolls have open socket type heads with card pates and open mouths.
- Their dolls can be recognised by the 'S H' lettering as well as by mould number. In 1920, they were bought by Kammer & Reinhardt.

An early 20thC Simon and Halbig 'Lady' doll, no. 1159.
12in (30.5cm) high

£700-750   **DE**

An early 1900s Simon and Halbig/Adolf Wislizenus toddler doll, all original.

£800-900   **DE**

A Simon & Halbig character-face child doll, mould 531.
c1890   *18in (45.5cm) high*

£850-950   **BEJ**

A Simon & Halbig shoulder-head 'fortune teller' doll.
c1890   *8in (20cm) high*

£350-450   **BEJ**

A Simon & Halbig child doll, for Kämmer & Reinhardt.
c1890   *9in (23cm) high*

£450-550   **BEJ**

A Simon and Halbig girl doll, with bisque socket-head, brown mohair wig and papier mâché/wood ball-jointed body.
5.25 (64cm) high

£500-550   **TK**

A Simon & Halbig tiny child doll, in an Orkney chair.
c1890   *7in (17.5cm) high*

£350-420   **BEJ**

A Simon & Halbig character boy, with fully-jointed composition body, blond mohair wig, dressed in vintage clothes, includes "1908 Baseball Fan" pin, incised "S&H 150/2".
21in (53.5cm) high

£16,000-18,000   **Ber**

A S.F.B.J Jumeau laughing toddler doll, no. 236.

£800-900   **DE**

S.F.B.J.

■ The 'Societe Francaise de Fabrication de Bébés & Jouets' was a group of French doll makers who joined together to challenge the threatening German doll industry.

■ They were based primarily at the Jumeau factory in France and were active from 1899-c1950. As they tried to control costs to produce less expensive dolls, quality was often compromised.

■ Dolls tend to be slim, with high cut legs and composition or wooden bodies. Their character dolls, made from 1911 onwards, were more successful.

A S.F.B.J. Bébé, mould 301.
c1900   18in (46cm) high

£1,100-1,300   **BEJ**

A S.F.B.J. Bébé, mould 301, all original.
c1900

£1,500-1,700   **BEJ**

An early S.F.B.J. Bru-like mould doll, with high forehead, incised "Depose SFBJ9".
21in (53.5cm) high

£800-1,200   **DE**

JUMEAU

■ Jumeau, based in France, were active from 1842-1899 and after releasing the first bébé, went on to produce portrait bébés from 1870 and 'Jumeau Triste', sad dolls, from c1880. The heads are marked clearly with the Jumeau name.

■ Pierre Francois Jumeau created the first 'bébé' doll, an idealised version of a chubby young girl, in 1885. It was a departure from previous dolls which were shaped to look like slim ladies.

■ Competition from less expensive dolls from Germany led to the decline of the company in its last decade.

A S.F.B.J. Bébé, with chair, mould 60.
c1900   *12.5in (31.5cm) high*

£600-700   **BEJ**

A S.F.B.J. Bébé, original outfit, mould 60.
c1900   *12.5in (31.5cm) high*

£600-650   **BEJ**

A Jumeau 'Portrait Fashion' doll, with pressed bisque socket-head on bisque shoulder plate, with blue paperweight eyes, closed mouth, pierced ears, original gusseted kid body, ivory net and lace dress, elaborate lace bonnet, chip to neck.
21in (53.5cm) high

£2,000-2,500   **Ber**

A Jumeau 'Tête' doll, with open mouth, original wig and cork pate, size 8, with red stamp on head.
19in (48.5cm) high

£1,800-2,300   **DE**

A Jumeau 'Tête' doll, with open mouth and creamy composition, size 9, red stamp on head.
21in (53.5cm) high

£2,000-2,500   **DE**

A Jumeau Bébé, size 8.

c1890 22in (56cm) high

£1,500-1,700 BEJ

A Jumeau Bébé, in chemise, size 7.

c1890 18in (46cm) high

£1,300-1,500 BEJ

A Jumeau Bébé, size 9.

c1885 24in (61cm) high

£2,500-2,800 BEJ

A Gebrüder Heubach German schoolboy.

c1900 16in (40.5cm) high

£850-950 BEJ

A Gebrüder Heubach pouty child, all original.

c1915 9.5in (24cm) high

£550-650 BEJ

A Gebrüder Heubach boy doll, with domed bisque socket-head, closed pouty mouth, intaglio eyes, blond moulded hair and composition baby's body, probably marked "0 68 96 Germany", blue ink stamp "19" or "13" and another mark "27", slight repairs.

1912 8.5in (22cm) high

£550-600 TK

A rare Heubach character child, with bisque socket-head and heavily moulded hair, painted intaglio eyes, open mouth with two painted teeth, and fully-jointed composition body, plaid linen dress with lace and ribbon trim, wool cape, red silk shoes.

The character dolls produced by the Thuringian company Gebruder Heubach (c1840-1945) are highly sought after for their visual appeal. Much effort was devoted to the heads, with well-painted moulded hair, rosy cheeks and extremely characterful faces. Their eyes were realistic with an indented pupil and an iris highlighted with a white dot.

19in (48.5cm) high

£16,500-17,500 Ber

An Ernest Heubach googly doll, all original.

£250-300 DE

A Kestner doll, with four upper teeth and mohair wig, with mâché/wood ball jointed body and red ink stamp "Germany 6", marked "L*made in Germany* 164".

28in (71cm) high

£550-650 TK

A Kestner doll, all-bisque on 'wrestler body', huge size.

c1885   *11in (28cm) high*

£2,750-3,500   **BEJ**

A Kestner Baby doll, with composition baby's body, bonnet marked "11".

1912   *13.75in (35cm) high*

£400-500   **TK**

A Kestner all-bisque googly doll, replaced legs.

7in (17.5cm) high

£200-250   **DE**

A German Max Oscar Arnold fashion doll, with shoulder-head and kid body.

c1890   *16in (40.5cm) high*

£500-600   **BEJ**

A French Belton doll, with Bru-like face, wooden body and straight wrists.

20in (51cm) high

£2,000-2,500   **DE**

A CLOSER LOOK AT A TWO-FACED DOLL

Bru Jeune & Cie (1866-1883) produced a number of very unusual and fine quality bébé dolls. These examples are much sought after, more so than those produced after 1899 when the company was taken over.

The 'two-faced' style was introduced by Jumeau and features a knob in the hair to turn the head round. The first face is crying, the second is smiling.

A Belton doll, with closed mouth, the body with moulded red stockings, the swivel flange neck of early design.

9in (23cm) high

£300-350   **DE**

An Ettiene Denamur French Bébé.

c1885   *11.5in (29cm) high*

£1,800-2,000   **BEJ**

A very rare two-faced Bru doll, with bisque cup-and-saucer head on bisque shoulder plate and gusseted kid body with bisque hands, first face has blue-painted intaglio eyes with finely stroked lashes, the open-closed mouth with tiny painted teeth, original bonnet flips to reveal second face of a crying child with closed-screaming mouth, narrow-painted eyes, furrowed brows and appropriately tinted red face, marked No.4.

15in (38cm) high

£12,000-13,000   **Ber**

A Bru Jne. & Cie Fashion doll, Paris, with pale bisque socket-head on bisque shoulder plate, gusseted kid body, blue paperweight eyes, finely painted eyelashes and brows, closed smiling mouth, human hair wig, wearing ivory cotton pique dress, undergarments, leather shoes, picture hat with flocked flowers on brim, chest stamp, blue oval "Au Nain Bleu, CHAUVERE, 27 Boule Parvoire", damage to kid arms.

18in (46cm) high

£2,000-3,000 Ber

A French Charles Marcoux Bébé, in rocking chair.

c1890 *16in (23cm) high*

£1,000-1,300 BEJ

A Porzellanfrabrik Mengersgereuth baby.

c1915 *9in (23cm) high*

£300-350 BEJ

A French fashion doll, by Francois Gaultier, incised "S".

1880-90 *20in (51cm) high*

£2,000-2,500 DE

A Kämmer & Reinhardt girl doll and doll bed, short human wig and composition body jointed at hip and shoulder.

c1930

£120-180 TK

A Bébé Mothereau, blonde wig and original fully-jointed body, wears period embroidered cotton and crocheted dress, straw hat and original leather boots.

12in (30.5cm) high

£7,500-8,500 Ber

A German Goebal fly-on-nose character doll.

c1900 *14in (35.5cm) high*

£900-1,000 BEJ

A French Damerval Laffranchy Bébé, with walking body.

c1900 *15in (38cm) high*

£1,000-1,100 BEJ

A rare pair of Rose O'Neill huggers.

3.25in (8.5cm) high

£200-250 SFel

A German Alt, Beck & Gottschalk shoulder-head lady, with kid body.

c1890 *21in (53cm) high*

£1,100-1,200 BEJ

A French Bébé Lanternier, with two original outfits.

c1900 *35in (89cm) high*

£4,500-5,000 BEJ

A German Hertwig Rose O'Neill-type Kewpie, with half the box (not shown).

c1910

£800-900 BEJ

A Rose O'Neill kewpie doll, original skirt, mint condition.

4.5in (11.5cm)

£80-100   **DE**

A German Schoenau & Hoffmeister doll, riding a tricycle, wearing a lamb outfit.

c1910

£350-400   **BEJ**

A German Hertel Schwab & Co. baby, unmarked.

c1915

£900-1,000   **BEJ**

A German Bruno Schmidt boy doll.

c1915   17in (43cm) high

£900-1,000   **BEJ**

A CLOSER LOOK AT A THULLIER BÉBÉ DOLL

A. Thullier of Paris (1875-1893) are a highly sought after name. Their fine quality dolls fetch good prices when sold.

Her enchanting face, clothing and wig are all in excellent condition.

Her wig and clothing are original. She has not been redressed.

At 21 inches this is a very large doll. Dolls this size are not at all common.

She retains her original shoes, which match the doll and were marked by the maker.

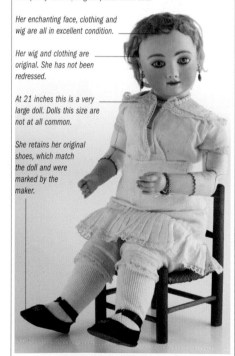

A French bisque Thullier bébé doll, with bisque socket-head, gusseted kid body, bisque lower arms, blue paperweight eyes, pierced ears, closed mouth, original mohair wig and marked head and shoulder plate, originally marked shoes with butterfly rosettes, original chemise, mint condition, incised "A.9.T."

21in (53.5cm) high

£40,000-45,000   **Ber**

A Limoges bébé.

Several of the well known porcelain factories at Limoges produced a wide range of bébé dolls of differing qualities between c1897 and c1925.

c1910   19in (48cm) high

£750-800   **BEJ**

An unmarked all-bisque googly doll, with extra clothing, boxed.

c1910   6in (15cm) high

£550-650   **BEJ**

A Jules Steiner doll, fully-jointed composition body, red mohair wig, fixed blue glass eyes, painted brows and eyelashes, closed mouth and pierced ears, dressed in ivory cotton and lace dress, tan wool overcoat, underwear, socks, brown leather shoes and silk bonnet, marked "Le Petit Parisien, BEBE STEINER", incised "Figure C No. 2, J. Steiner BTE S.G.D.G, Paris".

19in (42.5cm) high

£3,500-4,000   **Ber**

A late 19thC bisque-head doll, with cloth body and open mouth, in contemporary sailor dress, possibly marked "Alma".

12.5in (32cm) high

£50-60   **WHP**

A Lenci Maxette doll, with two tags near hem, mint condition.

Lenci was founded in Turin, Italy in 1918. Between 1920 and 1940, they produced a variety of sophisticated fabric dolls in elaborate costumes. The felt face is painted in a surprisingly expressive way. Clothes are usually brightly coloured. Lenci dolls must be clean with bright clothes. Dirty faced or worn examples with faded or damaged clothing will be worth a third to a half of the price of a clean and bright example. Correct tags add a premium if present.

£180-200   **DE**

A Lenci 'Mascotte' doll, with rare costume, labelled.

£180-200   **DE**

An Italian Lenci 'Schoolboy' felt doll, all original.

c1930   *17in (43cm) high*

£400-500   **BEJ**

A 1930s Lenci mechanical store display mannequin, from Lord & Taylor with Lord & Taylor tag, all original.

£750-800   **DE**

A 1930s Nora Wellings black doll, with painted plush velvet face, flirty glass eyes and smiling mouth.

£55-65   **WHP**

A Nora Wellings 'Mountie' doll.

9.75in (25cm) high

£15-25   **WHP**

A 1930s Empire-marked 'Sailor', often mis-sold as a Nora Wellings doll.

8in (20cm) high

£20-25   **BEJ**

A 1950s Invicta 'Marine' doll.

9in (23cm) high

£10-15   **DH**

A rare early Setti 'St. Nicholas' doll, handmade and painted by artist John R. Wright.

18in (45.5cm) high

£1,000-1,500   **DE**

Left: An early Setti 'Farmer' doll, handmade and painted by John R. Wright.

19in (48.5cm) high

£900-1,100   **DE**

Right: An early Setti 'Farmer's Wife' doll, handmade and painted by John R. Wright.

18in (45.5cm) high

£800-1,000   **DE**

A large size Steiff 'Pucki', with tag and money bag.

£160-180   **DE**

A British made Dutch boy, labelled "Allwin".

c1930   *18in (46cm) high*

£150-200   **BEJ**

A rare Steiff 'Golfer' doll.

£60-80   **DE**

A Macauley Culkin 'Home Alone' figure, some original clothing.

c1988   *19in (48cm) high*

£4-6   **WHP**

One of a pair of 'Raggedy Ann' doll, in rare dress, all original, Georgene label.

'Raggedy Ann' was based on a story by the American Johnny Gruelle. Gruelle's publisher was the first to mass produce these dolls from 1918, but other companies such as Georgene Averill of New York (1876-1963) also produced variations.

£200-250 (pair)   **DE**

A Käthe Kruse girl doll, with painted head, blonde human wig, swivel neck, cloth body and original red and white dress, slight rubbing to nose and left cheek.

Kathe Kruse of Germany made a very small range of cloth dolls between 1911 and 1956. Early dolls fetch a premium and can be recognised by having three hand-stitched pate seams on their heads.

c1953

£400-500   **TK**

Left: An American Izannah Walker cloth doll, with brown eyes, distinct mouth, brown painted short hair with wisps at sides, unmarked indicating early specimen.

Izannah Walker dolls are rare and like many early American cloth dolls, highly sought after. Based in Rhode Island, she patented her cloth dolls on November 4th 1873 with designs for oil painted features and stitched hands with separate thumbs. Later versions are marked with the patent date.

17in (43cm) high

£10,000-12,000   **Ber**

Right: A Columbian cloth doll, with hand-painted features, painted blue eyes and curly brown hair, wears ivory cotton dress and blue gingham checked bonnet over lace trimmed bonnet.

22in (56cm) high

£6,000-6,500   **Ber**

A Philadelphia painted cloth doll, with gusseted shoulder and knee joints, well-moulded features and stocking body.

22in (56cm) high

£2,000-2,500   **Ber**

An Alabama 'Indestructible' baby, with signed body.

18.5in (47cm) high

£2,000-2,500   **Ber**

MARY HOYER

- Mary Hoyer of the 'Mary Hoyer Doll Mfg Co.' of Reading Pennsylvania, USA, introduced her first doll in 1939. The first dolls did not bear marks, with composition being used until 1946 when the material changed to hard plastic.
- By the mid 1950s, Hoyer's dolls were being shipped all over the world. Markings read 'The Mary Hoyer Doll' or 'ORIGINAL Mary Hoyer Doll'.
- The production of marked hard plastic dolls ceased in 1960, and unmarked examples were made, but these soon ceased too. Production recommenced in 1990 with the 'Doll with the Magic Wand Collection', based on a story Hoyer had written in 1956.
- Vintage Hoyer dolls, made using original moulds, but not produced by the factory can be found. They are of lower quality, often with poorer quality painting over a red body using paint that flakes easily. They are not marked.
- Condition is paramount – dolls must be clean, undamaged and wear unfaded, original, tagged clothes in excellent condition. Boxed examples command a premium.

A very rare 1930s early Mary Hoyer doll, with twist waist, unmarked.

This was one of her first dolls.

£150-200 DE

A vintage Mary Hoyer doll, with tagged outfit, original shoes and replaced wig.

£280-330 DE

A vintage Mary Hoyer 'Southern Belle' doll.

£350-400 DE

A 1950s Mary Hoyer doll, with rare platinum blonde hair, doll marked and outfit tagged.

£600-700 DE

A vintage Mary Hoyer doll, in hard plastic with tagged dress, marked on back, all original.

£250-300 DE

A 1950s vintage Mary Hoyer doll, with factory-made clothes and hat, original shoes and socks.

14in (35.5cm) high

£250-300 DE

A 1950s Mary Hoyer doll, with a rare hairstyle and red hair, no tag on gown, marked and boxed.

The box adds to the value. Without it, this doll would be worth £450-500.

£600-700 DE

A vintage Mary Hoyer 'Rollerskating' doll.

£300-350 DE

A vintage Mary Hoyer 'School Time' doll.

$420-480 DE

A vintage Mary Hoyer 'At The Beach' doll, all original.

£420-480 DE

A B C D E F G H I J K L M N O P Q R S T U V W XYZ

A 1950s Mary Hoyer boy doll, with tagged shirt and pants, marked and boxed.

£550-600   **DE**

A 1950s vintage Mary Hoyer boy doll, with original clothes.

Boy dolls are hard to find.

£400-450   **DE**

PLASTIC DOLLS

- To be collectable, plastic dolls need to be in perfect condition, with the body and face fresh and clean. The hair must be set in the original style – look for examples with rare styles and colours.
- Damage, such as chewed hands and pulled hair or non-original parts will reduce the value considerably.
- Clothes must be original, clean and unfaded. Boxed plastic dolls will command a premium. These dolls were mass produced, so only those in as perfect condition as possible will be desirable to collectors. Dolls by named mid-20th century makers are the most collected, so look for names such as Barbie, Sasha, Terri Lee and Vogue.

A blonde-haired blue-eyed Sasha doll.

17in (43cm) high

£60-70   **WHP**

A dark-haired brown-eyed Sasha doll, with some original clothing and original Sasha wrist tag.

17in (43cm) high

£150-180   **WHP**

A brunette gingham 103 Sasha doll, in original clothing and box.

15.75in (40cm) high

£160-200   **WHP**

A Sasha boy, with brown hair and eyes, some original clothing and Sasha wrist tag.

17in (43cm) high

£100-150   **WHP**

An early 1950s Vogue Doll Company strung 'Ginny' doll, with tagged dress and later plastic Ginny shoes.

£250-300   **DE**

Two blonde-haired baby boy and girl Sasha dolls.

The girl doll is worth slightly more than the boy.

2.75in (32cm) high

£60-80 each   **WHP**

A Cheryl Vogue Doll Company 'Ginny' doll.

c1953

£350-400   **DE**

An April Vogue Doll Company composition strung 'Ginny' doll, all original.

c1953

£420-480   **DE**

An early rare Vogue 'Toddler Cowboy' doll, with lasso and signed shoe, all original, mint condition.

£300-350   **DE**

Two 1950s Rosebud Kewpie dolls.

Taller 10.25in (15cm) high

£40-50 (price for two)   **OACC**

An Alexander 'Sonja Henie' composition doll, all original.

c1939   *14in (35.5cm) high*

£550-650   **DE**

An Alexander 'Dr. Allen Defoe' composition doll.

This is a rare model.

1937-1939   *15in (38cm) high*

£1,000-1,300   **DE**

A 1930s Arranbee 'Nancy' composition doll, with all original clothes.

12in (30.5cm) high

£180-200   **DE**

A 1940s DeWees Cochran 'Cindy' Latex composition doll, with original clothes.

DeWees Cochran made one of a kind dolls based on photos of children and had a line of three dolls: 'Barbara', 'Cindy', and 'Sue'.

16in (40.6cm) high

£550-600   **DE**

A 1930s Effanbee 'Patsy' composition doll, all original.

14in (35.5cm) high

£180-200   **DE**

A German Schilling Regency young man doll, with kid body, all original.

c1870   *18in (46cm) high*

£750-850   **BEJ**

A British Pierotti wax baby, with inserted hair.

c1890   *7in (17.75in) high*

£600-700   **BEJ**

A German Schilling child, in wax on papier-mâché.

c1880   *11in (28cm) high*

£750-850   **BEJ**

A large German Schilling glazed papier-mâché doll.
c1880 *33in (84cm) high*

£1,500-1,800 **BEJ**

An American Schoenhut girl, with moulded painted brown hair, intaglio blue eyes, closed mouth, blue linen dress and original ivory leather shoes, model no. 102, stamped patented "JAN-17-11".
16.5in (42cm) high

£2,000-2,500 **Ber**

A Schoenhut No.205 character doll, with early carved hair, original clothes and older repro shoes.

These wooden dolls were sold as indestructible. They were inexpensive when new and often show signs of wear.
14in (35.5cm) high

£750-850 **DE**

A German Parian doll, with shoulder head, glass eyes, deep modelling to hair, black hairband and pierced ears.
20in (51cm) high

£750-850 **DE**

A German china doll, signed "Germany", mint condition, with original body and clothes.
1890s

£80-120 **DE**

A German Parian head Scottish boy, all original.
c1880 *12.5in (32cm)*

£300-350 **BEJ**

A Dutch doll, in contemporary costume with hoof feet and blue eyes.
11in (28cm) high

£20-25 **WHP**

A 19thC Dutch doll, with painted wooden face and blue eyes, some original clothing.
12in (30cm) high

£12-15 **WHP**

A wax head doll, with blue glass eyes, some original clothing, possibly French.
c1870 *14in (36cm) high*

£25-35 **WHP**

A composition baby doll, with sleepy blue glass eyes, open mouth with two upper teeth and stuffed cloth body, marked "Germany".
15in (38cm) high

£25-35 **WHP**

A 1920s mechanical black composition baby.

£80-100 **JPA**

A carved marble swaddling baby, in wooden black forest cradle, all original.
c1880 Cradle 5.5in (14cm) high

£200-250 **BEJ**

A doll, made from black lisle stockings, yarn hair, shoe button eyes, felt lips and calico dress.

c1910   15.5in (39.5cm) high

£120-180   **RAA**

A composition soft-bodied St. Trinian's girl, in original outfit.

c1920   16in (40.5cm) high

£250-350   **BEJ**

An early plastic googly-style doll, in original crêpe paper costume.

c1930   7in (18cm) high

£15-20   **WHP**

An early 1940s doll, all original.

£200-250   **DE**

A 1950s American 'Sweet Sue' character doll, all original.

15in (38cm) high

£80-100   **DE**

A group of three Gofun-head Chinese dancers.

c1890

£200-300   **BEJ**

A Japanese costume doll, with silk costume, Gofun-head, boxed, superior quality.

c1920   14in (35cm) high

£300-400   **BEJ**

An American 'Eloise' character doll, all original with label at right hip, designed by Bette Gould.

c1955

£220-280   **DE**

A Japanese Gofun-head man-doll, on stand.

6in (15cm) high

£100-150   **BEJ**

A pair of Edi walking Tyrolean figures with ball and thread mechanism.

c1940   6in (15cm) high

£30-50   **WHP**

A pair of 1920s Chinese plaster dolls, boxed, mint condition.

3in (7.5cm) high

£60-90   **BEJ**

A B C D E F G H I J K L M N O P Q R S T U V W XYZ

A mid-20thC papier-mâché clown.
1940-50

£150-200 BCAC

A pair of 20thC German-made Dutch art
dolls, all original outfits, unmarked.

10.5in (26.5cm) high

£250-300 BEJ

A pair of 20thC Swiss travel dolls.

£55-65 (pair) DE

Dolls' Clothes and Accessories

A 19thC muslin doll's dress,
museum mounted.

£250-300 BCAC

A Victorian doll's dress, in leaf
and flower print fabric, neck
and arms finished with tatting.
1870-80

£450-500 BCAC

A fashion doll's three-piece outfit, to fit a 21in (53cm) doll.
c1890

£150-200 BEJ

A print and calico doll's quilt, mounted.

9.75in (25cm) long

£220-280 BCAC

A late 19thC mounted postage stamp
doll's quilt, in pieced cotton.

6.75in (17cm) long

£220-280 BCAC

A late 19thC doll-sized tied quilt.

18in (46cm) long

£180-220 BCAC

A wooden doll's house bookcase, with wooden "books" on the shelves.

5.25in (13.5cm) high

£50-60 SFel

A Walterhausen doll's house bureau, with drop-down writing slope, good condition.

5.5in (14cm) high

£180-220 SFel

A rare 19thC Walterhausen doll's house desk.

4in (10cm) wide

£220-270 SFel

A doll's house chaise longue.

2.25in (5.5cm) long

£20-25 SFel

A 1930s dolls house painted wooden single bed with bed clothes.

4.25in (11cm) long

£20-30 SFel

A doll's house wooden armchair.

2in (5cm) high

£10-15 SFel

A pair of doll's house padded chairs (one shown).

2.75in (7cm) high

£25-30 SFel

A doll's house painted wooden crib.

2in (5cm) wide

£20-25 SFel

A 1930s doll's house sink.

3.25in (8cm) wide

£8-12 SFel

A 19thC German doll's house carved ivory gazebo, with a Stanhope lens set in the finial.

4.25in (10.5cm) high

£150-180 SFel

A hand-painted miniature vase, decorated with birds, with Japanese marks to base.

2in (5cm) high

£10-15 SFel

A hand-painted miniature vase, decorated with pagodas, with Japanese marks to base.

2in (5cm) high

£20-25   SFel

A miniature vase, with "New York Chinatown" on the side and "Made in Japan" on the base.

2.5in (6.5cm) high

£15-20   SFel

A miniature vase, marked "Made in Japan" on the base.

2.5in (6.5cm) high

£3-5   SFel

A doll's house turned ivory vase, with fabric flowers.

5.5in (14cm) high

£50-75   SFel

A doll's house mounted pheasant display.

1.75in (4.5cm) high

£10-15   SFel

A doll's house gilt-painted plastic jug.

2.5in (6cm) high

£50-80   SFel

A Limoges miniature coffee/tea set, marks to base.

c1910   *3.5in (9cm) wide*

£50-80   SFel

A doll's house carved ivory jardinière.

5in (12.5cm) high

£65-75   SFel

A doll's house oak longcase clock.

7.5in (18.5cm) high

£25-30   SFel

A mid-to late 19thC doll's house six-branch chandelier.

6in (15cm) high

£250-300   SFel

A doll's house globe on stand.

1.5in (4cm) high

£8-10   SFel

A terracotta bust of a man with a felt hat, smoking a pipe.

2.5in (6.5cm) high

£8-10   SFel

A 19thC doll's house frame, with inset engraving of Osbourne House.

3.25in (8cm) wide

£30-35 SFel

A Tri-Ang doll's house clothes mangle.

2.75in (7cm) high

£30-35 SFel

A doll's house sewing machine on stand.
c1900 *2.75in (7cm) high*

£60-100 SFel

A doll's house floor sweeper.

3in (7.5cm) high

£3-5 SFel

A painted tinplate step ladder.

2.25in (5.5cm) high

£8-12 SFel

A "Coronation" Smokers' Set, dated.
1911 *3in (7.5cm) wide*

£35-45 SFel

A Limoges doll's house foot bath, with gilt trim.

0.75in (2cm) long

£10-15 SFel

A doll's house metal coal shovel.

2.75in (5cm) long

£5-10 SFel

A ceramic doll's house bath.

2.25in (5.5cm) long

£10-12 SFel

A doll's house typewriter, painted green.

£30-35 SFel

A 1920s doll's house cloth "cook" doll, holding a knife and fork.

6.5in (16.5cm) high

£30-40 SFel

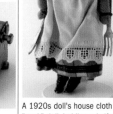

A 1920s doll's house cloth "maid" doll, holding a broom.

6.5in (16.5cm) high

£25-35 SFel

A CLOSER LOOK AT A TEDDY BEAR

Although unmarked, this bear shows many characteristics of early bears.

His snout is long – later bears made after World War II generally have shorter snouts.

His eyes are early 'boot buttons'. Glass was used after the late 1920s, with plastic being used from the 1950s onwards.

He is covered with mohair, later bears used a 'shinier' synthetic plush material.

His jointed arms are long and curved. Bears from the 1950s onwards usually have shorter arms.

An early 20thC teddy bear, the fully-jointed golden body stuffed with wood wool, with felt pads and black button eyes.

13in (33cm) high

£900-1,000   **DN**

Steiff bear, with mohair plush.

Steiff made their first bear in 1902, and their bears grew in popularity from 1905 onwards. They are now highly collectable, with age and condition deciding value. The famous 'button in the ear', which changed in shape and colour over the years, and the overall form, help to date Steiff bears.

c1907   *17in (43cm) high*

£850-1,000   **BEJ**

A 1930s/40s teddy bear, probably by Chiltern, the fully-jointed golden plush body with fabric pads and glass eyes, small patch on left arm.

15.75in (40cm) high

£200-250   **DN**

A Steiff bear, with no button, in mint condition.

c1950   *11in (28cm) high*

£375-450   **BEJ**

An early British bear, maker unknown, with glass eyes.

c1915   *18in (46cm) high*

£400-450   **BEJ**

A 1920s teddy bear, the fully-jointed golden plush body with worn velvet pads and glass eyes, the body containing an inoperative musical movement.

18.5in (47cm) high

£200-250   **DN**

A Steiff 'Zotty' bear, with bells in paw, original paper tag.

Zotty bears were introduced by Steiff in 1951. Their name comes from the German word 'zottig' which means 'shaggy'. These popular bears are characterised by their long shaggy mohair and open mouths.

12in (30.5cm) long

£150-200   **SI**

A Farnell bear, with long jointed arms and legs, humped back, and stitched claws.

J.K. Farnell were an early manufacturer of teddy bears in England. They were founded in 1840 and produced their first soft toys in the late 1890s.

c1912   *11in (28cm) high*

£700-800   **SFel**

A 1930s Merrythought teddy bear, the fully-jointed golden plush body with fabric pads and glass eyes, printed maker's label to right foot.

15in (38cm) high

£250-300   **DN**

A 1930s German Hermann open-mouth teddy bear, with growler.

20in (50cm) high

£400-450   **BEJ**

A British aubergine-coloured bear.

c1940   *15in (38cm) high*

£200-300   **BEJ**

A 1930s British Pedigree teddy, with label.

19in (48cm) high

£200-250   **BEJ**

A 1930s British Chad Valley teddy bear.

20in (50cm) high

£500-600   **BEJ**

A German bear, with round muzzle and growler.

c1950 18in (46cm) high

£400-450   **BEJ**

A British cubbie bear, with short limbs, maker unknown.

c1930   *14in (35.5cm) high*

£300-350   **BEJ**

A British glum bear cub, unmarked.

c1950   *11in (28cm) high*

£350-400   **BEJ**

A British Chiltern 'Hugmee' bear.

One of English company Chiltern's (1908-1967) most popular ranges was the Hugmee bear. It was introduced in 1923 and there were many different designs, including this one with its unusual unshaved muzzle. After the war Hugmees had shorter arms and legs to conserve materials. Chiltern bears typically have upturned paws.

c1930   *16in (40.5cm) high*

£400-600   **BEJ**

A British 'Monty' bear, with original outfit, maker unknown.

c1940

£250-300   **BEJ**

A
B
C
D
E
F
G
H
I
J
K
L
M
N
O
P
Q
R
S
T
U
V
W
XYZ

An early Schuco clockwork somersaulting bear.

The German company Schuco are very well known for their tinplate toys and wind-up mechanisms. They produced ingenious small monkeys and bears containing perfume bottles or with clockwork mechanisms like this one.

4.75in (12cm) high

£300-350　　　　　**SFel**

FIND OUT MORE...

*Puppenhaus Museum, Steineck-Foundation, Steinenvorstadt 1, 4051 Basle, Switzerland. www.puppenhausmuseum.ch.
A collection of over 2,000 teddy bears, mostly dating from before 1950.*

The Bethnal Green Museum of Childhood, London E2.

Pauline Cockrill, 'Teddy Bear Encyclopaedia', published by Dorling Kindersley, 2001.

SOFT TOYS

- Steiff, better known for its teddy bears, is the earliest and most popular manufacturer of soft toys. Steiff's patent dates back to 1892, although the founder Margarete Steiff made small animal-shaped pin cushions as presents for friends before then.

- Although somewhat overshadowed by the success of the teddy bear, ranges grew in the early 20th century. Other makers such as Schuco and the English companies 'Merrythought' and 'Chad Valley' also moved into this market.

- The period from the 1920s – 1950 is the 'golden age' of collectable soft toys. Toys from the 1960s onwards, especially from the Far East, are less well made and were made in vast quantities.

- The material used, the type of eyes and the label all help with identification and dating. Clothed animals often date from during the war, when mohair was scarce and other fabrics were used.

- Cartoon and character toys are popular across markets and tend to fetch high prices. Pre-war Disney related toys are better quality.

- Collectors should look for toys in good, unworn condition. Retention of the label is important. Steiff is the most collectable name, but their small bugs, insects and more unusual 'creatures' have not yet found widespread favour with collectors, so tend to be less valuable.

A 1950s Steiff 'Peggy' penguin.

13in (33cm) high

£150-200　　　　　**DE**

A Steiff mohair lamb, in mint condition.

c1950　　　11in (28cm) high

£250-350　　　　　**BEJ**

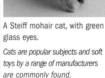

A Steiff mohair cat, with green glass eyes.

Cats are popular subjects and soft toys by a range of manufacturers are commonly found.

6in (15cm) long

£50-75　　　　　**DE**

A Steiff 'Jumbo' mechanical, limited edition number 1927 of 4000.

1988-90

£150-200　　　　　**DE**

A Steiff 'Snobby' grey jointed poodle, with collar and original paper tag, button in ear.

5in (13cm) high

£80-100　　　　　**SI**

A Steiff 'Mimic Tessie' arm puppet, with original paper label and button in ear, some fading to tongue and ruff of mouth.

12.5in (5cm) high

£250-300　　　　　**SI**

A Steiff 'Gaty' hand puppet, with original paper label and button in ear, model number 317.

£100-150　　　　　**SI**

A Steiff rabbit, with original paper tag and button in ear, model number 2965/20.

8in (20cm) long

£200-250　　　　　**SI**

A Steiff 'Snobby' black poodle hand puppet, with original paper label and button in ear.

£150-200   SI

A Steiff 'Gaty' hand puppet, with original paper label and button in ear, model number 317.

£100-150   SI

A Merrythought 'Jerry' mouse, in velveteen, with label.
c1930   *9in (23cm) high*

£200-250   BEJ

A 1930s German mohair clockwork kitten.

6in (14cm) high

£200-250   BEJ

A 1950s British Merrythought piglet, with label.

9in (23cm) high

£80-120   BEJ

A pale blue plush lamb, boxed, unmarked.
c1930

£100-150   BEJ

A 1960s Chad Valley Golly, with felt eyes and plastic suede-effect mouth and teeth, typically dressed in yellow waistcoat, striped trousers and blue jacket, with printed label.

2.5in (62cm) high

£25-35   DN

A British Golly, unmarked.

c1930   *14in (34cm) high*

£50-80   BEJ

A 1970s Wendy Boston Basil Brush.

15.75in (40cm) high

£25-35   WHP

TREEN

- Treen, meaning 'from the tree', is the descriptive term given to a huge range of items produced from turned or, more rarely, carved wood.

- Produced since medieval times until the late 19th century, these small items had a variety of domestic uses in the home or on the farm.

- Although treen was produced for such a long period, early pieces, which are usually very well modelled, are extremely scarce and command very high prices when found. The majority of pieces available to the collector will date from the 19th century.

- Woods used are always tightly grained and robust, often with good colours. Recognising a particular wood can be challenging.

- Treen from the 17th century is characteristically made from yew, fruitwoods, beech, elm and chestnut. The 18th century saw the use of imported boxwood, maple and pine. By the second quarter of the 18th century, exotic hardwoods such as lignum vitae, ebony and mahogany had become popular.

- Well modelled and finely formed pieces will always be popular, but pieces bearing dates, inscriptions and mottoes are also highly sought after.

- Condition is important as all of these pieces were made to be used and can show wear. Damage will seriously affect values unless the piece is rare. Patination is also important.

A 19thC English treen spice turret, in sycamore.

5.75in (14.5cm) high

£70-100   PC

A mid-19thC wooden chemist's jar.

7in (18cm) high

£25-35   OACC

A late19thC pine butter marker, with thistle mould.

4.75in (6.5cm) high

£10-15   PC

A Victorian olivewood string box.

c1860   3.75in (9.5cm) high

£40-60   MB

A 19thC English boxwood glove powdering flask.

6in (15cm) high

£40-50   PC

A mid/late 19thC American turned wood finial, classic shape, original finish.

13.5in (34.5cm) high

£15-20   TWC

A 19thC English nutmeg grater, carved from a coquilla nut.

The coquilla nut comes from the South American Attalea funifera tree. In Europe, these nuts have been carved since the 18thC.

4.5in (11cm) high

£400-500   PC

A butter pot, with excellent patination.

4in (10cm) diam

£30-40   PC

An American boxwood ink sander, with pierced Star of David design.

c1810   2.75in (7cm) high

£80-120   RAA

A 19thC English fruitwood double-cup measure.

From the W.J. Shepherd Collection STO 206. Chemists and apothecaries used these measures to make soda water. They were not designed, as is often thought, as a cup to hold a duck or a hen's egg.

3.75in (9.5cm) high

£50-60   PC

Two 19thC turned wood lamp stands.

7in (18cm) high

£350-450 SI

An 18thC American turned and incised burl mortar and pestle.

Provenance: The Society of the Cincinnati. The collection records state that the mortar and pestle were originally owned by Silas Kellogg, a Revolutionary War officer.

6.5in (17cm) high

£180-220 SI

An American tiger maple mandrill.

A tinsmith used this tool to make sized rings for bails and handles. This wood is highly desirable to collectors.

13.5in (34cm) high

£70-100 RAA

A pair of treen beakers, each clasped by a hand, carved from solid wood, one rim repaired.

7in (18cm) high

£280-320 GorL

A pair of 19thC turned walnut chambersticks.

9.5in (24.5cm) high

£220-280 OACC

FIND OUT MORE...

Edward Pinto, 'Treen and other Wooden Bygones: An Encyclopaedia and Social History', published by Bell, 1983.

Jonathan Levi & Robert Young, 'Treen for the Table: Wooden Objects Relating to Eating and Drinking', published by the Antique Collectors' Club, 1998.

A West Country thatcher's legget, used to pack the thatch tightly.

18in (46cm) long

£40-50 OACC

A pair of 19thC mahogany book markers, each carved in the shape of a book, with gilded 'pages' and applied turned handloo.

10.5in (26.5cm) long

£800-1,000 L&T

A Victorian truncheon, painted with crowned garter motto containing "PP" above initials "PW" and dated 1848, well worn.

17.5in (44.5cm) long

£40-50 W&W

A wooden nutcracker.

Just as corkscrews have become collectable, nutcrackers are also becoming increasingly desirable and sought after. Although they are not as easily classified as corkscrews and many examples do not bear patents or makers' names, the variety available to collectors is huge, with many decorative examples, and they are still comparatively reasonably priced. This is almost certainly an area to watch for in the future.

7in (18cm) high

£60-80 OACC

An 17thC English carved oak bible box, the front with scoop decoration, the moulded base carved with lunettes.

26in (65.5cm)

£600-700 SI

An 18thC Continental painted tortoiseshell box, probably French, rectangular with hinged cover, finely painted with 18thC figures in a landscape of classical architectural ruins.

3.5in (8.5cm) wide

£400-500 SI

An 18thC enamel-on-copper circular box, probably French, the hinged cover finely painted with a boat wharf scene, the base painted with colourful floral sprays.

5in (12.5cm) diam

£200-300 SI

A silver piqué and moss agate oval box.

c1780 *4in (10cm) wide*

£250-300 RdeR

A painted "Wilber Force" anti-slave box, lined with tortoiseshell, showing a slave in chains.

c1759-1833 3in (7.5cm) diam

£400-500 RdeR

One of a pair of George III crossbanded mahogany serpentine-front knife boxes, with herringbone borders, the hinged tops with engraved brass shield-shaped crests on ogee bracket feet, one with original fitted interior.

15in (38cm) high

£1,500-2,000 Clv

A late 18thC/early 19thC south Staffordshire green enamel patch box, the hinged cover painted with a Neo-classical building in a landscape and "Virtue is the greatest ornament of the fair", some damage and lacking the mirror.

1.5in (4cm)

£100-150 DN

Three late 18thC/early 19thC south Staffordshire enamel patch boxes, comprising one in yellow, the cover painted with an allegorical scene depicting an angel upon a cloud protecting a medallion of George III from arrows and "May no weapon form'd against him prosper, God save the King", one in pale blue, the cover painted with a dove and buildings and "As the dove so is my love", the other in royal blue, the cover "A present from Birmingham", all with chips and restoration.

Largest 2.5in (6cm) diam

£550-600 DN

A Victorian tortoiseshell rectangular pin box, plush-lined, lacks name plaque.

3.25in (8cm) wide

£70-100 BAR

A Regency blonde tortoiseshell casket, with dome top, paper-lined interior and on white glass bead feet, lacks thumb piece.

2.5in (6.5cm) wide

£80-120 **BAR**

An early 19thC tortoiseshell round box, with pique work scrolling borders, the cover with a monogram, chips and cracks.

3in (8cm)

£120-180 **DN**

An early 19thC miniature chest, mahogany-veneered with applied reeded edge above two short and three long drawers, fitted brass knob handles, on splay bracket feet.

8.75in (22.5cm) wide

£1,000-1,200 **WW**

An American early 19thC leather-covered dome top box, with bail handle, newspaper-covered interior, tooled leather with star and rotary designs, some loss to leather.

8.75in (22cm)

£80-120 **TWC**

An American Chippendale mahogany tea caddy, moulded hinged lid with cast brass handle over conforming case with moulded base, raised on bracket feet.

12.75in (32cm) wide

£150-200 **SI**

A 19thC black and gilt-decorated steel rectangular strong box, with loop handle and satin-lined interior, finely decorated with figures in landscapes.

8in (20.5cm) wide

£180-220 **LFA**

An American japanned and painted tin document box, probably New York State.

c1830

£800-1,000 **RAA**

An American basswood painters' box for painting materials.
c1830   *15in (38cm) long*

£800-1,000   **RAA**

A German pressed box, depicting Frederick the Great, tortoiseshell lined.
c1830   *3.25in (8cm) wide*

£150-200   **RdeR**

A 19thC inlaid mahogany and satinwood tea caddy, with fitted interior and ivory escutcheon, the brass pull engraved with the initials "L.A.A." and the letter "K", refinished.
12in (30.5cm) wide

£180-220   **SI**

An early Victorian mahogany and brass bound writing box, the hinged lid with a central cartouche, enclosing a fitted interior with leather inset slope above a side drawer and inset brass handles.
19.5in (49.5cm) wide

£200-300   **DN**

A Victorian totoiseshell card case.
c1840   4.25in (10.5cm) long

£100-150   **MB**

A Victorian mother-of-pearl card case.
c1850   4.25in (10.5cm) long

£70-100   **MB**

A 19thC tortoiseshell small canted rectangular box, the hinged cover with silver banding.
2.5in (6.5cm)

£180-220   **DN**

A 19thC tortoiseshell and brass-strung small rectangular box, on turned ivory feet.
3.5in (6.5cm)

£60-80   **DN**

A 19thC mahogany box, the hinged lid enclosing four square section glass decanters and three stoppers with gilt decoration, some damage to decanters.
8.75in (22.5cm) high

£400-500   **DN**

A 19thC French faience box, rectangular with hinged cover, painted floral sprays on a white ground, signed "VP".
5.5in (14cm) wide

£120-180   **SI**

A Victorian crossbanded figured walnut rectangular box, the hinged cover with brass plaque engraved 'Gloves and Handkerchiefs'.

10.5in (26.5cm) high

£150-200   **Clv**

A late Victorian tortoiseshell and silver-mounted cigarette box, the hinged cover with a central monogram and shaped panels at the corners, Birmingham hallmarks for "A. & J. Zimmerman".

1900   *7.5in (19cm) wide*

£350-400   **DN**

A silver cigar box, with engine-turned decoration and pull out ashtray, on ball feet, London hallmarks.

The drawer is an extremely rare feature, making this box more valuable than other silver cigar/cigarette boxes.

1920   *6in (15cm) wide*

£650-750   **Tag**

Two late 19thC French enamelled brass rectangular boxes, the larger with a light blue ground, the cover painted with amorous couple, both with raised "jewelled" decoration.

9.5in (24cm)

£1,300-1,800   **SI**

An early 20thC mahogany liqueur case, the fall front rectangular box with a mirrored lid, the case fitted to contain two cut glass decanters, a silver-plated shaker, a bitters bottle and six cut glass cordials.

14.25in (36.5cm) wide

£400-450   **SI**

A late Victorian silver gilt small circular box, the cover design by William Burges and made by Carl Krall, with plain surface except for the hinged cover engraved with "A Pelican in Piety" against a hatched silver ground, flanked by arched panels, four of which contain Lombardic script, with a "CK" punch to the base for the maker, "Krall" for the company and with London hallmarks.

In 'William Burges and the High Victorian Dream' by J. Mordaunt Crook, John Murry (publishers) Ltd, London 1981, illustration 209 we see the cover of a wafer box by Burges and part of a travelling communion set, probably made by Barkentin & Krall. The image on that cover is identical to this piece and is incidentally made by Carl Krall of that same company. Even though this piece was made 11 years after the death of Burges, the image on the cover is still considered to be by Burges.

1892

£1,000-1,500   **DN**

A Piero Fornasetti wooden box, with alphabet motif.

c1953   *11.75in (30cm) long*

£180-220   **FM**

A French shagreen cigar box, with ivory trim to the lid.

c1940   *8in wide*

£850-950   **Tag**

An 18thC rectangular tea chest on bun feet, with later gilt and black lacquer decoration, the oak interior with divisions, a secret drawer to one side containing an early Victorian silver engraved caddy spoon, the bowl with a split.

10in (25.5cm)

£200-250   **WW**

A late 18thC rectangular tea chest, with canted corners, veneered in burr-yew within chain circlets, feather-banded inlaid stringing and fluting, the interior with two lidded compartments.

10.5in (26.75cm)

£1,200-1,800   **WW**

A George III mahogany fan inlaid double tea caddy.

c1800   *7.5in (19cm) wide*

£200-250   **MB**

A George III oval tea caddy, veneered in harewood with marquetry inlay of crossed bow and arrow within a floral garland, an open escutcheon, the hinged cover with a flowerhead panel.

4.5in (11.5cm) high

£600-1,000   **WW**

A Regency cube shape tea caddy, veneered in satinwood with oval fan inlay and chequer stringing, the interior with a lid.

4.75in (12cm)

£250-300   **WW**

A Regency cube tea caddy, veneered in sycamore with painted penwork panels of Neo-classical figures and inlaid stringing.

5in (12.5cm) wide

£180-220   **WW**

A Victorian single canister rosewood tea caddy, with original bowl.

c1830   *7.25in (18.5cm) wide*

£150-200   **MB**

A 19thC ebony tea caddy, the sarcophagus shape mounted with ivory reel and bead bands and inlaid with flowers.

9.5in (24cm) wide

£120-180   **Chef**

A Victorian oval tea caddy, with a carved woven effect ivory body, an oval vacant cartouche with beaded edge, plated mounts and hinged cover with a ribbed bud finial, maker's mark Henry Wilkinson of Sheffield.

5.75in (14.5cm)

£550-650   **WW**

A Victorian tortoiseshell and mother-of-pearl tea caddy, of canted rectangular form, on bun feet.

4.25in (11cm) wide

£500-600   **DN**

A late Victorian oak tea chest, with plated metal mounts, handle and engraved hinged cover, with two lidded compartments, on brass baluster-turned feet.

8.5in (21.5cm)

£200-250   **WW**

A 19thC French novelty ebonized tea chest, no mixing bowl.

11.5in (29cm)

£180-220   **WW**

- The Black Forest is a mountainous region of Bavaria, Germany, and has been a popular holiday destination for centuries. Most Black Forest carvings date from the mid 19th century onwards and were bought as holiday souvenirs.
- Not all Black Forest items come from the eponymous Bavarian region. The title is applied to a style, with items being produced in Germany and Switzerland.
- As well as novelty items, cuckoo clocks are common, having been produced since the mid 18th century, as are larger items such as hall chairs and umbrella stands.
- Bears are the most common subjects, with dogs, birds, stags and other animals typical of the areas also being produced. Carvings are still being made, so collectors should look out for signs of age as modern examples only have a decorative value. Larger or functional pieces are very desirable.

A Swiss Black Forest bear, with moveable limbs.

c1860   8.75in (22cm) high

£100-150   **SS**

A Swiss Black Forest bear match holder.

c1860   5.5in (14cm) high

£100-200   **SS**

A late 19thC Black Forest carved wood smoker's compendium, modelled as a bear standing on its back legs, with a hinged head, the right arm raised supporting a leaf and branch quatreform top, with a brass ashtray, two lidded compartments, each with a bear and a third to the back.

34in (86.5cm) high

£2,600-3,000   **WW**

A Black Forest carved wood inkwell, modelled as a bear, feeding a cub from a bottle, the hinged head fitted with a glass well.

6.75in (17cm) high

£450-550   **WW**

A Black Forest carved wood inkwell, modelled as a sitting bear, with a hinged head fitted with a cut glass inkwell.

6.5in (16.5cm) high

£400-500   **WW**

A Black Forest carved wood model of a bear, and another, cracked.

13in (33cm) long

£620-680   **WW**

A Black Forest carved wood model of a bear, the base inscribed "St Moritz".

5.75in (14.5cm) high

£70-100   **WW**

A Black Forest carved wood model of a bear, with a thermometer.

5.25in (13.5cm) high

£70-100   **WW**

A Black Forest carved wood model of a bear, together with two similar models.

5.5in (14in) long

£70-100 | **WW**

A Black Forest carved wood model of a bear, seated behind a hollowed tree trunk, fitted with a brass liner.

5.5in (14cm) high

£80-120 | **WW**

A Swiss Black Forest basket box.

c1860   *7.5in (19cm) wide*

£100-200 | **SS**

A 19thC Black Forest carved limewood figure group, depicting an eagle on a rocky outcrop, wings outstretched and holding its prey, a young deer.

17.25in (44cm) high

£800-1,000 | **L&T**

A Swiss Black Forest inkwell, carved as birds and a nest on a leaf with acorns.

c1860   *11.5in (29cm) wide*

£200-260 | **SS**

A Swiss Black Forest pot, carved as a fox beside a tree stump.

c1860   *3in (8cm) high*

£100-150 | **SS**

A Black Forest clock, carved with two figures of St Bernard dogs on a base of entwined branches.

c1860   *23in (58cm) high*

£7,500-8,500 | **SS**

A pair of Black Forest vases, each carved with figures of stags and deer standing under a tree.

c1860   *18.5in (47cm) high*

£4,000-4,600 | **SS**

TUNBRIDGEWARE

■ The majority of Tunbridgeware is produced using a technique, known as 'stickwork', of cutting slim rods of differently coloured wood into thin slices. These small 'tiles' are then applied to the surface of objects in an intricate mosaic pattern. Geometric borders surround floral, landscape or further geometric designs.

■ Early pieces produced before the 19th century used traditional marquetry techniques, but 'stickwork' was faster and less expensive and dominated from the 1820s onwards.

■ The most common objects found are boxes, picture frames, rulers and other small domestic objects. Larger pieces such as sewing or work tables are scarce and fetch high prices when offered for sale.

■ It was made in and around the English spa town of Tunbridge Wells, often as souvenirs for visiting tourists.

■ Although the technique dates back to the 17th century, most of the Tunbridgeware available to collectors dates from the mid- to late 19th century until around 1930.

■ Tunbridgeware is difficult to repair so condition is important. Ensure tiles are not missing or that the surface is not warped or lifting. Wood colours were exploited by the makers, so look for good contrast and pleasing colours. Original labels or pieces marked with a maker's name will command a premium.

■ Due to its complexity, it is not often faked, but German strapwork and Sorrento ware resemble Tunbridgeware and are often mistaken for it.

A Victorian inlaid rosewood Tunbridgeware box.
c1870   3.75in (9.5cm) wide

£70-90　　　　**MB**

A Victorian rectangular Tunbridgeware box, the hinged cover with a panel of flowers.
4.5in (11cm) wide

£60-70　　　　**LFA**

An inlaid rosewood Tunbridgeware needle box.
c1870   2.5in (62cm) wide

£75-85　　　　**MB**

A Victorian square Tunbridgeware box, the cover with a spray of flowers and leaves.
2.75in (7cm) wide

£50-60　　　　**LFA**

A 19thC rectangular walnut and Tunbridgeware tea caddy, with flared base, the domed hinged lid enclosing two lidded compartments, on turned disc feet.
9.5in (24cm) wide

£120-180　　　　**L&T**

A 19thC rosewood Tunbridgeware box, the cover with unusual tessera bird in a tree panel within Vandyke crossbanding.
2.5in (6.5cm) wide

£250-350　　　　**B**

A square Tunbridgeware box, with geometric parquetry top.
3in (7.5cm)

£80-120　　　　**GorL**

A small Victorian rectangular Tunbridgeware sewing box, the sliding cover with a pin cushion.
2in (7cm) wide

£60-70　　　　**LFA**

A 19thC rosewood Tunbridgeware box, with perspective cube top.
2.5in (6.5cm) wide

£45-55　　　　**B**

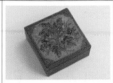

A 19thC rosewood Tunbridgeware stamp box, printed Edward VII Penny Red.
1.75in (4.5cm) wide

£90-100　　　　**B**

A 19thC oak Tunbridgeware stamp box, with mark of Royal Tunbridge Wells Ware, the top inlaid the with word 'Postage'.
3.5in (9cm) wide

£200-250　　　　**B**

A 19thC Tunbridgeware stamp box, depicting the head of the young Queen Victoria.
1.5in (4cm) wide

£200-250　　　　**B**

A 19thC Tunbridgeware rouge box, with tessera eight-pointed star.
1.75in (4.5cm) diam

£55-65　　　　**B**

A 19thC Tunbridgeware pomade pot, with eight-pointed star.
1.75in (4.5cm) diam

£55-65　　　　**B**

A 19thC cylindrical Tunbridgeware counter box, the threaded cover with eight-pointed star.
1.25in (3cm) diam

£55-65 B

A 19thC cylindrical Tunbridgeware counter box, the threaded cover with eight-pointed star and Vandyke crossbanding.
1.25in (3cm) diam

£60-70 B

A Victorian round Tunbridgeware box.

£30-40 LFA

A Victorian small, round Tunbridgeware box.

£180-220 LFA

An inlaid rosewood stickware Tunbridgeware sovereign box.
c1840 1.25in (3.2cm) diam

£40-60 MB

Two 19thC Tunbridgeware napkin rings.

£65-75 B

Left: A 19thC Tunbridgeware clothes brush, with perspective cube back.
6.5in (16.5cm) long

£45-55 B

Centre: A 19thC Tunbridgeware clothes brush, the back with perspective cube and the handle with tessera flowers.
9.5in (24cm) long

£65-75 B

Right: A 19thC Tunbridgeware clothes brush, with tessera floral back.
6.5in (16.5cm) long

£35-45 B

A Victorian Tunbridgeware wedge-shaped menu holder.

£30-40 LFA

A 19thC Tunbridgeware cribbage board, with half-square mosaic, restored condition.
9in (23cm) wide

£150-200 B

A 19thC rosewood Tunbridgeware paper knife, with tessera mosaic handle.

£50-70 B

Left: A 19thC rosewood Tunbridgeware paper knife, with tessera mosaic handle and blond wood blade.
8in (20cm) long

£50-60 B

Right: A 19thC rosewood Tunbridgeware paper knife, with tessera mosaic handle, with damage.
9.5in (24cm) long

£55-65 B

A 19thC Tunbridgeware ebonised photograph frame, with tessera banding.
6.5in (16.5cm) wide

£180-220 B

FIND OUT MORE...

Brian Austen, 'Tunbridgeware and Related European Decorative Woodwares', Published by Trans-Atlantic Publications, 1989.

Tunbridge Wells Museum, Civic Centre, Mount Pleasant, Royal Tunbridge Wells, Kent TN1 1JN, England.
www.tunbridgewells.gov.uk/museum/

MAUCHLINEWARE

- Mauchlineware is a form of souvenir ware including boxes and small domestic objects, such as sewing accessories. It would have been bought by 19th century tourists travelling around Scotland as a functional momento of their visit.

- It is usually made from the light wood of the sycamore and is characterised by a small 'decal' showing a local scene which is commonly applied as a transfer. Otherwise, surfaces are largely plain. Early pieces were hand painted or hand decorated with penwork, but these are comparatively scarce and fetch higher prices.

- It takes its name from the small Scottish town of Mauchline in Ayrshire, where it was produced primarily by W.A. Smith from the 1820s onwards. From the 1860s, it was also made in Lanark at the 'Caledonian Box Works' of Archibald Brown.

- Box production ceased in 1933, when the factory suffered a serious fire. Despite this, the range is highly diverse, so collectors may consider collecting a type, such as boxes or sewing accessories.

- The transfer scene and the entire piece are covered with layers of varnish meaning that they are usually intact, but collectors should beware scratched and dented pieces as these reduce the value considerably.

A Mauchlineware box, with a print of Gardens, Bournemouth.

4.25in (10.5cm) wide

£50-70   OACC

A Mauchlineware box, with a print of Lyndhurst.

5in (13cm) wide

£50-70   OACC

A Mauchlineware box, with a print of a Welsh market scene.

6.75in (17cm) wide

£80-120   OACC

A Mauchlineware glove box, with a print of Osbourne House in centre and Ventnor from the east and west on either side, catch broken but repairable.

Osborne House, on the Isle of Wight, was bought in 1845 by the Royal Family, but was not found to be large enough. Prince Albert embarked upon rebuilding the house in the style of an Italian villa and, upon its completion in 1851, it had grown enormously. Queen Victoria and Prince Albert enjoyed staying there greatly as it provided a fine escape from royal and public life, and Victoria spent much of her time there after Albert died. Victoria died there herself in January 1901.

9.75in (25cm) wide

£80-100   OACC

A Mauchlineware turned wood money box, with a print of Ravenscraig Castle, Dysart, with unusual turret design.

c1890   3.25in (8cm) high

£30-40   PC

A Mauchlineware money box, with a print of University College, Oxford.

3.25in (8cm)

£40-60   OACC

A circular Mauchlineware box, of George Square, Glasgow.

£40-50　　　　　　**OACC**

A circular Mauchlineware box, with a print of Windsor Castle.

1.25in (3cm) diam

£50-60　　　　　　**OACC**

A late 19thC Mauchlineware root snuff mull.

2.25in (5.5cm) wide

£450-550　　　　　　**PC**

A late 19thC Mauchlineware skittle, with a print of Sandown Bay, Isle of Wight.

3.25in (8cm) high

£45-55　　　　　　**PC**

Two Mauchlinware napkin rings, with a print of St Leonard's Church, Seaford, Lyndhurst.

£15-18 each　　　　　　**OACC**

A Mauchlineware sycamore napkin ring, with a print of Wells Cathedral.

1880　　　2in (5cm) diam

£20-25　　　　　　**MB**

A Mauchlineware egg timer, with a print of The Beach, Marblethorpe.

3.25in (8cm) high

£50-70　　　　　　**OACC**

A CLOSER LOOK AT A FERNWARE BOX

Ferns were very popular during the late 19th century, where their leaf shape was used as a decorative motif on ceramics, glass, wood, metal and in architecture. Fernware is a form of Mauchlineware and was produced from around 1870.

There were several techniques for achieving this subtle effect. These included attaching fern leaves to the item and using them as a 'stencil', whilst dye was spattered over the piece. Some leaves were then removed and the piece was spattered with dye again. This would happen several times before the final leaf was removed, leaving the lightest colour and almost an 'three dimensional' effect to the whole piece.

A late Victorian fernware vesta case.

c1890　　　1.25in (3cm) diam

£45-55　　　　　　**OACC**

FIND OUT MORE...

John Baker, Mauchline Ware and associated Scottish souvenir ware, Shire Books, Shire Album 140, 1985.

Princess Ira von Furstenberg, Tartanware: souvenirs from Scotland, Pavilion Books, 1996.

David Trachtenberg & Thomas Keith, The Collector's Guide to Mauchline Ware, Antique Collectors' Club, forthcoming.

Edward & Eva Pinto, Tunbridge and Scottish Souvenir Woodware, G.Bell & Sons, 1970.

Other methods used paper printed with a fern pattern or transfers. Joins are usually easy to spot on the paper-covered objects.

Fernware has become increasingly popular amongst collectors recently with the size of the object, unusual shapes and condition being primary factors for collectors to consider when building a collection.

A late Victorian fernware box.

c1890

3.5in (9cm) diam

£50-70　　　　　　**OACC**

TRIBAL ART

- Tribal art refers to the work of the Peoples of Africa, Oceania, South East Asia and the Americas. These traditional items were made for ceremonial and functional purposes, rather than as aesthetic objects. Every piece of tribal art, whether a mask, figure, currency, piece of jewellery or textile is a one-off.

- The climate and natural environment mean that a lot of very old primitive art has been destroyed. However, some of the most exquisite examples date from the late 19th and early 20th centuries.

- Generally speaking, tribal art is extremely difficult to date. Documented provenance with an object can help to ascertain an approximate age, and this will also add to the value. The pieces are often heavily patinated, making them look very old, but wear and usage will also have this effect. This does not affect the desirability. Tribal art is valued for its visual impact, cultural diversity and artistic expression.

- Unfortunately this area has been marred by an abundance of fakes. The surge in interest in tribal art in recent years has meant a huge increase in the number of imitations. However, the heavy patination and wear created by age and continued use is not easily replicated and a trained eye will be able to tell the difference. It is always advisable to visit a reputable dealer or auction house when buying tribal art.

An early 20thC Ingulia pig mask, with good patination.

12.25in (31cm) wide

£800-1,000   **GR**

An African Tshokwe mask, with oval face and coffee bean eyes, with scarification marks on cheeks, chin and forehead.

7.5in (19cm) high

£800-1,200   **GR**

A late 19th/early 20thC Ntoma Bambara mask, with detailed decoration covered by heavy patination.

This mask would originally have been applied with cowrie shells and iron rings.

12.5in (32cm) high

£2,800-3,200   **GR**

A Haya mask, from Tanzania, Africa.

10in (26cm) high

£450-500   **GR**

A Dan mask, with stylized protruding jaw, from the Ivory Coast, West Africa.

10in (26cm) high

£3,100-3,600   **GR**

An early 20thC Baule Kple Kple mask, of the Goli dance.

This is one of the most abstracted of African masks.

15.25in (39cm) high

£5,000-5,500   **GR**

A Chiwara headdress, with heavy patination, from the Bambara tribe, Mali.

15.75in (40cm) high

£1,500-2,000   **GR**

A Baule tribe mask, with a well-formed naturalistic human face, a delicate pouting mouth, finely drawn T-shaped nose and eyebrows, almond-slit eyes delineated with white, the simple cross-hatched hair balances a white crescent moon, from the West Coast of Africa.

17.75in (45cm) high

£2,800-3,200   **GR**

An Agbogho Mmwo or white maiden mask, from the Igbo tribe, Central Nigeria.

This mask defines female beauty and was used in masquerades and festivals. It is rare to find these masks in such perfect condition, including original fringe decoration.

28.75in (73cm) high

£3,500-4,000   **GR**

A very old Karli mask, showing Newan religious dualism between Hindu and Buddhist iconography.

15.75in (40cm) high

£650-750 GR

An Igorots Shaman's headdress, with monkey and snake skulls, possibly from the Longat or Kankani tribes in Northern Luzon, Phillippines.

11.5in (29cm) wide

£650-750 GR

An Indian tribal mask, depicting Ganesh, the Hindu elephant God.

31.5in (80cm) long

£600-700 GR

A 19thC tribal mask, depicting Ganesh, from Maharashtra district, India.

29.5in (75cm) long

£850-950 GR

An early 20thC Himalayan carved wood mask, with signs of kaolin, pitch and applied animal hair.

17in (43cm) high

£800-1,200 GR

A Sub-Himalayan mask, strong form with bold shapes and good patination.

11in (28cm) high

£650-750 GR

A Maprik Yam mask, in highly abstracted form, from Papua New Guinea.

Yam masks from the Maprik area of Papua New Guinea are used for ceremonial purposes during the yam harvest festival. The yams, which can grow up to 12ft (366cm) long, are decorated with these masks as well as flowers, fruit and leaves. The yams represent clan ancestor's spirits, and are believed to be present as seeing and hearing human beings. They are exchanged with traditional exchange partners. The partner with the biggest yam is said to have the most power.

18.5in (47cm) high

£300-400 GR

A Himalayan mask, with red and white bands.

13in (33cm) high

£800-1,200 GR

An Indonesian mask, depicting a Mahabharata or Rama character.

7.75in (20cm) high

£200-250 GR

A fine Kalimantan mask, with original paintwork and fibre hair, Borneo.

14in (36cm) high

£2,800-3,200 GR

A Bahay or Modang Dayak tribe pig mask, used in planting ceremonies, from north east Kalimantan, Borneo.

10.25in (26cm) high

£2,800-3,200 GR

A Bahay or Modang Dayak tribe pig mask, used in planting ceremonies, north east Kalimantan, Borneo.

13.75 (35cm) high

£2,800-3,200 GR

An Ikenga carving of a warrior, from eastern of Nigeria.

13in (33cm) high

£300-400 **GR**

A Bon-po carving, possibly from the Himalayas or Nepal.

20in (51cm) high

£1,000-1,500 **GR**

An excavated bronze of a warrior, holding a shield, India.

6.75in (17cm) high

£1,000-1,200 **GR**

A Shiva deity bronze votive, India.

2.75in (7cm) high

£40-50 **GR**

A 17thC primitive bronze, depicting a cow, from Kanataka, India.

5.75in (14.5cm) high

£480-520 **GR**

A Khond tribe votive bronze, from India.

2in (5cm) high

£40-50 **GR**

A Khond tribe votive bronze, from India.

2.75in (7cm) high

£50-60 **GR**

A Khond tribe votive bronze, from India.

2in (5cm) high

£40-50 **GR**

A Khond tribe votive bronze, from India.

2.25in (6cm) high

£40-50 **GR**

A Khond tribe votive bronze, from India.

2.5in (6.5cm) high

£80-100 **GR**

A tribal bronze figure, depicting a three-headed shiva, from Sub-Himalayas, India.

7.5in (19cm) high

£400-500 **GR**

A pair of Ifugao rice gods, both male and female deities, the male with one hand to his chin, the female supporting her head with both hands, from the Philippines.

9in (23cm) high

£400-500 pair **GR**

An excavated iron torque, from Chad, West Africa.

11in (28cm) high

£700-800 | **GR**

A m'bun status currency, in throwing knife form, from Gabon, Africa.

17in (43cm) high

£750-850 | **GR**

Three metal pendants, in female image, from Taraba, Africa.

£150-200 each | **GR**

Two Katanga crosses, from Africa.

9in (23cm) wide

£150-200 each | **GR**

A fine Chamba tribe rattle, with two small and one large bell, from Nigeria.

9.5in (24cm) high

£250-300 | **GR**

A Chamba rattle, with finely wrought detailing, from Nigeria.

22in (56cm) wide

£650-700 | **GR**

A Senufo tribe pulley, from West Africa.

6.5in (16.5cm) high

£450-500 | **GR**

A carved and painted wooden spoon, with a figure of a woman with elongated body, short strong legs, possibly Senufo tribe, from the Ivory Coast, West Africa.

18.5in (47cm) long

£300-350 | **GR**

Three ceremonial spoons, from Timor.

Tallest 11.75in (30cm) long

£650-700 | **GR**

A beautifully formed and eroded ceremonial ladder, from west Timor.

64.5in (164cm) high

£1,500-2,000 | **GR**

An rare early 20thC iron lamp, decorated with birds and with heavy patination, from Yoruba, Africa.

£1,500-2,000 | **GR**

A tribal cooking pot, from Africa.

6in (15cm) high

£150-200 | **GR**

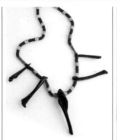

A Naga tribe necklace, made with glass beads and monkey bones, from the North Indian/Burmese border.
11.75in (30cm) diam

£150-200 GR

A Naga tribe necklace, made with conch shells.
11.75in (30cm) diam

£200-250 GR

A Naga tribe necklace, from the North Indian/Burmese border.
25in (64cm) long

£150-200 GR

A Naga tribe conch bead necklace, from Burma.
24.75in (63cm) diam

£800-850 GR

An excavated Naga tribe bronze bracelet.
3.5in (9cm) diam

£80-120 GR

An African ivory bracelet.
4in (10cm) diam

£350-400 GR

An ivory bracelet, from Yoruba, West Africa.
5in (13cm) wide

£200-250 GR

Two ivory rings, from South Sudan.
Largest 2in (5cm) long

L £90-120, R £180-220 GR

Three Ethiopian pendants.
Largest 3.75in (9.5cm) long

£80-120 each GR

A Miris tribe necklace, with blue and orange beads, from Arunachal Pradesh, India.
17.25in (44cm) diam

£250-300 GR

A necklace, from Misoram, India.
13.25in (34cm) diam

£50-60 GR

A brass tribal necklace.
16.5in (42cm) long

£850-900 GR

An early 20thC abstract raffia panel.

These pieces were used as status currency by the chiefs and nobles of the Shoowa tribe in the Kuba Kingdom of Zaire.

£500-550   **GR**

An early 20thC abstract raffia panel.

22.5in (57cm) high

£550-600   **GR**

An early 20thC abstract raffia panel.

22.5in (57cm) high

£650-700   **GR**

An early 20thC abstract raffia panel.

21.25in (54cm) high

£550-600   **GR**

An early 20thC abstract raffia panel.

24.5in (62cm) high

£600-650   **GR**

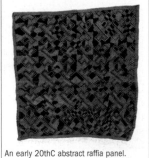

An early 20thC abstract raffia panel.

24in (61cm) high

£550-600   **GR**

An early 20thC abstract raffia panel.

31.5in (80cm) high

£550-600   **GR**

A red died ntshak, from the Bushong tribe in the Kuba Kingdom of Zaire.

Ntshak are dance skirts or ceremonial wraps worn by members of high status within the tribe.

36.25in (92cm) high

£550-600   **GR**

An early 20thC Nergede Kuba tribe panel, with appliquéd raffia status cloth.

38in (97cm) high

£550-600   **GR**

An early 20thC abstract raffia panel.

23.25in (59cm) high

£600-650   **GR**

POCKET WATCHES

- The most common types of pocket watch are open-faced watches, followed by 'hunters' and 'half-hunters'. Movements differ depending on the period. During the 19th century, the two most popular mechanisms were the cylinder escapement and the more efficient lever escapement, which dominated from the 1830s.

- By the 1870s an in-built winding mechanism was developed which meant that watches need not be wound with a key, as before.

- Collectors should ensure that the movement inside the watch matches the case and face. Movements are often signed and if they do not match, the value will be reduced. Pocket watches by noted manufacturers will fetch higher prices.

- Pocket watches with fine decoration, chronographs or extra dials showing moon phases, and calendars are more desirable. 14 carat gold pocket watches are American in origin.

- Lady's versions of pocket watches are smaller in overall size. Usually more ornately decorated than gentlemen's versions, they are often found hanging from a ribbon or short chain, mounted upside down so that they could be read easily when worn.

- The silver or gold chain that often accompanies a gentleman's pocket watch is known as an 'Albert' and they generally have an intrinsic value in themselves. The other end could hold useful accessories such as watch keys and pencils.

A 14K white gold open-faced keyless gentleman's pocket watch, by Hamilton, enamel dial with Roman numeral and seconds subsidiary, the 19-jewel movement no. 3051462
1925

£200-300   **FRE**

An 18ct gold slim Gubelin pocket watch, with Swiss 17-jewel movement, brushed silver dial with raised baton hands and numerals, case, dial and movement signed and a chain.
c1950   1.5in (4cm) diam

£200-250   **DN**

A 14K gold hunter keyless pocket watch, by Waltham, the white enamel dial with Roman numerals and seconds subsidiary, the movement no. 8733290, with gold cuvette, the case engine-turned with milled bezel, incorporating an initialled cartouche.

£200-300   **FRE**

A 19thC Swiss 18ct gold slim pocket watch, stamped 'B.M. - J.I.', six jewel cylinder movement with gold balance, unusual engine-turned three piece hinged case with offset bezel and dial, silvered and engine-turned dial with black Roman numerals.
1850

£200-300   **DN**

A 14K gold open-faced keyless pocket watch, the dial signed "Tavannes Watch Co." with Arabic numerals and seconds subsidiary, the 15-jewel movement no. 251956, with base metal cuvette, the case with engine-turned decoration.

£200-300   **FRE**

A gold and enamel lady's open-faced fob watch, with cylinder escapement.

£120-180   **FRE**

A 14K gold open-faced octagonal pocket watch, by Waltham, the white enamel dial with Arabic numerals, one hand missing.

£100-150   **FRE**

WALTHAM WATCH COMPANY

- The 'Waltham Watch Company' started as the 'Warren Mfg Co.' set up by Edward Howard, David Davis and Aaron Dennison in 1851. A factory was built at Waltham, Massachusetts in 1853, and the company name changed many times during the 1850s.

- After 1859, the name was changed finally to 'The American Waltham Watch Company' with pocket watches bearing the name 'Waltham' shortly afterwards.

- Many millions of inexpensive watches were produced by Waltham, who are credited with being the first mass-producer of watches in America.

- The company closed in 1957. Collectors particularly look out for early 'Waltham' pocket watches bearing the names of the three original founders or 'Appleton, Tracey & Co.' used in the late 1850s. All pocket watches are marked with a serial number which accurately dates them.

A lady's 18ct gold and grey guilloche enamel fob watch, textured gold effect dial with Arabic numerals, Swiss 17-jewel nickel bar movement with internal winding ratchet, and a small rose diamond seven stone engraved ribbon-bow fob.

c1920

£180-220 | **DN**

A 14K gold hunter keyless pocket watch, by Waltham, the white enamel dial with Roman numerals and seconds subsidiary, the three-quarter plate movement no. 4978010, the gold cuvette signed and dated, in bright-cut engraved case.

1898

£120-180 | **FRE**

A 14K gold hunter keyless pocket watch, by Waltham, the white enamel dial with Roman and Arabic numerals and seconds subsidiary, the movement no. 1498563, with gold cuvette, engine-turned oration, missing glass.

£150-200 | **FRE**

A French silver pair cased pocket watch, with Danish hallmarks, the movement signed "Lepine à Paris", lacking outer case.

£250-350 | **FRE**

An 18K gold and black enamel lady's fob watch, with white enamel dial, the case with engine-turned decoration and black enamel garter cartouche, one hand loose, glass badly cracked.

£100-150 | **FRE**

A Swiss gold and enamel lady's fob watch, by L. Muonier, the white enamel dial with Roman and Arabic numerals, the Geneva bar escapement with mono-metallic balance, the back of the case ornately decorated with coloured enamel with a portrait of a lady.

£200-300 | **FRE**

A gold and enamel lady's fob watch, by LeRoy à Paris, with signed gold cuvette, the enamel worn.

£200-300 | **FRE**

A silver and enamel Art Deco lady's pendant fob watch, the white enamel dial with Roman numerals, triangular fan-shaped form, broken loop.

c1930

£80-120 | **FRE**

A 14K gold pendant lady's fob watch, by G. Eckhardt, with gold lapel brooch, with 10-jewel movement.

£130-180 | **FRE**

A 10K gold and diamond set fob locket, with lion mask decoration.

£250-300 | **FRE**

A Victorian silver and agate-inset gentleman's Albert chain, fitted with a pencil holder.

£120-180 | **FRE**

WRIST WATCHES

■ Watches were first worn on the wrist in the early 20th century. Early wristwatches look like small pocket watches with thick wire at the top and bottom to hold the strap. They are always circular in shape and have unsigned silvered or enamel dials and chrome, silver or gold cases. Despite their early date, they are generally of comparatively low value.

■ It was not until the First World War that wristwatches began to become common when they were issued to servicemen. The style quickly took off and by the 1930s, wristwatches outnumbered pocket watches many times over.

■ Watches from the 1920s and 1930s took a range of styles, with square, rectangular and octagonal case shapes being popular. Many matched the Art Deco stylings of the period. Automatic watches were developed around 1926 and became more reliable during the 1930s.

■ The 1940s saw watch styles matching jewellery designs of the period. During the war, many noted manufacturers made standard issue watches for the armed forces which are characterised by robust steel construction, black dials and luminous numerals.

■ The 1950s saw a move towards futuristic styling, with technical innovations including the first electric battery powered watch being developed by Hamilton Watch Co in 1957.

■ Maker, complexity, materials and model can all add to the value, with sophisticated watches by renowned makers being the most desirable and valuable. Names to look for include Patek Philippe, Rolex, Cartier, Jaeger le Coultre and Audemars Piguet. Styling is also important and adds to desirability.

■ Wristwatches with extra features such as calendars, chronographs and moon phases are highly sought after.

■ Although quartz had been used for timepieces from the 1920s, it was not until the early 1970s that it was used for wristwatches.

A gentleman's 14ct gold wristwatch, by Hamilton, the dial with seconds subsidiary, 19-jewel movement No. M39777, no winder.

£200-250   **FRE**

A gentleman's 14ct gold automatic wristwatch, by Hamilton, the dial with centre seconds sweep hands, and calendar aperture, no winder.

£350-450   **FRE**

A gentleman's 14ct gold Masterpiece wristwatch, by Hamilton, the dial with seconds subsidiary, the back inscribed and dated.
1971

£200-250   **FRE**

A lady's steel and gilt Cartier, Panthere wristwatch, on conforming bracelet, with original box,

£2,000-3,000   **DN**

A gentleman's 14ct gold Thin-O-Matic Masterpiece wristwatch, by Hamilton, the dial with centre seconds sweep hand, the back of the case with presentation inscription and dated, lacks strap.

£120-180   **FRE**

A gentleman's 14ct white gold wristwatch, by Hamilton, the chapter ring with Roman numerals, 19-jewel movement no. 2901879.

£750-850   **FRE**

A lady's 14ct gold dress watch, by Hamilton, with 17-jewel movement.

£45-55   **FRE**

A 14ct gold Omega watch, with engine-turned bezel and alligator band.

£180-220   **FRE**

A gentleman's 18ct gold wristwatch, by Omega, the dial with seconds subsidiary.

£250-300 **FRE**

A gentleman's 14ct gold wristwatch, by Omega, the dial with seconds subsidiary.

£150-200 **FRE**

A gentleman's 14ct gold wristwatch, by Omega, broken strap.

£300-400 **FRE**

A gentleman's gold and steel automatic Miester Constellation chronograph wristwatch, by Omega, the dial with centre second sweep and calendar aperture, the 24-jewel movement no. 24757082.

£150-200 **FRE**

An 18ct yellow gold and stainless steel Rolex Prince.

Face 0.75in (2cm) wide

£4,200-4,800 **WG**

A CLOSER LOOK AT A ROLEX OYSTER

Rolex developed the world's first fully waterproof, dustproof and airtight watch case in 1926 and named it the 'Oyster'.

In 1927, it was successfully tested by Mercedes Gleitze, a young female swimmer as she swam across the English Channel.

An 18ct yellow gold and stainless steel Rolex Prince.

Face 0.75in (2cm) wide

£4,200-4,800 **WG**

A stainless steel Rolex Explorer, ref: 5504, with original lacquered dial.

c1959

£2,800-3,200 **WG**

A 1970s stainless steel Rolex Comex Sea Dweller, ref: 1665, with plastic face.

£8,000-12,000 **WG**

A stainless steel Rolex GMT Master, ref: 1675, with painted crown guard and dial with gold or gilt chapter ring.

c1961 1.5in (3.5cm) w

£2,000-3,000 **WG**

LONGINES

Longines was founded in 1832 at a watch making workshop in St Imier, Switzerland. The first factory was built at 'Es Longines' close to the town, hence the name. They used the 'winged hour glass' logo on many of their watches. Longines watches have sold very successfully, with a great many ranges being released. As such, they are currently very reasonably priced and make a good name to start a collection with.

A gentleman's 14K gold wristwatch, by Longines, the dial with seconds subsidiary, the 17-jewel movement no. 776829.

£300-400 **FRE**

A gentleman's 14ct gold wristwatch, by Longines, the dial with seconds subsidiary, the 17-jewel movement no. 8275833.

£120-180 **FRE**

A gentleman's 14ct gold wristwatch, by Longines, the dial with seconds subsidiary, the 17-jewel movement no. 8100554.

£300-400 **FRE**

A gentleman's 14ct gold wristwatch, by Longines, the dial with seconds subsidiary, lacking winder, band broken.

£100-150 **FRE**

A gentleman's 14ct gold wristwatch, by Longines, the dial with seconds subsidiary, the jewel movement no. 10113768, the back inscribed and dated. *1958*

£150-200 FRE

A platinum Breitling Navitimer 1461, no.8 from a limted edition of 25.

Face 1.5in (4cm) wide

£15,000-18,000 WG

A gentleman's alarm chronometer wristwatch, by Henri Giraux.

£120-180 FRE

A gentleman's 14K gold wristwatch, by Invicta, the dial with seconds subsidiary, 17-jewel movement.

£250-350 FRE

A CLOSER LOOK AT A JAEGER REVERSO WRIST WATCH

The Jaeger 'Reverso' was first introduced in 1937.

It was reputedly developed for polo players and sportsmen, who needed to protect the face from hard knocks. By flipping the watch over, the face and glass are protected by a metal back

Now very popular with collectors, it has been largely unparalleled, despite a short-lived attempt at a copy by Hamilton. It is still produced today by Jaeger le Coultre in various models.

The styling is strongly Art Deco, with a clean geometric form and linear details. Its popularity suffered somewhat during the Second World War and the following years.

A 1950s 18ct gold round International Watch Company dress watch, with calibre 83 movement and orginal dial.

Face 1.5in (3.5cm) wide

£1,000-1,400 WG

A 1940s Jaeger Reverso wristwatch, with Cartier-style dial.

Face 1in (2.5cm) wide

£3,000-4,000 WG

A 1950s Jaeger Le Coultre Automatic Memovox, with alarm, date and original tortoiseshell brown patina.

Face 1.5in (3.5cm) wide

£1,000-2,000 WG

A gentleman's 14ct gold wristwatch, by Movado, the dial with seconds subsidiary, the 15-jewel movement un-numbered, crack to glass.

£150-250 FRE

A 1950s 18ct gold rectangular Patek Philippe, ref: 2433, with original dial.

£3,800-4,200 WG

A gentleman's 14ct gold wristwatch, by Mathey Tissot, the dial with centre seconds sweep hand, back of case inscribed and dated, no winder.

1965

£80-120 FRE

A late 1940s/early 1950s 18ct gold oversized round Vacheron & Constantin watch, with original engine-turned guillouche dial.

Face 1.5in (3.5cm) wide

£3,800-4,200 WG

A gentleman's 14ct gold Premiere wristwatch, by Waltham, the dial with subsidiary seconds, the 17-jewel movement no. 74807, the back of the case engraved and dated, the minute hand loose.

1942

£100-150 FRE

A gentleman's 14ct gold wristwatch, by Zodiac, the dial with subsidiary seconds, 17-jewel movement.

£80-120 FRE

A Swiss gentleman's 14ct gold wristwatch, the dial with one hand missing.

£300-400 FRE

Novelty Watches

A Budweiser promotional wristwatch, by Jay Ward Productions, depicting Anheuser-Busch Inc, Budweiser on centre dial, with leather wristband, base metal bezel, stainless steel back, 12-jewel movement.

£40-50 FRE

An Energizer Bunny promotional wristwatch, by Hana Time, depicting the Energizer Brand Battery bunny on centre dial with leather wristband, case movement, assembled in China from Swiss parts, Hong Kong case complete in sleeve with original warranty.

£8-12 FRE

A Nestlé Little Hans promotional wristwatch, by Rega Industries, Ltd., depicting Little Hans of Nestlé on centre dial, eyes of character move in accordance with seconds, with leather wristband and complete with original shipping package and warranty.

c1972

£20-30 FRE

A 40th Anniversary Howdy Doody wristwatch, by NBC Inc and K.F.S Inc, depicting four profiles of Howdy Doody on the centre dial, leather wristband in original sleeve case and with warranty.

£35-45 FRE

A Ronald McDonald promotional wristwatch, by American Watch Service, depicting Ronald on centre dial, base metal bezel, stainless steel back, Swiss made, complete with original box and warranty.

McDonalds have recently expressed doubts about continuing to use Ronald McDonald as he is now seen as an 'outdated' character, no longer popular with children. If they decide to discontinue the clown, items showing him may increase in popularity.

c1974

£20-40 FRE

An "It's Howdy Doody Time" wristwatch, by NBC. "Say Kids, What Time is It? It's Howdy Doody Time!" with character depicted on centre dial, electronically timed, base metal, Swiss made, diamond tooled and unbreakable mainspring, with original sleeve case and warranty.

The Keebler Elf 'Ernie' promotional wristwatch, depicting Keebler Company elf Ernie on centre dial, with synthetic and leather wristband, base metal bezel, diamond tooled, stainless steel back, Swiss made.

£12-15   FRE

A Tony the Tiger says "They're Gr-r-reat" wristwatch, by Kellogg Company, depicting Tony the Tiger for Frosties on centre dial, with leather wristband.

c1976

£25-35   FRE

A "Hey, Kool-Aid" promotional wristwatch, by General Foods Corporation, depicting the Kool-Aid Man on centre dial, with fabric wristband corresponding in colour to the cherry flavoured drink, with original box.

£20-30   FRE

c1971

£60-80   FRE

A Mr Peanut promotional calendar wristwatch, depicting Mr Peanut of Planters on centre dial with choice of blue or yellow wristbands, anti-magnetic, base metal, electronically tested, Swiss made, with original advertisement, shipping package and warranty.

c1072

£20-30   FRE

A Ritz Crackers promotional wristwatch, by Continental Watches, depicting Ritz Crackers on centre dial, with leather wristband, base metal case, electronically tooled, steel back, Swiss made, with original shipping package and warranty.

c1976

£80-120   FRE

A "It's Bugs Bunny time" wristwatch, by Lafayette Watch Co., "I'm Bugs About Baseball" with character depicted on centre dial, base metal, Swiss-made, shock resistant, in original box with warranty.

c1972

£25-35   FRE

A Yellow Pages promotional wristwatch, depicting Yellow Pages on centre dial, with leather wristband, base metal bezel and stainless steel back.

£45-55   FRE

A Dick Tracy wristwatch, Swiss made and base metal, depicting Chester Gould's comic series character holding a movab le gun, fabric wristband.

£20-30   FRE

A Donald Duck wristwatch, by Bradley Time, Walt Disney Productions, precision Swiss movement, anti-magnetic, blue leather wristband, in original red case with warranty.

£30-40 | **FRE**

A Dr. Seuss "The Cat in the Hat Time Teller" wristwatch, by Lafayette Watch Co., Swiss made and base metal, with depiction on centre dial, red wristband, complete in original box.

c1972

£70-100 | **FRE**

A Mickey and Minnie Mouse wristwatch, by Walt Disney Productions, depicting a spirited tennis match between Mickey and Minnie, base metal bezel, stainless steel back, and Swiss made, leather band.

£20-30 | **FRE**

A Popeye the Sailorman "I Yam what I Yam" wristwatch, by Sheffeld Watch Corp., depicting Elzie Segar's comic strip character on centre dial, fabric wristband, with warranty.

c1972

£20-30 | **FRE**

A Porky Pig wristwatch, by Sheffeld Watch Corp., Swiss made and base metal, depicting the Loony Tunes classic character on centre dial, leather wristband, complete warranty.

c1972

£20-30 | **FRE**

A Scooby-Doo "Where Are You?" wristwatch, by NanRic Watch Co., base metal and Swiss made, depicting the famous canine sleuth on centre yellow dial, in original box with warranty.

With the current trend of comic book characters being made into feature films, original memorabilia relating to the characters in question should become more highly sought after, providing the films succeed in capturing the public's imagination.

c1970

£150-200 | **FRE**

A Sesame Street Big Bird wristwatch, by Bradley Time, depicting the well known Sesame Street character on the centre dial, base metal and Swiss-made, red wristband, in original box with warranty.

c1977

£20-30 | **FRE**

A Snoopy wristwatch, by United Features Syndicate, Swiss made and stainless steel back, depicting Snoopy from the Charles M. Schultz comic strip, complete in original box and warranty.

c1972

£20-30 | **FRE**

A Superman wirstwatch, by Bradley Time, depicting Jerry Siegel's classic hero of Action Comics on centre dial, fabric wristband, complete in original box.

c1973

£15-20 | **FRE**

A Woody Woodpecker wristwatch, by Walter Lantz Productions, Inc., the convex centre dial depicting Woody Woodpecker, waterproof and Swiss made, red wristband.

c1972

£20-30   FRE

A 1970s patriotic construction worker wristwatch, styled by Manfred, depicting male construction worker on centre dial, diamond-tooled, base metal case, electronically timed, Swiss made, fabric patriotic wristband, in original box.

£30-40   FRE

A President George Herbert Walker Bush wristwatch, by Sanders & Co., the president seated on a Republican elephant, leather wristband, in original velvet box with original sales receipt.

c1990

£20-40   FRE

A "Clinton - Gore" Presidential campaign wristwatch, stainless steel back and metal case red leather wristband.

1992

£8-12   FRE

A President Bill Clinton wristwatch, depicting Clinton on centre dial, leather wristband.

£12-15   FRE

A President Richard Nixon wristwatch, by Dirty Time Co., depicting "Dicky Dixon" diamond-tooled, electronically timed, base metal case, Swiss made, patriotic wristband, with warranty.

£80-120   FRE

An "I'm Not A Crook' Richard Nixon wristwatch, by Tru Time, a whimsical Nixon character on the centre dial, stainless steel back, with red, white and blue fabric wristband.

£80-120   FRE

A "Keep the Spirit of '76" bicentennial gentleman's wristwatch, by Bradley Time, base metal case and Swiss movement, depicting George Washington and fellow comrades waving the American flag, in original box with warranty.

c1976

£20-30   FRE

An offical "Philadelphia '76'" Bicentennial commemorative timepiece, electronically timed, diamond-tooled, Swiss movement, wristband, with original sleeve case and sales receipt, wear to brass case.

£8-12   FRE

A President Ronald Reagan wristwatch, by Timely Creations, depicting Regan seated on Republican elephant, base metal bezel, stainless steel back, on fabric wristband.

c1980

£8-12   FRE

A Statue of Liberty wristwatch, depicting the American flag and the Statue of Liberty, base metal, Swiss made, diamond-tooled, unbreakable mainspring, electronically timed, in original box with sales receipt.

£12-18   FRE

A 1970 "Uncle Sam" calendar watch, by Birmingham Watch Co., base metal bezel and stainless steel back, depicting Uncle Sam on centre dial, patriotic fabric wristband, in original shipping package with warranty.

£20-30   FRE

A Ghostbusters wristwatch game, by Nelsonic.

c1990   8.75in (22cm) long

£10-15   **HLJ**

A official E.T. wristwatch, by Nelsonic, anti-magnetic and stainless steel back, depicting the extraterrestrial character on centre dial, leather wristband, in original box.

c1982

£20-30   **FRE**

An official Star Wars wristwatch, by Bradley Time, depicting the droids R2-D2 and C-3PO on centre dial, precision Swiss movement, electronically timed and anti-magnetc, navy wristband, complete in original box with warranty.

c1977

£35-45   **FRE**

A "Forever Elvis" commemorative wristwatch, by Precision Watch Company Inc, depicting Elvis on one of his national tours on centre dial, with leather wristband, base metal back and Swiss made, complete in original box and with warranty.

£25-30   **FRE**

A "Keep Time with the Fonz" wristwatch, by Time Trends, depicting The Fonz from "Happy Days" TV series on centre dial with simulated fabric wristband, complete in original box with warranty.

c1976

£15-20   **FRE**

A Jack and Jill "Digital Tell Time" wristwatch, by Sutton Time Ltd, Swiss made, depicting nursery rhyme children Jack and Jill on centre dial, red leather wristband, in original box with warranty.

c1974

£150-200   **FRE**

The Evel Knievel wristwatch, by Bradley Time, depicting the motorcycle daredevil on centre dial, with leather and star-studded wristband, anti-magnetic, electronically timed, precision Swiss movement, complete in box with warranty.

c1975

£60-80   **FRE**

A Lucky Las Vegas wristwatch, depicting the lucky dice of Las Vegas above a green gaming background on centre dial, on leather wristband, electronically timed, base metal, Swiss manufactured, anti-magnetic.

£20-30   **FRE**

An original Laurel and Hardy wristwatch, by Dirty Time Company, depicting the comic legends on centre dial, with red leather band, wear and corrosion to bezel.

£15-20   **FRE**

A wristwatch commemorating the lunar landing, by Fashion Time, leather wristband, Swiss made, and complete with original box and warranty.

c1972

£80-120   **FRE**

A humorous bearded doll watch.

£8-12   **FRE**

CORKSCREWS

- The first recorded mention of using a 'screw to remove a cork' was in 1681, but they had been known and used before then. The 19th century saw the 'golden age' of inventions with many patents for new designs being issued.

- The 'screw' is known as a 'worm' or 'helix' and can be made from shaped wire or cast in shape. The first turn often had sharp edges, known as 'cyphered' edges to help with penetration into the cork.

- Corkscrews fall into two main categories, 'straight pull', where the force to extract the cork comes from the user, and 'mechanical', where a mechanism helps draw out the cork. Mechanical versions and early or finely made straight pulls are generally more desirable.

- Corkscrews with unusual mechanisms, those made from precious materials and those marked with desirable makers' names will fetch the highest prices.

- It is worth considering condition. Collectors should ensure that the corkscrew works and is complete. Rust or other marks should be carefully cleaned off and moving parts gently oiled. Repairs will devalue a corkscrew, as will serious damage to the worm.

A mother-of-pearl and silver pocket corkscrew, by Samuel Pemberton.

There are many designs for these early corkscrews with silver, often ornate, sheaths. They were mainly made in Holland.

c1810   3.25in (8.5cm) long

£200-250   **CSA**

A peg and warm steel corkscrew.

2.5in (6cm) long

£80-120   **BS**

A pocket corkscrew, the casing made from a British Lee Enfield .303 rifle cartridge.

c1918

£15-20   **CSA**

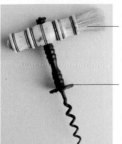

A steel corkscrew, with finger grip.

c1900   6in (15cm) long

£50-80   **BS**

A 19thC steel corkscrew, with bone grip, replaced brush, crack in bone.

6in (15cm) long

£120-180   **BS**

An American Williamson bell cap continuous action corkscrew.

c1910   7.5in (19cm) long

£35-40   **CSA**

A 1930s Schlitz Beer advertising corkscrew, with bell cap.

5in (12.5cm) long

£15-20   **CSA**

A CLOSER LOOK AT A PULL CORKSCREW

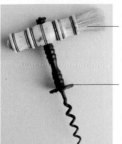

Brushes were inset into handles from the late 18thC until the late 19thC. They were used to brush deposits off the label or bottle top.

The first corkscrew patent, in 1795, used a 'button' at the top of the worm which prevented the worm moving further into the cork and also helped to 'unstick' the cork.

A Henshall button-type corkscrew, with bone handle and brush.

c1830   6in (15.5cm) long

£65-70   **CSA**

A 1930s San Benito advertising corkscrew.

5in (12.5cm) long

£12-15   **CSA**

A stainless steel Valenzina corkscrew, 1949 registration.

£20-25   **CSA**

A German plastic Sieger 600 continuous action corkscrew.
c1960   4.5in (11.5cm) long

£10-12   **CSA**

A 1960s American chrome barman's tool, with spirit measure and can opener.
6in (15.5cm) long

£5-8   **CSA**

A pair of English 1930s carved pinewood figural corkscrews, carved as a fighting cat and Scottie dog.
Dog 5in (12.5cm) wide

£15-20   **CSA**

A carved rosewood figural Chinaman corkscrew.
c1930   5in (12.5cm) high

£6-8   **CSA**

An American syrocowood "The Waiter" corkscrew.
Due to Prohibition, corkscrews had to be disguised. In this case, the head of the waiter lifts off and acts as the handle for the corkscrew.
c1910   8in (20.5cm) high

£75-95   **CSA**

A German celluloid mermaid corkscrew, with metallic painted scales, marked "GES GESCHULTZ".
c1900   4.25in (10.5cm) long

£300-400   **CSA**

A German celluloid covered lady's legs folding corkscrew, with half-length stockings.
These whimsical corkscrews are very popular with collectors and are reminiscent of debauched nights spent watching the can-can dancers at the Moulin Rouge, Paris. they come in large and small sizes with a variety of coloured full or half stockings.
c1880-90   2.5in (6.5cm) long

£120-150   **CSA**

A German celluloid lady's legs folding corkscrew, with pink-striped stockings.
c1880-90   2.5in (6.5cm) long

£120-150   **CSA**

An English eight-tool folding bow corkscrew, with hoof pick, leather hole punch, gimlet, grooved helical worm corkscrew, spike, auger, screw driver and button hook, stamped "B.B. Wells West Strand".
c1820 Closed 2.75in (7cm) long

£80-100   **CSA**

A 1920s steel corkscrew, with cast iron bottle opener.
5in (12.5cm) long

£30-50   **BS**

A bone-handled perfume corkscrew, for opening perfume bottles.
c1830   5in (12.5cm) long

£10-15   **CSA**

A cast brass two-finger figural spider and fly corkscrew.
c1930   6.5in (16.5cm) long

£12-14   **CSA**

A German cast brass key corkscrew.
c1930 *5in (12.5cm) long*

£12-14 **CSA**

An American Clough patent corkscrew, with wooden advertising sheath.
c1910 *4in (10cm) long*

£5-10 **CSA**

A German Monopol continuous action corkscrew.
c1910 *5in (12.5cm) high*

£15-20 **CSA**

A Converse N.Y. patent corkscrew.
c1899 *4.25in (10.5cm) long*

£20-25 **CSA**

An early 19thC steel corkscrew.
5.5in (14cm) long

£50-80 **BS**

A 1920s Bacchus corkscrew.
6.5in (16.5cm) long

£50-80 **BS**

A 1920s steel corkscrew.
5.75in (14.5cm) long

£40-60 **BS**

A French all-steel corkscrew, by Perille.

This corkscrew design was patented by Frenchman J. Perille in 1876.

c1910

£15-20 **CSA**

A 19thC brass corkscrew.
5in (12.5cm)

£120-180 **BS**

A bone and brass narrow rack 'King's Screw' corkscrew, by Robert Jones.

c1820　　7.5in (19cm) long

£150-200　　CSA

A wide rack King's Screw corkscrew, by Dowler, with gilt bronze barrel.

c1820　　7.5in (19cm) long

£400-450　　CSA

A four pillar steel 'King's Screw' corkscrew.

Turning the handle forces the worm into the cork. The side handle is then turned operating a 'rack and pinion' to remove the cork. Barrels may be open as with this example, but are more commonly closed.

c1820　　8in (20.5cm) long

£380-420　　CSA

FIND OUT MORE...

Bernard Watney & Homer Babbidge, 'Corkscrews for Collectors', published by Sotheby Parke Bernet, 1983.

Donald Bull, 'The Ultimate Corkscrew Book', published by Schiffer Publishing, 1999.

A CLOSER LOOK AT A MECHANICAL CORKSCREW

Turned bone and ivory handles with integral brushes are typical.

The 'Thomason type' was patented by Sir Edward Thomason in 1802.

They always take this form, but barrels may be ornately decorated or open which adds value. The motto 'Ne Plus Ultra' is also common.

A bone and brass Thomason-type double-action corkscrew, by Wilmot & Roberts.

c1810　　7in (17.5cm) long

£150-175　　CSA

A Weir's concertina type corkscrew, by Heeley & Sons, with gilt bronze finish.

The patent for this design was taken out in 1884 by Marshall Weir.

c1884　　6in (15.5cm) long

£45-60　　CSA

A Lund two-part lever corkscrew.

It is unusual to find the two parts together. This design was first registered by Edmund Burke of London in 1854. Lund's version, with a separate worm, was patented in 1855. Early examples are marked with his name and a 'milestone' motif.

c1880　　8in (20cm) wide

£60-70　　CSA

A French chrome-plated 'Zig-Zag' concertina corkscrew, with original box and instructions.

c1920　　6in (15.5cm) long

£55-65　　CSA

A James Heeley A1 double lever corkscrew.

c1890　　6in (15.5cm) long

£65-75　　CSA

A 1950s brass set of scales bottle opener.

4.5in (11.5cm) long

£2-4   **CSA**

A 1950s Australian aluminium hand bottle opener, marked "Made in Australia".

6.75in (17cm) long

£2-4   **CSA**

A 1950s Canadian souvenir bottle opener, by Century, decorated with a family of bears in a mountainous landscape.

3.75in (9.5cm) long

£2-4   **CSA**

A 1950s brass Eiffel tower souvenir bottle opener.

4in (10cm) long

£2-4   **CSA**

A 1950s heavy cast brass double sided horses head bottle opener.

4in (10cm) long

£2-4   **CSA**

A 1950s Johnnie Walker spirit pourer.

5.75in (14.5cm) long

£8-10   **CSA**

A Greek souvenir bottle opener, with a classic head and "EPMH" on one side and diaphanous figure and a cartouche with a deer and "NA 1947".

c1947   *3in (7.5cm)*

£6-8   **CSA**

A Booths spirit pourer.

c1935   *5.75in (14.5cm) long*

£8-10   **CSA**

A 1950s wooden man in morning suit bottle opener, with articulated arms.

5in (12.5cm) high

£2-4   **CSA**

A 1940s King George IV whisky spirit pourer.

5in (12.5cm) long

£8-10   **CSA**

A 1950s Burdon Sherry spirit pourer.

4in (10cm) long

£5-6   **CSA**

A 1940s King George IV whisky spirit pourer.

5in (12.5cm) long

£8-10   **CSA**

A 1960s pottery "Bob Cratchet" spirit pourer.

Bob Cratchet was a character in Charles Dickens' novel 'A Christmas Carol'.

A John Haig's whisky spirit pourer.

6.5in (16.5cm) long

£8-10   **CSA**

A 1960s Wade china Beefeater Gin cork.

£12-15   **CSA**

£15-20   **CSA**

Cocktail Shakers

A 1950s Italian Alps novelty carved wood articulated cork, carved as a drinking man.

5in (12.5cm) high

£8-10   **CSA**

A 1950s Italian Alps novelty carved wood articulated cork, carved as a kissing couple.

5in (12.5cm) high

£10-12   **CSA**

A silver-plated cocktail shaker, with spot-hammered decoration, marked "AM 0990" on the base.

c1935   11.5in (29cm) high

£500-600   **Tag**

A silver-plated cocktail shaker, in the shape of a hand bell, with wooden handle.

c1935   11.5in (29cm) high

£450-550   **Tag**

A silver-plated cocktail shaker, with gilt details, with cocktail ingredients marked on the exterior.

This is a very popular design, where the user twists the silver plated sleeve until an inscribed arrow points at his chosen cocktail. The series of windows then displays the ingredients for that cocktail.

c1935   4.5in (11cm) high

£850-950   **Tag**

A silver-plated cocktail shaker, in the shape of a bowling pin, with wooden handle.

c1935   15.5in (39.5cm) high

£550-650   **Tag**

A Mixit cut glass and silver-plated cocktail shaker, the silver-plated lid with revolving cocktail menu, including Martini, White Lady, Kicking Horse and Bacchante.

c1935   9.5in (24cm)

£450-550   **Tag**

A pair of silver wine coasters, by Chas T. Fox and Geo Fox.

Wine coasters became popular as table ware from the 1760s onwards. Solid silver wine coasters were phased out in favour of plated versions from the 1850s. Bases are made from robust woods such as lignum vitae and mahogany.

£4,000-5,000   **GS**

A pair of ornate silver wine coasters, by Joseph Craddock and William Reid, London.

£5,000-6,000   **GS**

A pair of silver-plated pierced wine coasters.

£300-400   **GS**

A pair of 18thC Old Sheffield Plate wine casters.

5in (12.5cm) diam

£200-250   **CSA**

A Sheffield Plate decanter wagon.

c1830   *19in (48.5cm) long*

£1,200-1,300   **CSA**

A silver wine funnel, by Hester Bateman, London.

1789

£2,000-3,000   **GS**

A silver wine funnel, by Joseph Preedy, London.

1791

£800-1,000   **GS**

A silver wine funnel, London.

1813

£900-1,100   **GS**

A silver wine funnel, London.

1872

£800-1,000   **GS**

A silver wine funnel, by Thomas Johnson, London hallmarks.

1823

£700-900   **GS**

A 19thC French silver tastevin.

c1870   *3in (7.5cm) diam*

£150-175   **CSA**

An 18thC French silver tastevin, engraved "M Sanson" on the handle.

A tastevin is a shallow dish, usually silver, used for tasting and examining the colour of wine.

3in (7.5cm) diam

£200-225   **CSA**

A silver-plated tastevin, marked "Marche aux vins Beaune".
c1900   *4in (10cm) wide*
£15-20   **CSA**

A 19thC French silver tastevin.
c1870   *3in (7.5cm) diam*
£150-175   **CSA**

A silver-plated tastevin, with pierced vine leaf handle.
c1880   *3.75in (9.5cm) wide*
£15-20   **CSA**

A Staffordshire pottery sherry barrel.
c1870   *11.5in (29.5cm) high*
£170-200   **CSA**

A Staffordshire pottery stirrup cup, shaped as a fox's head.

Stirrup cups have no base and were made to be used on horseback. They were popular between c1770 and c1830 and enjoyed a revival in the late 19thC.

c1830   *5in (12.5cm) long*
£500-600   **CSA**

A silver and trompe l'oeil whisky flagon, by Thornhill of London, Chester hallmarks.
1892
£250-275   **CSA**

A Swiss silver-plated sleigh bottle cradle.
c1880   *11.5in (29.5cm) long*
£250-270   **CSA**

A silver-plated wine bottle holder, dated.
1864   *8in (20.5cm) high*
£65-85   **CSA**

A 1920s French turned wood bottle corker.
     10in (25.5cm) high
£20-25   **CSA**

A Recency Scottish whisky dispenser, carved wood with detachable whiskey cask, on a wheeled base.

This dispenser would have been pushed along the dining table after the meal so that guests could fill their glasses as required.

     26in (66cm) high
£2,500-3,000   **CSA**

Six silver and enamel cocktail sticks, in the shape of umbrellas, Birmingham hallmarks.
1909   *2.75in (7cm) long*
£60-90   **CSA**

NEW COLLECTABLES

Today's arts and crafts will become the collectables of the future and it is well worth while searching for quality contemporary items to start a collection. In the past, items made by skilled people kept their value and often became more valuable once the artist was recognised. This applies to arts and crafts today. Look for high levels of craftsmanship and the use of quality materials. As with all collecting, buyers should choose pieces that appeal to them. Remember, however, that new designs are often innovative and may initially challenge personal perceptions of aesthetics.

Three 'Yunomis' (teabowls), by Takeshi Yasuda.

4in (10cm) high

£85 each CAA

'Le Bol', by Takeshi Yasuda.

4in (10cm) high

£275 CAA

'Unfolding Bowl', by Takeshi Yasuda.

13in (33cm) diam

£1,150 CAA

'Leaf Platter', by Takeshi Yasuda.

19.75in (50cm) diam

£1,150 CAA

Three 'Unfolding Vases', by Takeshi Yasuda.

Takeshi Yasuda was born in 1943 in Tokyo. He was a tutor in ceramics and applied art at the Royal College of Art during the late 1990s and has exhibited extensively in Japan, Germany, Denmark and New York.

17.75in (45cm) high

£1,150 (each) CAA

'Neptune 2', by Jane Blackman.

Jane Blackman combines form with painting, brushing expressive and instinctive marks on the interior of her pieces. Edges and boundaries that change how the viewer perceives the piece are of great interest to her.

6.75in (17cm) high

£400 CAA

'Round Bodied Form', by Betty Blandino.

9.75in (25cm) high

£370 CAA

'Eastellanus', by Jane Blackman.

9.5in (24cm) high

£460 CAA

'Asymmetric Form', by Betty Blandino.

Blandino studied at Goldsmith's College, London, from 1957-1958. Her work is typified by 'pregnant' rounded forms with thin walls. The clay surfaces remain natural.

7.75in (20cm) high

£370 CAA

'Vase', by Anna Silverton.

20.5in (52cm) high

£370 CAA

'Brown Vessel', by Anna Silverton.

Silverton transcends original indigenous ceramic designs with her personal style. All vases are wheel-thrown in two pieces which are joined together and finished afterwards. In order to retain the natural burnished shine, brown vases, which are made from black earthenware clay, are not varnished and are not waterproof.

20.5in (52cm) high

£370 CAA

'Black Caddy on base', by Julian Stair.

Caddy 6in (16cm) high

£1,500   **CAA**

Three 'Cups on Bases', by Julian Stair.

4.5in (11.5cm) high

£285 (each)   **CAA**

'Large Bowl', by Andrew Wicks.

7.5 in (19cm) high

£285   **CAA**

'Small Round Vase', by Andrew Wicks.

5in (12.5cm) high

£60   **CAA**

'Fruit', by Felicity Aylieff.

£920   **CAA**

'Large Caddy', by Richard Batterham.

7.75in (20cm) high

£225   **CAA**

'Layers III', by Robert Cooper.

15in (38cm) high

£1,260   **CAA**

'Tall Yellow Vessel', by Gabrielle Koch.

17in (43cm) high

£1,260   **CAA**

'Ocean I' and 'Ocean II', by Emmanuel Cooper.

Largest 7.75in (20cm) high

£370 (each)   **CAA**

'Large Black and White Bowl', by Sophie Lowe.

£345   **CAA**

Two 'Spotted Flasks', by Malcolm Martin and Gaynor Dowling.

Tallest 17.25in (44cm) high

£450 (each)   **CAA**

'New World Order', by Carol McNicoll.

8.75in (22.5cm) high

£1,140   **CAA**

Three 'Cylindrical Vessels', by Sue Paraskeva.

Tallest 3.25in (8.5cm) high

£100-250 (each)   **CAA**

'Round Vessel', by David Roberts.

12.75in (32.5cm) high

£1,145   **CAA**

'Sraffito', large bowl by Rupert Spira.

16.5in (42cm) diam

£2,200   **CAA**

Three pieces by Edmund de Waal, including from left to right, 'Bowl Red Seal', 'Small Jar', and 'Offering Dish'.

6in (15.5cm) high

£320-£400 (each)   **CAA**

'Catching the Cock', by Michael Flynn.

Michael Flynn, born in 1947, is known for his figurative work using raku techniques and porcelain. They display an energetic and bizarre feeling, inspired by theatre, dance and mythology. He has exhibited throughout Europe and in the U.K. and has undertaken many private and public commissions.

15.75in (40cm) high

£1,950   **CAA**

'White Form', by Mo Jupp.

14.5in (37cm) high

£690   **CAA**

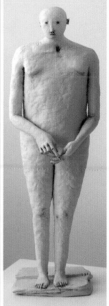

'Standing Figure', by Clair Curneen.

28.25in (72cm) high

£1,700   **CAA**

A brooch, by Anna Gordon.

Born in 1971, Gordon studied at the Edinburgh College of Art. Her style is highly minimalist, using classical shapes such as the square and circle. Influences, apart from the shapes themselves, come from architecture. She works primarily in gold, silver and platinum.

4.25in (11cm) long

£290   **CAA**

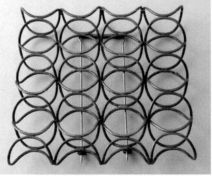

A brooch, by Anna Gordon.

3in (7.5cm) wide

£390   **CAA**

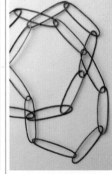

A necklace, by Anna Gordon.

24in (63cm) diam

£230   **CAA**

A feather necklace, by Kate Wilkinson.

14.5in (37cm) long

£73   **CAA**

A pair of black earrings, by Kate Wilkinson.

1in (3cm) diam

£70   **CAA**

A pair of pink earrings, by Kate Wilkinson.

1in (3cm) diam

£70   **CAA**

A feather bracelet, by Grainne Morton.

7in (18cm) long

£225 CAA

A brooch, by Grainne Morton.

2in (5cm) diam

£425 CAA

A necklace, by Elizabeth Bone.

11in (28cm) long

£986 CAA

A wrap necklace, by Loekie Heintzberger.

28.75in (73cm) long

£900 CAA

A necklace, by Daphne Krinos.

18.5in (47cm) long

£575 CAA

A necklace, by Emma Gale.

9in (23cm) diam

£275 CAA

A necklace, by Adam Paxon.

24in (61cm) long

£218 CAA

A bracelet, by Catherine Hills.

8.25in (21cm) long

£1,210 CAA

'Shoveller Duck Box', in wood with egg, by Nicola Henshaw.

£860 CAA

'Burr Oak Vessel', by Anthony Bryant.

7.75in (20cm) high

£860 CAA

MURANO GLASS

The production of the many famous glassworks at Murano, near Venice, Italy, has always been popular, with many vintage pieces now becoming increasingly sought after. Although the factories at Murano continue to produce many high quality pieces, collectors should look for quality pieces from up and coming glassmakers, or pieces by established makers who may not yet be recognized.

A contemporary and unique Vittorio Ferro murano 'Murrine' vase, in blown glass, signed.

10.25in (26cm) high

£1,000-1,300 FM

A contemporary and unique Vittorio Ferro pale blue glass vase, signed.

£800-1,200 FM

A contemporary and unique Vittorio Ferro vase, in red and blue hand-blown glass.

11.25in (28.5cm) high

£800-1,200 FM

A contemporary and unique Vittorio Ferro polychrome vase, signed.

£800-1,200 FM

VITTORIO FERRO

- Vittorio Ferro is part of a well known glass-making family. He started working at the renowned Fratelli Toso in Murano at the age of 14 and was promoted to glass master at 20.
- He studied under his uncles, the Zuffi brothers, and Professor Ansolo Zuga, and produced a great many of the designs at Fratelli Toso until its closure in 1981, when he was immediately offered a position as a Master at the de Majo glassworks.
- His passion lies in 'murrine', where many rectangles or circles of differently coloured glass made from cut rods are gathered and fused together into a mosaic pattern and applied to the exterior of a clear glass vessel.
- He won the Borselle d'Oro prize in 1969 and the 'Altino' prize in 1993 and was included in a book on famous glass masters in 1994.
- He retired in 1994 and is now working at the Fratelli Pagnin workshop, directing production of his own creations using murrine and many other historic techniques.

A contemporary and unique Vittorio Ferro yellow glass vase, signed.

10.25in (26cm) high

£1,000-1,500 FM

A contemporary handmade turquoise glass vase, designed by Riccardo Licata.

16.25in (41cm) high

£600-700 FM

A contemporary G. Michello blown glass vase.

9in (23cm) high

£1,000-1,500 FM

A contemporary handmade blue glass vase, designed by Riccardo Licata.

16.25in (41cm) high

£600-700 FM

A contemporary glass piece 'Espanol vinas hez', by Soumero.

10.5in (27cm) high

£900-1,000 FM

RICCARDO LICATA

- Born in Turin in 1929, Licata studied at the Liceo Artistico and the Accademia di Belle Arte and produced designs for numerous Murano glassmakers, who used blanks and painted mirrors.
- In 1952, he designed a popular range known as 'Aquarium' for Gino Cendese amongst many other commissions for various important glassmakers.
- From 1957, he was a professor at the 'Ecole des Beaux Arts' in Paris and also worked on projects including set designs and book illustrations.

A

Acid Etching A technique using acid to decorate glass to produce a matt or frosted appearance.

Albumen print Photographic paper is treated with egg white (albumen) to enable it to hold more light sensitive chemicals. After being exposed to a negative, the resulting image is richer with more tonal variation.

Ambrotype A glass negative plate treated with chemicals and mounted on a dark background to show the image.

Autographic A feature used by Kodak between 1914 and 1932 that allowed the user to 'write' directly onto the film, using a stylus via a hinged door on the back of the camera.

Applied Refers to a separate part that has been attached to an object, such as a handle.

B

Baluster A curved form with a bulbous base and a slender neck.

Bébé The French term for a doll that represents a baby rather than an adult.

Bisque A type of unglazed porcelain used for making dolls from c1860 to c1925.

Boards The hard covers of a book.

Brassing On plated items, where the plating has worn off to reveal the underlying base metal.

Broderie Anglaise Meaning 'English embroidery', white thread is embroidered onto a white cloth, used after the 1820s.

C

Cabochon A large, protruding, polished, but not faceted, stone.

Cameo Hardstone, coral or shell that has been carved in relief to show a design in a contrasting colour.

Cameo glass Decorative glass made from two or more layers of differently coloured glass, which are then carved or etched to reveal the colour beneath.

Cartouche A framed panel, often in the shape of a shield or paper scroll, which can be inscribed.

Celadon A distinctive grey/green or blue/green glaze derived from iron and used to imitate jade in China for over 2,000 years.

Character doll A doll with a face that resembles a real child rather than an idealized one.

Charger A large plate or platter, often for display, but also for serving.

Cloisonne A decorative technique using small cells created by soldering thin strips of metal to an object which are then filled with coloured enamels.

Clubhouse Signature A player's signature that was not actually signed by the player, but by one of his colleagues such as a batboy.

Composition A mixture including wood pulp, plaster and glue and used as a cheap alternative to bisque in the production of dolls' heads and bodies.

Compote A dish, usually on a stem or foot, to hold fruit for the dessert course.

Craze A network of fine cracks in the glaze caused by uneven shrinking during firing.

Cultured pearl A pearl formed when an irritant is artificially introduced to the mollusc.

D

Daguerrotype A 'positive' image photographed directly onto a metal plate which is then usually mounted into a decorative case. The first practical photography process and used from c1839 until the 1850s.

Diecast Objects made by pouring molten metal into a closed metal die or mould.

Ding A very small dent in metal.

DQ Standing for 'diamond quilted', where a repeated pattern of diamond shapes cover the surface.

E

Earthenware A type of porous pottery that requires a glaze to make it waterproof.

Ebonized Wood that has been blackened with dye to resemble ebony.

Escapement The mechanical part of the clock or watch that regulates the transfer of energy from the weights or spring to the movement of the clock or watch

F

Faience Earthenware that is treated with an impervious tin glaze. Popular in France from the 16th century and reaching its peak during the 18th century.

Fairing A small porcelain figure made in Eastern Germany and given away as prizes or sold inexpensively at fairs. They usually have an amusing subject and title.

Ferrotype Similar to an ambrotype but black enamelled tin, not glass, is used. The quality of the image is usually inferior to that of an ambrotype.

Finial A decorative knob at the end of a terminal, or on a lid.

Flatware The term for any type of cutlery.

Foliate Leaf and vine motifs.

G

Guilloché An engraved pattern of interlaced lines or other decorative motifs, sometimes enamelled over with translucent enamels.

IJKL

Inclusions Used to describe all types of small particles of decorative materials embedded in glass.

Iridescent A lustrous finish that subtly changes colour depending on how light hits it. Often used to describe the finish on ceramics and glass.

Kutani Japanese porcelain made at Kutani, in the Kaga province of Japan, in the 17th and 18th centuries.

Lambrequins A shaped decoration derived from the hanging fringes on tents at a jousting competition. Used to describe similarly shaped borders on ceramics, silver and furniture.

MNO

Meiji A period in Japanese history dating from 1868-1912.

Mon A Japanese family crest. A common example is the 16 petal chrysanthemum flower.

M.O.P. Mother of pearl. The shiny and coloured interior of some shells.

Netsuke A small toggle, usually carved from ivory or wood, used to secure pouches and boxes (known as sagemono) hung on cords through the belt of a kimono. They are most often carved as figures or animals.

Opalescent An opal-like, milky glass with subtle gradations of colour between thinner more translucent areas and thicker, more opaque areas.

P

Paisley A soft woollen fabric with a stylized design based on pinecones.

Paste (Jewellery) A hard, bright glass cut the same way as a diamond and made and set to resemble them.

Patera An oval or circular decorative motif often with a fluted or floral centre.

Penwork Black japanned items were decorated with white japanned patterns, with details and shading being applied using Indian ink and a pen. Popular in England during the 18th and 19th centuries.

Pique A decorative technique where small strips or studs of gold are inlaid onto ivory or tortoiseshell on a pattern and secured in place by heating.

Pontil A metal rod to which a glass vessel is attached when it is being worked. When it is removed it leaves a raised disc-shaped 'pontil mark'.

Pounce pot A small pot made of wood (treen), silver or ceramic. Found on inkwells or designed to stand alone, it held a gum dust that was sprinkled over parchment to prevent ink from spreading. Used until the late 18th century.

Pressed (Press Moulded) Ceramics formed by pressing clay into a mould. Pressed glass is made by pouring molten glass into a mould and pressing it with a plunger.

R

Reeded A type of decoration with thin raised, convex vertical lines. Derived from the decoration of classical columns.

Repoussé A French term for the raised, 'embossed', decoration on metals such as silver. The metal is forced into a form from one side causing it to bulge.

S

Satsuma Collective term for potteries on the island of Kyushu, Japan, which made items for export to the West. Their ware is typified by a clear, yellowish glaze, often decorated with coloured figures and flowers and gilt decoration.

Sweet Spot The area of a baseball between the two curving lines of stitching where it is most desirable to find a player's autograph.

Stoneware A type of ceramic similar to earthenware and made of high-fired clay mixed with stone, such as feldspar, which makes it non-porous.

Suzuribako A Japanese writing box containing tools such as brushes, inkpots and ink slabs.

T

Tazza A shallow cup with a wide bowl, which is raised up on a single pedestal foot.

Tooled Collective description for a number of decorative techniques applied to a surface. Includes engraving, stamping, punching and incising.

Tsuba A Japanese sword guard. An often ornate disc placed between the blade and the handle to protect the hand from the blade.

V

Vermeil Gold-plated silver.

Vesta case A small case or box, usually made from silver, for carrying matches.

W

White metal Precious metal that is possibly silver, but not officially marked as such.

Whitework Decorative white embroidery on white fabric, usually cotton. Often said to be the forerunner of lace.

Y

Yellow metal Precious metal that is possibly gold, but not officially marked as such.

KEY TO ILLUSTRATIONS

EVERY COLLECTABLE ILLUSTRATED in *Collectables Price Guide 2003-4* by Judith Miller has a letter code that identifies the dealer or auction house that sold it. The list below is a key to these codes. In the list, auction houses are shown by the letter Ⓐ and dealers by the letter Ⓓ. Some items may have come from a private collection, in which case the code in the list is accompanied by the letter Ⓟ. Inclusion in this book in no way constitutes or implies a contract or a binding offer on the part of any of our contributors to supply or sell the goods illustrated, or similar items, at the prices stated.

ACM Ⓓ
Antiques of Cape May
Tel: 001 800 224 1687

AGI Ⓐ
Aurora Galleries International
30 Hackamore Lane, Suite 2,
Bell Canyon, California 91307 USA
Tel: 001 818 884 6468
Fax: 001 818 227 2941
vjc@auroragalleriesonline.com
www.auroragalleriesonline.com

AMM Ⓓ
Automatomania
Shop 124, Grays Antiques Market,
58 Davies Street, London W1K 5LP
Tel: 020 7495 5259
07790 719097
www.automatomania.com

AnA Ⓓ
Ancient Art
85 The Vale, Southgate,
London N14 6AT
Tel: 020 8882 1509
Fax: 020 8886 5235
ancient.art@btinternet.com
www.ancientart.co.uk

AS&S Ⓐ
Andrew Smith & Son Auctions
Hankin's Garage, 47 West Street,
Alresford, Hampshire
Tel: 01962 842 841
Fax: 01962 863 274
auctions@andrewsmithandson.
fsbusiness.co.uk

ATM Ⓓ
At the Movies
17 Fouberts Place, Carnaby,
London W1F 7QD
Tel: 020 7439 6336
Fax: 020 7439 6355
info@atthemovies.co.uk
www.atthemovies.co.uk

B Ⓐ
Bracketts Fine Art Auctioneers
Auction Hall, The Pantiles,
Tunbridge Wells, Kent TN2 5QL
Tel: 01892 544 500
Fax: 01892 515 191
sales@bfaa.co.uk
www.bfaa.co.uk

BA Ⓓ
Branksome Antiques
370 Poole Road, Branksome,
Poole, Dorset BH12 1AW
Tel: 01202 763 324/679 932
Fax: 01202 763 643

BAC Ⓓ
Burlwood Antique Center
Route 3, Meredith,
NH 03253 USA
Tel: 001 603 279 6387
rckhprant@aol.com
www.burlwood-antiques.com

BAR Ⓐ
Bristol Auction Rooms
St John's Place, Apsley Road,
Clifton, Bristol BS8 2ST
Tel: 0117 973 7201
Fax: 0117 973 5671
info@bristolauctionrooms.co.uk
www.bristolauctionrooms.co.uk

BCAC Ⓓ
Bucks County Antique Center
Route 202, Lahaska
PA 18931 USA
Tel: 001 215 794 9180

BEJ Ⓓ
Bébés & Jouets
C/o Post Office,
165 Restalrig Road,
Edinburgh EH7 6HW
Tel: 0131 332 5650
bebesetjouets@u.genie.co.uk

Ber Ⓐ
Bertoia Auctions
2141 Demarco Drive,
Vineland NJ 08360 USA
Tel: 001 856 692 1881
Fax: 001 856 692 8697
bill@bertoiaauctions.com
www.bertoiaauctions.com

BG Ⓐ
**Bob Gowland International
Golf Auctions**
The Stables, Claim Farm,
Manley Road, Frodsham,
Cheshire WA6 6HT
Tel/Fax: 01928 740 668
bob@internationalgolfauctions.com
www.internationalgolfauctions.com

Bib Ⓓ
Biblion
1/7 Davies Mews,
London W1K 5AB
Tel: 020 7629 1374
Fax: 020 7493 7158
info@biblion.com
www.biblion.com

BonS Ⓐ
Bonhams, Sevenoaks
49 London Road, Sevenoaks,
Kent TN13 1AR
Tel: 01732 740 310
Fax: 01732 741842
info@bonhams.com
www.bonhams.com

BS Ⓐ
Below Stairs of Hungerford
103 High Street,
Hungerford, Berkshire
RG17 0NB
Tel: 01488 682 317
Fax: 01488 684 294
hofgartner@belowstairs.co.uk
www.belowstairs.co.uk

MSC Ⓟ
Mark Slavinsky Collection

CAA Ⓓ
Contemporary Applied Arts
2 Percy Street, London
W1T 1DD
Tel: 020 7436 2344
Fax: 020 7436 2446
www.caa.org.uk

CA Ⓐ
Chiswick Auctions
1-5 Colville Road,
London
W3 8BL
Tel: 020 8992 4442
Fax: 020 8896 0541

CB Ⓓ
Colin Baddiel
Stand B25,
Stand 351-3,
Grays Antique Market,
South Molten Lane, London
W1Y 2LP
Tel: 020 7408 1239
Fax: 020 7493 9344

CHAA Ⓐ
**Cowan's Historic
Americana Auctions**
673 Wilmer Avenue,
Cincinnati,
OH 45226 USA
Tel: 001 513 871 1670
Fax: 001 513 871 8670
Info@HistoricAmericana.com
www.historicamericana.com

Chef Ⓐ
Cheffins
The Cambridge Saleroom,
2 Clifton Road,
Cambridge CB1 4BW
Tel: 01223 213 343
Fax: 01223 413 396
fine.art@cheffins.co.uk
www.cheffins.co.uk

Clv Ⓐ
Clevedon Salerooms
Herbert Road,
Clevedon,
Bristol BS21 7ND
Tel: 01275 876 699
Fax: 01275 343 765
clevedon.salerooms@cableinet.co.uk
www.clevedon-salerooms.com

CO Ⓐ
Cooper Owen
10 Denmark Street,
London,
WC2H 8LS
Tel: 020 7240 4132
Fax: 020 7240 4339
info@cooperowen.com
www.cooperowen.com

ColC Ⓓ
Collectors Cameras
PO Box 16, Pinner,
Middlesex HA5 4HN
Tel: 020 8421 3537

CR Ⓐ
Craftsman Auctions
333 North Main Street,
Lambertville,
NJ 08530 USA
Tel: 001 609 397 9374
Fax: 001 609 397 9377
info@ragoarts.com
www.ragoarts.com

CRIS Ⓓ
Cristobal
26 Church Street,
London NW8 8EP
Tel/Fax: 020 7724 7230
steven@cristobal.co.uk
www.cristobal.co.uk

CS Ⓓ
Christopher Seidler
Stand G13,
Grays Mews Antiques Market,
London W1K 5AB
Tel: 020 7629 2851

CSA Ⓓ
Christopher Sykes Antiques
The Old Parsonage, Woburn,
Milton Keynes MK17 9QL
Tel: 01525 290 259/290 467
Fax: 01525 290 061
sykes.corkscrews@sykes-
corkscrews.co.uk
www.sykes-corkscrews.co.uk

CVS Ⓓ
**Cad Van Swankster at
The Girl Can't Help It**
Alfies Antique Market,
Shop G100 & G116,
Ground Floor, 13-25 Church
Street, Marylebone,
London NW8 8DT
Tel: 020 7724 8984
Fax: 020 8809 3923

DAC Ⓓ
**Dynamite Antiques
& Collectibles**
Tel: 001 301 652 1140
bercovici@erols.com

DE Ⓓ
The Doll Express
P.O. Box 367,
1807 North Reading Road,
Reamstown, PA 17567 USA
Tel: 001 717 336 2414
Fax: 001 717 336 1262
thedollexpress@thedollexpress.com
www.thedollexpress.com

DH Ⓓ
David Huxtable
11 & 12 The Lipka Arcade,
288 Westbourne Grove,
London W11
07710 132 200
david@huxtins.com
www.huxtins.com

DN Ⓐ
Dreweatt Neate
Donnington Priory Salerooms,
Donnington, Newbury,
Berkshire RG14 2JE
Tel: 01635 553 553
Fax: 01635 553 599
fineart@dreweatt-neate.co.uk
www.auctions.dreweatt-
neate.co.uk

DO Ⓓ
DODO
Alfies Antique Market,
1st floor (F071,2 & 3),
13-25 Church Street,
Marylebone, London
NW8 8DT
Tel: 020 7706 1545

DRA Ⓐ
Rago Modern Auctions
333 North Main Street,
Lambertville, NJ 08530 USA
Tel: 001 609 397 9374
Fax: 001 609 397 9377
info@ragoarts.com
www.ragoarts.com

Duk Ⓐ
Hy. Duke and Son
The Dorchester Fine Art
Salerooms, Weymouth Avenue,
Dorchester, Dorset DT1 1QS
Tel: 01305 265 080
Fax: 01305 260 101
enquiries@dukes-auctions.com
www.dukes-auctions.com

FA Ⓐ
Fraser's Autographs
399 The Strand, London WC2R 0LX
Tel: 020 7836 9325
Sales@frasersautographs.co.uk
www.frasersautographs.com

FFA Ⓓ
Finesse Fine Art
Empool Cottage, West Knighton,
Dorset DT2 8PE
Tel: 01305 854 286
Fax: 01305 852 888
Mob: 07973 886 937
tony@finessefineart.com
www.finessefineart.com

FFM Ⓓ
Festival
136 South Ealing Road,
London W5 4QJ
Tel: 020 8840 9333
info@festival1951.co.uk

FLA Ⓓ
Fayne Landes Antiques
593 Hansell Road,
Wynnewood, PA 19096 USA
Tel: 001 610 658 0566

FM Ⓓ
Francesca Martire
Stand f. 131-137, First Floor,
13-25 Alfies Antiques Market,
13 Church Street,
London NW8 0RH
Tel: 020 7723 1370
www.francescamartire.com

Fra Ⓓ
France Antique Toys
Tel: 001 631 754 1399

FRE Ⓐ
Freeman's
1808 Chestnut Street,
Philadelphia, PA 19103 USA
Tel: 001 215 563 9275
Fax: 001 215 563 8236
info@freemansauction.com
www.freemansauction.com

G Ⓐ
Guernsey's Auctions
108 East 73rd Street,
New York, NY 10021 USA
Tel: 001 212 794 2280
Fax: 001 212 744 3638
guernsey@guernseys.com
www.guernseys.com

GA Ⓓ
Gentry Antiques
c/o Rod & Line Shop,
Little Green, Polperro,
Cornwall PL13 2RF
Tel: 07974 221 343
info@cornishwarecollector.co.uk
www.cornishwarecollector.co.uk

GG Ⓓ
Guest & Gray
1-7 Davies Mews,
London W1K 5AB
Tel: 020 7408 1252
Fax: 020 7499 1445
info@chinese-porcelain-art.com
www.chinese-porcelain-art.com

GorB Ⓐ
Gorringes
Terminus Road,
Bexhill-on-Sea,
East Sussex TN39 3LR
Tel: 01424 212 994
Fax: 01424 224 035
bexhill@gorringes.co.uk
www.gorringes.co.uk

GorL Ⓐ
Gorringes
15 North Street,
Lewes, East Sussex
BN7 2PD
Tel: 01273 472 503
Fax: 01273 479 559
auctions@gorringes.co.uk
www.gorringes.co.uk

GR Ⓓ
Gordon Reece Galleries
16 Clifford Street,
London W1X 1RG
Tel: 020 7439 0007
Fax: 020 7437 5715
www.gordonreecegalleries.com

Gro Ⓓ
**Mary Wise and
Grosvenor Antiques**
Grosvenor Antiques,
27 Holland Street,
London W8 4NA
Tel: 020 7937 8649
Fax: 020 7937 7179

GS Ⓓ
Goodwins Antiques Ltd
15 & 16 Queensferry Street,
Edinburgh
EH2 4QW
Tel: 0131 225 4717
Fax: 0131 220 1412

H&G Ⓓ
Hope and Glory
131A Kensington
Church Street,
London
W8 7LP
Tel: 020 7727 8424

HA Ⓐ
Hunt Auctions
75 E. Uwchlan Ave,
Suite 130, Exton,
PA 19341 USA
Tel: 001 610 524 0822
Fax: 001 610 524 0826
info@huntauctions.com
www.huntsauctions.com

HamG Ⓐ
Hamptons
Baverstock House,
93 High Street,
Godalming, Surrey
GU7 1AL
Tel: 01483 423 567
Fax: 01483 426 392
fineart@hamptons-int.com
www.hamptons.co.uk

HC Ⓓ
Heritage Comics
Heritage Plaza,
100 Highland Park Village,
2nd Floor, Dallas, Texas
75205-2788 USA
Tel: 001 800 872 6467 /
001 214 528 3500
Fax: 001 214 520 6968
www.heritagecomics.com

HLJ Ⓓ
Hugo Lee-Jones
Tel: 01227 375 375
Mob: 07941 187 2027
electroniccollectables@hotmail.com

J&H Ⓐ
**Jacobs and Hunt
Fine Art Auctioneers**
26 Lavant Street,
Petersfield, Hampshire
GU32 3EF
Tel: 01730 233 933
Fax: 01730 262 323
auctions@jacobsandhunt.co.uk
www.jacobsandhunt.co.uk

JBC Ⓟ
James Bridges Collection

JBS Ⓓ
John Bull Silver
139A New Bond Street,
London W1Y 9FB
Tel: 020 7629 1251
Fax: 020 7495 3001
elliot@jbsilverware.com
www.jbsilverware.co.uk

JDJ Ⓐ
James D Julia Inc
PO Box 830,
Fairfield, Maine 04937 USA
Tel: 001 207 453 7125
Fax: 001 207 453 2502
jjulia@juliaauctions.com
www.juliaauctions.com

JPA Ⓓ
Jessica Pack Antiques
Chapel Hill,
North Carolina USA
Tel: 001 919 408 0406
jpantiques1@aol.com

Koz Ⓓ
Bill and Rick Kozlowski
Tel: 001 215 997 2486

L&T Ⓐ
Lyon and Turnbull Ltd.
33 Broughton Place,
Edinburgh EH1 3RR
Tel: 0131 557 8844
Fax: 0131 557 8668
info@lyonandturnbull.com
www.lyonandturnbull.com

LB ⓓ
Linda Bee
Grays in The Mews
Antiques Market, 1-7 Davies
Mews, London W1K 5AB
Tel/Fax: 020 7629 5921
07956 276384

LC Ⓐ
Lawrence's Fine Art Auctioneers
South Street, Crewkerne, Somerset
TA18 8AB
Tel: 01460 73041
Fax: 01460 74627
enquiries@lawrences.co.uk
www.lawrences.co.uk

LFA Ⓐ
Law Fine Art Ltd.
Firs Cottage, Church Lane,
Brimpton, Berkshire RG7 4TJ
Tel: 0118 971 0353
Fax: 0118 971 3741
info@lawfineart.co.uk
www.lawfineart.co.uk

MA ⓓ
Manic Attic
Stand S011, Alfies Antiques
Market, 13 Church Street,
London NW8 8DT
Tel: 020 7723 6105
Fax: 020 7724 0999
manicattic@alfies.clara.net

MB ⓓ
Mostly Boxes
93 High Street,
Eton, Windsor, Berkshire
SL4 6AF
Tel: 01753 858 470
Fax: 01753 857 212

Men ⓓ
**Mendes Antique Lace
and Textiles**
Flat 2, Wilbury Lawn, 44 Wilbury
Road, Hove, BN3 3PA
Tel: 01273 203 317
www.mendes.co.uk

MH ⓓ
Mad Hatter Antiques
Unit 82, Admiral Vernon Antique
Market, 141-149 Portobello Rd,
London W11
Tel: 020 7262 0487
Mob: 07931 956 705
madhatter.portobello@virgin.net

MHC ⓟ
Mark Hill Collection
Mob: 07798 915 474
stylophile@btopenworld.com

MHT ⓓ
Mum Had That
Tel: 01442 412 360
info@mumhadthat.com
www.mumhadthat.com

MM Ⓐ
Mullock Madeley
The Old Shippon, Wall-under-
Heywood, Church Stretton,
Shropshire, SY6 7DS
Tel: 01694 771 771
Fax: 01694 771 772
info@mullockmadeley.co.uk
www.mullock-madeley.co.uk

NBen ⓓ
Nigel Benson
20th Century Glass,
58-60 Kensington Church Street,
London W8 4DB
Tel: 020 7938 1137
Fax: 020 7729 9875
Mob: 07971 859 848

OACC ⓓ
**Otford Antiques and
Collectors Centre**
26-28 High Street, Otford, Kent
TN15 9DF
Tel: 01959 522 025
Fax: 01959 525 858
www.otfordantiques.co.uk

PB ⓓ
Petersham Books
Unit 67, 56 Gloucester Rd,
Kensington,
London SW7 4UB
Tel/Fax: 020 7581 9147
ks@modernfirsts.co.uk
www.modernfirsts.co.uk

PC ⓟ
Private Collection

PJC ⓟ
Peter Jackson Collection

PR ⓓ
Paul Reichwein
2321 Hershey Avenue, East
Petersburg, PA 17520 USA
Tel: 001 717 569 7637
paulrdg@aol.com

PSA Ⓐ
Potteries Specialist Auctions
271 Waterloo Road, Cobridge,
Stoke-on-Trent ST6 3HR
Tel: 01782 286 622
Fax: 01782 213 777
enquiries@potteriesauctions.com
www.potteriesauctions.com

PSpA ⓓ
Pantiles Spa Antiques
4-6 Union House, The Pantiles,
Tunbridge Wells TN4 8HE
Tel: 01892 541 377
Fax: 01435 865 660
psa.wells@btinternet.com
www.antiques-tun-wells-kent.co.uk

PTA ⓓ
Past-Tyme Antiques
Tel: 001 703 777 8555
pasttymeantiques@aol.com

QUAD ⓓ
Quadrille
146 Portobello Rd,
London W11 2DZ

RAA ⓓ
Axtell Antiques 1 River Street,
Deposit, New York 13754 USA
Tel: 001 607 467 2353
Fax: 001 607 467 4316
rsaxtell@msn.com
www.axtellantiques.com

RB ⓓ
Roger Bradbury
Church Street, Coltishall, Norwich,
Norfolk, NR12 7DJ
Tel: 01603 737 444

RBL ⓓ
Richard Ball Lighters
richard@lighter.co.uk

RdeR ⓓ
Rogers de Rin
76 Royal Hospital Road, Paradise
Walk, Chelsea, London SW3 4HN
Tel: 020 7352 9007
Fax: 020 7351 9407
rogersderin@rogersderin.co.uk
www.rogersderin.co.uk

Ren ⓓ
Rennies
13 Rugby Street,
London WC1 3QT
Tel: 020 7405 0220
info@rennart.co.uk
www.rennart.co.uk

RG ⓓ
Richard Gibbon
34/34a Islington Green,
London N1 8DU
Tel: 020 7354 2852
neljeweluk@aol.com

RH ⓓ
Rick Hubbard Art Deco
3 Tee Court, Bell Street, Romsey,
Hampshire SO51 8GY
Tel/Fax: 01794 513 133
rick@rickhubbard-artdeco.co.uk
www.rickhubbard-artdeco.co.uk

Rox ⓓ
Roxanne's
Tel: 001 888 750 8869 /
001 215 750 8868
gemfairy@aol.com

S&T ⓓ
Steinberg and Tolkien
193 King's Road Chelsea,
London SW3 5ED
Tel: 020 7376 3660
Fax: 020 7376 3630

SCG ⓓ
**Gallery 1930 – Susie Cooper
Gallery**
18 Church Street, Marylebone,
London NW8 8EP
Tel: 020 7723 1555
Fax: 020 7735 8309
gallery1930@aol.com
www.susiecooperceramics.com

SFel ⓓ
Sandra Fellner
Grays Antiques Market, Davies
Street/Davies Mews/
South Molton Lane,
London W1Y 5AB
Tel: 020 8946 5613

SI Ⓐ
Sloans
4920 Wyaconda Road,
N Bethesda, MD 20852 USA
Tel: 001 301 468 4911
Fax: 001 301 468 9182
www.sloansauction.com

SM ⓓ
**Sparkle Moore at The Girl
Can't Help It**
Alfies Antique Market, Shop G100
& G116, Ground Floor, 13-25
Church Street, Marylebone,
London NW8 8DT
Tel: 020 7724 8984
Fax: 020 8809 3923
Mob: 07958 515 614
sparkle.moore@virgin.net
www.sparklemoore.com

SN ⓓ
Sue Norman at Antiquarius
Stand L4, Antiquarius,
135 King's Road, Chelsea,
London SW3 4PW
Tel: 020 7352 7217
Fax: 020 8870 4677
sue@sue-norman.demon.co.uk
www.sue-norman.demon.co.uk

SRA Ⓐ
Sheffield Railwayana
43 Little Norton Lane,
Sheffield S8 8GA
Tel/Fax: 0114 274 5085
ian@sheffrail.freeserve.co.uk
www.sheffieldrailwayana.co.uk

SSc ⓟ
Sue Scrivens Collection

SSp ⓓ
Sylvie Spectrum
Stand 372, Grays Antiques
Market, 58 Davies Street,
London W1Y 2LB
Tel: 020 7629 3501
Fax: 020 8883 5030

Tag ⓓ
Tagore Ltd
Stand 302, Grays Antiques
Market, 58 Davies Street, London,
W1Y 2LP
Tel: 020 7499 0158
Fax: 020 7499 0158

TK Ⓐ
Auction Team Köln
Postfach 50 11 19,
Bonner Str. 528-530,
D-50971 Köln, Germany
Tel: +49/ 0221 38 70 49
Fax: +49/0 221 37 48 78
Auction@Breker.com
www.Breker.com

TR ⓓ
Terry Rodgers & Melody LLC
30 & 31 Manhattan Art and
Antiques Center, 1050 2nd
Avenue,
New York, NY 10022
Tel: 001 212 758 3164
Fax: 001 212 935 6365

Trio ⓓ
Trio
Stand L24, Grays Antiques
Market, 1-7 Davies Mews,
London W1Y 2LP
Tel: 020 7493 2736
Fax: 020 7493 9344
www.trio-london.fsnet.co.uk

TWC Ⓐ
T W Conroy
36 Oswego St,
Baldwinsville, NY 13027
Tel: 001 315 638 6434
Fax: 001 315 638 7039
www.twconroy.com

V ⓓ
Ventisemo
4Unit S001, Alfies Antique Market,
13-25 Church Street,
Marylebone, London NW8 8DT
Mob: 07767 498 766

VE ⓓ
Vintage Eyeware
Tel: 001 917 721 6546
www.vintage-eyeware.com

Vec ⓓ
Vectis Auctions Limited
Fleck Way, Thornaby,
Stockton on Tees TS17 9JZ
Tel: 01642 750 616
Fax: 01642 769 478
enquiries@vectis.co.uk
www.vectis.co.uk

W&W Ⓐ
Wallis and Wallis
West Steet Auction Galleries,
Lewes, East Sussex BN7 2NJ
Tel: 01273 480 208
Fax: 01273 476 562
grb@wallisandwallis.co.uk
www.wallisandwallis.co.uk

WG ⓓ
The Watch Gallery
129 Fulham Road,
London,
SW3 6RT
Tel: 020 7581 3239
Fax: 020 7584 6497

WHP Ⓐ
WH Peacock
26 Newnham Street, Bedford
MK40 3JR
Tel: 01234 266 366
Fax: 01234 269 082
info@peacockauction.co.uk
www.peacockauction.co.uk

Wim ⓓ
Wimpole Antiques
Stand 349, Grays Antiques
Market, 58,
Davies St, London, W1K 2LP
Tel: 020 7499 2889
Fax: 020 7493 9344

WO ⓓ
Wiseman Originals
34 West Square, Lambeth,
0 London SE11 4SP
Tel: 020 7587 0747
Fax: 020 7793 8817
wisemanoriginals@compuserve.com
www.wisemanoriginals.com

WoS ⓓ
Wheels of Steel
Unit B10-11, Grays Mews
Antiques Market, 1/7 Davies
Mews, London W1Y 2LP
Tel: 020 7629 2813
Fax: 020 7493 9344
wheels-of-steel@grays.clara.net

WW Ⓐ
Woolley and Wallis
51-61 Castle Street, Salisbury,
Wiltshire SP1 3SU
Tel: 01722 424 500
Fax: 01722 424 508
enquiries@woolleyandwallis.co.uk
www.woolleyandwallis.co.uk

NOTE

IF YOU WISH to have any item valued, it is advisable to contact the dealer or specialist in advance to check that they will carry out this service and whether there is a charge. While most dealers will be happy to help you with an enquiry, do remember that they are busy people. Telephone valuations are not possible. Please mention *Collectables Price Guide 2003-4* by Judith Miller when making an enquiry.

DIRECTORY OF SPECIALISTS

ADVERTISING
David Huxtable
11 & 12 The Lipka Arcade,
288 Westbourne Grove,
London W11
Tel: 07710 132 200
david@huxtins.com
www.huxtins.com

ANTIQUITIES
Ancient Art
85 The Vale, Southgate,
London N14 6AT
Tel: 0208 882 1509
Fax: 0208 886 6235
ancient.art@btinternet.com
www.ancientart.com

Oxford Forum of Ancient Art
3 North Parade,
Banbury Rd,
Oxford OX2 6LX
Tel: 01865 316 366
Fax: 01865 316 969
vpurcell@oxfordforum-
ancientart.com
www.oxfordforum-
ancientart.com

Rupert Wace Ancient Art Ltd
14 Old Bond St, London
W1X 3DB
Tel: 0207 495 1623
Fax: 0207 495 8495
rupert.wace@btinternet.com

AUTOGRAPHS
Fraser's Autographs
399 The Strand, London WC2R 0LX
Tel: 0207 836 9325
sales@frasersautographs.co.uk
www.frasersautographs.co.uk

Ink Quest Autographs
Alfies Antiques Market,
Stand G058,
13-25 Church St,
London NW8 8DT
Tel: 07973 135 906

AUTOMOBILIA
Autodrome Almshouse Arcade,
Chichester PO19 4JL
Tel: 01243 778 126

C.A.R.S.
4-4a Chapel Terrace Mews,
Kemp Town, Brighton
BN2 1HU
Tel: 01273 601 690
cars@kemptown-
brighton.freeserve.co.uk
www.carsofbrighton.com.uk

Finesse Fine Art
Empool Cottage, West Knighton,
Dorset DT2 8PE
Tel: 01305 854 286
Fax: 01305 852 888
tony@finesse-fine-art.com
www.finesse-fine-art.com

BOOKS
Biblion
Gray's Mews Antiques Market
1-7 Davies Mews,
London W1K 5AB
Tel: 0207 629 1374
Fax: 0207 493 7158
info@biblion.com
www.biblion.com

Petersham Books
2 Petersham Lane,
London SW7 5PY
Tel/Fax: 0207 581 9147

Henry Sotheran Ltd
2/5 Sackville St,
London W1X 2DP
Tel: 0207 439 6151
sotherans@sotherans.co.uk
www.sotherans.co.uk

Shapero Rare Books
32 St George St,
London W1S 2EA
Tel: 0207 493 0876
rarebooks@shapero.com
www.shapero.com

CAMERAS
Collectors Cameras
P.O. Box 16, Pinner,
Middx HA5 4HN
Tel: 0208 428 4773

Vintage Cameras
256 Kirkdale, Sydenham,
London SE26 4NL
Tel: 0208 778 5416
info@vintagecameras.co.uk
www.vintagecameras.co.uk

CANES
Michael German Antiques
38b Kensington Church St
London W8
Tel: 0207 937 2771

CERAMICS
Andrew Dando
34 Market St, Bradford-on-
Avon, BA15 1LL
Tel: 01225 422 702
Fax: 01225 310 717
andrew@andrewdando.co.uk
www.andrewdando.co.uk

Beth Adams
Alfies Antiques Market, Stand
G43/44, 13-25 Church St,
London NW8
Tel: 0207 723 5613
Fax: 0207 262 1576

Beverly
30 Church St, London NW8
Tel: 0207 262 1576

**Gallery 1930 –
Susie Cooper Gallery**
18 Church St, London
NW8 8EP
Tel: 0207 723 1555
Fax: 0207 735 8309

Festival for Midwinter
136 Sth Ealing Rd,
London W5 4QJ
Tel: 0208 840 9333
sj@festival1951.demon.co.uk

Gentry Antiques
C/o Rod & Line Shop,
Little Green, Polperro,
Cornwall PL13 2RF
Tel: 07974 221 343
info@cornishwarecollector.couk
www.cornishwarecollector.co.uk

Jacqueline Oosthuizen
23 Cale St, London SW3 3QR
Tel: 0207 352 6071

Mad Hatter
Admiral Vernon Antiques
Market, Unit 83, 141-149
Portobello Rd,
London W11
Tel: 0207 262 0487
madhatter.portobello@virgin.net

Rick Hubbard Art Deco
3 Tee Court, Bell St, Romsey,
Hampshire SO51 8GY
Tel: 01794 513133
www.rickhubbard-artdeco.co.uk

Stockspring Antiques
114 Kensington Church St,
London W8 4BH
Tel/Fax: 0207 727 7995
stockspring@antique-
porcelain.co.uk
www.antique-porcelain.co.uk

Sue Norman
Antiquarius, Stand L4,
135 King's Rd, London
SW3 4PW
Tel: 0207 352 7217
Fax: 0208 870 4677
sue@sue-norman.demon.co.uk
www.sue-norman.demon.co.uk

**The Emporium Antiques &
Collectibles Centre**
138-140 Upper Wickham Lane,
Welling DA16 3DP
Tel: 0208 855 8308

**Mary Wise & Grosvenor
Antiques**
27 Holland St, London W8 4NA
Tel: 0207 937 8649
Fax: 0207 937 7179
info@artnetwork.co.uk
www.art-network.co.uk
Sylvia Powell Decorative Arts

18 The Mall, Islington,
London N1 0PD
Tel: 0207 354 2977
dpowell909@aol.com
www.sylvia-powell.com

CLOCKS & WATCHES
**Keith Stones Grandfather
Clocks**
5 Ellers Drive, Doncaster,
South Yorks DN4 7DL
Tel: 01302 535 258
clocks@kstones.fsnet.co.uk
www.kstones.fsnet.co.uk

Kleanthous Antiques
144 Portobello
Rd, London W11 2DZ
Tel: 0207 727 3649
antiques@kleanthous.com
www.kleanthous.com

The Watch Gallery
129 Fulham Rd,
London SW3 6RT
Tel: 0207 581 3239
Fax: 0207 584 6497

COMICS
Book & Comic Exchange
14 Pembridge Road,
London W11
Tel: 0207 229 8420

**Tilley's Vintage
Magazine Shop**
281 Shoreham St, Sheffield
Tel: 01142 752 442
tilleys281@aol.com
www.tilleysmagazines.com

COMMEMORATIVE
WARE
Hope & Glory
131a Kensington
Church St, London W8 7LP
Tel: 0207 727 8424

Recollections 5 Royal Arcade,
Boscombe BH1 4BT
Tel: 01202 304 441

COSTUME JEWELLERY
Cristobal
26 Church St, London NW8 8EP
Tel: 0207 724 7230
steven@cristobal.co.uk
www.cristobal.co.uk

Richard Gibbon
34/34a Islington Green,
London N1 8DU
Tel 0207 354 2852
neljeweluk@aol.com

William Wain
Antiquarius, 131-141 King's Rd
London SW3 4PW
Tel: 0207 351 5353

EPHEMERA
Iain Campbell
1 Barrowmore Estate,
Chester CH3 7JA
Tel: 01829 741 499

Quadrille 146 Portobello Road,
London W11 2DZ

FIFTIES & SIXTIES
Francesca Martire
Alfie's Antiques Market, Stand
F131-7, 13-25 Church St,
London NW8 8DT
Tel: 0207 723 1370

Manic Attic
Alfie's Antiques Market, Stand
S011, 13-25 Church St,
London NW8 8DT
Tel: 0207 723 6105
Fax: 0207 724 0999
manicattic@alfies.clara.net

Ventisemo
Alfie's Antiques Market,
Unit S001
13-25 Church St.,
London NW8 8DT

Zoom
Arch 65, Cambridge Grove
London W6 0LD
Tel: 07000 9666 2001
eddiesandham@hotmail.com
www.retrozoom.com

GENERAL
**Otford Antiques and
Collectors Centre**
26-28 High St, Otford,
Kent TN15 9DF
Tel: 01959 522 025
Fax: 01959 525 858
www.otfordantiques.co.uk

Pantiles Spa Antiques
4-6 Union House, The Pantiles,
Tunbridge Wells, Kent TN4 8HE
Tel: 01892 541 377
Fax: 01435 865 660
psa.wells@btinternet.com
www.antiques-tun-wells-
kent.co.uk

**Woburn Abbey
Antiques Centre**
Woburn Abbey, Woburn,
Bedfordshire MK17 9WA
Tel: 01525 290 350
Fax: 01525 292 102

GLASS
Andrew Lineham Fine Glass
The Mall, Camden Passage,
London N1 8ED
Tel/Fax: 01243 576 241
andrew@andrewlineham.co.uk
www.andrewlineham.co.uk

Frank Dux Antiques
33 Belvedere, Bath BA1 5HR
Tel/Fax: 01225 312 367
antique.glass@bath.co.uk
www.antique-glass.co.uk

Jeanette Hayhurst Fine Glass
32a Kensington Church St,
London W8
Tel: 0207 938 1539

Mum Had That
Tel: 01442 412 360
info@mumhadthat.com
www.mumhadthat.com

Nigel Benson 20th Century
Glass, 58-60 Kensington
Church St, London W8 4DB
Tel: 0207 938 1137
Fax: 0207 729 9875

JEWELLERY
Joseph Bonnar
72 Thistle St, Edinburgh EH2 1EN
Tel: 0131 226 2811

N. Bloom & Son
The Bond Street Antiques
Centre,124 New Bond St,
London W1S 1DX
Tel: 0207 629 5060
nbloom@nbloom.com
www.nbloom.com

Sylvie Spectrum
Gray's Antiques Market, Stand
372, 58 Davies St, London W1Y
2LB
Tel: 0207 629 3501
Fax: 0208 883 5030

Wimpole Antiques
Gray's Antiques Market,
Stand 349,
58 Davies St, London W1K 5LP
Tel: 0207 499 2889
Fax: 0207 624 7628

KITCHENALIA
Appleby Antiques Geoffrey Van
Arcade, Stand 18, 107
Portobello Rd, London W11
Tel: 01453 753 126
applebyantiques@aol.com
www.applebyantiques.com

Below Stairs of Hungerford
103 High St, Hungerford,
Berkshire RG17 0NB
Tel: 01488 682 317
Fax: 01488 684 294
hofgartner@belowstairs.co.uk
www.belowstairs.co.uk

Kitchen Bygones
Alfie's Antiques Market, Stand
B51-53, 13-25 Church St,
London NW8 8DT
Tel: 0207 258 3045

Ann Lingard
Rope Walk Antiques, 18-22
Rope Walk, Rye, Sussex TN31 7NA
Tel: 01797 233 486
Fax: 01797 224 700

MECHANICAL MUSIC
Mayflower Antiques
105 High St, Dovercourt
CO12 3AP
mayflower@anglianet.co.uk

Terry & Daphne France
Tel: 01243 265 946
Fax: 01243 779 582

The Talking Machine
30 Watford Way,
London NW4 3AL
Tel: 0208 202 3473
talkingmachine@gramophones.n
direct.co.uk
www.gramophones.ndirect.co.uk

MILITARIA
Anthony Goodlad
26 Fairfield Rd, Brockwell,
Chesterfield S40 4TP
Tel: 01246 204 004

Boscombe Militaria
86 Palmerston Rd,
Boscombe, Bournemouth
BH1 4HU
Tel: 01202 733 696

Christopher Seidler
Gray's Mews Antiques Market
South Molton Lane, London
W1K 5AB
Tel: 0207 629 2851

Q&C Militaria
22 Suffolk Rd,
Cheltenham GL50 2AQ
Tel: 01242 519 815
john@qcmilitaria.freeserve.
co.uk
www.qcmilitaria.com

**The Armoury of
St James' Military
Antiquarians**, 17 Piccadilly
Arcade, Piccadilly, London
SW1Y 6NH
Tel: 0207 493 5082
welcome@armoury.co.uk
www.armoury.co.uk

Chelsea Military Antiques
Antiquarius, Stand N13/14
131/141 King's Road,
London SW3
Tel: 0207 352 0308

ORIENTAL & ASIAN
Roger Bradbury
Church St, Coltishall, Norwich
Norfolk NR12 7DJ
Tel: 01603 737 444

Justin Garrard
Dolphin Arcade, 155
Portobello Rd
London W11
Tel: 0208 847 2349

Guest & Gray
Gray's Mews Antiques Market,
1-7 Davies Mews, London
W1K 5AB
Tel: 0207 408 1252
Fax: 0207 499 1445
info@chinese-porcelain-
art.com
www.chinese-porcelain-
art.com

Japanese Gallery
23 Camden Passage,
London N1 8EA
Tel: 0207 226 3347
Fax: 0207 229 2934

Ormonde Gallery
156 Portobello Rd, London
W11 2EB
Tel: 0207 229 9800
ormondegall@aol.com

Patricia Cater Oriental Art
Gloucestershire GL56 0QW
Tel: 01451 870 126
patriciacaterorg@aol.com
www.patriciacater-
orientalart.com

PLASTICS
Noe & Chiesa
Alfie's Antiques Market,
Stand G87-8, 13-25
Church St,
London NW8 8DT
Tel: 0207 723 0449

POSTERS
At The Movies 17 Fouberts
Place, London W1F 7QD
Tel/Fax: 0207 439 6355
info@atthemovies.co.uk
www.atthemovies.co.uk

Barclay Samson
65 Finlay St,
London SW6 6HF
Tel: 0207 731 8013
richard@barclaycamson.com

DODO
Alfies Antiques Market, Shop
F071, 13-25 Church St,
London NW8 8DT
Tel: 0207 706 1545

Rennies
13 Rugby St,
London WC1 3QT
Tel: 0207 405 0220
info@rennart.co.uk
www.rennart.co.uk

MODERN PRINTS
Images
248 Verulam Court,
Woolmead Ave,
London NW9 7AZ
Tel: 0208 202 7949
Fax: 0208 202 8014
sales@images-art.co.uk
www.images-art.co.uk

Wiseman Originals
34 West Square,
London SE11 4SP
Tel: 0207 587 0747
Fax: 0207 793 8817
wisemanoriginals@compuserv
e.com
www.wisemanoriginals.com

PENS & WRITING
Battersea Pen Home
P.O. Box 6128,
Epping CM16 4CG
Tel: 0870 900 1888
Fax: 0970 909 9888
info@penhome.com
www.penhome.com

Henry The Pen Man
Admiral Vernon Antiques
Market Portobello Rd,
London W11
Tel: 0208 530 3277

ROCK & POP
More Than Music
P.O. Box 2809, Eastbourne,
Sussex BN21 2EA
Tel: 01323 649 778
Fax: 01323 649 779
www.mtmglobal.com

Tracks
P.O. Box 117, Chorley,
Lancashire, PR6 0UU
Tel: 01257 269 726
Fax: 01257 231 340
sales@tracks.co.uk
www.tracks.co.uk

SCENT/PERFUME BOTTLES
Linda Bee
Gray's Mews Antiques Market,
107 Davies Mews,
London, W1Y 2LP
Tel: 0207 629 5921
Fax: 0207 629 5921

Lynda Brine Antiques
Assembly Antiques Centre,
5-8 Saville Row, Bath,
Somerset
Tel: 01225 448 488
lyndabrine@yahoo.co.uk
www.scentbottlesandsmalls.
co.uk

Tom Clarke
Admiral Vernon Antiques
Centre, Unit 36, Portobello
Rd, London W11
Tel/Fax: 0208 802 8936

Trio
Gray's Antiques Market,
Stand L24,1-7 Davies Mews,
London W1Y 2LP
Tel: 0207 493 2736
Fax: 0207 493 9344

SCIENTIFIC & TECHNICAL, INCLUDING OFFICE, MEDICAL, OPTICAL
Arthur Middleton
12 New Row, Covent Garden,
London WC2N 4LF
Tel: 0207 836 7042
Fax: 0207 497 2486

Branksome Antiques
370 Poole Rd, Branksome,
Dorset BH12 1AW
Tel: 01202 763 324
Fax: 01202 769 932

**The Classic Telephone
Company**
Antiques on High, 85 High St,
Oxon OX1 4BG
Tel: 01865 251 075

On the Air Ltd
The Vintage Technology
Centre, The Highway,
Hawarden CH5 3DN
Tel: 01244 530 300
www.vintageradio.co.uk

Stuart Talbot
P.O. Box 31525,
London W11 2XY
Tel: 0208 969 7011
talbot.stuart@talk21.com

SEWING & NEEDLEWORK
Thomas & Pamela Hudson
9 Watermore Rd, Cirencester
GL7 1JW
Tel: 01285 652 972
www.pwhudson.demon.co.uk

SILVER
John Bull Silver
139a New Bond St,
London W1Y 9FB
Tel: 0207 629 1251
Fax: 0207 495 3001
elliot@jbsilver.co.uk
www.jbsilver.co.uk

Goodwins Antiques
15 & 16 Queensferry St
Edinburgh EH2 4QW
Tel: 0131 225 4717
Fax: 0131 220 1412

Jeffrey Neal & Tim Evans
The Portobello Antiques Store,
79 Portobello Rd,
London W11 2QB
Tel: 0207 229 8202

Peter Gaunt
Gray's Antiques Market,
Stand 120, South Molton Lane,
London W1Y 2LP
Tel: 0207 629 1072

The London Silver Vaults
Chancery House, 53-64
Chancery Lane,
London WC2A 1QS
Tel: 0207 242 3844

SMOKING
Richard Ball
richard@lighter.co.uk
www.lighter.co.uk

Tagore
Gray's Antiques Market, Stand
302, 58 Davies St,
London W1Y 2LB
Tel: 0207 499 0158

Tom Clarke
Admiral Vernon Antiques
Centre, Unit 36,
Portobello Rd, London W11
Tel/Fax: 0208 802 8936

SPORTING MEMORABILIA
Fiona Taylor
Jubilee Hall Antiques Centre,
Oak St, Lechlade GL7 3AE
Tel: 01367 253 777

Manfred Schotten
109 High St, Burford,
Oxon OX18 4RH
Tel: 01993 822 302
enquiries@schotten.com
www.schotten.com

Old Troon Sporting Antiques
49 Ayr St, Troon KA10 6EB
Tel: 01292 311 822
Fax: 01292 313 111

Sean Arnold
1 Pembridge Villas,
London W2 4XE
Tel: 0207 221 2267
Fax: 0207 221 5464

Simon Brett Creswyke House,
Moreton-in-Marsh GL56 0LH
Tel: 01608 650 751

Vintage Picatoriana
Westbourne Antiques Arcade,
Stand 27a, 113 Portobello Rd,
London W11

Warboys Antiques
Old Church School, High St,
Warboys PE28 2SX
Tel: 01487 823 686
john.lambden@sportingantiques.
co.uk
www.sportingantiques.co.uk

Yesterday's Tackle & Books
42 Clingan Rd, Boscombe East
BH6 5PZ
Tel: 01202 476 586

TEXTILES & COSTUME
**Cad van Swankster at
The Girl Can't Help It**
Alfies Antiques Market, Shop
G100 & G115, 13-25 Church St,
London NW8 8DT
Tel: 0207 724 8984
Fax: 0208 809 3923

**Mendes Antiques
Textiles & Lace**
Flat 2 Wilbury Lawn,
44 Wilbury Road,
Hove BN3 3PA
lace@mendes.co.uk
www.mendes.co.uk

Old Hat
66 Fulham High St,
London SW6 3LQ
Tel: 0207 610 6558

**Sparkle Moore at The Girl
Can't Help It**
Alfie's Antiques Market,
Shop G100 & G116, 13-25
Church St,
London NW8 8DT
Tel: 0207 724 8984
Fax: 0208 809 3923
sparkle.moore@virgin.net
www.sparklemoore.com

Steinburg & Tolkien
193 King's Rd, London
SW3 5ED
Tel: 0207 376 3660
Fax: 0207 376 3630

Witney Antiques 96-100 Corn
St, Witney, Oxon OX2 6BU
lel: 01993 703 902
Fax: 01933 779 852
witneyantiques@commumity.
co.uk
www.witneyantiques.com

TOOLS
The Tool Shop
78 High St, Needham Market,
Suffolk IP6 8AW
Tel: 01449 722 992

TOYS, GAMES & DOLLS
Automatomania
Gray's Antiques Market, Shop 124,
58 Davies St, London W1K 5LP
Tel: 0207 495 5259
www.automatomania.com

Bébés & Jouets C/o Post
Office, 165 Restalrig Rd,
Edinburgh EH7 6HW
Tel: 0131 332 5650

**Collectors Old Toy Shop
& Antiques**
89 Northgate, Halifax,
North Yorkshire, HX1 1XF
Tel: 01422 360 434

Colin Baddiel
Gray's Antique Market, Stand
B25, South Molton Lane,
London W1Y 2LP
Tel: 0207 629 7352
Fax: 0207 493 9344

Garrick Coleman
75 Portobello Rd, London W11
Tel: 0207 937 5524
coleman-antiques-antiques-
london@compuserve.com
www.antiquechess.co.uk

Hugo Lee-Jones
Tel: 01227 375 375
Tel: 07941 187 2027
electroniccollectables@hotmail.com

Sandra Fellner
Gray's Antiques Market,
58 Davies St., London W1
Tel: 0208 946 5613

Sue Pearson 12 1/2 Prince
Albert St,
Brighton, East Sussex BN1 1HE
Tel: 01273 329 247
www.sue-pearson.co.uk

The Vintage Toy & Train Shop
Sidmouth Antiques & Collectors'
Centre, All Saints' Rdm,
Sidmouth EX10 8ES
Tel: 01395 512 588

Tim Armitage 99 Welsh Row,
Nantwich CW5 5ET
Tel: 01270 626 608

Victoriana Dolls
101 Portobello Rd,
London W11 2BQ
Tel: 01737 249 525
Fax: 01737 226 254
heather.bond@totalserve.co.uk

Wheels of Steel (Trains)
Gray's Mews Antiques Market,
Stand 349, 58 Davies St,
London W1Y 2LP
Tel:0207 629 2813

TREEN & BOXES
Becca Gauldie Antiques
Scottish Antiques & Arts Centre
Abernyte, Scotland PH14 9SJ
Tel: 01828 686 401

**June & Tony Stone Fine
Antique Boxes**
75 Portobello Rd, London,
W11 2QB
Tel: 01273 579 333
jts@boxes.co.uk
www.boxes.co.uk

Mostly Boxes
93 High St, Eton, Windsor,
Berkshire SL4 6AF
Tel: 01753 858 470

Pauline Parkes
Durham House Antiques Centre,
Sheep St, Stow-on-the-Wold
GL54 1AA
Tel: 01451 870 404
durhamhouse@compuserve.com

Polly de Courcy-Ireland
P.O. Box 29, Alresford,
Hampshire SO24 9WP
Tel: 01962 733 131

Rogers de Rin
76 Royal Hospital Road,
Paradise Walk, London SW3 4HN
Tel: 0207 352 9007
rogersderin@rogersderin.co.uk
www.rogersderin.co.uk

Susan Shaw Period Pieces
Solihull West, Midlands
Tel/Fax: 0121 709 1205

Peter Gibbons Jubilee Hall
Antiques Centre, Oak St,
Lechlade GL7 3AY
Tel: 01367 253777

TRIBAL
Elms Lesters
The Painting Rooms,
Flitcroft St, London WC2H 8LS
Tel: 0207 836 6747
www.elms-lesters.demon.co.uk

Gordon Reece
16 Clifford St, London W1X 1RG
Tel: 0207 439 0007
Fax: 0207 437 5715
www.gordonreecegalleries.com

Pacifica Block 7, 479 Park West
Place,Edgware Rd, London W2
Tel: 0207 402 6717

WINE & DRINKING

Bacchus Lombard St,
Petworth GU28 0AG
Tel: 01798 342844
Fax: 01798 342634

Christopher Sykes Antiques
The Old Parsonage, Woburn,
Milton Keynes MK17 5AB
Tel: 01525 290 259
Fax: 01525 290061

sykes.corkscrews@sykes-
corkscrews.co.uk
www.sykes-corkscrews.co.uk

Tagore Ltd
Gray's Antiques Market, Stand
302, 58 Davies St, London, W1Y
2LB
Tel: 0207 499 0158

NEW COLLECTABLES

Contemporary Applied Arts
Mary La Trobe-Bateman,
2 Percy St,
London W1T 1DD
Tel: 0207 436 2344
Fax: 0207 436 2446
www.caa.org.uk

Crafts Council Gallery Shop
44a Pentonville Rd, Islington,
London N1 9BY
Tel: 0207 806 2559
www.craftscouncil.org.uk

Vetro & Arte Gallery
Calle de Cappeller 3212,
Dorsoduro 30123, Venezia, Italia
Tel: 0039 041 5229 525
contact@venicewebgallery.com
www.venicewebgallery.com

DIRECTORY OF AUCTIONEERS

THIS IS A LIST OF AUCTIONEERS that conduct regular sales. Auctioneers who
wish to be listed in this directory for our next edition, space permitting, are
requested to email info@thepriceguidecompany.com

LONDON

Angling Auctions
PO Box 2095,
London W12 8RU
Telephone: 0208 749 4175
Fax: 0208 743 4855
neil@anglingauctions.demon.
co.uk

Bloomsbury Book Auctions
3 & 4 Hardwick Street,
London EC1R 4RY
Tel: 0207 833 2636
Fax: 0207 833 3954
info@bloomsbury-book-
auct.com
www.bloomsbury-book-
auct.com

Bonhams
101 New Bond Street,
London W1S 1SR
Tel: 0207 393 3900
Fax: 0207 393 3905
www.bonhams.com
info@bonhams.com

Chiswick Auctions
1-5 Colville Road,
London W1S 1SR
Tel: 020 8992 4442
Fax: 020 8896 0541

Christies (South Kensington)
85 Old Brompton Road,
London SW7 3LD
Tel: 0207 581 7611
Fax: 0207 321 3311
www.christies.com
info@christies.com

Cooper Owen
10 Denmark Street, London
WC2H 8LS
Tel: 0207 240 4132
Fax: 0207 240 4339
auctions@cooperowen.com
www.cooperowen.com

Fraser's Autographs
399 The Strand,
London WC2R 0LX
Tel: 020 7836 9325
Sales@frasersautographs.co.uk
www.frasersautographs.com

Sotheby's 34-35 New Bond
Street, London W1A 2AA
Tel: 0207 293 5000
Fax: 0207 293 5989
www.sothebys.com
info@sothebys.com

Rosebery's
74-76 Knights Hill, West
Norwood, London, SE27 0JD
Tel: 0208 761 2522
Fax: 0208 761 2524

BEDFORDSHIRE

W. & H. Peacock The Auction
Centre, 26 Newnham Street,
Bedford, MK40 3JR
Tel: 01234 266366
Fax: 01234 269082
www.peacockauction.co.uk
info@peacockauction.co.uk

BERKSHIRE

Cameo Kennet Holme Farm,
Bath Road, Midgham, Reading,
Berkshire, RG7 5UX
United Kingdom
Telephone: 0118 971 3772
Fax: 0118 971 0330
cameo-auctioneers@lineone.net

Dreweatt Neate
Donnington Priory, Donnington,
Nr. Newbury, RG14 2JE
Tel: 01635 553553
Fax: 01635 553599
www.auctions.dreweatt-
neate.co.uk
info@dreweatt-neate.co.uk

Law Fine Art Ltd
Firs Cottage, Church Lane,
Brimpton RG7 4TJ
Tel: 0118 971 0353
Fax: 0118 971 3741
info@lawfineart.co.uk
www.lawfineart.co.uk

Special Auction Services
The Coach House, Midgham
Park, Reading, RG7 5UG
commemorative@aol.com

BUCKINGHAMSHIRE

Amersham Auction Rooms
125 Station Road, Amersham,
Buckinghamshire, HP7 0AH
Tel: 01494 729292
Fax: 01494 722337
info@amershamauctionrooms.
co.uk
www.amershamauctionrooms.
co.uk

CAMBRIDGESHIRE

Cheffins The Cambridge
Saleroom, 2 Clifton Rd,
Cambridge, CB1 4BW
Tel: 01223 213343
Fax: 01223 413396
fine.art@cheffins.co.uk
www.cheffins.co.uk

Hyperion Auctions Ltd
Station Road, St Ives
PE27 5BH
Tel: 01480 464140
Fax: 01480 497552
enquiries@hyperionauctions.co.uk
www.hyperionauctions.co.uk

CHANNEL ISLANDS

Martel Maides
40 Cornet Street, St Peters Port,
Guernsey, Channel Islands GY1
1LF United Kingdom
Telephone: 01481 722700
Fax: 01481 723306
auctions@martelmaides.co.uk
www.martelmaides.co.uk

CHESHIRE

Frank R. Marshall & Co.
Marshall House, Church Hill,
Knutsford, WA16 6DH
Tel: 01565 653284
Fax: 01565 652341
antiques@frankmarshall.co.uk
www.frankmarshall.co.uk

Halls Fine Art (Chester)
Booth Mansion, 30 Watergate
Street, Chester, Cheshire, CH1
2LA United Kingdom
Telephone: 01244 312300
Fax: 01244 312112
general@halls-auctioneers.ltd.uk
www.halls-auctioneers.ltd.uk

**Bob Gowland International
Golf Auctions**
The Stables, Claim Farm,
Manley Road
Frodsham, Cheshire, WA6 6HT
Tel/Fax: 01928 740668
bob@internationalgolfauctions.com
www.internationalgolfauctions.com

CLEVELAND

Vectis Auctioneers Fleck Way,
Thornaby, Stockton-on-Tees,
TS17 9JZ
Tel: 01642 750616
Fax: 01642 769478
enquiries@vectis.co.uk
www.vectis.co.uk

CORNWALL

Jeffreys 5 Fore Street,
Lostwithiel, Cornwall, PL22 0BP
Tel: 01208 872245
Fax: 01208 873260
Jeffreys.lostwithiel@btinternet.com

W.H. Lane & Son
Jubilee House, Queen Street,
Penzance, TR18 4DF
graham.bazley@excite.com

David Lay
The Penzance Auction House,
Alverton, Penzance, Cornwall,
TR18 4RE United Kingdom
Tel: 01736 361414
Fax: 01736 360035
dlay@pzsw.fsnet.co.uk

CUMBRIA

James Thompson
64 Main Street, Kirkby,
Lonsdale, LA6 2AJ
Tel: 01524 271555
Fax: 01524 272939
sales@jthompsonauctioneers.
co.uk
www.jthompsonauctioneers.co.uk

Mitchells Auction Co.
Furniture Hall, 47 Station Road,
Cockermouth, Cumbria, United
Kingdom CA13 9PZ
Tel: 01900 828557
Fax: 01900 828073
MFineart@aol.com

Penrith Farmers' & Kidds
Skirsgill Saleroom, Skirsgill,
Penrith, CA11 0DN
Tel: 01768 890781
Fax: 01768 895058
penrith.farmers@virgin.net

DERBYSHIRE

Noel Wheatcroft & Son
Matlcok Auction Gallery,
The Old Picture Palace, Dale
Road, Matlock DE4 3LU
Tel: 01629 57460
Fax: 01629 57956
www.wheatcroft-noel.co.uk

DEVON

Bearne's St Edmund's Court,
Okehampton Street,
Exeter, EX4 1LX
Tel: 01392 207000
Fax: 01392 207007
enquiries@bearnes.co.uk
www.bearnes.co.uk

Bonhams Dowell Street,
Honiton EX14 1LX
Tel: 01404 41872
Fax: 01404 43137
honiton@bonhams.com
www.bonhams.com

Taylor's
Honiton Galleries, 205 High
Street, Honiton, Devon, EX14
8LF United Kingdom
Telephone: 01404 42404
Fax: 01404 46510
sales@honitongalleries.com

DORSET

Charterhouse
Back Lane, Sherborne, Dorset
DT9 3JE, United Kingdom
Telephone: 01935 812277
Fax: 01935 389387
enquiry@charterhouse-
auctions.co.uk
www.charterhouse-auctions.co.uk

HY Duke & Sons
Weymouth Avenue, Dorchester,
Dorset, DT1 1QS United Kingdom
Telephone: 01305 265080
Fax: 01305 260101
enquiries@dukes-auctions.com
www.thesaurus.co.uk/
hyduke&son

Martin Spencer Thomas
43a Rolle St., Exmouth,
Devon EX8 2SN
Tel: 01395 267403
Fax: 01395 222598
martin@martinspencerthomas.co.uk
www.martinspencerthomas.co.uk

Riddetts of Bournemouth
177 Holdenhurst Road,
Bournemouth, BH8 8DQ
Tel: 01202 555686
Fax: 01202 311004
auctions@riddetts.co.uk
ww.riddetts.co.uk

Semley Auctioneers
Station Road, Semley, Nr
Shaftesbury, Dorset SP7 9AN,
United Kingdom
Tel: 01747 855122
Fax: 01747 855222
semley.auctioneers@btinternet.com
www.semleyauctioneers.com

ESSEX

Ambrose Ambrose House, Old
Station Road, Loughton, Essex
IG10 4PE United Kingdom
Telephone: 0208 502 3951
Fax: 0208 532 0833
info@ambroseauction.co.uk
www.ambroseauction.co.uk

G.E. Sworder & Sons
14 Cambridge Road, Stansted
Mountfitchet, Essex CM24 8DE
United Kingdom
Telephone: 01279 817778
Fax: 01279 817779
auctions@sworder.co.uk
www.sworder.co.uk

GLOUCESTERSHIRE

BK The Tithe Barn, Southam,
Cheltenham, Gloucestershire
GL52 3NY, United Kingdom
Telephone: 01242 573904
Fax: 01242 224463
artantiques@bkonline.co.uk
www.bkonline.co.uk

Bristol Auction Rooms
St Johns Place, Apsley Road,
Clifton, Bristol BS8 2ST
United Kingdom
Telephone: 0117 973 7201
Fax: 0117 973 5671
info@bristolauctionrooms.com
www.bristolauctionrooms.com

Cotswold Auction Co.
Chapel Walk Saleroom,
Chapel Walk, Cheltenham,
Gloucestershire GL50 3DS
United Kingdom
Tel: 01242 256363
Fax: 01242 571734
info@cotswoldauction.co.uk
www.cotswoldauction.co.uk

Mallams (Cheltenham)
26 Grosvenor Street,
Cheltenham, Gloucestershire,
GL52 2SG United Kingdom
Telephone: 01242 235712
Fax: 01242 241943
cheltenham@mallams.co.uk
www.mallams.co.uk

HAMPSHIRE

Andrew Smith & Sons
Hankin's Garage, 47 West
Street, Alresford, Hampshire
Tel: 01962 842841
Fax: 01962 863274
chrisjarrey@andrewsmithandson.
fsbusiness.co.uk

Jacobs and Hunt
Fine Art Auctioneers
26 Lavant Street,
Petersfield,
Hampshire GU32 3EF
Tel: 01730 233 933
Fax: 01730 262 323

Odiham Auction Sales
Unit 4, Priors Farm, West Green
Road, Mattingley, Hampshire
RG27 8JU United Kingdom
Telephone: 01189 326 824
Fax: 01189 326 797
auction@dircon.co.uk
www.thesaurus.co.uk/odiham

HEREFORDSHIRE

Brightwells The Fine Art
Saleroom, Ryelands Road,
Leominster, Herefordshire,
HR6 8NZ
Tel: 01568 611122
Fax: 01568 610519
www.brightwells.com

HERTFORDSHIRE

**Brown & Merry –
Tring Market Auctions**
Brook Street, Tring, HP23 5EF
Tel: 01442 826 446
Fax: 01442 890 927

ISLE OF WIGHT

Ways The Auction House,
Garfield Road, Ryde, PO33 2PT
Tel: 01983 562255
Fax: 01983 565108
ways@wayauctionrooms.fsbusine
ss.co.uk
www.waysauctionrooms.fsbusine
ss.co.uk

KENT

Bonhams 49 London Road,
Sevenoaks, Kent, TN13 1AR
Tel: 01732 740310
Fax: 01732 741832
sevenoaks@bonhams.com
www.bonhams.com

Bracketts The Auction Halls,
Linden Park Road, Pantiles,
Tunbridge Wells, Kent, TN2 5QL
United Kingdom
Telephone: 01892 544500
Fax: 01892 515191
sales@bfaa.co.uk
www.bfaa.co.uk

Hogben Auctioneers
Unit C, Highfield Estate, off
Warren Road, Folkestone, Kent,
CT19 6DD, United Kingdom
Telephone: 01303 246810
Fax: 01303 246256
hogbenauctions@btconnect.com

LANCASHIRE

Capes Dunn & Co.
The Auction Galleries, 3
8 Charles Street,
Manchester, M1 7DB
Tel: 0161 273 1911
Fax: 0161 273 3474

LEICESTERSHIRE

Gilding's Roman Way Market,
Harborough, LE16 7PQ
Tel: 01858 410414
Fax: 01858 432956
sales@gildings.co.uk
www.gildings.co.uk

Heathcote Ball & Co.
Castle Auction Rooms,
78 St Nicholas Circle,
Leicester, LE1 5NW
Tel: 0116 2536789
Fax: 0116 2538517
heathcoteball@clara.net

LINCOLNSHIRE

Golding Young & Co.
Old Wharf Road, Grantham,
Lincolnshire, NG31 7AA
United Kingdom
Telephone: 01476 565118
Fax: 01476 561475
enquiries@goldingyoung.com
www.goldingyoung.com

Marilyn Swain
The Old Barracks, Sandon Road, Grantham, Lincolnshire, NG31 9AS, United Kingdom
Telephone: 01476 568861
Fax: 01476 576100
swain.auctions@virgin.net

MERSEYSIDE

Cato, Crane & Co 6 Stanhope Street, Liverpool, L8 5RE
Tel: 0151 709 5559
Fax: 0151 707 2454
www.cato-crane.co.uk

NORFOLK

Keys 8 Market Place, Aylsham, Norfolk, NR11 6EH, United Kingdom
Telephone: 01263 733195
Fax: 01263 732140
mail@aylshamsalerooms.co.uk
www.aylshamsalerooms.co.uk

Knights Sporting Auctions
The Thatched Gallery, The Green, Aldborough, Norwich, Norfolk, NR11 7AA
Tel: 01263 768488
Fax: 01263 768788
www.knights.co.uk

Horners Auctioneers Acle Salerooms, Main Road, Acle, Norfolk
Tel:0800 975 4416
Fax: 01493 750 506
auction@horners.co.uk
www.horners.co.uk

NORTHAMPSTONSHIRE

Heathcote Ball & Co. Albion Auction Rooms, Commercial Street, Northampton, NN1 1PJ
Tel: 01604 622735

NOTTINGHAMSHIRE

Mellors & Kirk Fine Art Auctioneers
Gregory Street, Nottingham, NG7 2NL
Tel: 0115 9790000
melkirk@dircon.co.uk
www.mellors-kirk.co.uk

Neales 192-194 Mansfield Road, Nottingham, NG1 3HU
Tel: 0115 9624141
Fax: 0115 9856890
fineart@neales.co.uk
www.neales.co.uk

T. Vennett-Smith 11 Nottingham Road, Gotham, Nottingham, NG11 0HE
Tel: 0115 9830541
Fax: 0115 9830114
info@vennett-smith.co.uk
www.vennett-smith.co.uk

OXFORDSHIRE

Mallams Pevensey House, 27 Sheep Street, Bicester, Oxfordshire, OX6 7JF
United Kingdom
Telephone: 01869 252901
Fax: 01869 320283
bicester@mallams.co.uk
www.mallams.co.uk

Mallams (Oxford) Bocardo House, St Michaels Street, Oxford, Oxfordshire, OX1 2EB, United Kingdom
Telephone: 01865 241358
Fax: 01865 725483
oxford@mallams.co.uk
www.mallams.co.uk

Soames Country Auctions
Pinnocks Farm Estate, Witney, Oxfordshire, OX8 1AY
Tel: 01865 300626
soames@email.msn.com
www.soamesauctioneers.co.uk

SHROPSHIRE

Halls Fine Art (Shrewsbury)
Welsh Bridge Salerooms, Shrewsbury, Shropshire, SY3 8LA, United Kingdom
Telephone: 01743 231212
Fax: 01743 246191
fineart@halls-auctioneers.ltd.uk
www.halls-auctioneers.ltd.uk

Walker Barnett & Hill
Cosford Auction Rooms, Long Lane, Cosford, TF11 8PJ
Tel: 01902 375555
Fax: 01902375556
wbhauctions@lineone.net
www.walker-barnett-hill.co.uk

Mullock & Madeley
The Old Shippon, Wall-under-Heywood, Nr Church Stretton, Shropshire, SY6 7DS
United Kingdom
Telephone: 01694 771771
Fax: 01694 771772
info@mullockmadeley.co.uk
www.mullock-madeley.co.uk

Walker, Barnett & Hill
Cosford Auction Rooms, Long Lane, Cosford, TF11 8PJ
Tel: 01902 375555
Fax: 01902 375556
wbhauctions@lineone.net
www.walker-barnett-hill.co.uk

SOMERSET

Aldridges Newark House, 26-45 Cheltenham Street, Bath, BA2 3EX
Tel: 01225 462830
Fax: 01225 311319

Clevedon Salerooms Herbert Road, Clevedon, Bristol, BS21 7ND, United Kingdom
Telephone: 01275 876699
Fax: 01275 343765
clevedon.salerooms@cableinet.co.uk

Gardiner Houlgate
The Bath Auction Rooms, 9 Leafield Way, Corsham, Bath, Somerset SN13 9SW
United Kingdom
Telephone: 01225 812912
Fax: 01225 811777
auctions@gardiner-houlgate.co.uk
www.invaluable.com/gardiner-houlgate

Lawrence's Fine Art Auctioneers Ltd
South Street, Crewkerne, TA18 8AB
Tel: 01460 73041
Fax: 01460 74627
enquiries@lawrences.co.uk
www.lawrences.co.uk

STAFFORDSHIRE

Potteries Specialist Auctions
271 Waterloo Road, Cobridge, Stoke-on-Trent, ST6 3HR
Tel: 01782 286622
Fax: 01782 213777
enquiries@potteriesauctions.com
www.potteriesauctions.com

Richard Winterton
School House Auction Rooms, Hawkins Lane, Burton-on-Trent, DE14 1PT
Tel: 01283 511224
Fax: 01283 568650
adrianrathbone@btconnect.com

Wintertons Lichfield Auction Centre, Fradley, Lichfield, WS13 8NF
Tel: 01543 263256
Fax: 01543 415348
enquiries@wintertons.co.uk
www.wintertons.co.uk

Stockton on Tees Vectis Auctions Limited, Fleck Way, Thornaby, Stockton on Tees, TS17 0JZ
Tel: 01642 750 616
Fax: 01642 769 478
enquiries@vectis.co.uk
www.vectis.co.uk

SUFFOLK

Diamond Mills 117 Hamilton Road, Felixstowe, Suffolk, IP11 7BL, United Kingdom
Telephone: 01394 282281
Fax: 01394 671791
diamondmills@easynet.co.uk

Neal Sons & Fletcher
26 Church Street, Woodbridge, IP12 1DP
Tel: 01394 382263
Fax: 01394 383030
enquiries@nsf.co.uk
www.nsf.co.uk

SURREY

Barbers The Mayford Centre, Smarts Heath Road, Woking, Surrey, GU22 0PP
United Kingdom
Telephone: 01483 728939
Fax: 01483 762552
www.thesaurus.co.uk/barbers

Clark Gammon Guildford Auction Rooms, Bedford Road, Guildford, Surrey, GU1 4SJ, United Kingdom
Telephone: 01483 880915
Fax: 01483 880918

Ewbank Auctioneers The Burnt Common Auction Rooms, London Road, Send, Woking, Surrey, GU23 7LN, United Kingdom
Telephone: 01483 223101
Fax: 01483 222171
antiques@ewbankauctions.co.uk
www.ewbankauctions.co.uk

Hamptons Auctioneers
93 High Street, Godalming, Surrey GU7 1AL United Kingdom
Telephone: 01483 423567
Fax: 01483 426392
fineart@hamptons-int.com
www.hamptons.co.uk

P.F. Windibank Dorking Halls, Reigate Road, Dorking, RH4 1SG
Tel: 01306 884556
Fax: 01306 884669
sjw@windibank.co.uk
www.windibank.co.uk

EAST SUSSEX

Edgar Horns 46-50 South Street, Eastbourne, East Sussex, BN21 4QJ, United Kingdom
Telephone: 01323 410419
Fax: 01323 416540
sales@edgarhorns.com
www.edgarhorns.com

Gorringes Terminus Road, Bexhill-on-sea, TN39 3LR
Tel: 01424 212994
Fax: 01424 224035
bexhill@gorringes.co.uk
www.gorringes.co.uk

Gorringes 15 North Street, Lewes, BN7 2PD
Tel: 01273 472503
Fax: 01273 479559

auctions@gorringes.co.uk
www.gorringes.co.uk

Raymond P. Inman The Auction
Galleries, 35 & 40 Temple Street,
Brighton, BN1 3BH
Tel: 01273 774777
Fax: 01273 735660
r.p.inman@talk21.com

Wallis & Wallis West Street
Auction Galleries, Lewes, East
Sussex, BN7 2NJ
Tel: 01273 480208
Fax: 01273 476562
grb@wallisandwallis.co.uk
www.wallisandwallis.co.uk

WEST SUSSEX
John Bellman New Pound
Wisborough Green, Billingshurst
RH14 0AZ
Tel: 01403 700858
Fax: 01403 700059
enquiries@bellmans.comuk
www.bellmans.co.uk

Denhams The Auction Galleries,
Warnham, Nr Horsham,
RH12 3RZ
Tel: 01403 255699
Fax: 01403 253837
denhams@lineone.net

Rupert Toovey Star Road,
Partridge Green, Horsham,
RH13 8RA
Tel: 01403 411744
Fax: 01403 711919
auctions@rupert-toovey.com
www.rupert-toovey.com

TYNE & WEAR
Anderson & Garland
Marlborough House,
Marlborough Crescent,
Newcastle Upon Tyne, Tyne And
Wear NE1 4EE United Kingdom
Telephone: 01912 326278
Fax: 01912 618665
agarland@compuserve.com

Corbitts 5 Mosley Street,
Newcastle-upon-Tyne, NE1 1YE
Tel: 0191 232 7268
Fax: 0191 261 4130
collectors@corbitts.com
www.corbitts.com

WEST SUSSEX
Denhams Horsham Auction
Galleries, Dorking Road,
Warnham, Nr Horsham
West Sussex RH12 3RZ
United Kingdom
Telephone: 01403 255699
Fax: 01403 253837
denhams@lineone.net
www.thesaurus.co.uk/denhams

John Beilman New Pound,
Wisborough Green, Billingshurst,
West Sussex RH14 0AY
United Kingdom
Telephone: 01403 700858
Fax: 01403 700059
enquiries@bellmans.co.uk
www.bellmans.co.uk

WARWICKSHIRE
Locke & England 18 Guy
Street, Leamington Spa,
Warwickshire CV32 4RT
United Kingdom
Telephone: 01926 889100
Fax: 01926 470608
info@leauction.co.uk
www.leauction.co.uk

WEST MIDLANDS
Biddle & Webb
Icknield Square, Ladywood
Middleway, Birmingham, West
Midlands B16 0PP United
Kingdom
Tel: 01214 558042
Fax: 01214 549615
antiques@biddleandwebb.freeser
ve.co.uk

Bonhams The Old House,
Station Road, Knowle,
Solihull, B93 0HT
Tel: 01564 776151
Fax: 01564 778069
knowle@bonhams.com
www.bonhams.com

Fellows & Sons, Augusta
House, 19 Augusta Street,
Hockley, Birmingham B18 6JA
Tel: 0121 212 2131
Fax: 0121 212 1249
info@fellows.co.uk
www.fellows.co.uk

Walker, Barnett & Hill
Waterloo Road, Salerooms,
Clarence Street, Wolverhampton
WV1 4JE
Tel: 01902 773531

WILTSHIRE
Dominic Winter Auctions The
Old School, Maxwell Street,
Swindon, Wiltshire SN1 5DR
United Kingdom
Telephone: 01793 611340
Fax: 01793 491727
info@dominicwinter.co.uk
www.dominic-winter.co.uk

Finan & Co The Square, Mere,
Wiltshire BA12 6DJ
United Kingdom
Telephone: 01747 861411
Fax: 01747 861944
post@finanandco.co.uk
www.finanandco.co.uk

Henry Aldridge & Sons The
Devizes Auctioneers, Unit 1,
Bath Road Business Centre,
Devizes, Wiltshire SN10 1XA
United Kingdom
Telephone: 01380 729199
Fax: 01380 730073
andrew.aldridge@virgin.net
www.henry-aldridge.co.uk

Hamptons 20 High Street,
Marlborough SN8 1AA
Tel: 01672 516161
Fax: 01672 515882
saleroom@hamptons-int.com
www.hamptons.co.uk/services/f
ine_art_auction/index.asp

Woolley & Wallis 51-61 Castle
Street, Salisbury SP1 3SU
Tel: 01722 424500
Fax: 01722 424508
enquiries@woolleyandwallis.co.uk
www.woolleyandwallis.co.uk

WORCESTERSHIRE
Andrew Grant St Mark's House,
St Mark's Close, Cherry Orchard,
Worcester, Worcestershire WR5
3DJ United Kingdom
Telephone: 01905 357547
Fax: 01905 763942
fine.art@andrew-grant.co.uk
www.andrew-grant.co.uk

Phillip Serrell, The Malvern
Saleroom, Barnards Green Road,
Malvern WR14 3LW
Tel: 01684 892314
Fax: 01684 569832
www.serrell.com

EAST YORKSHIRE
Dee, Atkinson & Harrison
The Exchange Saleroom,
Driffield, East Riding of Yorkshire
YO25 7LJ United Kingdom
Telephone: 01377 253151
Fax: 01377 241041
exchange@dee-atkinson-
harrison.co.uk
www.dee-atkinson-
harrison.co.uk

NORTH YORKSHIRE
David Duggleby The Vine Street
Salerooms, Scarborough, North
Yorkshire YO11 1XN United
Kingdom
Telephone: 01723 507111
Fax: 01723 507222
auctions@davidduggleby.com
www.davidduggleby.com

Morphets 6 Albert Street,
Harrogate, HG1 1JL
Tel: 01423 530030
Fax: 01423 500717
enquiries@morphets.co.uk
www.morphets.co.uk

Tennants, The Auction Centre,
Leyburn, DL8 5SG
Tel: 01969 623780
Fax: 01969 624281
enquiry@tennants-ltd.co.uk
www.tennants.co.uk

SOUTH YORKSHIRE
A. E. Dowse & Sons Cornwall
Galleries, Scotland Street,
Sheffield, South Yorkshire S37
7DE
United Kingdom
Telephone: 0114 272 5858
Fax: 0114 249 0550
aedowse@talk21.com

BBR Auctions Elsecar Heritage
Centre, 5 Ironworks Row,
Wath Road, Elsecar, Barnsley,
South Yorkshire
S74 8HJ United Kingdom
Telephone: 01226 745156
Fax: 01226 361561
sales@bbrauctions.co.uk
www.bbrauctions.co.uk

Sheffield Railwayana 43 Little
Norton Lane, Sheffield, S8 8GA
Tel: 0114 274 5085
Fax: 0114 274 5085
ian@sheffrail.freeserve.co.uk
www.sheffieldrailwayana.co.uk

WEST YORKSHIRE
Andrew Hartley Fine Arts
Victoria Hall Salerooms, Little
Lane, Ilkle, LS29 8EA
Tel: 01943 816363
info@andrewhuntleyfinearts.co.uk
www.andrewhuntleyfinearts.co.uk

SCOTLAND
Bonhams Edinburgh
65 George Street, Edinburgh
EH2 2JL
Tel: 0131 225 2266
Fax: 0131 220 2547
edinburgh@bonhams.com
www.bonhams.com

Loves Auction Rooms 52-54
Canal Street, Perth, Perthshire,
PH2 8LF
Tel: 01738 633337
Fax: 01738 629830

Lyon & Turnbull
33 Broughton Place, Edinburgh
EH1 3RR United Kingdom
Telephone: 0131 557 8844
Fax: 0131 557 8668
info@lyonandturnbull.com
www.lyonandturnbull.com

Lyon & Turnbull 4 Woodside Place, Glasgow, G3 7QF
Telephone 0141 353 5070
Fax 0141 332 2928
info@lyonandturnbull.com
www.lyonandturnbull.com

McTears
Clydeway Business Centre, 8 Elliot Place, Glasgow, G3 8EP
Tel: 0141 221 4456
Fax: 0141 204 5035
enquiries@mctears.co.uk
www.mctears.co.uk

Thomson, Roddick & Medcalf Ltd
42 Moray Place, Edinburgh, EH3 6BT
Tel: 0131 220 6680
Fax: 0131 441 7455
mark.medcalf@virgin.net
www.thomsonroddick.com/trm/.index.html

WALES
Bonhams Cardiff 7-8 Park Place, Cardiff, Glamorgan, CF10 3DP
Tel: 02920 727 980
Fax: 02920 727 989
cardiff@bonhams.com
www.bonhams.com

Peter Francis Curiosity Salerooms, 19 King Street, Carmarthen, South Wales
Tel: 01267 233456
Fax: 01267 233458
www.peterfrancis.co.uk

Welsh Country Auctions
2 Carmarthen Road, Cross Hands, Llanelli, Dyfed, SA14 6SP
Tel/Fax: 01269 844428

IRELAND
HOK Fine Art
4 Main Street, Biackrock, Co Dublin, Dublin, Eire, Ireland
Tel: 00 353 1 2881000
fineart@hok.ie

Mealy's
The Square, Castlecomer, County Kilkenny, Republic of Ireland
Telephone: 00 353 56 41229 /41413
Fax: 00 353 56 41627
info@mealys.com
www.mealys.com

CLUBS AND SOCIETIES

AUTOGRAPHS
International Autograph Collectors Club & Dealers' Alliance 4575 Sheridan St., Ste. 111, Hollywood, FL 33021-3515
Tel: 561 736 8409
www.iacc-da.com

Universal Autograph Collectors Club
P.O. Box 6181, Washington DC 20044
Tel: 202 332-7388
http://www.uacc.com

CAMERAS
Photographic Collectors Club of Great Britain 5 Station Industrial Estate, Prudhoe, Northumberland, NE42 6NP
Tel: 0117 9831839
mpritchard@cix.compulink.co.uk
www.nmsi.ac.uk/nmpft/pccgb.htm

CERAMICS
Belleek Collectors Group
5 Waterhall Avenue, Chingford, London E4 6NB
Tel: 0208 529 0510

The Bunnykins Collectors Club 6 Beckett Way, Lewes, East Sussex, BN7 2EB
Tel: 01273 479 056

Carlton Ware Collectors' International PO Box 161, Sevenoaks, TN15 6GA
Tel: 01474 853630
Fax: 01474 854385
cwciclub@aol.com
www.carltonwarecollectorsinternational.com

Chintz World International
Tel 01525 220272
Fax 01525 222442
www.chintzworld-intl.com

Clarice Cliff Collectors Club
Fantasque House, Tennis Drive, The Park, Nottingham, NG7 1AE
www.claricecliff.com

Cornish Collectors' Club
PO Box 18, Glossop SK13 8FA
Tel 01457 864833

Friends of Blue (Blue & White Pottery)
PO Box 122, Didcot OX11 0YN
Website www.fob.org.uk

Goss Collectors Club
ailsa@schofieldhouse.fsnet.co.uk
http://www.gosschina.com

Keith Murray Collectors Club
Fantasque House, Tennis Drive, The park, Nottingham NG7 1AE
www.keithmurray.com

Kevin Francis Guild 28 Liverpool Street, Stoke-on-Trent, Staffs ST4 1BJ
Tel: 01782 848 002

Mabel Lucie Attwell Abbey Antiques,63 Great Whyte, Ramsey, Huntingdon PE26 1HL
Tel: 01487 814753

Moorcroft Collectors' Club
Sandbach Road, Burslem, Stoke-on-Trent ST6 2DQ
Tel 01782 820500
Fax 01782 820501
cclub@moorcroft.com
www.moorcroft.com

Pendelfin Family Circle
Cameron Mill, Howsin Street, Burnley, Lancs BB10 1PP
Tel: 01282 432 301

Poole Pottery Collectors Club The Quay, Poole BH15 1RF
Tel: 01202 666200
Fax: 01202 682894
www.poolepottery.co.uk

Royal Doulton International Collectors' Club Minton House, London Road, Stoke-on-Trent ST4 7QD
Tel: 01782 292292
Fax: 01782 292099
enquiries@royal-doulton.com
www.royal-doulton.com/collectables

Royal Winton International Collectors Club Dancers End, Northall, Beds LU6 2EU
Tel: 01525 220 272
Fax: 01525 222 442

Shelley Group 12 Lilleshall Road, Clayton, Newcastle-Under-Lyme, Staffordshire, ST5 3BX

Spode Society PO Box 1812, London, NW4 4NW
Tel: 0208 203 1769
Fax: 0208 203 1769
ros.marl@tesco.net
www.spode.co.uk

Susie Cooper Collectors Group
Panorama House, 18 Oaklea Mews, Aycliffe Village, County Durham DL5 6JP
www.susiecooper.co.uk

The Sylvac Collectors Circle
174 Portsmouth Road, Horndean, Waterlooville, Hants

Official International Wade Collectors Club Wade Ceramics Limited, Royal Works, Westport Road, Stoke-on-Trent, ST6 4AP
Tel: 01782 255255
Fax: 01782 575195
club@wade.co.uk
www.wade.co.uk

The Wedgwood Society
Tel: 0171 628 7268

COMMEMORATIVE WARE
Commemorative Collectors Society
The Gardens, Gainsborough Road, Winthorpe, nr Newark, NG24 2NR
Tel: 01636 671377
chris@royalcoll.fsnet.co.uk
www.royalcoll.fsnet.co.uk/collectors.htm

COMICS
Association of Comic Enthusiasts
L'Hopiteau, St Martin du Fouilloux, 79420, France
Tel: 00 33 549 702 114

Comic Enthusiasts Society 80 Silverdale, Sydenham, London, SE26 4SJ

EPHEMERA
The Ephemera Society
PO Box 112, Northwood, HA6 2WT, United Kingdom
www.ephemera-society.org.uk

FILM & TV

James Bond 007 Fan Club & Archive
P.O. Box 007, Surrey KT15 IDY
Tel: 01483 756007

GLASS

Carnival Glass Society PO Box 14, Hayes, Middx UB3 5NU

The Glass Association
Broadfield House Glass Museum, Compton Drive, Kingswinford, DY6 9NS
Tel: 01384 812745
hian@turnermel.ssnet.co.uk
www.glassassociation.org.uk

Pressed Glass Collectors Club
4 Bowshot Close, Castle Bromwich B36 9UH
Tel: 0121 681 4872
www.webspawner.com/users/pre
ssedglass

MECHANICAL MUSIC

Musical Box Society of Great Britain
PO Box 299, Waterbeach, Cambridge CB4 4PJ

The British Vintage Wireless Society
59 Dunsford Close, Swindon, Wilts SN1 4PW
Tel:01793 541 634
www.bvws.org.uk

The City of London Phonograph and Gramophone Society
2 Kirklands Park, Fyfe KY15 4EP
Tel: 01334 654 390

METALWARE

Antique Metalware Society
P.O. Box 63, Honiton, Devon EX14 1HP
amsmemsec@yahoo.coouk

MILITARIA

Military – Crown Imperial
37 Wolsey Close, Southall, Middlesex UB2 4NQ

Military Historical Society
National Army Museum, Royal Hospital Road, London SW3 4HT

Orders & Medals Research Society
123 Turnpike Link, Croydon CR0 5NU

ORIENTAL

Oriental Ceramics Society
30b Torrington Square, London WC1E 7JL
Tel: 020 7636 7985
Fax: 020 7580 6749

Snuff Bottle Society 1 Tollard Court, West Hill Rd, Bournemouth BH2 5EH
Tel/Fax: 01202 292867

PENS & WRITING

Writing Equipment Society
Pastures Edge, Tregenna Road, Blisland, Bodmin, Cornwall PL30 4JS
wes.membershipsec@virgin.net
www.wesoc.co.uk

PERFUME/SCENT BOTTLES

The UK Perfume Bottle Collectors Club
Assembly Antiques Centre, 5-8 Saville Row, Bath BA1 2QP
Tel: 01225 448 488

RAILWAYANA

Railwayana Collectors Journal
7 Ascot Road, Moseley, Birmingham B13 9EN

SCIENTIFIC, TECHNICAL & MEDICAL

Opthalmic Antiques International Collector's Club
frankbarraclough@cs.com
www.college-
optometrists.org/college/
museum/oaicc

Scientific Instrument Society
31 High Street, Stanford in the Vale, Farringdon SN7 8LH
www.sis.org.uk

SMOKING

Lighter Club of Great Britain
Richard Ball
richard@lighter.co.uk
www.lighter.co.uk

The Society for Clay Pipe Research
2 Combe Avenue, Portishead, Bristol BS20 6JR

SPORTING

Cricket Memorabilia Society
29 Highclere Road, Crumpsall, Manchester M8 4WH
Tel: 0161 7403714
Fax: 0161 7403714

**Fishing Tackle -
The Collectors Register**
16 Pleshey Close, Worle, Weston Super Mare, Somerset
Tel: 01934 416 492

TEXTILES, COSTUME & FASHION

British Compact Collector's Club
PO Box 131, Woking, Surrey GU24 9YR

Fan Circle International
Cronk-Y-Voddy, Rectory Road, Coltishall NR12 7HF
jdm@coltishall.freeserve.co.uk

Headscarf Collectors Society
brenda@osmetic.fsnet.co.uk

The Lace Guild The Hollies, 53 Audnam Stourbridge, West Midlands DY8 4AE

TOOLS

Tools and Trades History Society 60 Swaley Lane, Swaley, Kent BR8 7JG
Tel: 01322 662 271

TOYS & DOLLS & TEDDY BEARS

British Doll Collectors Club
'The Anchorage', Wrotham Road, Culverstone Green, Meopham, Kent. DA13 0QW
www.britishdollcollectors.com

The British Model Soldier Society
44 Dayemead, Hoddesdon, Herts EN11 9LU

British Teddy Bear Association
PO Box 290, Brighton Sussex
Tel: 01273 697 974

Corgi Collectors Club PO Box 323, Swansea, Wales SA1 1BJ

Doll Club of Great Britain, PO Box 154, Cobham, Surrey KT11 2YE

The Fashion Doll Collectors Club of GB
PO Box 133, Lowestoft, Suffolk NR32 1WA
Tel: 07940 248127
voden@supanet.com

Hornby Collectors

Club PO Box 35, Royston, Herts SG8 5XR
Tel/Fax: 01223 208 308
hsclubs.demon.co.uk
www.hornby.co.uk

Matchbox International Collectors' Association 13A Lower Bridge Street, Chester CH1 1RS
Tel: 01244 346297
Fax: 01244 340437
mo@matchboxclub.com
www.matchboxclub.com

Historical Model Railway Society
59 Woodberry way, London E4 7DY

Merrythought International Collectors Club Ironbridge, Telford, Shrops TF8 7NJ
Tel: 01952 433 116

Pelham Puppets Collectors Club
46 The Grove, Bedford MK40 3JN
Tel: 01234 363 336

Steiff Club Office
Margaret Steiff GmbH, Alleen Strasse 2, D-89537 Giengen/Brenz, Germany

William Britain Collectors Club
PO Box 32, Wokingham RG40 4XZ
Tel: 01189 737080
Fax: 01189 733947
ales@wbritaincollectorsclub.co
m
www.britaincollectorsclub.com

TREEN & BOXES

The Mauchlinware Collectors' Club
Unit 37, Romsey Industrial Estate Greatbridge Road, Romsey, Hants SO51 0HR

WATCHES

British Watch & Clock Collectors Association 5 Cathedral Lane, Truro TR1 2QS
Tel 01872 264010
Fax 01872 241953
tonybwcca@cs.com
www.timecap.com

Using the Internet

THE INTERNET HAS REVOLUTIONISED the trading of collectables. Compared to a piece of furniture, most collectables are easily defined, described and photographed. Shipping is also comparatively easy, due to average size and weight. Prices are also generally more affordable and accessible than for antiques and the internet has provided a cost effective way of buying and selling, away from the overheads of shops and auction rooms. Many millions of collectables are offered for sale and traded daily, with sites varying from global online marketplaces, such as eBay, to specialist dealers' websites.

When searching online, remember that some people may not know how to accurately describe their item. General category searches, even though more time consuming, and even purposefully misspelling a name, can yield results. Also, if something looks too good to be true, it probably is. Using this book to get to know your market visually, so that you can tell the difference between a real bargain and something that sounds like one, is a good start.

As you will understand from buying this book, colour photography is vital – look for online listings that include as many images as possible and check them carefully. Beware that colours can appear differently, even between computer screens.

Always ask the vendor questions about the object, particularly regarding condition. If there is no image, or you want to see another aspect of the object – ask. Most sellers (private or trade) will want to realise the best price for their items so will be more than happy to help – if approached politely and sensibly.

As well as the 'e-hammer' price, you will probably have to pay additional transactional fees such as packing, shipping and possibly regional or national taxes. It is always best to ask for an estimate for these additional costs before leaving a bid. This will also help you tailor your bid as you will have an idea of the maximum price the item will cost if you are successful.

As well as the well known online auction sites, such as eBay, there are a host of other online resources for buying and selling, such as fair and auction date listings.

INTERNET RESOURCES

icollector

www.icollector.com
customerservices@icollector.com
A free service which allows users to search selected auction house catalogues in Europe, the U.S.A and the United Kingdom. Through its unique connection with eBay, users can bid live into salerooms as auctions happens. Users can also leave absentee bids through the internet and search an archive of auction catalogues dating back to 1994.

invaluable.com

www.invaluable.com
sales@invaluable.com
A subscription service which allows users to search selected auction house catalogues from the United Kingdom and Europe. Also offers an extensive archive for appraisal uses.

The Antiques Trade Gazette

www.atg-online.com
The online version of the UK trade newspaper, comprising British auction and fair listings, news and events.

Maine Antiques Digest

www.maineantiquesdigest.com
The online version of America's trade newspaper including news, articles, fair and auction listings and more.

Auctionnet.com

www.auctionnet.com
Simple online resource listing over 500 websites related to auctions online.

AuctionBytes

www.auctionbytes.com
Auction resource with community forum, news, events, tips and a weekly newsletter.

Go Antiques/Antiqnet

www.goantiques.com
www.antiqnet.com
An online global aggregator for art, antiques and collectibles dealers who showcase their stock online, allowing users to browse and buy.

eBay

www.ebay.com
Undoubtedly the largest and most diverse of the online auction sites, allowing users to buy and sell in an online marketplace with over 40 million registered users. Collectors should also view eBay Live Auctions (www.ebayliveauctions.com) where traditional auctions are combined with realtime, online bidding allowing users to interact with the saleroom as the auction takes place.

ACKNOWLEDGMENTS

DORLING KINDERSLEY would like to thank the following people for their assistance in producing this book:
Philip Gilderdale, Caroline Hunt, Julian Gray, Kelly Meyer, Martin Dieguez, Scott Stickland